This catalogue is published on the occasion of the exhibition:

The Great War

As Recorded through the Fine and Popular Arts

Morley Gallery

Morley College,
61 Westminster Bridge Road,
London, SE1 7HT

September 5 - October 2, 2014

Organised by:

LISS FINE ART

With the participation of David Cohen Fine Art

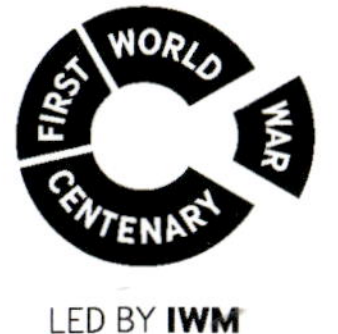

LED BY **IWM**

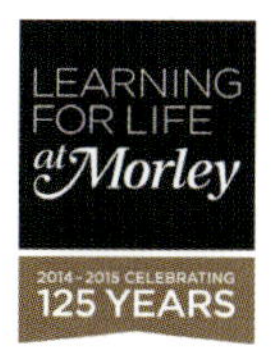

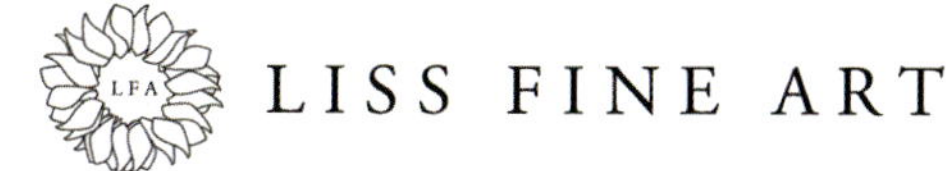

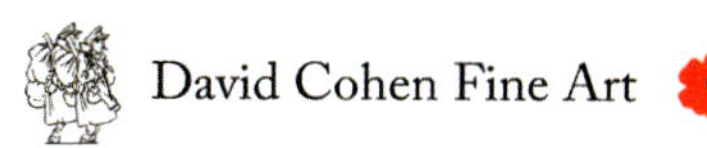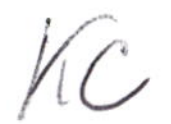

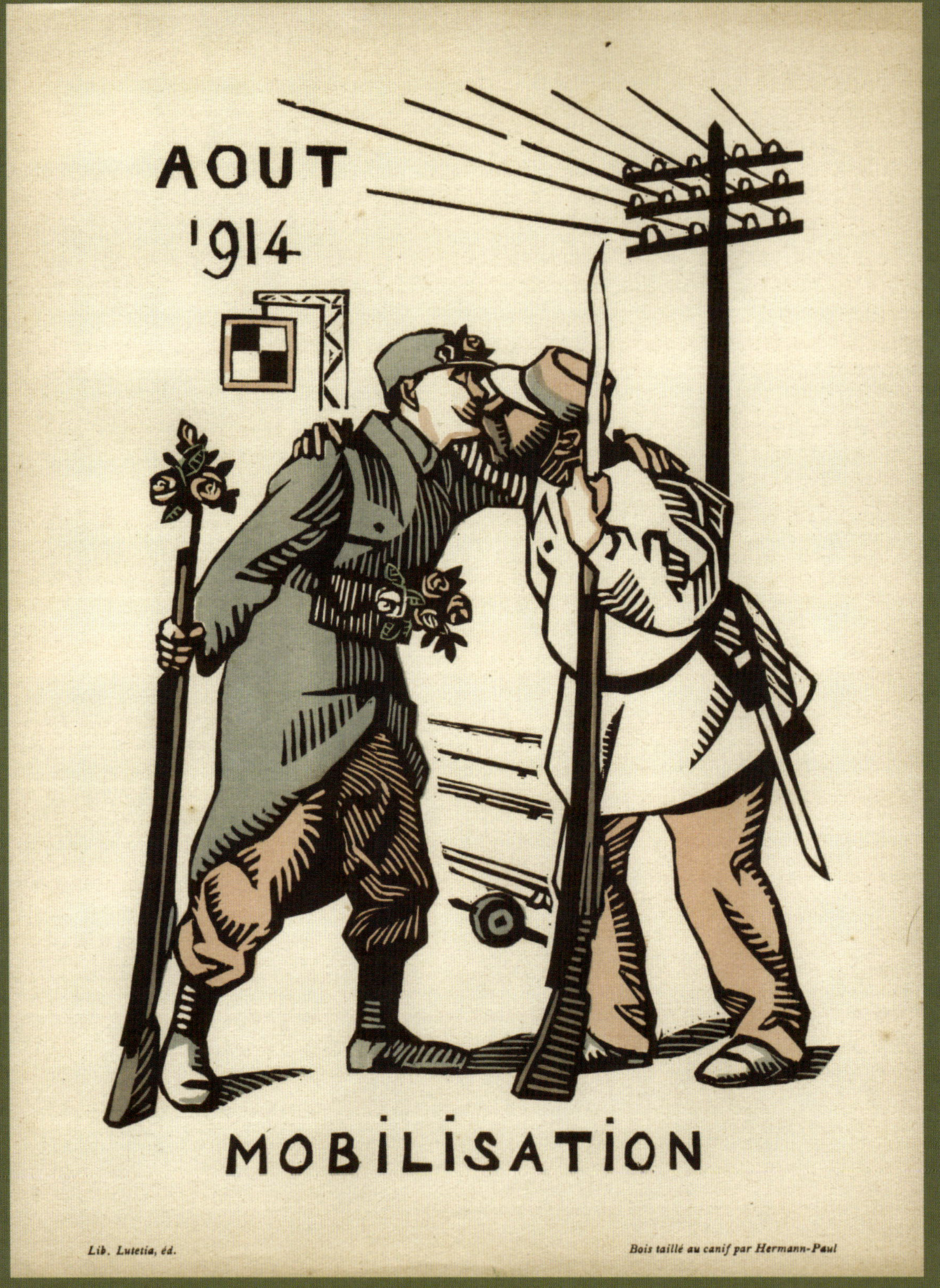

René Georges Hermann-Paul   (1864-1940)

148 – *Août 1914* from *Calendrier de la Guerre (1ère année – août 1914-juillet 1915)*, 1916,
Coloured woodcuts, 17 ¾ x 13 ¾ in. (45 x 35cm) each, published by Librarie Lutetia [A. Ciavarri, Directeur]

Two soldiers from different units who are preparing to embark for the Front, embrace during a chance encounter on a railway platform. The soldier in blue is decorated with flowers, momentoes from women who have bid him adieu. The first months of the war were by far the most bloody, and these friends may never meet again. (see pages 170-173)

The Great War

As Recorded through the Fine and Popular Arts

Edited by Sacha Llewellyn & Paul Liss

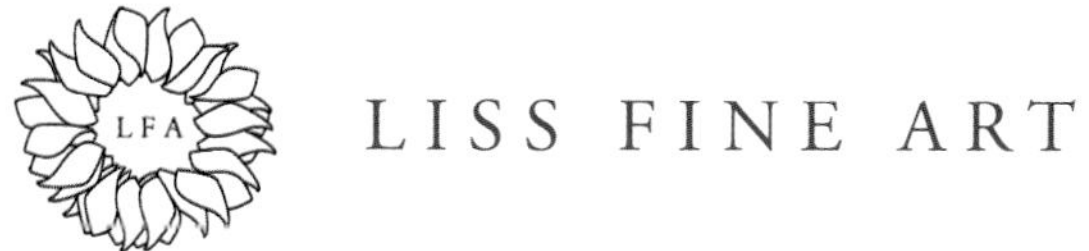

LISS FINE ART

ACKNOWLEDGEMENTS

We are especially grateful to Ela Piotrowska (Principal), Nick Rampley (Vice-Principal) and Jane Hartwell (Gallery Manager) of Morley College for giving us the opportunity to stage this exhibition, and also the Imperial War Museum for allowing this project to be part of a wider series of IWM-led First World War Centenary Initiatives.

We are also especially grateful to David and Judith Cohen for sharing their expertise with us over many years and proof-reading this catalogue.

Jonathan Black, Nick Bosanquet, Andrew Cormack, Paul Gough, Kenneth McConkey and Peyton Skipwith have all made invaluable comments on the form and content of this catalogue.

Libby Horner has been especially generous in providing information on Frank Brangwyn.

This catalogue would not have been possible without, additionally, the support of :

Elaine Andrews	Neil Jennings
Michael Barker	Stuart Last
Susan and Quentin Bone	Marc Lefebvre
Nicola Gordon Bowe	Marion and Barrie Liss
Ruth Bubb	Emma Mawdsley
Sarah Bull	Harry Moore-Gwyn
Michael Campbell	Conor Mullan
Francis Carline	Jonathan Rosenthall
Gill Clarke	Neil Sandberg
Stuardt-Mikhail Clarke	Jackie Setter
Peter Coulson	Nicola Shane
Daniel Dullaway	Christine Sheppard
Andy Ellis	Adrian Swire
Geoff Hassall (artbiogs.co.uk)	Sam Swire
www.hermann-paul.org	Anthony Thompson
Niall Hobhouse	Richard Thompson
Martin Humphries	Robert Upstone
Hermione Hunter	Christopher Whittick
Ian Jack	Micky Wolfson

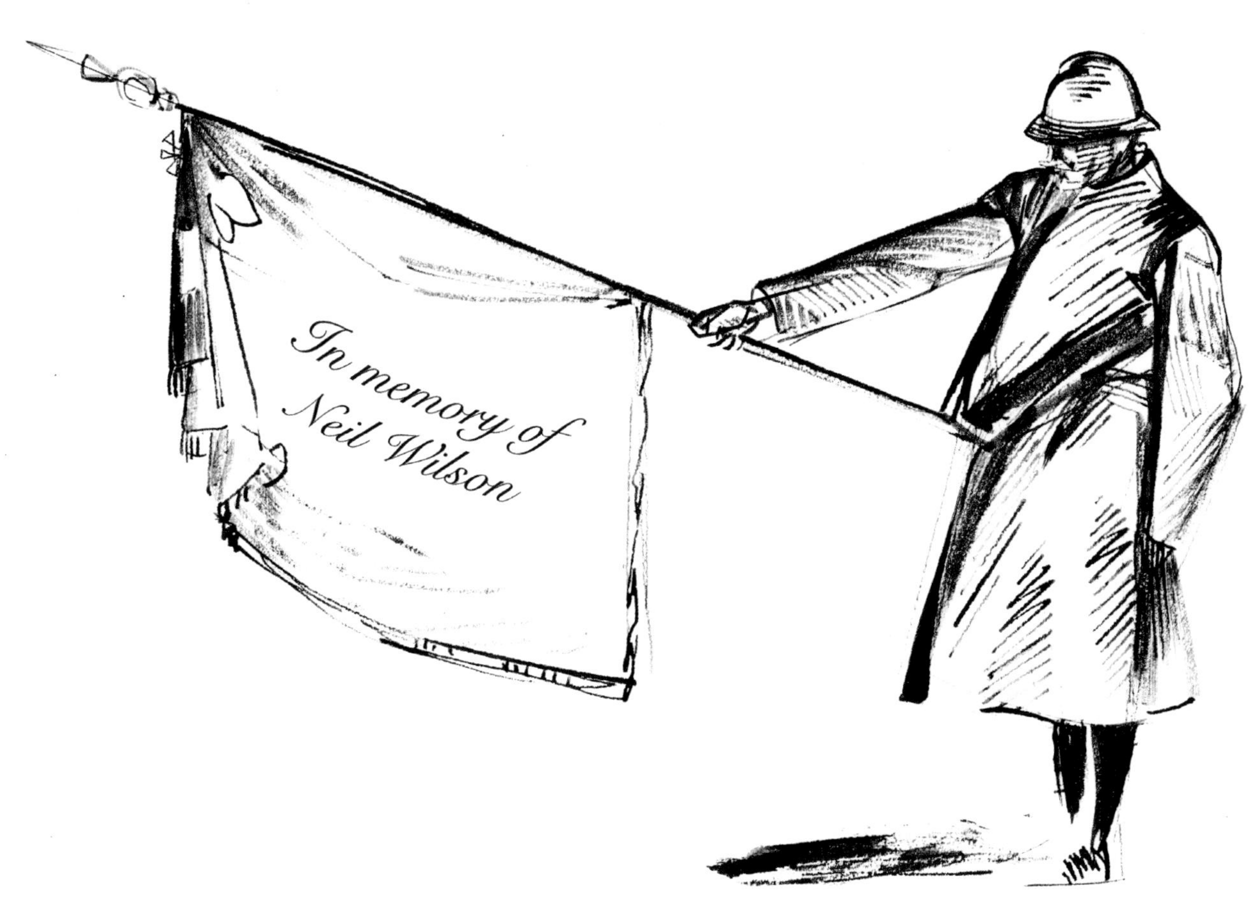
In memory of
Neil Wilson

CONTENTS

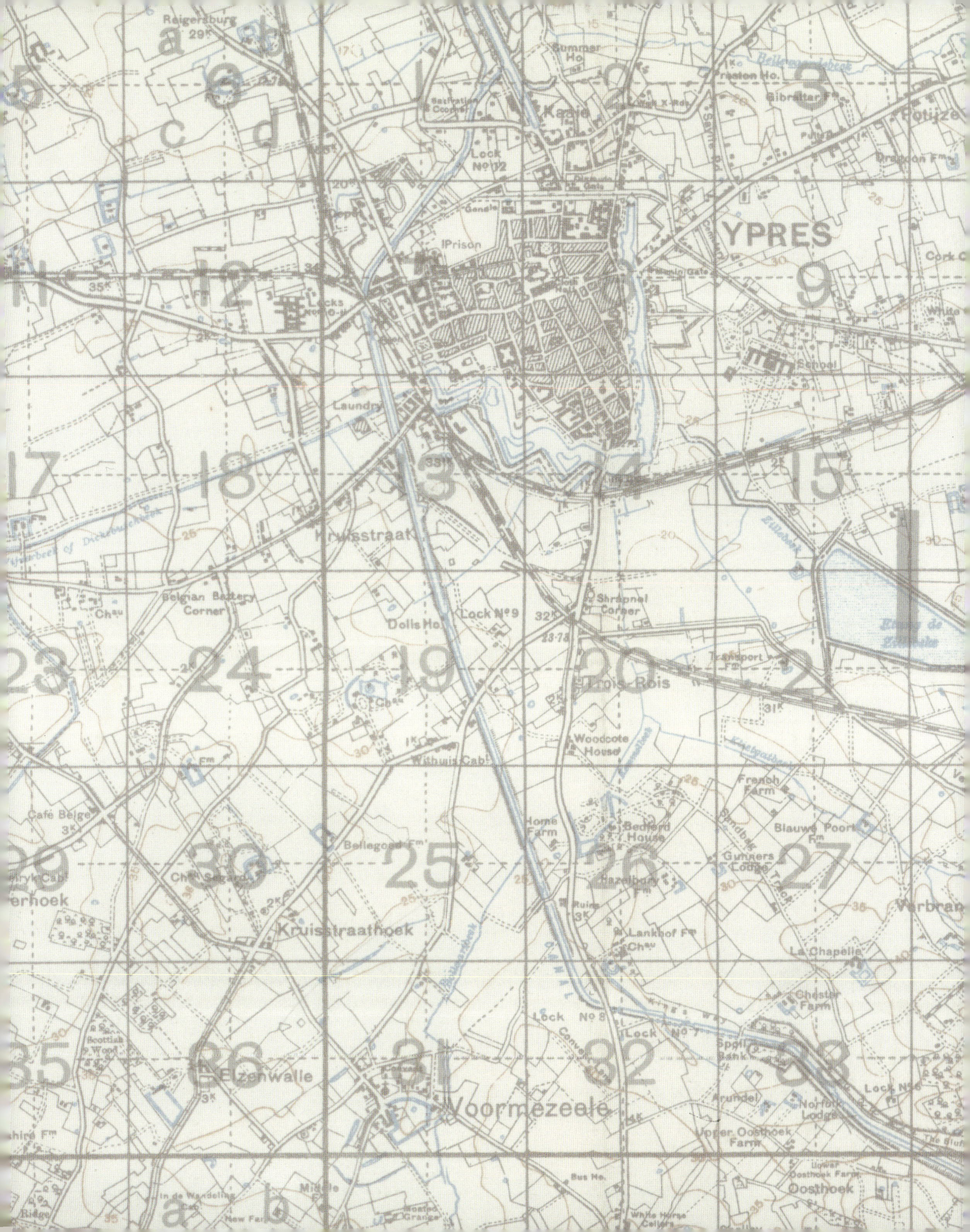

Reigersburg
Kasic
YPRES
Cork C.
9
Prison
Summer Ho.
Preston Ho.
Gibraltar F.
Potijze
Dragoon Fm
Canal
Lille Gate
White
School
Laundry
Kruisstraat
Belgian Battery Corner
Chau.
Dolls Ho.
Lock No 9
Shrapnel Corner
Transport Fm
Etang de Zillebeke
Trois Rois
Woodcote House
French Farm
Café Belge
Bellegoed Fm
Home Farm
Bedford House
Blauwe Poort Fm
Gunners Lodge
Verbran
erhoek
Chau. Segard
Hazelbury
Lankhof Fm
La Chapelle
Kruisstraathoek
Chester Farm
Scottish Wood
Lock No 8
Lock No 7
Elzenwalle
Voormezeele
Arundel
Norfolk Lodge
Upper Oosthoek Farm
Lower Oosthoek Farm
Oosthoek
Bus Ho.
New Farm
White Horse Cellars

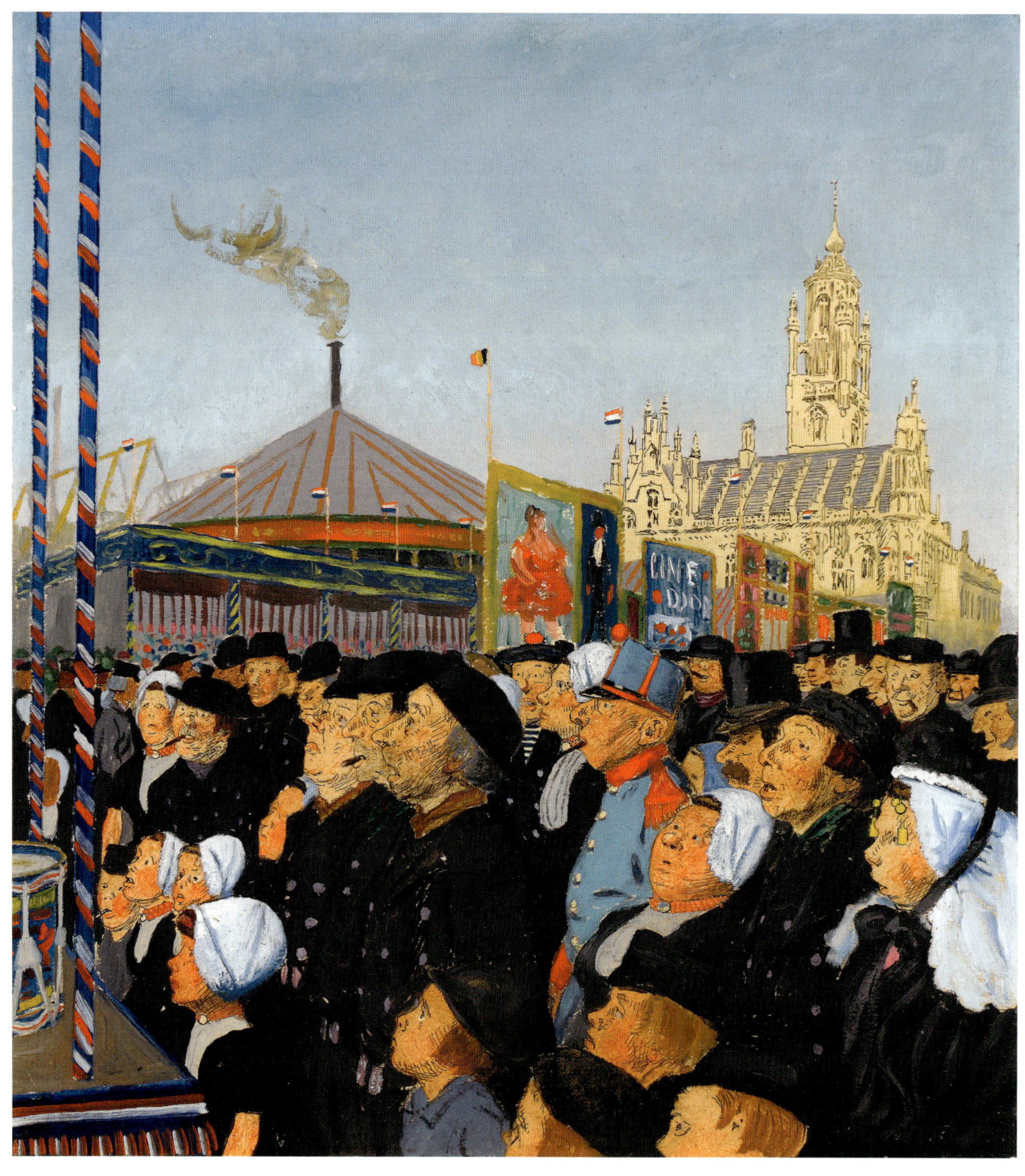

1 – Charles Pears (1873-1958)

At Middleburg: The Kermis, 1913, inscribed on reverse: 'full page in Punch',
Oil on card, 11 ⅜ x 9 ⅞ in. (29 x 25 cm)

Within a year of painting this colourful scene of the annual August festivities in Middleburg, Charles Pears would be commissioned as an Officer in the Royal Marines. His sombre wartime paintings of naval engagements (38) and freighters passing through an anti-submarine boom (40) seem far removed from the gaeity of this fin de la Belle Époque vignette.

FOREWORD

This catalogue – *The Great War As Recorded through the Fine and Popular Arts* – is published on the occasion of an exhibition of the same title held at Morley Gallery (September 5 - October 2, 2014). It offers a visual compendium of the war in the Centenary of the year in which it started.

This catalogue presents a view of the First World War through a multifarious record of two and three dimensional works of art: paintings, drawings, prints, sculpture, reliefs, posters, postcards, photographs, silhouettes and ceramics appear in the following pages. The material has been grouped into 14 subsections under the general headings of Combat, The Home Front and The Aftermath. These groupings highlight the themes that inspired both the fine and popular arts, although some are looser in association than others, and none are mutually exclusive. The introduction gives a more general survey of the underlying factors that influenced or determined the visual responses to the First World War. Although outside the remit of this catalogue, the accompanying exhibition includes other wartime objects from the collection of David and Judith Cohen, including trench art, commemorative ware, sweetheart brooches, games, puzzles and miniatures.

The content of the catalogue and accompanying exhibition concentrates on the Allies, with a particular bias towards British Art, though with the inclusion of some work from other participating nations. While it would be fascinating to tell the story of this global event from every point of view, this would have turned an already Herculean task into a near-impossible one.

Certain British artists – and the celebrated images they produced – are especially associated with The Great War. Whilst some of these artists – Henry Tonks, Eric Kennington, Christopher Nevinson, Colin Gill, Spencer Pryse and Muirhead Bone – feature in this catalogue, we have not attempted to present something which only the Imperial War Museum can do comprehensively. In the process of research undertaken over the last ten years, we have been fortunate to discover a number of previously unrecorded paintings by both Official War Artists and artists working independently. Surprisingly it is perhaps in the Popular Arts that we have found some of the most poignant and unfamiliar images of the First World War.

This exhibition follows on from our 2006 *Damn the War* catalogue. We are delighted to be collaborating with Morley College, drawing on shared resources and knowledge. We are grateful to the Imperial War Museum for allowing this project to be part of their wider series of IWM-led First World War Centenary Initiatives.

Sacha Llewellyn & Paul Liss

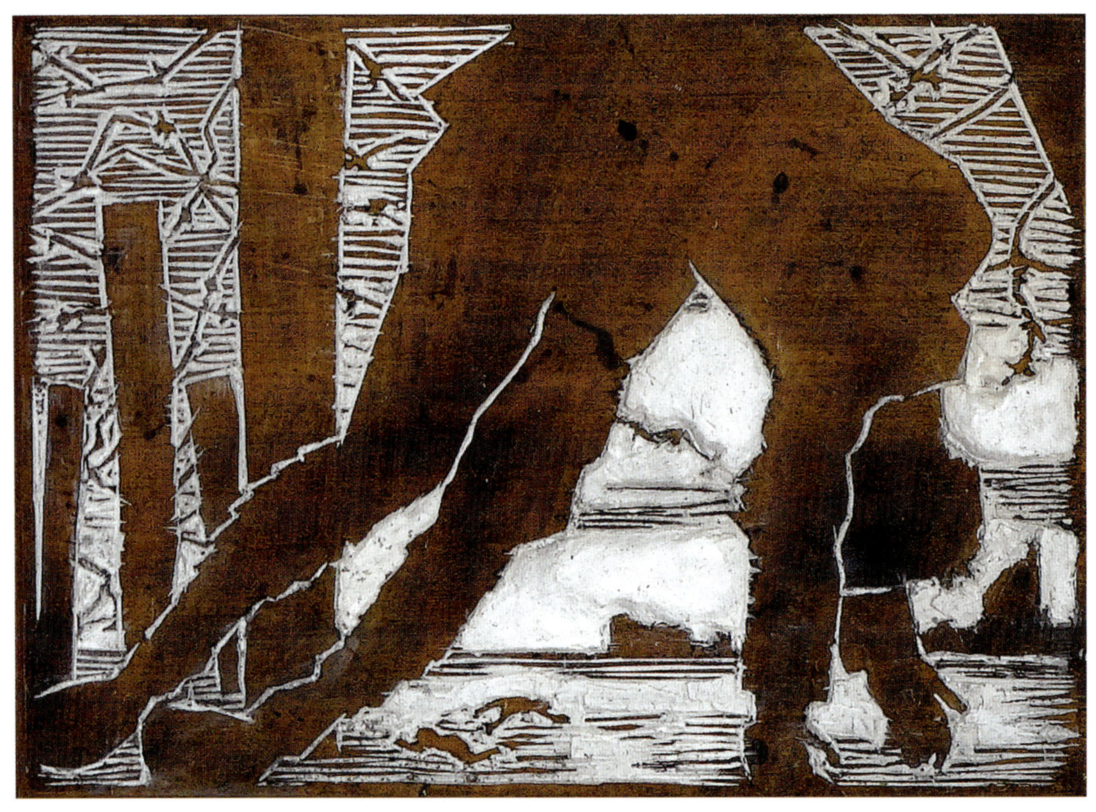

2 – John Moody (1906-1993)
War, 1928, the original woodblock, 3 x 4 in. (7.6 x 10.2 cm)

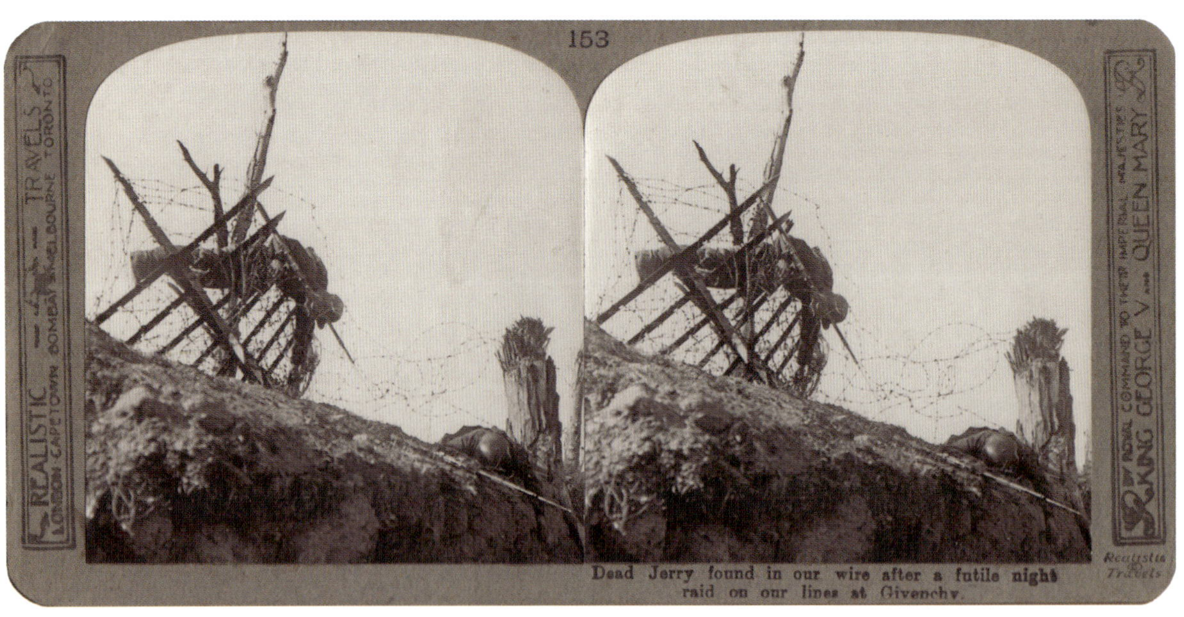

3 – Stereoscopic print: *Dead Jerry found in our wire after a futile night raid on our lines at Givenchy,*
3 ½ x 7 in. (9 x 18 cm), published by Realistic Travels

INTRODUCTION

Sacha Llewellyn

'Its Own Truths': The Great War as Recorded through the Fine and Popular Arts

> *"War does not purify, it intensifies – that's all. The material man becomes more material, the spiritual man more spiritual, and the true artist more passionately an artist."*
>
> Charles Lewis Hind, *Landscape Painting from Giotto to the Present Day*, Vol. 2, (London: Scribner's 1924), p.317

A century on, the events of 1914-18 are still difficult to comprehend. The first truly global conflict, the war's toll in human terms resulted in over 9 million soldiers and 6 million civilians killed and 21 million wounded. Countless towns and cities were destroyed or devastated, the countryside poisoned and ruined, resources expended. The Great War, as it was known, has a vast and varied literature: standard histories and detailed area studies and unit histories describe and interpret the significant events and massive undertakings. The first 'total' war, the role played by the men, women and children on what came to be called the Home Front has been appraised. The rich and diverse genre of war poetry, along with memoirs, diaries and notebooks, has come to dominate First World War memory. The visual response to the Great War, which was unprecedented in the history of conflict, provides yet another perspective for approaching this momentous subject.

John Moody's woodblock *War* (1928), (2) depicting a dead soldier slumped over a barbed-wire entanglement, is a defining image of the Great War. Created in the year of the 10th anniversary of the Armistice, *War* reflects a growing movement in Britain towards imagery of a darker nature, as the extent of the human suffering could no longer be denied. This is especially reflected in the flood of literary and autobiographical accounts of the war which appeared around this time, including Siegfried Sassoon's *Memoirs of a Fox-Hunting Man* (1928) and *Memoirs of an Infantry Officer* (1930), Robert Graves' *Goodbye to All That* (1929), Richard Aldington's *Death of a Hero* (1929) and Erich Maria Remarque's *All Quiet on the Western Front* (1929). On the day before the nationwide 10th anniversary celebrations took place, the Bishop of Manchester asked 'what the war means and should mean…for year by year the solemnity deepens, the direction of thought and feeling remains indefinite'.[1]

Born in 1906, Moody had been too young to participate in the war, but had suffered its consequences. As such, *War* can be read as both myth and allegory, a conscious reshaping of experience in memory. A stereoscopic print recording the same grim subject is presented as a contemporary factual record. (3) The caption leaves us in no doubt that the 'Dead Jerry' – no hero – has met the ignominious end he deserves. While offering two different perspectives, both images convey with equal power the bitter truth of shattered lives. By combining and contrasting different art forms, this catalogue and accompanying exhibition aim to enrich our overall understanding of the diverse nature of the visual imagery that developed as a result of, and in response to the war. (4, 5)

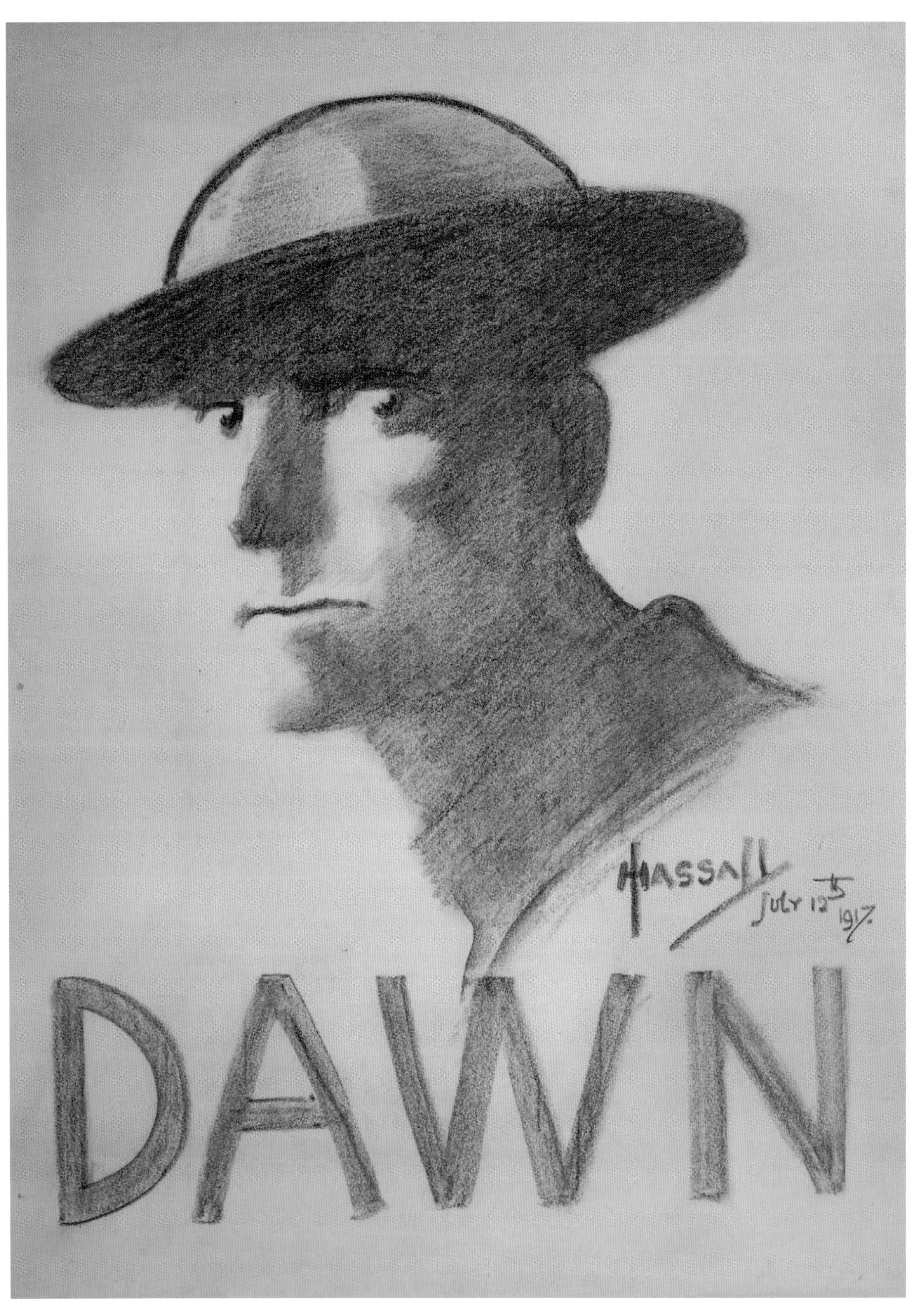

4 – John Hassall (1868-1948)
DAWN, 1917, signed inscribed with title and dated July 12, 1917,
Black chalk on paper, 32 x 23 in. (81 x 58.5 cm)

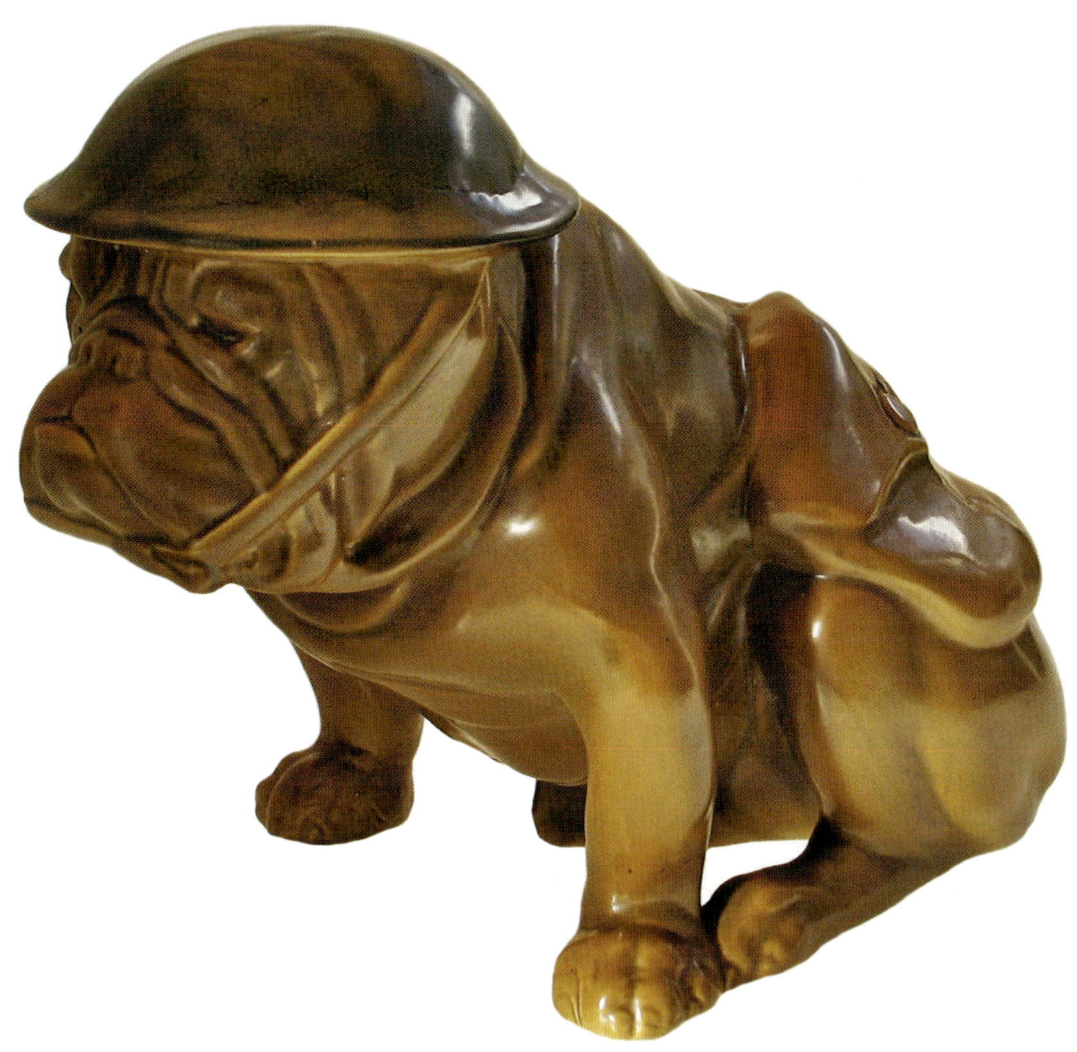

5 – Commemorative ware:
British bulldog wearing a Steel Helmet and equipment, 1917,
China, height : 6 ½ in. (15.5 cm), length: 8 in. (20 cm)

*   *   *   *   *

In 1971, the artist, designer and writer Barbara Jones (1912-1978) and collector Bill Howell published a book titled *The Popular Arts of the First World War*. (6) In the introduction, the popular arts are defined as 'the things that the ordinary people who were involved made for themselves or that were made in their taste'.[2] For the authors, this included posters and postcards, models and medals, crested china and brass work, war-toys and games and various forms of trench art. In her book *The Unsophisticated Arts*, 1951, Jones had already questioned the cultural heritage that attached greater value to 'academic art' (drawing, painting, printmaking and sculpture) over the 'arts of everyday life'.[3] In her radical exhibition of the same year, *Black Eyes & Lemonade*, she sought to provoke established ideas about museum and gallery culture, and the value attached to particular kinds of objects.[4]

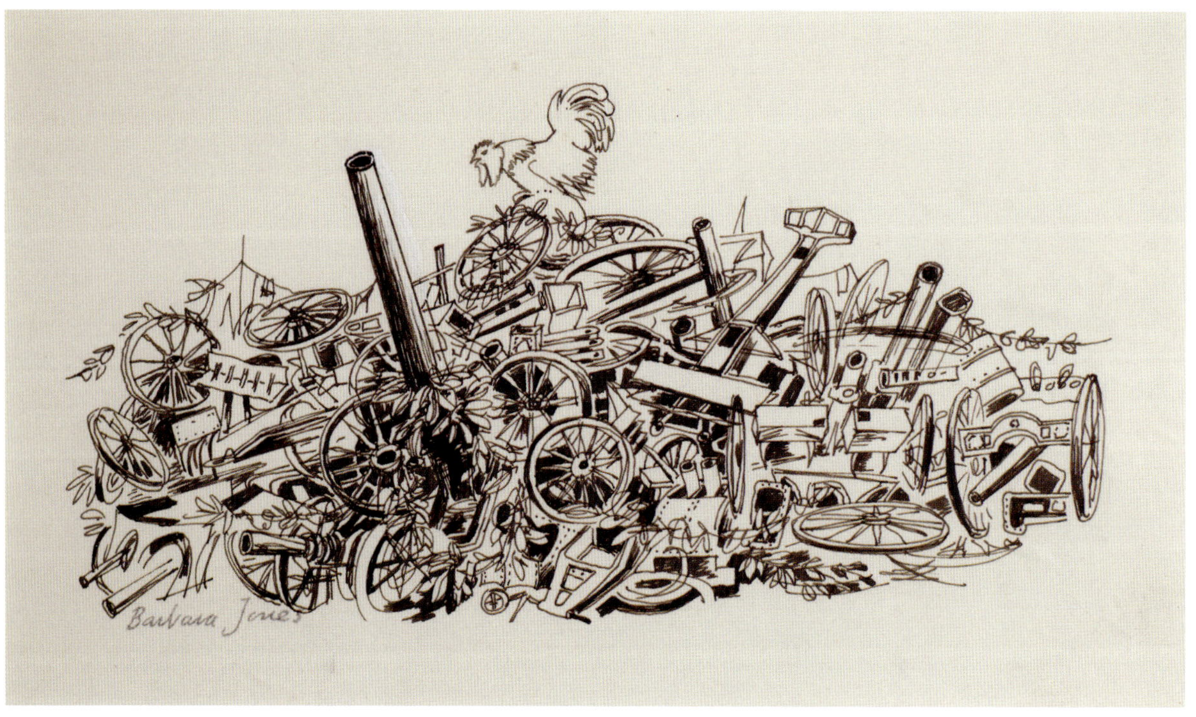

6 — Barbara Jones (1912-1978)
A pile of captured guns, aeroplanes and other detritus of war piled up in a Paris Street and crowned by a triumphant French cockerel, original drawing for *The Popular Arts of the First World War* (B. Jones & B Howell), c.1972, p.156, Pen & ink on paper laid on to card, 5 x 8 ⅝ in. (13 x 22 cm) sight size, provenance: the artist's studio

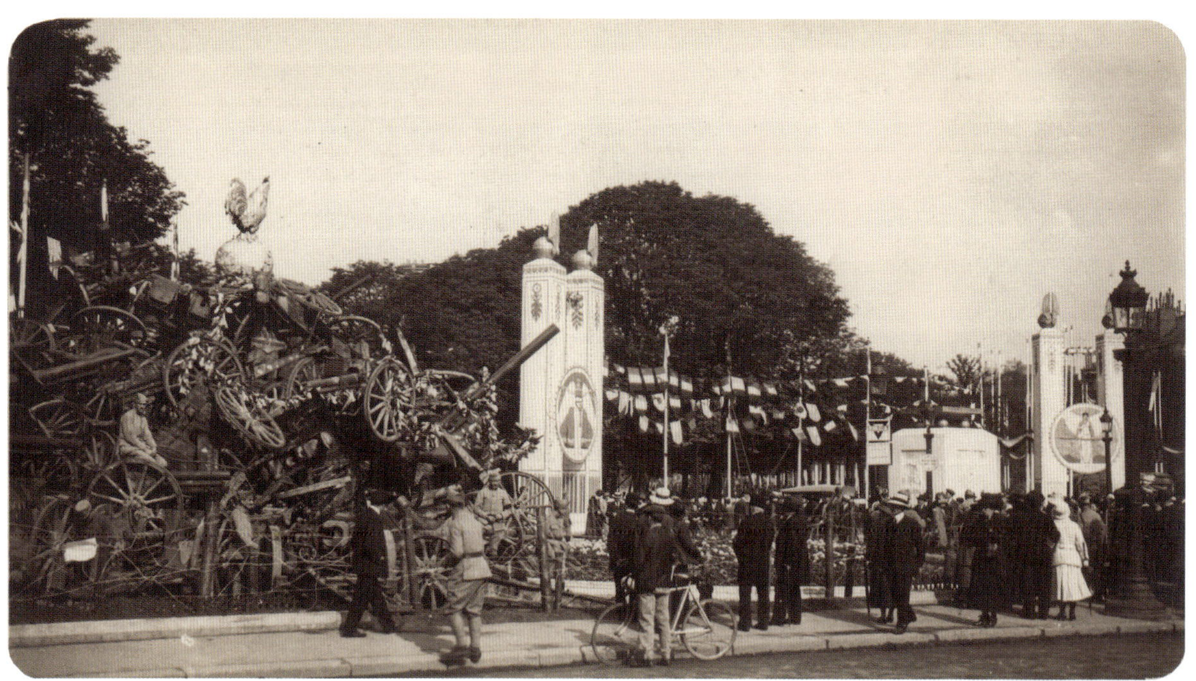

7 – The photograph which possibly inspired Jones' drawing, black & white photograph, 2 ½ x 4 ¼ in. (6.2 x 10.9 cm)

The general tone of *The Popular Arts of the First World War* is celebratory, and should be understood in the context of the wave of nostalgia that peaked in 1968, the 50th anniversary of the end of the war. In the English mass media, the war was portrayed as 'a popular melodrama in which causes were evaded and lessons concealed'.[5] Yet leafing through the pages of the book, it is, in part, possible to comprehend the authors' sanguine perspective, for so much of the popular arts of the First World War was created as a fantasy counterpart to reality and imbued with a gloss that obscured the war's terrible cruelty. According to the authors, this aspect of the popular arts, which served to channel public emotions along a different path, 'contained its own truths':

> 'If we set what they made beside the songs which Joan Littlewood collected in *Oh, What a Lovely War* and the slang and recitations that Eric Partridge and John Brophy recorded in *The Long Trail*, we begin to understand more of the Great War than if we only read the histories, visit museums or look at photographs and official paintings.'[6]

*　*　*　*　*

What role did art play during the Great War? During the early months of the war, the critic and writer Clive Bell (1881-1964) noted a general feeling of antagonism towards artistic practice: 'From every quarter comes the same cry – "This is no time for art!"'. Bell argued, however, that 'in times of storm and darkness it is the part of artists and philosophers to tend the lamp… because they alone can project their thoughts and feelings far beyond the frontiers of states and empires'.[7]

From early 1916, the notion that art could play a significant role in recording a nation at war began to gain currency. In May of that year, *The Times* published an editorial called 'Artists and the War' which questioned whether 'these great events and emotions in the midst of which we are living ought not to be left without being recorded in the best possible way'. There was a myriad of subjects to depict, such as 'the fighting line by day and night…the supply bases with their marvellous organization, there are the training-camps, the transport, the field dressing-stations, and a hundred other centres of interest varied and profound'.[8]

In that same month, Charles Masterman (1873-1927), head of the British War Propaganda Bureau situated at Wellington House, London, appointed Muirhead Bone (1876-1953) as Britain's first official war artist to provide eye-witness images intended for propaganda publications. When the Bureau was redesignated as the Department of Information in February 1917 it developed higher and more artistic aims, creating an official war artists' programme to chronicle every aspect of the conflict. In February 1918 the Department of Information became the Ministry of Information and under the direction of Lord Beaverbrook a British War Memorials Committee was established. This altered the direction and tone of official war art, to create a comprehensive legacy and a memorial collection of great art.[9]

The official war art schemes were an unprecedented act of government sponsorship of the arts. According to *A Concise Catalogue of Paintings, Drawings and Sculpture of the First World War 1914-1918* issued by the IWM in 1963, 'Specially Employed' war artists numbered 72 and a further 89, who served 'with the various forces' and were known as 'contributors', produced work which was purchased additionally under the official war art schemes.[10] By 1920, the combined war art schemes had resulted in the production of approximately 3000 contemporary paintings, drawings and sculptures.[11]

Official war artists had to conform to official requirements – on August 8, 1914 the Defence of the Realm Act (DORA) was passed which aimed to control the ways in which the war could be reported in pictures and words. However, works produced under the official war art schemes were varied in style and quality ranging from poetic evocations of the war to exacting factual records. Artists working independently had relative freedom to follow their own artistic and political agendas and by looking outside the frame of official commissions a greater understanding of the extent and diversity of artistic responses to war emerges. This catalogue takes an inclusive approach to war art, encompassing official war artists (Muirhead Bone, Richard Carline, Colin Gill, Eric Kennington, Spencer Pryse, Ellis Martin, Christopher Nevinson, Charles Pears, Charles Sims, Henry Tonks), 'contributors' (for example Edward Handley-Read, P.J. Hill, Ernest Procter) and the many artists who worked independently of the official government schemes (for example Rodo Pissarro, Mary Ethel Hunter, Stanhope Forbes, Ugo Matania).

Considering the work of unofficial artists raises interesting questions about the creative role of women and their response to the war. As Kathleen Palmer has shown, although several female artists were approached either by the British War Memorials Committee or the Ministry of Information, none of them completed commissions for the official schemes.[12] The Women's Work Sub-Committee (WWS), which had been set up at the end of the war to record the varied contributions of women to the war effort, did commission nine female artists, one photographer and several female sculptors. However, in the 1919 exhibition *The Nation's War Pictures* at Burlington House, of the 925 exhibits just 15 paintings and a small number of sculptural models were by women.[13] In the accompanying catalogue, Dorothy Coke and Anna Airy are the only female artists whose work is illustrated.[14]

Many female artists worked independently away from government aegis, responding to their experience of the conflict in powerfully individual works. Touring the towns and cities of France during the height of the war in 1917, Mary Ethel Hunter (1878-1936) has left a remarkable record of everyday life away from the Front. (8, 111). Margaret Wrightson (1877-1976) produced figures in bronze recording women's war work (142) and in 1922 received a commission for a remembrance and war memorial at Cramlington, Northumberland. In America, Clarence Underwood (1871-1929) produced some of the most evocative posters of the entire campaign. (138)

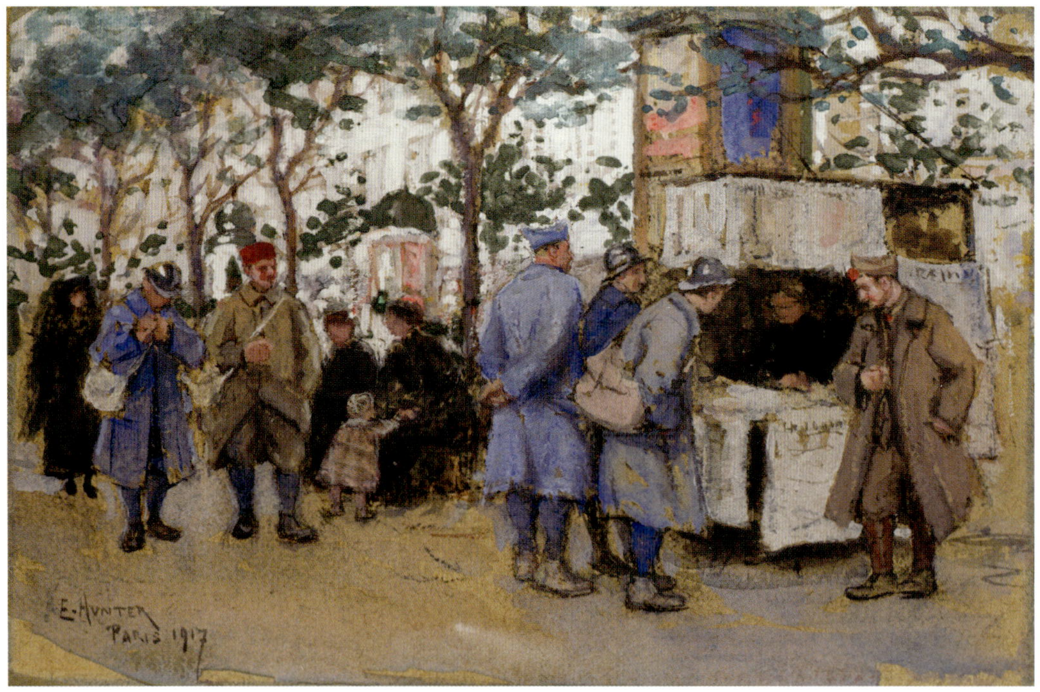

8 – Mary Ethel Hunter (1878-1936)
French soldiers and Bouquinistes along the Seine, 1917, signed, inscribed Paris and dated,
Watercolour on textured buff-coloured paper, 6 ¾ x 10 in. (17 x 25.5 cm)

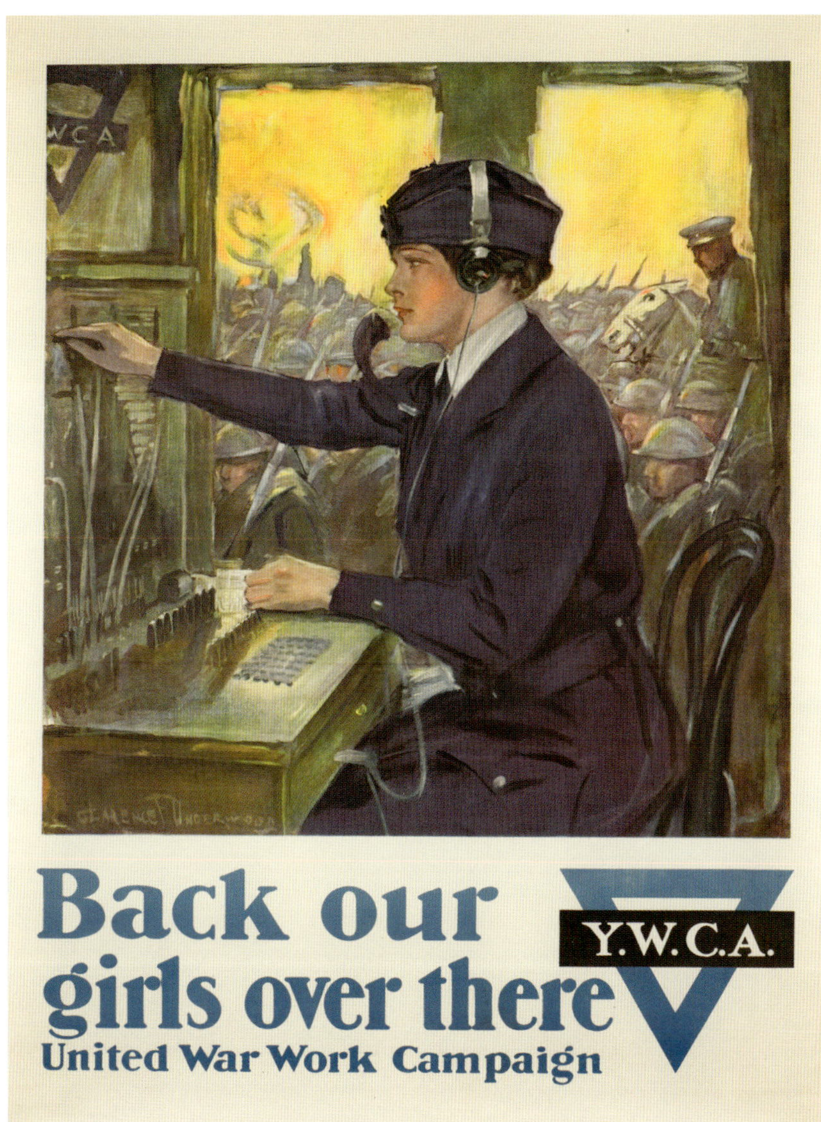

138 –
Clarence F. Underwood
(1871-1929)
Back our girls over there, 1918,
Signed in the plate,
Lithographic poster,
26 ⅝ x 19 in. (67.7 x 48.2 cm)
(see pages 160-161)

For all artists, the pressing question was how to find an appropriate language to represent the war. During the early months, Walter Sickert (1860-1942) had based his paintings, including *The Integrity of Belgium* (1914) and *Soldiers of King Albert the Ready* (1914) on newspaper photographs.[15] But as the war progressed, value was increasingly placed on the representation of immediacy and truthfulness, qualities which could only be in the grasp of those that had witnessed the conflict at first hand or had been present in its immediate aftermath. The paintings on war themes at the Royal Academy Summer Exhibition of 1916 were widely criticised:

> 'Whatever other merits these paintings may possess they are in no sense true war pictures...artists should be given the opportunity to see things with their own eyes and to bring their own emotional perceptions to bear upon the grim and noble realities of war, instead of being restricted to mere hearsay for their material.'[16]

Ugo Matania (1888-1979), along with his better known cousin Fortunino (1881-1963), contributed many pictures to the weekly 'War Numbers' issues of *The Sphere* between 1914 and 1919. (88) The editors valued the technical accuracy of the cousins' work in the knowledge that they had been given frequent access to the war zones in France and Belgium.[17]

In France, Le Rousseur claimed to be representing the frustration of the Poilus (French soldiers) with the lack of 'sincerity' in so many visual representations of the war:

> "To represent the war in both painting and literature one must have experienced it...one must have waded through mud, run beneath showers of shells; one must have heard the screams of the wounded, and witnessed the long rows of hideous corpses...only then is it possible to translate the sufferings, anxieties and failures of men thrown into the terrible ordeal of modern battle!"[18]

The series of lithographs by Pierre Abadie-Landel (1896-1972) depicting the delightful past-times of soldiers when off-duty, explores this notion with poignancy and sarcasm. (113)

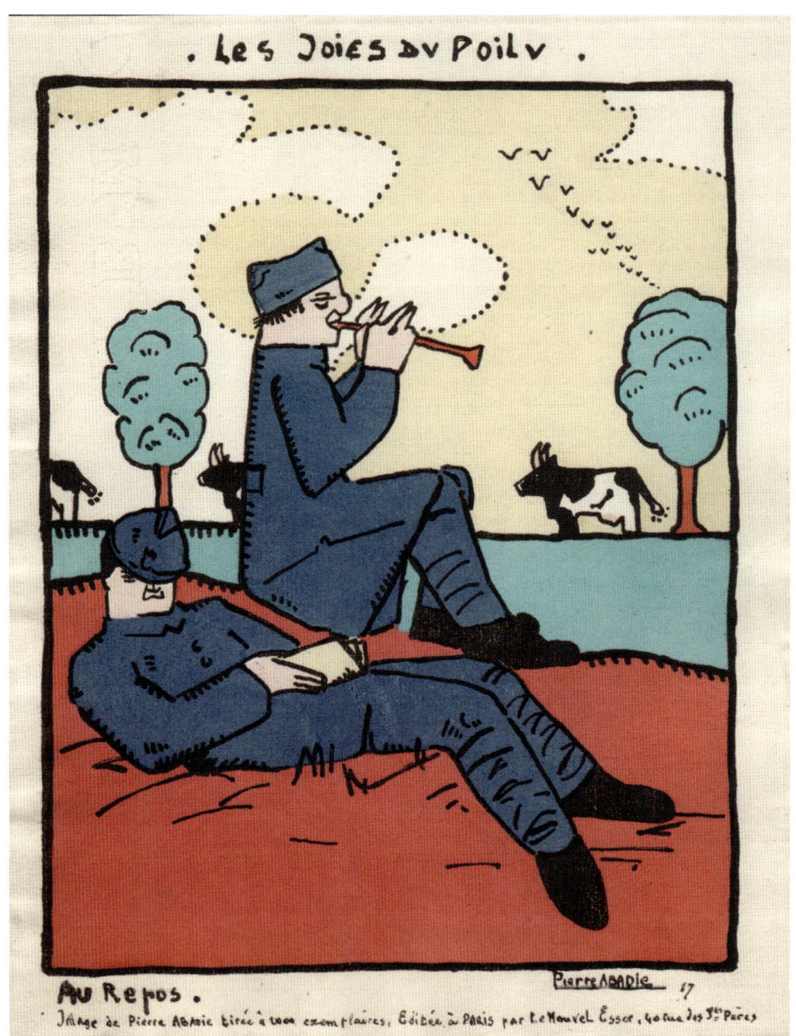

113 – Pierre Abadie-Landel
Les Joies du Poilu
[The Pleasures of the Poilu],
Au repos, 1917
Lithograph,
12 ¼ x 9 ¾ in. (31.1 x 24.7 cm)

(see pages 136-137)

Many artists responded to their experience of war with individual allegorical images intended to broaden meaning beyond the particular event to a wider context. Often melancholic in mood, painters frequently made use of religious and mythological references to disguise hidden and sometimes controversial meanings. In his maquette for an altarpiece, Percy Jowett (1882-1955), who served with the Royal Garrison Artillery and suffered shell shock, explores the theme of sacrificial love set between the wider dichotomy of physical death and nostalgic notions of chivalry. (9) The sombre and ravaged landscape sits adjacent to the fertile hills beyond which, along with tufts of green grass around the Crucifix, promise renewal after the devastation of war. In Hal Hurst's (1865–1938) *The Hero* (1915), Christ carries the dead soldier away from the flames of destruction to spiritual rejuvenation symbolised by a golden light. (49) In war poetry of the period, the Crucifixion was often symbolically identified with the sacrificial deaths of the soldiers. In her poem 'What the Moon Saw' (1914) Olive Lindsay wrote, 'Christ in the field? Yea, many Christs'.[19] The imagery of the Crucifix was also used symbolically by artists as evidence of the futility of war. In *Canadian Observation Post* (1920) (Canadian War Museum), Colin Gill's harrowing scene of exhausted and shell shocked soldiers is dominated by a fallen crucifix. Writing about his statue *Risen Christ* (1917-20) (National Galleries Scotland), Jacob Epstein explained that 'it stands and accuses the world of its grossness, inhumanity, cruelty and beastliness, for the World War and for the new wars'.[20] By identifying the war dead with Christ's sacrifice and other devices such as blasted trees, artists could challenge the rules of censorship which forbade the depiction of dead British or Allied troops. In November 1917, the War Office famously forbade Nevinson to exhibit or reproduce his painting *Paths of Glory* portraying dead Tommies.

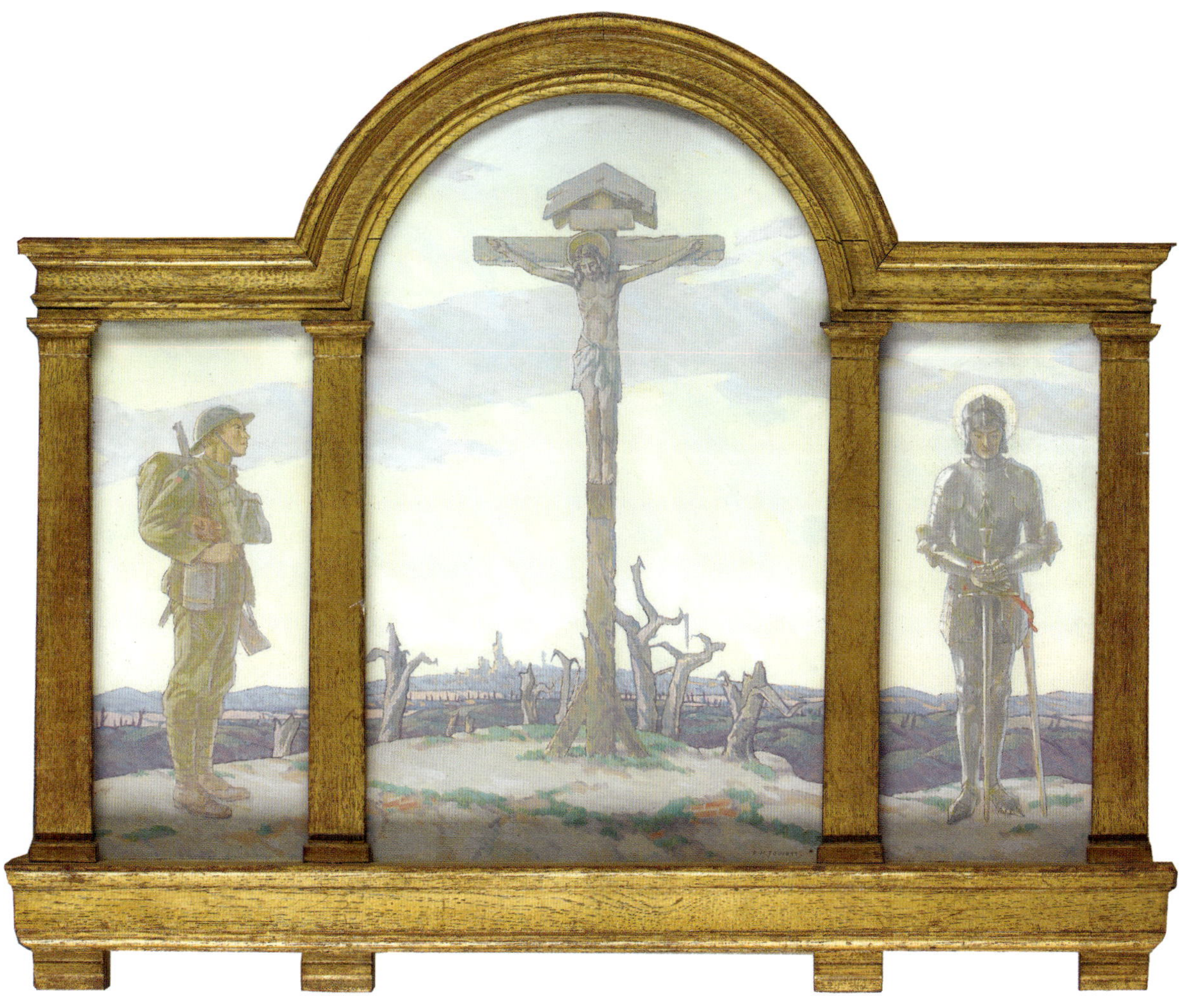

9 – Percy Jowett (1892-1955)
England (triptych), c.1918, tempera on board, 25.2 x 29.9 in. (64 x 76 cm) overall

In the years leading up to the war, radically new ideas and practices in the visual arts had been introduced into Britain through a series of key exhibitions in London, notably Roger Fry's two Post-Impressionist exhibitions at the Grafton Galleries (1910-11, 1912), Italian Futurist Painters at the Sackville Gallery (1912) and Post Impressionist and Futurist Exhibition at the Doré Gallery (1913).[21] The spirit of bellicosity and aggression that characterised the European

Avant-Garde was seen to be articulated in Britain by the Vorticist group headed by Wyndham Lewis and in the Futurist paintings of Christopher Nevinson. With the outbreak of war, the burgeoning Modernist movement was dealt a heavy blow by the suspicion that it was anti-patriotic, even anti-British and there was a widespread return to earlier conventions as people looked to traditional and reassuring values. 'You would think', Wyndham Lewis wrote in 1915, 'that the splendid war army of England were fighting to reinstate the tradition of Sir Frederick Leighton".[22]

However, if the radical language of the Modernist avant-garde seemed out of step with the country's mood, the formal experimentation of pre-war British modernism could be seen as an appropriate way of conveying the increasingly destructive narrative of modern total war. Reviewing the exhibition of *The Nation's War Pictures* at Burlington House (1919-20), C. J. Holmes, the Director of the National Gallery, considered that the war had heralded 'the arrival of a new artistic movement' and praised as more relevant the 'decorative experiments' and

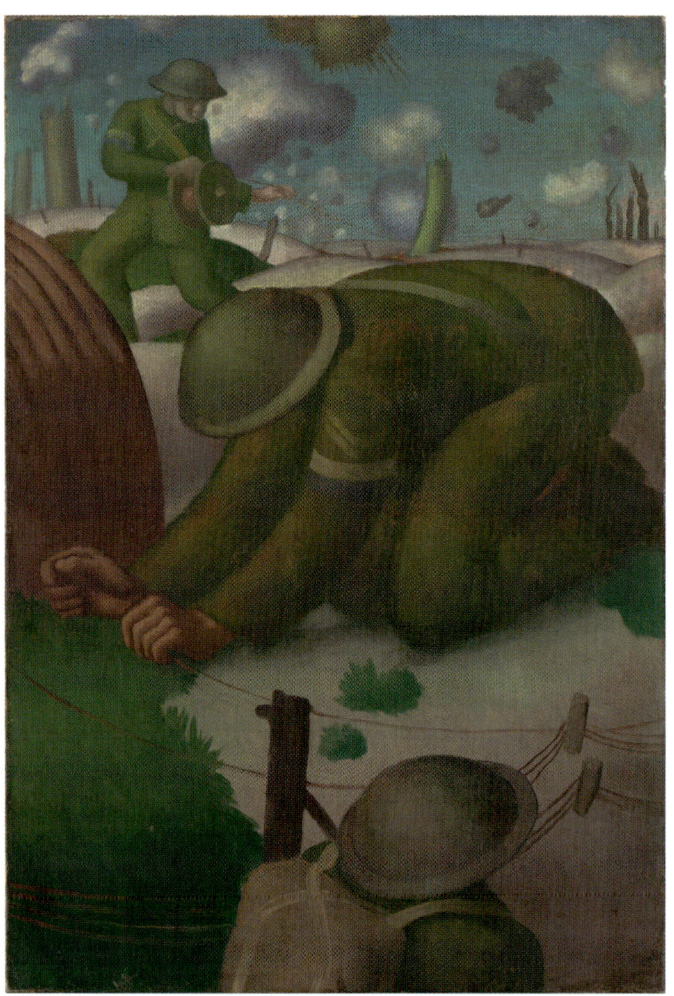

72 – Colin Gill (1892-1940)
Laying Telephone Wire, c.1918,
Oil on canvas, 24 x 16 in. (61 x 40.7 cm),
(see pages 90-91)

'pictorial beauty' of the works by the younger and more radical artists above the more traditional representations of war.[23]

These dual approaches, avant-garde and reactionary, modern and traditional, are evident in the works in this catalogue. Colin Gill's *Laying Telephone Wire* (c.1918), depicting crouching soldiers laying new lines of communication through a desolate war-torn landscape, makes use of decorative design motifs to incorporate a modernist vocabulary. (72) In *Ypres after the 1st Bombardment* (1916),

Christopher Nevinson (1889-1946) conveys the feeling of abandoned desolation and random destruction in what the *Manchester Guardian* referred to as a 'Futurist experiment on a lucid basis of realism'.[24] (101) These works contrast with the traditional treatment of Spencer Pryse's *Retreat from Ypres 1917* that draws on the 19th Century tradition of processional battle scene painting. (64) For his series of lithographs titled *Autumn Campaign* (1914), Pryse, an officer decorated for his service in the trenches, insisted on working *in situ* as the battle raged around him. This allowed him to produce what he described as 'an exact record of particular events, not embellished in any way'.

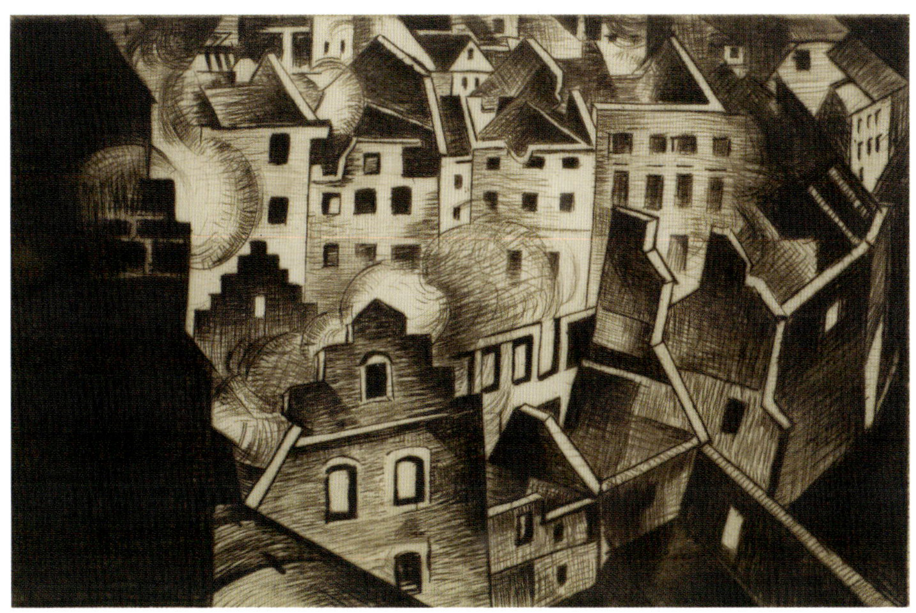

101 – Christopher Richard Wynne Nevinson (1889-1946) (see pages 118-119)
Ypres after the 1st Bombardment, 1916, signed in pencil,
Drypoint print on watermarked cream laid paper, 6 x 9 in. (15 x 22.5 cm)

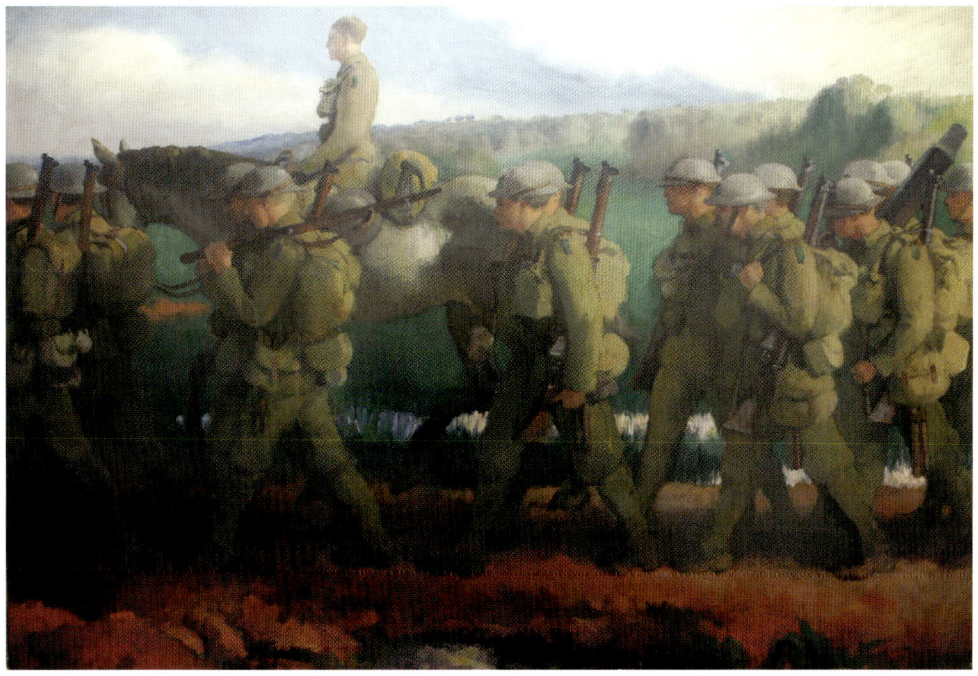

64 – Gerald Spencer Pryse, M.C. (1882-1956) (see pages 81-83)
The Retreat from Ypres, c.1917, oil on canvas, 42 x 50 in. (106.7 x 127 cm)

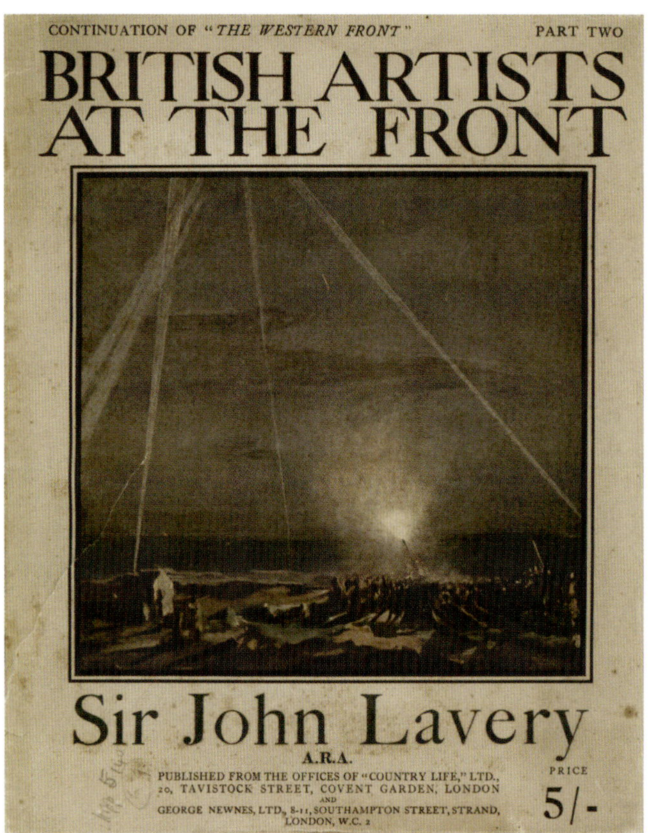

10 – Cover of one of the publications from *Country Life's* series *British Artists at the Front*, 1916-17, 12 ⅜ x 9 ⅜ in. (31.6 x 23.8 cm)

War artists' work achieved recognition through a series of prominent wartime exhibitions, many of which took place at commercial galleries.[25] When the DOI commissioned 18 artists to produce 66 propaganda lithographs under the collective title of *Britain's Efforts and Ideals*, they were exhibited at the Fine Art Society before touring the provinces and appearing in shows in Paris, New York and Los Angeles. Images were additionally widely circulated through reproduction. In 1916 and 1917, *Country Life*, 'with the permission of the War Office', editioned over two hundred of Muirhead Bone's drawings in a ten-part series titled *The Western Front*. (45, 52, 79, 152, 153) In 1918, the work of Nevinson, Paul Nash, Kennington and Lavery was reproduced in a further *Country Life* series of publications called *British Artists at the Front*. (10)

Official war artists were contractually obliged to allow their work to be used as the commissioning bodies saw fit. Other artists, in allowing their images to be widely exhibited and reproduced, displayed their patriotism and desire to help the war effort. This mass reproduction of pictures using the purely photomechanical means of offset lithography (first introduced commercially by I. W. Rubel in 1904) resulted in an unprecedented circulation of images during the war. Frank Brangwyn (1867-1956) produced a large number of posters, leaflets, advertisements and stamps for a variety of charitable and propaganda causes.[26] (42, 102, 130) In 1916, Bone gave permission for his drawings to appear not only on a set of postcards, but also as transfer printed designs on a set of plates. This transmutation of imagery contributed to a further blurring of the traditional demarcations that defined the fine and popular arts.

This evolution is particularly noticeable in the field of poster design. Posters were produced by government institutions, private organizations and individuals and were the result of collaborations between artists, designers, printers and advertising agents. Posters were produced on a vast scale, ranging from special editions commissioned by the DOI from established fine artists drawing directly onto the lithographic stone and editioned in small numbers,

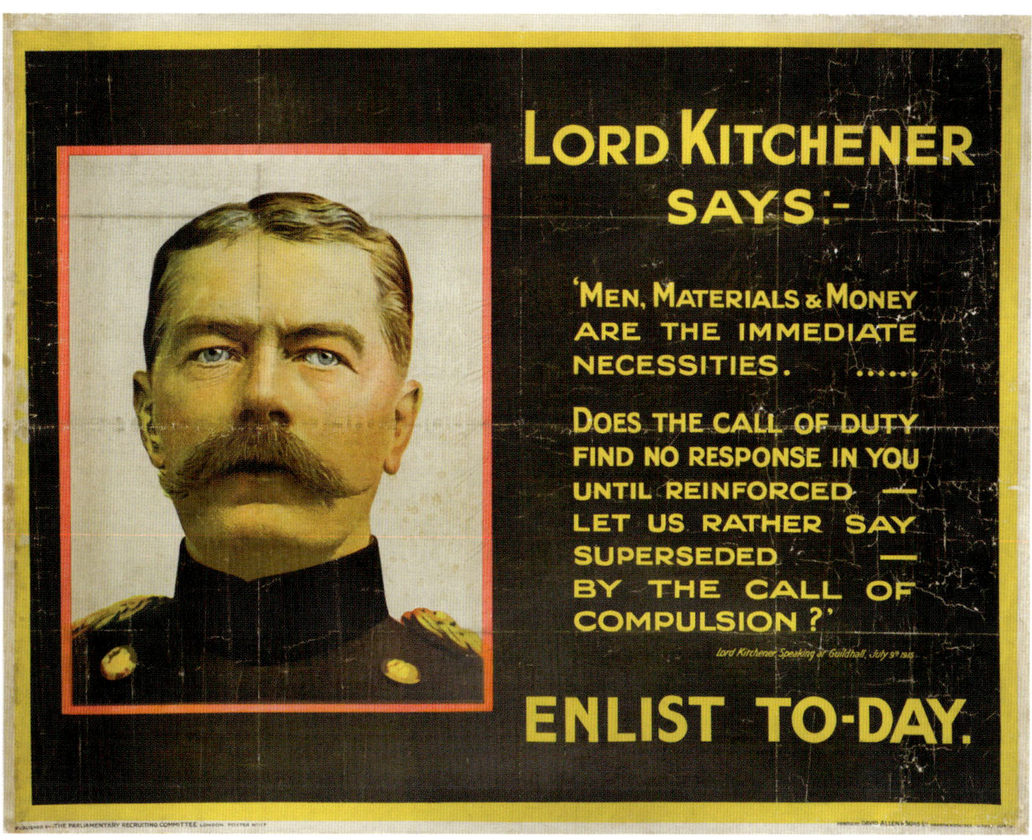

129 – English School, *Lord Kitchener Says... Enlist Today*, 1915, (see page 152)
Lithographic poster, 40 x 50 inches (102 x 127 cm), printed by David Allen & Sons,
Published by The Parliamentary Recruiting Committee, London, poster no 117

to photomechanically mass-produced anonymous images. The creators of some of the most
familiar wartime posters are today unknown – the image on the celebrated poster 'Lord Kitchener
Says Enlist Today' is produced from a photograph by Alexander Bassano, but the designer of the
poster remains unidentified. (129)

By the time war broke out, the poster was already well established as a powerful advertising tool
and artistic medium. The nations which participated in First World War issued posters to inspire,
inform and persuade, communicating notions of patriotism and service to a mass audience. In
his book, *War Posters issued by Belligerent and Neutral Nations* (1920), Martin Hardie, a former
Captain in the Infantry, recorded the important role played by posters in First World War history:

> "They had their story to tell and message to deliver. Their business was to waylay
> and hold the passersby and to impose their meaning upon them."[27]

Certain themes in posters were exploited by different countries, such as the need for recruitment
in the British Empire before 1916, and in the USA during the call for volunteers in 1917. (See
'Propaganda', pages 148-159) In countries where conscription existed (France, Austria, Germany)
recruitment was not such a pressing need, and posters were aimed at other aspects of the war such
as finance. (41, 80, 170, 171) As the war dragged on, all countries launched massive campaigns
for 'Liberty Loans', 'Emprunts de la Defense Nationale' or 'Kriegsanleihe'. Mythicized or mythical
figures were used as national symbols: Uncle Sam for the United States, John Bull and Britannia
for England, Marianne and Joan of Arc for France. After the war, the theme of reconstruction was

widely developed, particularly in France, to promote building activity and to encourage farming on lands that had been lain to waste. (154)

Imagery of life at the Front and the military deployment of modern technology were counterbalanced by images of rural life and the family. *L'Emprunt National 1918*, (11) with its picturesque portrayal of haymaking, conveys the ideal world remote from the trenches that soldiers believed they were fighting to preserve. By glorifying the common soldier, factory and agricultural worker or housewife, posters motivated the military and civilian populations to participate in the war.

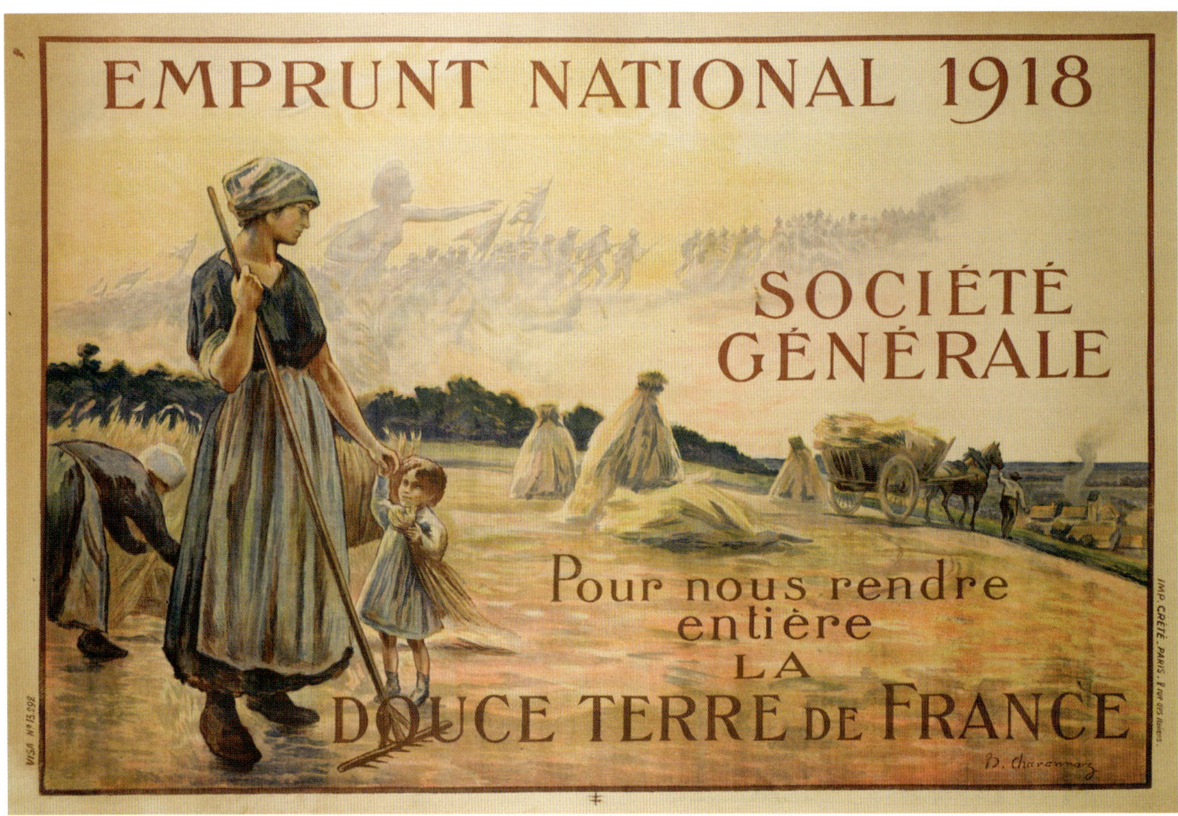

11 – B. Chavannaz
EMPRUNT NATIONAL 1918 SOCIÉTÉ GÉNÉRALE – Pour nous rendre entière la douce terre de France,
Lithographic poster, 31 ⅜ x 47 in. (79.7 cm x 119.3 cm), printed by Imprimerie Crété, Paris

The iconography of women in posters reflects the complexity of their dual roles during the war. They can be represented as traditional mothers and wives and damsels in distress, but also as nurses, telephone operators, drivers, agricultural and factory workers. Posters depicting women were used as part of the recruitment campaign. In the iconic 'Women of Britain say Go!', published by the Parliamentary Recruiting Committee, the women of Britain, who are portrayed as defenceless and in need of protection, incite their men to enlist (see page 29). Many posters reinforced traditional gender roles by portraying women as old-fashioned mothers and wives protecting the values of the home in the absence of sons and husbands. Posters such as 'The Kitchen is the Key to Victory Eat Less Bread' equate women's role as housekeeper to the contributions of men in the line of fire.[28] Many posters, however, persuaded women to leave behind the traditional realm of the home to take up an active role by serving through relief organisations such as the Young Women's Christian Association or the Red Cross, through government jobs in industry and on the land. The Y.W.C.A.'s poster 'For Every Fighter a Woman Worker' classifies the working woman as 'our second line of defence'. (140, 141)

Photography played an important role in poster design (146), but was also widely used in its own right for surveying and mapping territory, for official photographs and for personal mementoes. As early as September 1915, a writer in *The Manchester Guardian* recognised the importance of the photograph to both the war effort and the historian:

> 'In the aeroplane the present war has seen a new arm perfected and placed at the service of the Commander-in-Chief; in the camera the historian of the war, present and future, has found an ally as new and as valuable to his own task. The multitude of photographs which have been taken since August last have dealt with every phase and front of this tremendous struggle, and while many of them have been, perhaps, of merely transitory interest, a great proportion have constituted a quite irreplaceable record of historical detail which could have been secured in no other way.'[29]

As Jane Carmichael has explained in her book *First World War Photographers*, there were three categories of photographer during the war: official, press and amateur.[30] The role of official photographers was to compile authorized material to document the conflict both on the battlefields and on the Home Front. Their photographs reflect the planning, censorship and continuous need to generate public support for the war. On the Western Front, official photographers were usually integrated into the army and while their photographs were subject to censorship, they were assured a wide distribution in the home press and in propaganda material, as well as providing official military records. (12) Horace Nicholls (1867-1941) was appointed as 'official photographer of Great Britain' in July 1917, and produced a memorable series of scenes on the Home Front, primarily in munitions and ordnance factories.

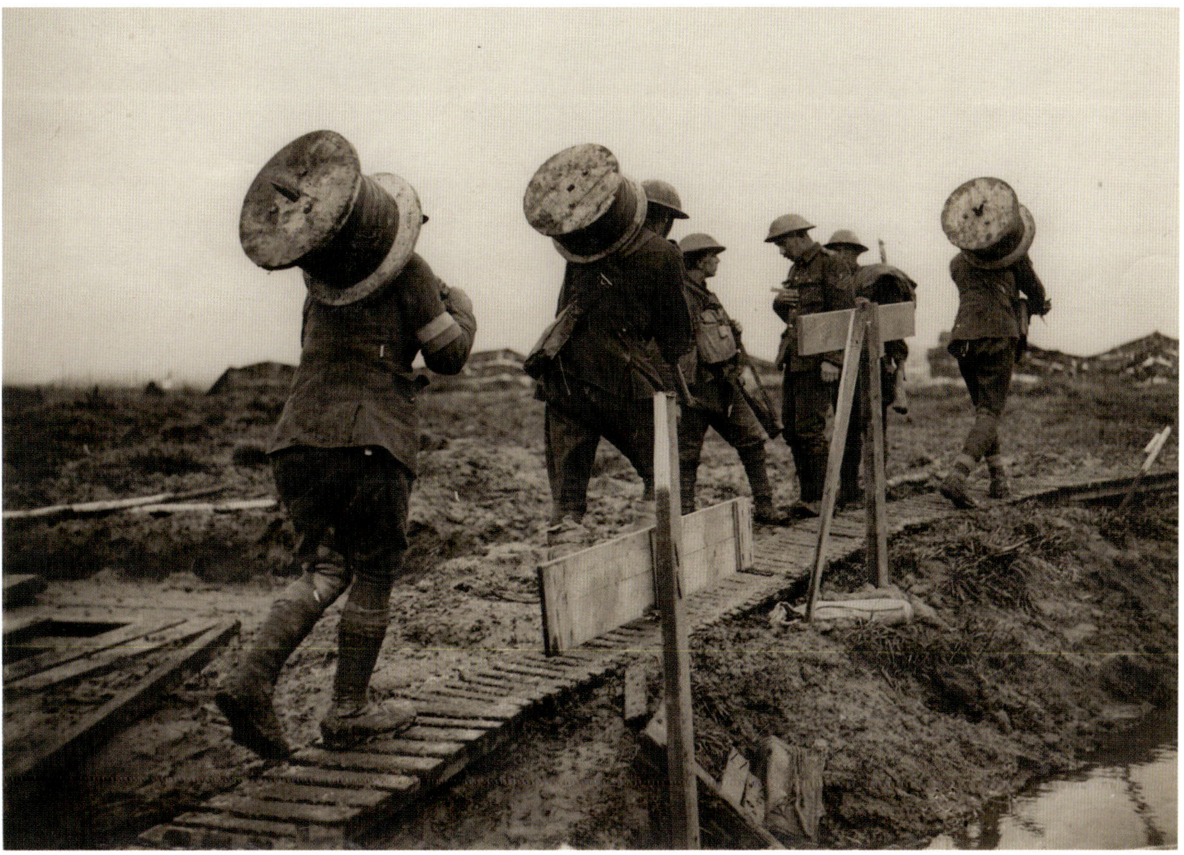

12 – Official photograph taken on the Western Front
"D 2114. The Battle of the Bridges. Telegraph wire going up for No Man's Land. Signallers on the way to establish communications.", black & white photograph, 6 x 8 in. (15.2 x 20.3 cm)

In France La Section Photographique de l'Armée (S.P.A.), founded in 1915 by Le Ministère de la Guerre, produced a vast number of photographs depicting the different Fronts, French victories, official celebrations and views of ruins, many of which were published and sold in albums for the price of one franc.

Press photographers tended to be anonymous and their work was rigorously restricted, especially in the zones of recent combat. As a result, many turned their attention to civilian activities in support of the war effort. The war inspired a wave of amateur photography as Officers and some soldiers took advantage of recently introduced portable and relatively affordable Kodak cameras to record their daily lives.[31] (13) While the legacy of the public image of war has proved more lasting, amateur photographs, where they have survived, can provide a more personal and faithful insight into war. The photographs of Charles Lansiaux (1855-1939), recently exhibited at Les Galeries des Bibliothèques de la Ville de Paris, show a vision of Paris far removed from the patriotic spirit so evident in French official photography.[32]

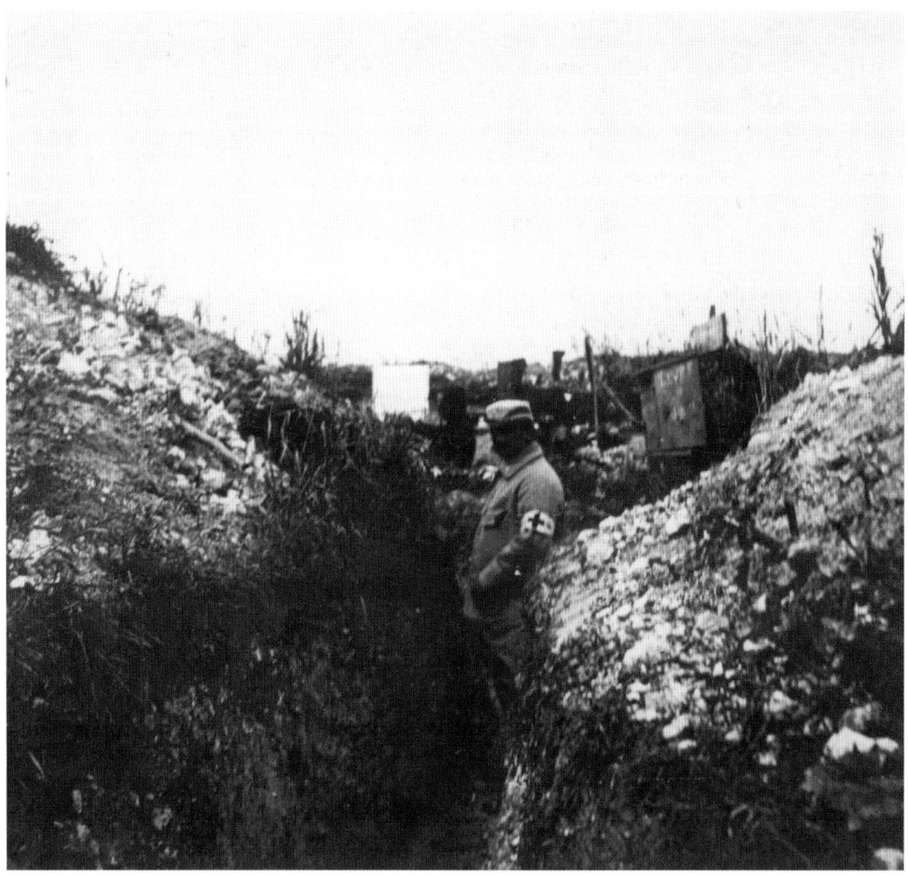

13 – Letterbox to the right of a soldier in one of the trenches,
Black & white photograph, 3 ½ x 6 ⅝ in. (8.8 x 17 cm)

While the higher end of the British press preferred to maintain their literary traditions, the more popular press welcomed the inclusion of photographs, using the half-tone process developed in the 1880s which allowed high quality photographs to be mass printed.[33] Throughout the war, the shortage and poor quality of photographs from the frontline was a consistent problem for newspapers trying to fulfil the public's voracious appetite for the latest images of the conflict and they offered handsome sums for amateur photographs. In April 1915, for example, *The Daily Mirror* advertised, '£1,000, £250 and £100 for the first, second and third most interesting war photographs from amateurs received and published between now and July 31'.[34]

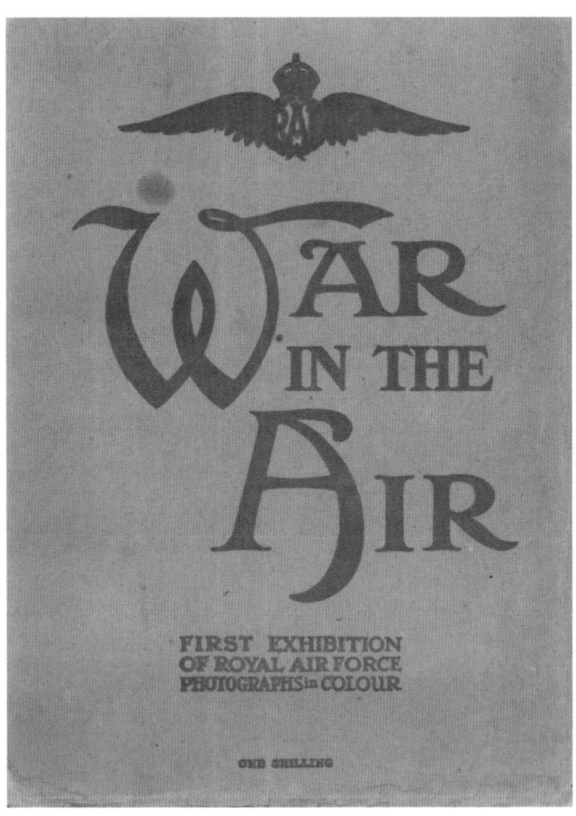

14 – *War in the Air, First Exhibition of Royal Air Force Photographs in Colour*, c.1918, 11 ¾ x 8 ⅜ in. (29.7 x 21.5 cm)

During the course of the war, the number and circulation of illustrated journals exploded, as people attempted to glean a more tangible sense of life at the Front. In England, *The War Illustrated, A Record of the Conflict of the Nation*, was first released in August 1914 and regular issues continued throughout the war. In France, the circulation of the weekly *Le Miroir de la Grande Guerre*, which was entirely illustrated with photographs, increased from 300,000 in 1914 to 1,000,000 in 1918. There was also a great demand for photographic souvenirs. Companies like Stevenard in Dunkirk and G. Lelong in Amiens began producing postcards and stereoscopic prints of official photographs and in England in 1918 the Photographic Bureau of the Ministry of Information opened a shop selling official photographs to the public.

Exhibitions of war photographs proved extremely popular with the public. The Royal Air Force's exhibition of aerial photographs, *War in the Air* (1918) attracted visitors with the claim that they would witness 'the story of the giant strides made in airmanship …which reads like a romance'.[35] (14) The exhibition of war photographs at the Grafton Galleries in March 1918 was planned 'for the purpose of bringing before the British peoples a vivid record of the work of our troops on all fronts in the world war'. In addition to the general public, the exhibition was also widely visited by soldiers on leave, 'who seemed amazed at the photographs, which one of them quaintly described as "better than oil paintings"'.[36]

During the First World War, the cinematograph as a media of war reporting and propaganda was recognised by the Government early in the conflict. In 1915, the British Topical Committee for War Films, sponsored by the War Office, was established with Charles Urban as its chairman. On December 29, 1915 Urban's documentary film, *Britain Prepared*, was released and showed the extent of Britain's contribution to the war effort in Allied countries. In August 1916, *The Battle of the Somme*, using the film footage of the cinematographers Malins and McDowell, went on view nationwide and as the first cinematographic document of actual fighting on the Front it had an enormous impact.[37] H. D. Girdwood was another photographer and cinematographer who in July 1915 was given permission to film on the Western Front. His film *With the Empire's Fighters*, showing the Indian Corps in action, was shown to the public in September 1916. In 1908 Girdwood had set up a company called Realistic Travels to distribute stereoscopic prints. One of these shows Girdwood discussing cinematography with the Prince of Wales. (15)

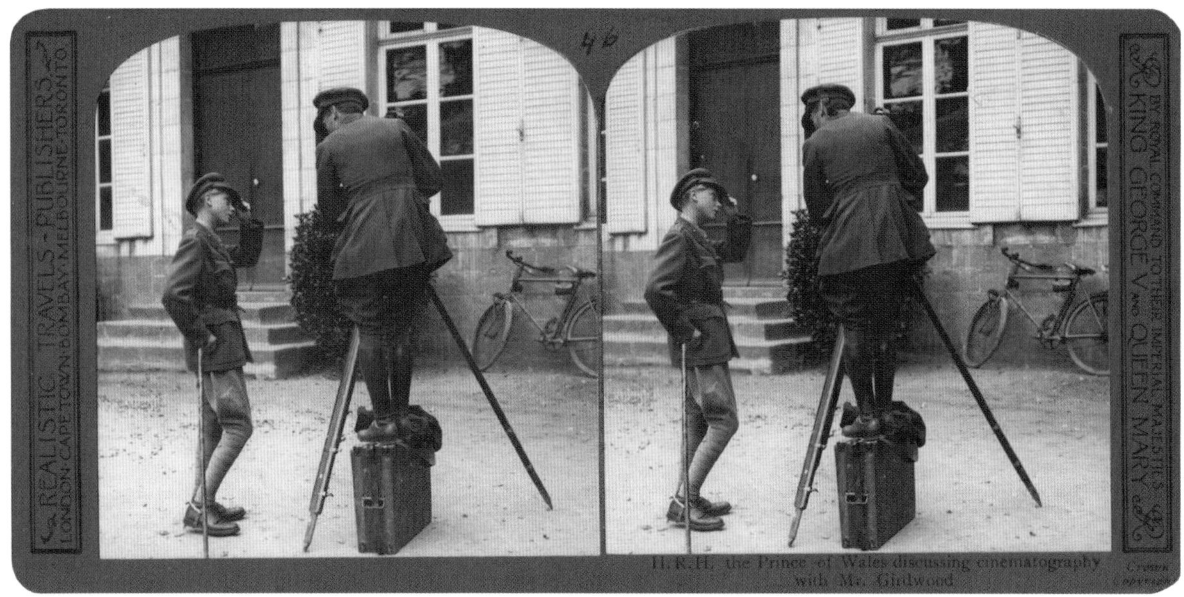

15 – Stereoscopic print: *H.R.H. the Prince of Wales discussing cinematography with Mr. Girdwood.*, 3 ½ x 7 in. (9 x 18 cm), published by Realistic Travels

The picture postcard was by far the most dominant visual medium through which the First World War was perceived. It is also perhaps the art form whose value for historians of the war has been the least explored. The artist Richard Carline, who was employed as an Official War Artist, wrote in his book *Pictures in the Post* (1959):

> 'With the outbreak of the Great War in 1914, when the cinematograph was still in its infancy, and broadcasting belonged to the distant future, the picture postcard proved of immense service in keeping up the spirits of the people, in reinforcing the messages carried by posters and in recording the events of the war'.[38] (16, 44)

During the period 1895-1915, which has been called 'the golden age of the picture postcard', between 200 and 300 billion postcards were produced and sold worldwide.[39] From the earliest days of the war, as millions of individuals became separated from their families and home communities, the postcard became a popular and rapid way of corresponding: Le Bureau de la Poste Militaire in France alone handled more than 1.5 million postcards per day during the period of the war. As a result of this demand, 250,000 workers were employed in the production of postcards in France, with a further 50,000 women working from home hand-colouring the cards.[40]

Postcard publishers were quick to seize the opportunity presented by the war and used a mixture of drawing, photography and photomontage to adapt their postcards to the culture of conflict. Regardless of nationality, postcard imagery explored shared themes: patriotism, victory, sacrifice and sentimentality. Heads of state, politicians and military leaders were celebrated as victorious heroes while ordinary soldiers were depicted dreaming of home or their loved ones, receiving medals or engaged in acts of heroism. Women are portrayed in the traditional roles of mother, lover and protector, while children represent both bravery and suffering. Models frequently borrowed the heroic poses and iconography previously associated with history painting. The use of tanks, incendiary shells, guns, aeroplanes and boats as decorative motifs represent the increasing mechanisation of war, while the frequent depiction of the trench is used to symbolise the troglodyte life of the soldier. Many of the early French and British cards lampooned the Germans and Kaiser Wilhelm in particular (28), and depicted Germany as a country outside the community of civilized nations. These were soon banned when it was 'discovered that when such productions have been found on prisoners or wounded soldiers they have...rendered themselves liable to summary treatment, and in some cases they have been maltreated or even shot'.[41]

While exploring similar themes, postcards could reflect differing attitudes and national mood sand as a result resonate deeply individual cultural meanings. British postcards, for example, were less sentimental and understated, and gently humorous, whilst French postcards were heavy in sentiment, frequently emphasising the solidarity of the Allies. On erroneously receiving a French postcard in August 1915, a man from Perth complained that British postcards were dull in comparison:

> 'The French Government goes one better than ourselves to a Field Army post card. The British one is now well-known brown khaki, that of France a nice stiff white card with the whole of the flags of the Allies in monogram'.[42]

When in 1916 a Russian tobacconist in Leeds was accused of selling indecent wartime postcards, he complained 'I am a Russian and I take a different view of these things to an Englishman'.[43] (17)

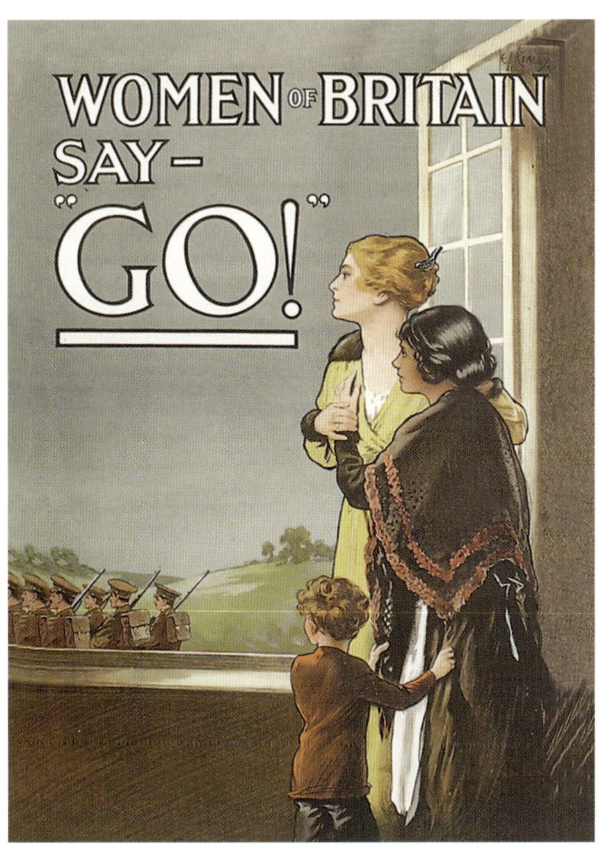

16 – Postcard version of poster : *Women of Britain Say "GO"*,
5 ½ x 4 ¼ in. (10.8 x 13.7 cm)

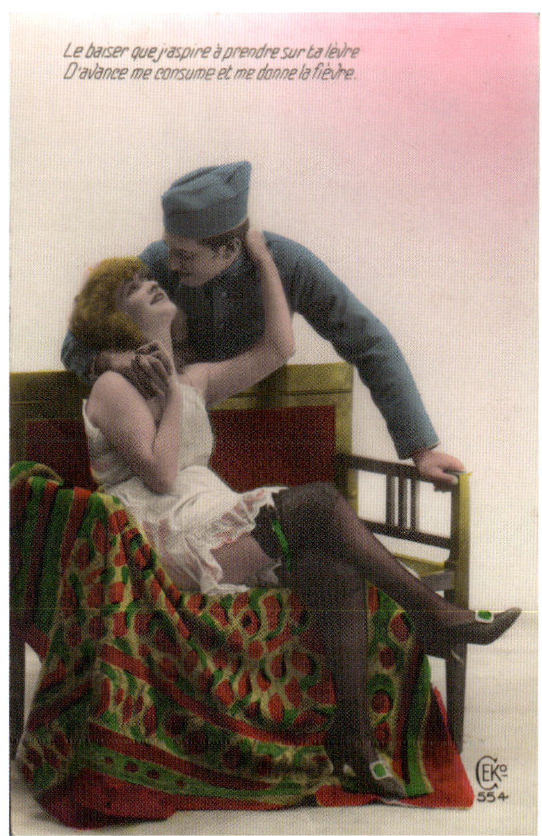

17 – French postcard – *Le baiser que ...*
5 ½ x 3 ½ in. (8.7 x 13.7 cm)

In their use of photomontage to create a fantastical wartime scene, often combining the opposing and unlikely themes of caring sentiment with weapons of destruction, postcards anticipate the photomontage art works of Berlin Dada. Indeed, Raoul Hausmann, the co-founder of the group in 1918, argued that photomontage was 'a mirror wrenched from the chaos of war and revolution, as new to the eye as it was to the mind'.[44] With their ambiguous meanings, these picture postcards convey, perhaps as strongly as any of the visual media produced during the war, the degree to which normal points of reference had become obscured in the chaos of destruction. A German soldier lies dead as a French nurse comforts the wounded hero under the inscription 'Pour l'Humanité!'. (18); Meowing kittens look adoringly on as a *Poilu* embraces his loved one in a trench-like void. (19)

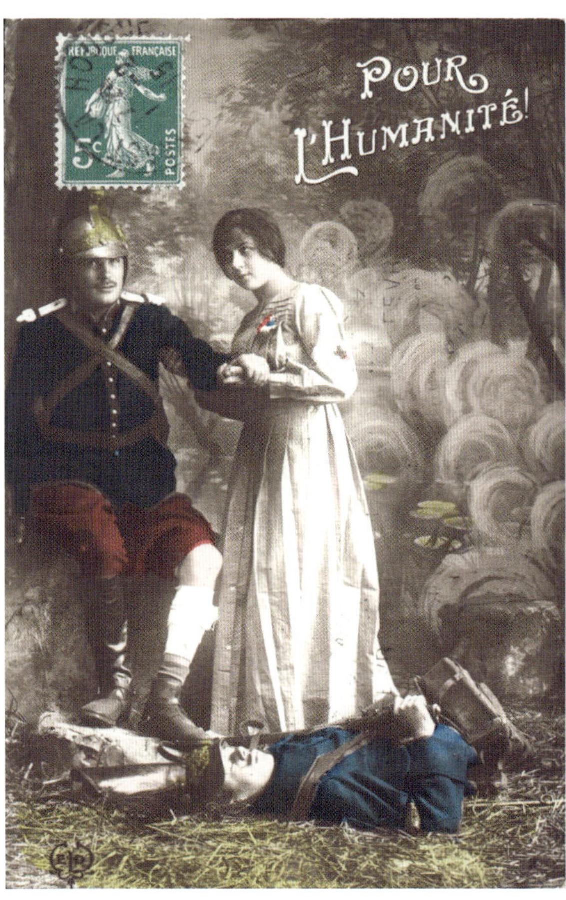

18 – French postcard
Pour l'Humanité!
5 ½ x 3 ½ in. (13.7 x 8.7 cm)

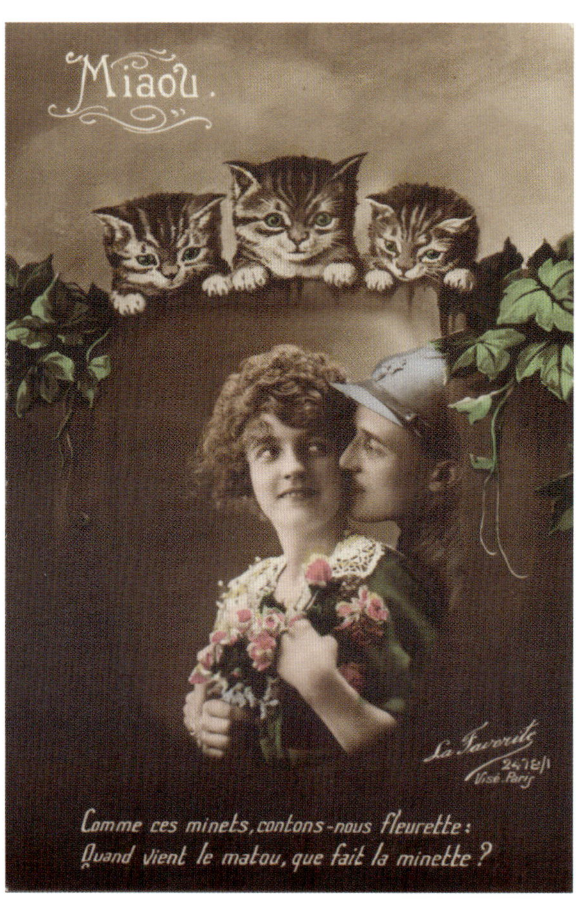

19 – French postcard – '*Miaou*'
Comme ces minets, contons-nous fleurette:
Quand vient le matou, que fait la minette?
5 ½ x 3 ½ in. (13.7 x 8.7 cm)

Because the war was such an integral part of everyone's life, almost any representation of it was automatically popular. In 1917 *The Bystander* gave Grimwades of Stoke permission to produce Bruce Bairnsfather's *Fragments from France* cartoons on a range of pottery including butter dishes, teapots and tobacco jars. (20) These were an immediate success, and thousands of pieces were produced during the remainder of the war. Other potteries produced tanks, guns, patriotic busts and figurines of the heroes and villains of war. Some had a sinister aspect, such as Carlton's Savoy China Grotesque, depicting a conscientious objector. (157) At the end of hostilities, there was an outpouring of mugs, bowls and plates bearing emblems of peace. (175)

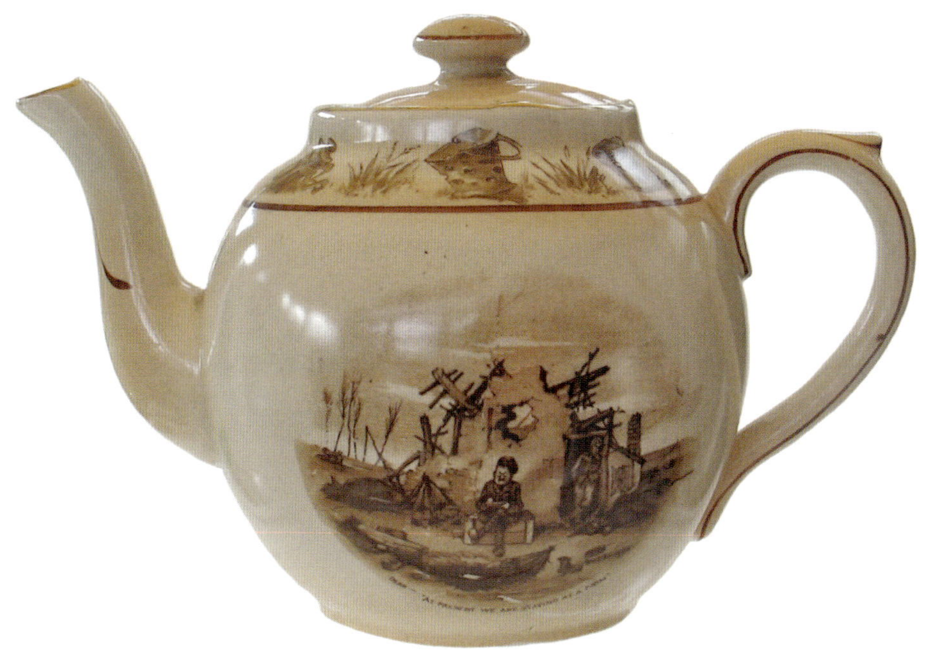

20 – Bairnsfather Ware *(Fragments from France)*, teapot, 8 x 6 ½ in. (20 x 16.5 cm),
Transfer reads: "Dear... 'At present we are staying on a farm.'"

For children, games and puzzles (21) that reflected the latest war events filled the shelves in toy shops, the most popular of which were *Spy!* and *Trench Football*, the latter including Allied and German political and military characters. Sweetheart brooches, many made of precious metals, precious stones and colourful enamels were given by servicemen to their loved ones as keepsakes.

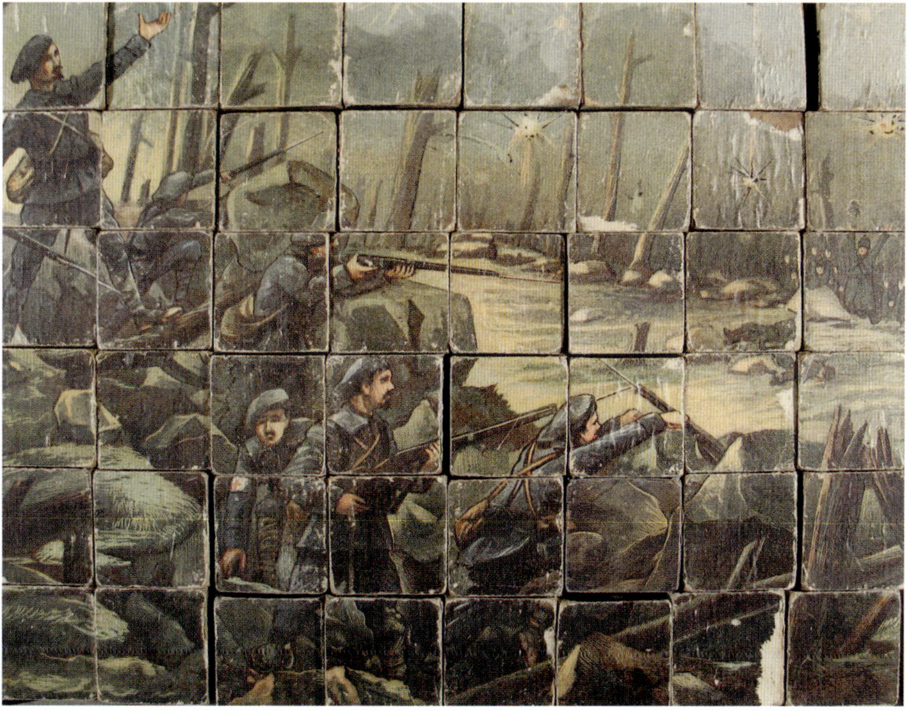

21 – Block Puzzle of a First World War French battle scene,
Wood and printed paper, 10 x 13 ½ in. (24.5 x 34.5 cm)

War mementoes crafted by soldiers, civilians, the wounded and prisoners of war from battlefield debris or pieces of military equipment are loosely categorized as 'trench' and 'commemorative' art. Shells and bullet casings were frequently decorated, and everyday objects such as lighters, cigarette boxes (22), jewellery boxes, walking sticks as well as military figurines and religious objects were crafted. While some of the objects are simple and relatively crude others, produced by skilled craftsmen, goldsmiths, engravers, coppersmiths etc., demonstrate a high degree of aptitude. For many, creating these objects was a reminder of a pre-war occupation and as such helped to preserve a feeling of self and humanity in a war that increasingly dehumanised men.

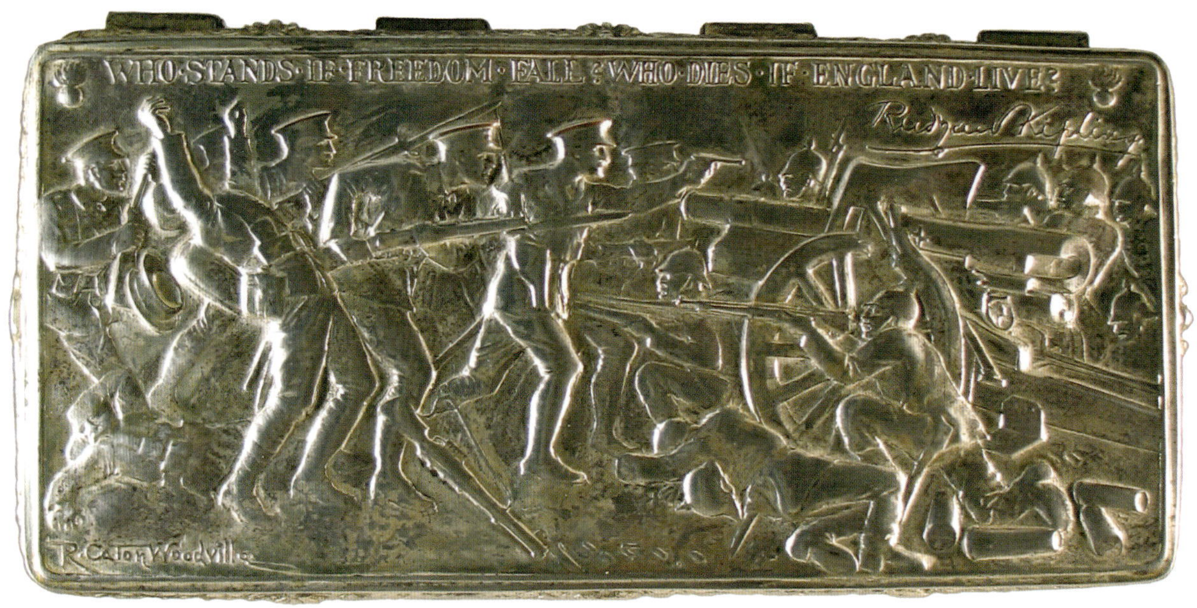

22 – Silver plated Cigarette Box, 1916-17,
On lid: a relief of a battle scene after Richard Caton Woodville with portrait heads of Allied leaders around the sides.
Inscribed with a quote from Rudyard Kipling's poem, "For all we have and are" (1914),
Inscribed on base "Wallacefield Auxiliary Hospital, Croydon. 1916 – 23rd October – 1917."
7 ½ x 3 ½ x 2 in. (19 x 9 x 5 cm)

* * * * *

The visual imagery of the First World War is loaded with meaning. Not only do the images say much about the people who created them and their own personal response to the war, but also about the lives of the men, women and children immersed in the unfolding drama. During the war, the rich and diverse visual media, which was promoted through exhibitions and publications or for sale as collectibles, shaped the attitudes of a war generation desperately searching for meaning in the midst of a cataclysm that even then was hard to comprehend. In January 1918, the *Pottery Gazette* commented that 'it is almost inevitable that most people will want to put by pieces of this [Bairnsfather] ware as a reminder to their children and children's children of the most stressful period in the world's history'.[45]

ENDNOTES

1 *Manchester Guardian*, November 10, 1928.

2 Barbara Jones & Bill Howell, *Popular Arts of the First World War,* (London: Studio Vista, 1972), p.7.

3 Barbara Jones, *The Unsophisticated Arts,* (London: Architectural Press, 1951).

4 *Black Eyes and Lemonade*, an exhibition of popular art, opened at the Whitechapel Art Gallery in the summer of 1951 as part of the Festival of Britain.

5 David Kunzle, Review, 'Popular Arts of the First World War by Barbara Jones; Bill Howell', *The Art Bulletin*, Vol. 55, No. 4 (Dec. 1973), p.647.

6 Barbara Jones & Bill Howell, p.167.

7 Clive Bell, 'Art and War', *International Journal of Ethics*, vol. 26, no.1 (Oct., 1915), p.8.

8 *The Times*, May 5, 1916.

9 The paintings commissioned by the British War Memorials Committee were intended for a Hall of Remembrance devoted to 'fighting subjects, home subjects and the war at sea and in the air'. In the event, because of lack of funding after the war, the Hall of Remembrance was never built, and the collection of paintings was given to the IWM.

10 *A Concise Catalogue of Paintings, Drawings and Sculpture of the First World War 1914-1918*, IWM Catalogue, 1963, pp.332-336.

11 Sue Malvern, *Modern Art, Britain and the Great War*, (Paul Mellon Centre for Studies in British Art: 2004) p.13.

12 Kathleen Palmer, *Women War Artists*, (London: Tate Publishing, 2011), p.2.

13 ibid.

14 *War Pictures, Official Illustrated Record*, (Exhibition catalogue issued by the authority of the IWM, 1919).

15 Paul Moorhouse, *The Great War in Portraits*, (NPG exhibition catalogue 2014), p.78.

16 Anonymous Slade School student, *UCL Union Magazine*, May 1916, p.275.

17 Paul Gough, *A Terrible Beauty, British Artists in the First World War*, (Bristol: Sansom & Co. Ltd., 2010), p.44.

18 Le Rousseur, 'Les dessins de la guerre', *Le Crapouillot*, 2e année, IX, avril 1917, p7.

19 Quoted in Nosheen Khan, *Women's Poetry of the First World War*, (Kentucky: University Press of Kentucky, 1988), p.51.

20 Jacob Epstein, *Epstein, An Autobiography*, (New York: Arno Press, 1975), p.102.

21 For a full chronology of the modern art exhibitions that took place in London during this period, see A. G. Robins, *Modern Art in Britain, 1910-1914*, (London: Merrell Holberton in association with Barbican Art Gallery, 1997), pp.181-185.

22 Wyndham Lewis, *Blast*, no.2, July 1915, p.23.

23 *Manchester Guardian*, December 12, 1919.

24 *The Observer*, March 14, 1915.

25 These include the Leicester Galleries, The Agnew Galleries, The Goupil Gallery and the Fine Art Society. For more on war time exhibitions, see Sue Malvern, pp.37 and 41.

26 Libby Horner, *Brangwyn at War*, (London: Horner & Goldmark, 2014).

27 Martin Hardie and Arthur Sabin, *War Posters Issued by Belligerent and Neutral Nations 1914-1919*, (London: A & C Black, 1920), p.4.

28 This poster, published by the Ministry of Food, is in the collection of the IWM no. 6541.

29 *The Manchester Guardian*, September 3, 1915.

30 Jane Carmichael, *First World War Photographers,* (Oxford: Routledge, 1989), p.1.

31 For the restrictions imposed on amateur photography, see ibid. p.11.

32 *La guerre au quotidian, Photographies de Charles Lansiaux*, Galerie des bibliothèques de la Ville de Paris, January 15 - June 15, 2014.

33 Jane Carmichael, p.V.

34 *Daily Mirror*, April 9, 1915.

35 *War in the Air,* (Exhibition catalogue, Royal Air Force, 1918), p.1.

36 *The Times*, March 1, 1918.

37 Paul Moorhouse, pp.38-42.

38 Richard Carline, *Pictures in the Post*, (London: Gordon Fraser, 1971), p.113.

39 Bjarne Rogan, 'An Entangled Object: The Picture Postcard as Souvenir and Collectible, Exchange and Ritual Communication' in *Cultural Analysis*, Volume 4, 2005, p.1.

40 I am grateful to Marc Lefebvre for this information.

41 *The Manchester Evening News*, December 4, 1914.

42 *The Perthshire Advertiser*, August 11 1915.

43 *The Liverpool Echo*, October 31, 1916.

44 Raoul Hausmann (1931), 'Photomontage', in C. Phillips (ed.), *Photography in the Modern Era*, (New York: Aperture 1989), p.179.

45 *The Pottery Gazette*, January 1918.

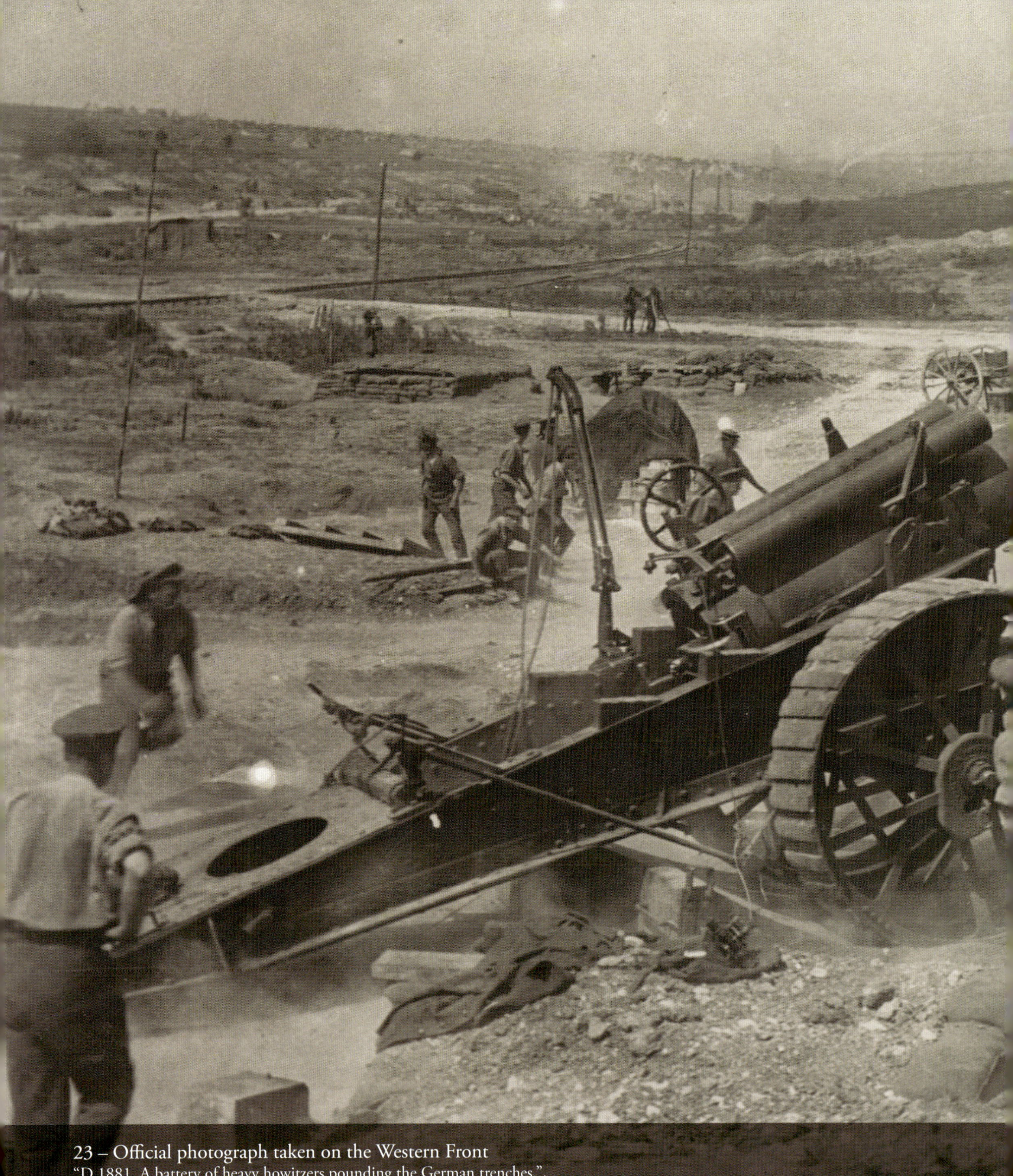

23 – Official photograph taken on the Western Front
"D.1881. A battery of heavy howitzers pounding the German trenches.",
Black & white photograph, 6 ⅝ x 8 ½ in. (17 x 21.6 cm)

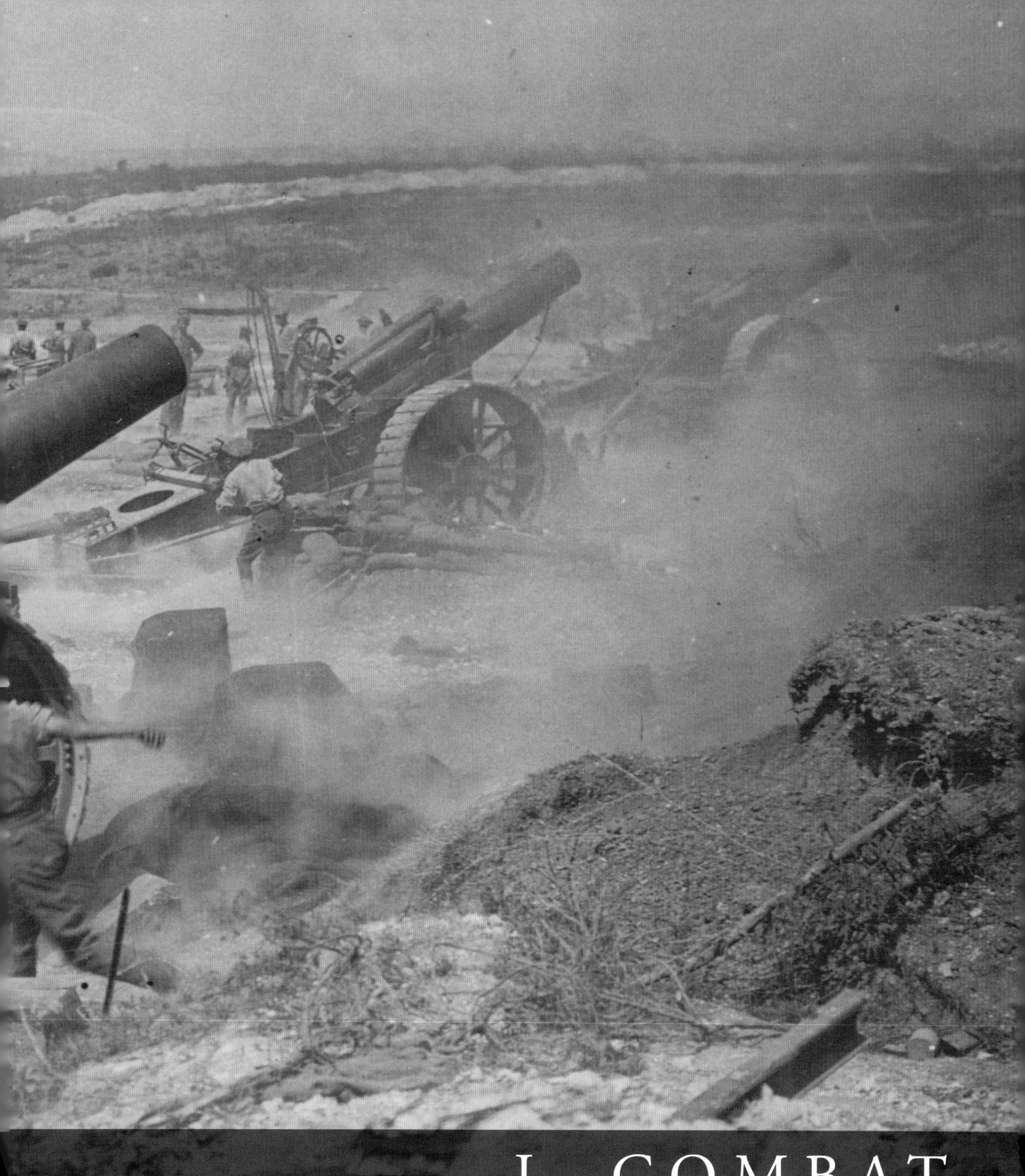

I COMBAT

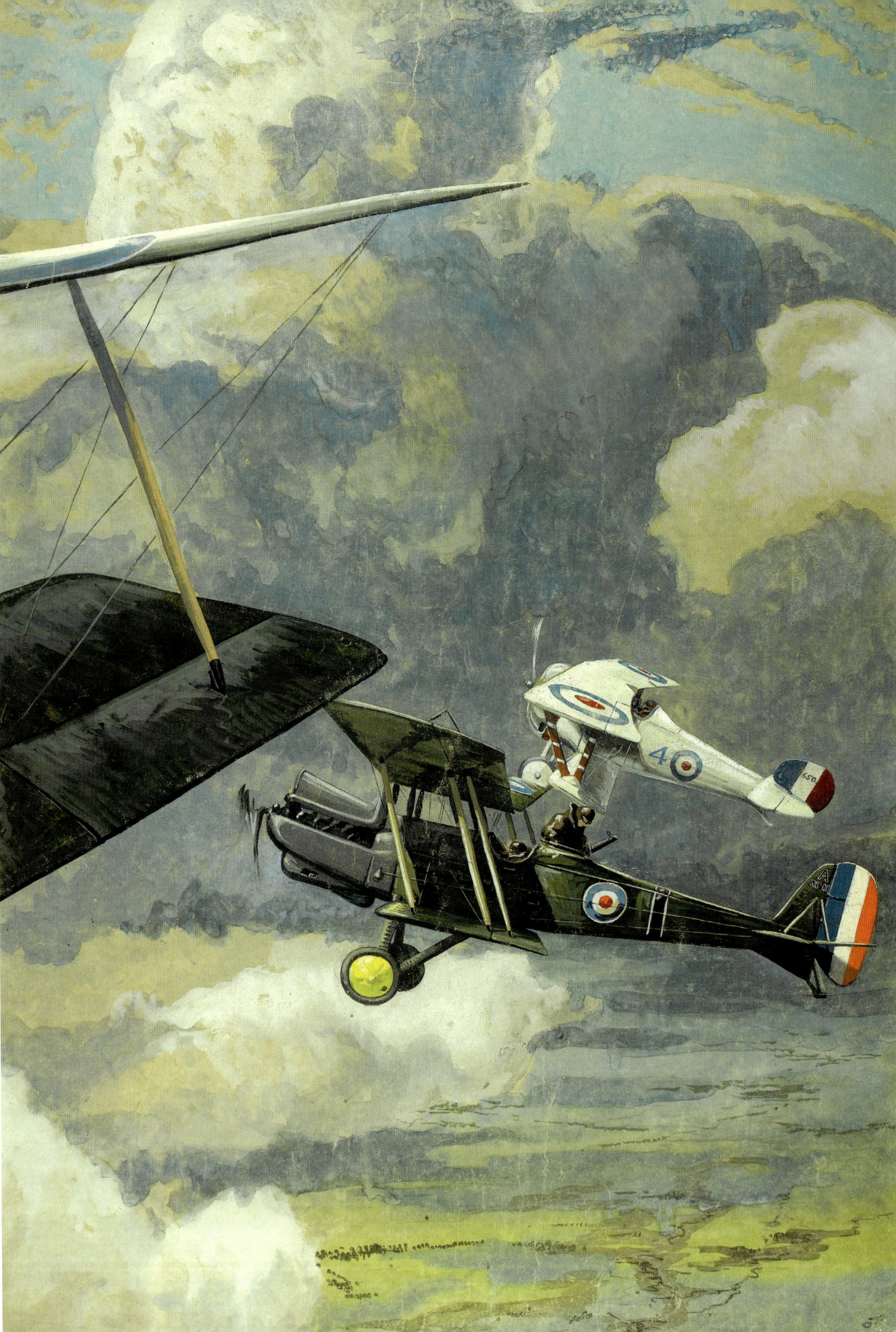

"Won't it be nice when all this beastly killing is over, and we can enjoy ourselves and not hurt anyone? I hate this game."

Captain Albert Ball, RFC, 'the Ace of English Aces', in a letter to Flora Young, May 5, 1917.
He died in action the following day.

"The heavens were the grandstands and only the gods were spectators. The stake was the world, the forfeit was the player's place at the table, and the game had no recess. It was the most dangerous of all sports and the most fascinating. It got in the blood like wine. It aged men forty years in forty days. It ruined nervous systems in an hour."

Elliott White Springs, U.S. Air Service, quoted in *US Air Services*, Volume 13, (1928)

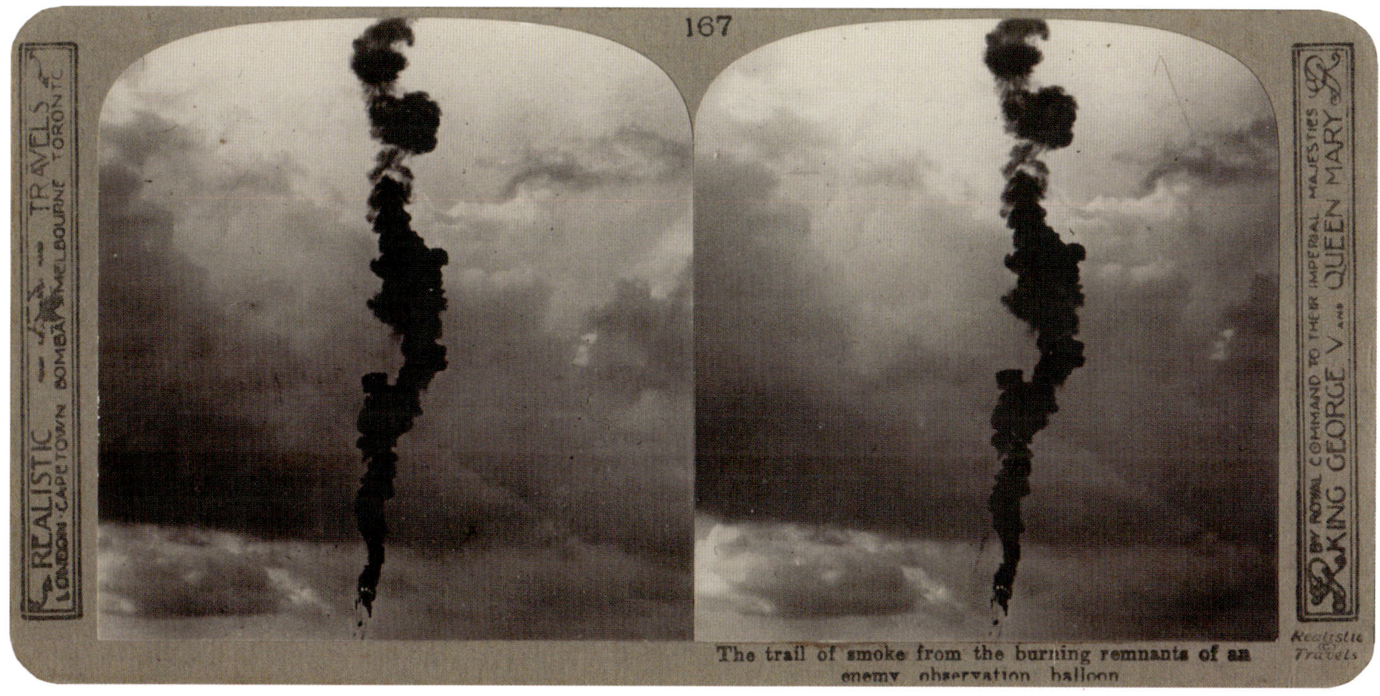

25 – Stereoscopic print: *The trail of smoke from the burning remnants of an enemy observation balloon.*
3 ½ x 7 in. (9 x 18 cm), published by Realistic Travels

24 – Lt. Richard Barrett Talbot Kelly (1896-1971)

An RE8 with a French Nieuport 27 fighter escort, c.1916,
Signed with initials, watercolour on paper, 40 ½ x 27 in. (103 x 68.5 cm) Provenance: The artist's daughter
This composition shows a British RE8, (a two-seat biplane reconnaissance aircraft), with a black band on the fuselage, escorted by a cream coloured Nieuport 27 (a French fighter aircraft).
Similar compositions by Kelly are in the collection of the RAF Museum, Hendon, though this is his largest recorded work. In 1980 *'A Subaltern's Odyssey' - A Memoir of the Great War, 1915-1917* was published based on Talbot Kelly's diaries.

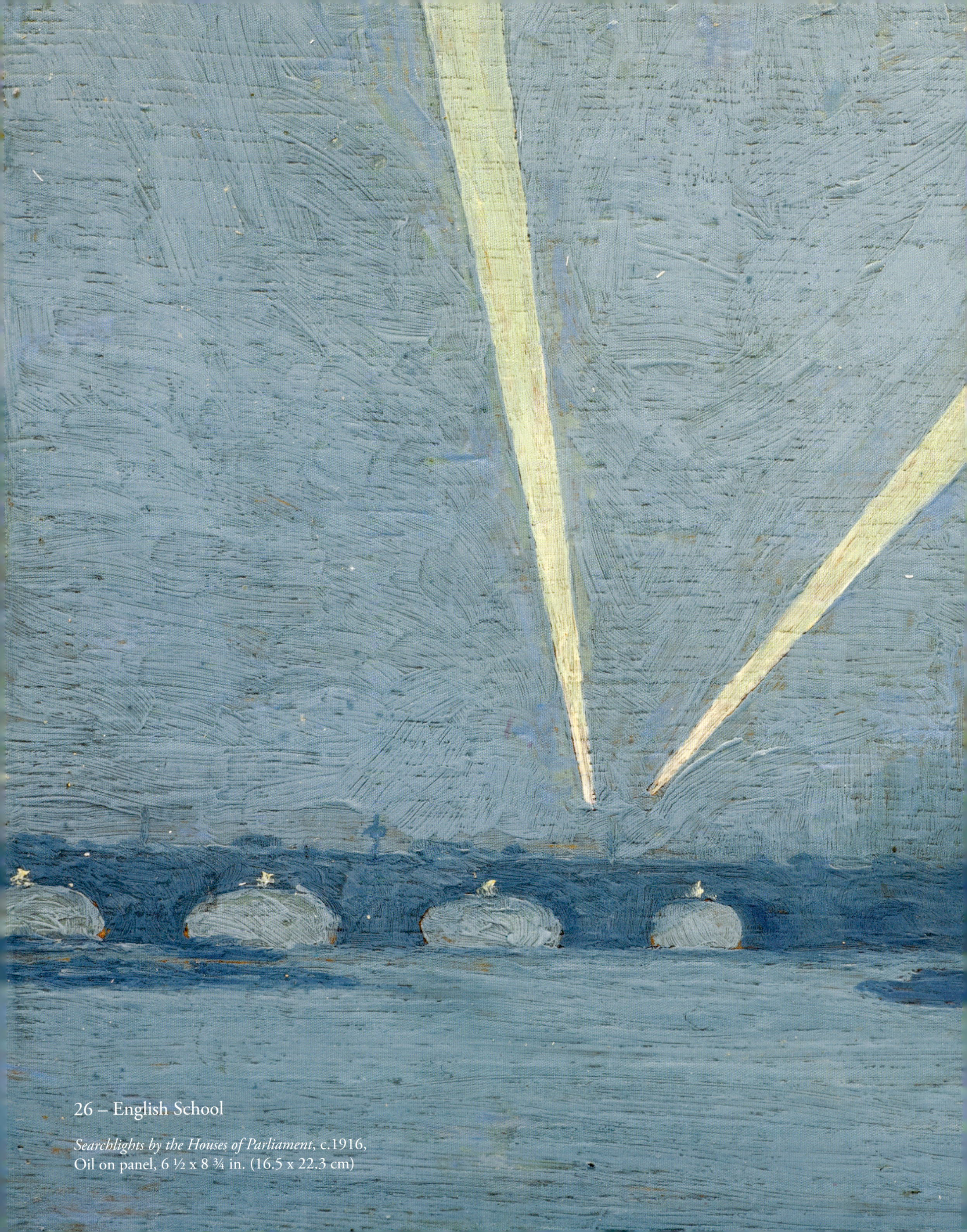

26 – English School

Searchlights by the Houses of Parliament, c.1916,
Oil on panel, 6 ½ x 8 ¾ in. (16.5 x 22.3 cm)

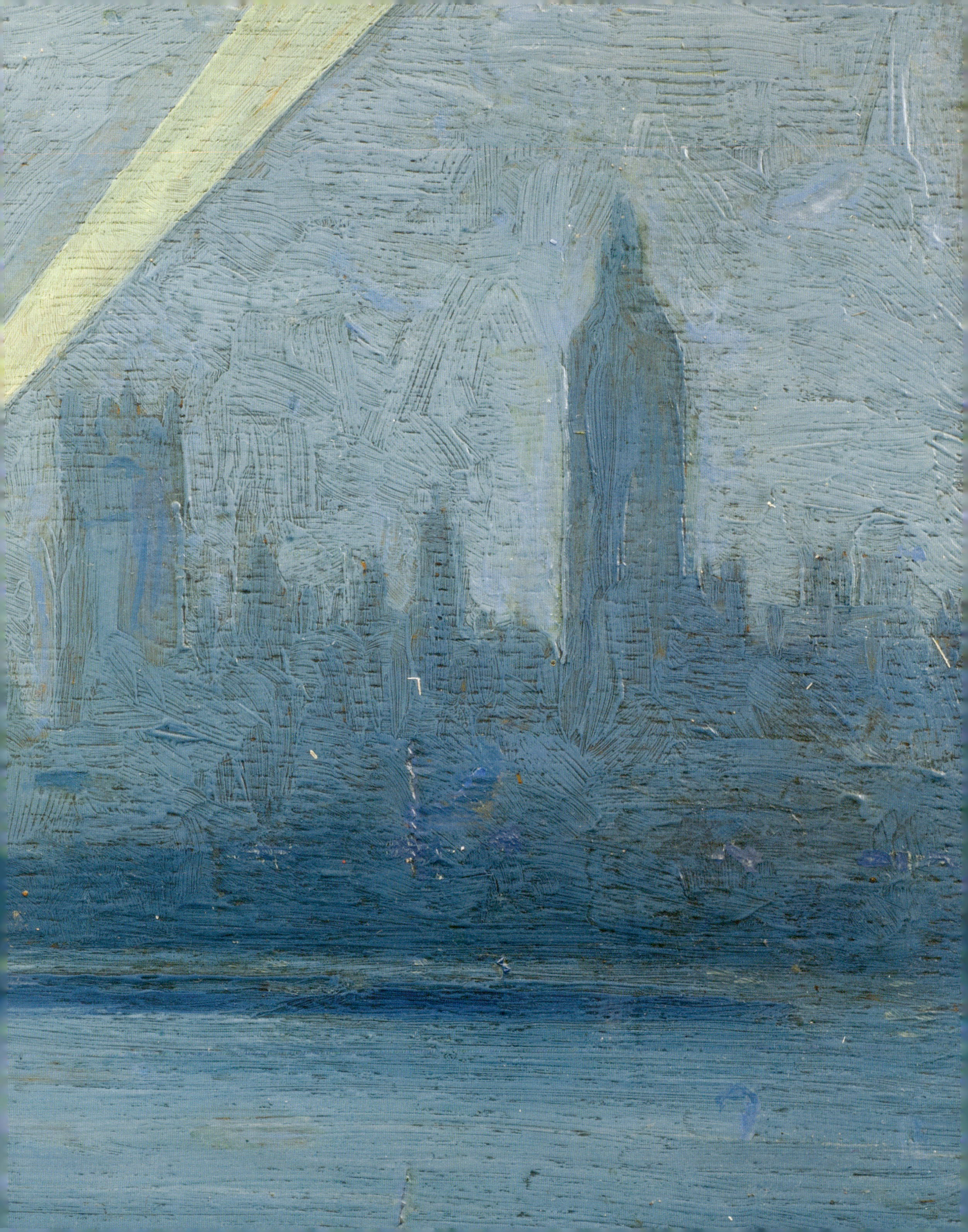

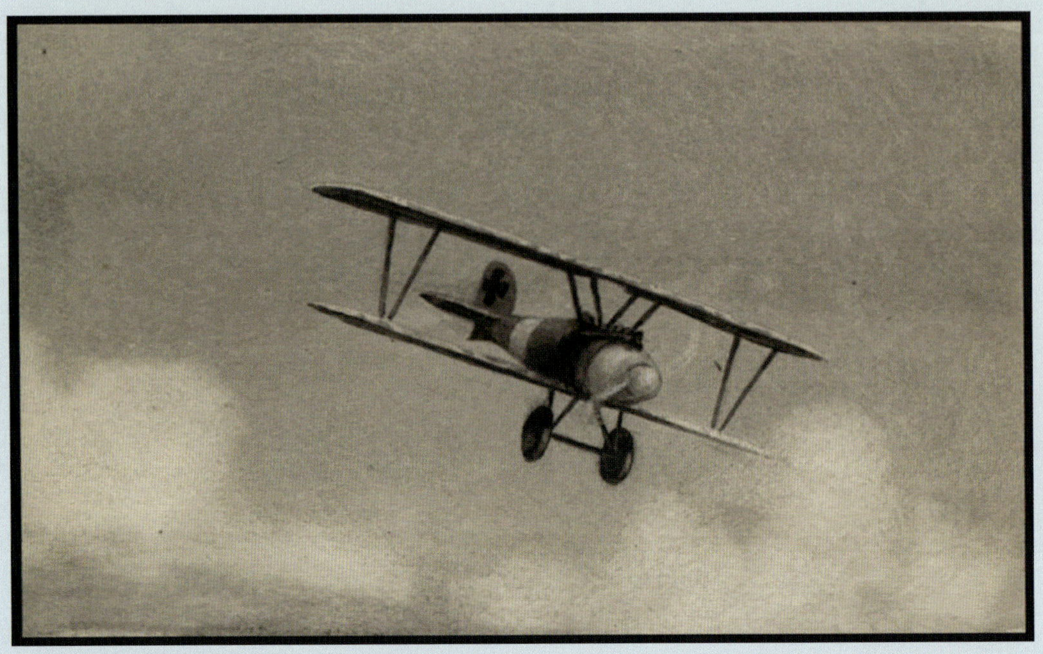

27 – Lt. Richard Barrett Talbot Kelly (1896-1971)

German Albatros D. III , c.1917,
Watercolour on paper, 3 x 4 ¾ in. (7.5 x 12 cm)

The Albatros D. III was a biplane fighter aircraft used by the Imperial German Army Air Service and the Austro-Hungarian Air Service. Talbot Kelly served in France as part of the Divisional Artillery of 9th (Scottish) Division. He was wounded on August 5 during a bombardment and was invalided home. Talbot Kelly wrote, "one does not hear the shell that gets one. If the ground had not been a bog and as soft as it is, it is absolutely certain that I would have been blown to bits." (*'A Subaltern's Odyssey' – A Memoir of the Great War, 1915-1917*, 1980.)

28 – British postcard

Coming down!
Image of "Kaiser Bill" in the guise of a Zeppelin, coming down in flames,
5 ½ x 3 ½ in. (13.8 x 8.7 cm)

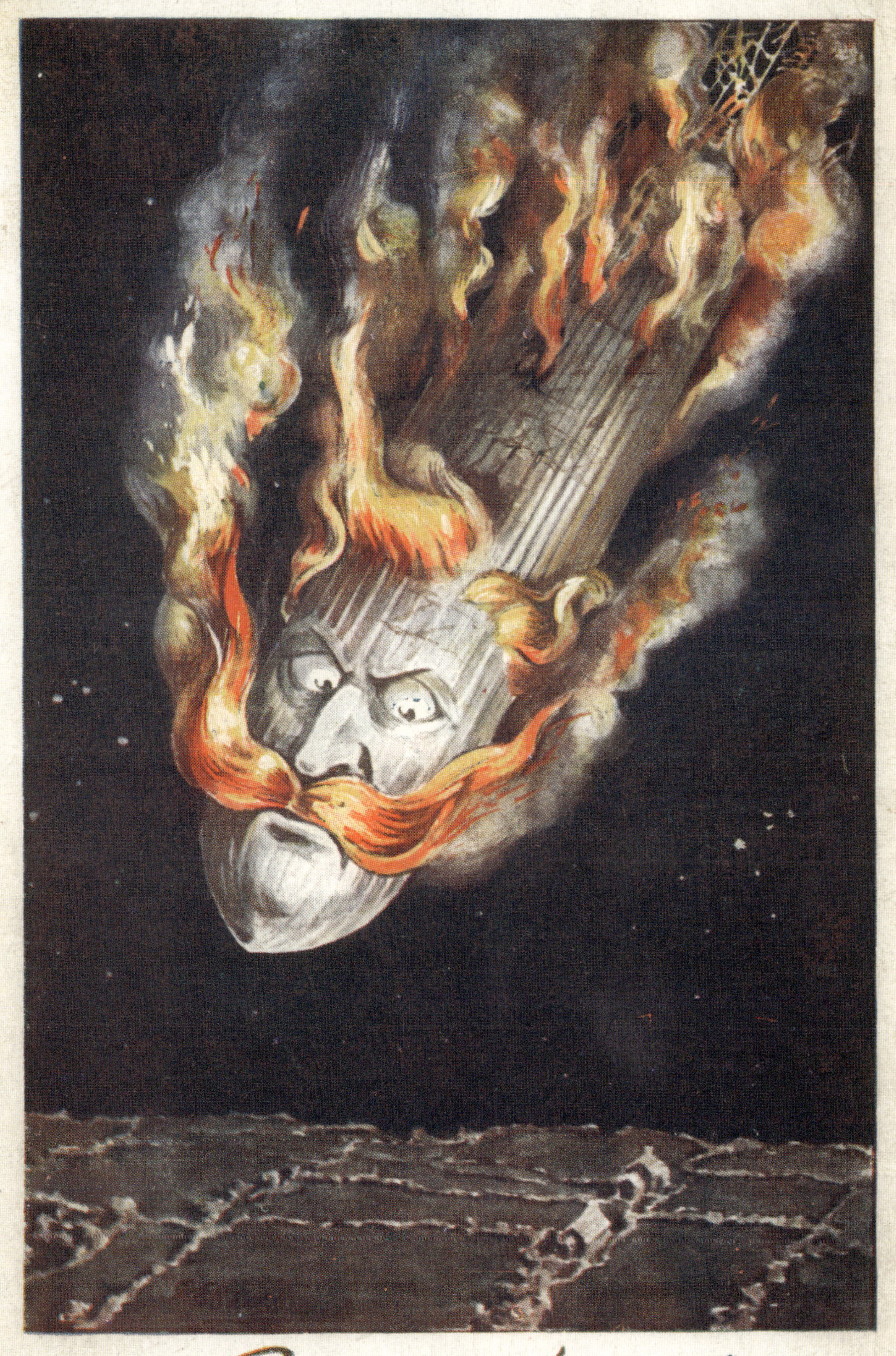

Coming down!

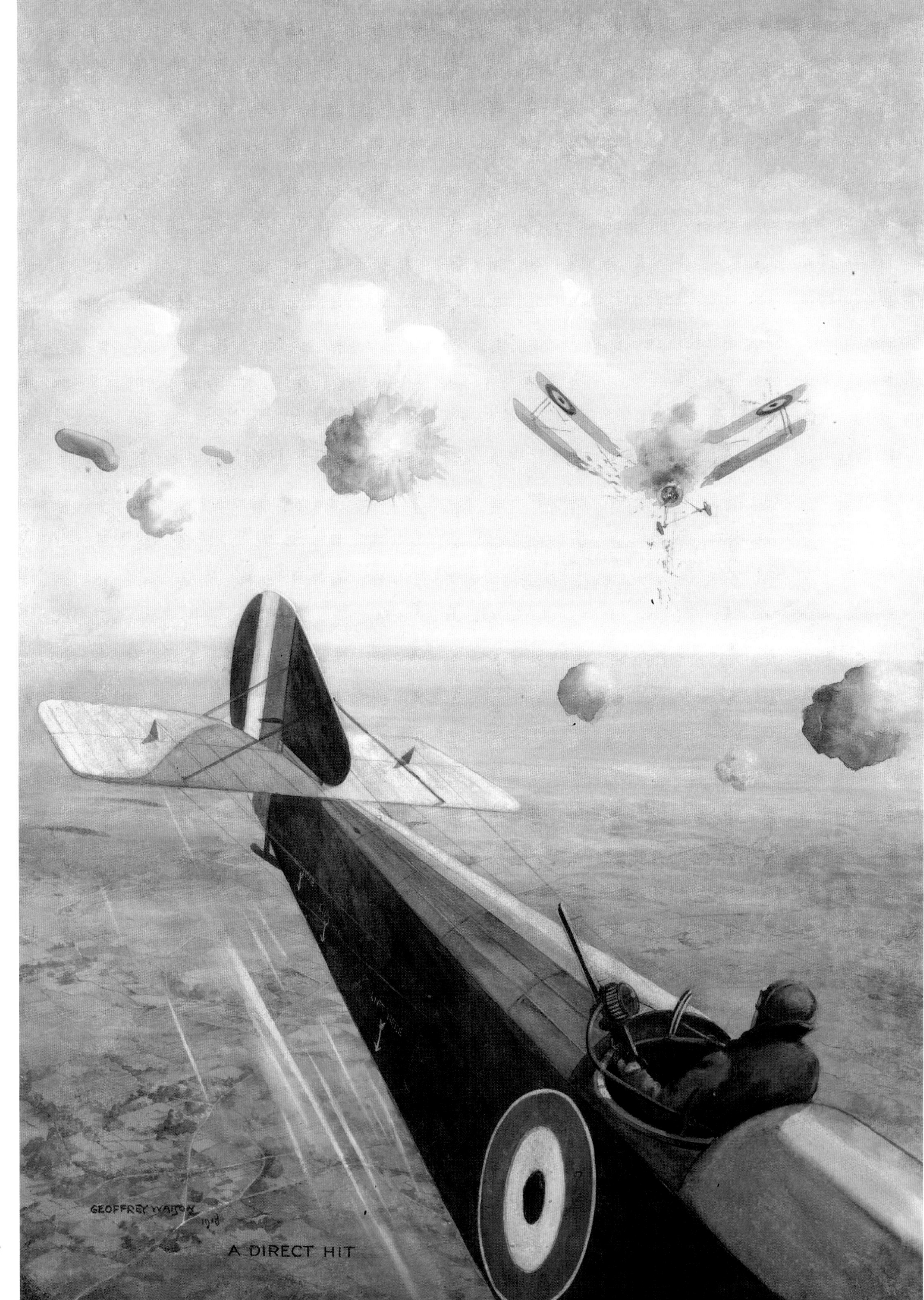

A DIRECT HIT

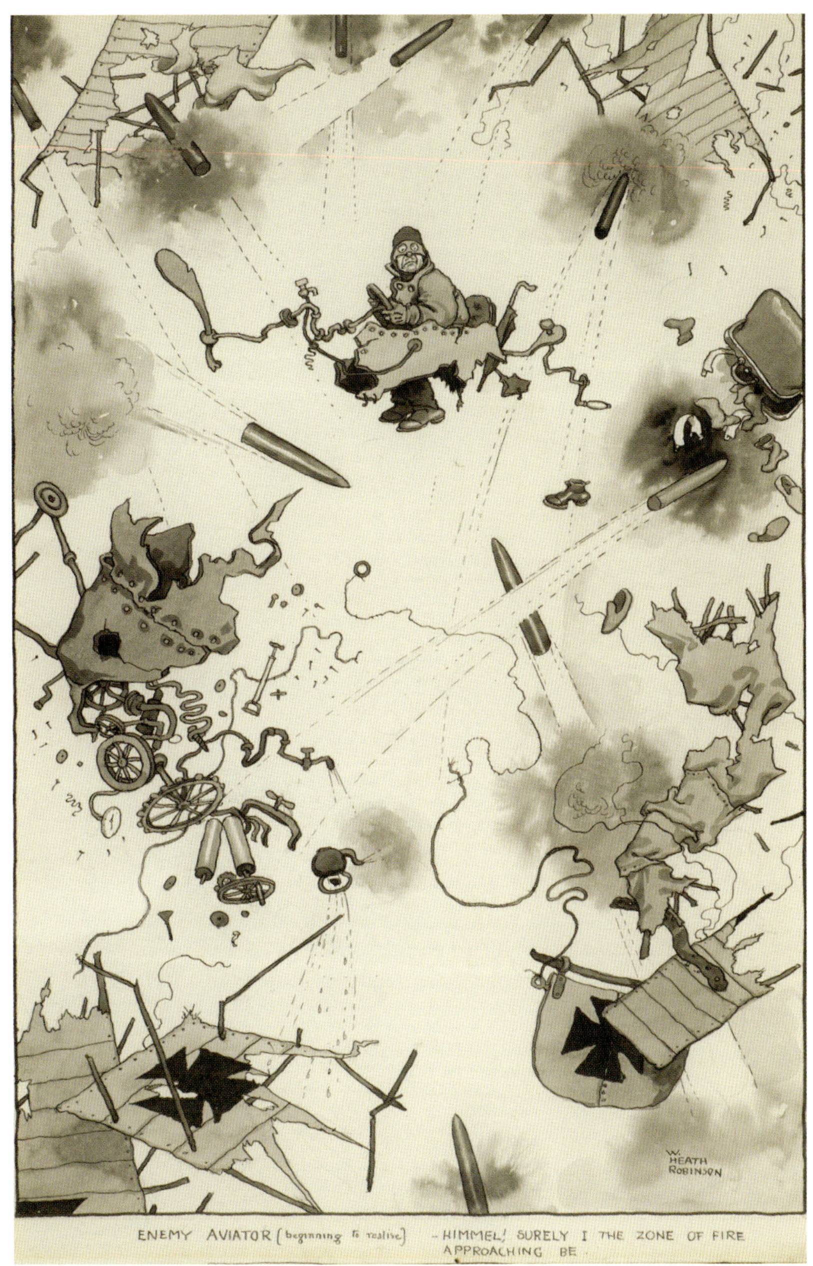

30 – William Heath Robinson (1872-1944)

A Nice Conclusion, c.1918,
Pen and ink, 17 x 10 in. (43 x 25.5 cm),
Inscribed with caption: "Enemy Aviator (beginning to realise) 'Himmel ! Surely I the zone of fire approaching be.' "Or
the English version - "Aviator (beginning to realise) 'Surely I must be approaching the zone of fire.' "

Heath Robinson's style of illustration was so original that his name has become a byword for a design or construction that is 'ingeniously or ridiculously over-complicated' (Oxford English Dictionary). Known by the popular press as the 'Gadget King', his illustrations evolved around his invention of contraptions that mocked the products of the industrial age.

29 – Geoffrey Watson (1894-1979)

A Direct Hit, 1918, signed, titled and dated,
Monochrome watercolour with gouache, 20 ½ x 14 ¼ in. (52 x 36 cm)

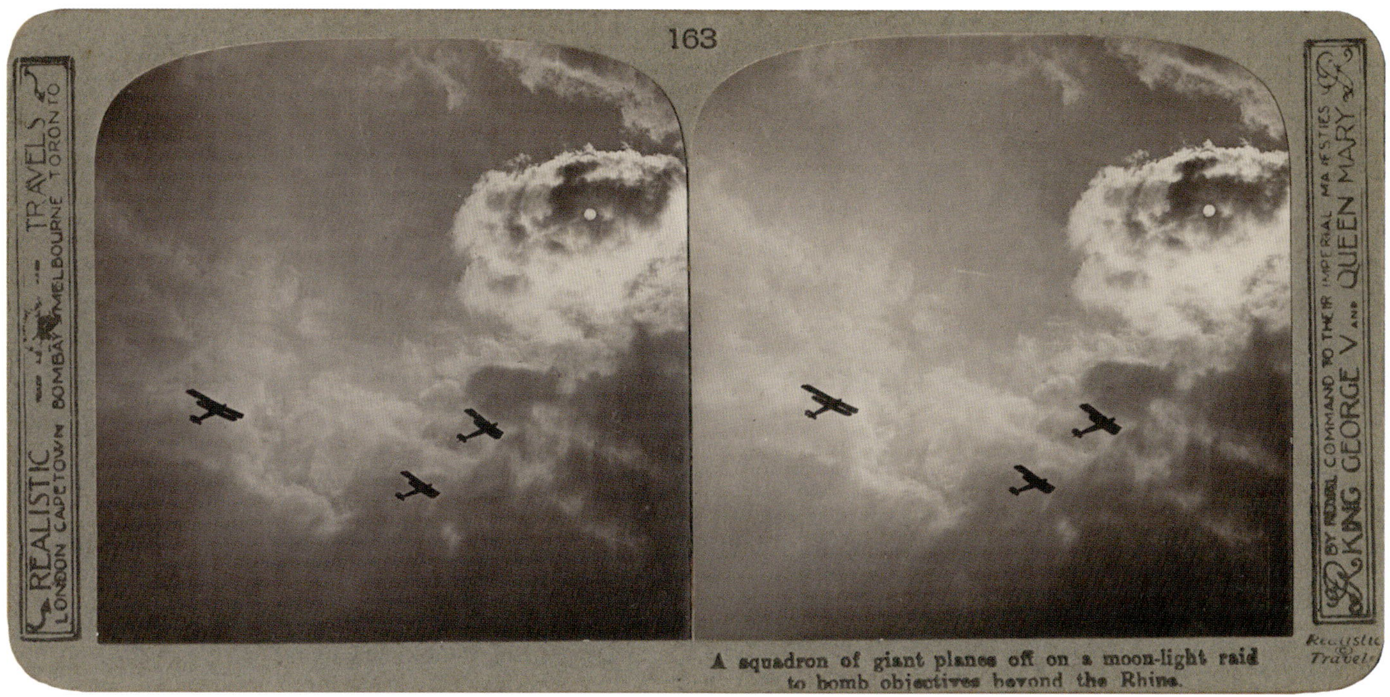

31 – Stereoscopic print: *A squadron of giant planes off on a moon-light raid to bomb objectives beyond the Rhine.*
3 ½ x 7 in. (9 x 18 cm), published by Realistic Travels

Realistic Travels, founded in 1908 by Dr. H.D. Girdwood, was one of the most prodigious producers of stereoviews during the First World War. Boxed sets of 'Great War Stereoviews' were sold in editions of 600, 500, 400, 300, 200 and 100. Stereoview production was a two-step process: a blank mount was imprinted with the company logo, title, copyright information, and sequence number. Next, the left and right photos were glued on. The Realistic Travels stereoviews were almost wholly Anglocentric, portraying the global nature of the conflict only insofar as it involved troops of the British Empire.

32 – Paul Colin (1892-1985)

Pilotes D'Avions, c.1920,
Signed in the plate,
Lithograph, published by: Hachard & Cie, Paris,
45 ¾ x 28 ½ in. (116.2 x 72.4 cm)

The text of the poster reads: Republic of France / Ministry of War / Military Aviation / Young Frenchmen: You can accomplish your compulsory military service as an AIRPLANE PILOT upon receiving preliminary instruction in a civil pilots' school at the expense of the State. Candidates are admitted from the age of 17 ½. Ask for more information from the Ministry of War, 12e Direction,4e Bureau. 231 Bd. St. Germain, Paris. This poster must not be covered over, destroyed or sold.

This poster design predates the Colin design for the Revue Nègre (1925), which helped to launch the career of Josephine Baker (who became his mistress) and immediately made Colin into one of the most famous poster designers of his age.

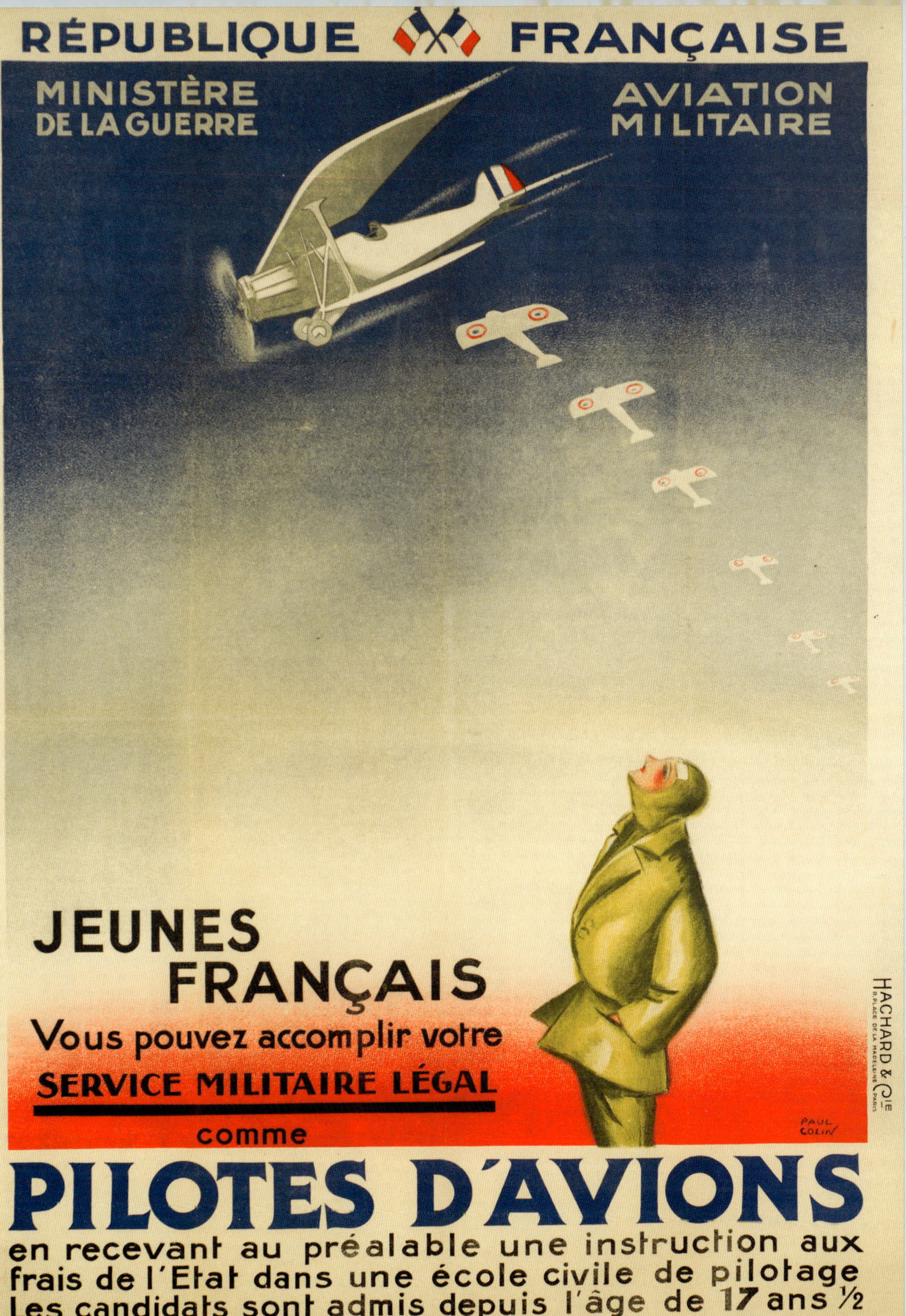

RÉPUBLIQUE FRANÇAISE
MINISTÈRE DE LA GUERRE
AVIATION MILITAIRE
JEUNES FRANÇAIS
Vous pouvez accomplir votre
SERVICE MILITAIRE LÉGAL
comme
PILOTES D'AVIONS
en recevant au préalable une instruction aux frais de l'Etat dans une école civile de pilotage
Les candidats sont admis depuis l'âge de 17 ans ½
Demandez les renseignements complémentaires au Ministère de la Guerre, 12e Direction, 4e Bureau, 231, Bd St Germain, Paris.
CETTE AFFICHE NE DOIT ÊTRE NI RECOUVERTE, NI DÉTRUITE, NI VENDUE.
PAUL COLIN
HACHARD & Cie

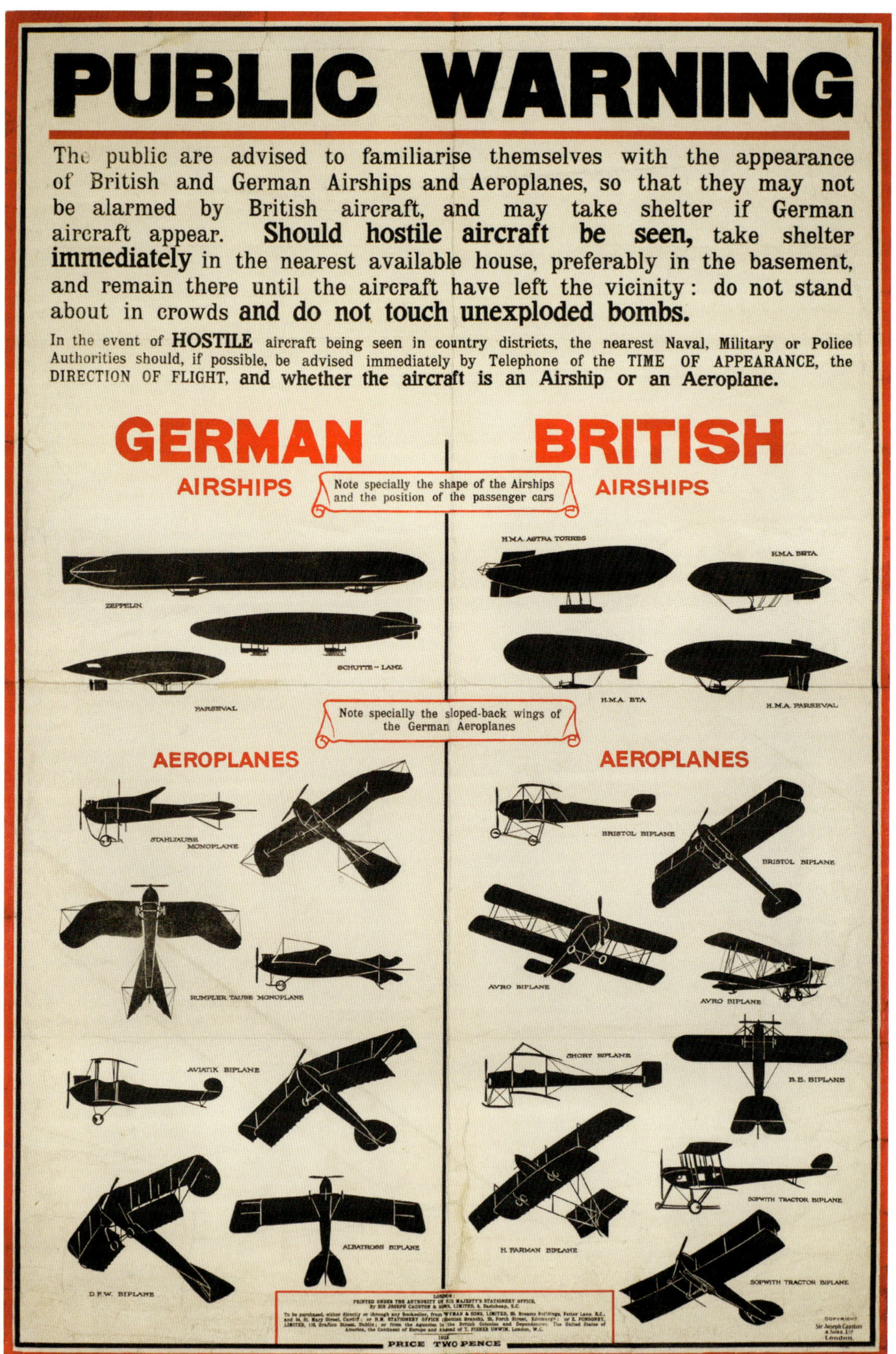

33 – English School

Public Warning – German airships & British airships, 1914-1918, 30 x 19 ⅝ in. (76.5 x 49.8 cm)
This information poster illustrates German and British aircraft and advises the public to familiarise themselves with their appearance.

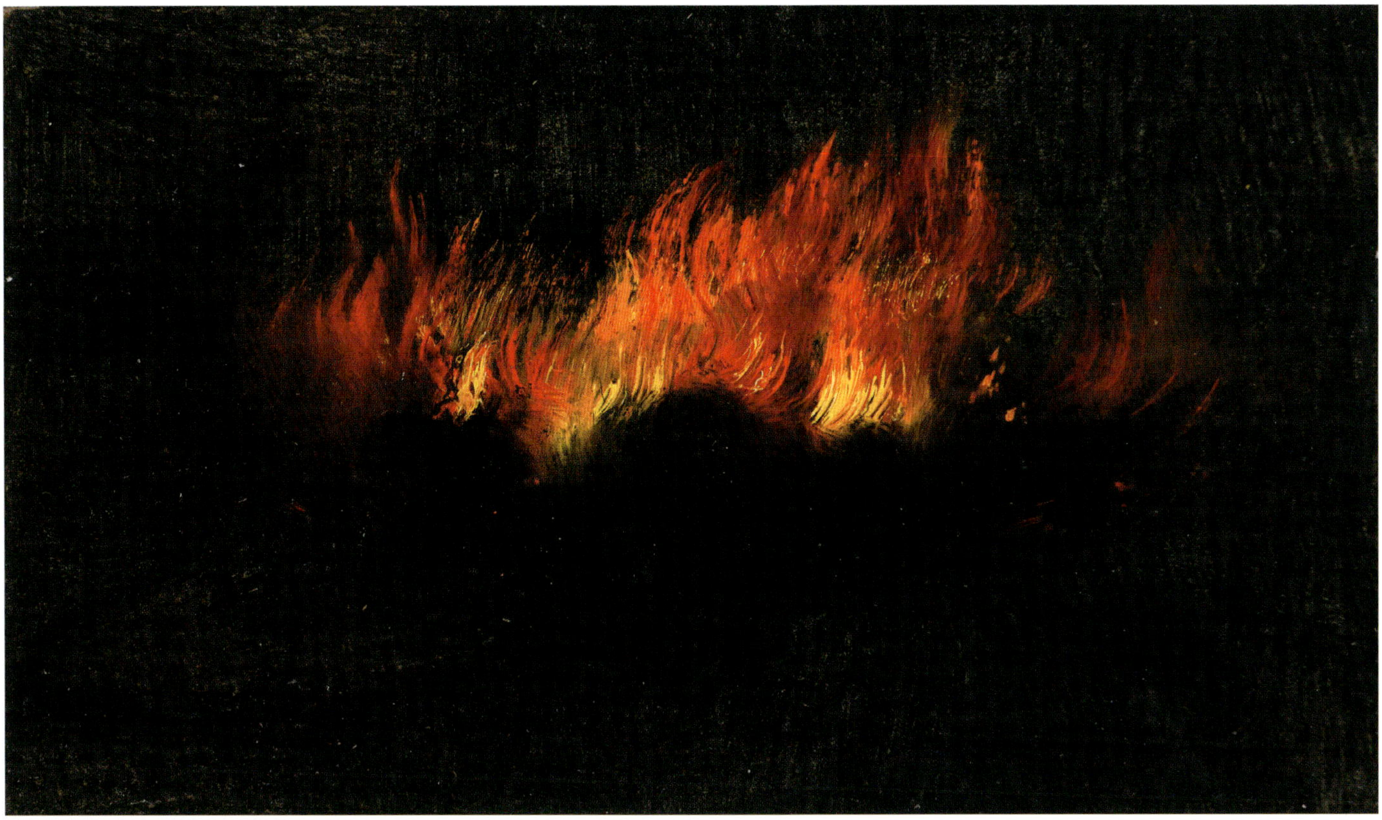

34 – Walter Hunt (1861-1941)

Schütte-Lanz aiship shot down by Captain William Leefe Robinson, V.C. on September 3, 1916, signed, inscribed on the reverse:
"Zeppelin in flames as seen through telescope from Southfields, September 3rd 1916.",
Oil on card, 4 x 6 in. (10 x 15 cm)
Schütte-Lanz aiships were made of wood, unlike Zeppelins which were made of duralumin.

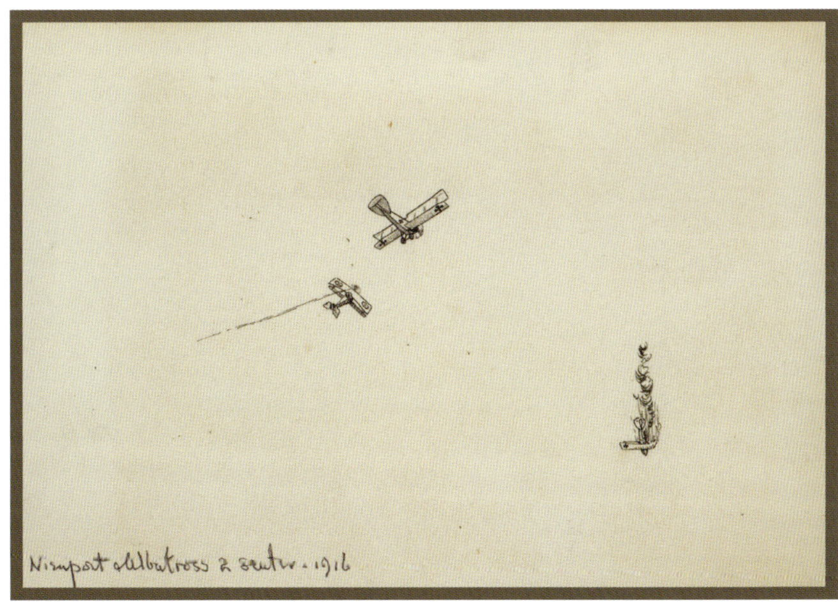

35 – Lt. Richard Barrett Talbot Kelly (1896-1971)

Aerial Combat – A French Nieuport and German 2-seater Albatros, 1916,
Inscribed with title, pen and ink on paper, 5 x 7 in. (12.7 x 17.7 cm)

SEA

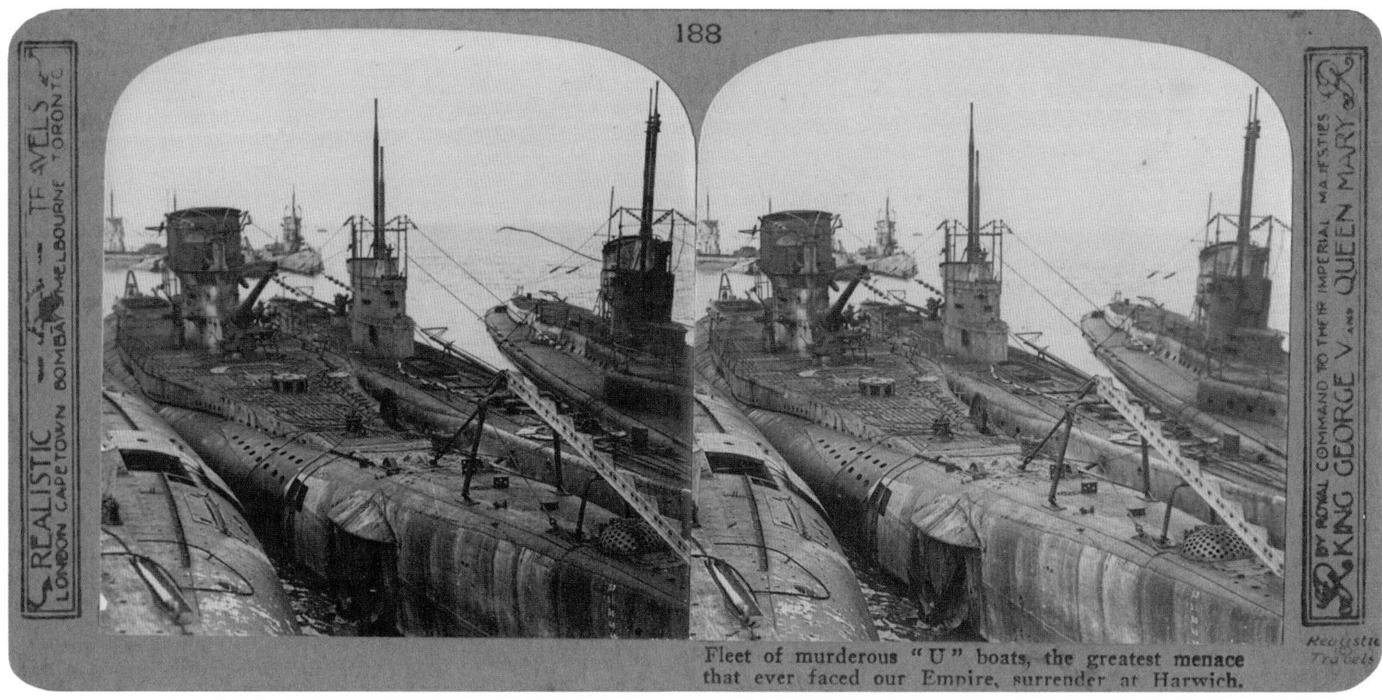

36 – Stereoscopic print: *Fleet of murderous "U" boats, the greatest menace that ever faced our Empire, surrender at Harwich.*
3 ½ x 7 in. (9 x 18 cm), published by Realistic Travels

At the outset of the First World War, German U-boats, though numbering only 38, achieved notable successes against British warships. However, because of the reactions of neutral powers (especially the United States), Germany hesitated before adopting unrestricted U-boat warfare against merchant ships. The decision to do so in February 1917 was largely responsible for the entry of the United States into the war.

37 – Harold M. Brett (1880-1955)

A Destroyer on a night time encounter, c.1917, signed,
Oil on panel, 27 ¾ x 19 ¾ in. (70.5 x 50 cm)

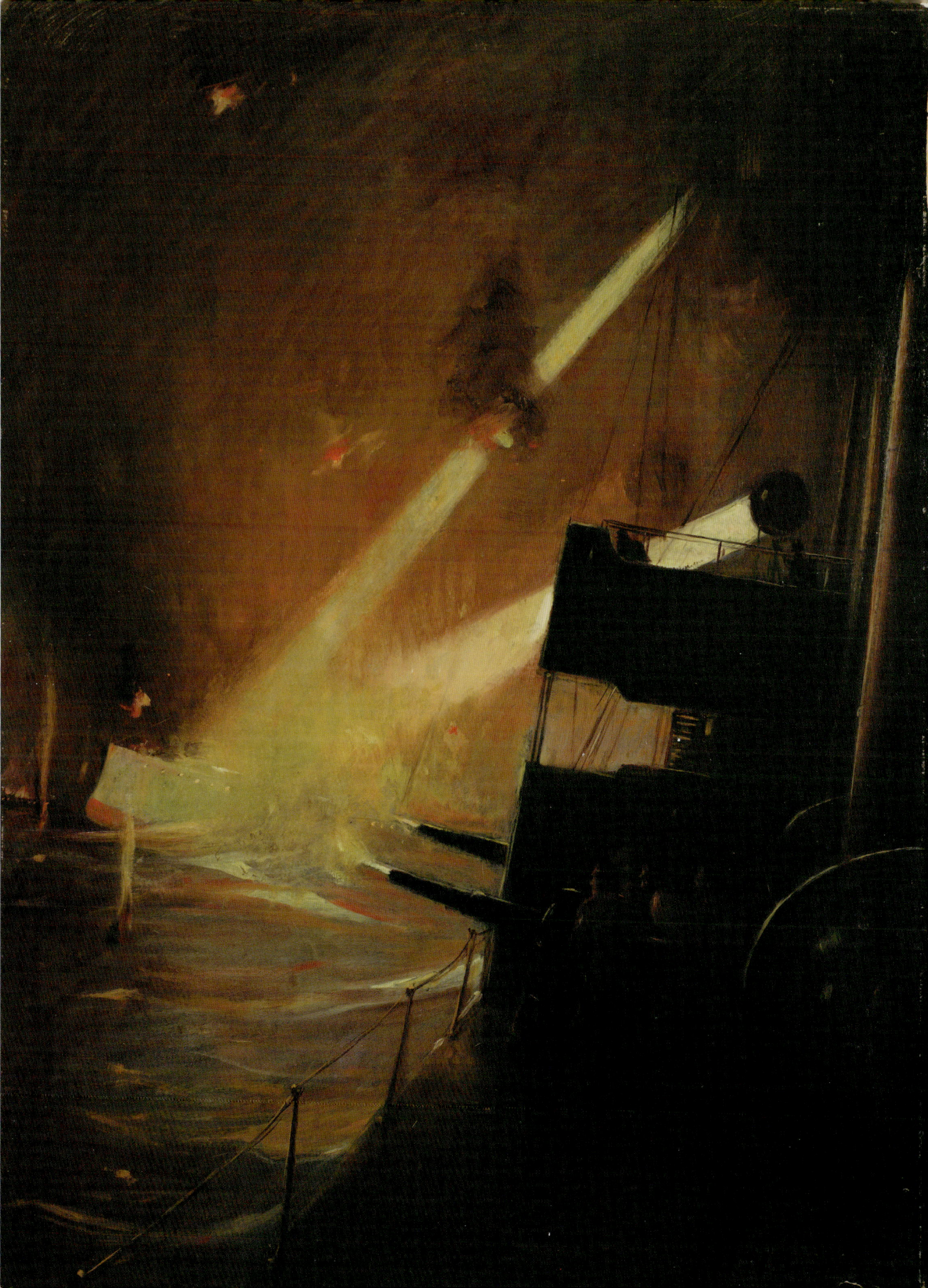

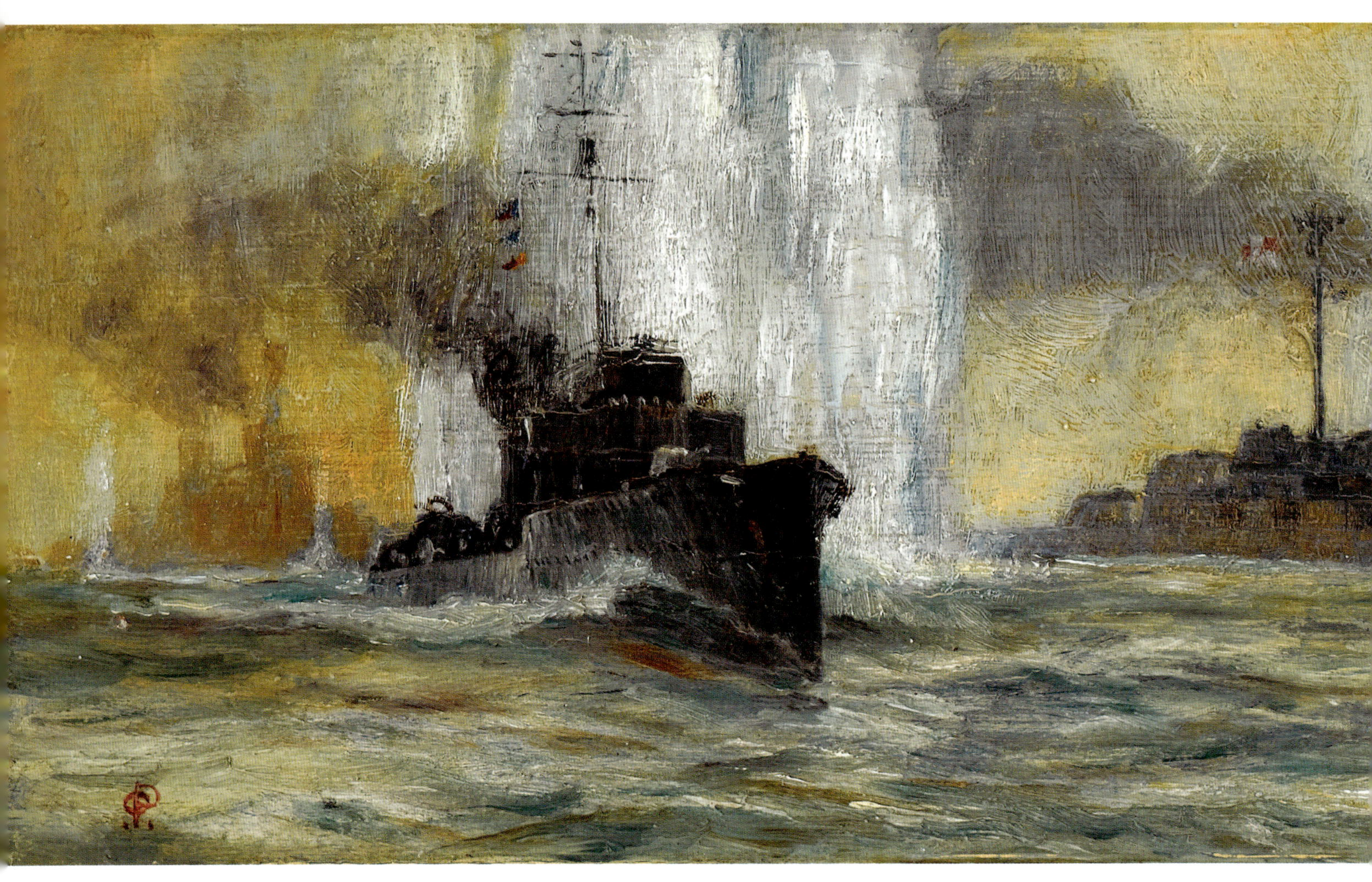

38 – Charles Pears (1873–1958)

Naval Encounter (possibly The Battle of Dogger Bank),
Signed with monogram and dated 1915,
Oil on panel, 5 ½ x 17 ⅜ in. (14 x 44 cm)

This panel possibly depicts the Battle of Dogger Bank of January 24, 1915, which was a clear-cut British
victory, with light British and heavy German casualties.

39 – Stereoscopic print: *Triumph of our Navy. Surrendered battleships and cruisers of the German fleet at Scapa Flow.*
3 ½ x 7 in. (9 x 18 cm), published by Realistic Travels

After the Armistice, seventy-four ships of the German High Seas Fleet were ordered into Scapa Flow to be interned.

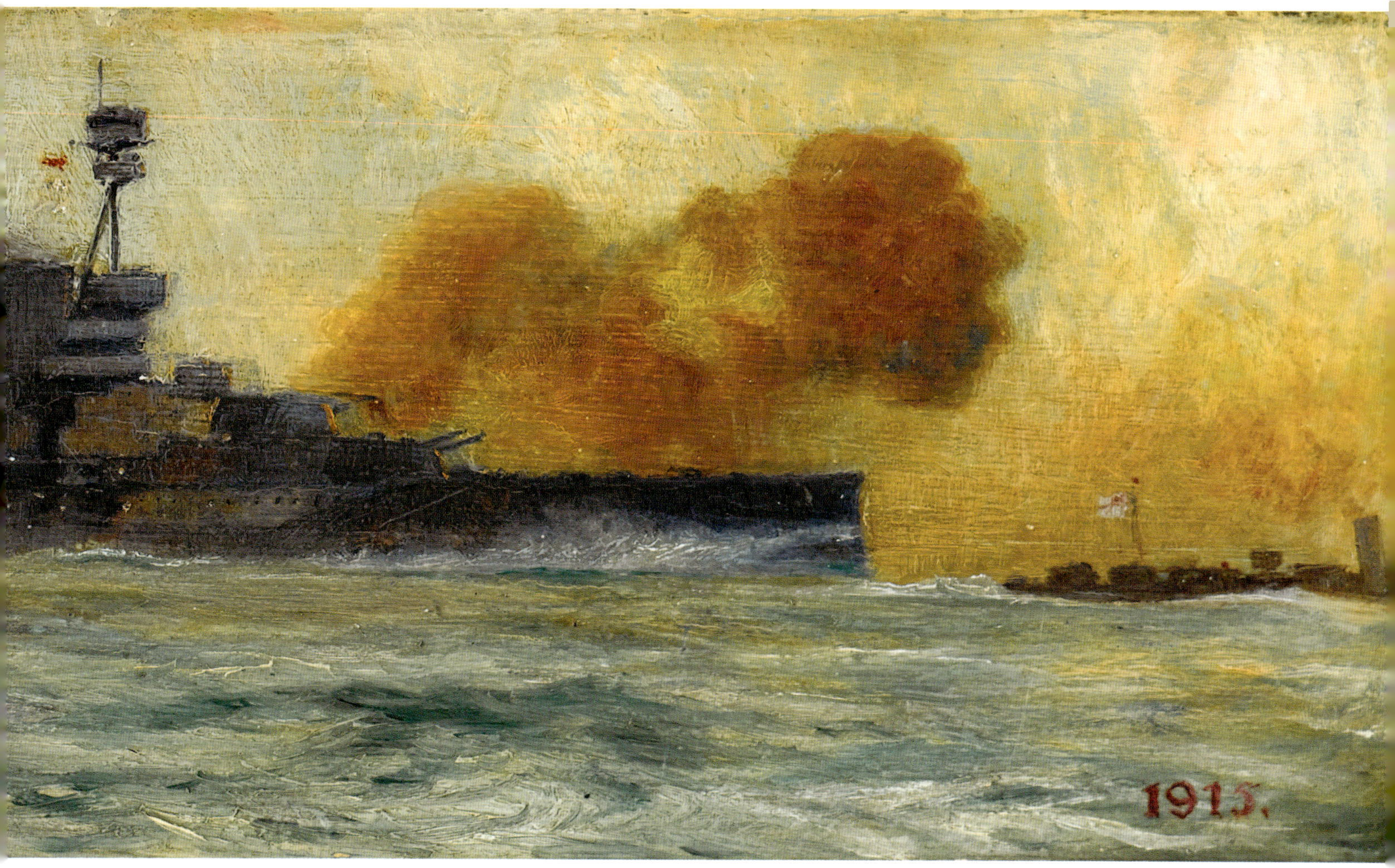

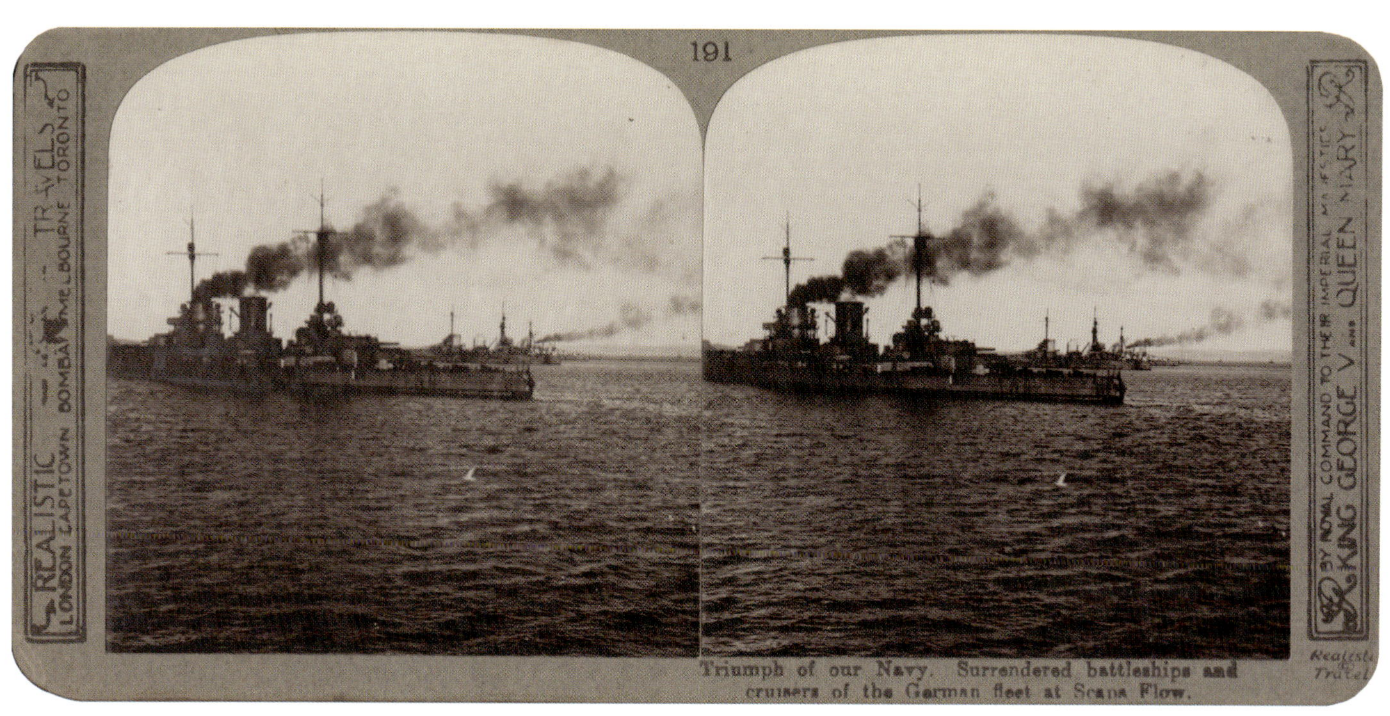
191
REALISTIC
LONDON CAPETOWN BOMBAY MELBOURNE TORONTO
TRAVELS
BY ROYAL COMMAND TO THEIR IMPERIAL MAJESTIC
KING GEORGE V AND QUEEN MARY
Triumph of our Navy. Surrendered battleships and
cruisers of the German fleet at Scapa Flow.

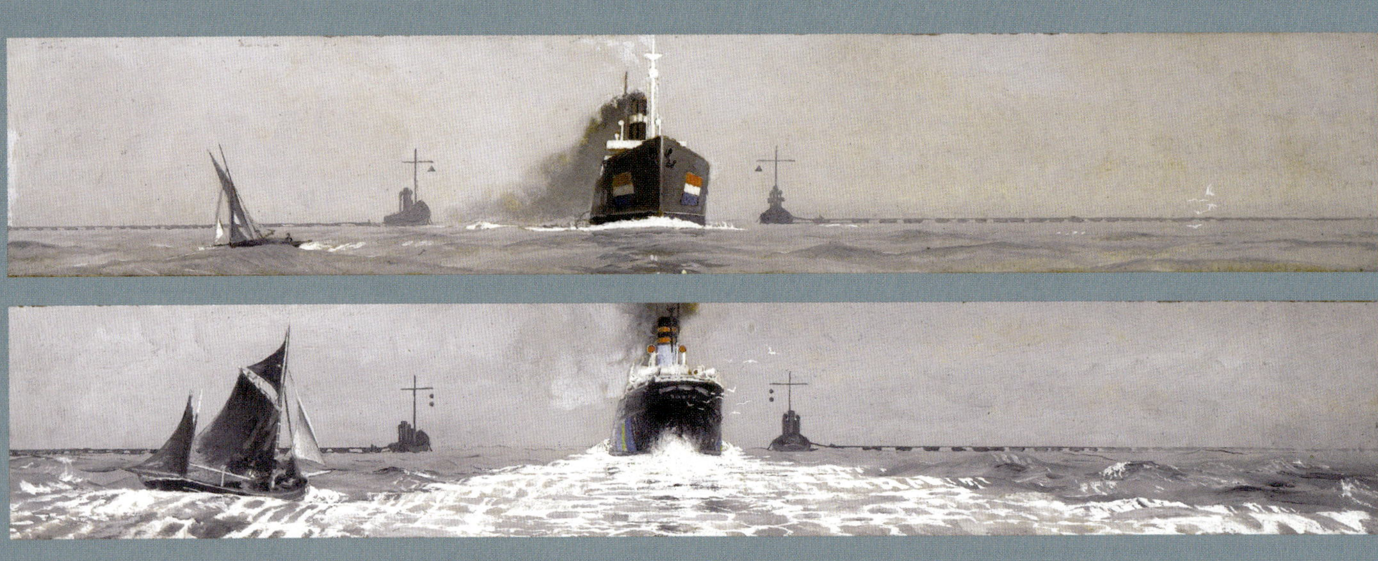

40 – Charles Pears (1873-1958)

Freighters passing through an anti-submarine boom, signed,
Gouache on paper, 13 ½ x 24 in. (8 x 43 cm)
Provenance: The Forbes Collection, Old Battersea House

These three images depict freighters passing through the entrance/exit of an anti-submarine defence called a boom – a series of wire nets suspended underwater from buoys which reach out from either side of an estuary, with a gap left for shipping in the middle that can be closed if/when a submarine attack is expected. In the picture the boom is the dark broken line on the horizon, extending from side to side. The two freighters steaming forwards have flags painted on the bow – of the Netherlands and Norway – to indicate to the war's combatants that they belong to neutral nations and should not be attacked. Judging by the Thames sailing barges also in the picture, this could be the Thames estuary, the Medway, or the Orwell.

41 – Adolph Treidler (1886-1981)

Shoot Ships to Germany and help America Win, 1917
Lithograph, printed by Thomsen-Ellis Baltimore for the
Publications Section, United States Shipping Board, Emergency Fleet Corporation, 1917
25 x 18 ¾ in. (64 x 48 cm)

The United States was a formal participant in the First World War from April 6, 1917 until the war's end on November 11, 1918. Before entering the war, the US had remained neutral, though it had been an important supplier to Britain and other Allied powers. During the war, the US mobilized over 4,000,000 military personnel and suffered 110,000 deaths, including 43,000 due to the influenza pandemic.

The poster shows two ships at sea, the larger one painted in dazzle camouflage, with text quoting Charles M. Schwab, an American steel magnate who on April 16, 1918 was made the Director General of the Emergency Fleet Corporation.

Dazzle camouflage, whose invention is generally credited to the artist Norman Wilkinson, consisted of complex patterns of geometric shapes in contrasting colours, interrupting and intersecting each other. Unlike other forms of camouflage, dazzle works not by offering concealment, but by making it difficult to estimate a target's range, speed and direction.

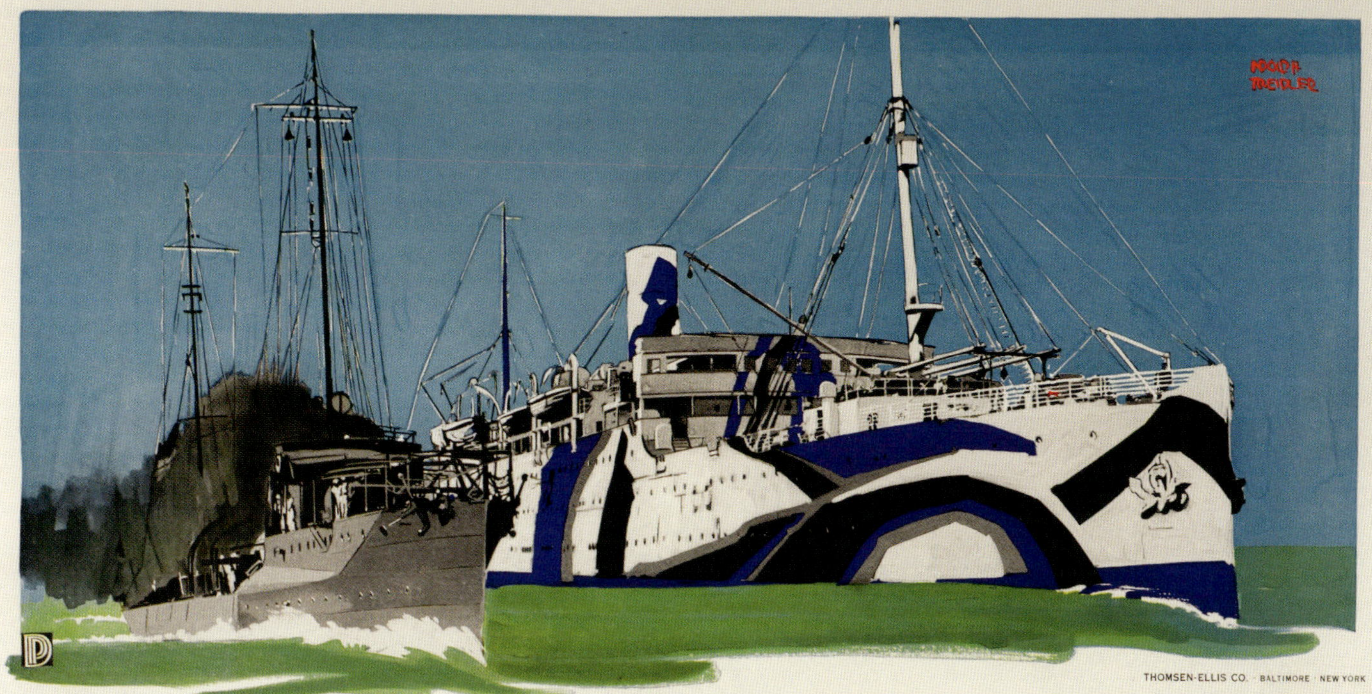

Shoot Ships to Germany and help AMERICA WIN—*Schwab*

At this Shipyard are being built ships to carry to our men "Over There"—Food, Clothing, and the Munitions of War.

Without these ships our men will not have an equal chance to fight.

The building of ships is more than a construction job—it is our chance to win the war.

He who gives to his work the best that is in him does his bit as truly as the man who fights.

Delays mean danger.

Are you doing your bit?

Are you giving the best that is in you to help your son, brother, or pal who is "OVER THERE"?

UNITED STATES SHIPPING BOARD EMERGENCY FLEET CORPORATION

ISSUED BY PUBLICATIONS SECTION, EMERGENCY FLEET CORPORATION, PHILADELPHIA

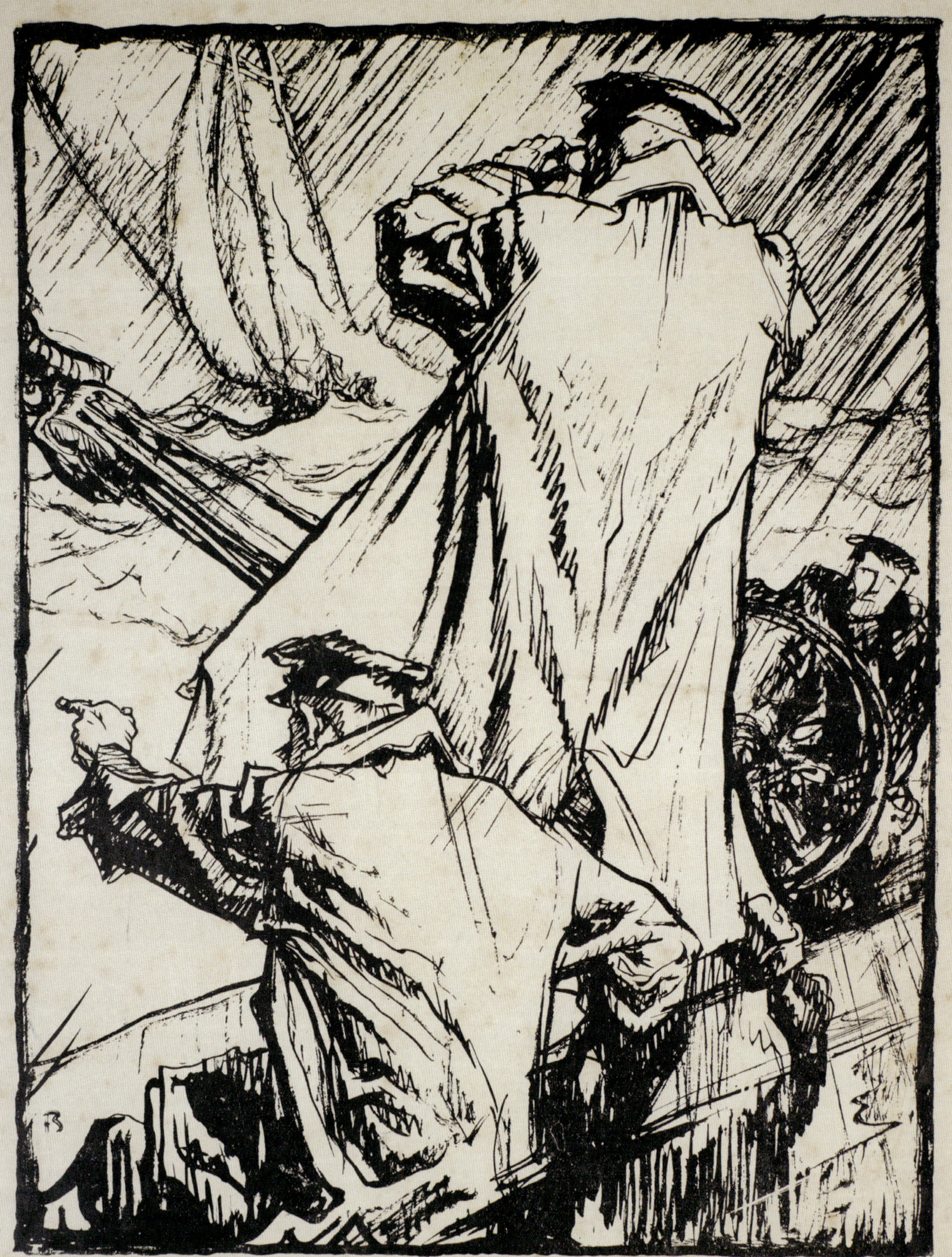

42 – Sir Frank Brangwyn (1867-1956)

Lookout – design for Zambrene Trench Coats (P3560),
Signed with initials in pencil,
Unlettered lithographic proof, 15 x 9 ½ in. (38 x 24 cm),
Provenance: Father Jerome Esser
Literature: Libby Horner, *Brangwyn at War!*, (Horner and Goldmark, 2014) p.134

Zambrene Ltd. 151 City Road, London EC1, were makers of Officer's trench coats.

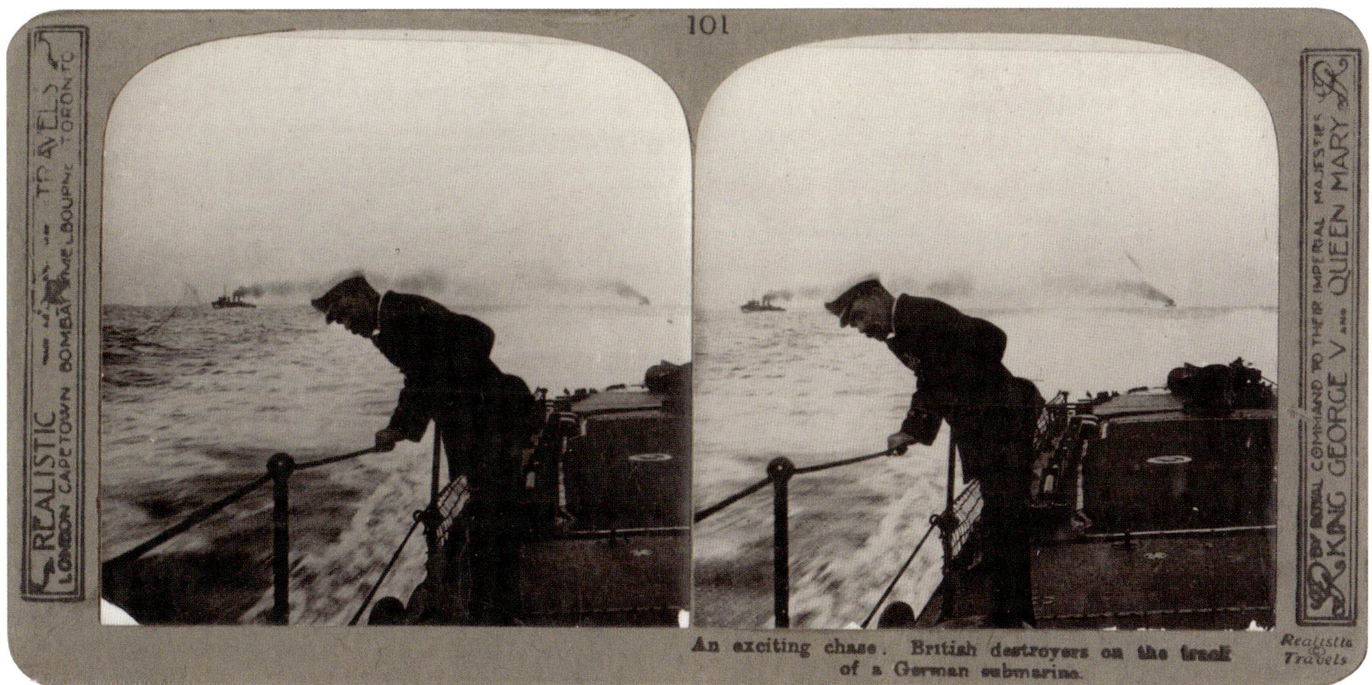

43 – **Stereoscopic print:** *An exciting chase. British destroyers on the track of a German submarine*
3 ½ x 7 in. (9 x 18 cm), published by Realistic Travels

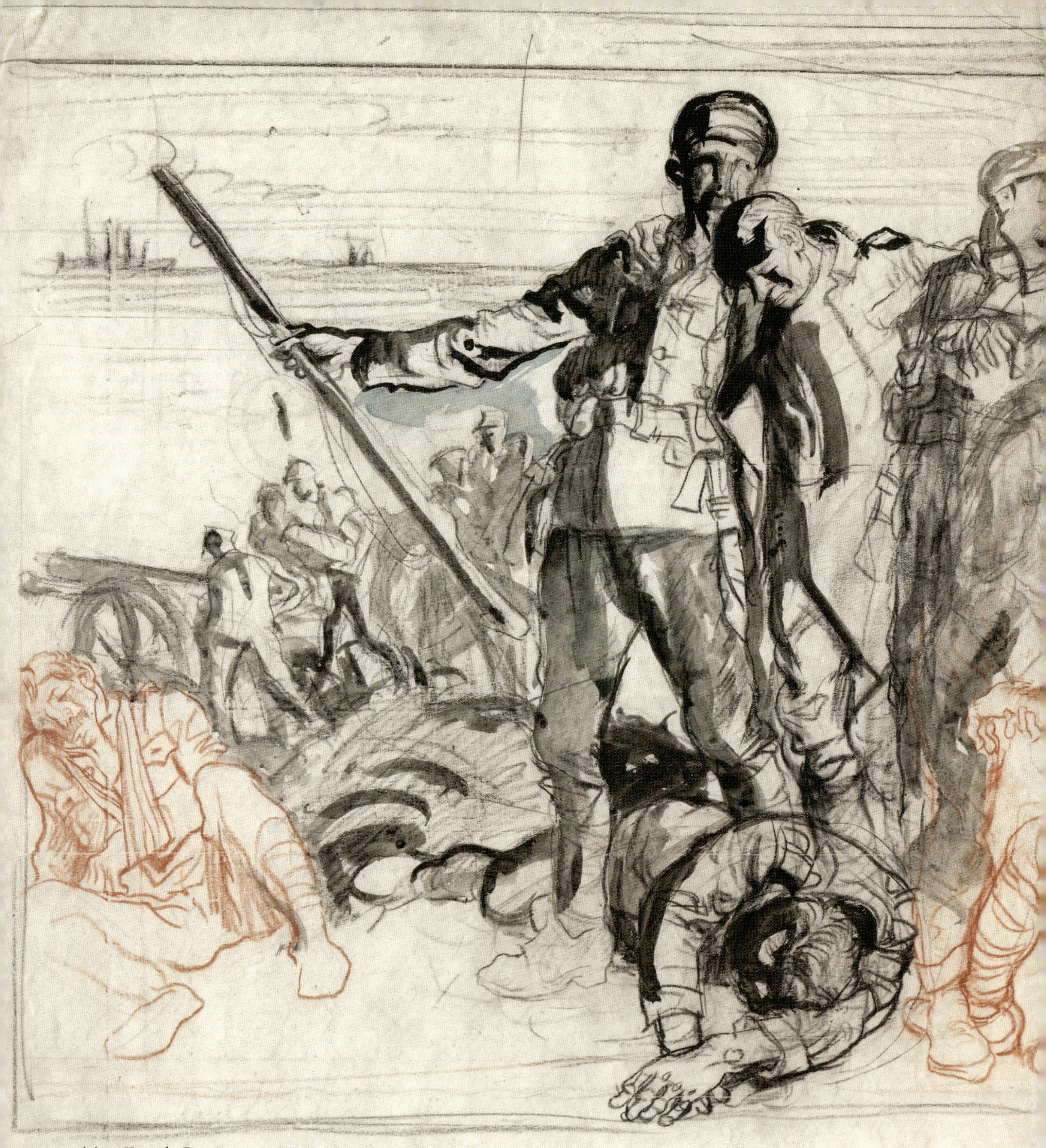

44 – Frank Brangwyn (1867-1956)

Landing Men from a Naval Fight (W1845); study for a poster, postcard and stamp,
Pencil, black & red chalk, wash and watercolour on paper,
20 ¼ x 16 ⅜ in. (51.5 x 41.7 cm),
Literature: Libby Horner, *Brangwyn at War!*, (Horner and Goldmark, 2014), p.36

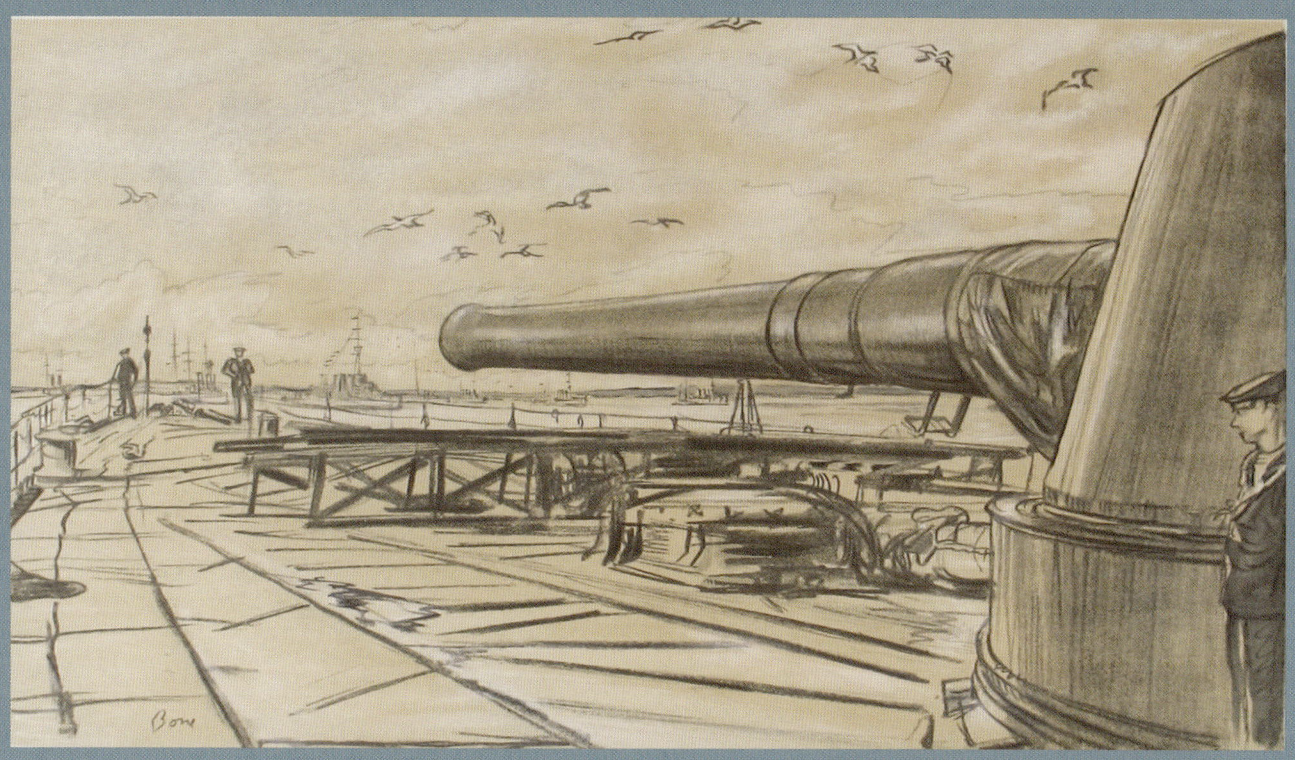

45 – Muirhead Bone (1876-1953)

On Board a Battleship : A Gun Turret on HMS Repulse, Firth of Forth, March 1917, signed in the plate,
Coloured lithograph, 8 x 14 in. (20 x 35.5 cm),
Published by *Country Life*, 1917

This was one of the sixty 'War Drawings' published with 'the authority of the War Office' *by Country Life*, 1917. The series constituted six volumes with ten images in each volume. H M S *Repulse* was one of the most famous British ships. This lithograph shows a gun turret viewed from the deck.

In May 1916, Charles Masterman (1873-1927), head of the British War Propaganda Bureau situated at Wellington House, appointed Muirhead Bone as Britain's first official war artist to provide eye-witness images intended for propaganda publications.

Following pages:

46 – Claude Muncaster (1903-1974)

Convoys in Peril, signed,
Inscribed on the reverse : "Convoys in Peril, chapter 1, A Searchlight flashed over them for an instant....then it left them, pulling blindly into the night....",
Wash on paper, 10 ¼ x 14 ½ in. (26 x 37 cm)

This picture shows a British freighter dead in the water after a torpedo attack. At the rear a black gash pierces the dazzle camouflage of the hull and a cloud of black smoke billows out of it. The crew are escaping by lifeboats, possibly to another ship in the convoy that has briefly lit the scene with its searchlights.

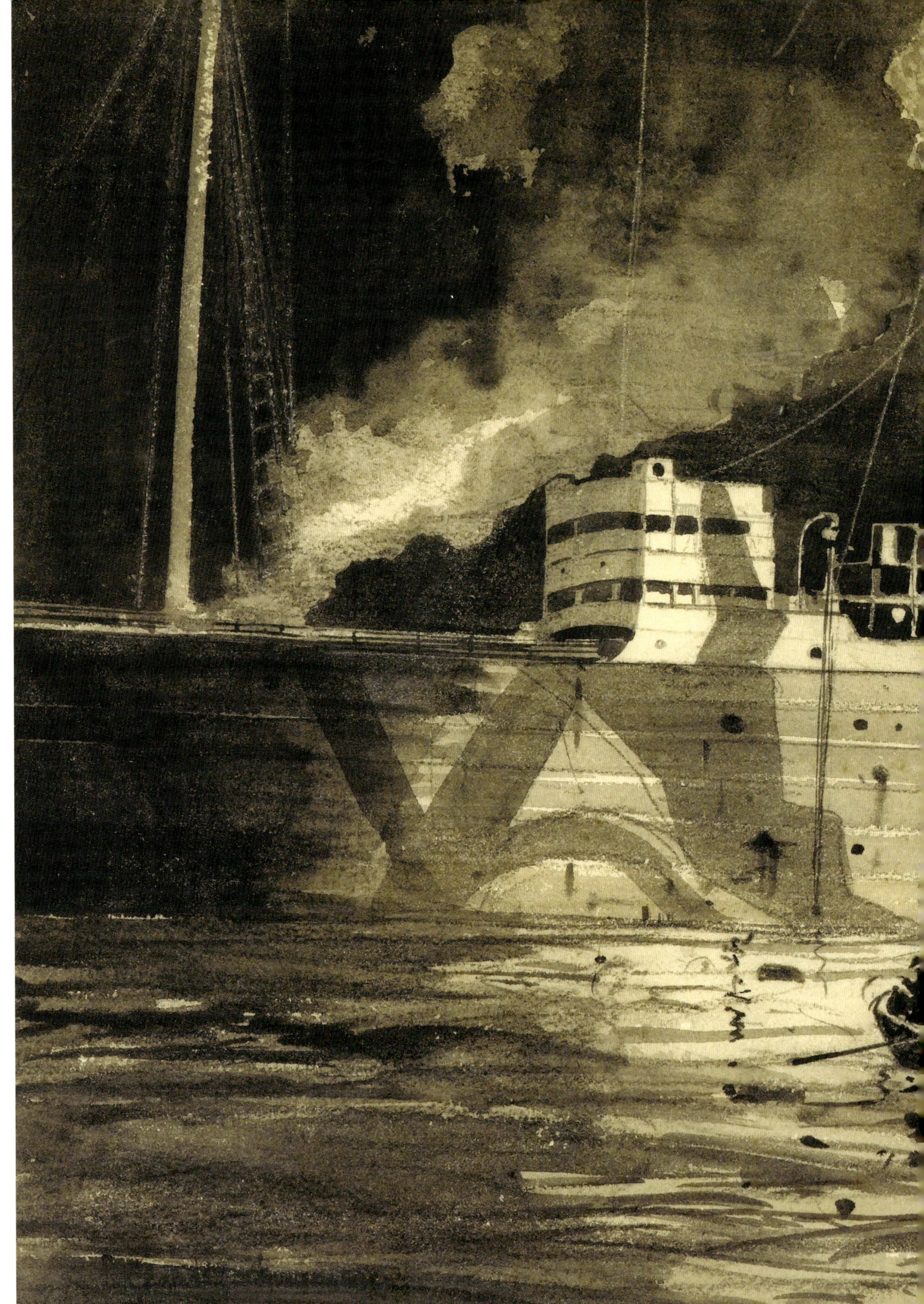

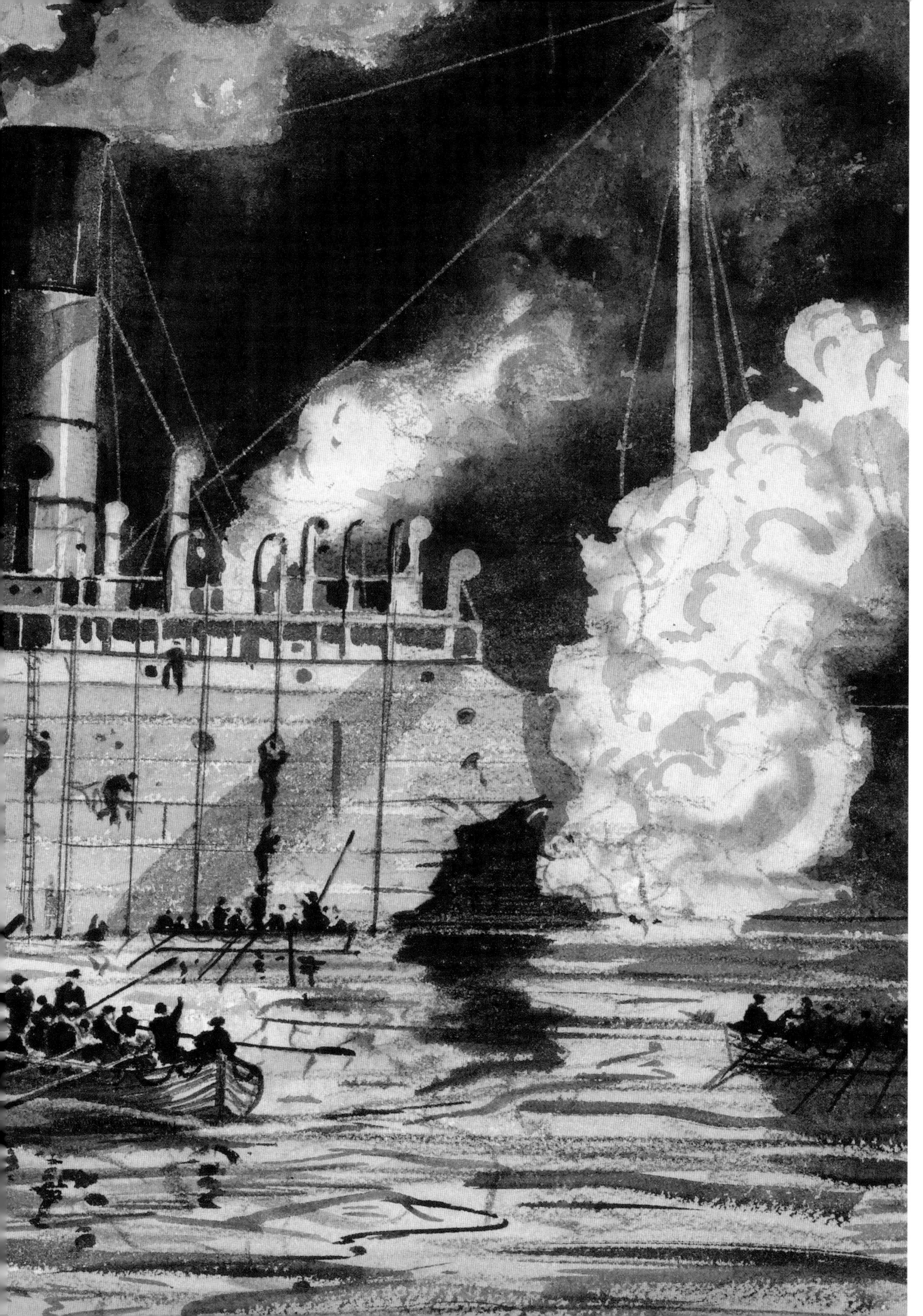

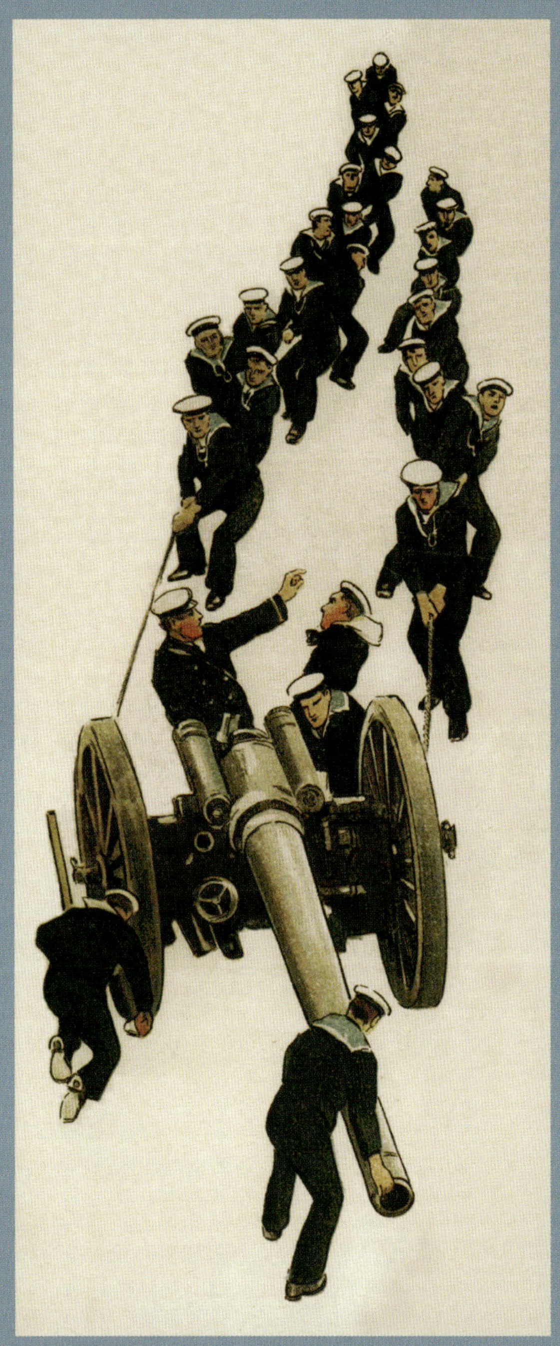

47 – Bert Thomas (1883-1966)

Naval images of our Allies, c.1914, signed in ink, lithograph, 57 ½ x 5 ½ in. (146 x 14 cm)

This vertical panorama shows a Non-Rigid Airship, a Seaplane and other aeroplanes, an armoured car and naval gun team together with an assortment of naval troops of British, French, Belgian and Russian nationalities. A pair to this print showing aircraft, airship, Lancers, Royal Field Artillery and an assortment of troops of British, Belgian, French, Russian and Indian nationalities is in the National Army Museum.

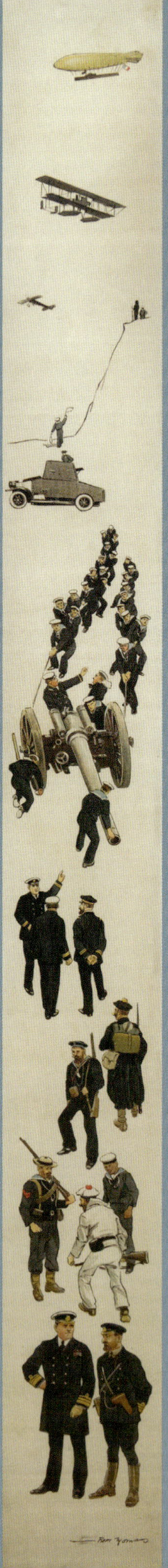

S.—1320 b. (Established—May, 1900.)
(Revised—January, 1917.) *Copy*

NAVAL SIGNAL.

| P.O. of Watch— |
| Read by— **B** |
| Reported by— |
| Passed by— |
| Logged by— |
| System— W/T |
| Date 21-11-18 |
| Time— 1045 |

From—

Commander-in-Chief Grand Fleet.

To—

Admiralty

The Grand Fleet met this morning at 0900 five Battle-Cruisers, nine Battle Ships seven Light-Cruisers and forty-nine Destroyers of the High Sea Fleet, which surrendered for internment and are being brought to the Firth of Forth.

(1005)

M. 1704/00.
Sta. 6/14.
Sta. 596/16.

[6222] 12009/D912 100m pads 12/17ss G & S 109 156

48 – Naval Signal Announcing the Surrender of the German Fleet, 21.11.1918

Wilfrid J. Jenkins – H.M.S. Mersey
Copy of Naval Signal, dated 11.11.18 sent at 10.56 a.m. from Navy Office (Southend) to General System W/T (Wireless Transmission),
containing a message from The Admiralty concerning the Armistice

The telegram relates to the surrender of the German High Seas Fleet to the British Grand Fleet under the command of Admiral Beatty. (see 39) The German ships had sailed by arrangement to a meeting place with the British fleet in the North Sea, from where they were escorted to an anchorage in the Firth of Forth. On the day he sent his telegram to the Admiralty (November, 21 1918), Beatty signalled the German ships: 'The German flag will be hauled down at sunset today and will not be hoisted again without permission'. But the next year at Scapa Flow the Germans scuttled most of their ships to prevent their use by their former enemy.

SOLDIERS & LAND

"The angel of the Lord on the traditional white horse and clad all in white with flaming sword, faced the Germans at Mons and forbade their further progress."

Brigadier General John Charteris, Chief Intelligence Officer, British Expeditionary Force, Western Front, September 5, 1914. (J. Charteris, *At GHQ,* Cassell & Co., 1931, p.25)

"This paper is to be considered by each soldier as confidential and to be kept in his Active Service Pay Book: You are ordered abroad as a soldier of your King to help our French comrades against the invasion of a common enemy. You have to perform a task which will need your courage, your energy, your patience. Remember that the honour of the British Army depends on your individual conduct. It will be your duty not only to set an example of discipline and steadiness under fire but also to maintain the most friendly relations with those whom you are helping in this struggle. In this new experience you may find temptations in both wine and women. You must entirely resist both temptations, and, while treating all women with perfect courtesy you should avoid any intimacy. Do your duty bravely. Fear God. Honour the King."

Earl Kitchener, Field Marshal, British Army / British Secretary of State for War, August 1917

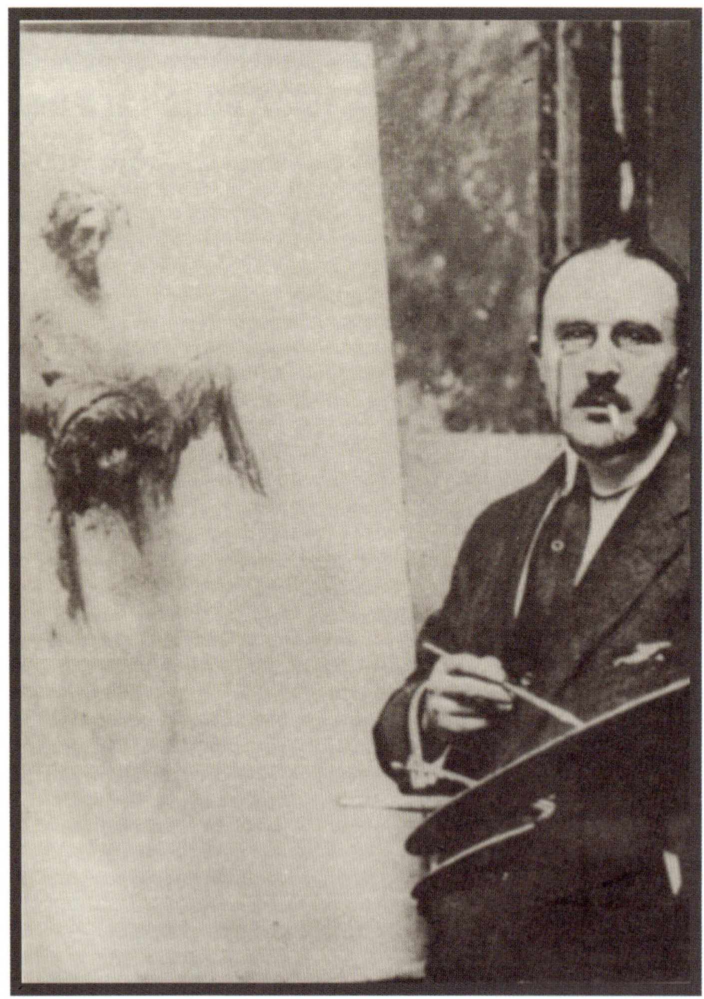

"The Popular English Artist, Hal Hurst, at Work on 'The Hero'."
New York Times, April 22, 1915

49 – Hal Hurst (1865–1938)

The Hero, 1915, signed,
Oil on canvas, 45 x 30 in. (114 x 76 cm)

In this picture, Christ carries the dead soldier away from the flames of destruction to spiritual rejuvenation symbolised by a golden light.

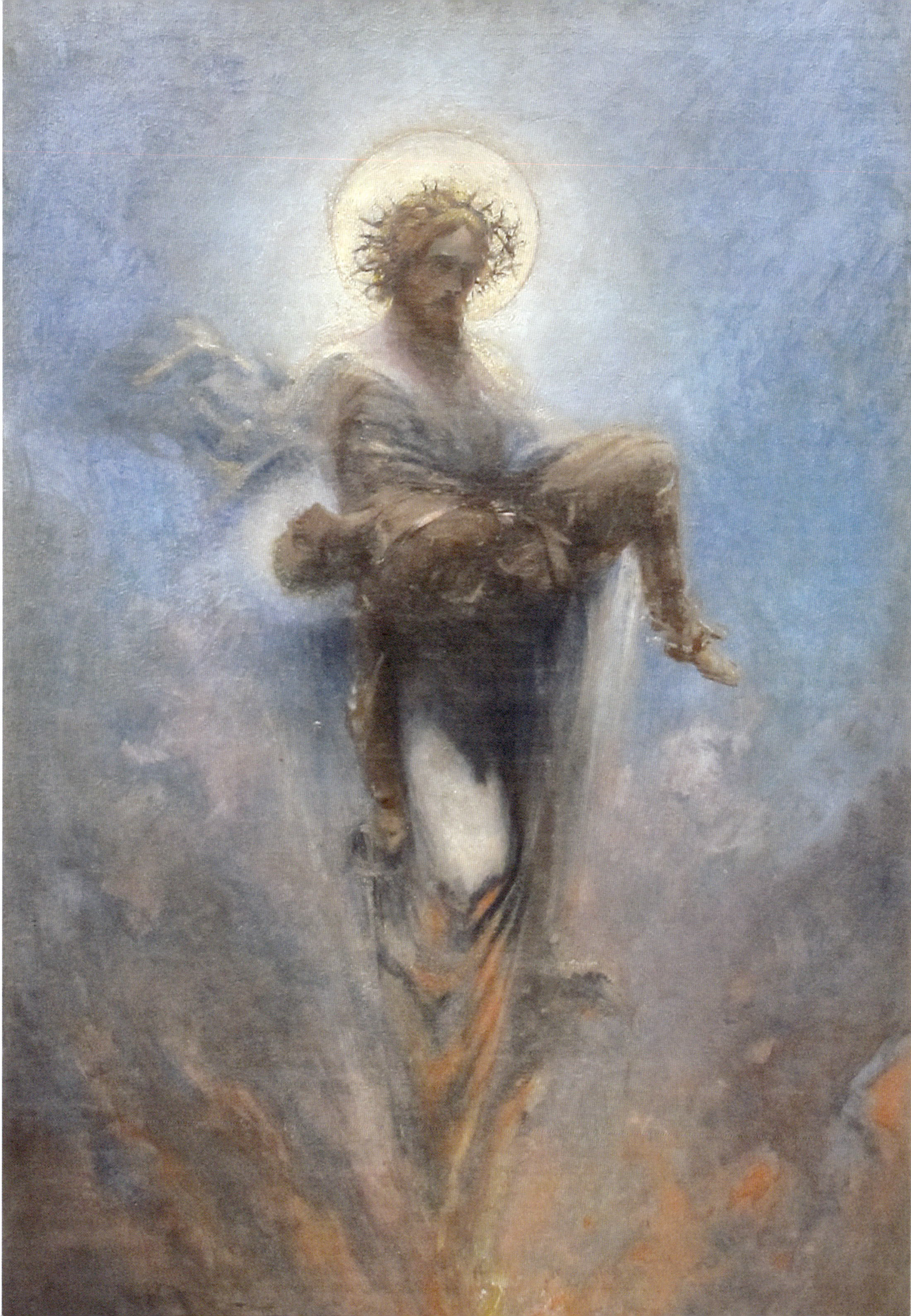

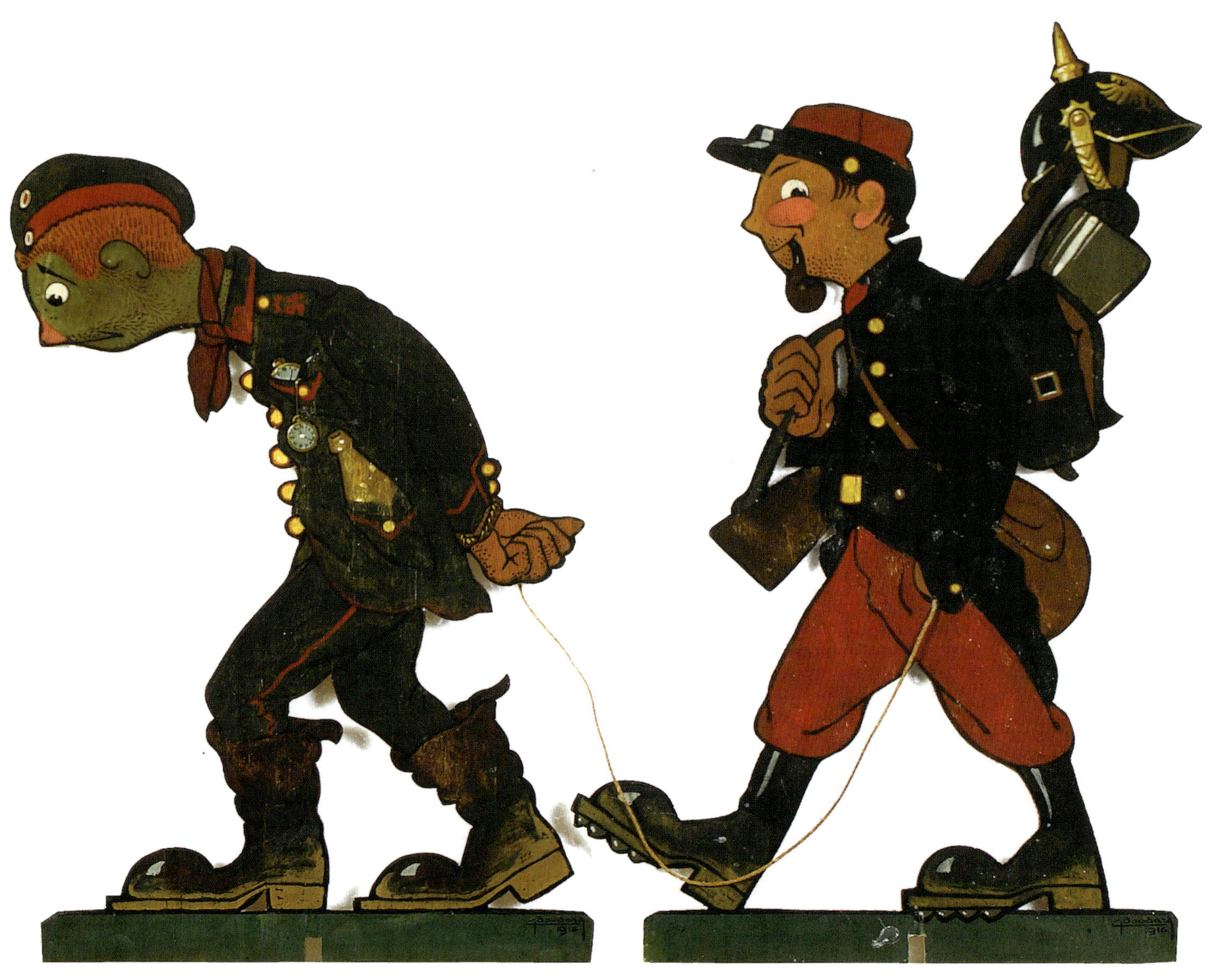

50 – G. Boudard

Le retour de la chasse, 1916,
A set of four painted figures cut in silhouette, each signed and dated - one inscribed Kamarad !!!!!! - and signed with initials on the reverse and inscribed 'reproduction interdite'.
Oil on fruit wood, each 17 ¾ x 11 ¾ in. (45 x 30 cm) with a cross bar support

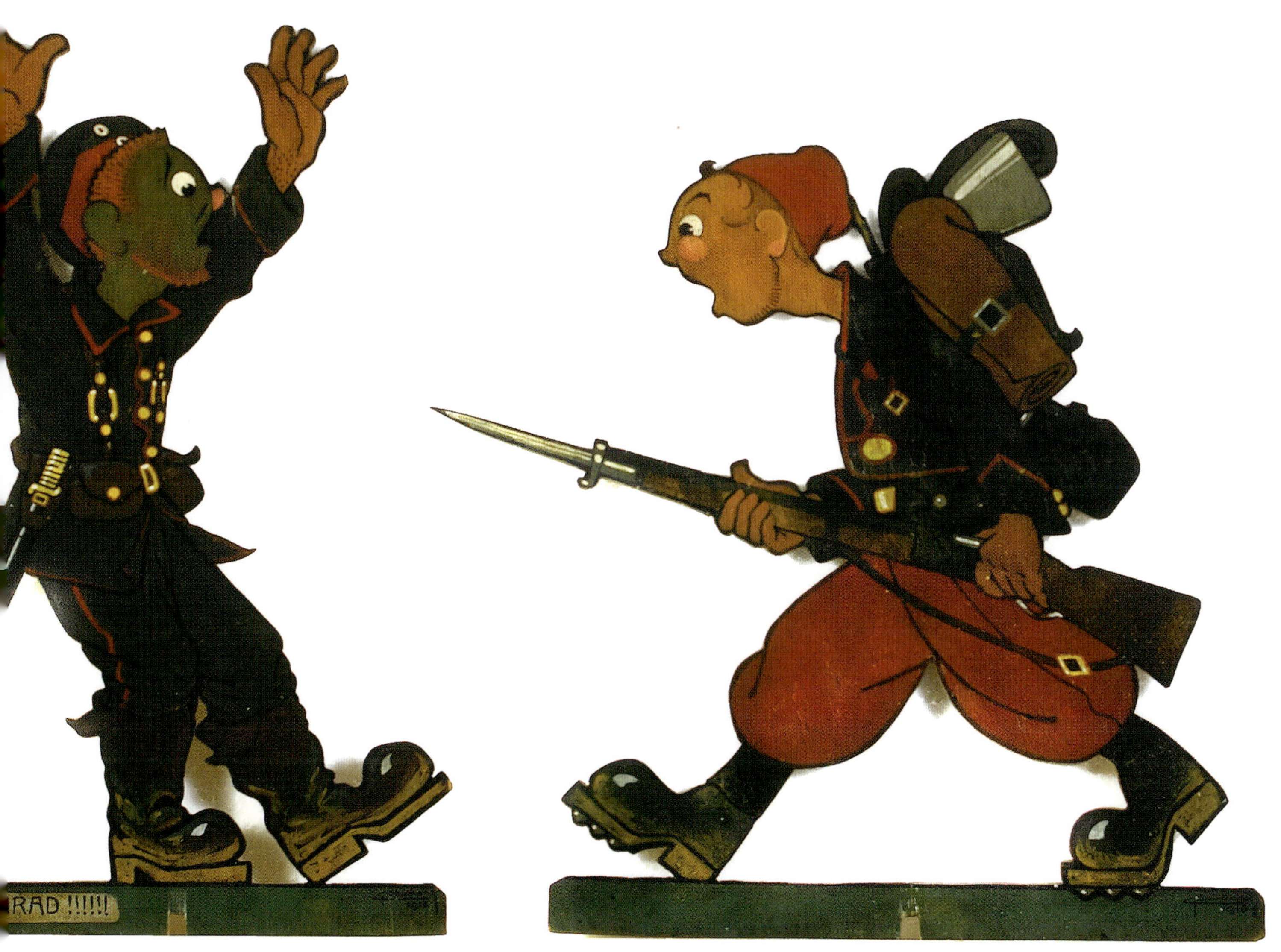

Boudard is recorded as having been wounded in the right hand at the First Battle of the Marne in September 1914. He subsequently worked at one of the 'Écoles des blessés' (24, Bd des Capucines, Paris) producing painted wooden figures in silhouette of French and German soldiers, two examples of which are in the collection of the Imperial War Museum, (dating to 1917) and one is at the Historial de la Grande Guerrre, Peronne (dating to 1916). A further set can be seen at The Musée de l'Armée in Paris.

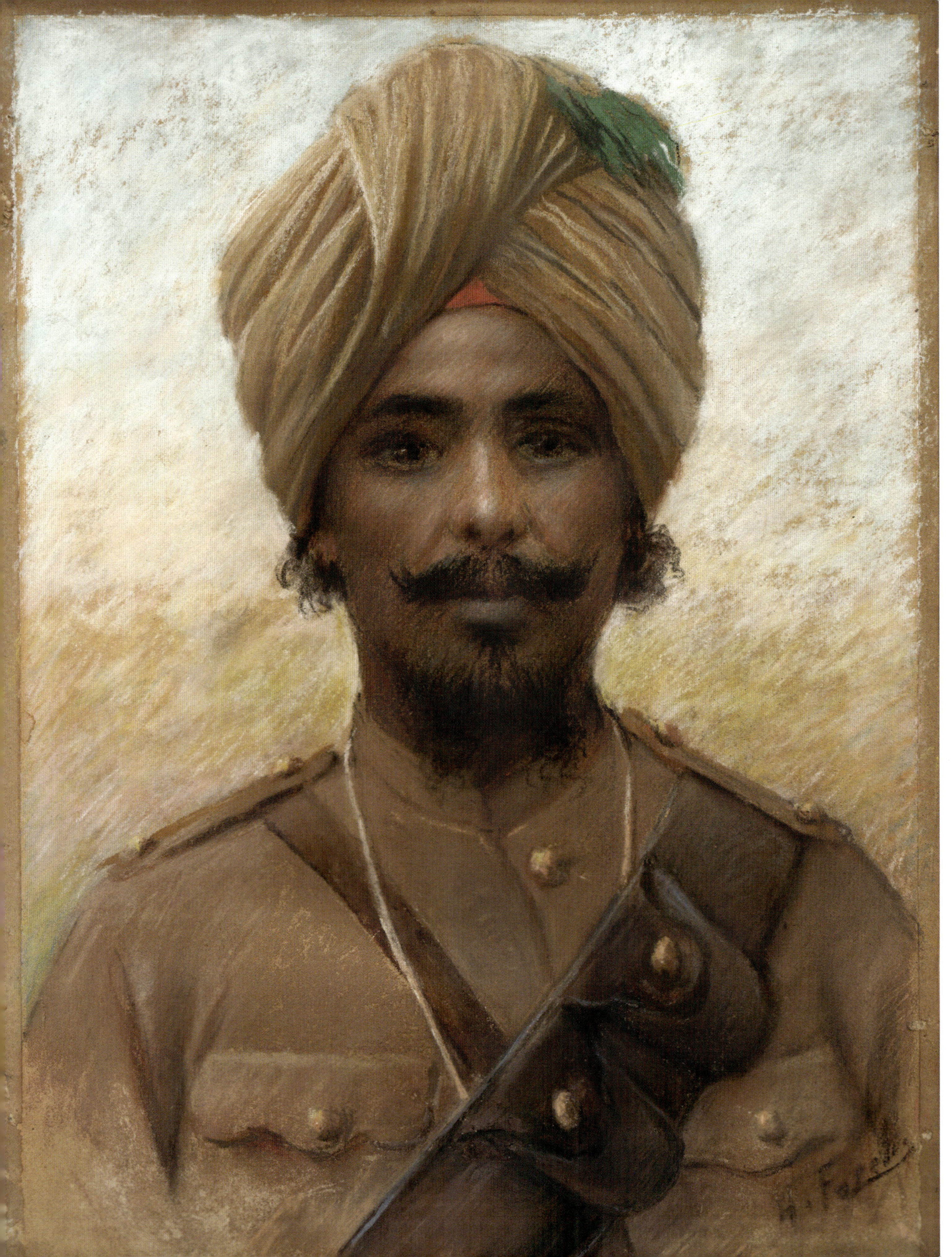
H. Fazee

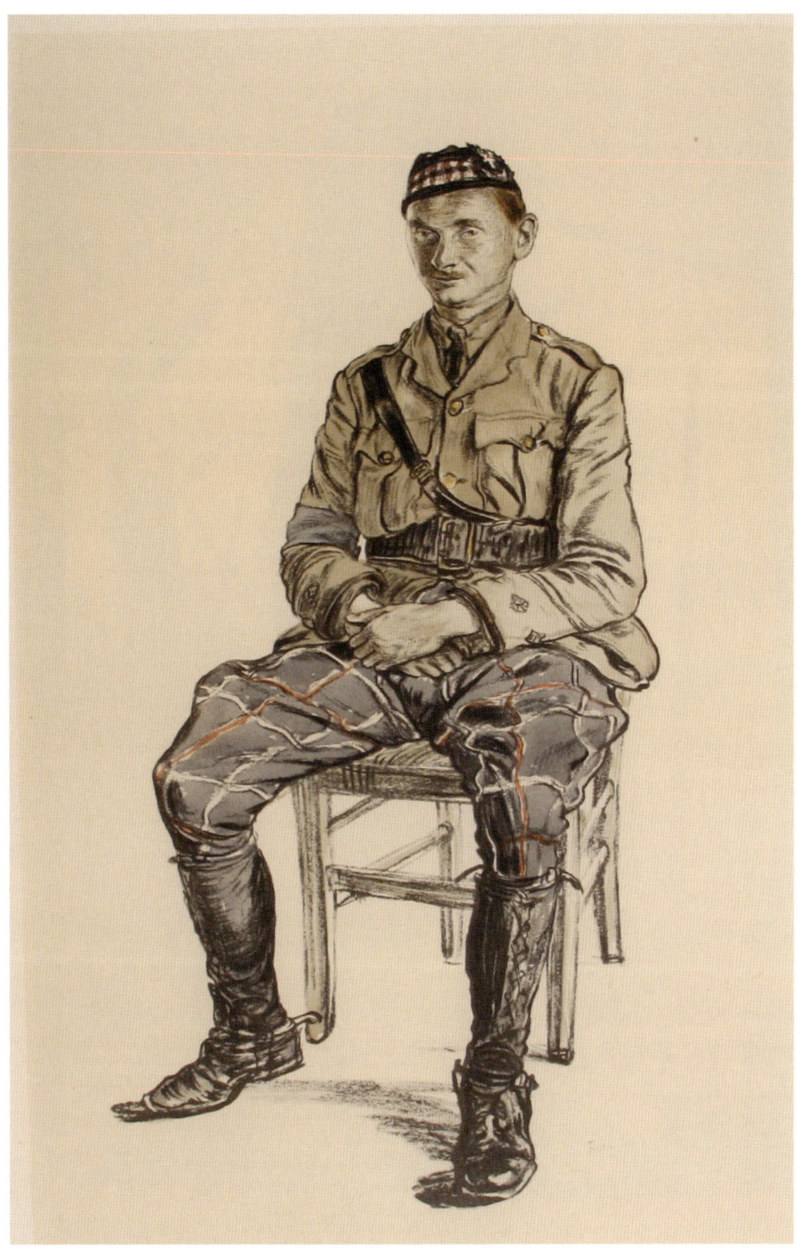

52 – Muirhead Bone (1876-1953)

Highland Officer – Lieutenant D.H. Georgeson, Seaforth Highlanders, Intelligence Officer 44th Brigade Headquarters, signed within the plate,
Coloured lithograph, 17 ½ x 12 ½ in. (44 x 32 cm)

This print appeared as one of the sixty 'War Drawings' published by *Country Life*, 1917.

51 – Albert Fossard (1867-1947)

Hindou, inscribed on verso: 'Guerre de 1914 – Hindou – Offert par M. Forcella en 1917 à M. P.P.',
Pastel on paper, 14 ⅜ x 10 ⅝ in. (36.5 x 27 cm)

1.2 million men from the Indian Army fought for Britain in the First World War and 140,000 of them fought on the Western Front. Of these, 90,000 served in the infantry and cavalry and as many as non-combatant labourers. The majority of these men came from Punjab, Garwahl, Nepal, Madras and Burma. Of the combatants, over 8,550 were killed and as many as 50,000 more were wounded. Almost 5,000 of the dead who have no known grave are commemorated on the Menin Gate at Ypres and at Neuve Chapelle.

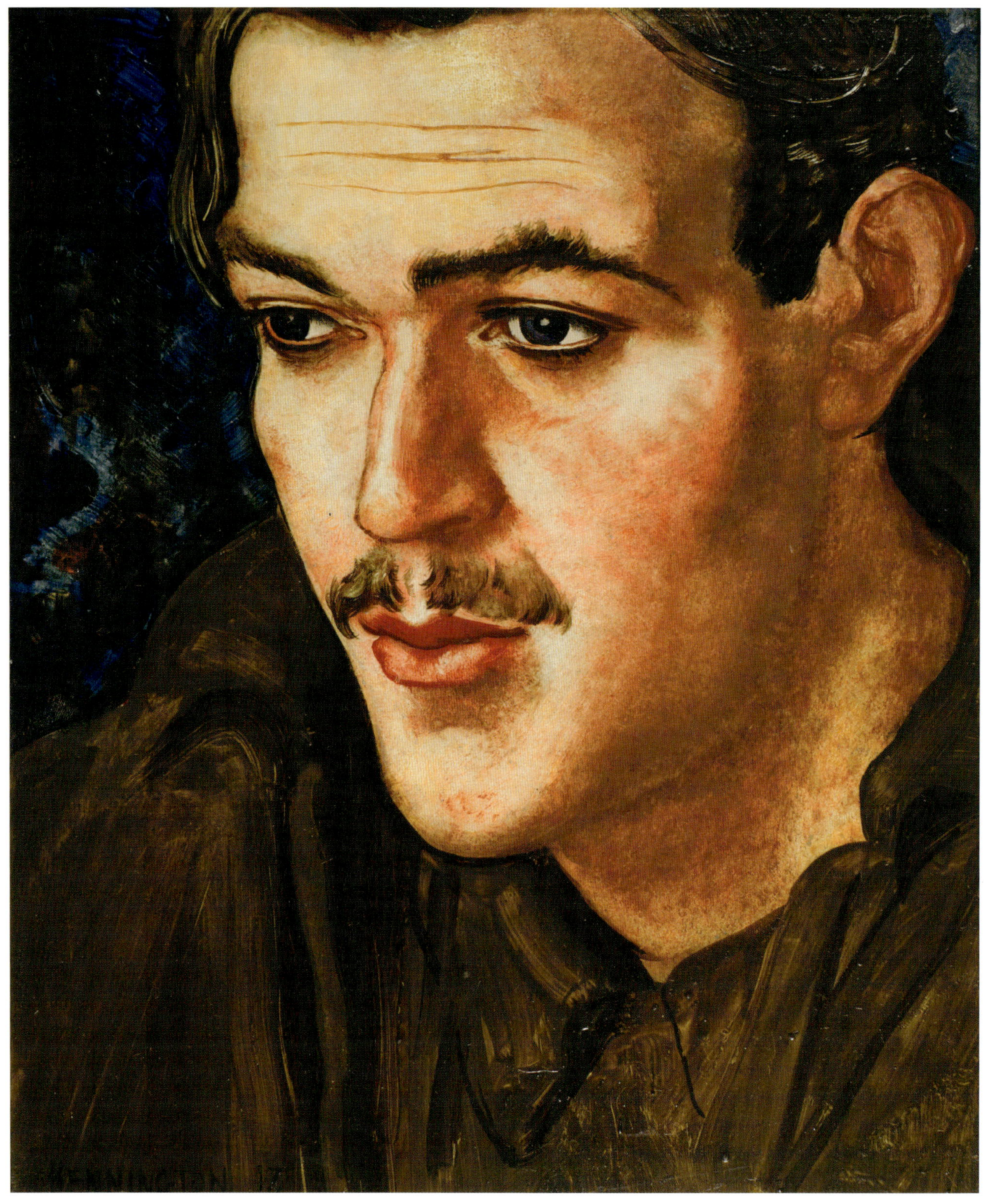

53 – Eric Kennington (1888-1960)

Portrait of Cosmo Clark, 1917, signed and dated,
Oil on panel, 12 x 9 7/8 in. (30.5 x 25 cm.)
Provenance: Jean and Cosmo Clark's daugher, Julia Rhys
Cosmo Clark and Eric Kennington – childhood neighbours – were life-long friends and during the First World War both
served with the Middlesex Regiment, to which Kennington was attached as an Official War Artist.

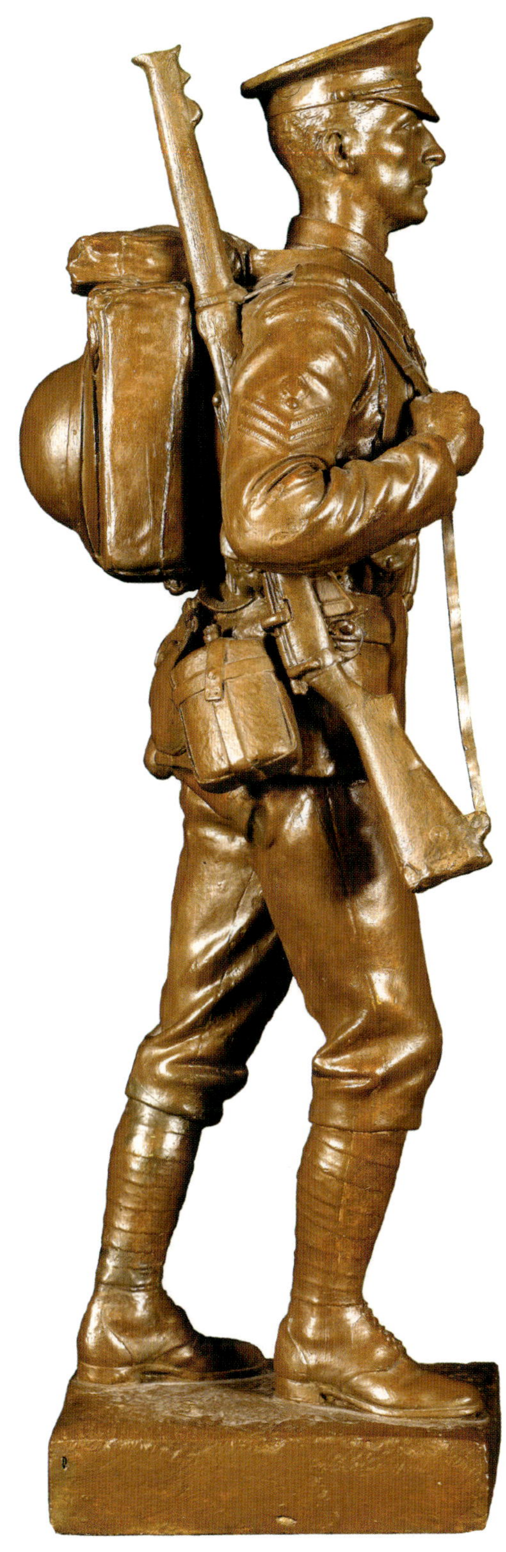

54 – George Edward Wade (1853-1933)

Sergeant of the Grenadier Guards in Marching Order,
The original plaster patinated with bronze finish, 17 in. (43 cm) high, provenance: the Artist's family

Wade produced numerous sculptures to commemorate the First World War including a Peace Memorial at Quarry Bank, Staffordshire, 1931, and an equestrian statue of Earl Haig, 1923, once a familiar landmark on Castle Hill, Edinburgh but now relocated within the Castle grounds.

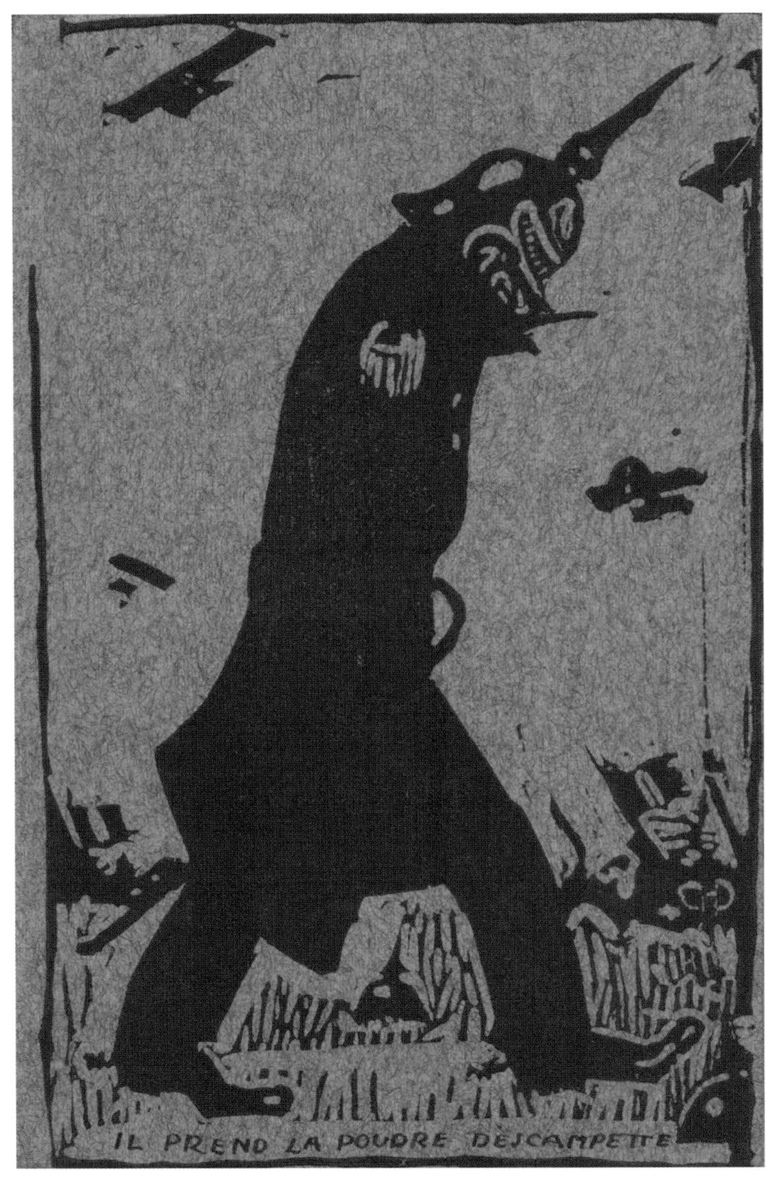

55 – Theophile-Alexandre Steinlen (1859-1923)

Il prend la poudre, signed with monogram,
Woodcut on grey paper, 5 ½ x 3 ½ in. (14 x 9 cm)

The monogram PP (Petit Pierre) was one of several pseudonyms used by Steinlen. Artists like Steinlen, who usually worked under contracts demanding exclusivity, used pseudonyms to allow themselves to undertake commissions from other (rival) publishers without being able to be directly identified.

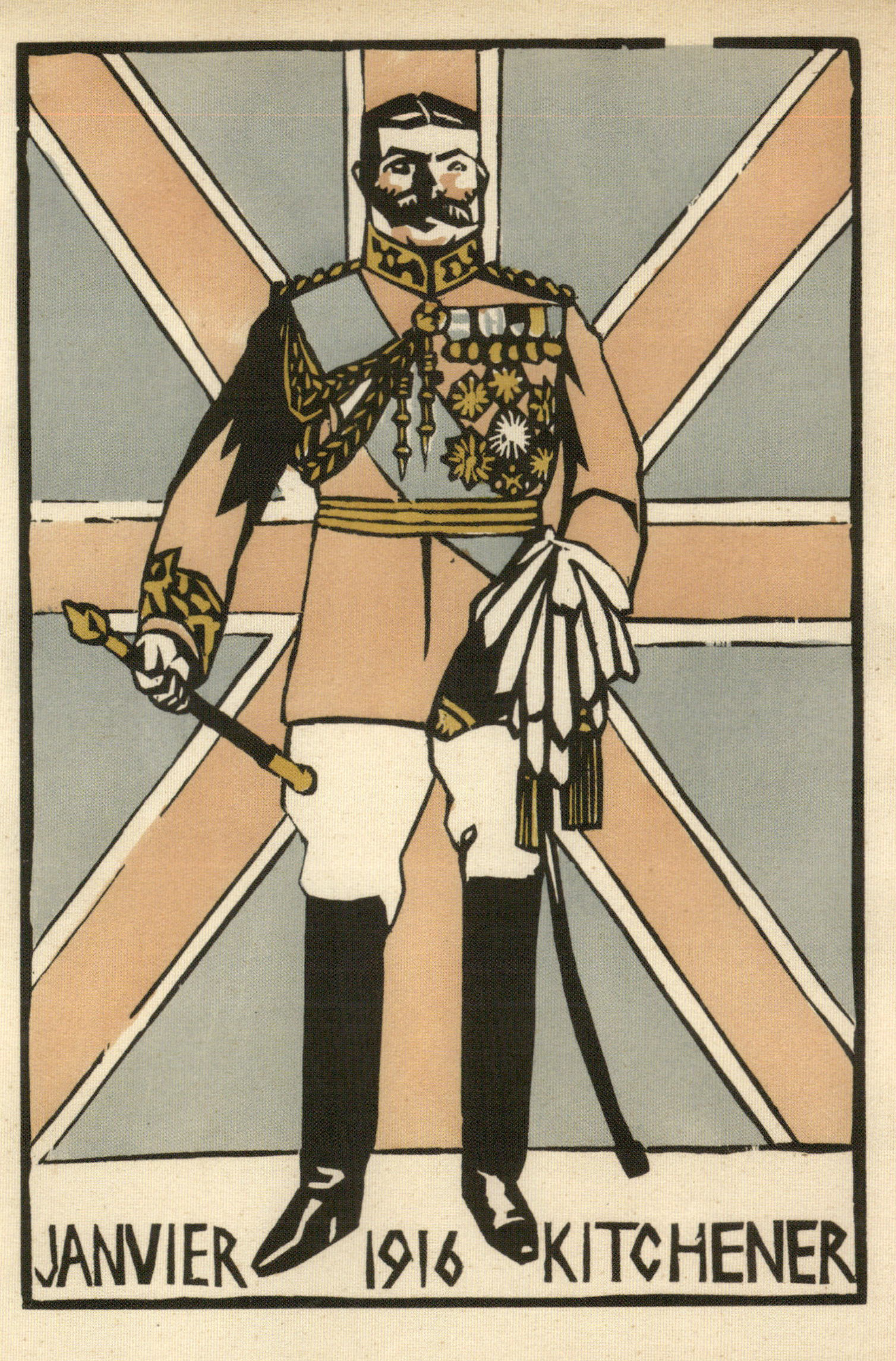

56 – René Georges Hermann-Paul (1864-1940)

Janvier 1916 – Kitchener from *Calendrier de la Guerre (2ème année – août 1915-juillet 1916),* 1916,
Coloured woodcuts, 17 ¾ x 13 ¾ in. (45 x 35cm)
Published by Librarie Lutetia [A. Ciavarri, Directeur]

See full calendar on following pages

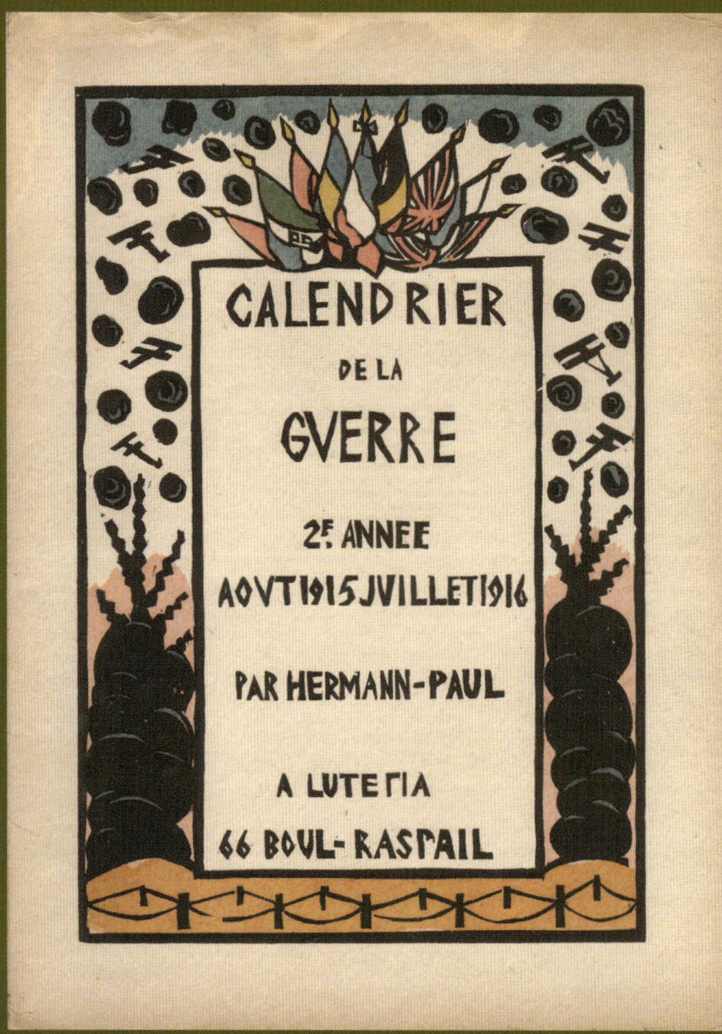

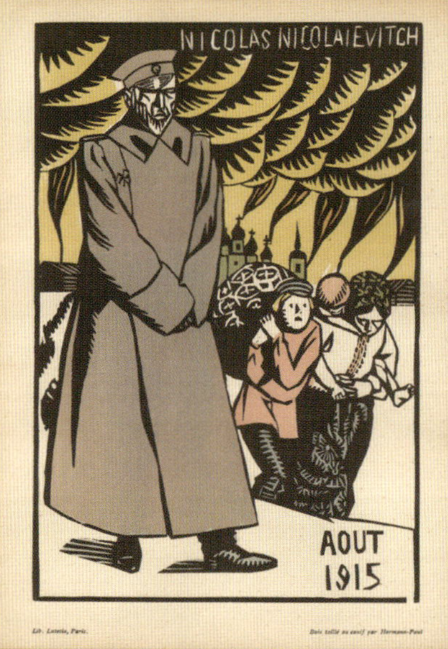

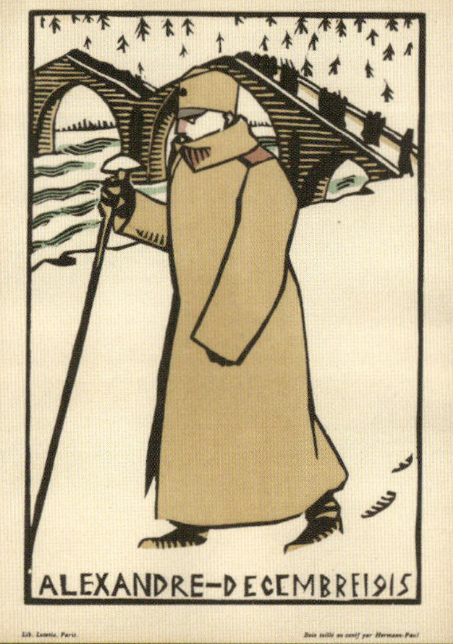

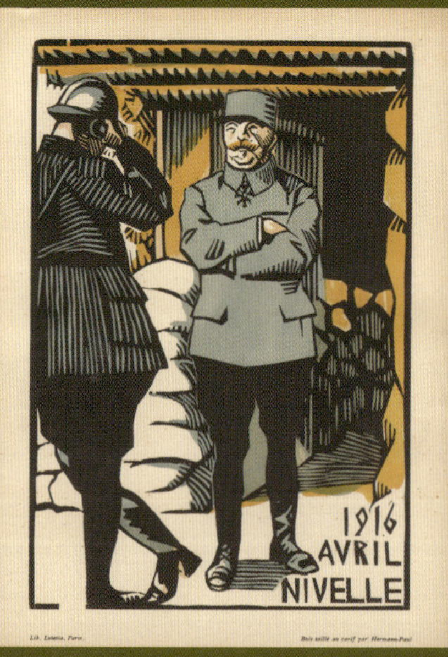

56 – René Georges Hermann-Paul (1864-1940)

Calendrier de la Guerre (2ème année – août 1915-juillet 1916), 1916,
Coloured woodcuts, 17 ¾ x 13 ¾ in. (45 x 35cm) each
Published by Librarie Lutetia [A. Ciavarri, Directeur]

This complete set includes twelve colored woodcuts each representing
a month of the second year of the Great War from August 1915 until
July 1916. Each month is represented by leaders and personalities of
the period.
Hermann-Paul was an illustrator whose art appeared in literary journals
and news weeklies. Before the First World War, Hermann-Paul's graphic
arts were mostly done as lithographs, etchings and dry points but after
war broke out, and metal became scarce, the artist turned to wood.

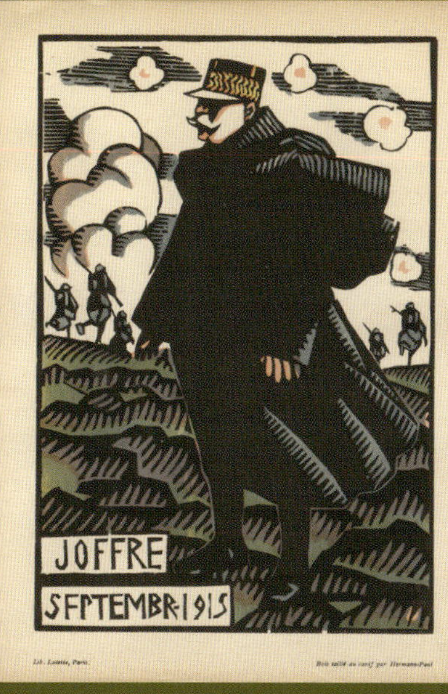
JOFFRE
SEPTEMBR 1915
Lib. Lemia, Paris.
Bois taillé au canif par Hermann-Paul

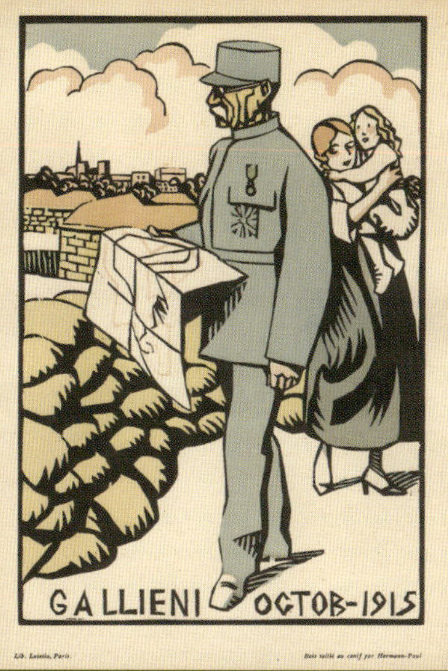
GALLIENI OCTOB-1915
Lib. Lemia, Paris.
Bois taillé au canif par Hermann-Paul

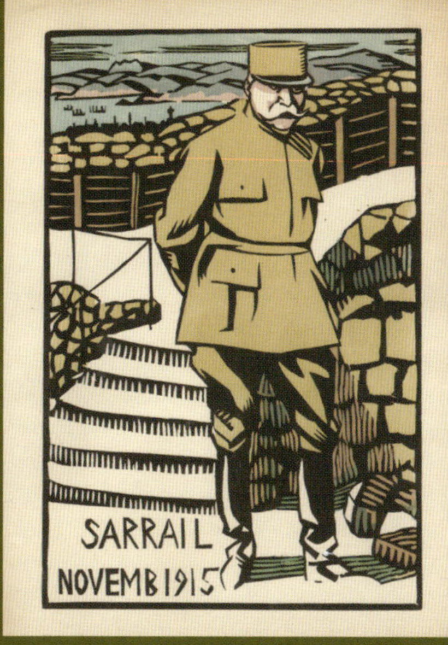
SARRAIL
NOVEMB 1915

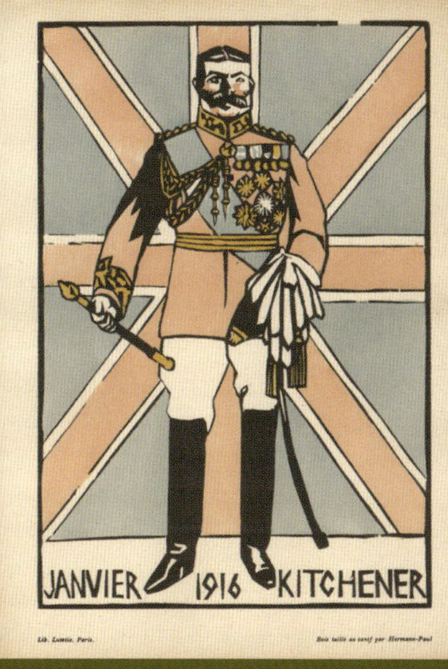
JANVIER 1916 KITCHENER
Lib. Lemia, Paris.
Bois taillé au canif par Hermann-Paul

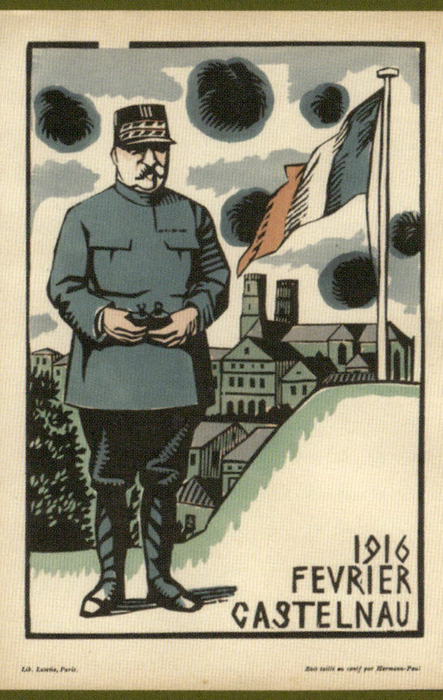
1916
FEVRIER
CASTELNAU
Lib. Lemia, Paris.
Bois taillé au canif par Hermann-Paul

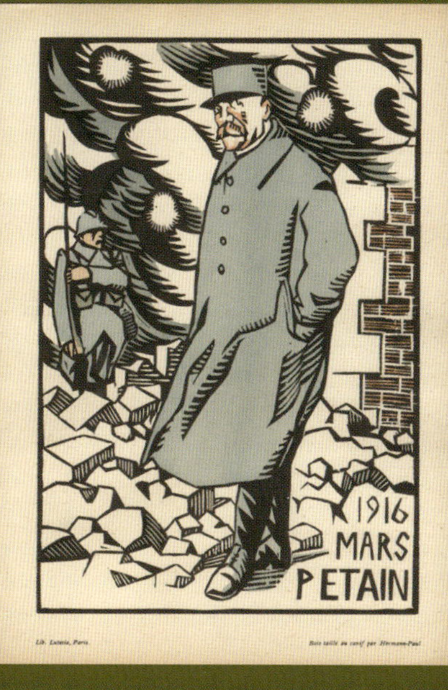
1916
MARS
PETAIN
Lib. Lemia, Paris.
Bois taillé au canif par Hermann-Paul

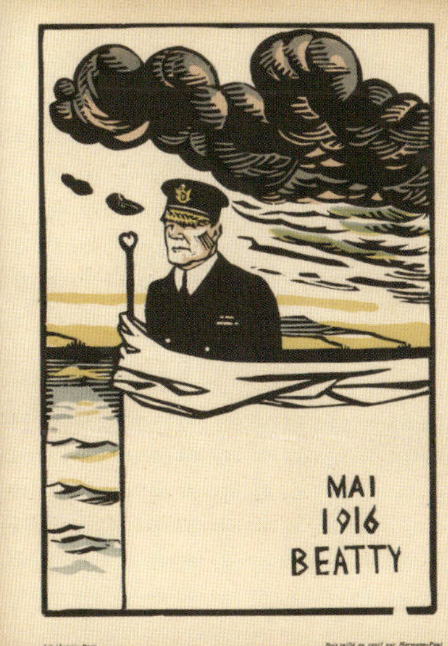
MAI
1916
BEATTY
Lib. Lemia, Paris.
Bois taillé au canif par Hermann-Paul

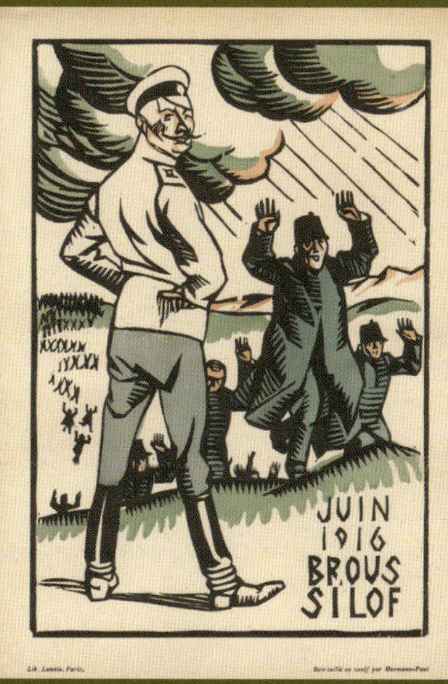
JUIN
1916
BROUS
SILOF
Lib. Lemia, Paris.
Bois taillé au canif par Hermann-Paul

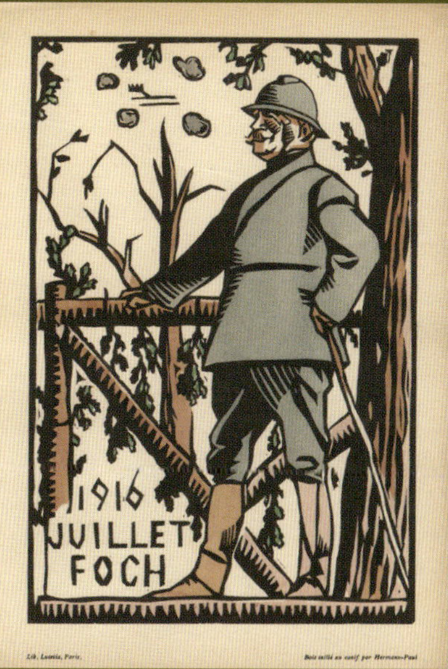
1916
JUILLET
FOCH
Lib. Lemia, Paris.
Bois taillé au canif par Hermann-Paul

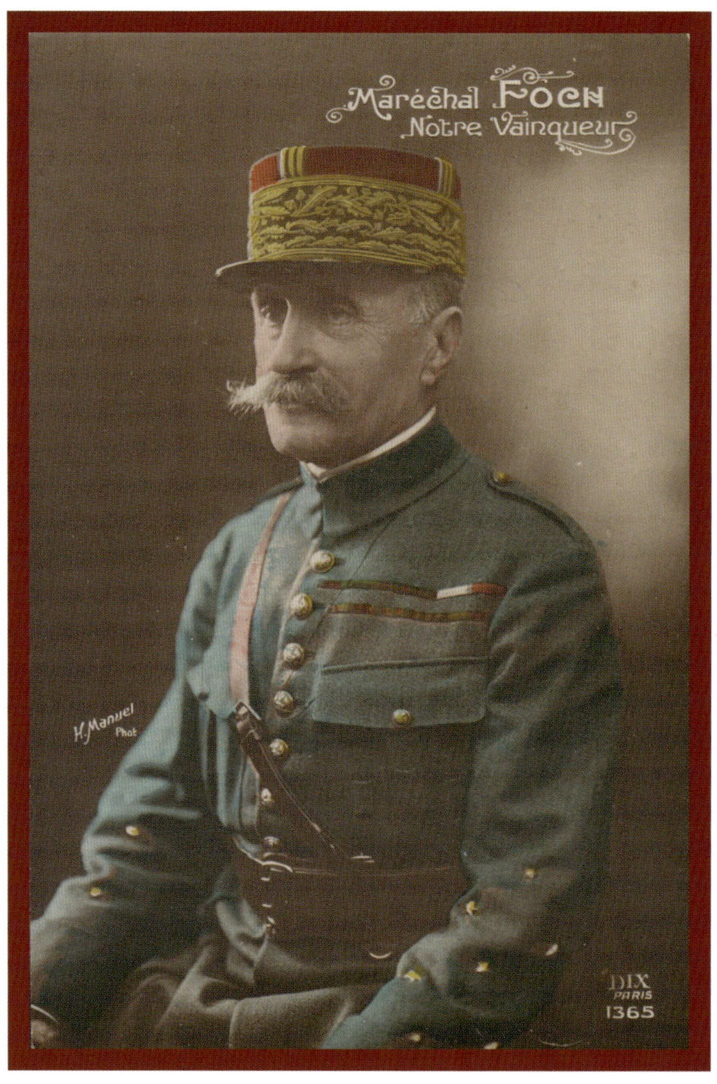

57 – French postcard

Maréchal Foch – Notre Vainqueur
Printed by DIX, Paris
5 ½ x 3 ½ in. (13.7 x 8.7 cm)

Born in 1851 Foch had already secured his reputation before the war as a soldier and military theorist. Foch's prestige soared as a result of the victory at the Marne, for which he was widely credited as a chief actor while commanding the French Ninth Army. He was then promoted again to command Army Group North, in which role he was required to co-operate with the British forces at Ypres and the Somme. In 1917, Foch was appointed Chief of the General Staff and in the spring of 1918 as Commander-in-Chief of the Allied Armies. He played a decisive role in halting a renewed German advance on Paris in the Second Battle of the Marne (July, 15-August 6, 1918), after which he was promoted to Marshal of France.

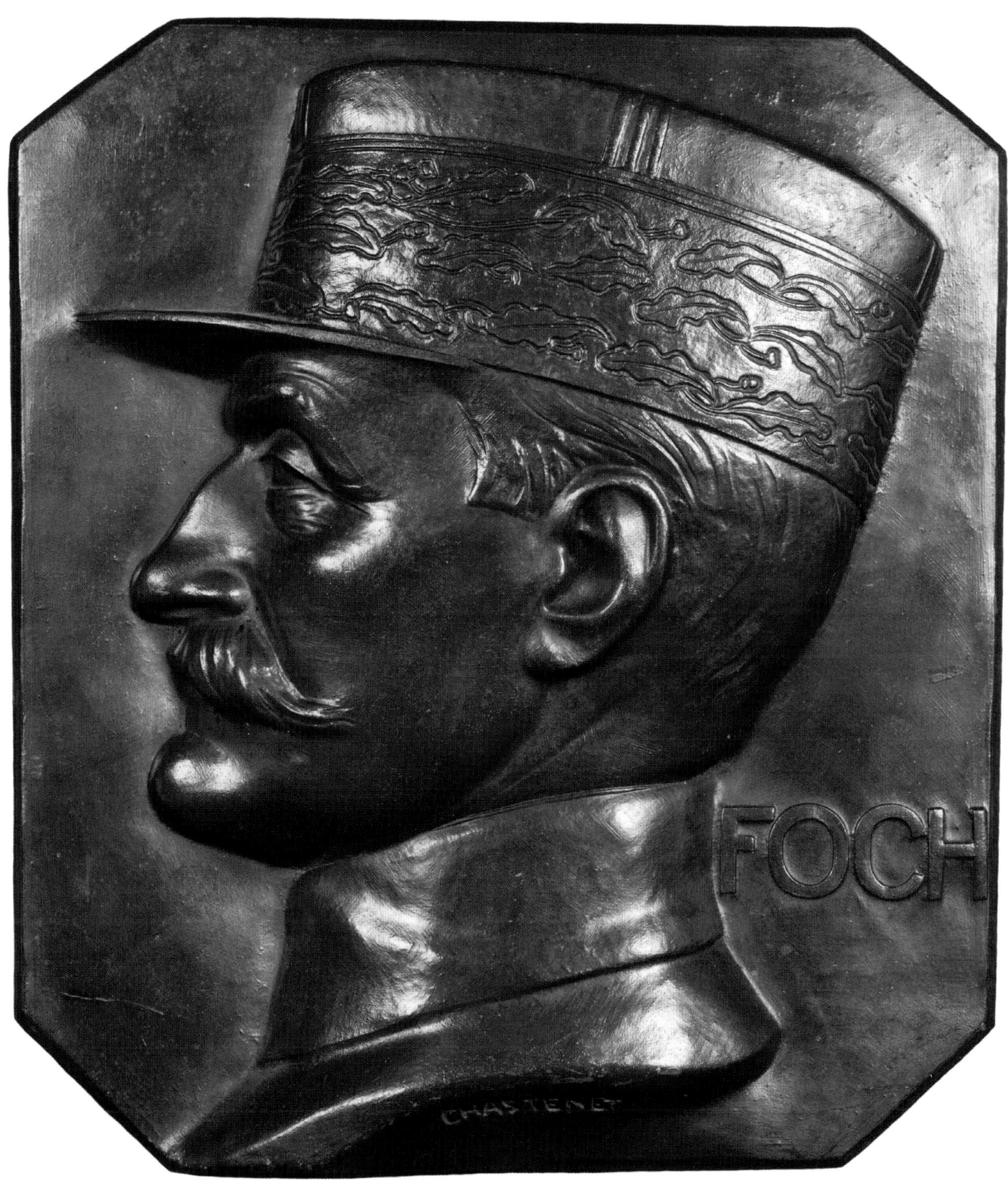

58 – André de Chastenet (1879-1961)

Profile portrait of Ferdinand Jean Marie Foch, 1912,
Signed and inscribed with title, dated 3rd April 1912 in pen and ink on the reverse and inscribed 'no 61'.
Bronze 9 ⅞ x 8 ¼ in. (25 x 21 cm), mounted on a mahogany panel

During the First World War the cult of heroes and leaders was very popular in all participating nations and was used for every purpose from private devotion to public propaganda. From 1904 Chastenet, a well-known portrait sculptor, regularly exhibited at the Salon of La Société Nationale des Beaux-Arts alongside Maillol, Carpeau, Rodin and Bourdelle.

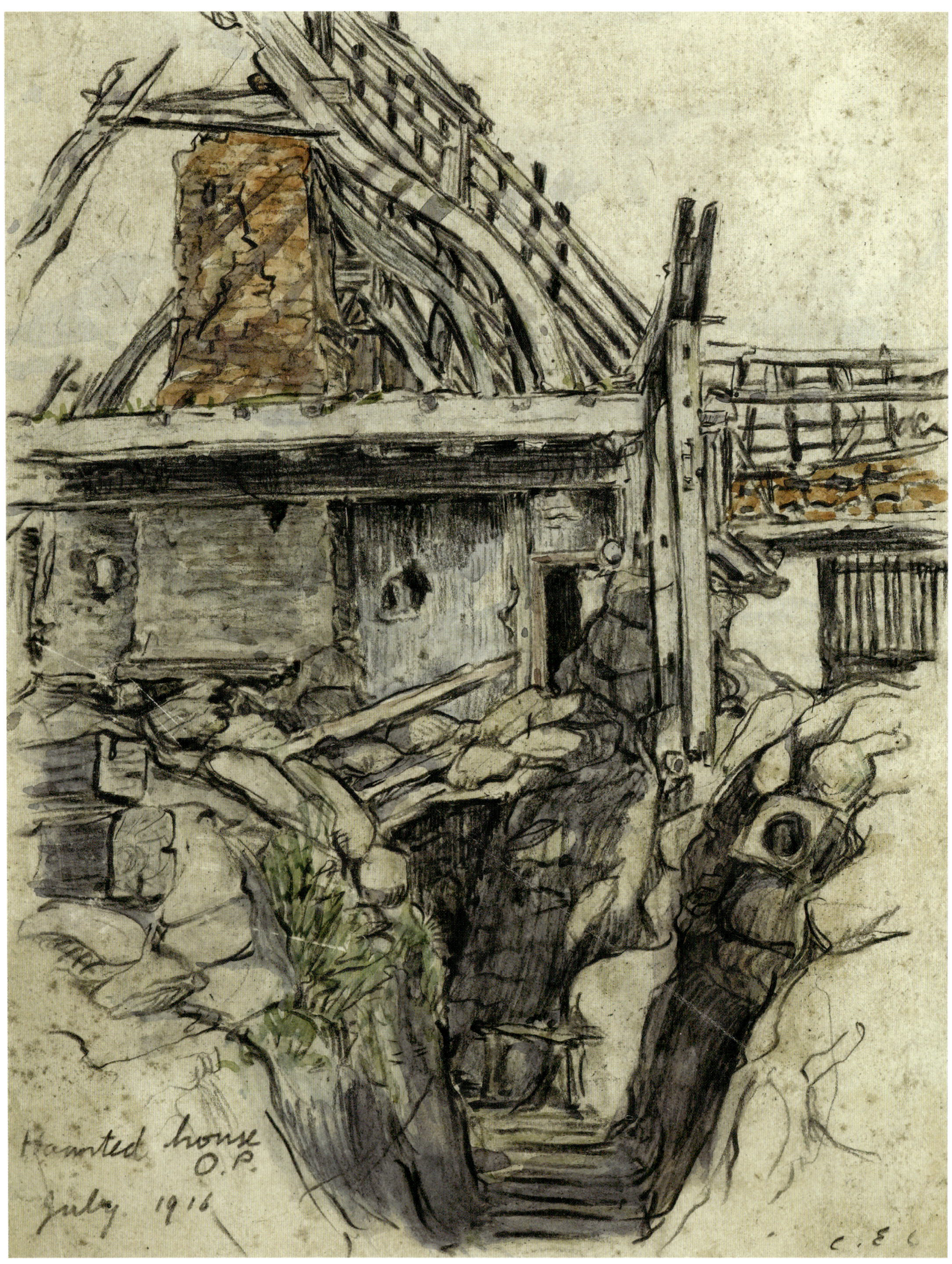

Haunted house
O.P.
July 1916
C.E.

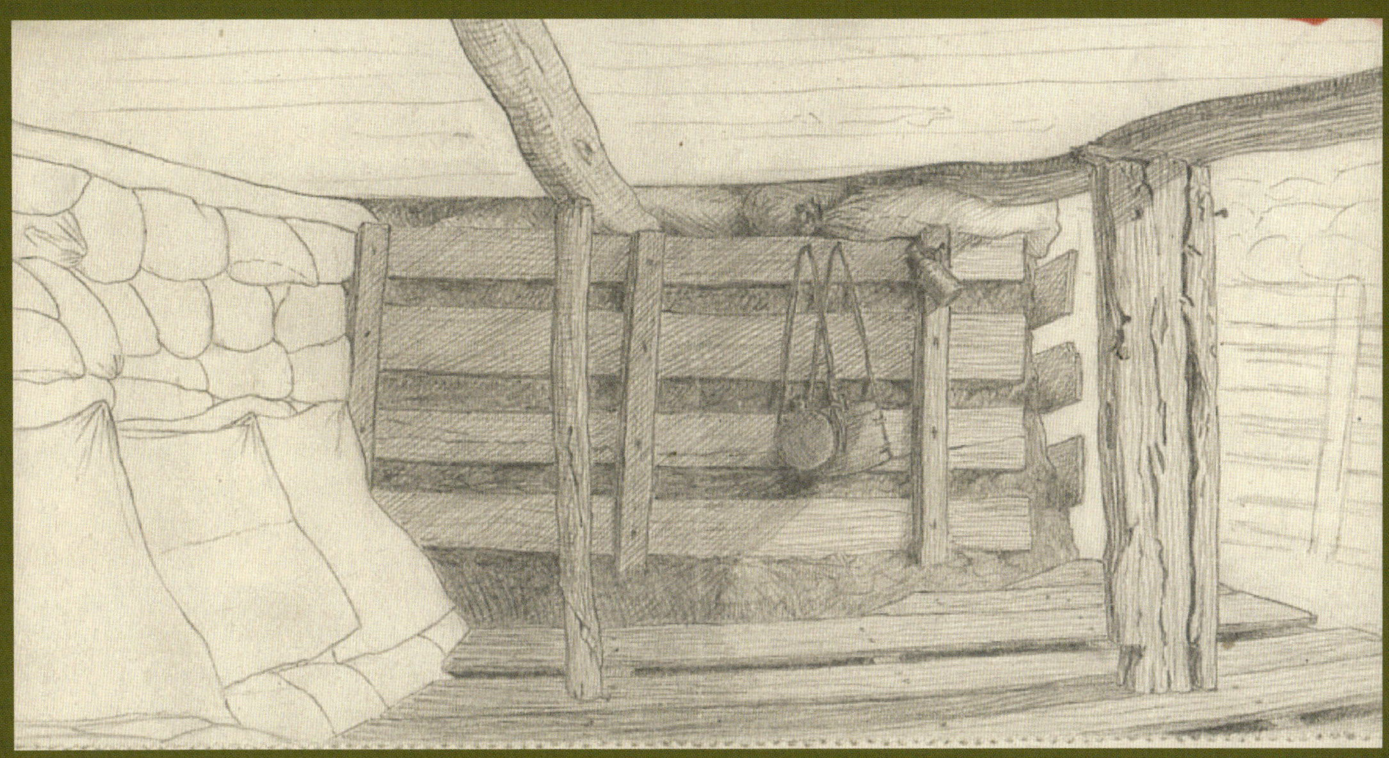

60 – Lt. Richard Barrett Talbot Kelly (1896-1971)

Forward Observation Dugout, Indian Village, Festubert, June 1915,
Pencil on paper, 6 x 3 ⅛ in. (15 x 8 cm)

As a Lieutenant in the Divisional Artillery of the 9th (Scottish) Division, Kelly spent long periods in the trenches. This is the original sketch for a watercolour in the collection of The National Army Museum showing Kelly's own *Forward Observation Post Dugout at the Indian Village, Festubert, June 1915*. The Battle of Festubert (May 15-25, 1915) was an attack by the British Army in the Artois region of France on the Western Front.

59 – Charles Cundall (1890-1971)

Haunted House, 1916,
Signed with initials, inscribed 'Haunted House, O.P.' and dated July 1916,
Coloured pencil and pencil on paper, 6 ½ x 5 in. (16.5 x 12.5 cm)

In the 450 mile-span between the English Channel and Switzerland, a network of approximately 25,000 miles of trenches was constructed during the war. Siegfried Sassoon wrote, "When all is done and said, the war was mainly a matter of holes and ditches." (Siegfried Sassoon, *Memoirs of an Infantry Officer*, 1930)

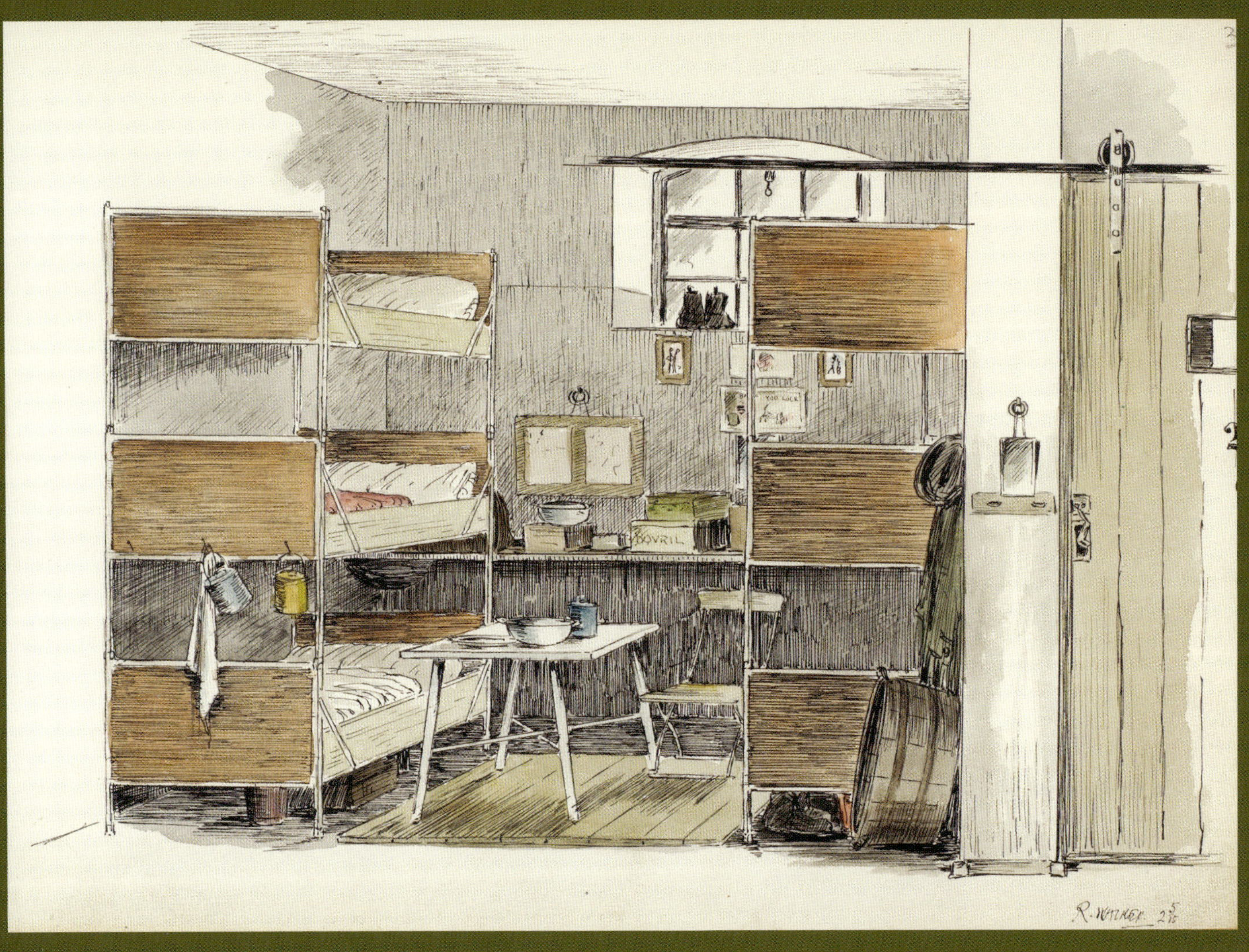

61 – Robert Walker

Horse box, 1915, signed and dated,
Pen & ink and watercolour on paper, 7 ¾ x 11 ½ in. (19.7 x 29.2 cm)

Robert Walker was an internee at Ruhleben Civilian Internment Camp, a former racecourse situated 10km to the west of Berlin. In 1917, he is recorded as having exhibited humorous drawings in the Studio in Ruhleben, alongside fellow artists Frank Wade and Percy Wood (*Ruhleben Camp Magazine*, June 1917). A similar drawing is in the collection of the Imperial War Museum (9496 Misc 60 (915))

62 – Richard Carline (1896-1980)

A dug-out at Ovilliers, 1918, signed, dated and inscribed "Ovillers",
Wash on paper, 16 x 12 ¼ in. (40.5 x 31 cm)

Carline was a Lieutenant in the Royal Air Force. Towards the end of the war he was appointed an Official War Artist and with his brother Sydney he became noted for aerial views.

Ovillers, a village about 5 kilometres north-east of the town of Albert, was attacked on the first day of the Battle of the Somme (1st July 1916). It was lost during the German advance in March 1918, but retaken on August 24 by the 38th (Welsh) Division.

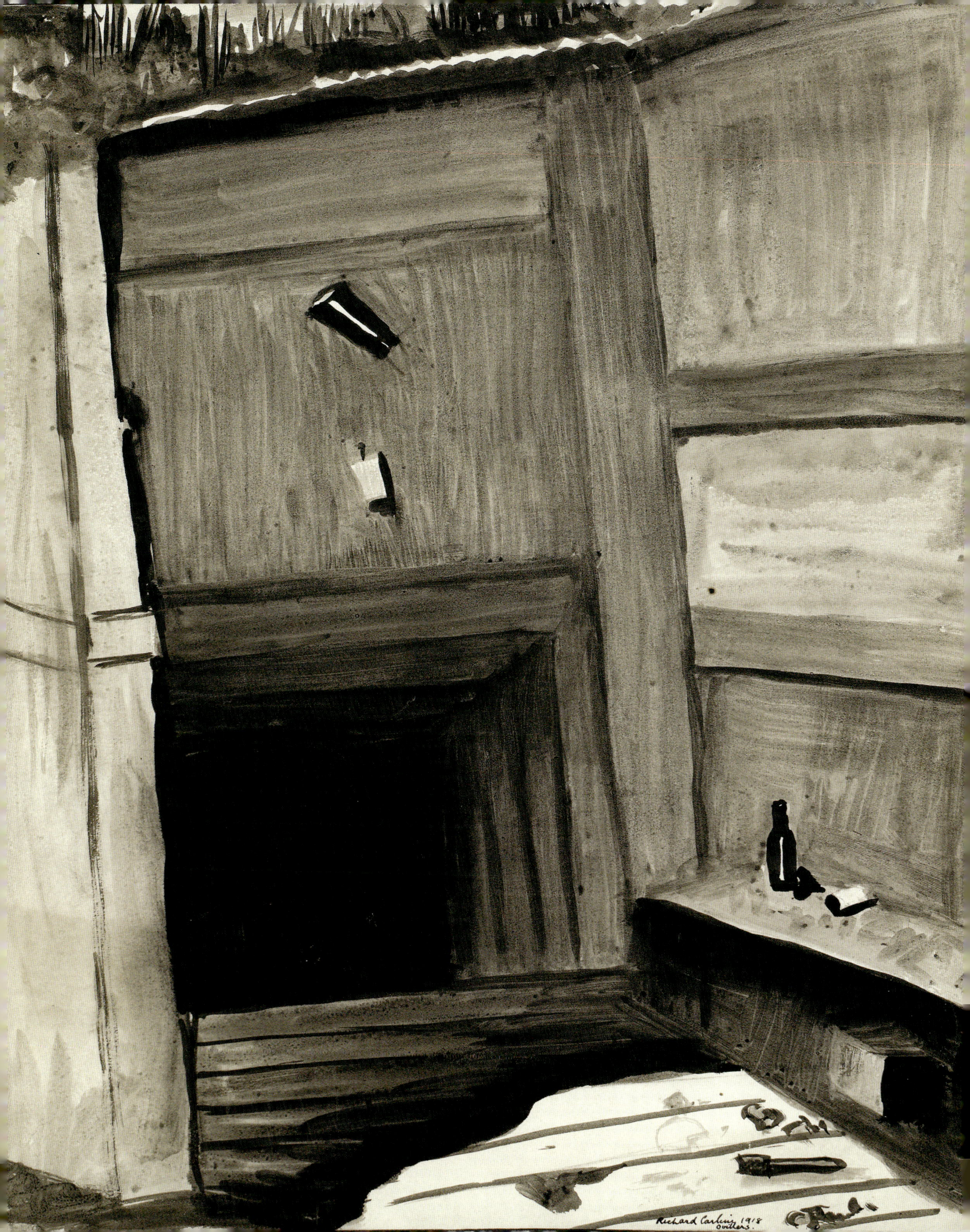

Richard Carline 1918
Ovillers.

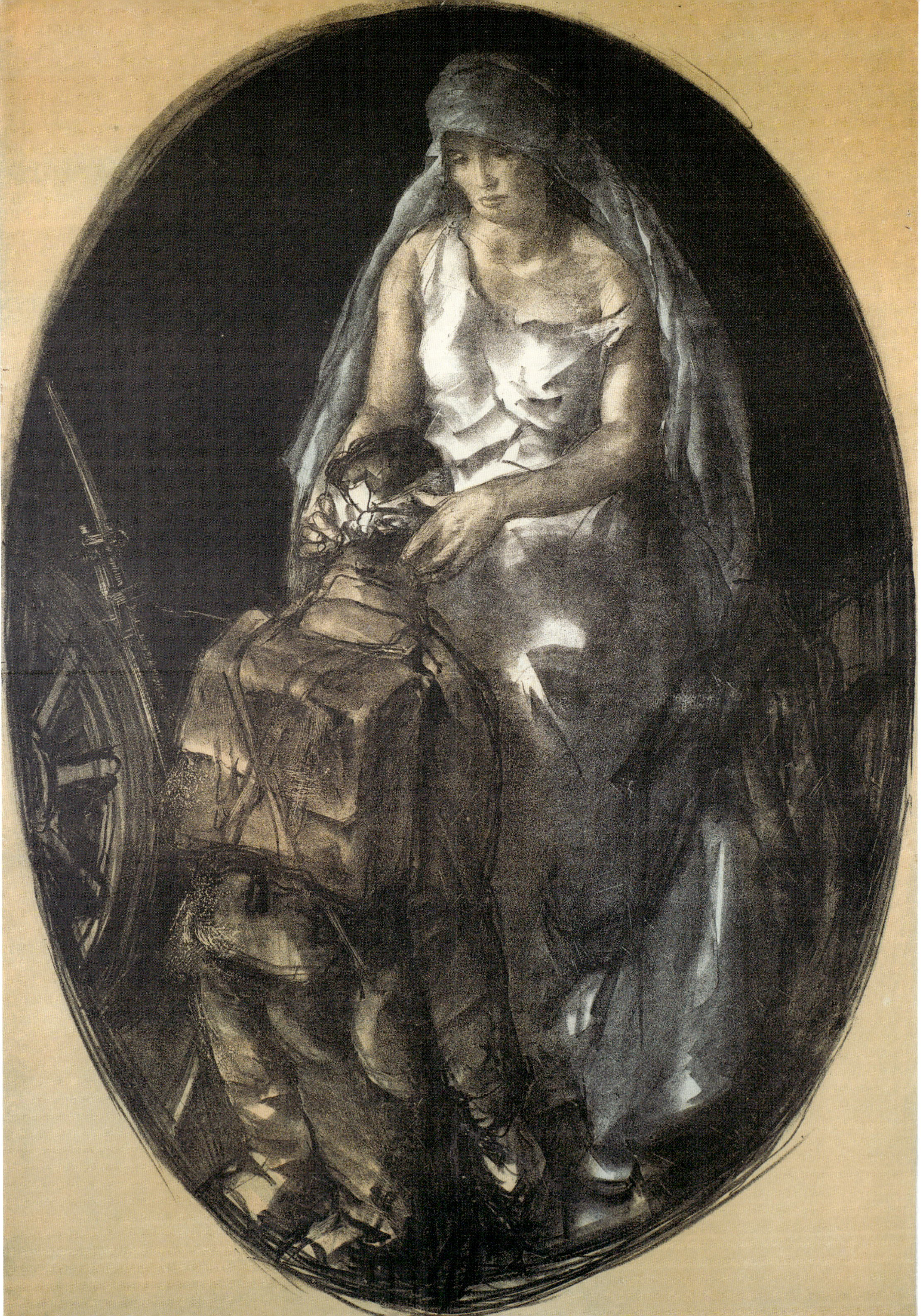

63 – Gerald Spencer Pryse, M.C. (1882-1956)

Poster (without the lettering) for The Nation's Fund for Nurses – 'A Thank-Offering from the British Empire to British Nurses', c.1915,
Lithographic poster printed by Vincent Brooks Day & Sons Ltd., London,
30 x 20 ins. (76 x 51 cm.)

During the war, Pryse designed a number of posters including several published by Frank Pick for the Underground Electric Railway in London, as well as for the Labour Party, The British Red Cross, and for the Empire Marketing Board.

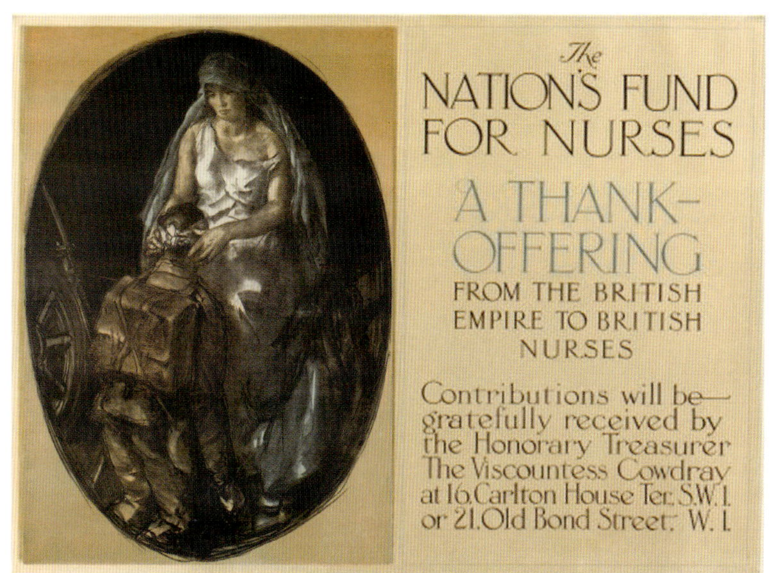

Following pages:

64 – Gerald Spencer Pryse, M.C. (1882-1956)

The Retreat from Ypres, c.1917,
Oil on canvas, 42 x 50 in. (106.7 x 127 cm)

Provenance: Stuart Cooper,
Exhibited: *Home Lad, Home, The War Horse Story*, St Barbe Museum & Art Gallery, Lymington, Hampshire, March 1- April 25, 2014,
Literature: Upper Grosvenor Galleries Memorial Exhibition catalogue of works by Gerald Spencer Pryse (1962)

Pryse served as an Officer in Queen Victoria's Rifles and was twice wounded, losing the sight of one eye. He had a distinguished service career and was awarded the Military Cross in the Third Battle of Ypres in 1917. *The Retreat from Ypres*, shows a column of infantry marching with their officer mounted on his horse and was a direct response to his own first-hand experience. A related subject, *The Retreat of the 7th Division and 3rd Cavalry at Ypres*, was produced by Pryse as a lithograph.

During the Great War, Pryse produced a considerable body of lithographic work, some of it in colour under the title *Autumn Campaign* (1914). This was based on his time in France and Belgium at the beginning of the war when he drove around in a Mercedes carrying lithographic stones in the boot. Many of his drawings appeared in the *Illustrated London News*. In 1917 he was appointed an Official War Artist. He served as a dispatch rider for the Belgian government and was present at the Siege of Antwerp. The artist wrote a wartime memoir entitled *Four Days: an account of a journey in France made between 28 and 31 August 1914,* published by John Lane in 1932.

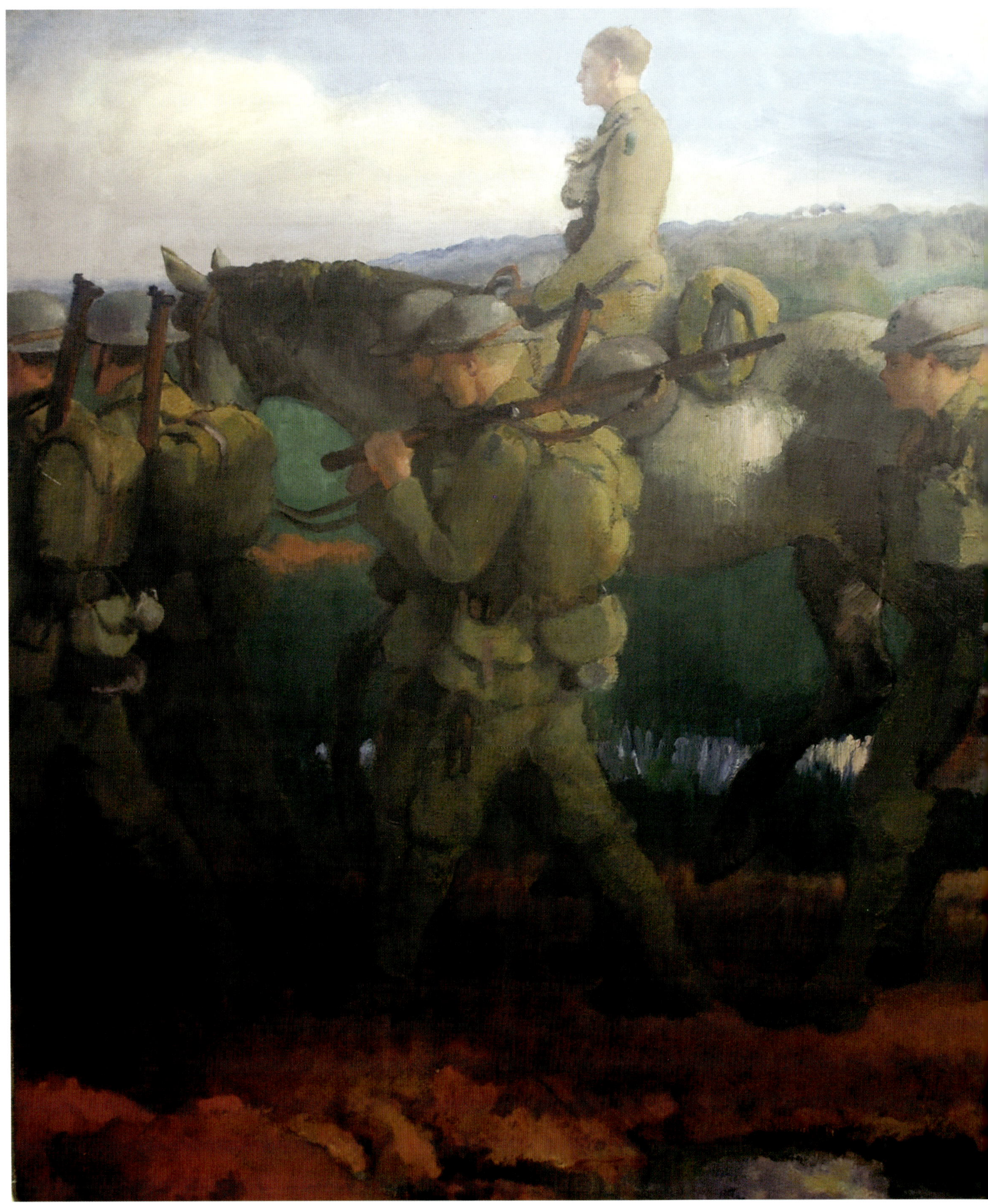

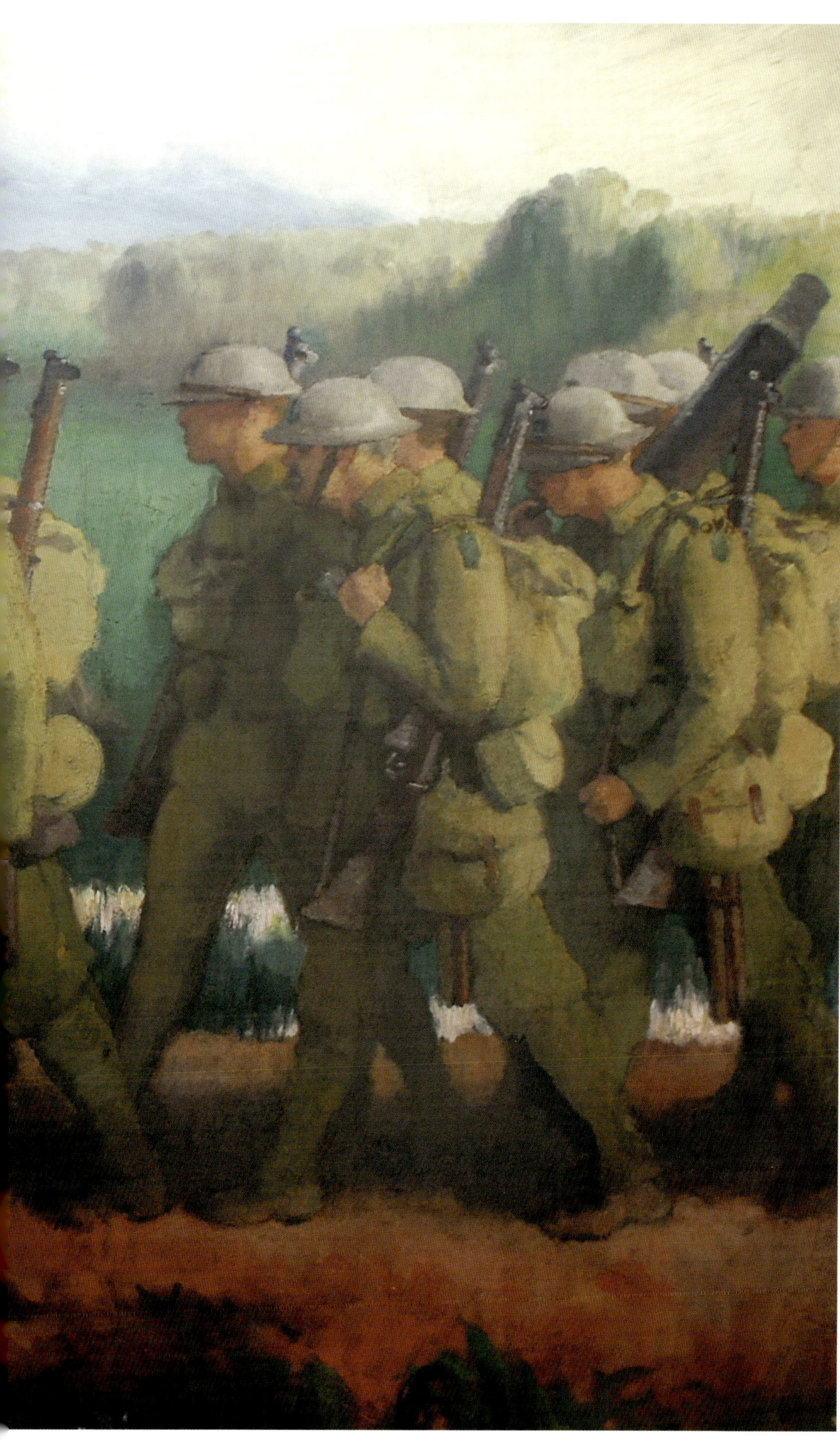

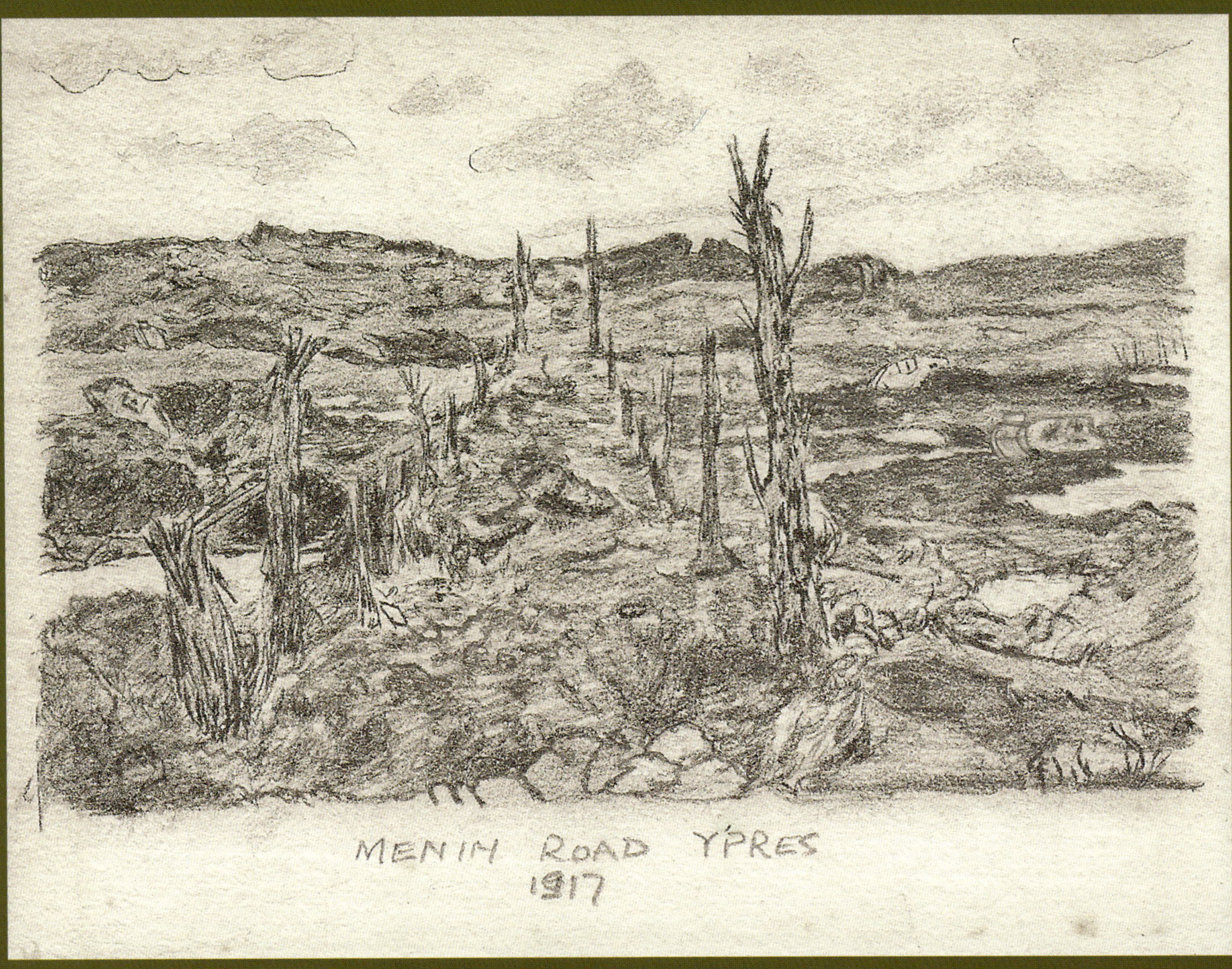

William Hugh Duncan Arthur (1892-1962)

65 – *Menin Road, Ypres*, 1917,
Inscribed: "*Menin Road, Ypres 1917*",
Charcoal and pencil on paper, 4½ x 5 ½ in. (11.5 x 14 cm)

This drawing shows a number of disabled British tanks at the Battle of Ypres.
William Hugh Duncan Arthur was a 2nd Lieutenant in the 9th Battalion South Staffordshire
Regiment. He had previously served as 35602 Private in the Royal Army Medical Corps.

66 – *The Old German Front Line, Arras*, c.1916,
Charcoal and pencil on paper, 4 ½ x 8 ¼ in. (11.5 x 21 cm)
This composition is identical to Charles Sims' painting, *The Old German Front Line, Arras, 1916*,
(*The Edwardians*, Fine Art Society Catalogue, 2011, p.69)

67 – *Bosch Dugouts, Hill 60 Sector*
(showing deserted German block house with table and chairs outside),
Charcoal and pencil on paper, 4 ½ x 5 in. (11.5 x 12.5 cm)

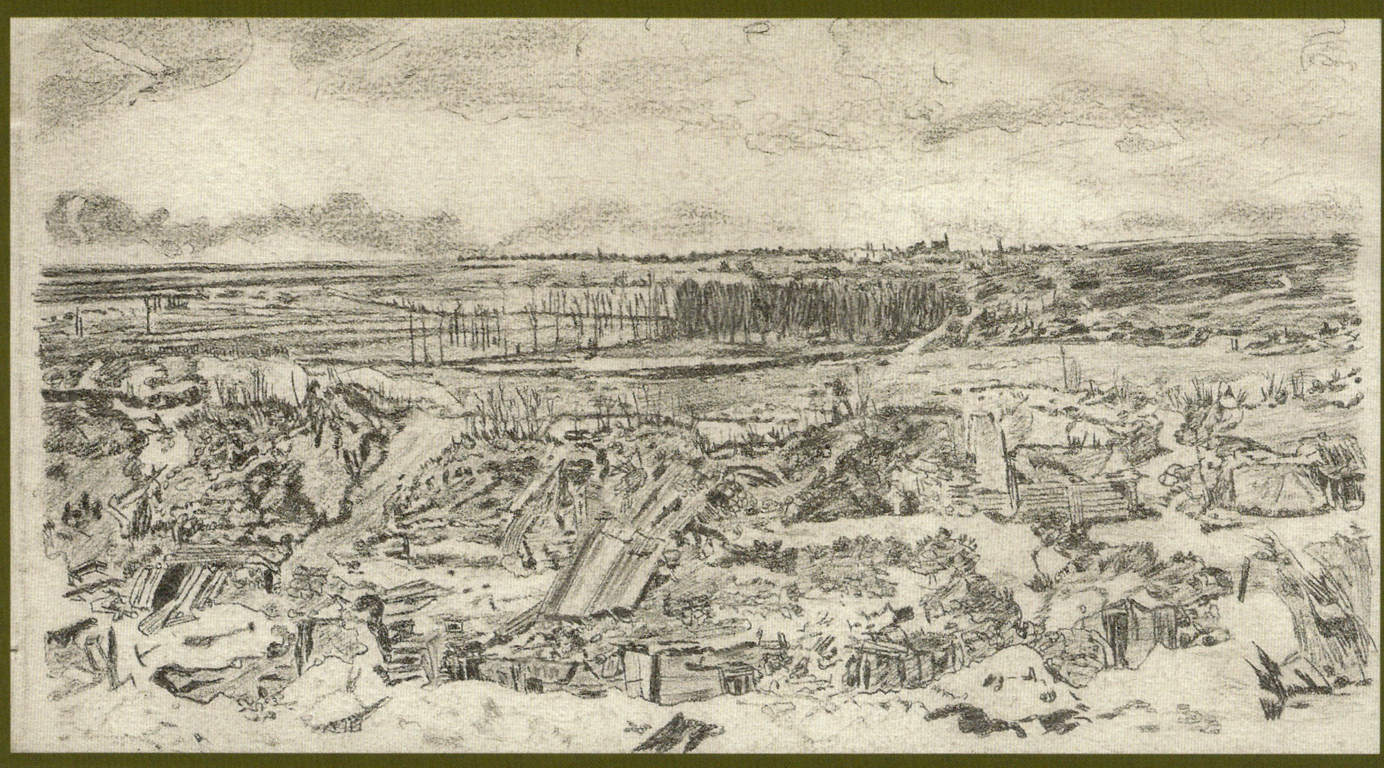

66

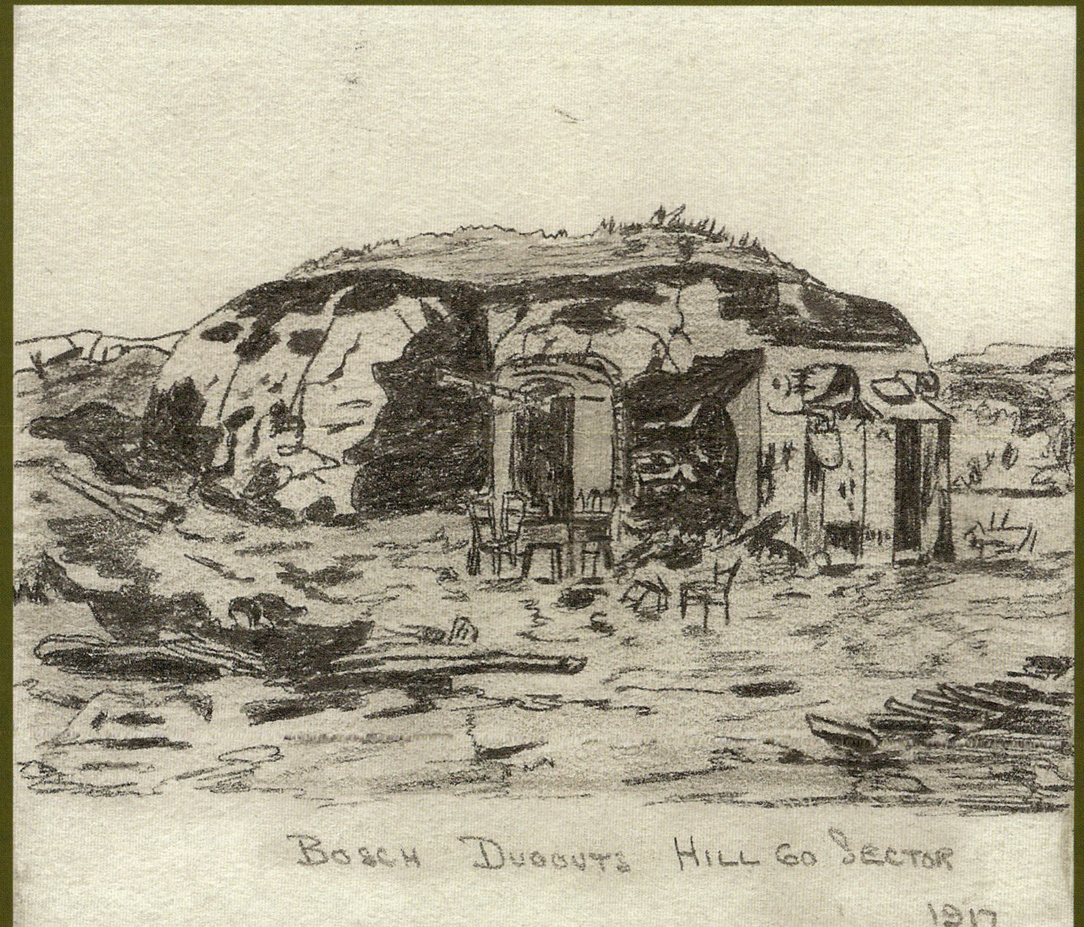

67

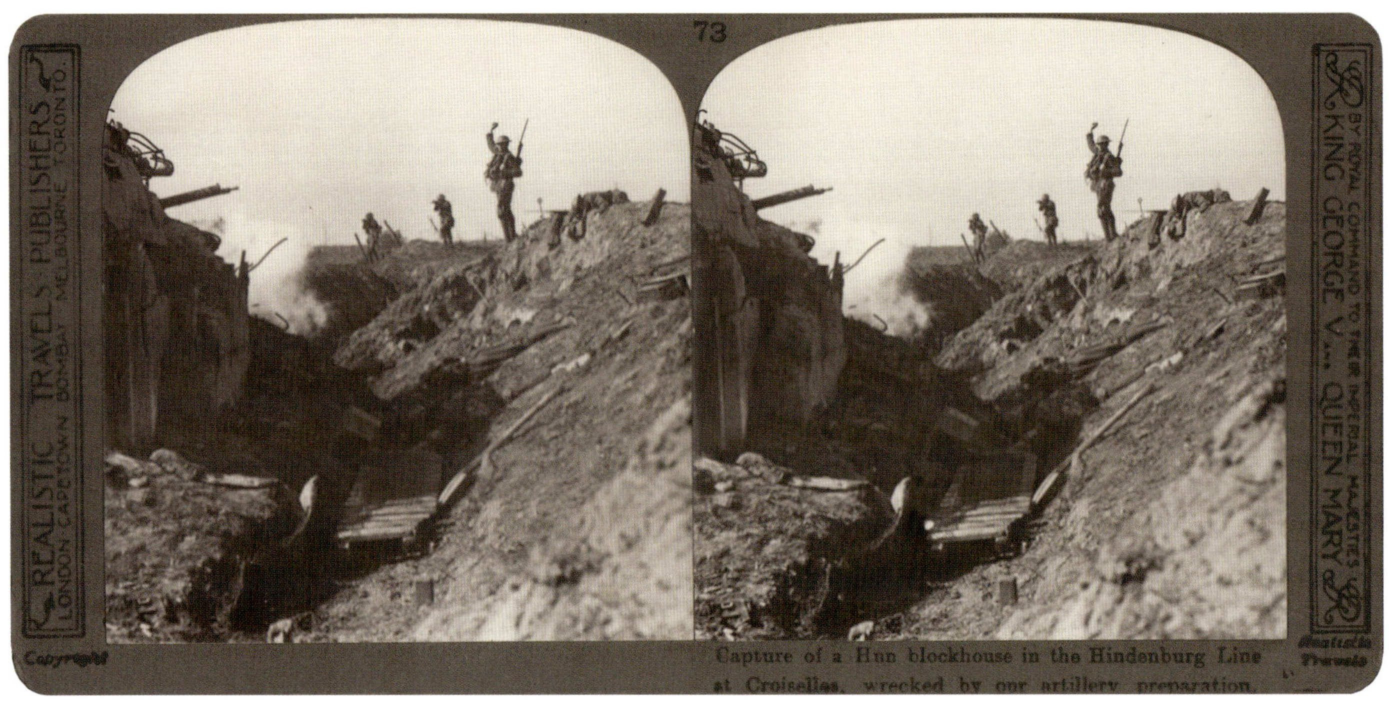

68 – Stereoscopic print: *Capture of a Hun blockhouse in the Hindenburg Line at Croiselles, wrecked by our artillery preparation.*
3 ½ x 7 in. (9 x 18 cm), published by Realistic Travels

The Siegfriedstellung (Hindenburg Line) was a German defensive position built during the winter of 1916-1917 on the Western Front, from Arras to Laffaux, near Soissons on the Aisne.

69 – Espinasse

Silhouette of a Tommy in marching order, c.1916, signed,
Silhouette, pen and ink on paper, 4 x 2 ¾ in. (10 x 7 cm)

The Steel Helmet, with its distinctive silhouette, was first issued to soldiers in early 1916.

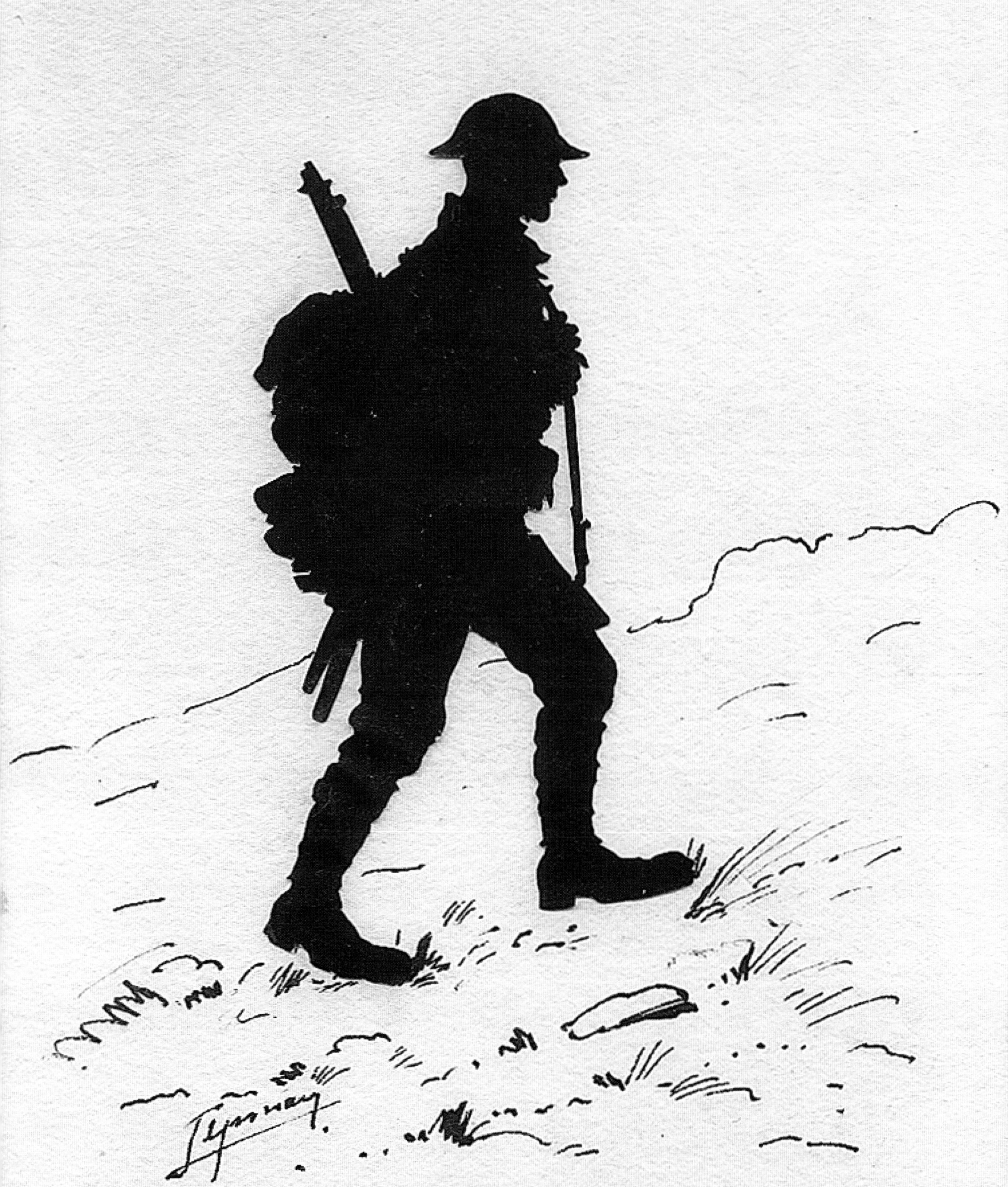

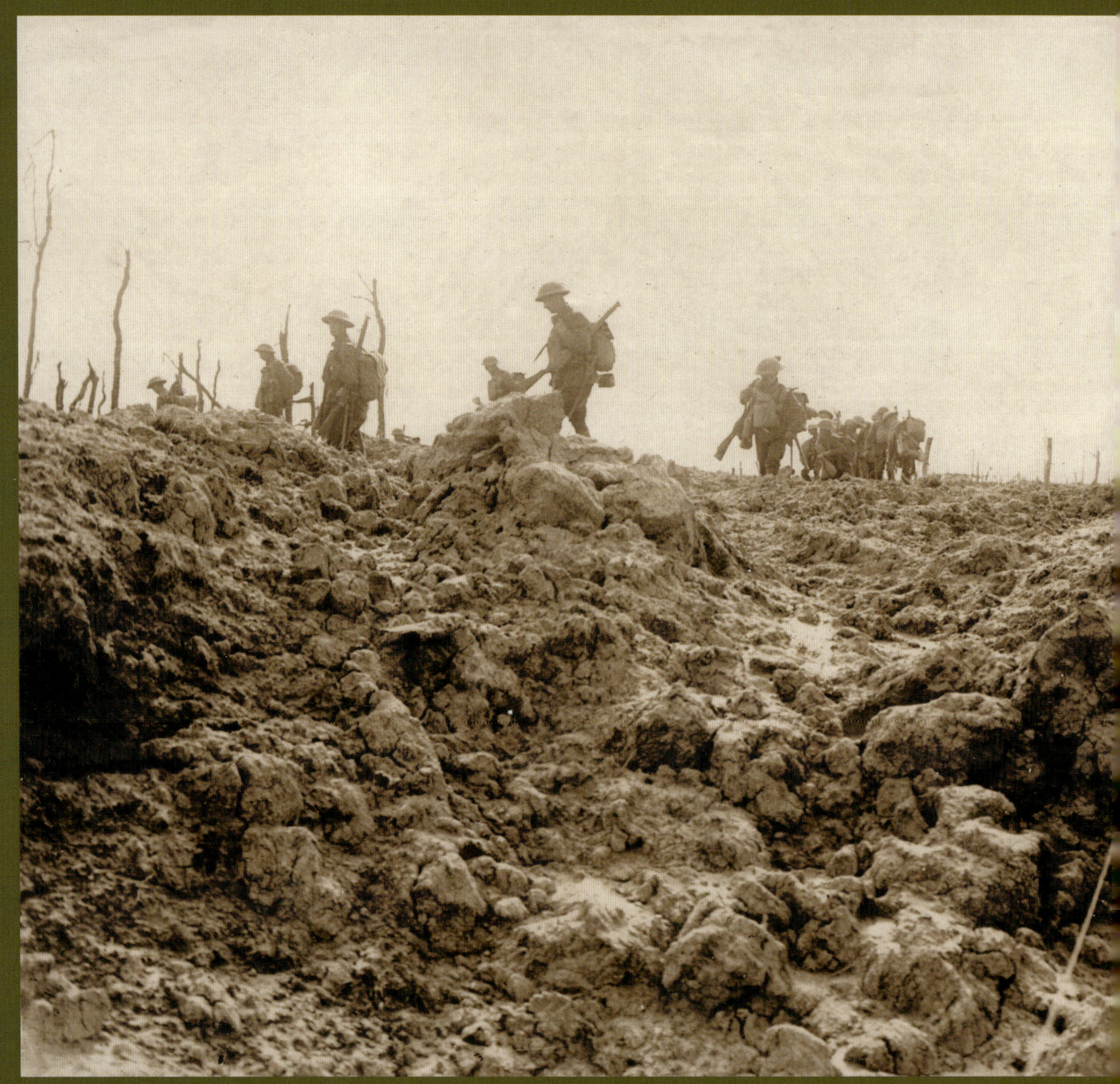

70 – Official photograph taken on the Western Front

Inscribed to the reverse: "C. 2224 The Battle of Flanders. British troops moving forward over ground churned up by shell fire."
Black & white photograph, 6 ½ x 8 ½ in. (16.7 x 21.5 cm)

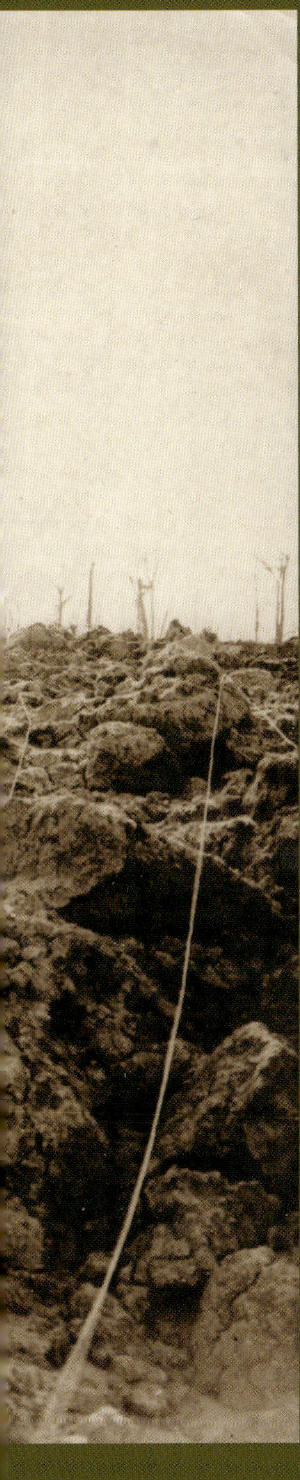

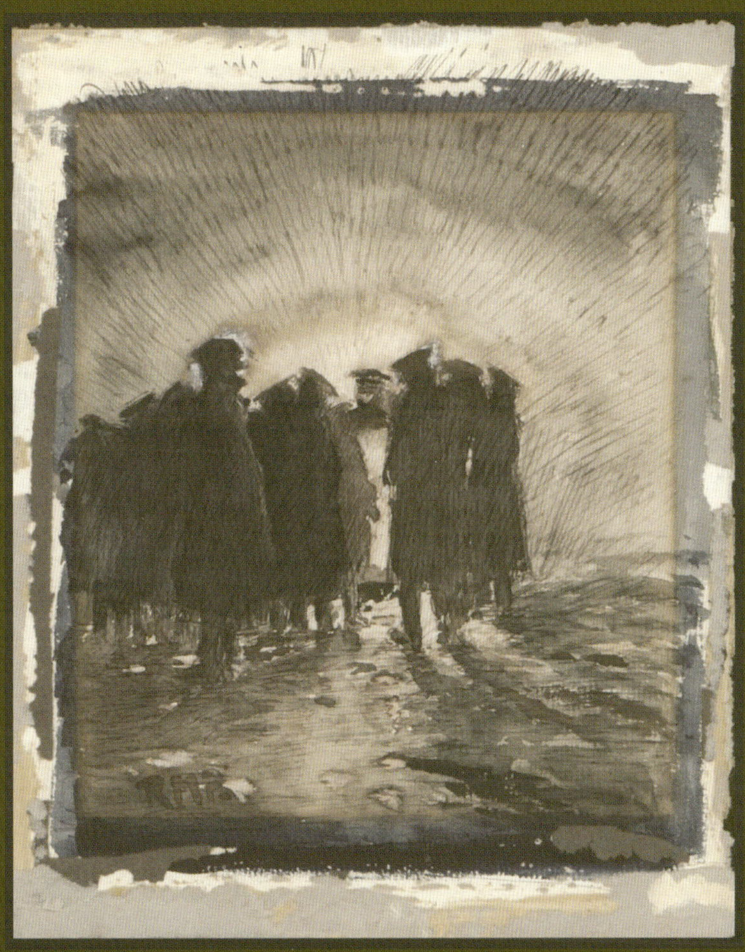

71 – English School

Officers by trenches meeting at dusk, signed with initials,
Pen and ink, 6 ⅞ x 5 ⅝ in. (17.5 x 15 cm)

COMMUNICATIONS & WEAPONS OF WAR

"Something was brought near the reserve trench, camouflaged with a big sheet. We didn't know what it was and were very curious and the Captain got us all out on parade, He said, 'You are wondering what this is. Well it's a tank' and he took the covers off and that was the very first tank."

Private Charles Coles, No. 12245, 4 Platoon, 1st Coy., 1st Btn., Coldstream Guards 1916

"Cambrai has become the Valmy of a new epoch in war, the epoch of the mechanical engineer."

Colonel J.F.C. Fuller, 1917.

72 – Colin Gill (1892-1940)

Laying Telephone Wire, c.1918,
Oil on canvas, 24 x 16 in. (61 x 40.7 cm),
Provenance: until 1972 this painting was attributed to Paul Nash on the basis of an old inscription on the canvas;
1972 sold at Christies (as unattributed); private collection until 2004; private collection from 2014

In December 1914, four months after Britain had declared war on Germany, Gill suspended his Rome Scholarship in Decorative Painting to volunteer for the Royal Garrison Artillery and by October 1915 he had been sent to the Front as a Second Lieutenant of the 17th Heavy Battery. In 1916 he was seconded to the Royal Engineers to work as a Camouflage Officer before being invalided out with gas poisoning in April 1918. After spending several months convalescing at the Hospital for Officers on the Isle of Wight, Gill requested an appointment as an Official War Artist: 'My name is Lieutenant Colin Gill of the Royal Engineers – my age 26; before the war I was a painter and studied at the Slade School of Art, London University. In 1913, I was awarded the Rome Scholarship in painting. I joined the army in 1914, went to France in 1915 and have been in the line ever since. I have had nearly three years first-hand experience of this line and feel capable of recording my impressions in pictures which would be of assistance to the work of the Ministry of Information.' (Letter to the Ministry of Information, May 22,1918) By June 25th Gill had been given a six-month appointment as an Official War Artist, and had received a letter from the Ministry reminding him that every work executed 'becomes the property of the Nation.' For this reason war paintings by Gill, outside the sixteen in the collection of the Imperial War Museum, are scarce. This painting can be compared to one of identical size and similar subject in the Imperial War Museum – *Observation of Fire: Gunner Officers Correcting Their Battery Fire by Field Telephone from a Disused Trench in No-Man's-Land*. Gill resumed his Scholarship at The British School at Rome in 1919. A photograph of Gill in his Rome studio, circa 1920, shows a First World War helmet as a studio prop. It is known that Gill completed his epic *Canadian Observation Post* (Canadian War Museum) in Rome and it is possible that this canvas was also completed at this time.

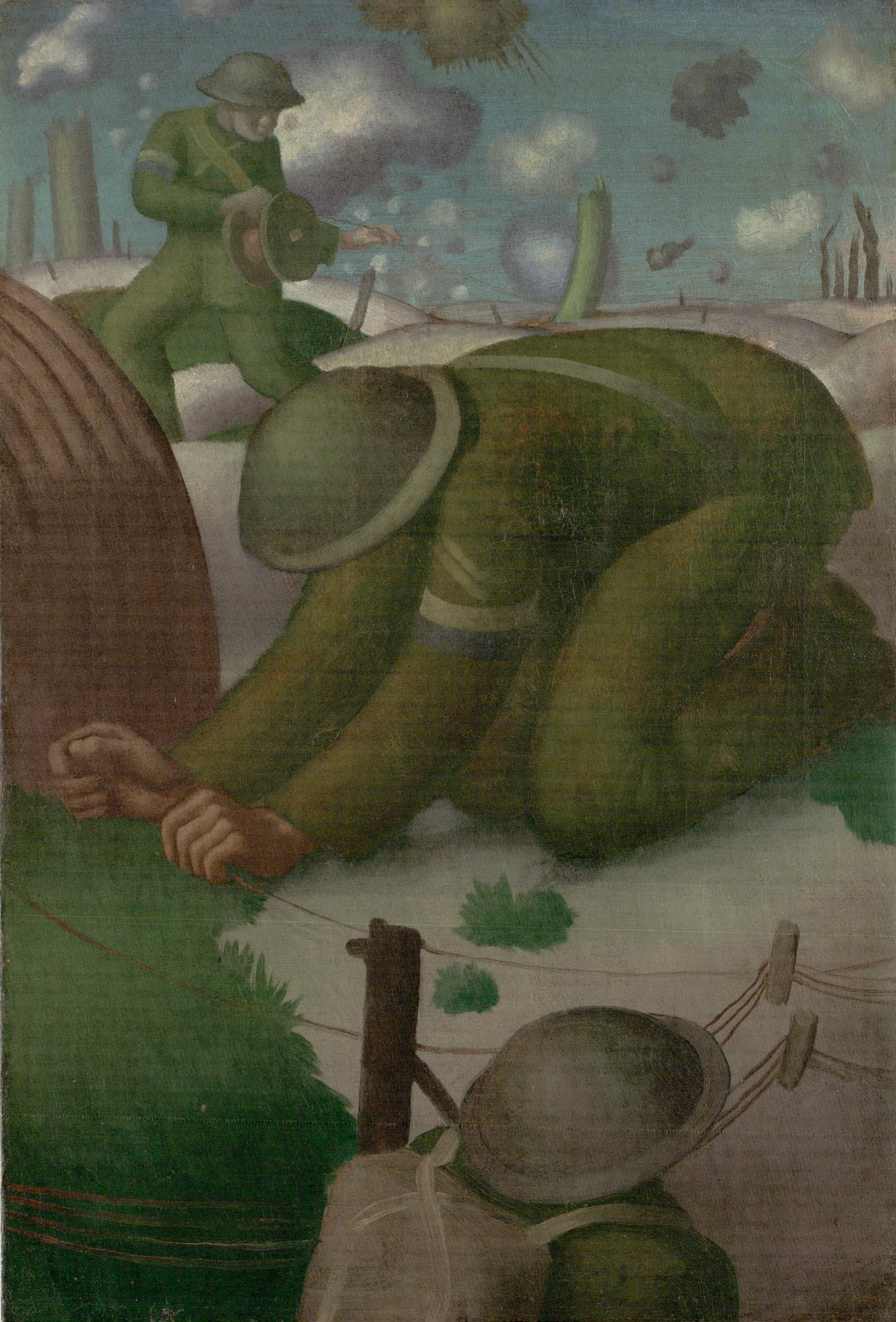

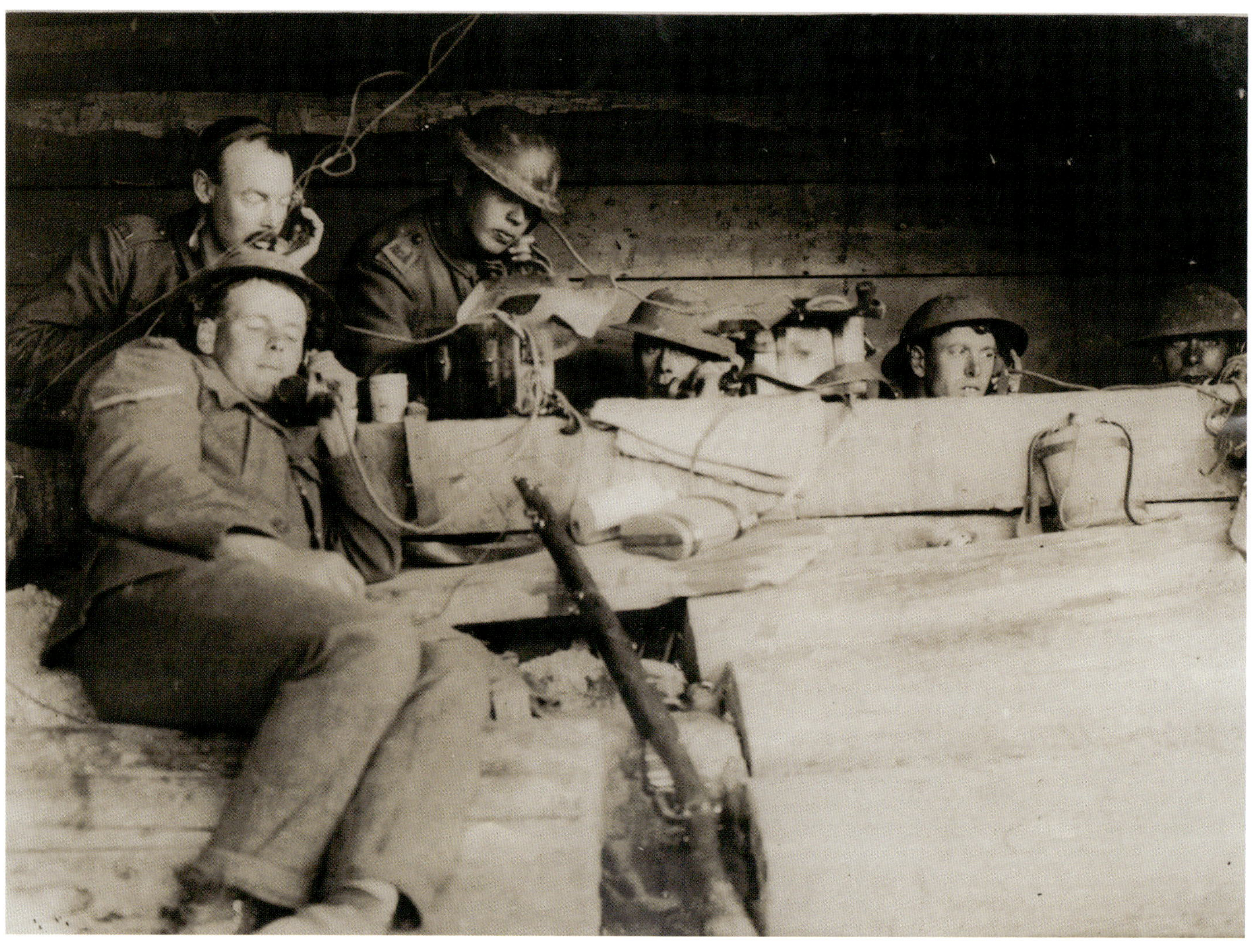

73 – Official photograph issued by the Press Bureau

Inscribed on reverse: *"Great British Advance in the West*, C.2266. Within 500 yards of the Boche and in one of their concrete dug-outs, these men are transmitting the orders of the Observation Officers and altering the range for the batteries.",
Black & white photograph, 6 ⅝ x 8 ½ in. (16.8 x 21.5 cm)

Field telephones were first used in the First World War to direct troops. They replaced flag signals and the telegraph as an efficient means of communication, but they depended on the laying of land lines. The first field telephones had a wind-up generator, used to power the telephone's ringer and batteries to send the call.

74 – Canadian School

"Send More Men – Won't YOU Answer the Call", 1915
Lithographic poster, 38 x 24 ¾ in. (97 x 63 cm),
Printed by Stone Ltd, commissioned by the Central Recruiting Committee No. 2 Military Division, Toronto

The British declaration of war automatically brought Canada into the war. As a British dominion, however, the Canadian government had the freedom to determine the country's level of involvement. Canada lost 67,000 men with 250,000 wounded, out of a total mobilisation of 620,000.

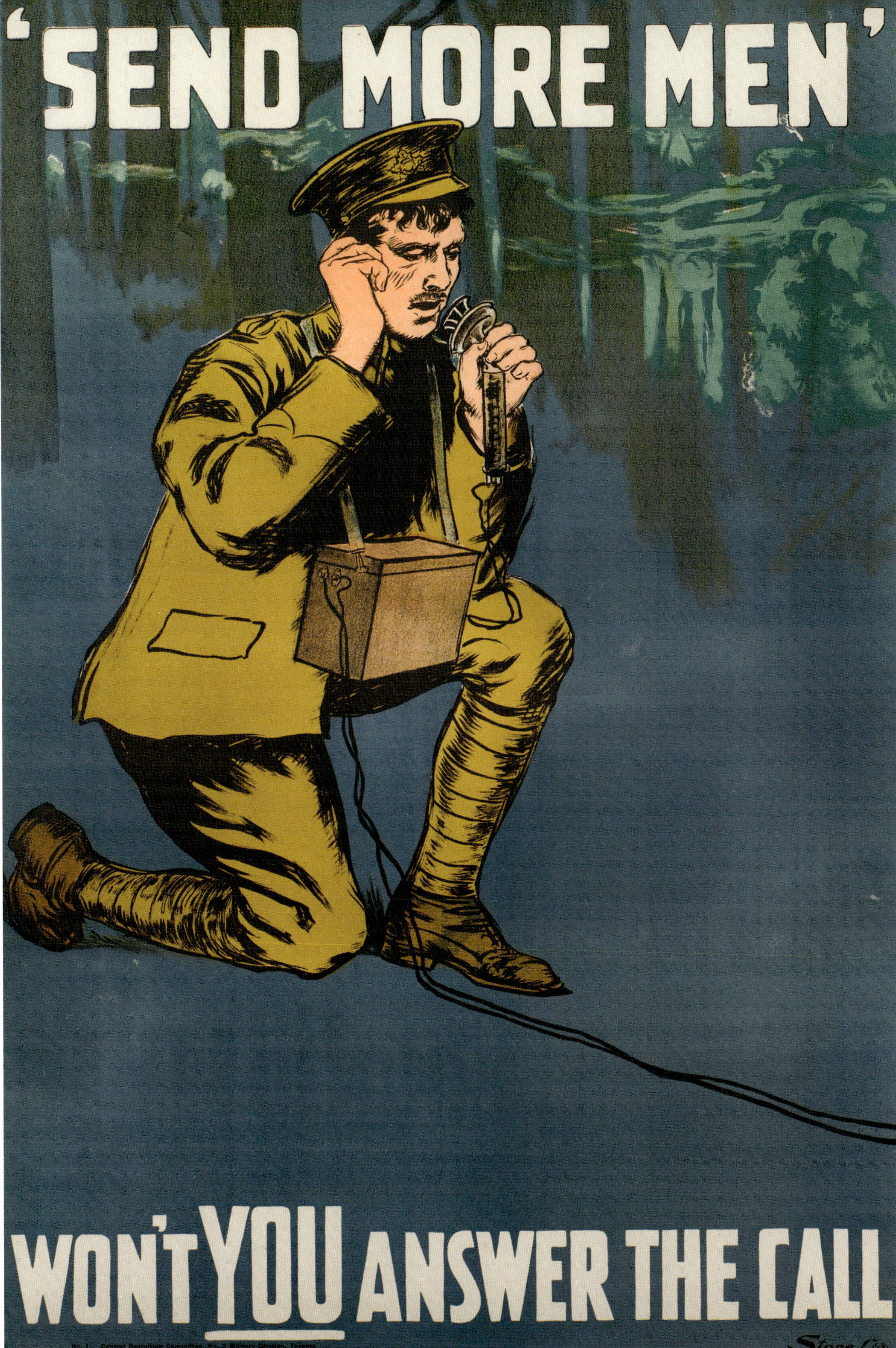

'SEND MORE MEN'
WON'T YOU ANSWER THE CALL
Stone Ltd
No. 1   Central Recruiting Committee, No. 2 Military Division, Toronto.

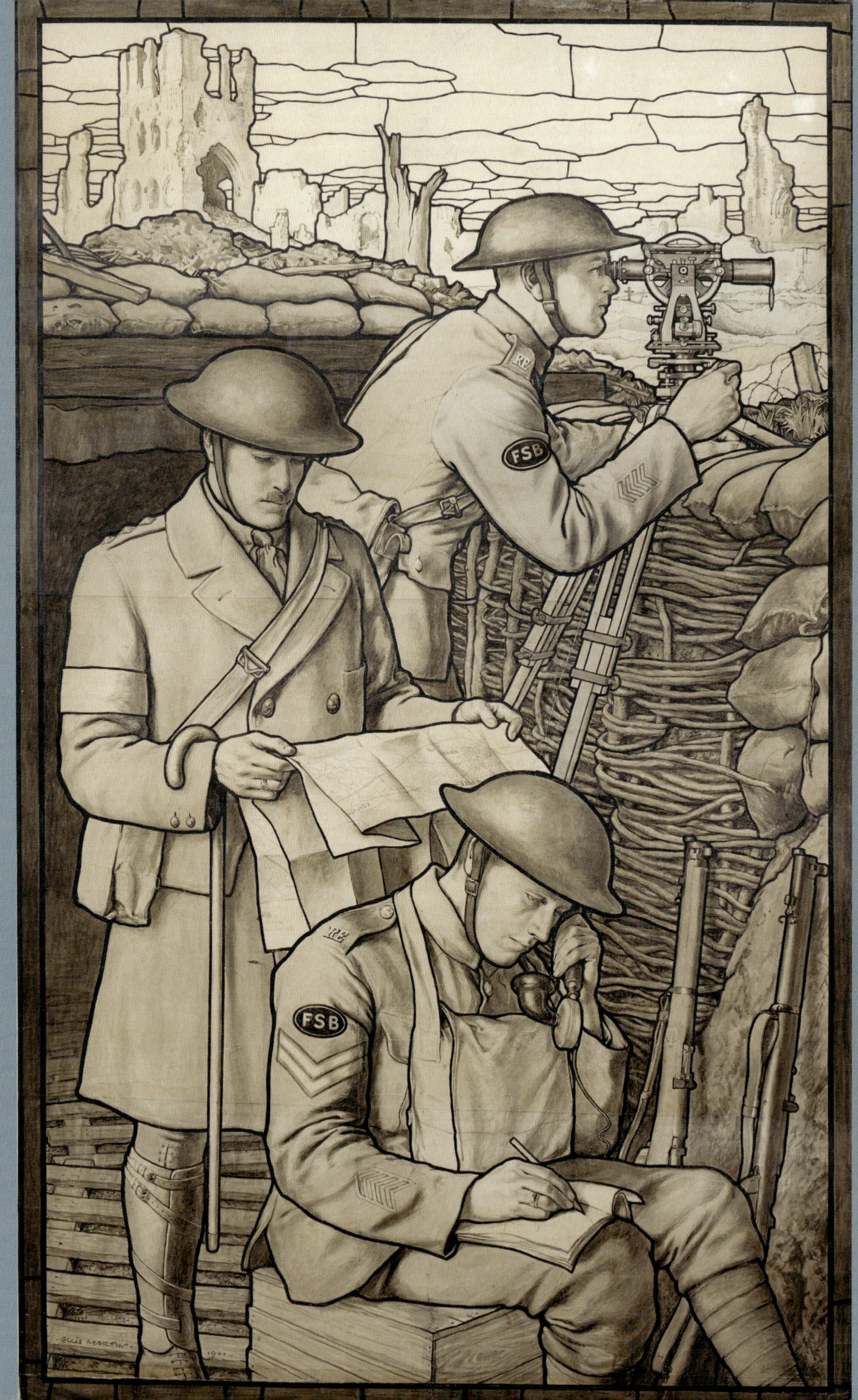
FSB
FSB
ELLIS MARTIN

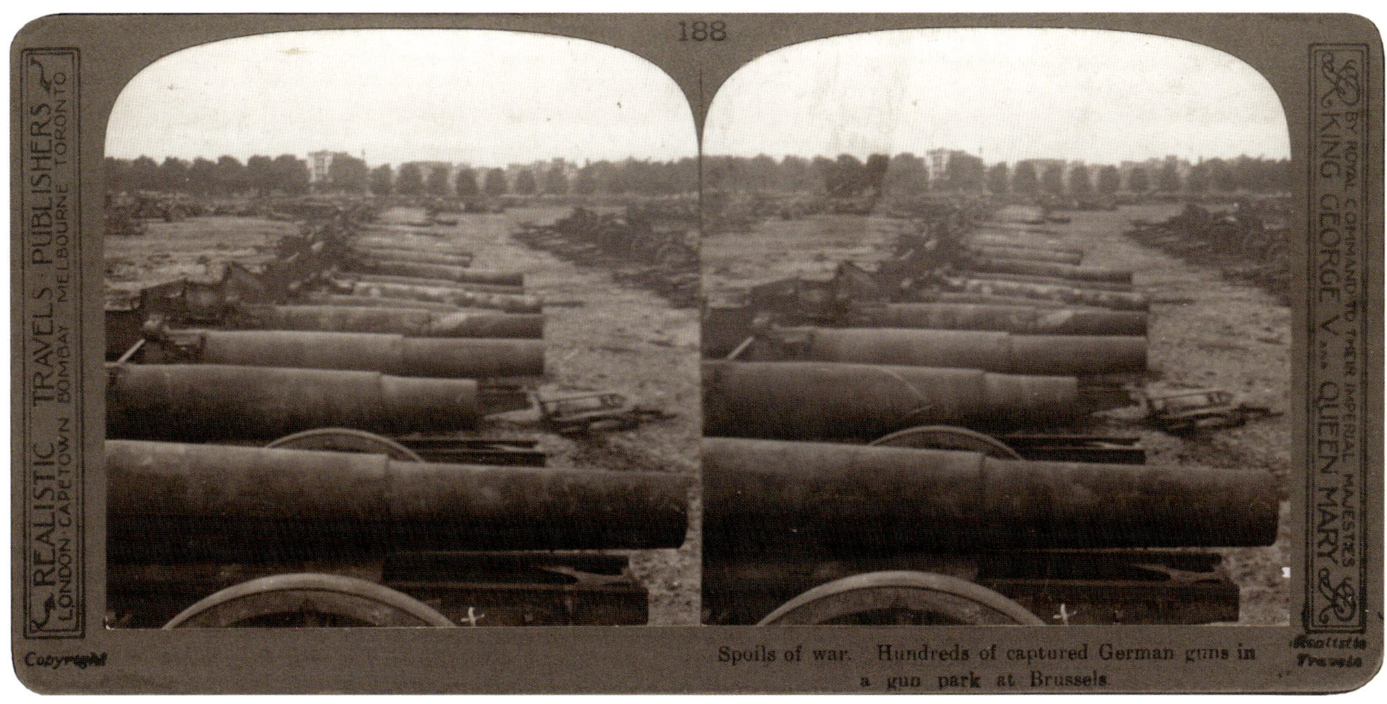

76 – Stereoscopic print: *Hundreds of captured German guns in a gun park at Brussels.*
  3 ½ x 7 in. (9 x 18 cm), published by Realistic Travels

75 – Ellis Martin (1881-1977)

The Field Survey Battalion – design for a stained glass memorial window, 1921, signed and dated,
Pen, ink, and monochrome wash on heavy paper, 59 ½ x 35 ½ in. (151 x 90.5 cm)

This design depicts three Royal Engineers in a trench, each with a badge marked 'FSB" (Field Service Battalion), comprising a Captain reading a map of Ypres, a Corporal communicating, and a Private looking through a theodolite. By mid-1918, there were five Field Survey Battalions in France. Ellis Martin was a commercial artist who, before the First World War, produced posters and advertising designs for firms such as Selfridges and W.H. Smith. When the First World War broke out he went to France with the Royal Engineers and the Tank Corps, as an artist sketching the landscapes over which the army and its heavy vehicles would have to move. When the war ended, Martin joined the Ordnance Survey.

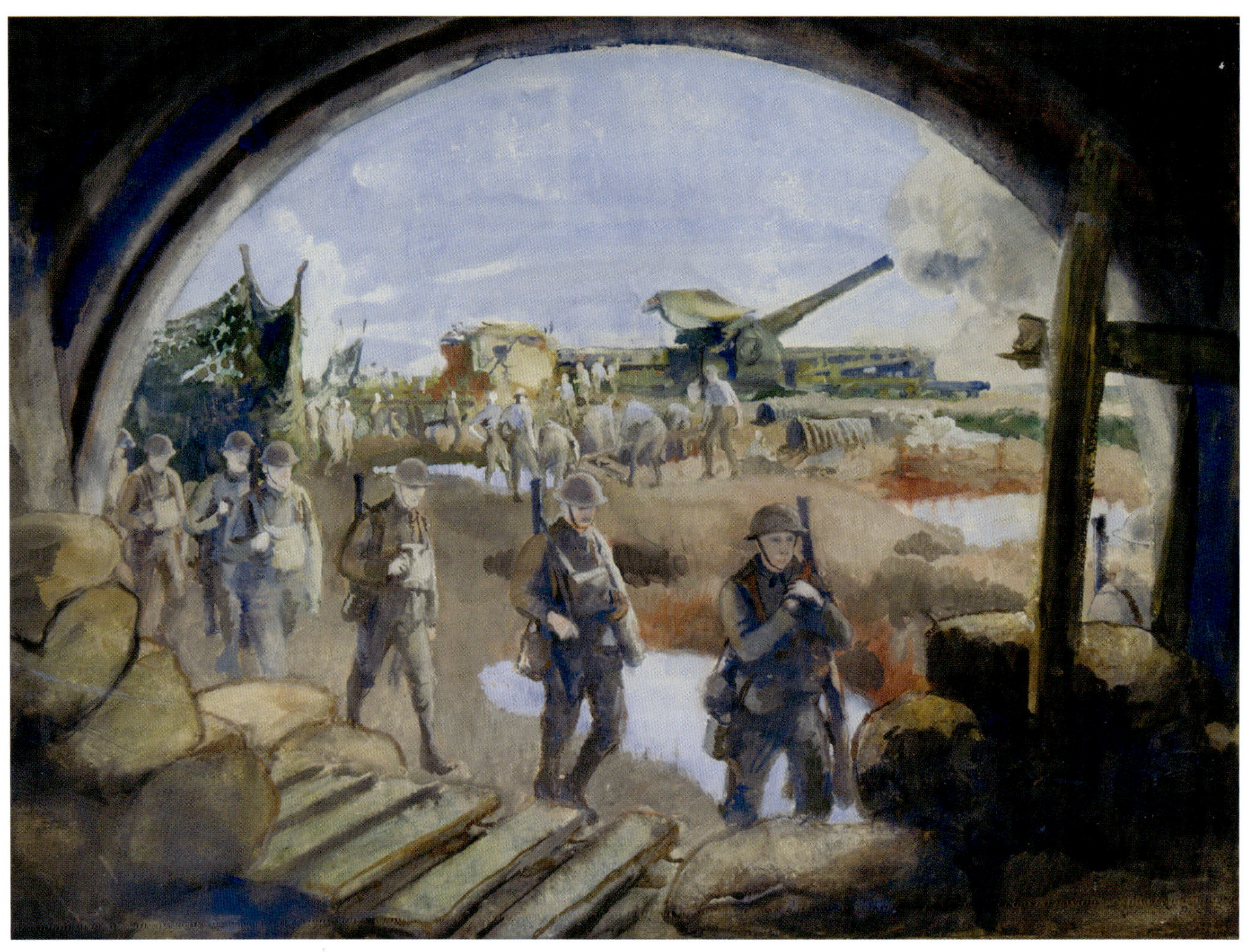

77 – English School

A Breech-loading 9.2" railway gun in action, France, c.1916,
Gouache on paper laid on card, 23 x 31 in. (68.5 x 78.5 cm)

This composition shows Infantry moving up to the Front, passing a corrugated roofed ammunition store. Shell holes, camouflage netting and men feeding a railway gun – which has just been fired – can be seen in the background.

The outbreak of the First World War caught the French with a shortage of heavy field artillery. In compensation, large numbers of large static coastal defence guns and naval guns were moved to the Front, but these were typically unsuitable for field use and required some kind of mounting. The railway gun, which was mounted on, transported by, and fired from a specially designed railway wagon, provided the obvious solution. By 1916, both sides were deploying railway guns. No Allied guns, however, were as powerful as the much feared German 16" Big Bertha, a super-heavy howitzer developed by the armaments manufacturer Krupp on the eve of the First World War.

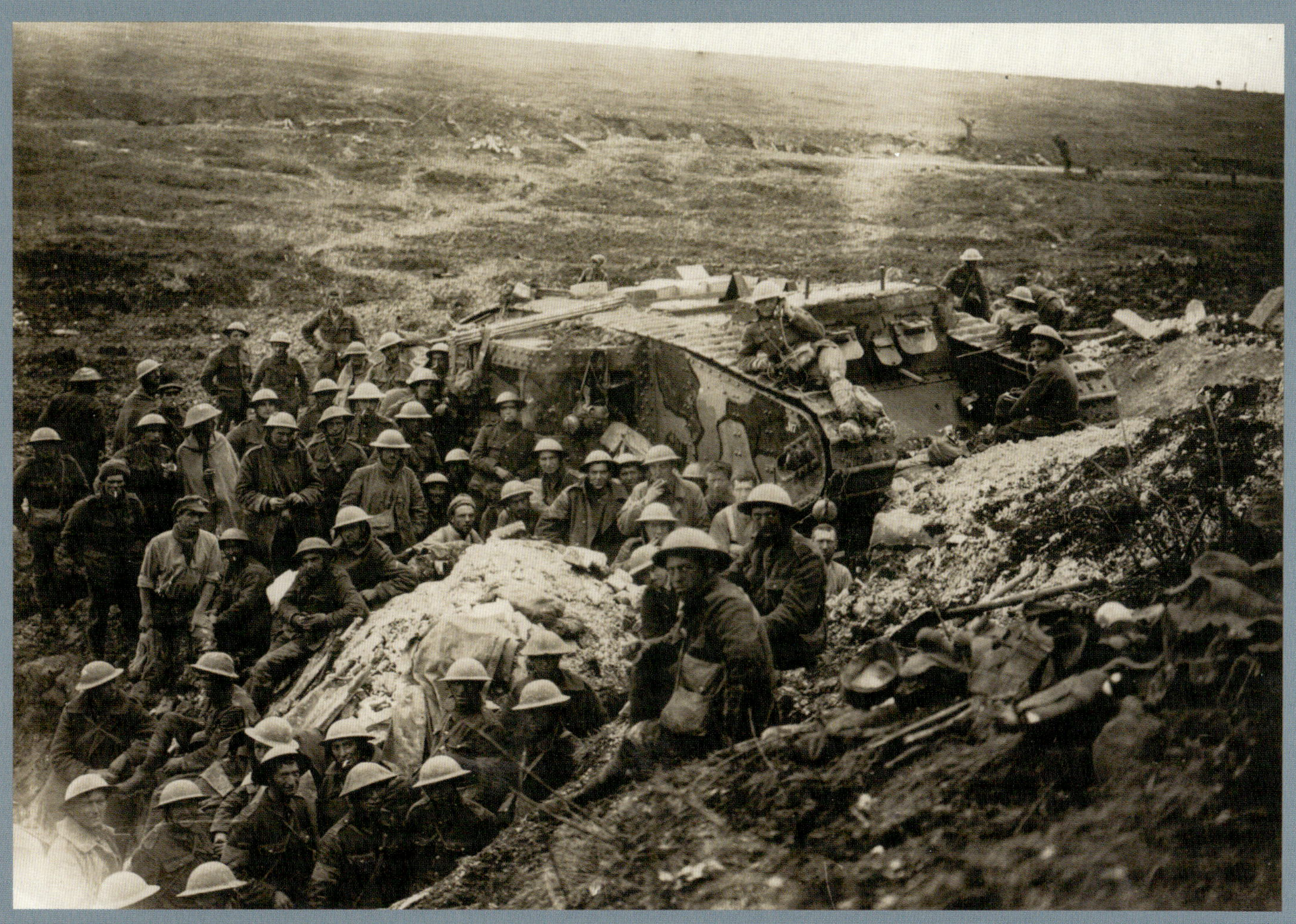

78 – Official photograph taken on the Western Front

Inscribed to the reverse:"D 1641. One of our Tanks at FLERS."
Black & white photograph, 6 x 8 in. (15.2 x 20.3 cm)

Flers-Courcelette was a battle within the Franco-British Somme Offensive which took place in the summer and autumn of 1916.
During this battle, the tank was deployed for the first time.

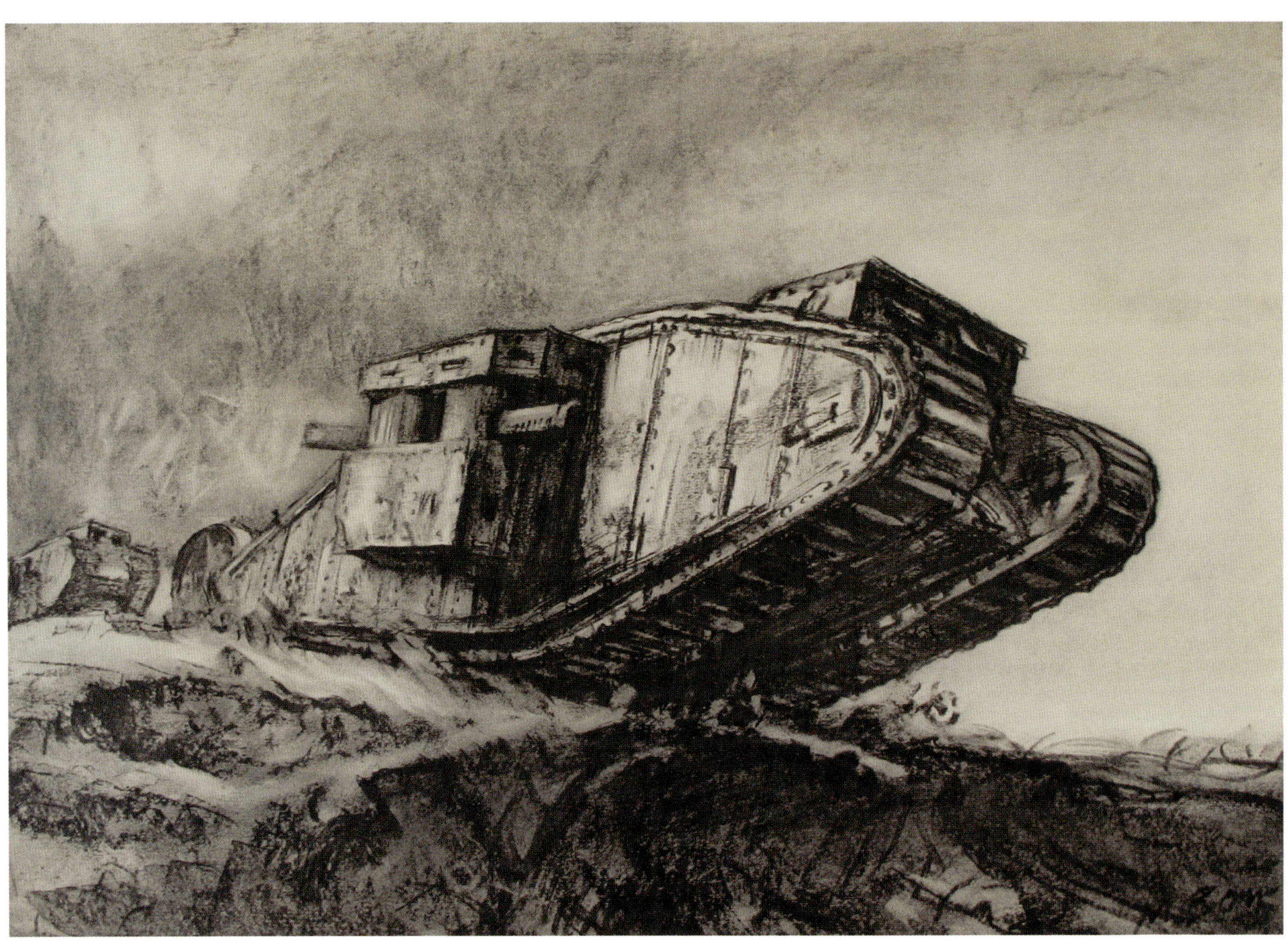

79 – Muirhead Bone (1876-1953)

A female Mark I tank is crossing No Man's Land, 1916, signed in the plate,
Lithographic reproduction from the series of war drawings published by *Country Life*, 1917,
13 x 17 ½ in. (33 x 44.4 cm)

The tank was originally designed as a special weapon to solve an unusual tactical situation, the stalemate of the trenches. They first appeared at the Battle of Flers-Courcelette in September 1916 when the British deployed 49 tanks. By 1918 Britain and France had produced 6,506 tanks between them, while Germany had produced just 20. Germany learnt to deal with tanks effectively. During the Battle of Amiens in 1918 72% of Allied tanks were disabled in just 4 days. Six days before the end of the war the British Tank Corps only had 8 tanks left. The tank became one of the great icons of the war. Responding to its distinctive geometry, Charles Sims, Frank Brangwyn and Muirhead Bone were just some of the artists who produced major compositions focusing on tanks in action.

80 – Irma Karoly Simay (1874-1955)

Souscrivez à l'emprunt de la libération. Lloyds Bank et National Provincial, 1918,
Lithographic poster, 47 ¼ x 31 ½ in. (120 x 80 cm),
Printed by Imprimerie Crété, Paris

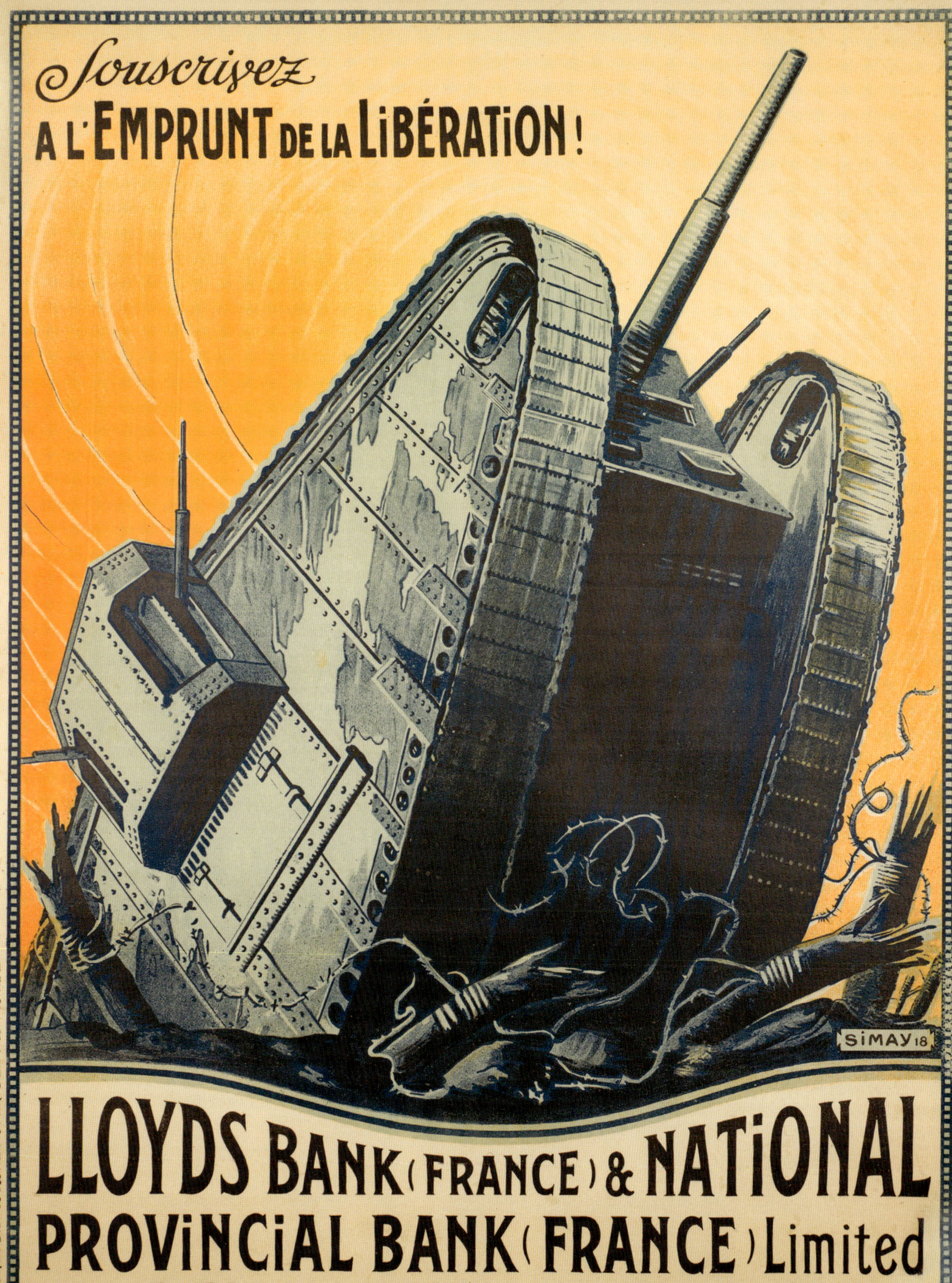

Souscrivez
A L'EMPRUNT DE LA LIBÉRATION !
SIMAY 18
Imp. CRÉTÉ 2,rue des Italiens PARIS == Visa n°13.312 ==
LLOYDS BANK (FRANCE) & NATIONAL
PROVINCIAL BANK (FRANCE) Limited
3, Place de l'Opéra _ PARIS

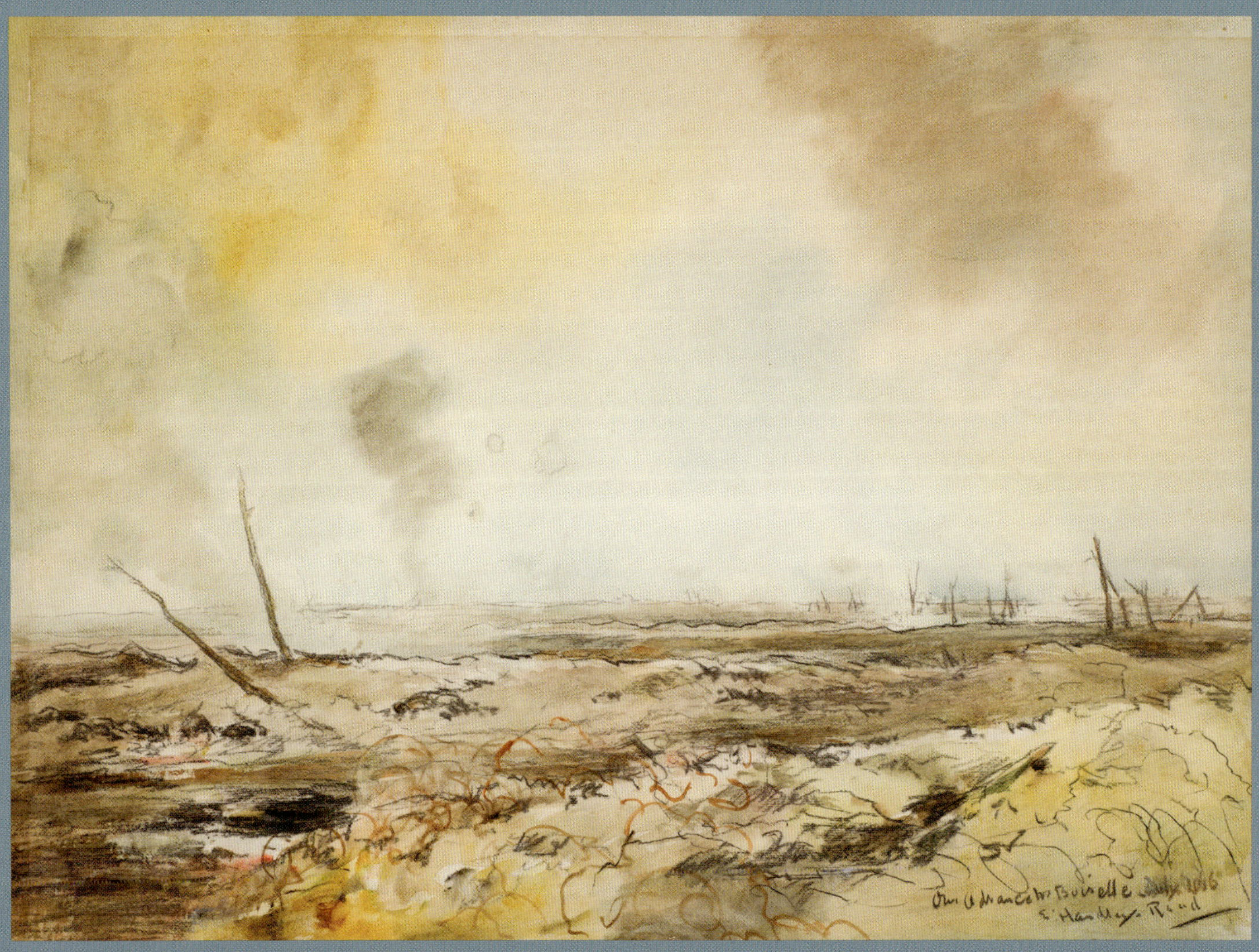

81 – Captain Edward Handley-Read (1869-1935)

Our Advance to (La) Boiselle - July 1916, signed, dated and inscribed with title,
Watercolour on paper, 18 ⅞ x 24 ½ in. (48 x 62.5 cm)

This painting represents a view from Keats Redan looking across Mash Valley towards the ruins of Contalmaison. It was here, on July 1, that the detached C & B Companies of the 23rd Battalion Northumberland Fusiliers attacked the German positions. The records of the Royal Army Medical Corps show that on July 17-18 there was a German gas bombardment and it is likely that this incident is recorded here. The mixture of chlorine (yellow/grey/green cloud) and phosgene would have diluted the clouds sufficiently to produce the effect shown in the painting.

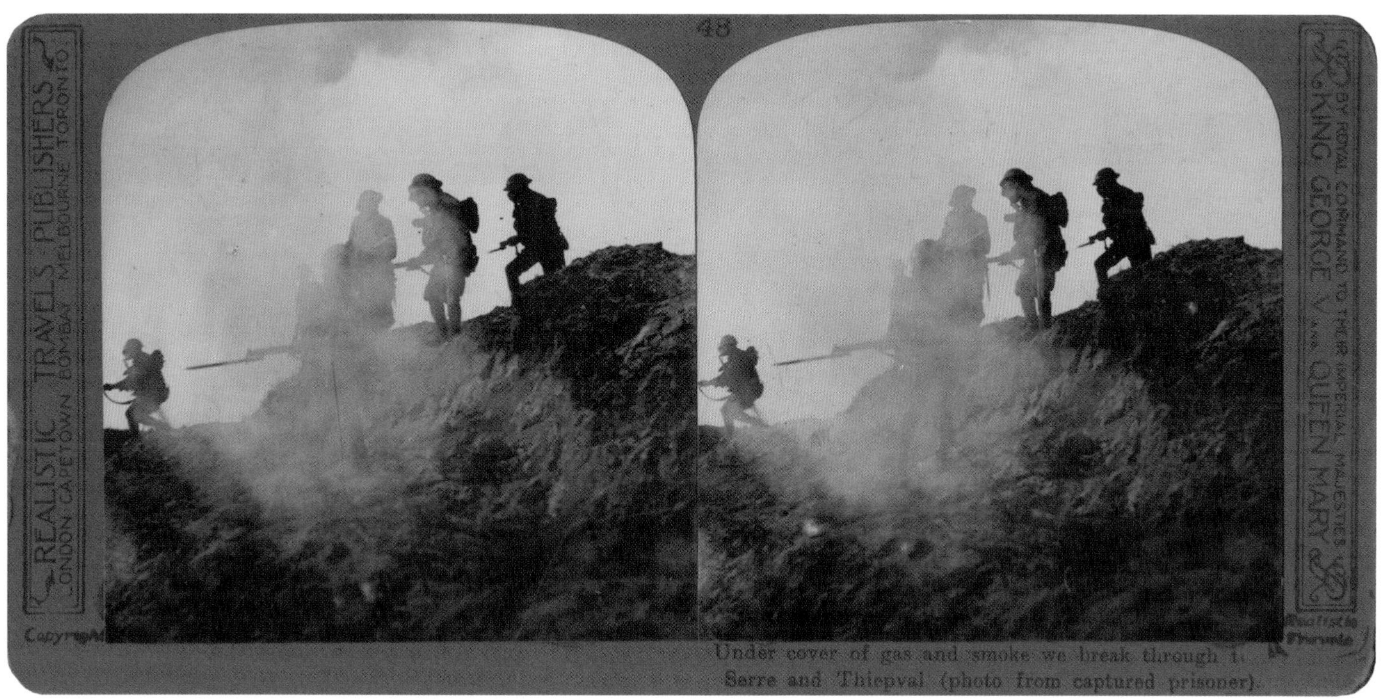

82 – **Stereoscopic print:** *Under cover of gas and smoke we break through to the Serre and Thiepval (photo from captured prisoner).*
3 ½ x 7 in. (9 x 18 cm), published by Realistic Travels

Gas was used by both sides from 1915 as an agent of mass destruction, and was one of the most feared weapons of the war, though it actually killed nothing like as many combatants as machine guns or artillery. During the First World War, the Germans released about 68,000 tons of gas, and the British and French released 51,000 tons. In total, 1,200,000 soldiers on both sides were gassed, of which 91,198 died horrible deaths. Gas might be released near the enemy, either from canisters or by shells, but no-one could control the wind direction and a number of gas attacks ended up blowing back on those who had instigated them. The horror of gas lay largely in the lingering death or permanent injury it inflicted.

France was the first country to use gas against enemy troops, firing the first tear gas grenades (xylyl bromide) in August 1914.

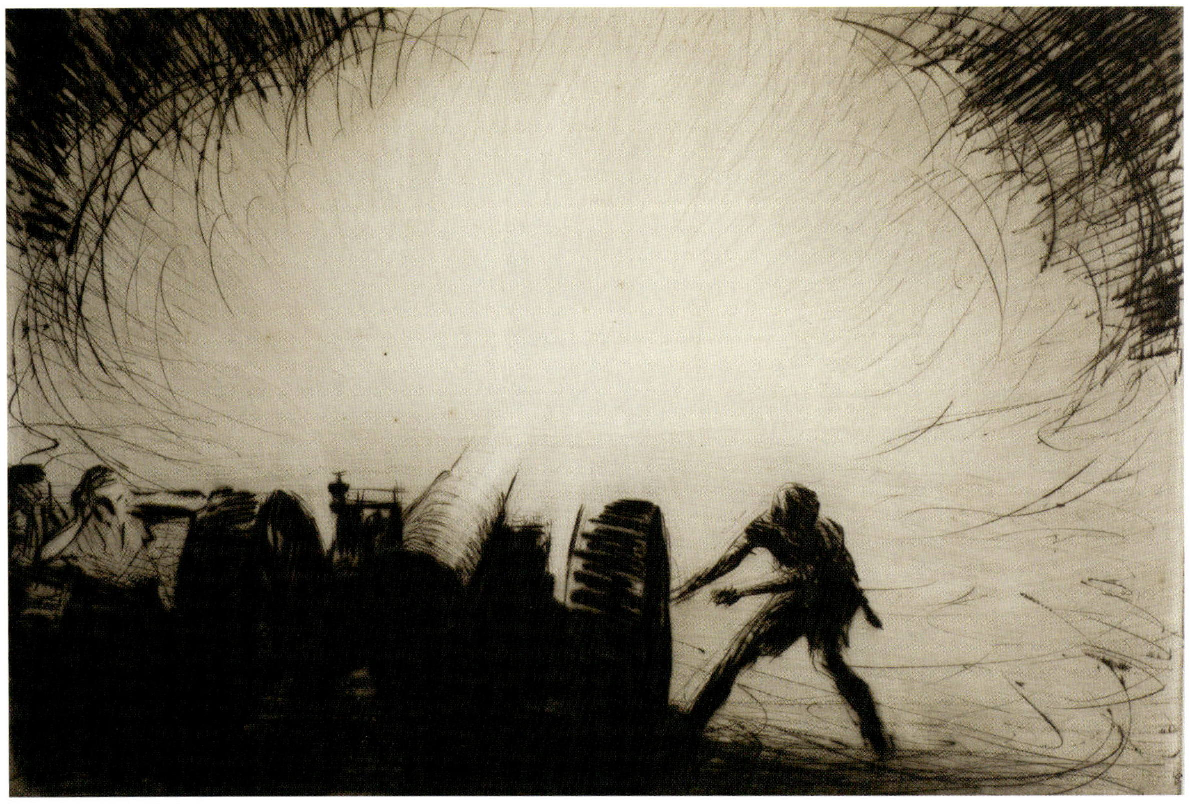

83 – James McBey (1883-1959)

"Zero". A Sixty-Five Pounder Opening Fire, 1920, signed in ink,
Drypoint print, 8 ¼ x 11 ¾ in. (21 x 30.2 cm), printed on 18th Century laid paper and inscribed Trial Proof V,

Hardie describes this print as follows: '*One of the guns near Jelil* [Palestine] is *opening fire at the 'zero' hour before dawn in the surprise bombardment on the morning of September 19th, 1918. The gun is in the foreground to left, silhouetted against the flash of light. On the extreme left are two men, one of whom holds his hand to his ears.*' (M. Hardie, *James McBey Catalogue Raisonne, 1902-1924*, London, 1925, No. 201.)

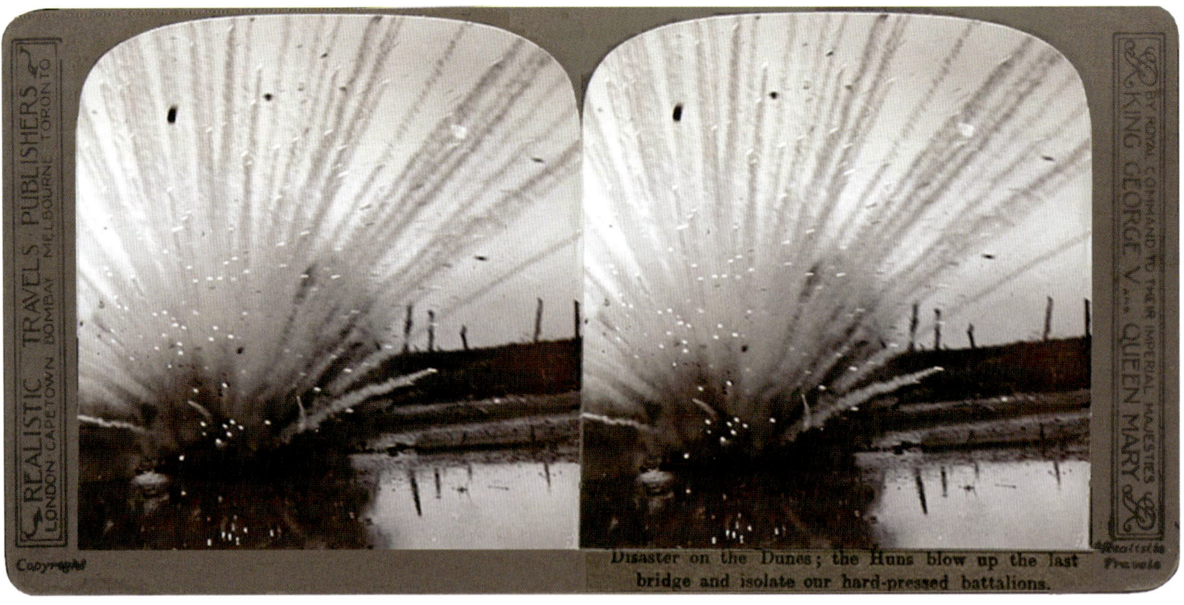

84 – **Stereoscopic print:** *Disaster on the Dunes; the Huns blow up the last bridge and isolate our hard-pressed battalions.*
   3 ½ x 7 in. (9 x 18 cm), published by Realistic Travels

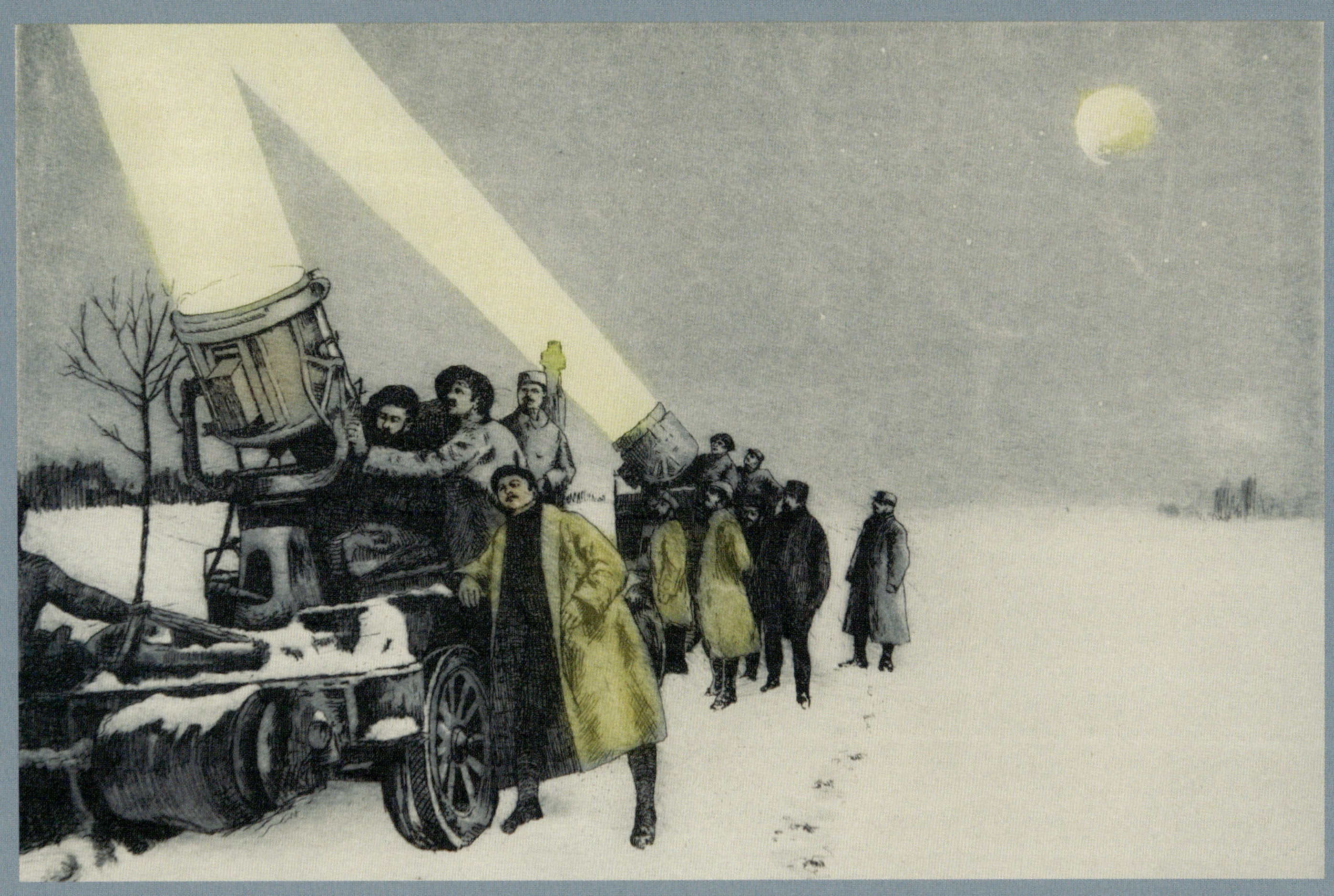

85 – Marcel Augis

Projecteurs en Action, Nuit d'Hiver 1917,
Signed and dated, inscribed with title,
Print (aquatint) : 7 x 9 in. (17.5 x 23 cm)

During the war, Marcel Augis produced many prints of the battles, battlefields and everyday life of the Allied troops. Many of these prints were purchased by soldiers returning home after the war or during the many battlefield remembrance tours that took place in the 1920s.

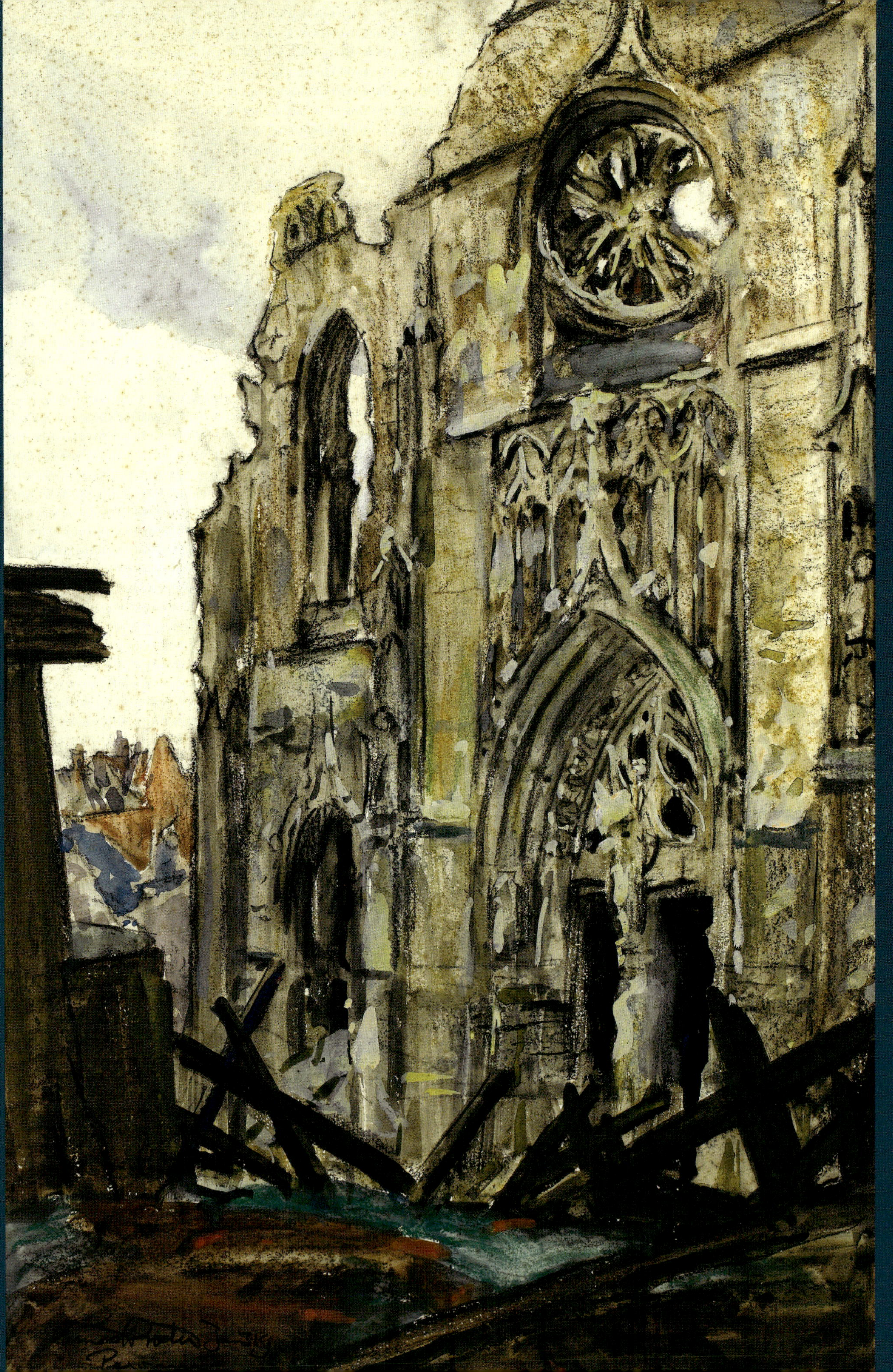

"Men will curse as they kill, yet accomplish deeds of self-sacrifice, giving their lives for others; poets will write with their pens dipped in blood, yet will write not of death but of life eternal; strong and courteous friendships will be born, to endure in the face of enmity and destruction. And so persistent is this urge to the ideal, above all in the presence of great disaster, that mankind, the wilful destructor of beauty, must immediately strive to create new beauties, lest it perish from a sense of its own desolation."

Radclyffe Hall, *The Well of Loneliness*, London 1928, p.331

"And all this madness, all this rage, all this flaming death of our civilization and our hopes, has been brought about because a set of official gentlemen, living luxurious lives, mostly stupid, and all without imagination or heart, have chosen that it should occur rather than that any one of them should suffer some infinitesimal rebuff to his country`s pride."

Bertrand Russell, *The Autobiography of Bertrand Russell (1967–1969)*, Vol. II, London 1968, p.265

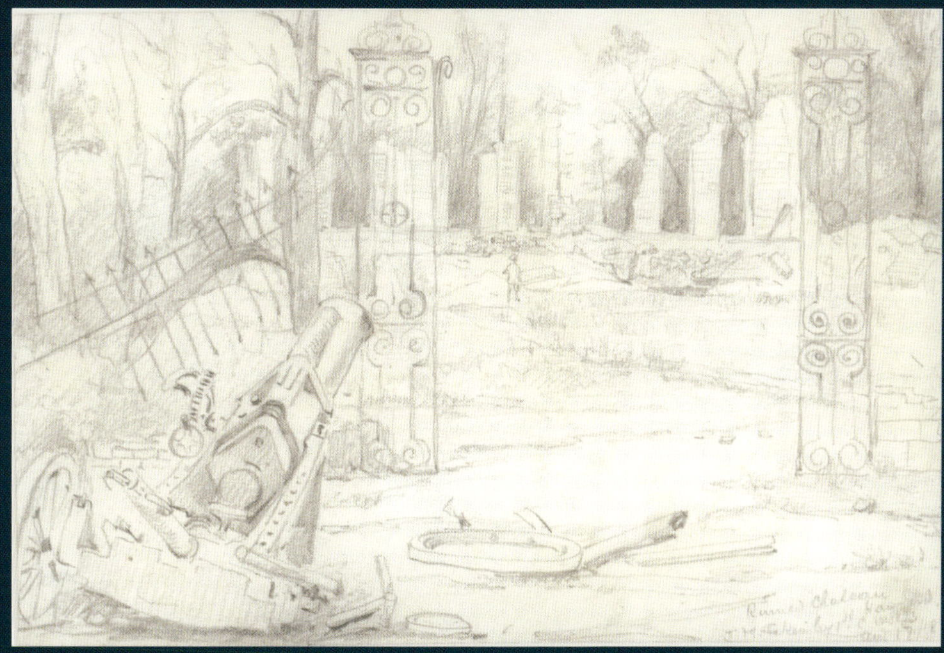

87 – Vivian John Cummings (b.1875)

Knocked out German trench mortar at the gates of the ruined chateau at Hangard, taken by
1st Canadian Mounted Rifles – August 17th 1918, inscribed,
Pencil on paper, - 7 x 10 in. (18 x 25.5 cm)

86 – Ernest Procter (1886-1935)

Péronne, Jan 3.1919, signed, dated, inscribed with title,
Crayon and gouache on paper, 19 ½ x 12 ½ in. (49.5 x 31.8 cm)

Initially working with the British Red Cross in Dunkirk, Procter later served on the Western Front with two units of the Section Sanitaire Anglaise, at Nieuport Bains and at Verdun. He was appointed Official War Artist for the Ministry of Information from 1918–19. Péronne, in northern France. is close to where the Battles of the Somme took place. This watercolour shows the flamboyant Gothic west front of the Église Saint-Jean-Baptiste which by 1917, like most of the town, had been almost entirely destroyed.

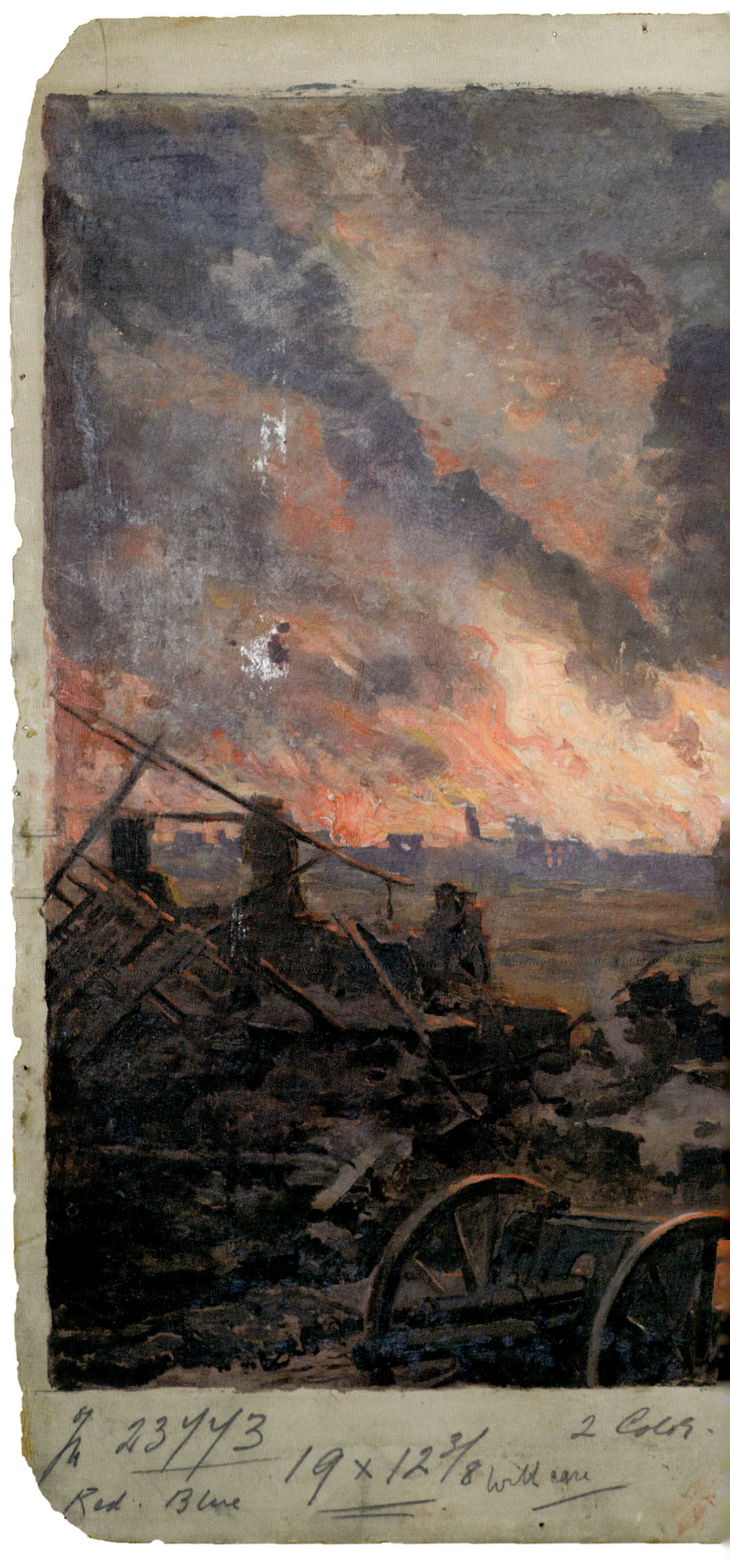

88 – Ugo Matania (1888-1979)

Gunners passing burning buildings, 1917,
Illustration for *The Sphere* 26/5/1917,
Signed with initials, dated, inscribed with measurements
and printing instructions, '2 cols, this is still wet',
Oil on card, 15 x 23 ½ in. (38.1 x 59.7 cm)

Ugo Matania, along with his cousin Fortunino (1881-1963) was considered to be one of the foremost illustrators of the war contributing many drawings to the weekly 'War Numbers' issues of *The Sphere* between 1914-1919 and the *London Magazine*. While some of his images were partly based on photographs and eye-witness accounts, he also made several trips to the war zones in France and Belgium.

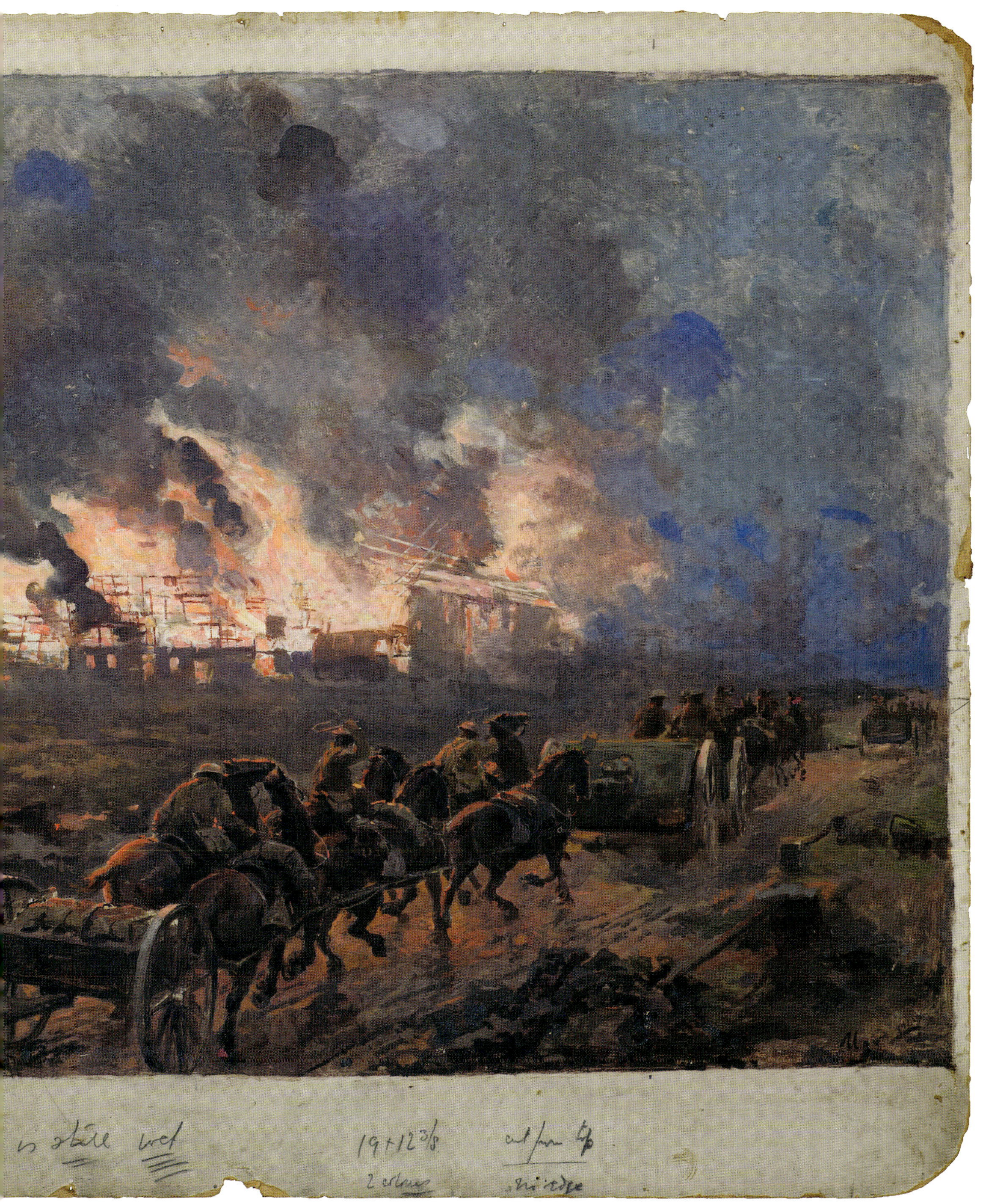
is still wet
19 + 12 3/8
2 colrs
cut from t/p
this edge

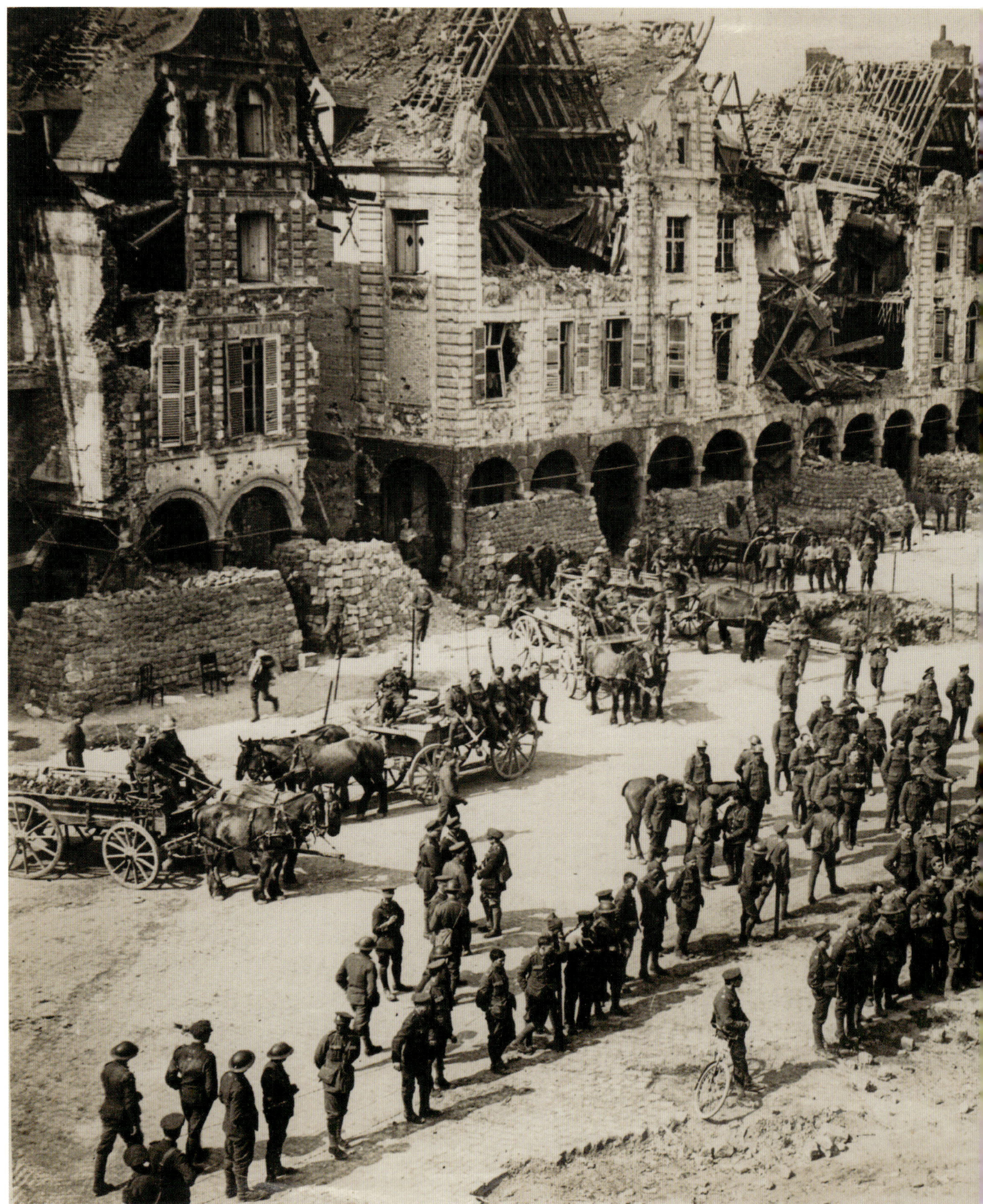

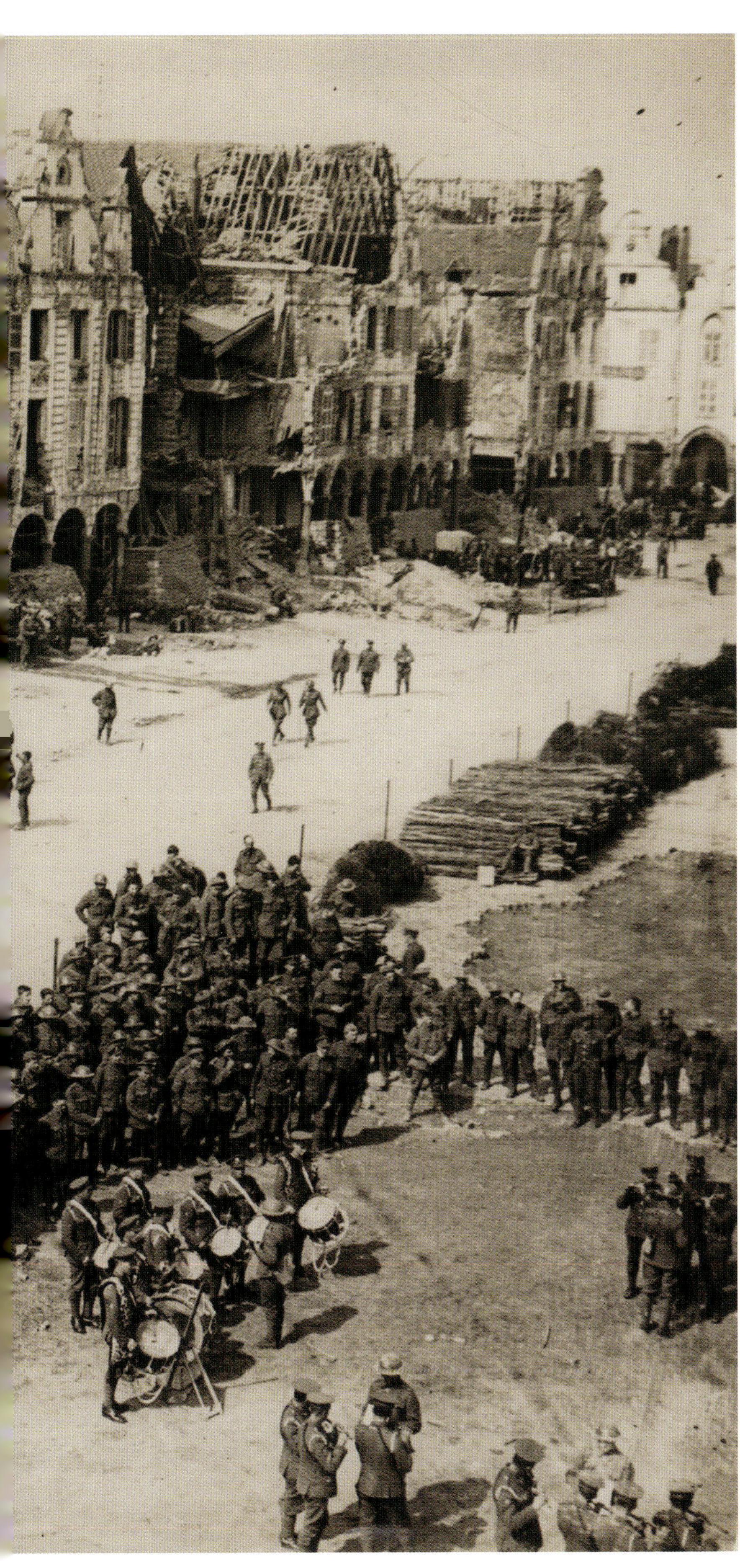

89 – Official photograph issued by Associated Illustration Agencies, Ltd.

Inscribed to the reverse:
"D 2475. View of one of the squares in Arras showing wrecked houses and a band playing."
Black & white photograph,
6 ½ x 8 ½ in. (16.5 x 21.5 cm)

Arras was ten kilometers behind the Allied Front Line, and a series of battles were fought around the city and nearby at Vimy Ridge. After the war three quarters of Arras had to be rebuilt – the City Hall was destroyed on October 7, 1914, the Belfry later in the same month and the Cathedral was severely bombed on July 6, 1915.

The Battle of Arras, a British offensive, lasted from April 9 to May 16, 1917. British, Canadian, New Zealand, Newfoundland, and Australian troops attacked German defences near the city. There were major gains on the first day, followed by stalemate. The battle cost nearly 160,000 British casualties and 125,000 German casualties.

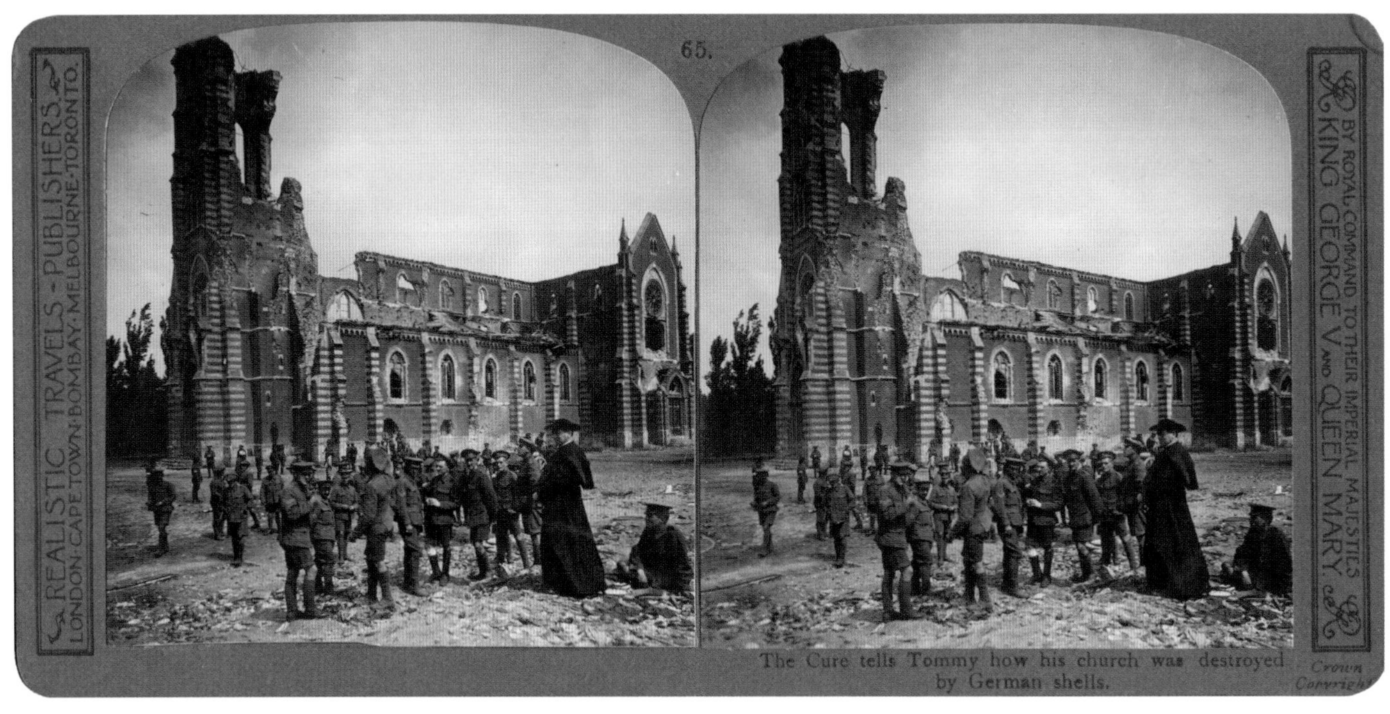

90 – Stereoscopic print: *The Curé tells Tommy how his church was destroyed by German shells.*
3 ½ x 7 in. (9 x 18 cm), published by Realistic Travels

Denys Wells (1881-1973)

91 – Shell damaged buildings Northern France, c.1918,
Oil on paper, 4 ⅞ x 8 ¼ in. (12.3 x 21.2 cm)

92 – Shell damaged buildings Northern France, c.1918,
Oil on paper, 5 x 8 ½ in. (12.7 x 21.5 cm)

In 1914 Wells joined the Artist's Rifles as a Commissioned Officer and served in France for
the duration of the war.

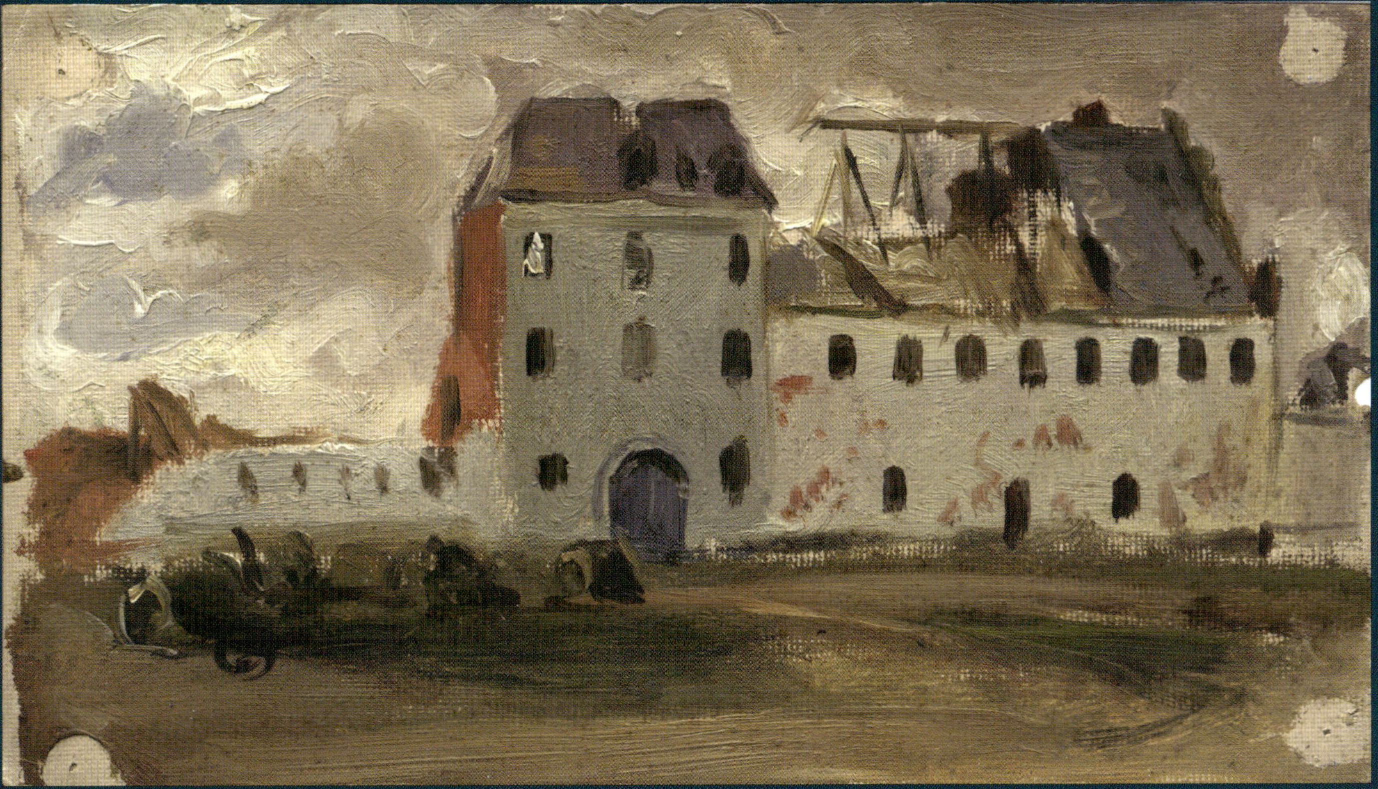

91

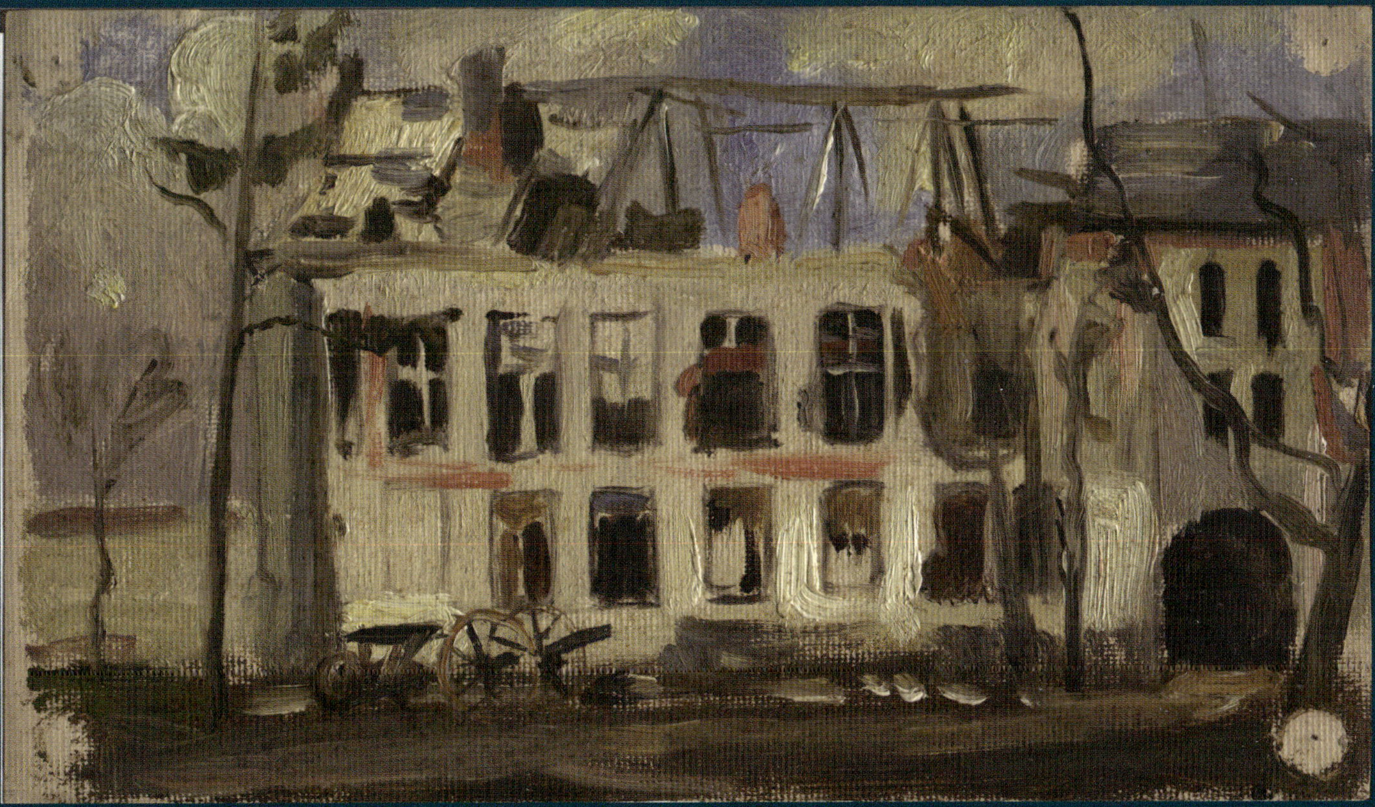

92

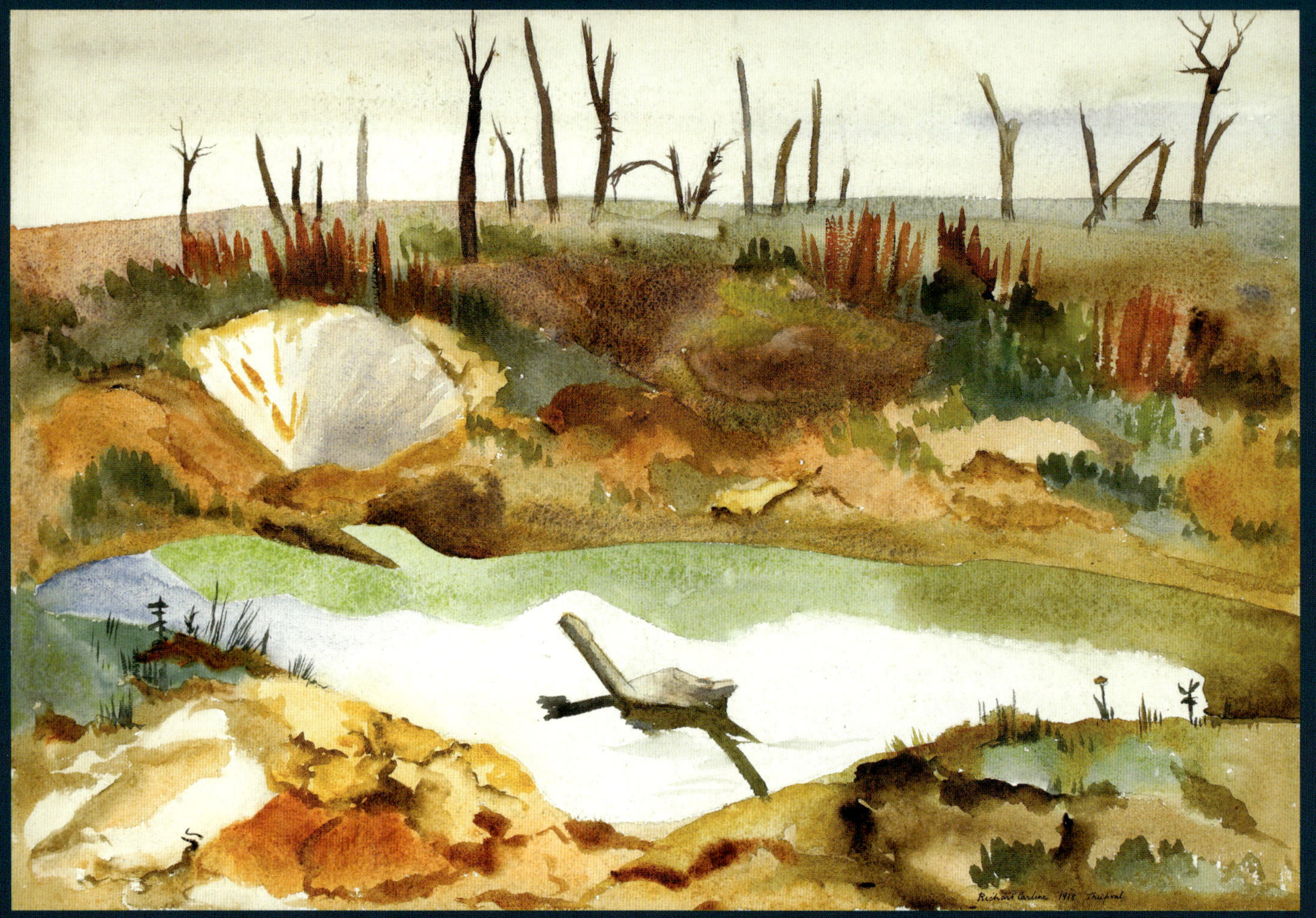

93 – Richard Carline (1896-1980)

'Thiepval', Pond, 1918, signed and dated, inscribed with title,
Watercolour on paper, 14 ⅞ x 20 ⅜ in. (37.8 x 52.3 cm)

During the war, the Western Front was transformed into a landscape of blasted trees, barbed wire and shell craters and trenches filled with mud and stagnant water. This painting shows the landscape near the village of Thiepval, 7km north of Albert in the Somme Department in Northern France. The original village was totally destroyed during the war. The present town, which occupies a location a short distance to the southwest of the former settlement, is home to Lutyen's Franco-British Memorial and the Thiepval Memorial to the Missing of the Somme.

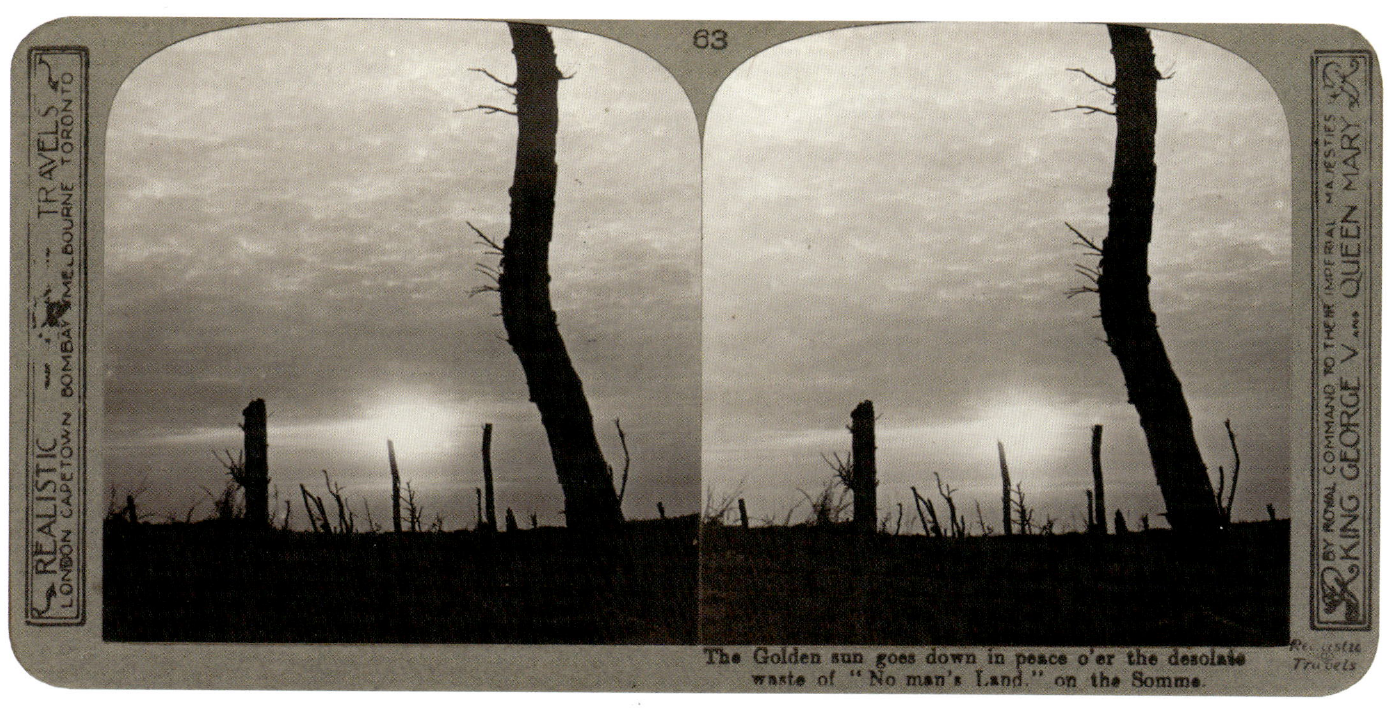

94 – **Stereoscopic print:** *The Golden sun goes down in peace o'er the desolate waste of "No man's Land" on the Somme.* 3 ½ x 7 in. (9 x 18 cm), published by Realistic Travels

Frank Brangwyn (1867-1956)

95 – Original design for the woodcut *Damn the War* (V1484),
Black wash on paper, 3 x 2 ½ in. (7.5 × 6.4 cm)

The dramatic gesture of the principal figure echoes the
stance of the innocent victim in Francisco de Goya's *The
Third of May 1808* (1814).

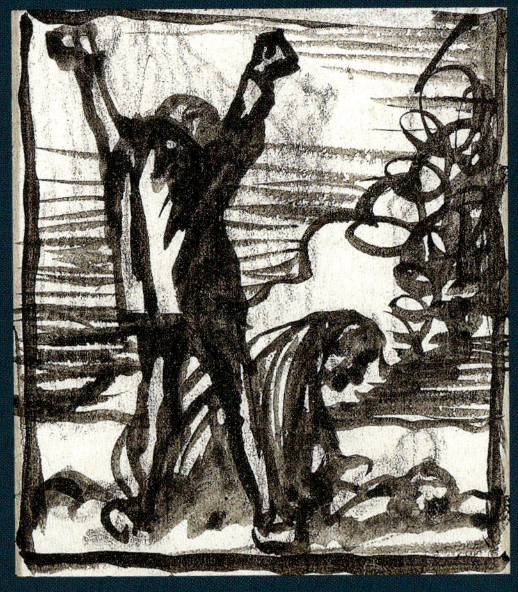

96 – Original design for the woodcut *Horresco* (V2125),
Black wash on paper, 3 x 2 ½ in. (7.5 × 6.4 cm)

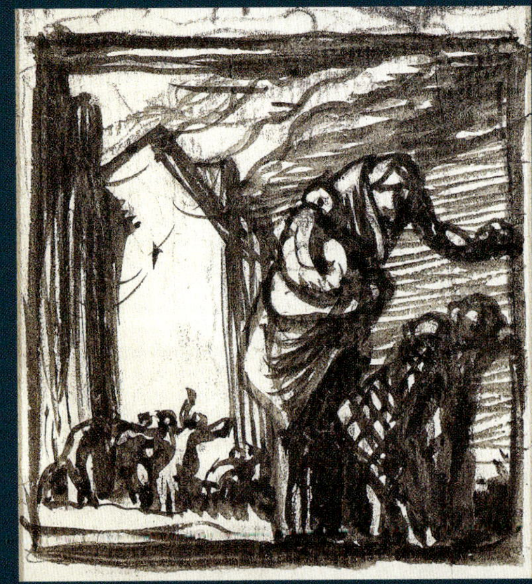

97 – Original design for the woodcut *The Fire/ Tragedy of
Dixmude* (V1482),
Black wash on paper, 3 x 2 ½ in. (7.5 × 6.4 cm)

The Fire was used as the cover design for the *Tragedy of
Dixmude* (1921), a catalogue of paintings and drawings
of Dixmude, near Ostend, donated to the town in
commemoration of the First World War. The Dixmude
trenches, otherwise known as the Trenches of Death, were
held by the Belgians for more than four years during the
Battles of the Yser against German forces often just a
hundred yards away. Brangwyn was the Chairman
of the English Committee for Dixmude.

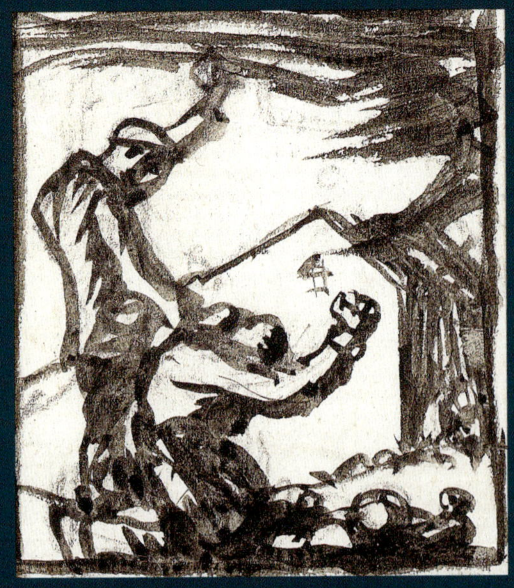

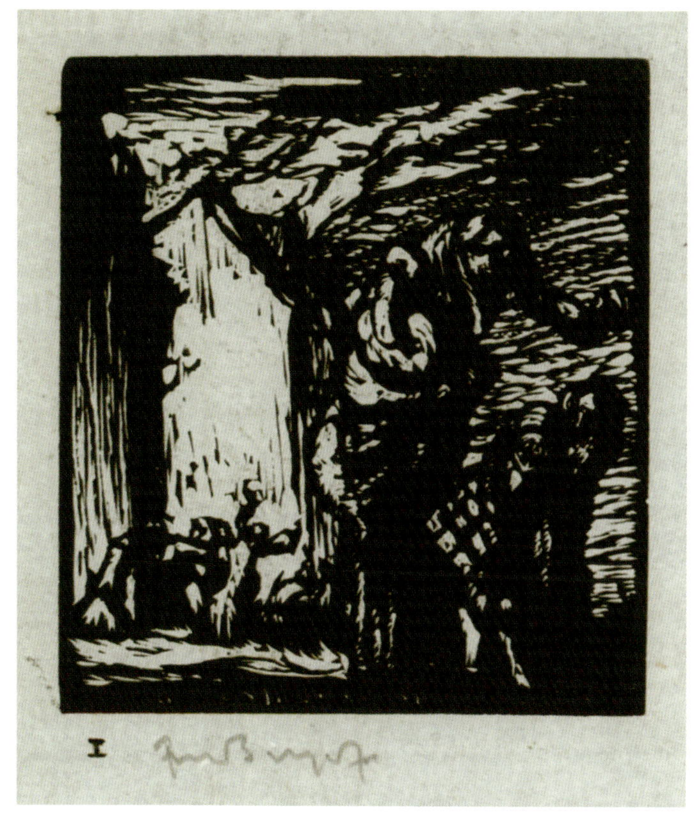

98

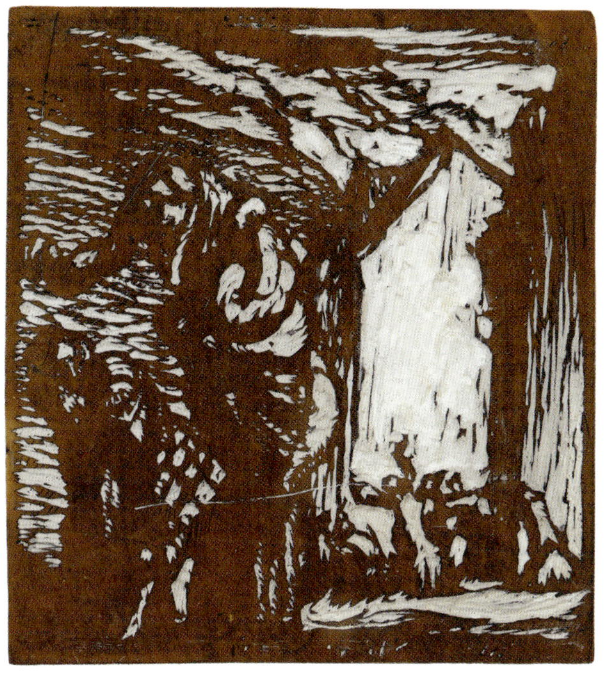

99

Horresco, 1919,
98 – Print, signed, approx. 6 ½ x 5 in. (16.5 x 12.7 cm)
99 – Original Woodblock, 3 ½ x 3 in. (9 x 7.6 cm)

Horresco is a reference to the Latin phrase 'horresco referens': I shudder as I tell the story.

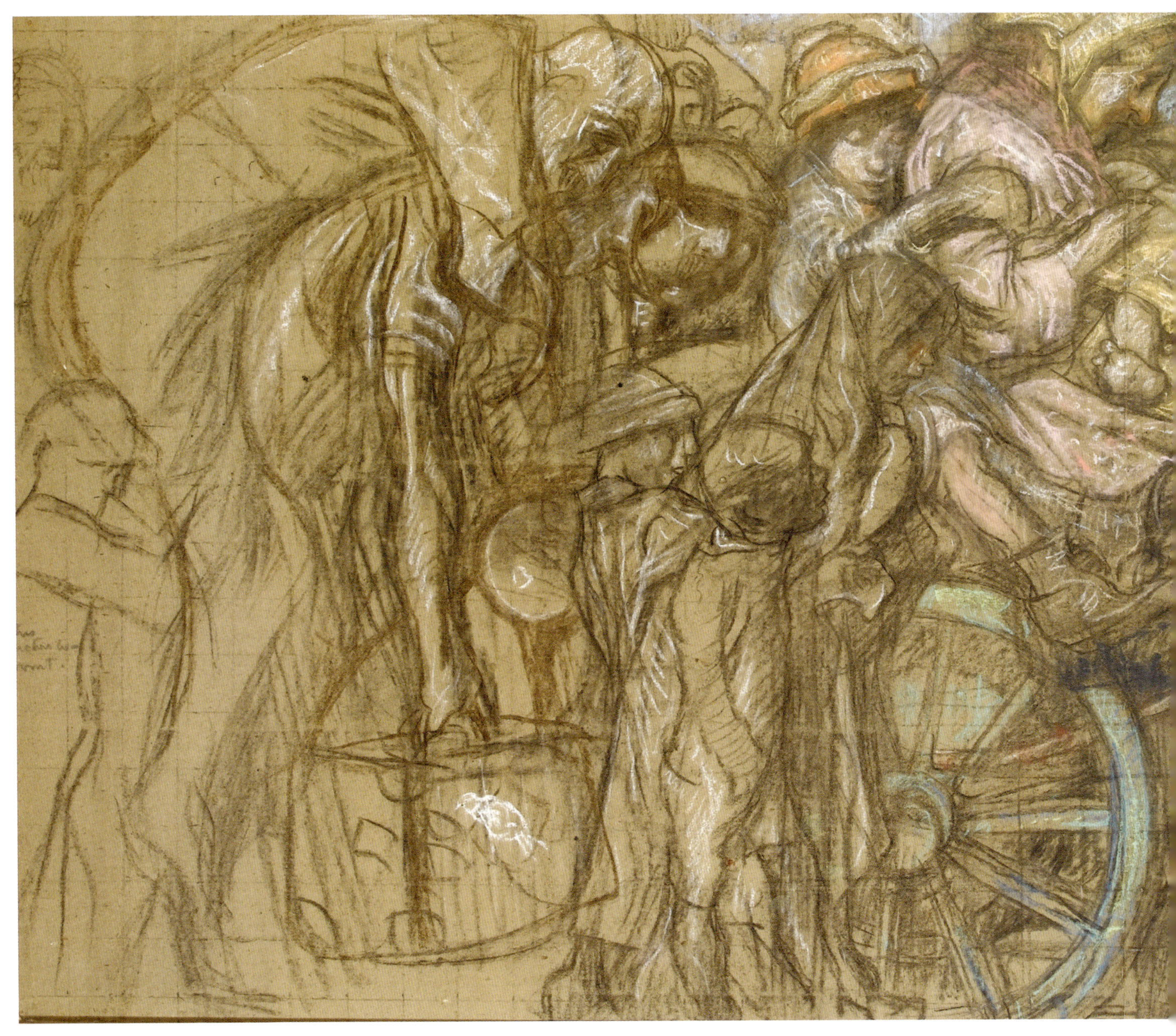

100 – Frank Brangwyn (1867-1956)

Study for *Exodus* (O283), c.1918,
Charcoal and coloured chalks on paper, 50 x 126 cm
Provenance: acquired directly from Brangwyn by Raymond Sheppard c.1950; private collection Canada since 2010,
Exhibited: *Frank Brangwyn*, The National Museum of Western Art, Tokyo, February 2010, cat 62

Ignoring Belgium's neutrality at the beginning of the war, the German Army engaged in numerous atrocities against the civilian population. 'The Rape of Belgium', as it became known, resulted in 6,000 Belgians killed, 25,000 homes and other buildings in 837 communities destroyed. One and a half million Belgians (20% of the entire population) fled. Brangwyn, Belgian by birth, was one of a number of artists who responded by creating powerful propaganda images demonstrating outrage at Germany's aggression.

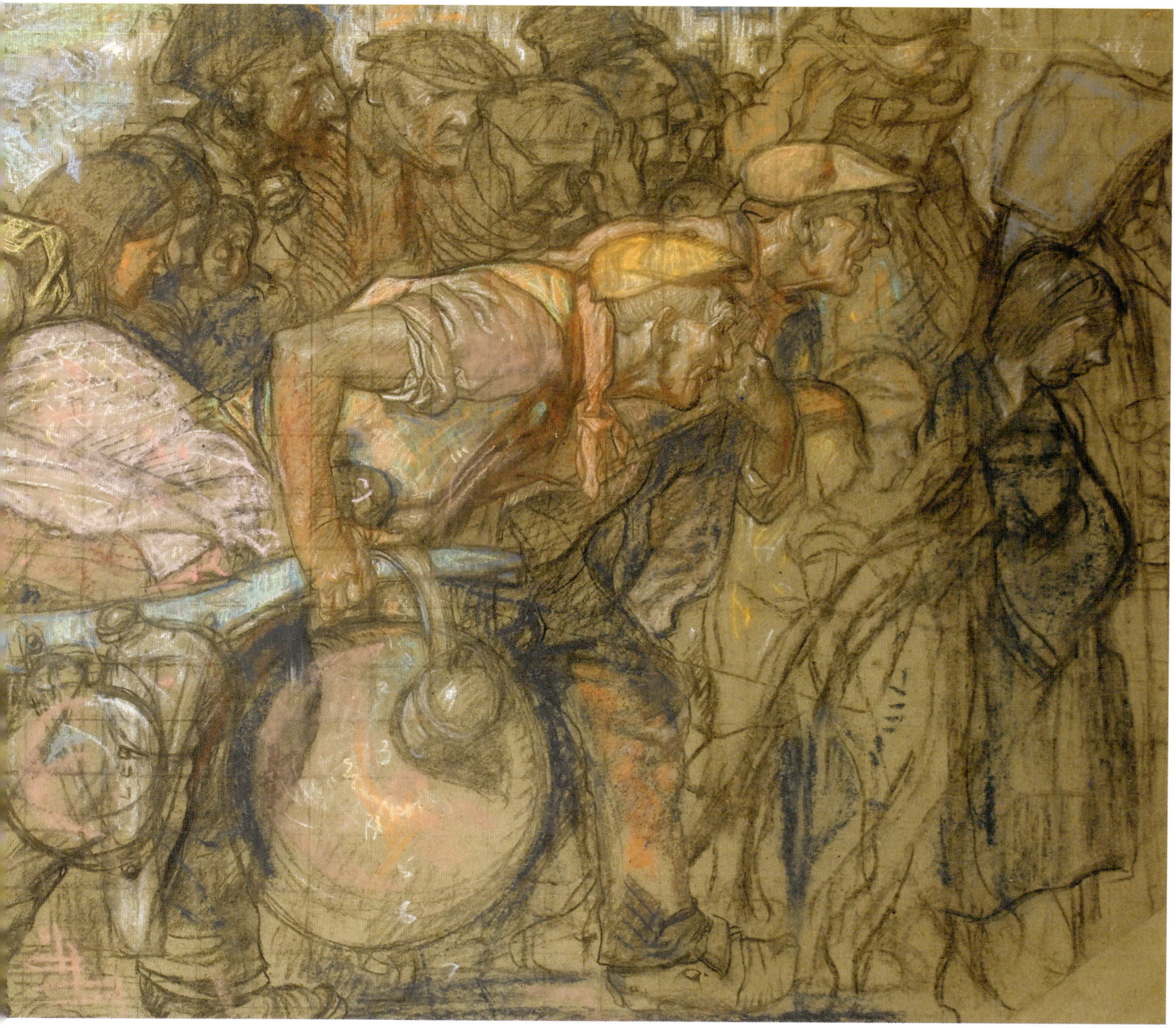

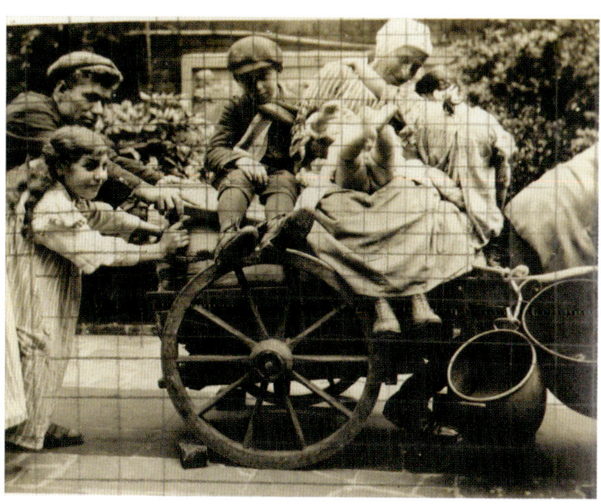

Squared photograph Brangwyn used for *Exodus*

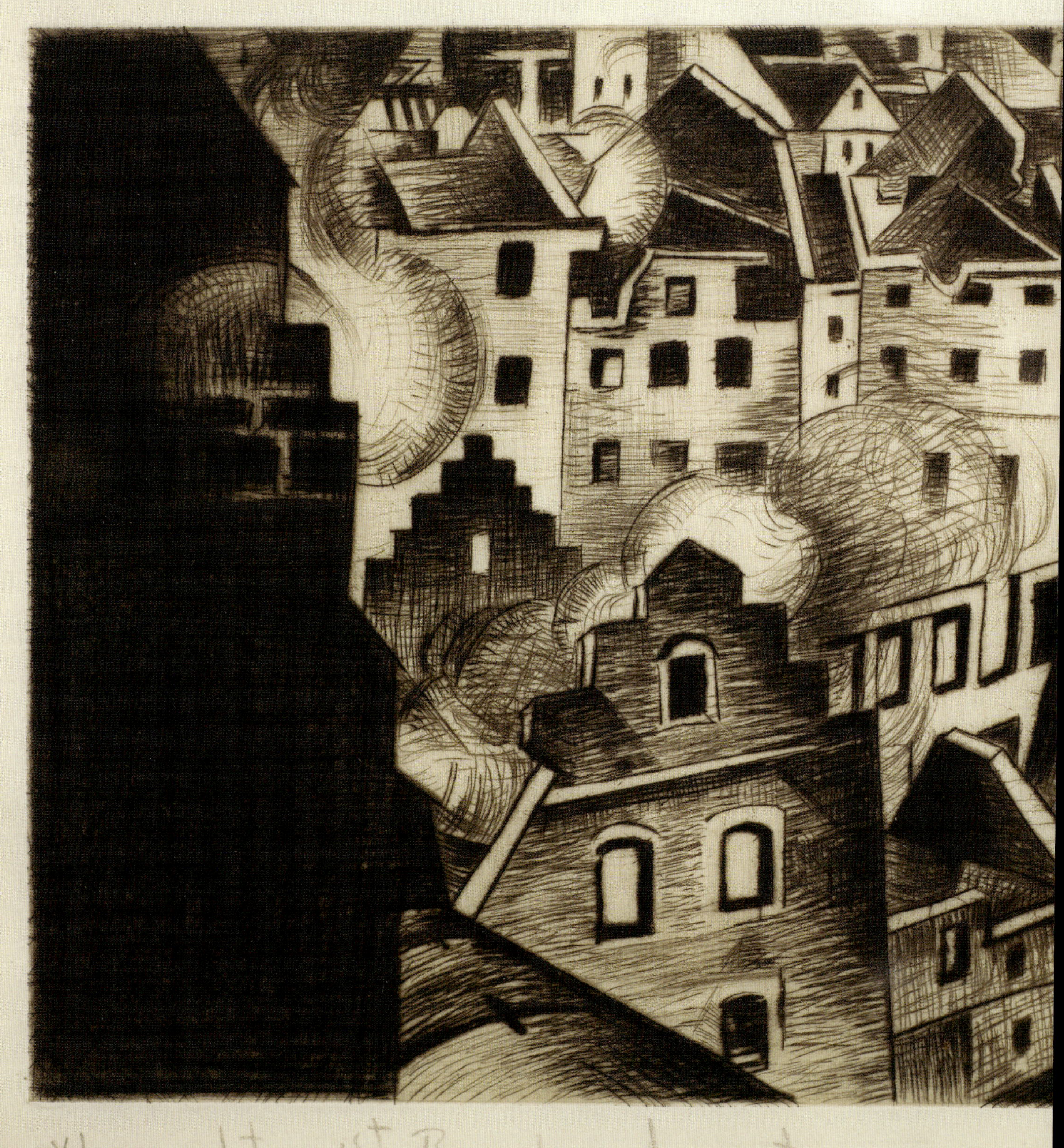

Ypres after 1st Bombardment.

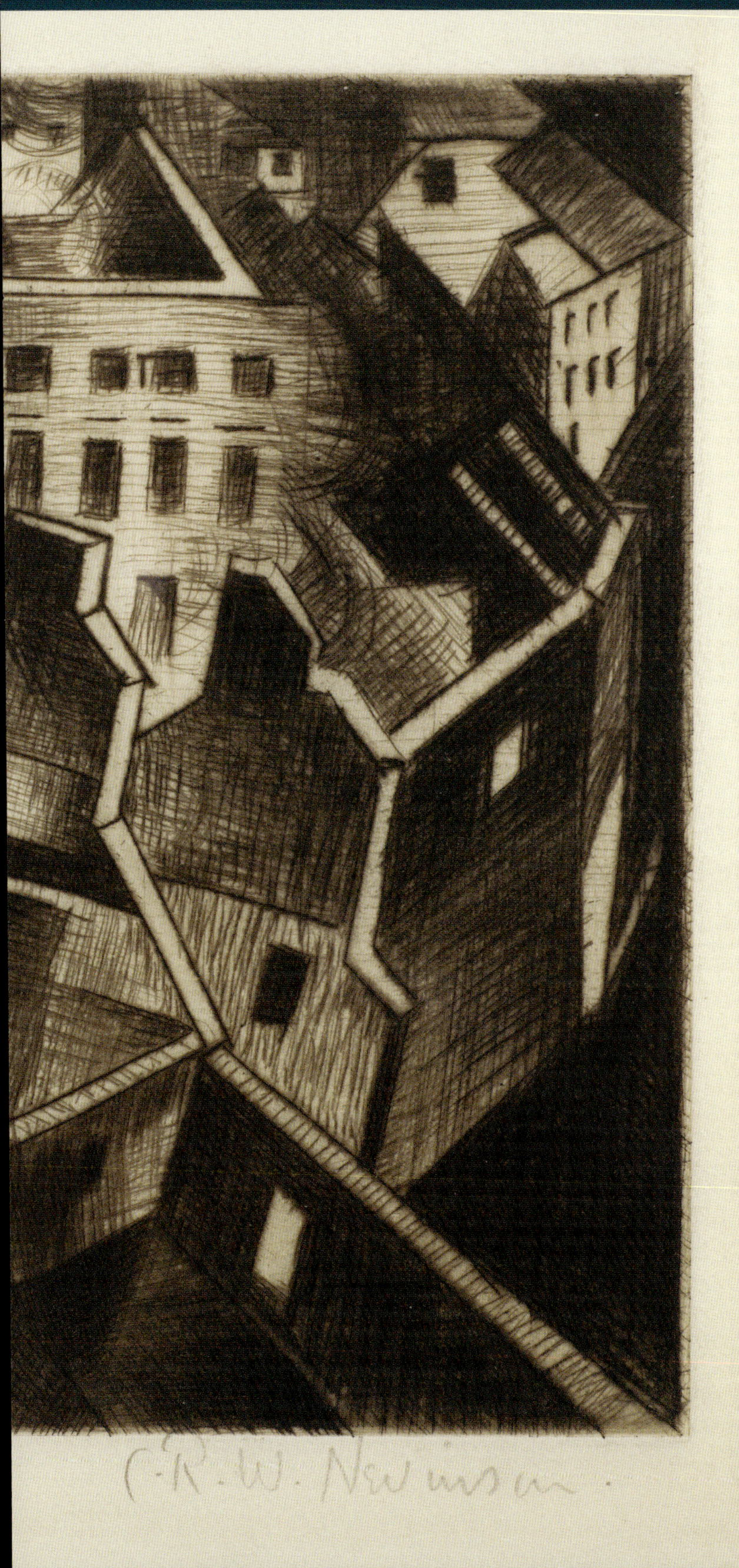

101 – Christopher Richard Wynn Nevinson (1889-1946)

Ypres after 1st Bombardment, 1916, signed in pencil,
Drypoint print on watermarked cream laid paper,
6 x 9 in. (15 x 22.5 cm)

This drypoint was made in the summer of 1916 – a print version of an oil painting exhibited at the London Group in early March 1915. Nevinson probably saw quite a bit of the much-shelled Ypres during the second half of November 1914 when he was driving a Mors motor ambulance from the Friends' Ambulance Unit base hospital at Malo-les-Bains (east of Dunkirk) to pick up wounded from a forward dressing station in Ypres and from the small town of Woesten to the north-west of the city. The First Battle of Ypres was coming to an end by late November 1914, but there were still periods of intense shelling in the area – during one of these Nevinson's ambulance was partially destroyed by a near miss while it was parked in the yard of the dressing station at Woesten. In later life Nevinson gave the impression he was actually driving the ambulance when the back part was demolished by a shell-burst. After his ambulance was written off Nevinson was transferred to work as a ward medical orderly at the Malo-les-Bains hospital from early December 1914 to the end of January 1915. The oil of *Ypres after the 1ˢᵗ Bombardment* was most likely painted in February 1915 – it is one of his few First World War designs executed in his Futurist manner. The drypoint, first exhibited in Nevinson's first solo exhibition at the Leicester Galleries (September-November 1916), so impressed Paul Nash that while he was at the Front in Flanders in March 1917, he wrote to his wife Margaret asking her to buy one if possible. Having recently visited Ypres, Nash thought Nevinson's print had really caught its feeling of abandoned desolation and random destruction.

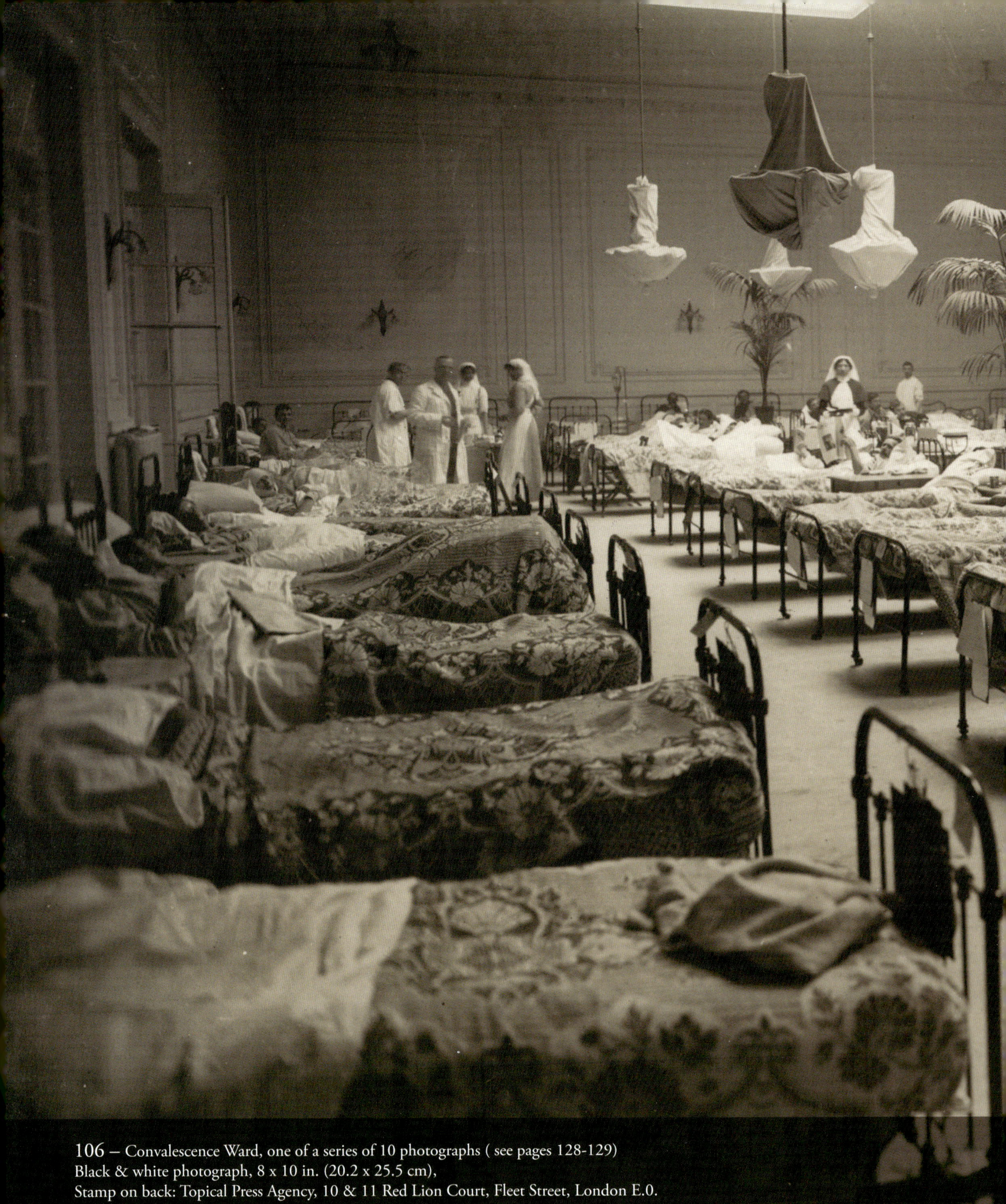

106 – Convalescence Ward, one of a series of 10 photographs (see pages 128-129)
Black & white photograph, 8 x 10 in. (20.2 x 25.5 cm),
Stamp on back: Topical Press Agency, 10 & 11 Red Lion Court, Fleet Street, London E.0.

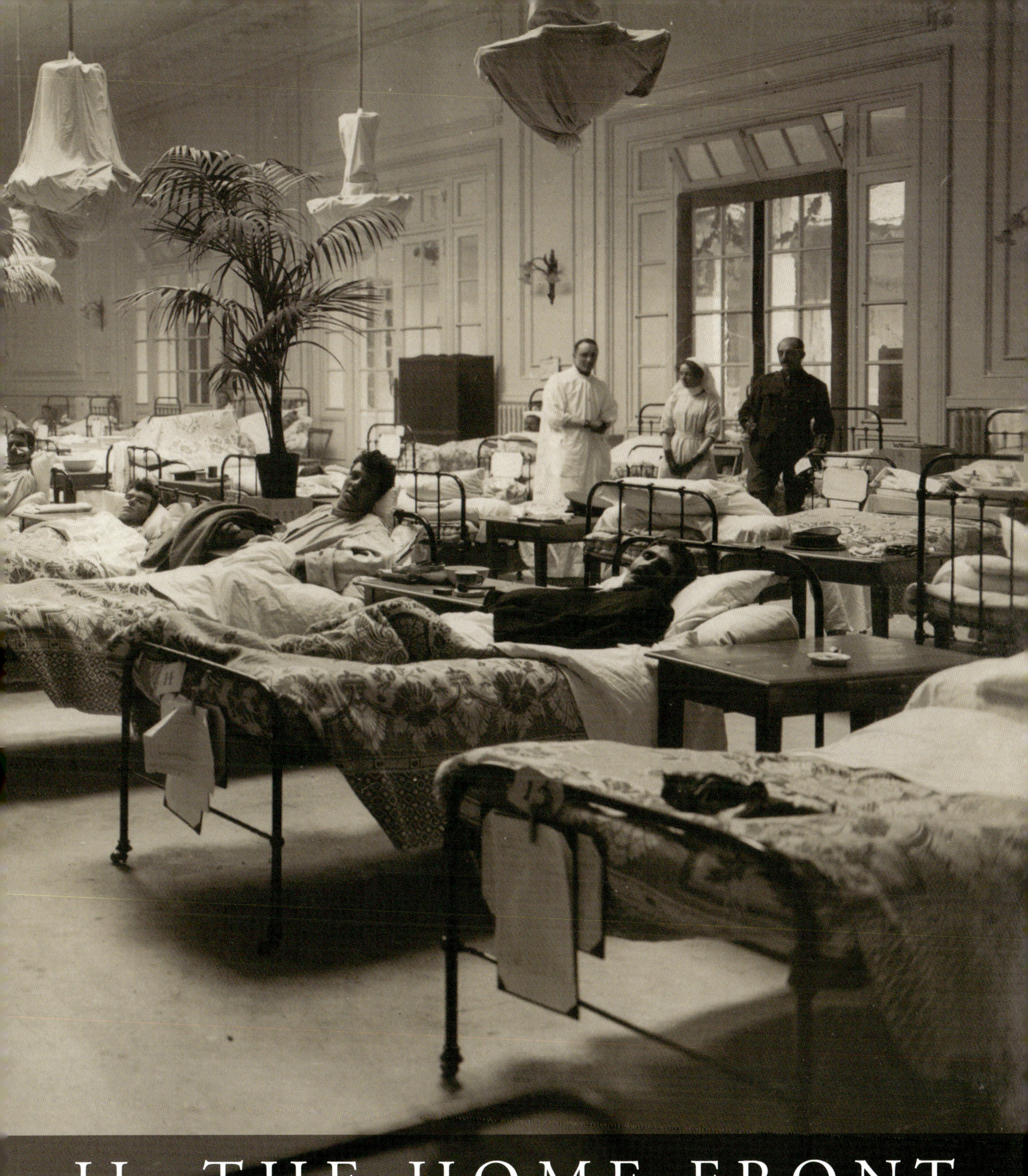

II THE HOME FRONT

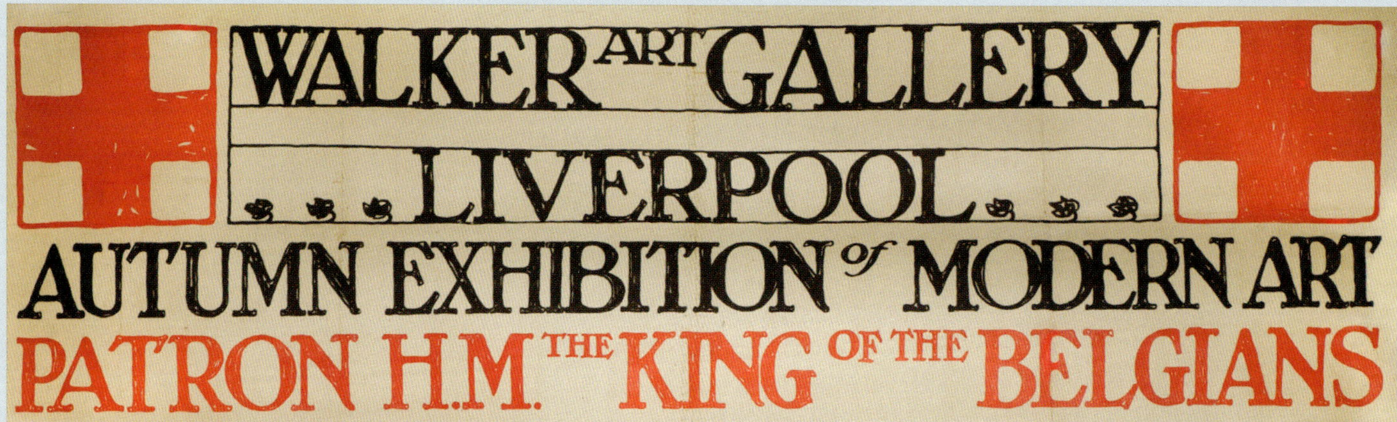

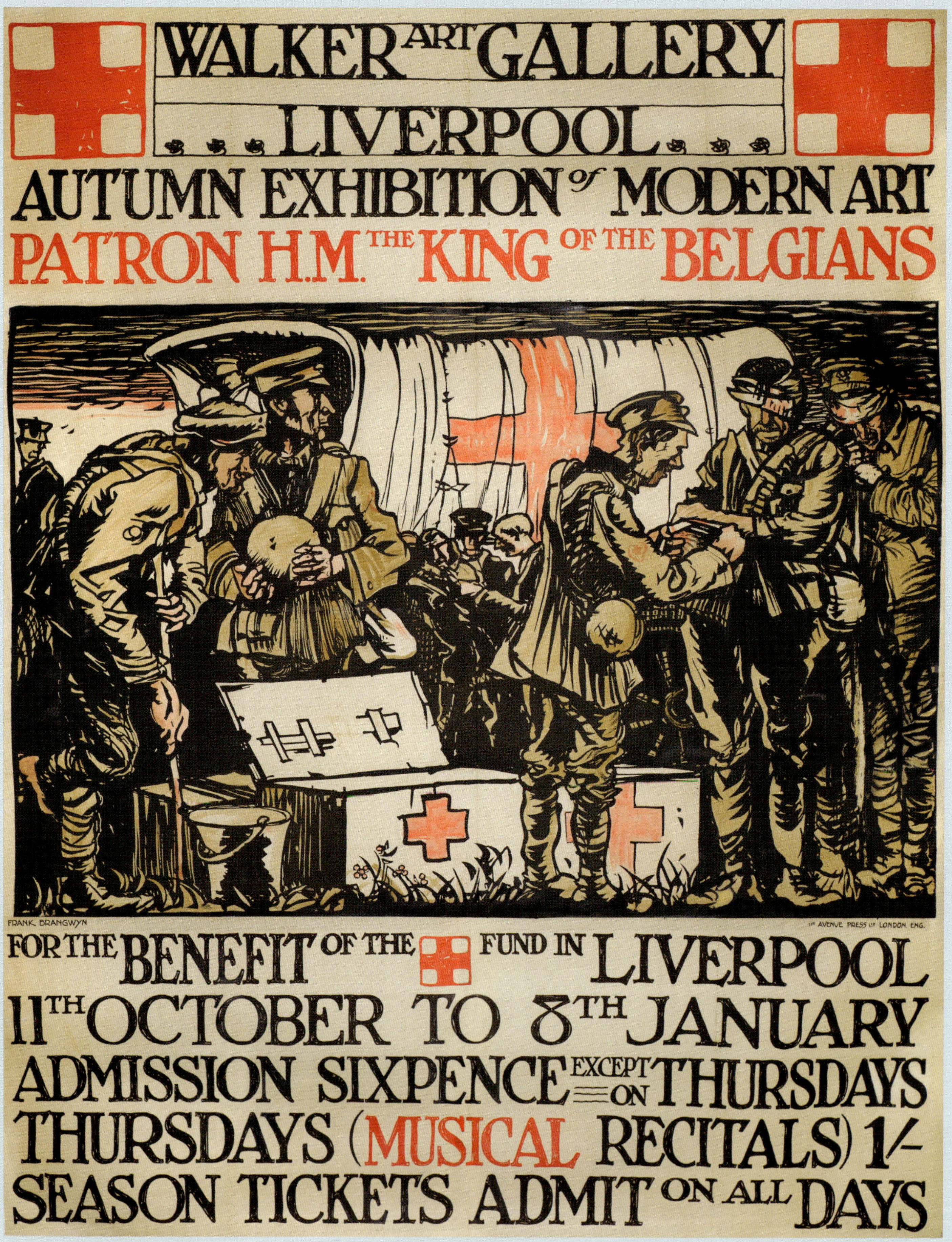

WALKER ART GALLERY
LIVERPOOL
AUTUMN EXHIBITION of MODERN ART
PATRON H.M. THE KING OF THE BELGIANS
FRANK BRANGWYN
1ST AVENUE PRESS LT LONDON ENG.
FOR THE BENEFIT OF THE FUND IN LIVERPOOL
11TH OCTOBER TO 8TH JANUARY
ADMISSION SIXPENCE EXCEPT ON THURSDAYS
THURSDAYS (MUSICAL RECITALS) 1/-
SEASON TICKETS ADMIT ON ALL DAYS

"In no circumstances whatever will the expression 'shell-shock' be used verbally or be recorded in any regimental or other casualty report, or in any hospital or other medical document."

British Army General Routine Order No. 2384, issued on June 7, 1917 in France

"Before an attack, the platoon pools all its available cash and the survivors divide it up afterwards. Those who are killed can't complain, the wounded would have given far more than that to escape as they have, and the unwounded regard the money as a consolation prize for still being here."

Robert Graves, *Good-bye to All That*, 1929

102 – Frank Brangwyn (1867-1956)

Field Hospital in France (W3749), signed in the plate,
Original lithographic poster, 78 ¾ x 59 in. (200 x 150 cm)
Printed by the Avenue Press,
Literature: Libby Horner, *Brangwyn at WAR!* (Horner and Goldmark, 2014) p.145

This is the only known surviving version of the poster accompanied by its two banners *For the Benefit of the Red Cross Fund in Liverpool*.

The vehicle in the background, which might be a horse-drawn or motor ambulance, was used for transporting wounded. A field hospital was a large mobile medical unit, or mini hospital, that temporarily took care of casualties before they could be moved to permanent hospital facilities.

Avenue Press, titling the work *Field Hospital in France*, also produced 15 lithographic prints on extra quality paper, 38 x 58 in. (96.5 x 147.5cm), printed in black, red and buff, each signed copy selling for 15 guineas in May 1916. Poster prints 40 x 60 in. (101.5 x 152.5 cm) cost one guinea each. Lettering sheets for the top and bottom, designed by Brangwyn and limited to 50 sets, sold for 5 shillings.

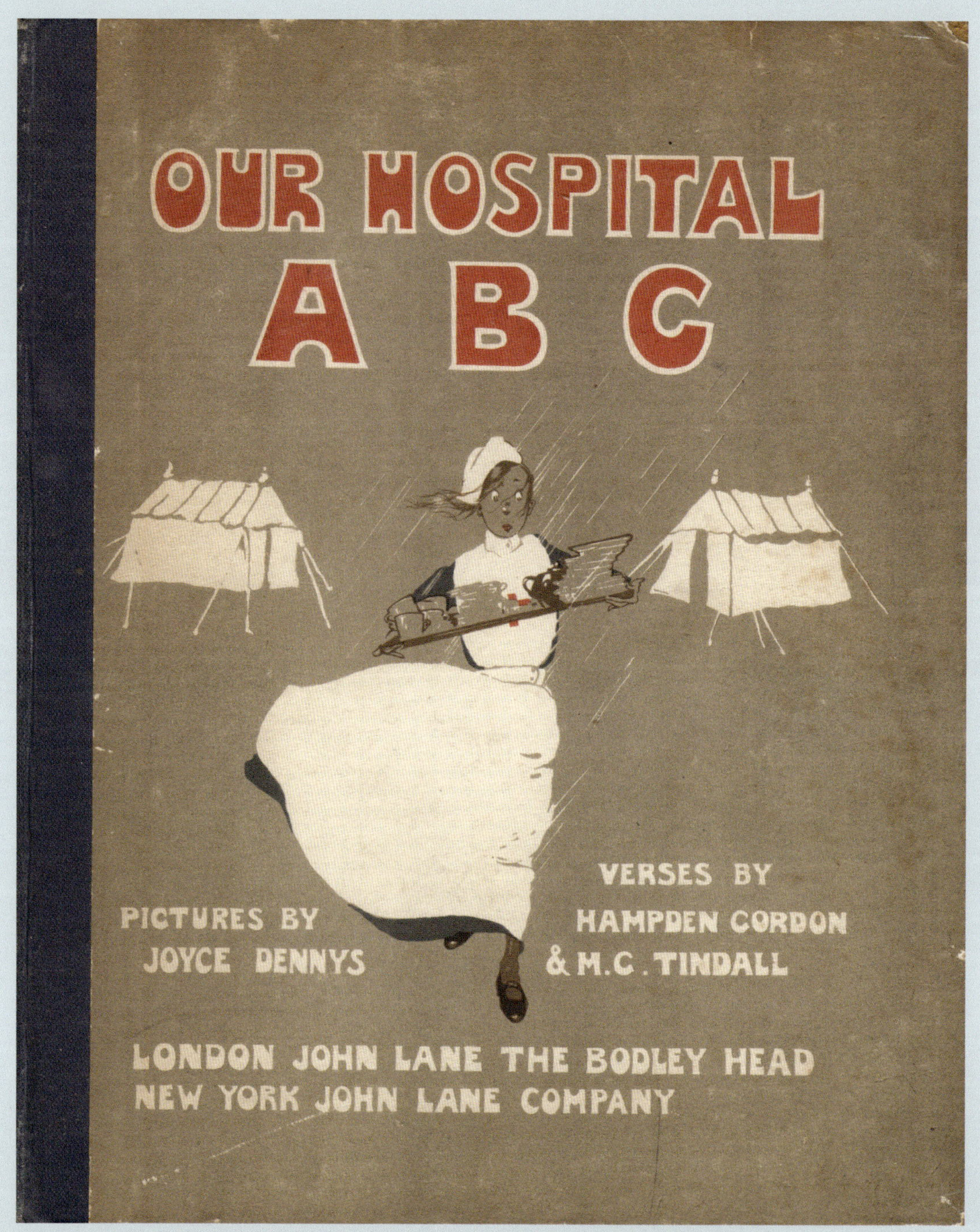

103 – *Our Hospital ABC*, 1916

Published by John Lane, London, pictures by Joyce Dennys, verses by Hampden Gordon & M.C. Tindall
60 pages, 9 ½ x 7 ½ in. (24 x 19 cm)

"Mr. John Lane, of the Bodley Head, Vigo Street, W., has just published a charming illustrated book of verses, entitled: "Our Hospital A.B.C.," the very spirited and delightful pictures being by Joyce Dennys and the verses by Hampden Gordon and M.C. Tindall. The letters A.B.C. stand for Anzac, British, Canadian. The clever drawings are for most part skits on the members of Voluntary Aid Detachments, but neither the Matron nor the Sisters have escaped ridicule. As a medicine label on the fly-leaf announced that the contents are "not to be taken seriously," this may be legitimate, but we could wish that the authors had also paid a passing tribute to the splendid work done by these highly skilled officers....
The book is sure to be popular, and deservedly so; it would be a most acceptable Christmas gift. The cost is 3s. 6d. and we advise our readers to secure a copy forthwith. From the pretty cover of red, white and blue on a grey background, to the last page, they will get, in amusement, full value for their money." (*The British Journal of Nursing*, December 9, 1916.)

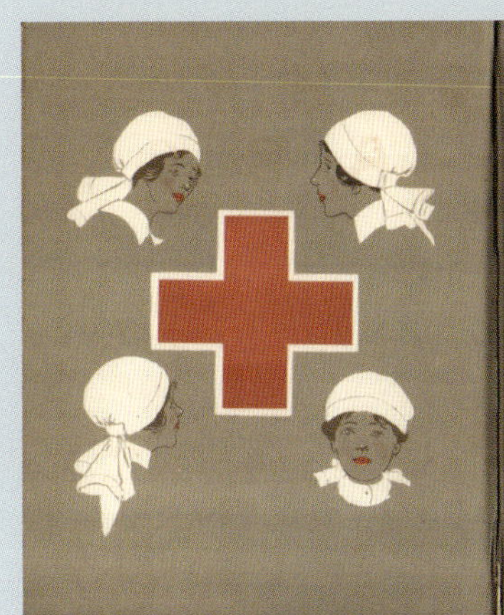

OUR HOSPITAL
A B C
ANZAC **B**RITISH **C**ANADIAN

PICTURES BY JOYCE DENNYS
VERSES BY HAMPDEN GORDON
& M. C. TINDALL

LONDON JOHN LANE THE BODLEY HEAD
NEW YORK JOHN LANE COMPANY
TORONTO   S. B. GUNDY

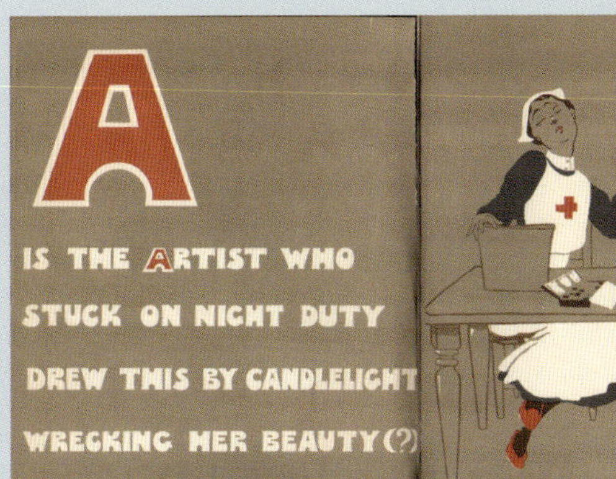

A

IS THE **A**RTIST WHO
STUCK ON NIGHT DUTY
DREW THIS BY CANDLELIGHT
WRECKING HER BEAUTY (?)

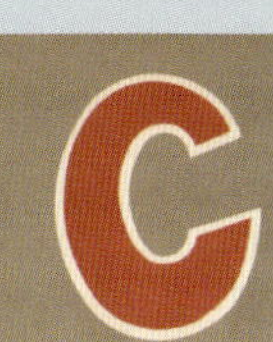

C

IS FOR **C**ANADA
GALLANT AND TRUE
WHOSE SONS MAKE THE HUNS
LOOK DECIDEDLY BLUE

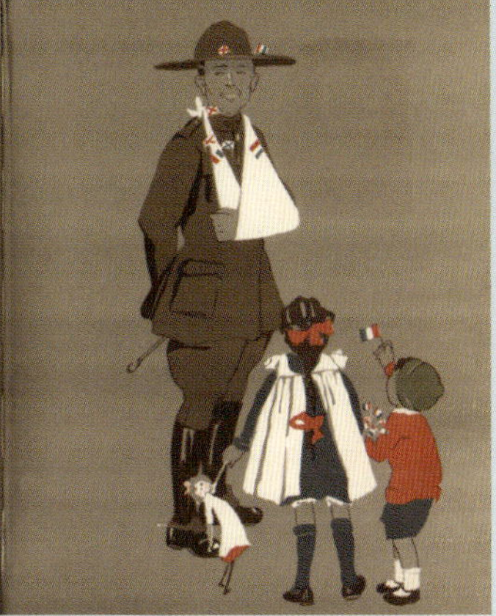
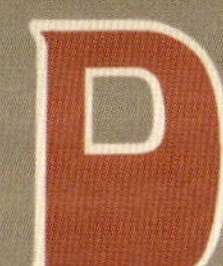

D

THE **D**ISPENSER
EXCUSE MY EMOTION
BUT O! WITH WHAT SKILL
DOES SHE MIX YOU A LOTION

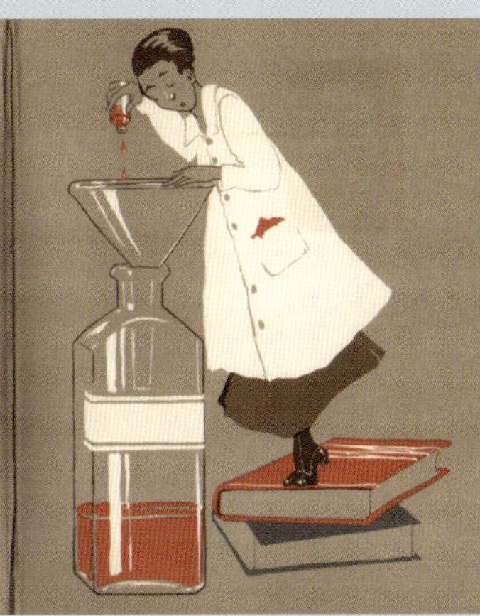

H

IS OUR **H**OSPITAL
NEVER MIND WHERE
OF COURSE IT'S THE BEST
IN THE LAND, WE ARE THERE

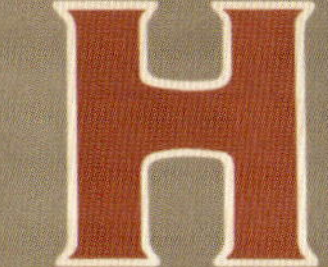

I

IS FOR **I**ODINE
THERE IS "SOME" MESS
IF AN ORDERLY SPILLS IT
ALL OVER YOUR DRESS

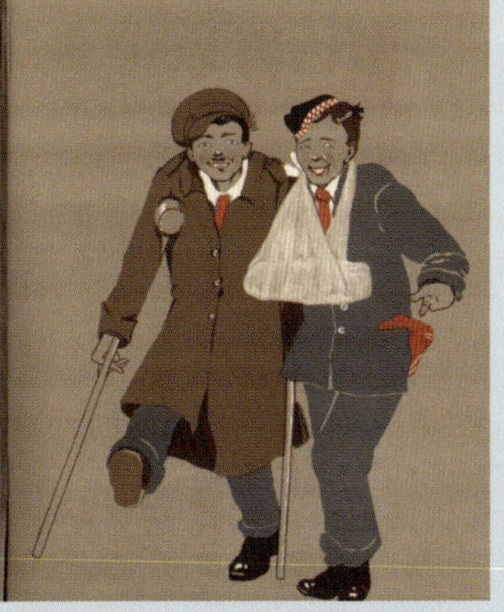
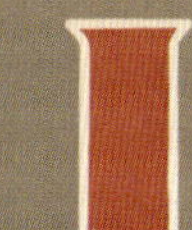
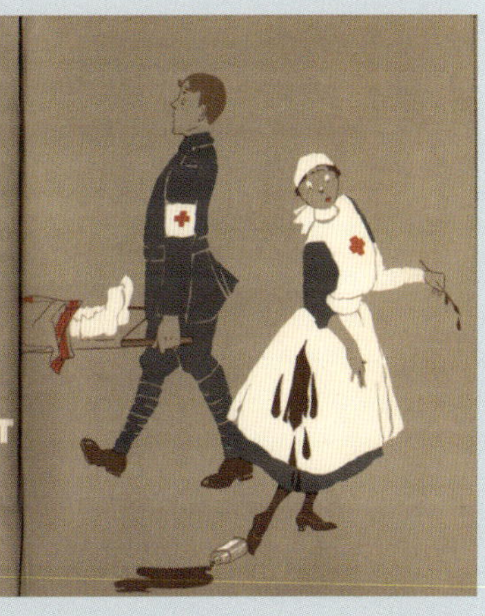

X

THE **X**- RAY
IF BY ANY ILL LUCK
YOU SWALLOW A SIXPENCE
IT SHOWS WHERE IT'S
STUCK

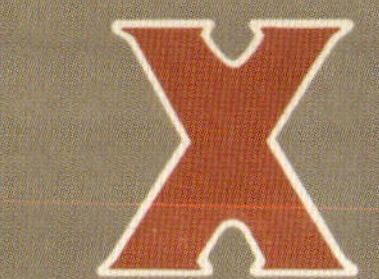
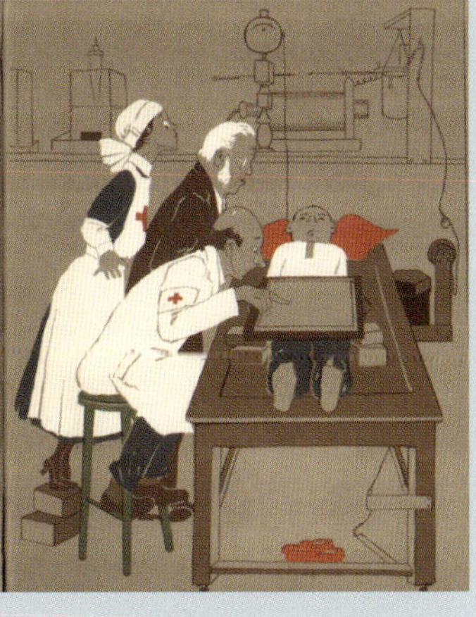
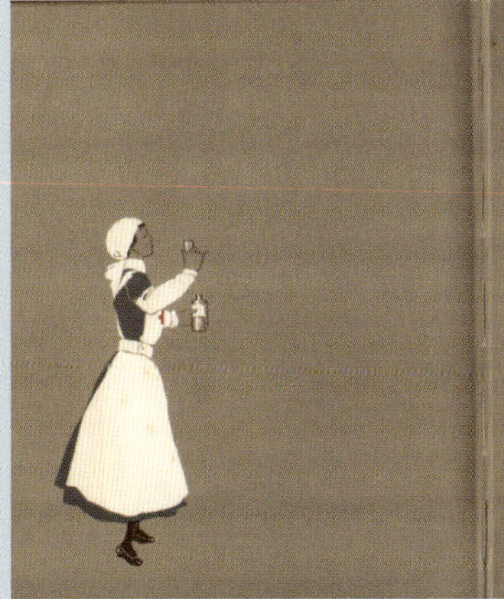
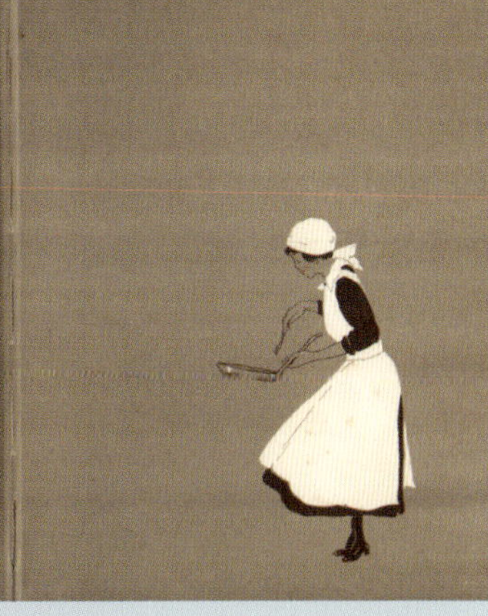

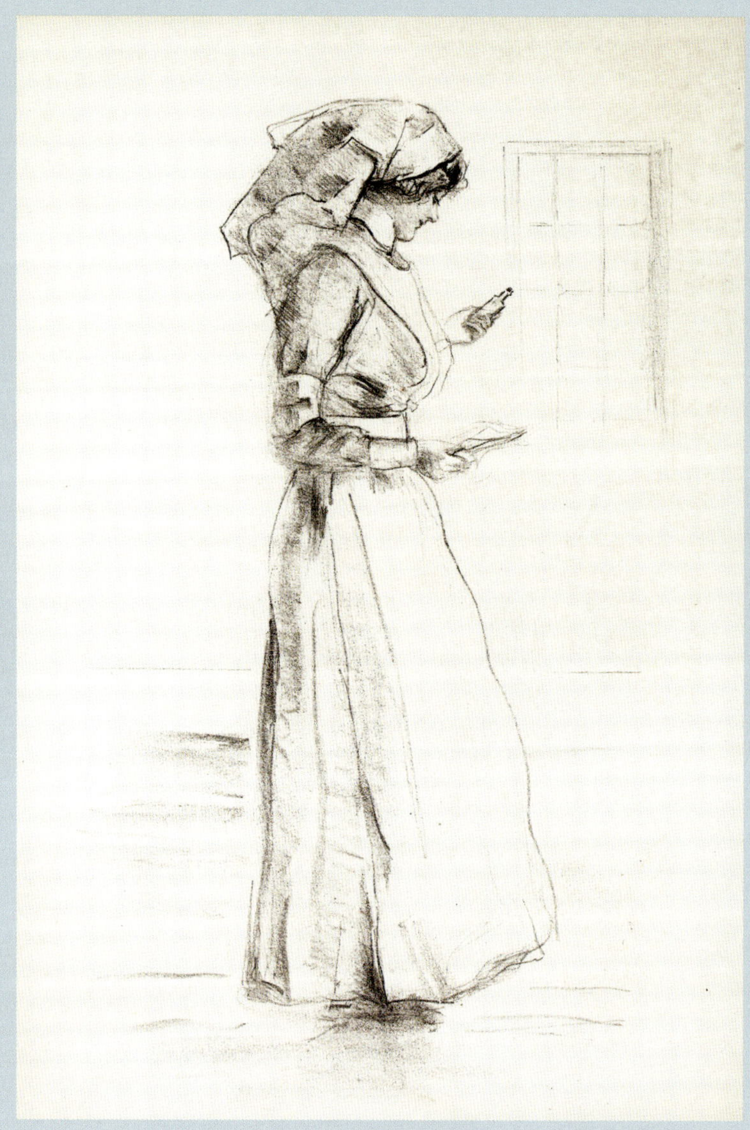

104 – Albert de Belleroche (1864-1944)

Nurse,
Lithograph, 22 x 15 in. (56 x 38 cm)

105 – Henry Tonks (1862-1937)

Study for 'An Advanced Dressing Station in France', 1918
Pastel on paper, 20 x 14 in. (50.5 x 35.5 cm)

The First World War created major problems for the Army's medical services. Ideally, the wounded first made it to a Regimental Aid Post, then on to a mobile Advanced Dressing Station. Here, often in appalling conditions, injuries might be cleaned and dressed, injections given and emergency amputations carried out. The next stop was a Casualty Clearing Station (CCS), where more substantial aid could be given several miles behind the Front Line. In 1918, the Ministry of Information commissioned Tonks to paint a large single picture, *An Advanced Dressing Station in France*, now in the collection of the Imperial War Museum, for which this is a study. Tonks had been both a surgeon and art teacher at the Slade before the war. In the early years of the war he was a civilian doctor in France and Italy. In 1916 he joined the Royal Army Medical Corps, working in Sidcup with Sir Harold Gillies, one of the pioneers of plastic surgery.

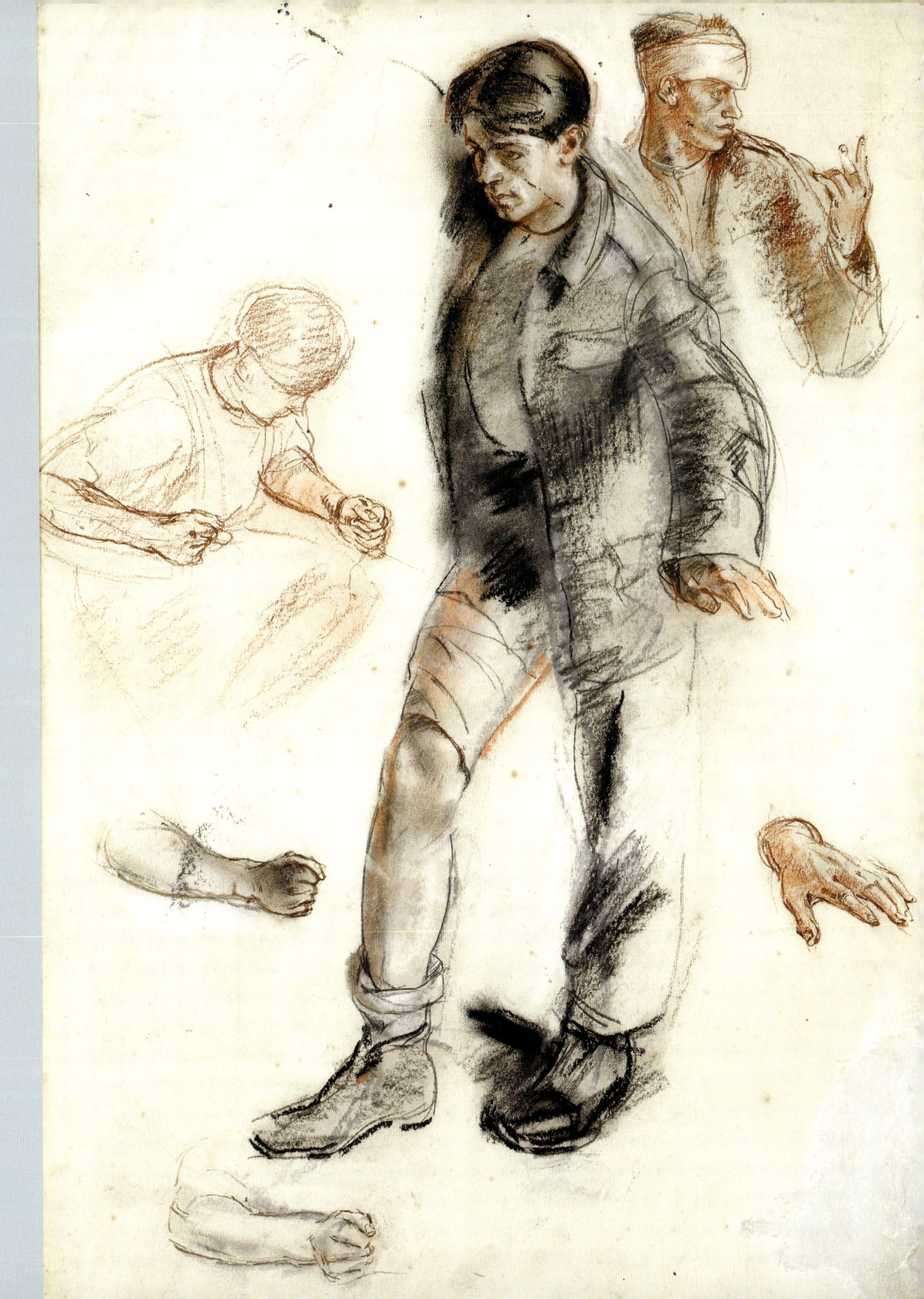

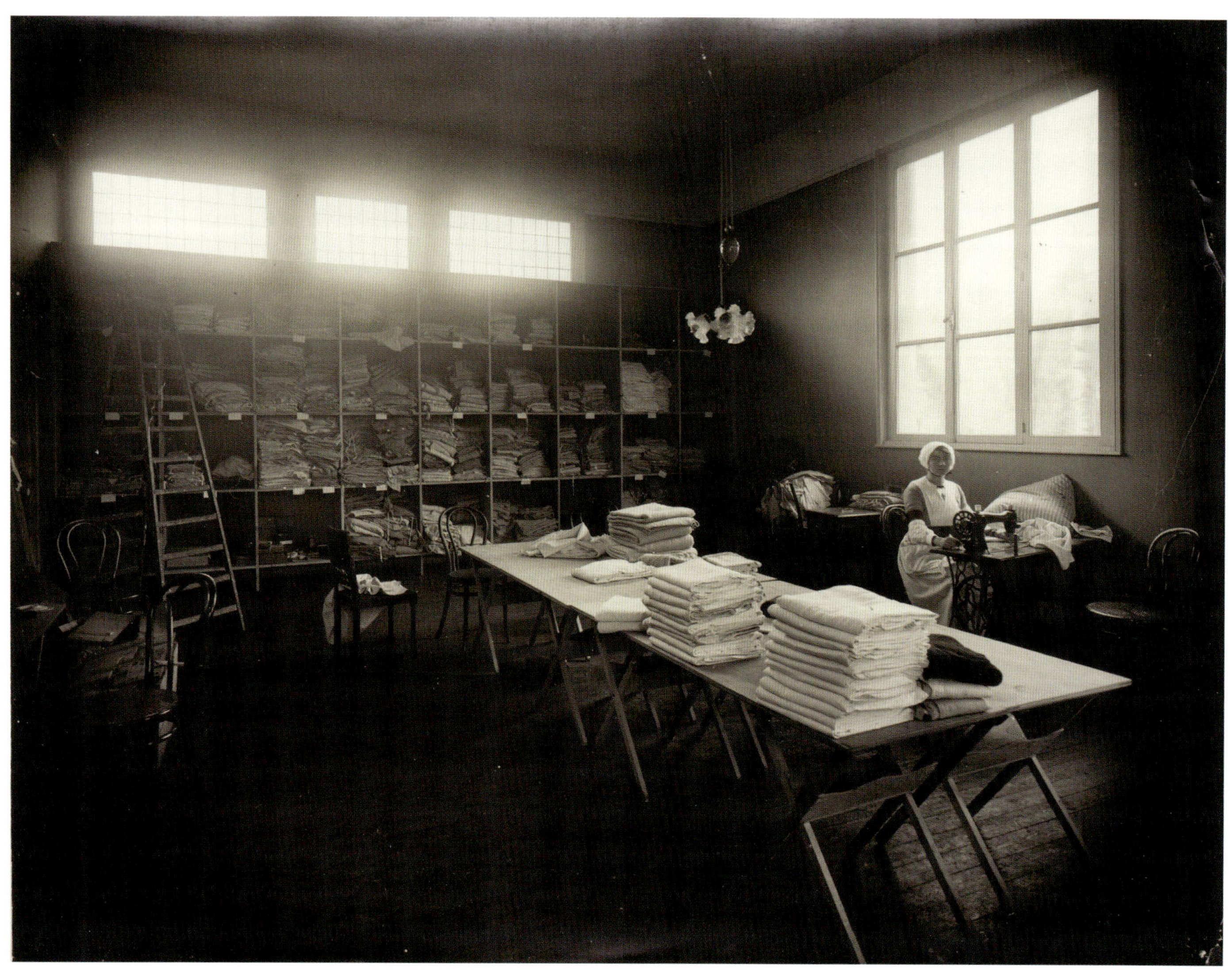

106 – No. 1 British Red Cross Society Hospital

Black & white photograph, 8 x 10 in. (20.2 x 25.5 cm) each
Stamp on back: Topical Press Agency, 10 & 11 Red Lion Court, Fleet Street, London E.0.

A series of ten original images for the *Illustrated War News* relating to No. 1 British Red Cross Society Hospital, (commonly known as The Duchess of Westminster's Hospital, named after its founder). The hospital was on the French coast at Le Touquet, housed in a building which, prior to the war, had been a Casino. Two of the photographs show Ward 2, the chandeliers covered with canvas. There is a group photograph of the Duchess (wearing a crucifix and large belt buckle) with the nursing staff of the hospital and a similar group shot of the Medical Officers posing outside the front of the hospital, (Charles Gordon Watson, Commandant and Chief Surgeon, standing at the very front). The Duchess is shown again, this time a solitary figure at work, in the linen room. An image showing an X-Ray taking place includes a medical orderly wearing an armband displaying the letter X. Another image shows an operation in progress with a medical orderly wearing an armband displaying the letter T (Technician). Another photograph shows a nurse at the dispensary which in peacetime had been the Casino bar. Ambulances can be seen parked outside the hospital in the snow. J. R. R. Tolkien stayed at the hospital while recovering from trench fever.

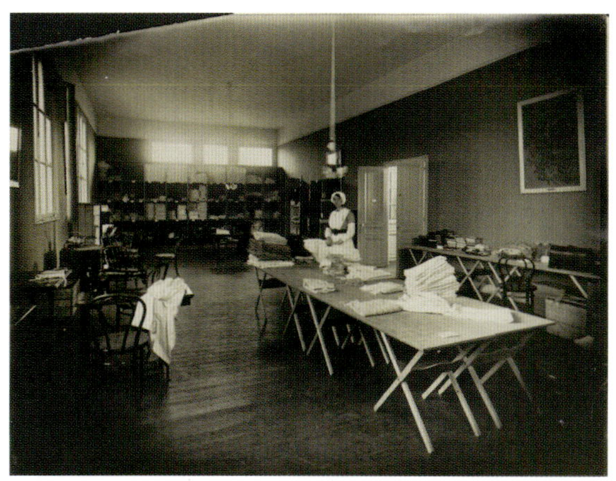
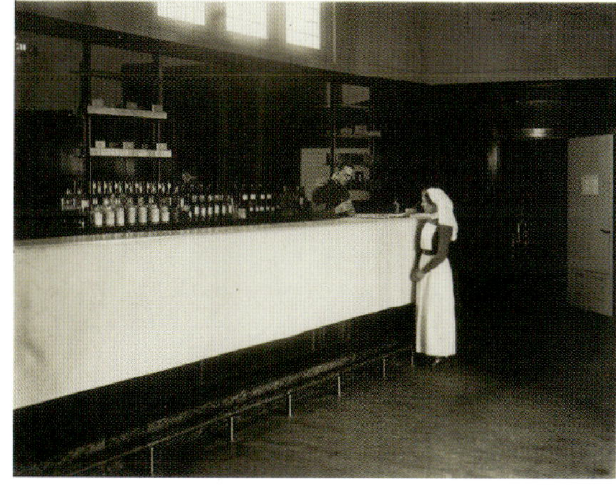
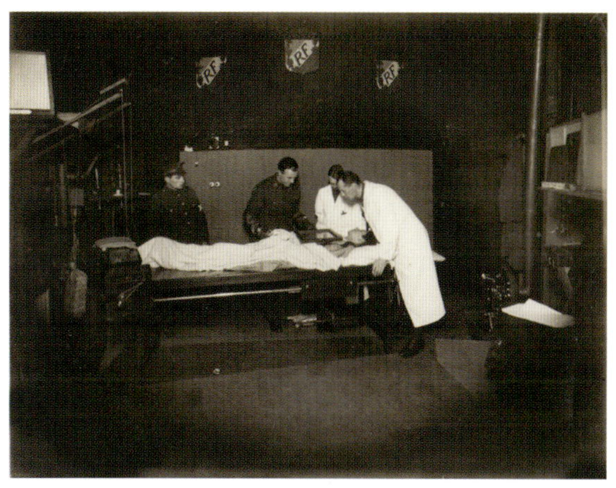
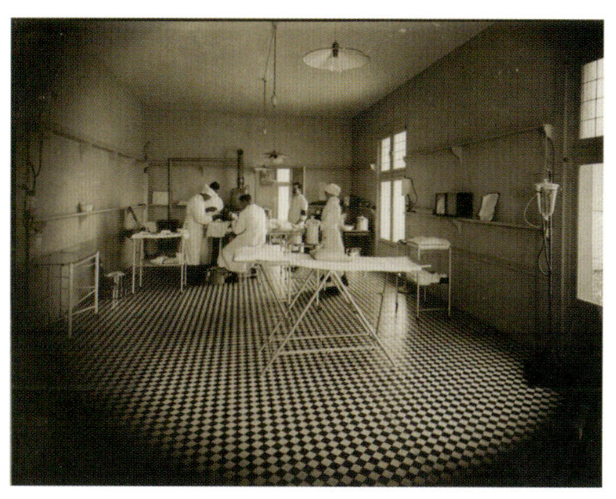
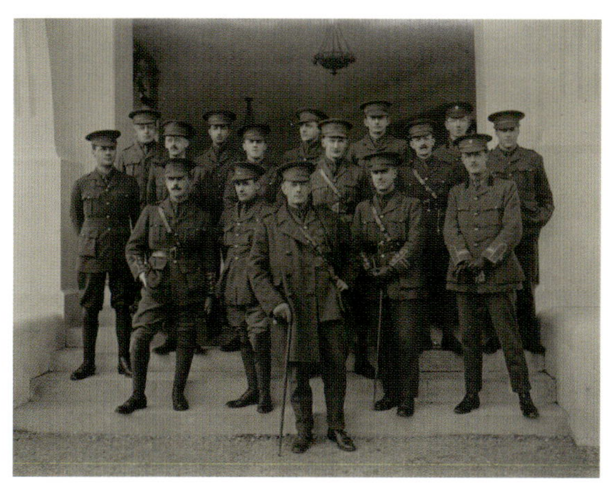
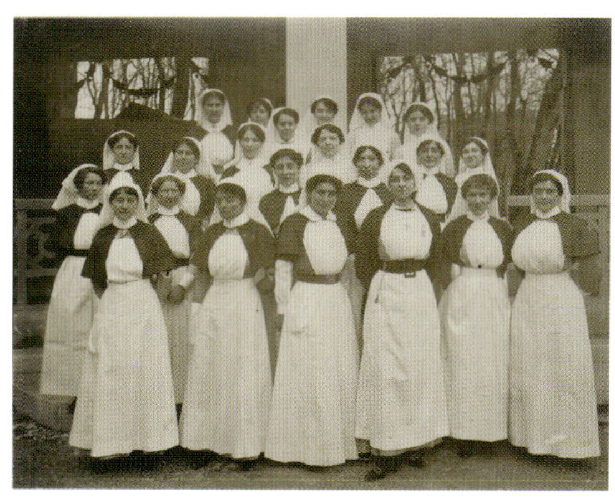
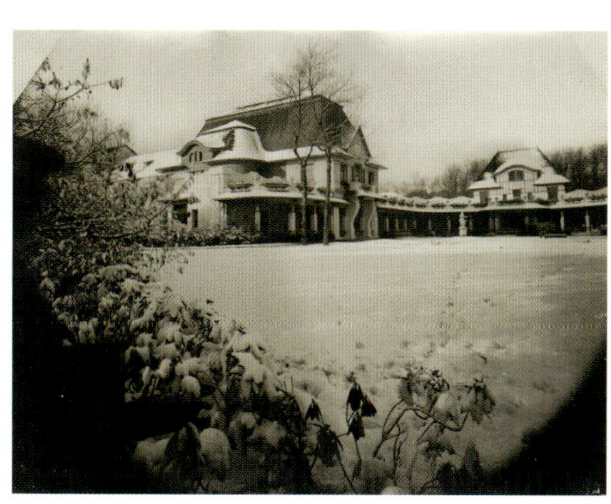
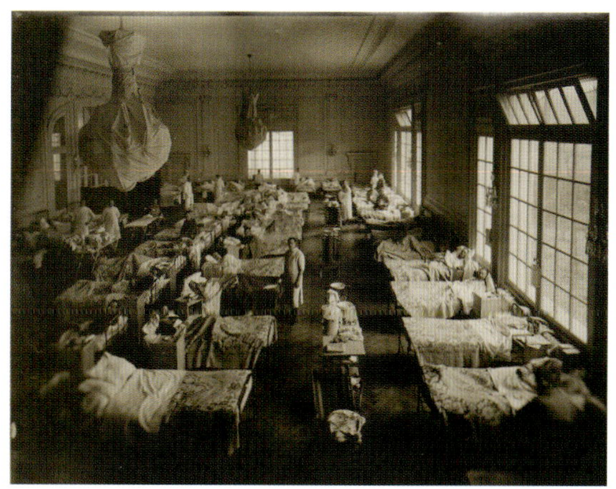

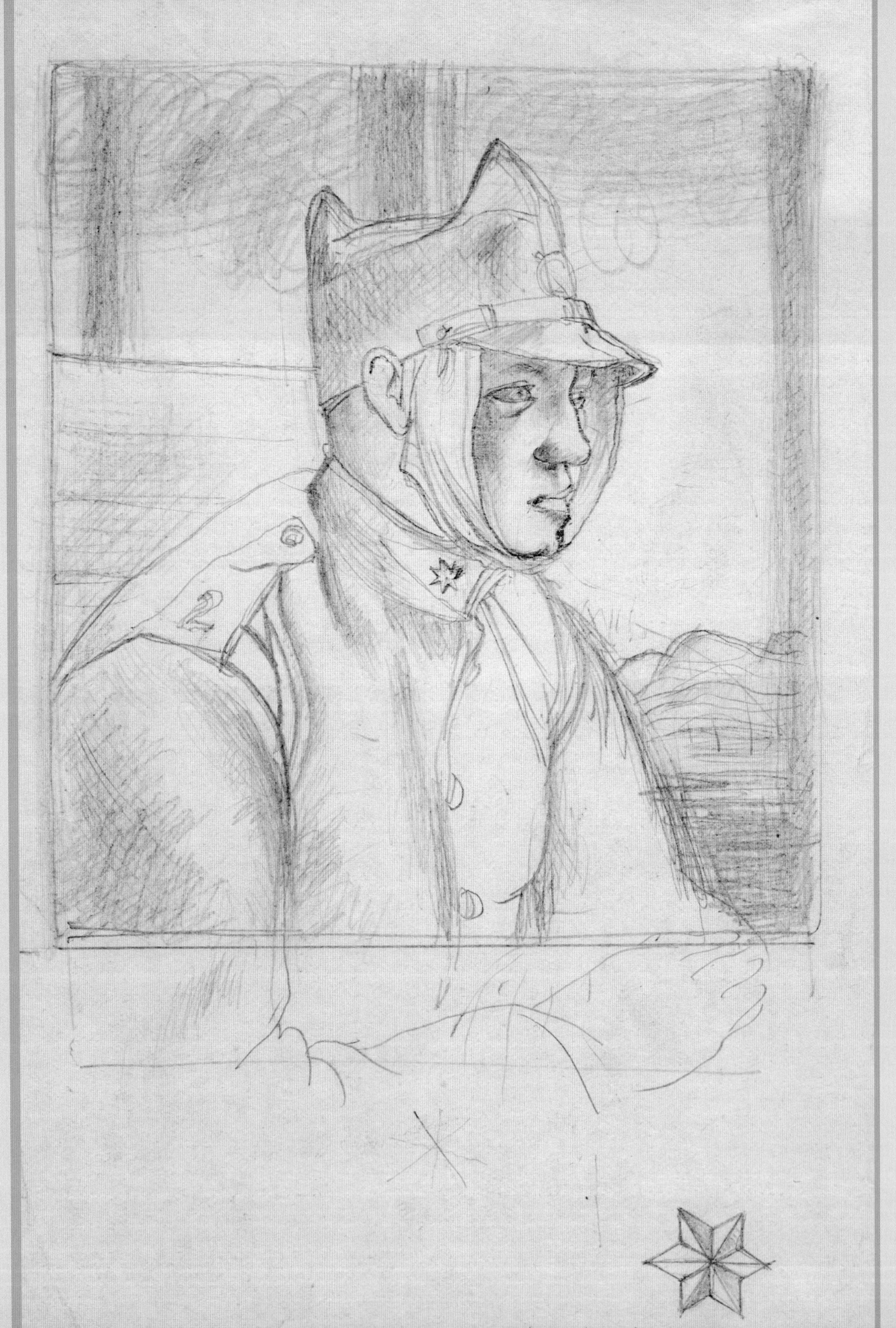

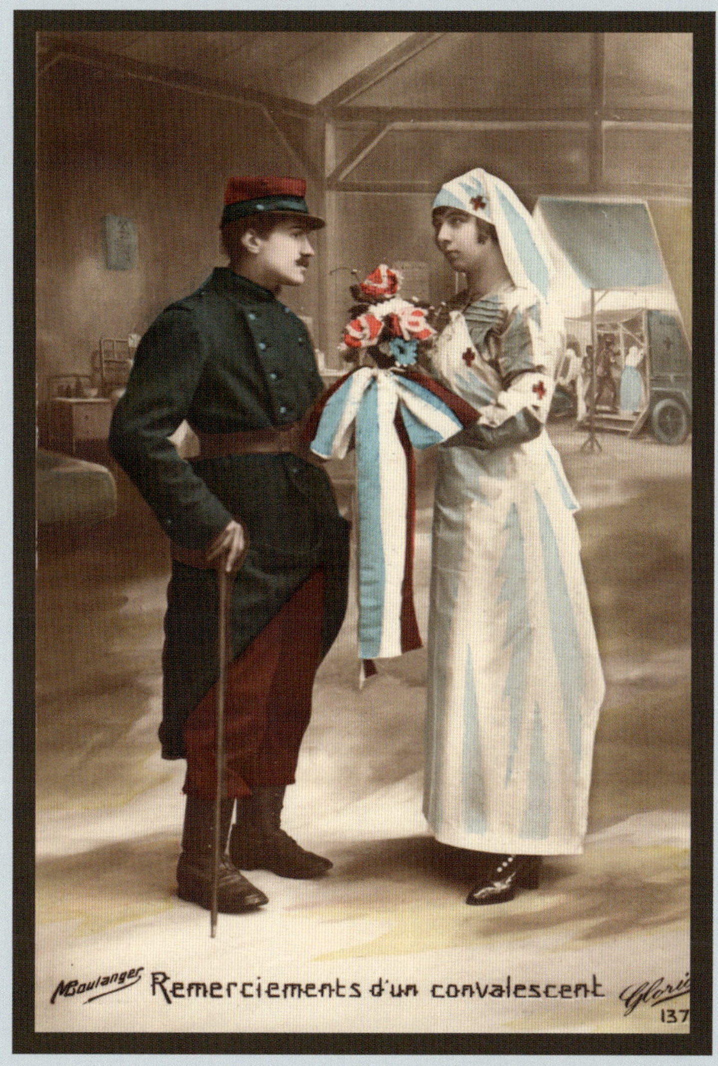

108 – French postcard

Remerciements d'un convalescent,
Printed by Gloria,
5 ½ x 3 ½ in. (13.7 x 8.7 cm)

107 – Robert Sargeant Austin (1895-1973)

Shell-shocked Italian soldier with bandage, travelling in a railway compartment, c.1918,
Pencil on paper, 8 x 5 in. (20 x13 cm),
Provenance: The Artist's brother Frederick Austin; thence by descent

During the First World War Austin served in the Royal Garrison Artillery as a gunner. He had been at the Royal College of Art for a brief spell before the outbreak of the war and resumed his studies afterwards. Millions of soldiers suffered "shell shock," or post-traumatic stress disorder due to the horrors of trench warfare. Shell-shocked men often had uncontrollable diarrhoea, insomnia, stopped speaking and twitched uncontrollably. While some soldiers recovered, for others the symptoms continued for the rest of their lives.

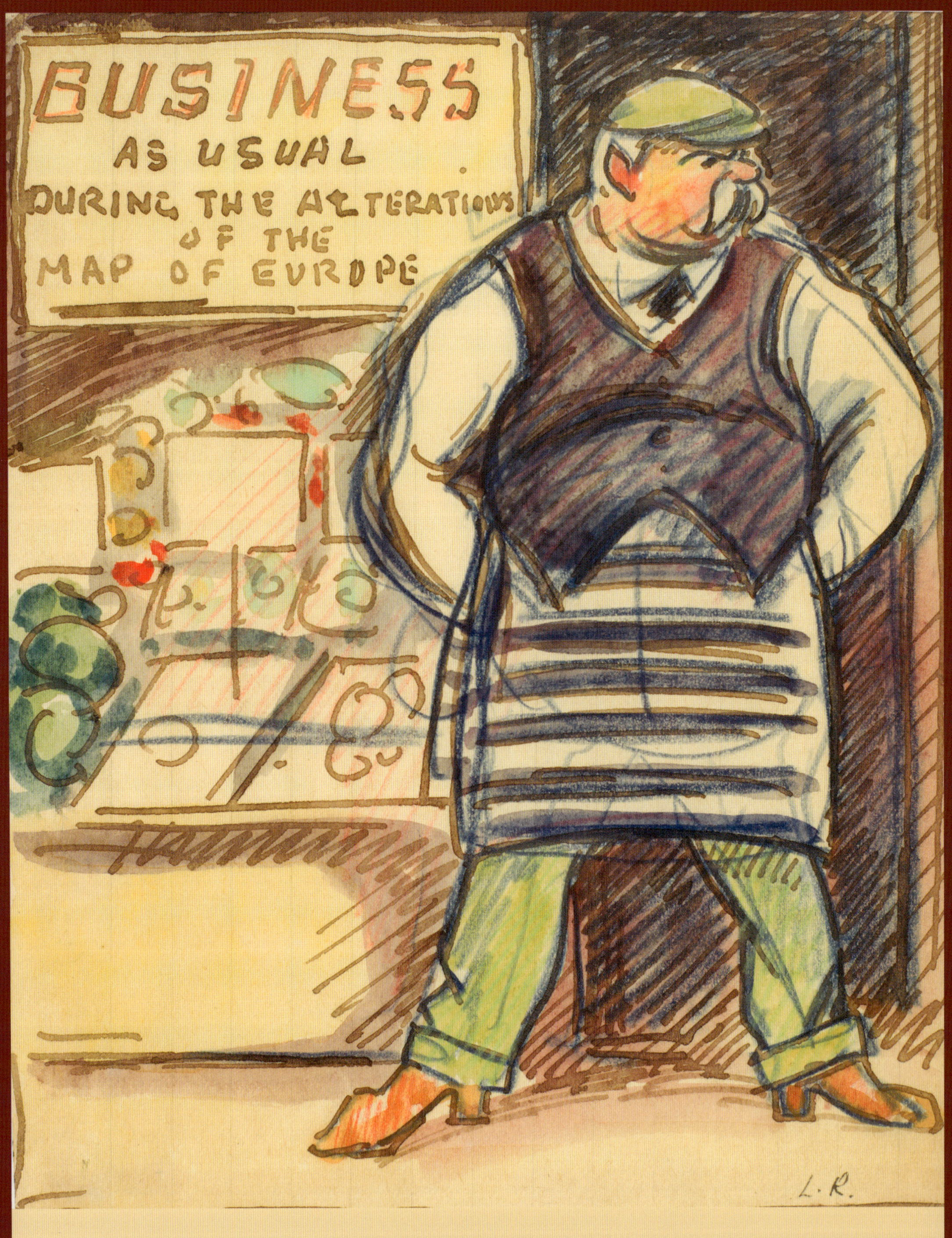

BUSINESS
AS USUAL
DURING THE ALTERATIONS
OF THE
MAP OF EUROPE
L.R.

"The maxim of the British people is 'Business as usual'."

Winston Churchill, speaking at Guildhall, November 9, 1914

"We said goodbye to a whole epoch
Furious giants were looming over Europe
The eagles were leaving their eyries expecting the sun
Voracious fishes were swimming up from the abysses
Nations were rushing together to know each other through and through
The dead were trembling with fear in their dark dwellings"

Guillaume Apollinaire, *The Little Car*, August 31, 1914

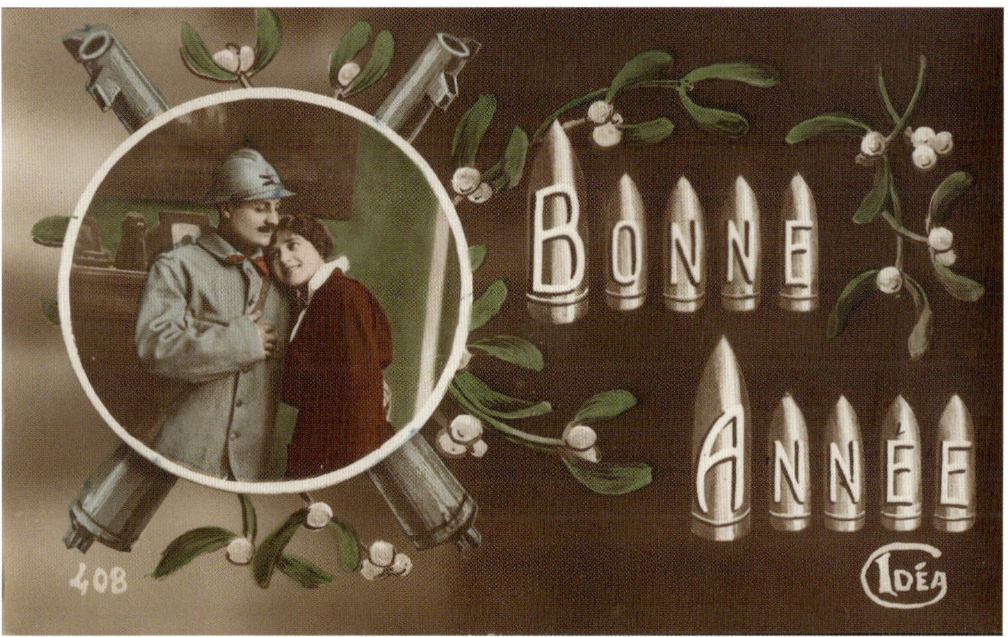

110 – French postcard

Bonne année,
Printed by Idéa, 3 ½ x 5 ½ in. (8.7 x 13.7 cm)

109 – Ludovic-Rodolphe (Rodo) Pissarro (1878-1952)

Business as Usual During the Alterations of the Map of Europe, c.1915, signed with initials,
Watercolour on paper, 6 ⅝ x 5 ⅜ in. (17 x 13.5 cm)

One of a series of scenes that Ludovic Pissarro observed whilst living in London during the war, this watercolour shows a defiant greengrocer outside his shop window in which a poster pronounces 'Business as Usual During the Alterations of the Map of Europe'. Although food shortages did occur at the start of the war due to panic buying, Britain continued to successfully import food (mostly from America and Canada) with merchant ships travelling in relative safety across the Atlantic. However, in 1917, the Germans introduced unrestricted submarine warfare and merchant ships were sunk with great frequency, causing the shortages that led to the imposition of rationing in February 1918.

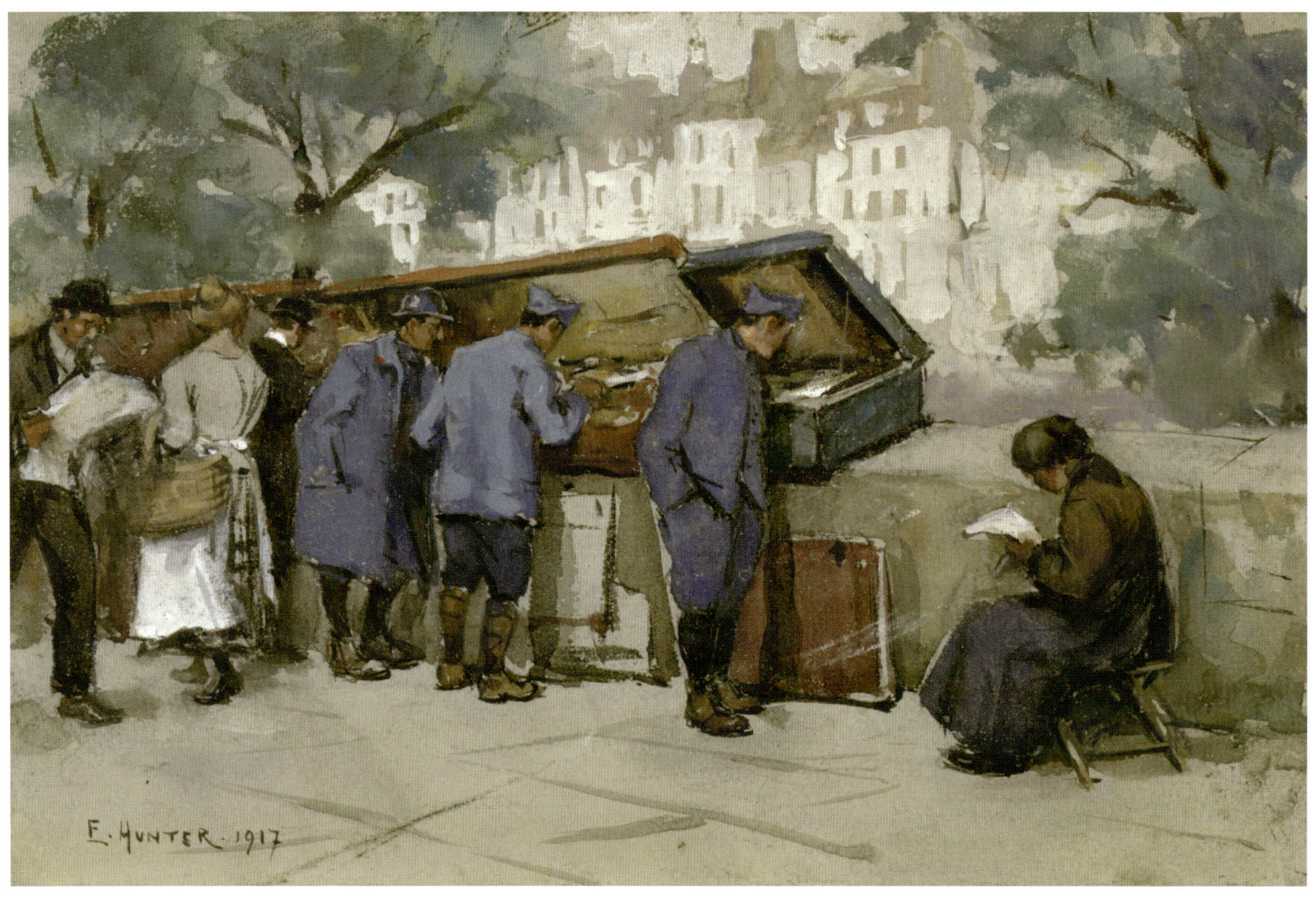

111 – Mary Ethel Hunter (1878-1936)

French soldiers and Bouquinistes along the Seine, 1917, signed and dated,
Watercolour on paper, 6 ½ x 9 ½ in. (16.5cm x 24cm)

Touring the towns and cities of France during the height of the war in 1917, Mary Ethel Hunter left a remarkable record of life away from the Front.

112 – Fred Pegram (1870-1937)

Nervous Young Officer to Bus Conductor 'First Single to Oxford Circus', 1916, signed, titled to label,
Pen and ink on paper, 17 x 10 in. (43 x 25.5 cm)

This drawing was reproduced in the February 16, 1916 issue of *Punch* magazine (page 123). During the First World War Pegram served as a Special Constable at Buckingham Palace and during this period he produced a large number of cartoons for various magazines.

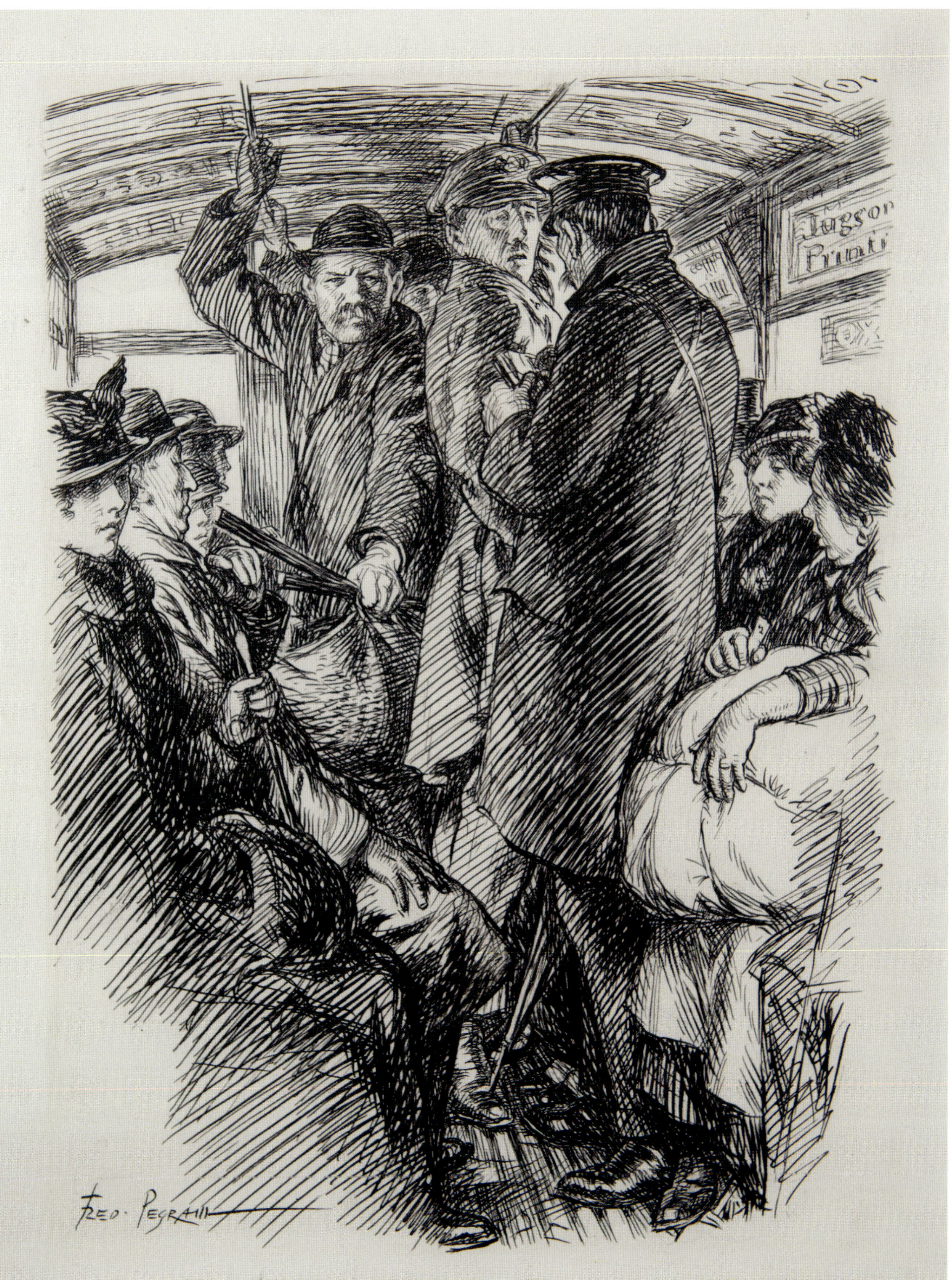

Jugson
Prints
FRED· PEGRAM

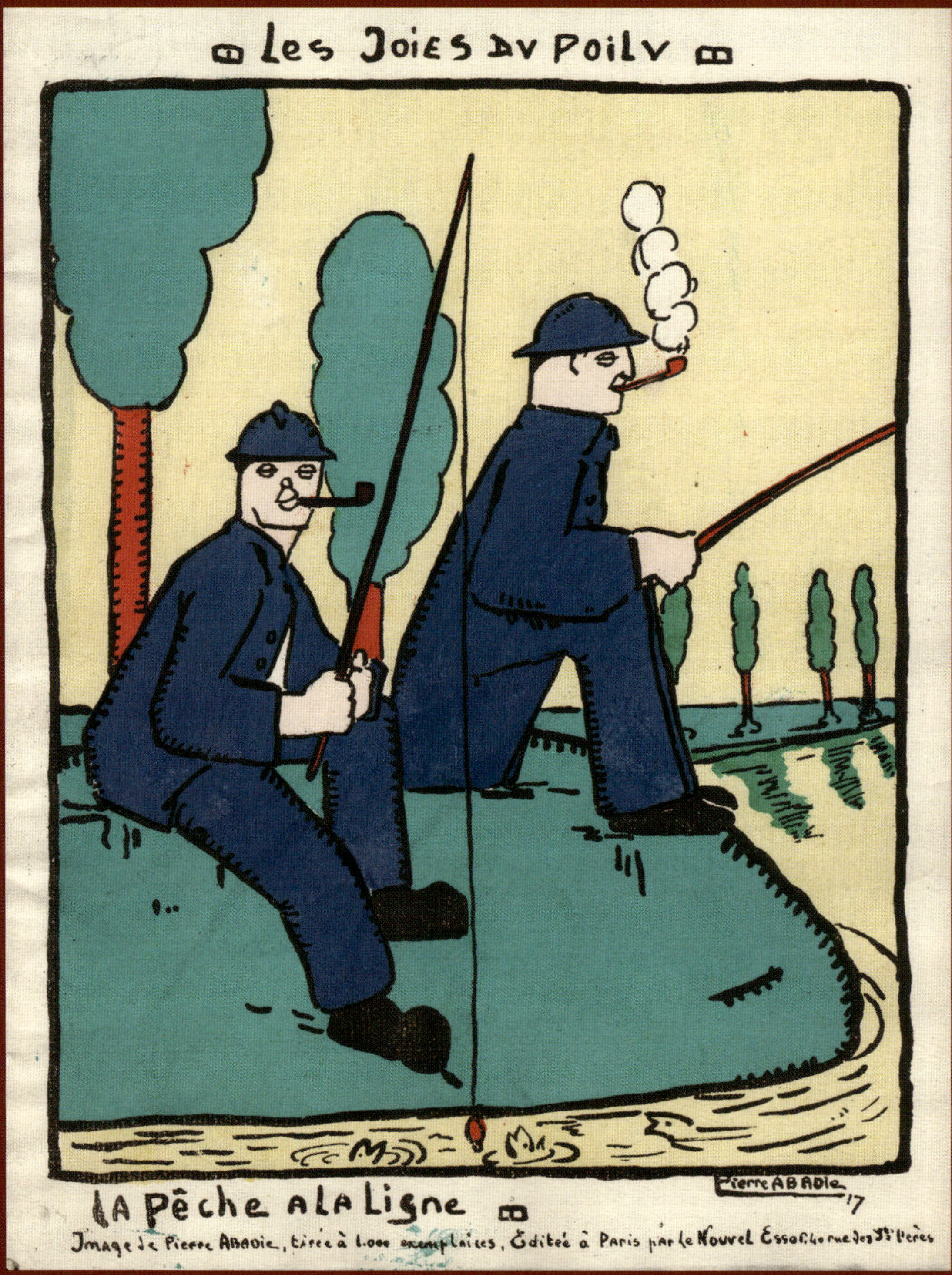

113 – Pierre Abadie-Landel (1896-1972)

Les Joies du Poilu [The Pleasures of the Poilu], 1917,
Series of six humorous images of les *poilus* (French soldiers) on leave,
Lithographs, each 12 ¼ x 9 ¾ in. (31.1 x 24.7 cm), printed by Le Nouvel Essor, Paris

Abadie-Landel's set of images are inspired by the 19th-century tradition of the 'Images d'Epinal', prints on popular subjects rendered in bright sharp colours.

a *Le départ pour la permission* / b *La pêche à la ligne* / c *Le bain* / d *Au repos* / e *Le pinard* / f *Le colis*

LES JOIES DU POILU
Le Départ pour la Permission.

a

LES JOIES DU POILU
La Pêche à la Ligne

b

LES JOIES DU POILU
Le Bain

c

LES JOIES DU POILU
Au Repos.

d

LES JOIES DU POILU
Le Pinard

e

LES JOIES DU POILU
Le Colis

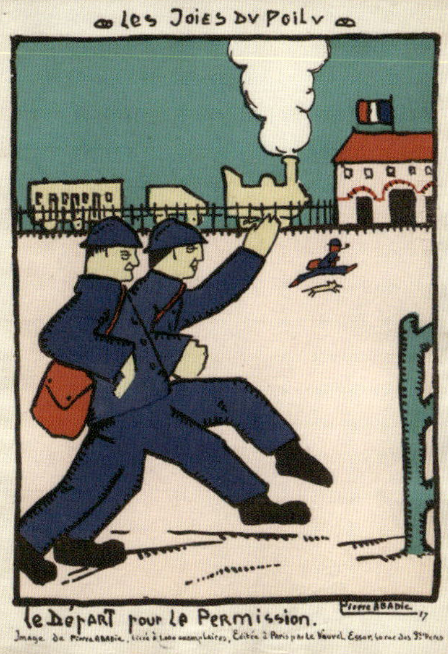

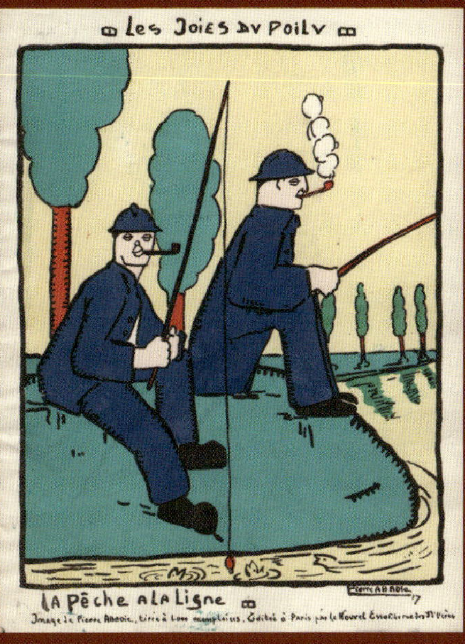

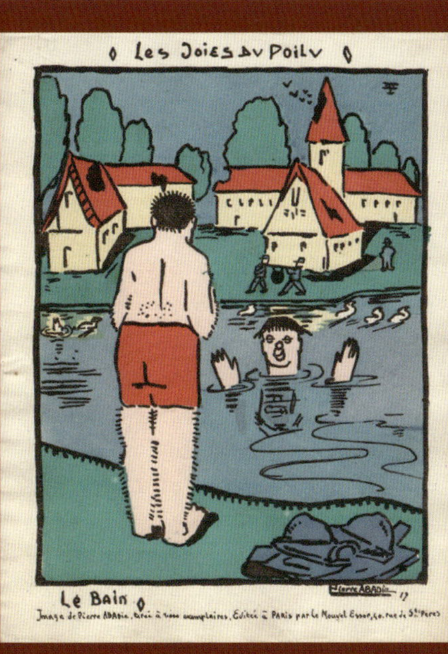

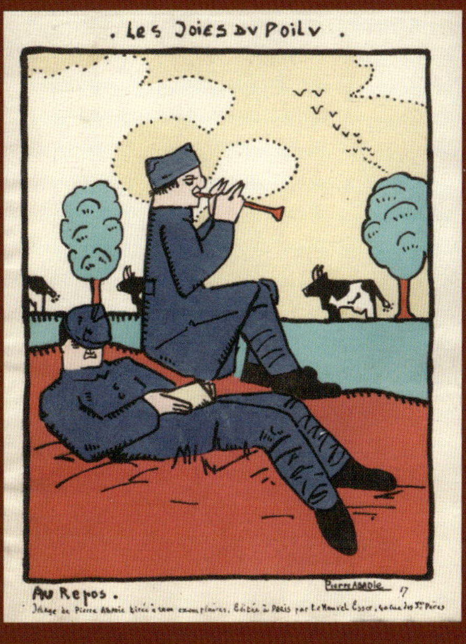

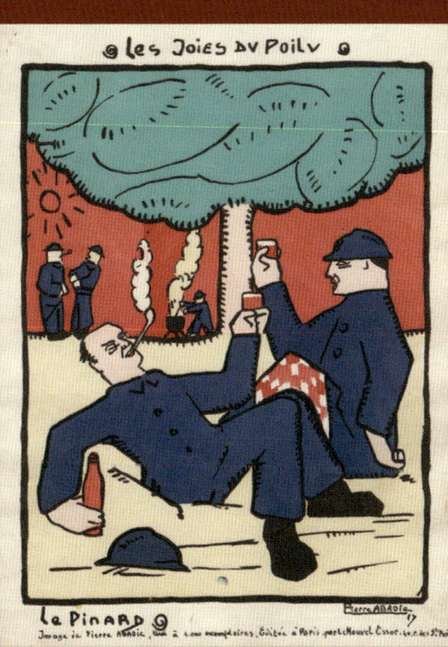

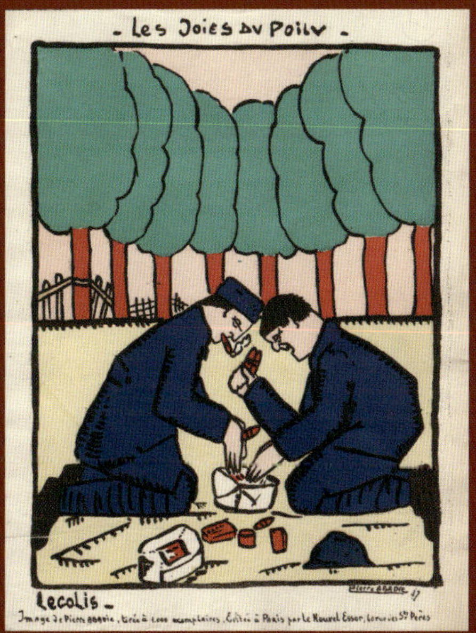

f

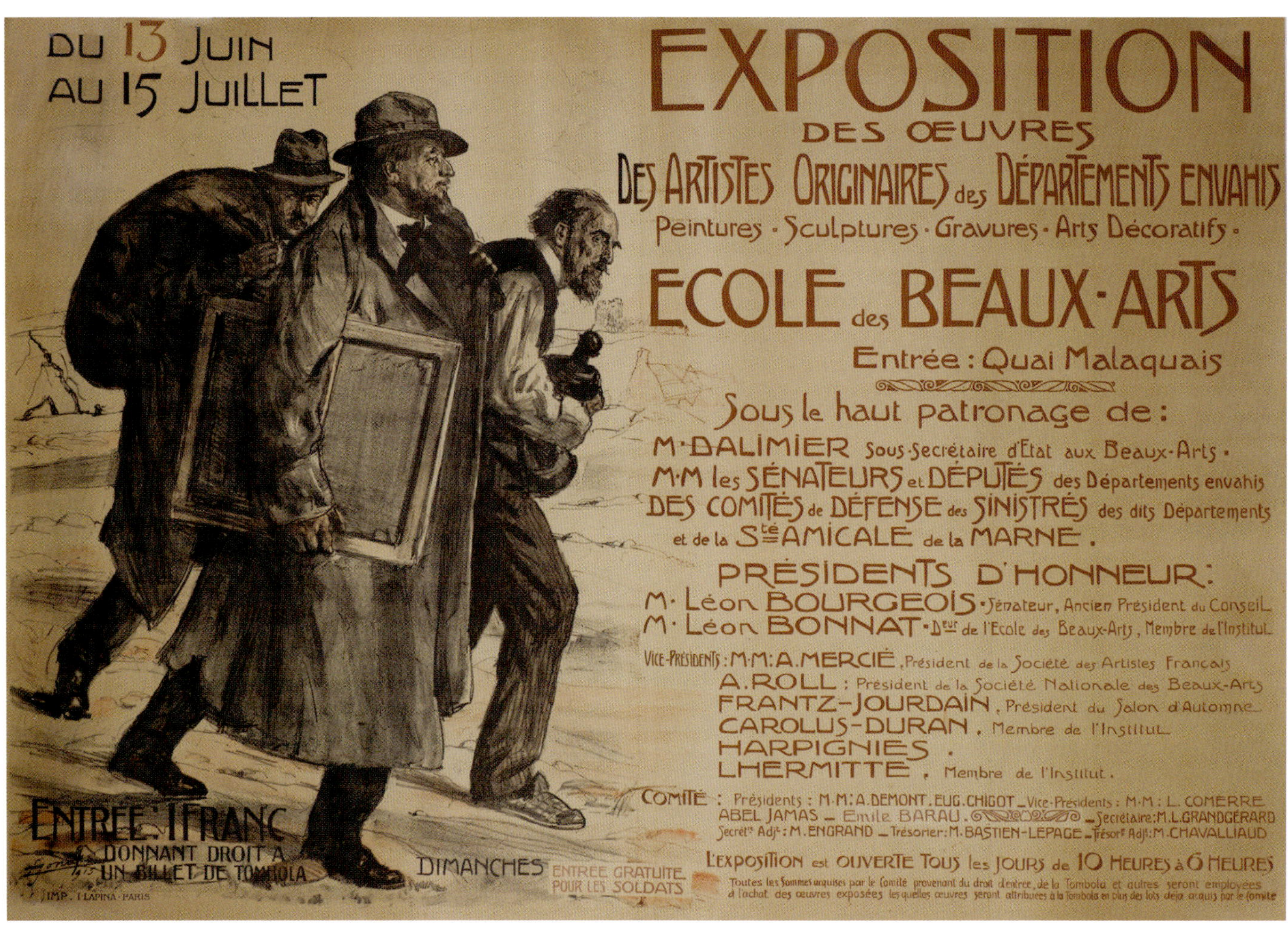

114 – Lucien Jonas (1880-1947)

Exposition des oeuvres des artistes originaires des Départements envahis – École des Beaux-Arts, 1915,
Lithographic poster, 29 ½ x 41 ¾ in. (75 x 106 cm), published by Lapina, Paris

Three artists, the sculptor Léon Joseph Chavaillaud (1858-1921), the sculptor Georges Engrand (1852-1936) and the painter Lucien Grangérand (1880-1970) flee the invaded territories with their artworks.

115 – Robert Randoll (1864-1946)

War Searchlights over Westminster Bridge, 1917, signed and titled on a label on the reverse,
Pastel on paper, 9 ½ x 6 ½ in. (24.1 x 16.5 cm)

The main German bombing campaign against England started in January 1915 under the cover of darkness. Initially these raids were by airships but by 1917, the date of this pastel, attacks were largely from aeroplanes. Eventually blackouts ensured that targets were harder to identify and landmarks were heavily protected through the use of search lights and barrage balloons.

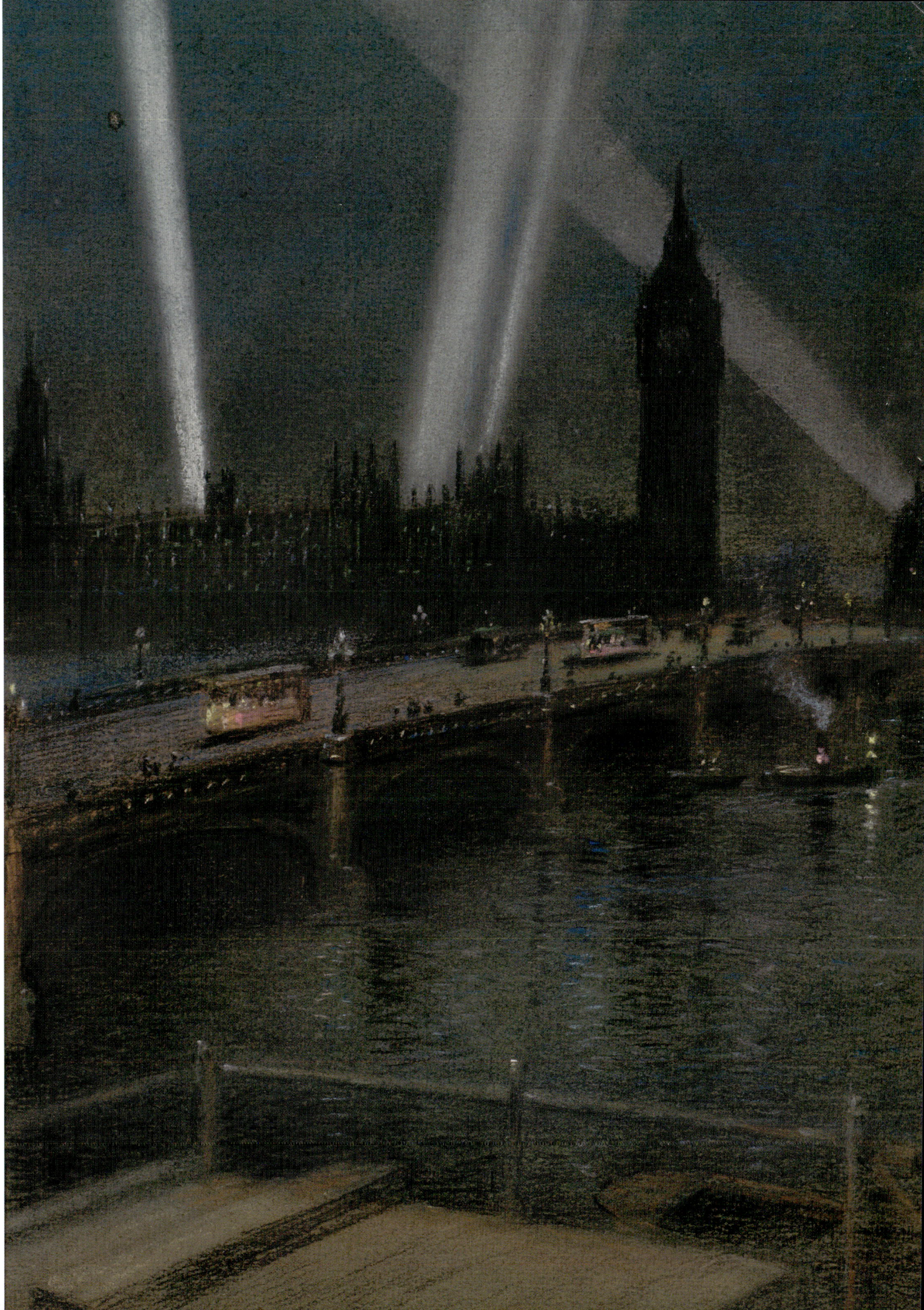

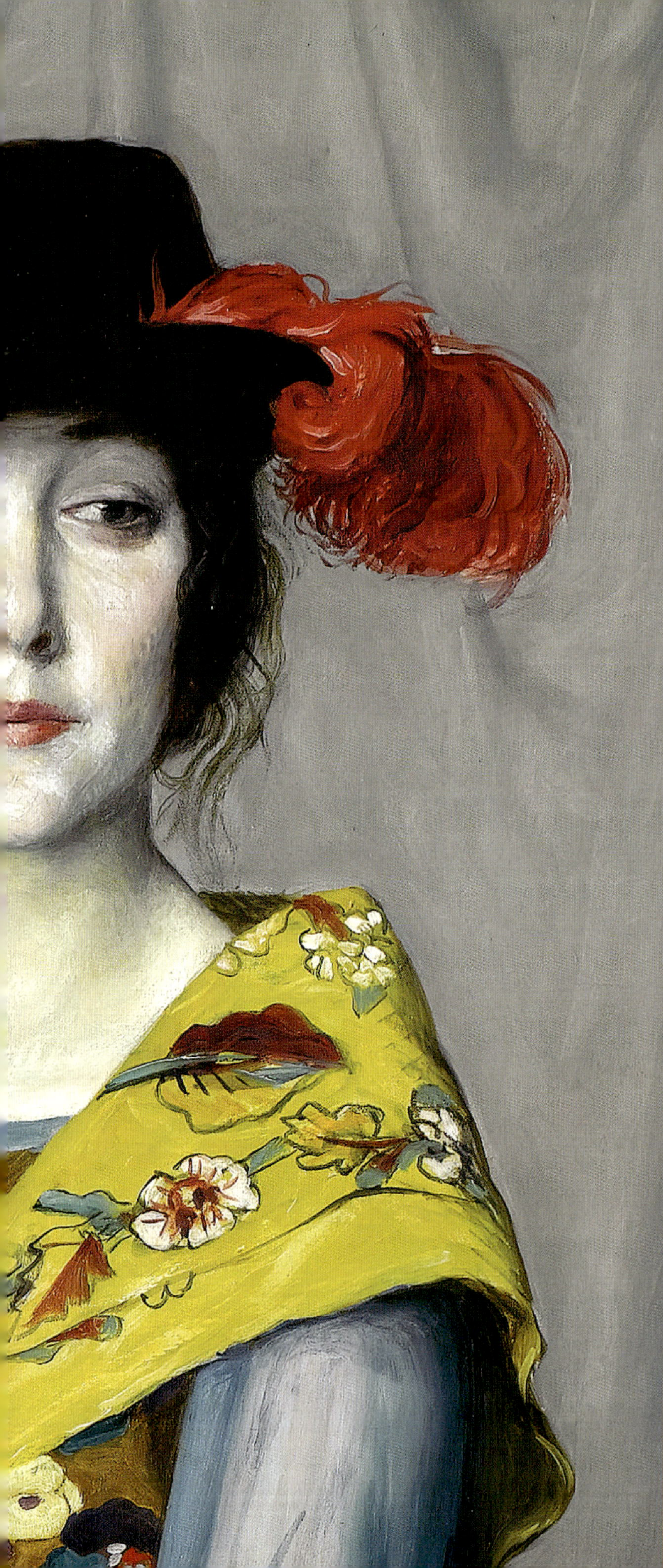

Aged 55 when war broke out, Strang was too old to enlist. His four sons, however, served in France. Many of his paintings from this period engaged with aspects of life on the Home Front.

Buffets were held throughout the war as fund-raising events. P.G. Konody singled out *The Buffet* when reviewing 'The exhibition of the International Society of Sculptors, Painters and Gravers', Grosvenor Gallery, (*The Observer*, June 17, 1917) as one of a few works that made 'an unusually striking display': 'The charm and refinement that have so often been found lacking in Mr. Strang's works are conspicuously present in the figure of a woman with piquant features, in a gay print dress of the type vaguely called 'futurist' with light blue gauzy sleeves and a bright yellow neckerchief.' Red feathers, traditionally associated with war and courage, became a fashionable accessory for women during the war; white feathers were associated with peace (or cowardice). From a portrait of the same woman in the Manchester City Art Gallery, dating to 1916, the model can be identified as Panchita Zorolla.

C.R. Ashbee, who sat for Strang, recalled that: 'in each of his portraits there is some touch of his sitters' ugliness revealed in the beauty of the draughtsmanship....those of us who.....have sat for our portraits and prize the results....are also grimly conscious of an unpleasant something in ourselves that we don't mention but that our love of truthfulness would not have us conceal.' (C.R. Ashbee, unpublished typescript of memories, Victoria and Albert Museum, vol IV, p. 71, quoted in Athill, *William Strang*, 1981, p. 22)

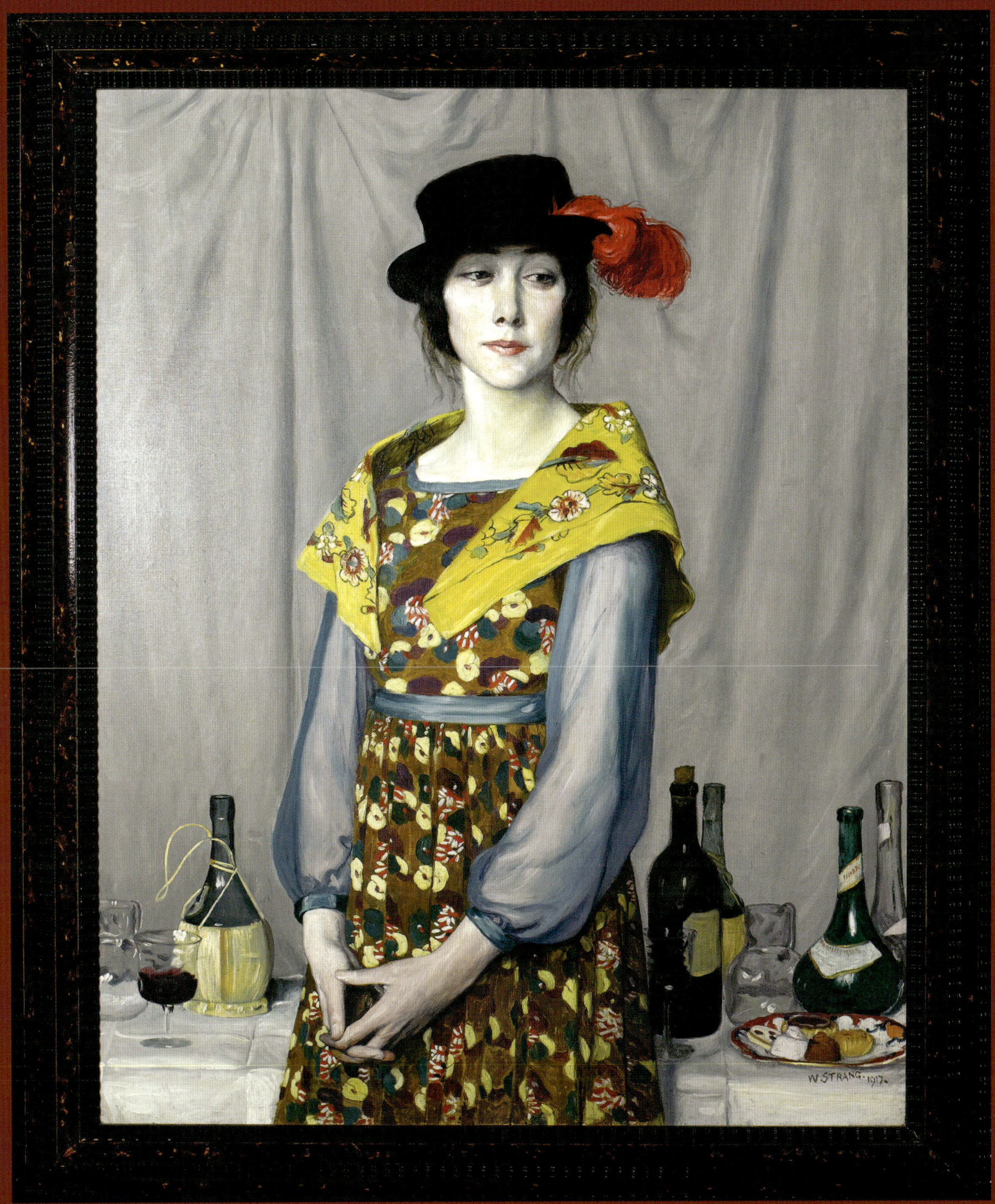

116 – William Strang (1859-1921)

The Buffet, 1917,
Signed and dated 1917, inscribed on a label attached to the reverse of the canvas
Oil on canvas, 40 x 30 in. (101.6 x 76.2 cm.)

Exhibited: The exhibition of the International Society of Sculptors, Painters and Gravers, Grosvenor Gallery, June 1917;
The Carnegie Institute, 1917

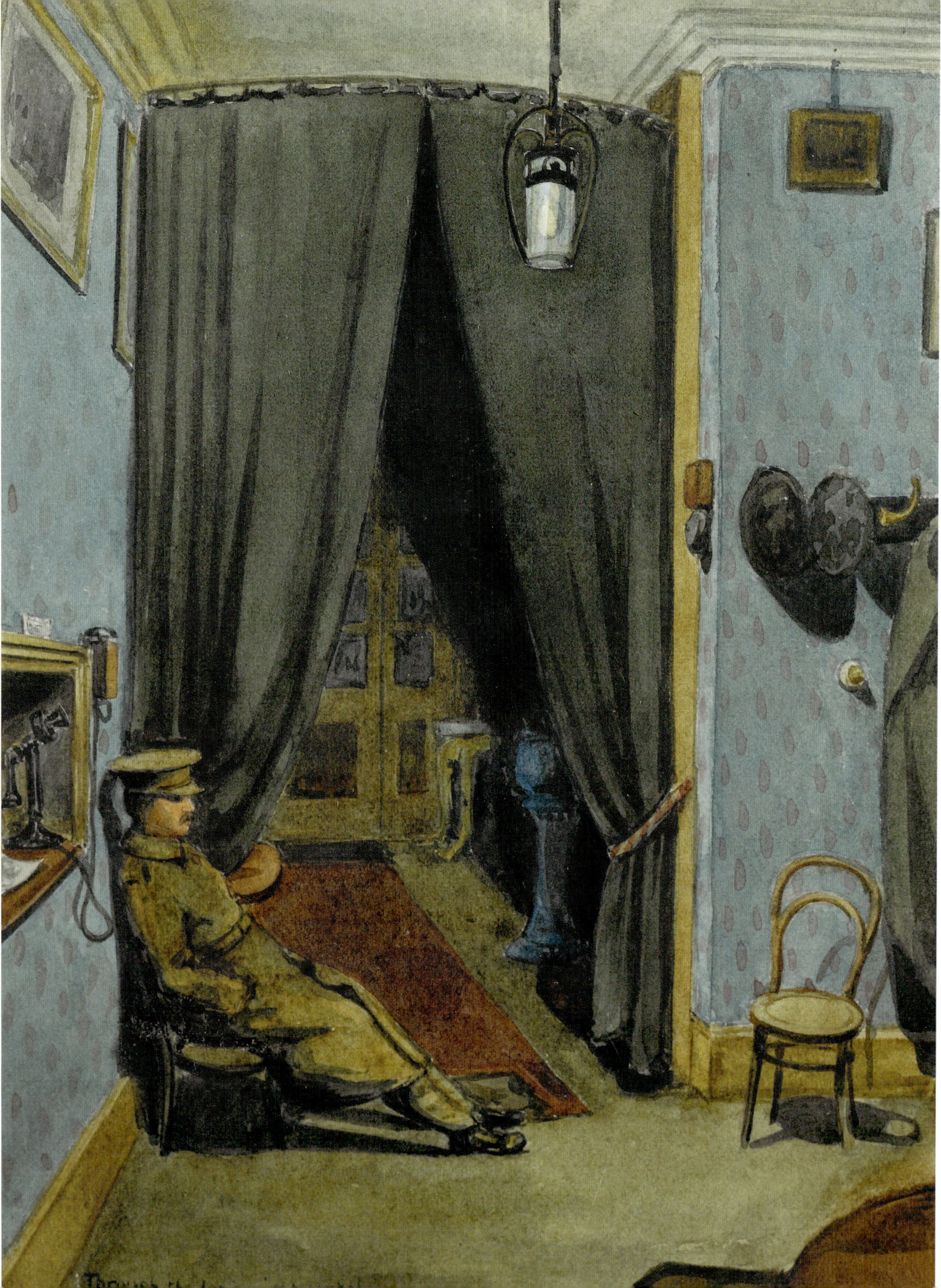

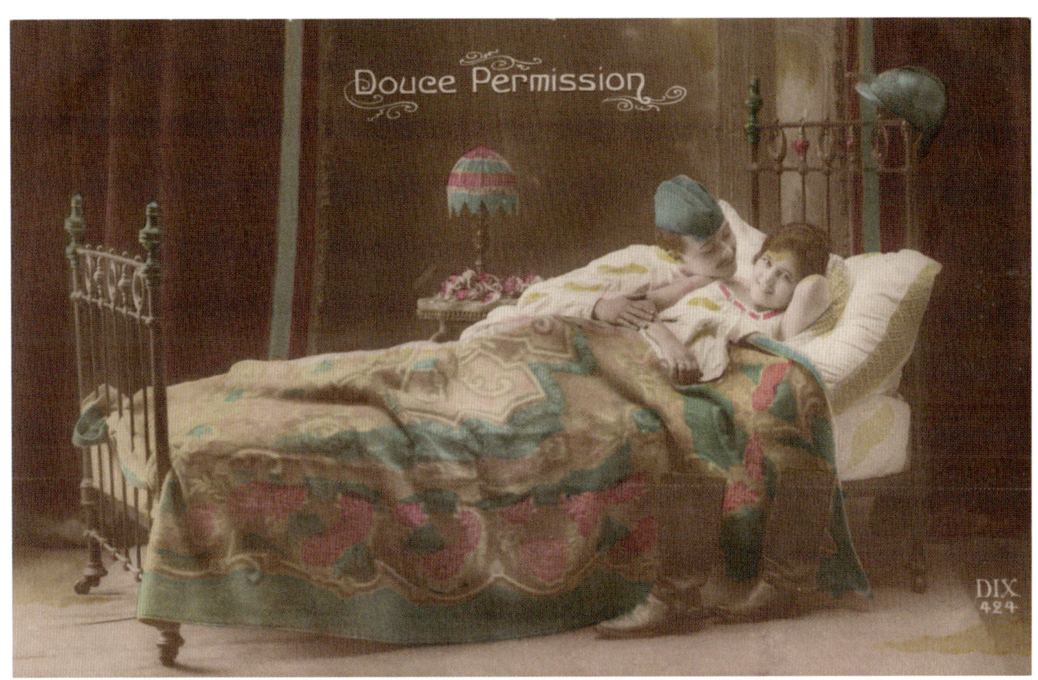

118 – French Postcard

Douce Permission,
3 ½ x 5 ½ in. (8.7 x 13.7 cm)
Printed by DIX

117 – P. J. Hill

Through the long night watches, telephone duty at White Horse Hotel, 1916,
Inscribed with title, watercolour on paper, 6 ¾ x 4 ¾ in. (17 x 12 cm)

21017 Private P. J. Hill served with the 36th Company (D), 20th City of London Battalion of The County of London Regiment. This was a Home Front-only training battalion, and not intended for duty abroad, though some of the men would later be transferred to battalions overseas. Hill would have been well into his forties in 1915 and too old to serve abroad. In each battalion there were approximately five companies consisting of 220 men whose responsibilities would have been to look after local areas, together with daily training.

Fatigues (duties) would have been part of a daily routine – in this case looking after and protecting the landline and telephone exchange – the only means of communication in the local hotel where the officers were billeted.

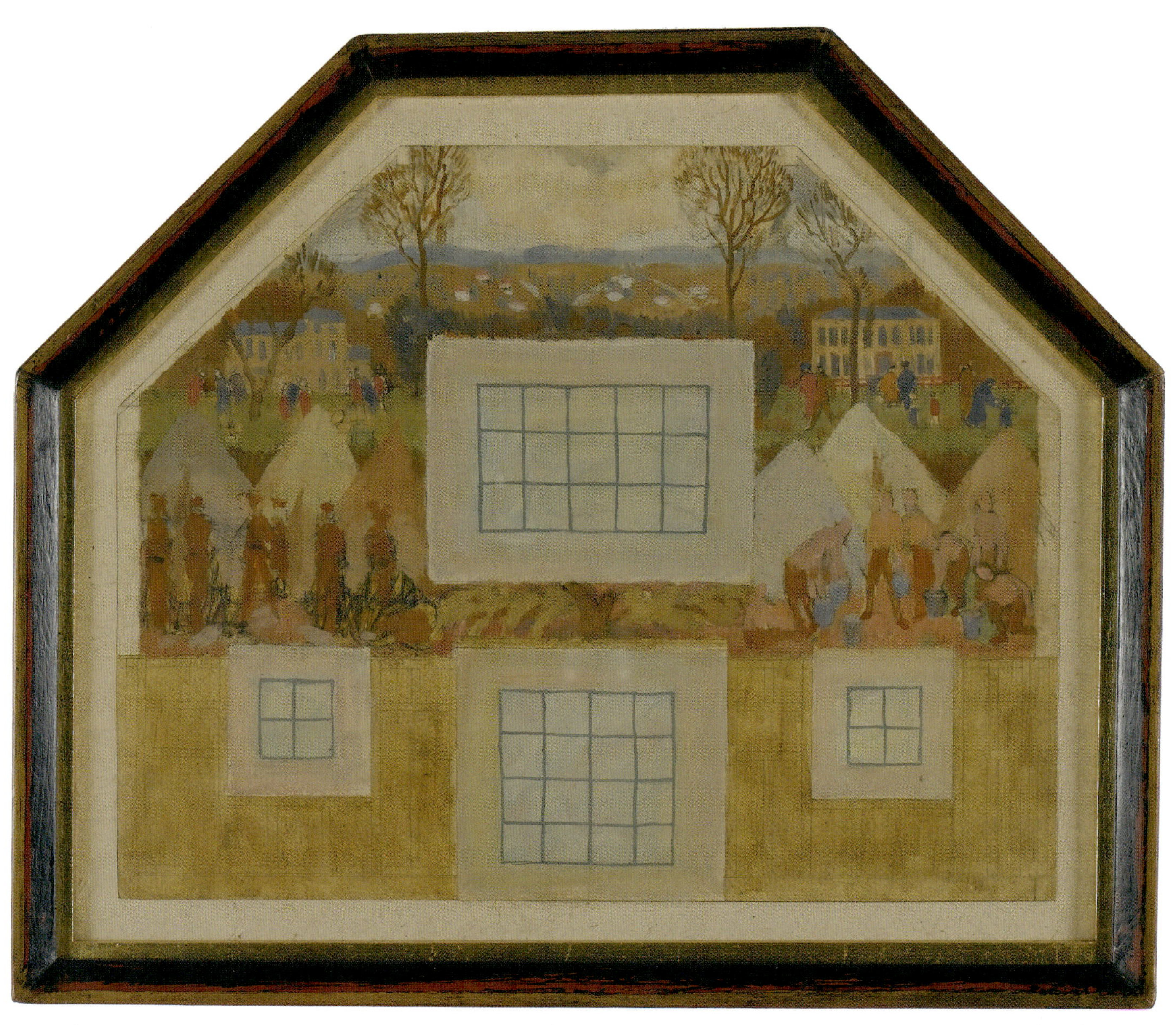

119 – Charles Mahoney (1903-1968)

Encampment,
Oil on paper, 13 x 15 ⅜ in. (33 x 39 cm)

120 – Sir Herbert James Gunn (1893-1964)

Interior Scene, Memories of James Pryde, c. 1915-16, signed,
Oil on board, 18 ½ x 14 ½ in. (46.5 x 36.5 cm)

This painting has been described by Professor Kenneth McConkey. as 'a poetic envoi to a life interrupted by the call to arms for in 1915 Gunn joined the Artists' Rifles and after training was transferred to Northern France.' (*The Edwardians: The Golden Years Before the War*, published by The Fine Art Society, December 2011.)

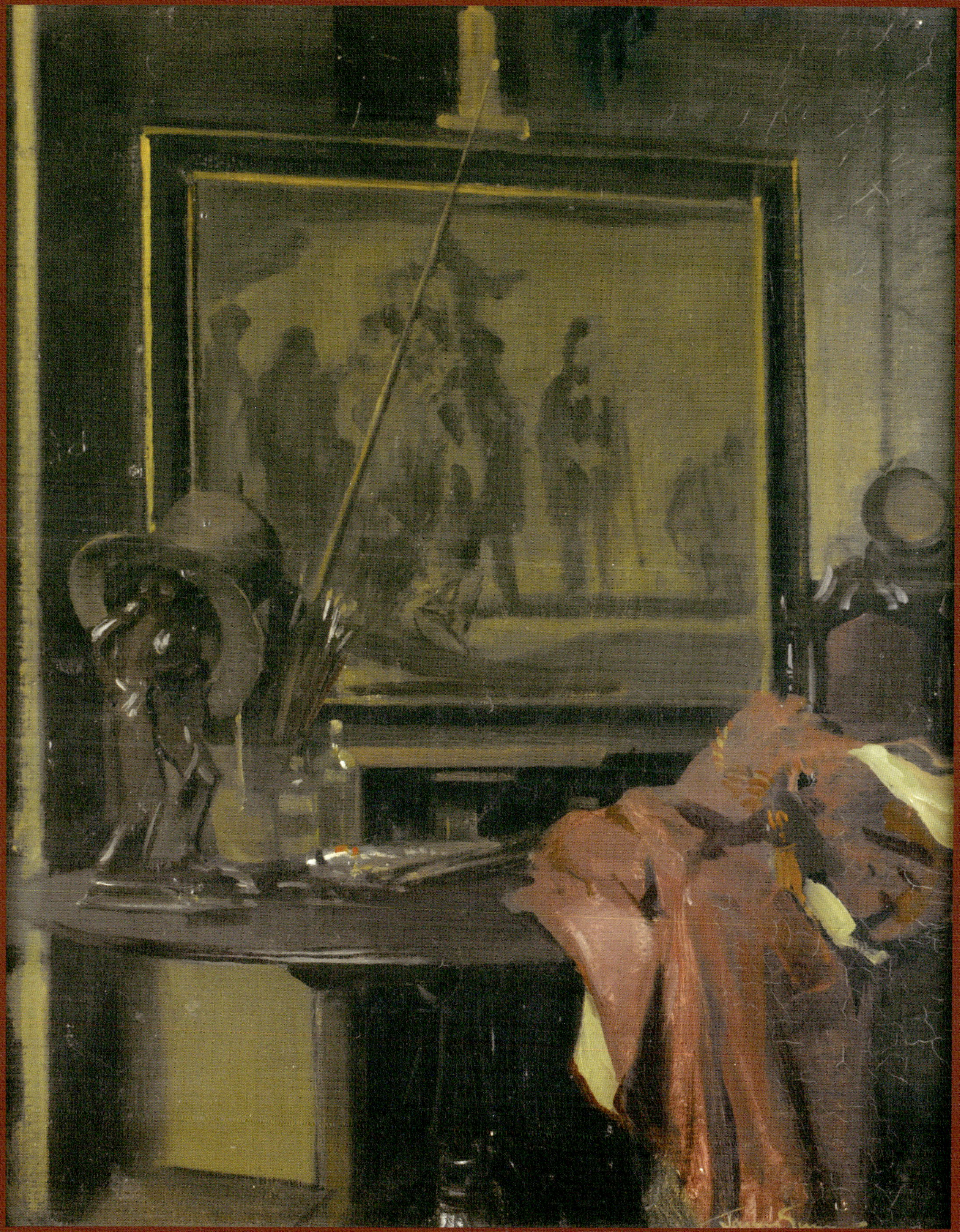

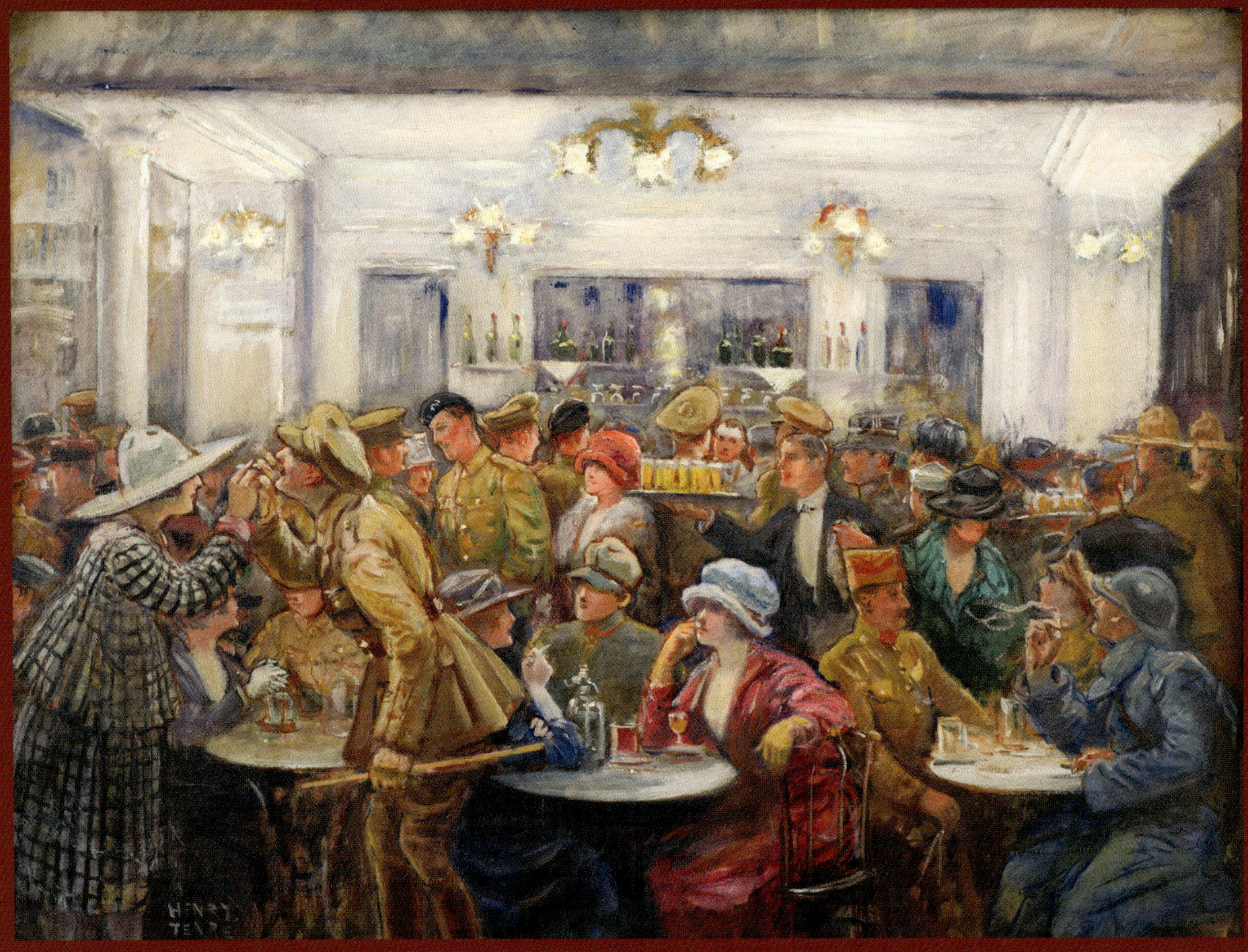

121 – Charles Henry Tenré (1864-1926)

L'abreuvoir de L'Olympia pendant un entr'acte, c.1918,
Signed and inscribed with title on the reverse,
Oil on canvas on board, 18 ¾ x 23 ¾ in. (47 x 60 cm)

The scene shows drinks during an interval at the Olympia Music Hall in Paris. Notably Tenré has included Allied soldiers of all nationalities – British (including Scottish), French, Belgian, American, Italian and Serbian – as well as a mixture of soldiers of different ranks ranging from the Officer in the foreground having his cigarette lit, to a Tommy and a *Poilu* gazing into the eyes of a glamorous Parisienne.

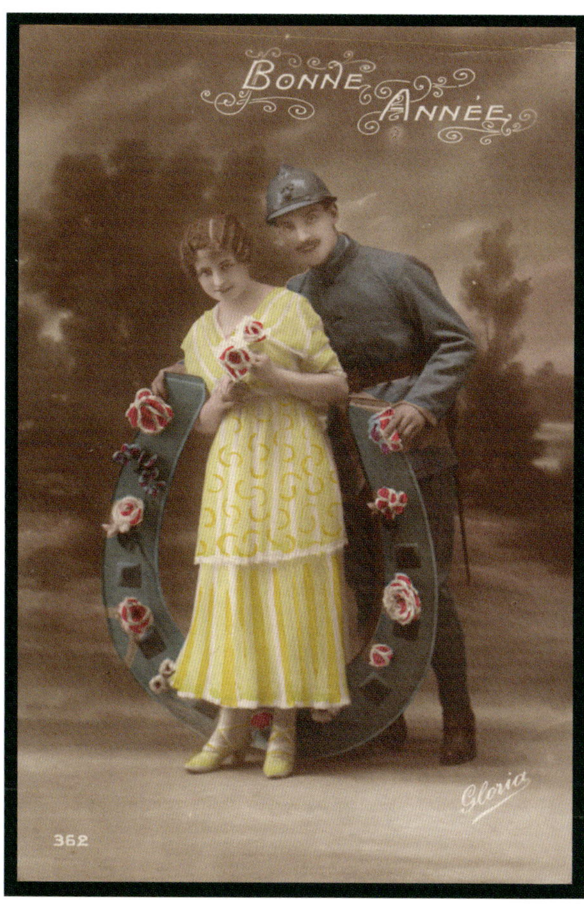

122 – French Postcard

Bonne Année,
5 ½ x 3 ½ in. (13.7 x 8.7 cm)
Printed by Gloria

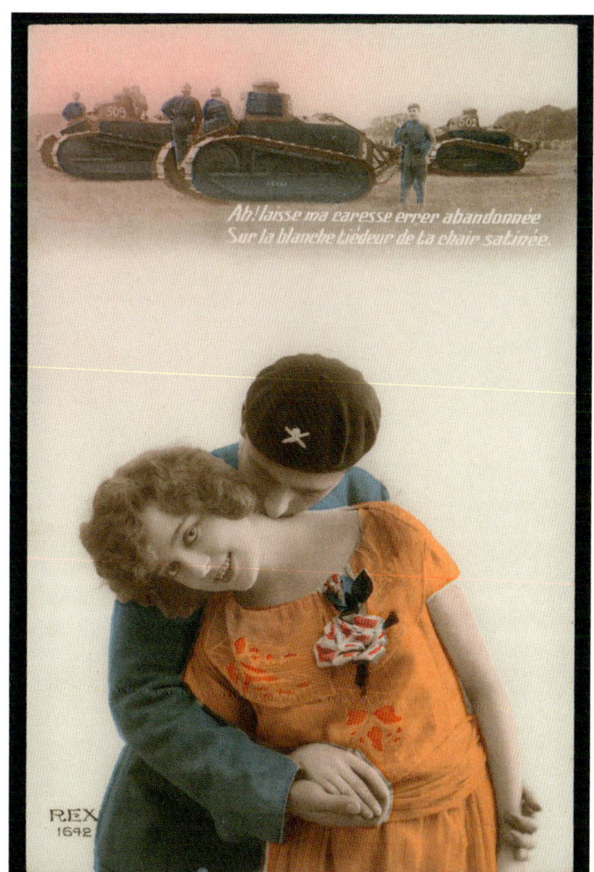

123 – French Postcard

*"Ah! laisse ma caresse errer abandonnée
sur la blancheur de la chair satinée",*
5 ½ x 3 ½ in. (13.7 x 8.7 cm)
Printed by la Sociète anonyme de papéteries
de Levallois-Clichy, "les cartes luxe REX"

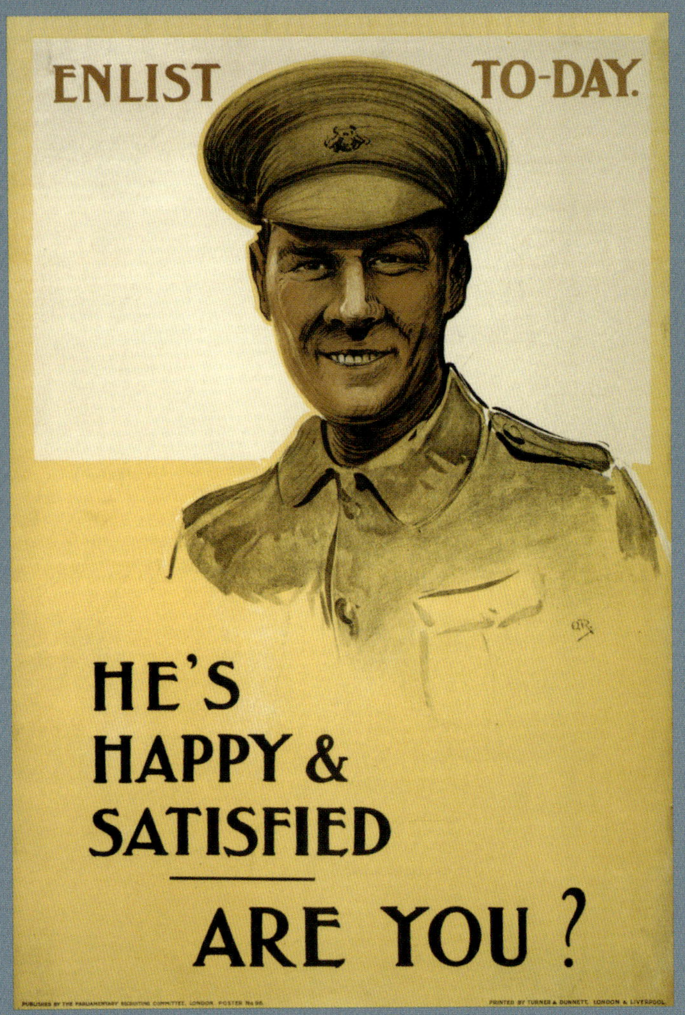

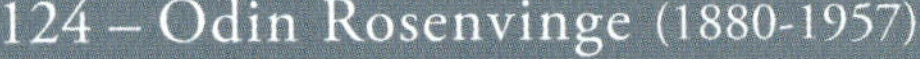

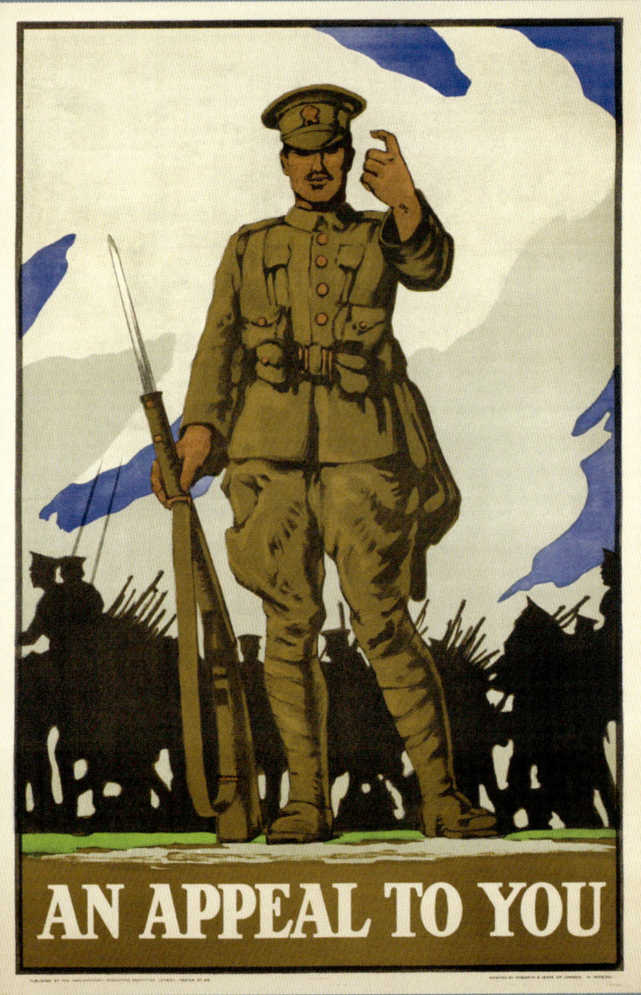

124 – Odin Rosenvinge (1880-1957)

Enlist Today, He's Happy & Satisfied – Are You?, 1915,
Lithographic poster, 30 x 20 in. (76 x 51 cm),
Original Parliamentary Recruiting Committee Poster No 96,
Printed by Turner & Dunnett, London and Liverpool

Rosenvigne had a background in commercial art, working for various firms in Leeds and Liverpool. During the war he served in the Middle East. After the war he became a highly reputed designer of posters and postcards.

125 – Alfred Leete (1882-1933)

An Appeal to You, April 1915,
Lithographic poster published by the Parliamentary Recruiting Committee (PRC # 88), 39 x 25 in. (102 x 63 cm),
Printed by Roberts & Leete, London

" [The First World War] was the most colossal, murderous, mismanaged butchery that has ever taken place on earth. Any writer who said otherwise lied. So the writers either wrote propaganda, shut up, or fought."

Ernest Hemingway, quoted in Robert Hughes, *The Shock of the New*, (Knopf, 1980), p.58

"In war-time the word patriotism means suppression of truth."

Siegfried Sassoon, *Memoirs of an Infantry Officer*, 1930

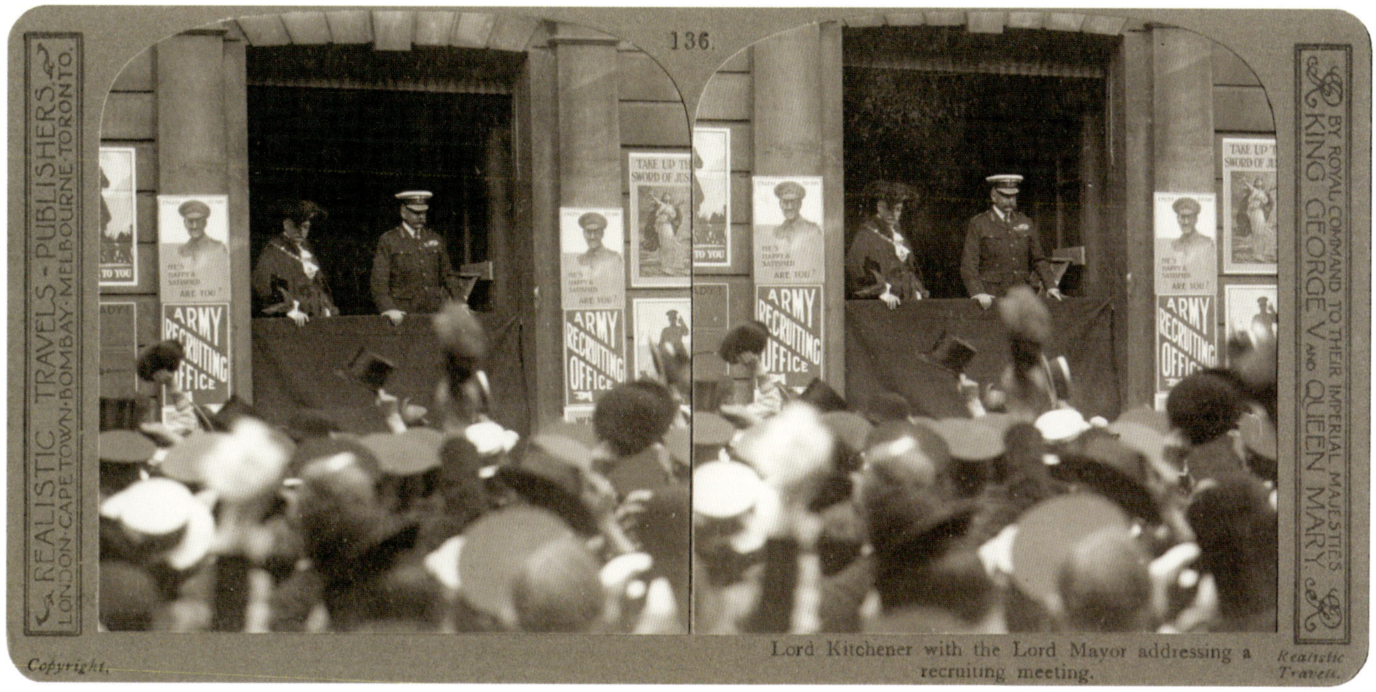

126 – Stereoscopic print: *Lord Kitchener with the Lord Mayor addressing a recruiting meeting.*
    3 ½ x 7 in. (9 x 18 cm), published by Realistic Travels

Amongst the recruiting posters visible are *An appeal to You* and *He's Happy & Satisfied, Are You?* (see opposite).

Fifty-four million copies of some two hundred different posters were produced and distributed by the Parliamentary Recruiting Committee over the course of the war. Millions more were produced by other wartime (often private) organizations. As one Londoner observed in January 1915: "Posters appealing to recruits are to be seen on every hoarding, in most shop windows, in omnibuses, tramcars, and commercial vans. The great base of Nelson's pillar is covered with them." (Catc Haste, *Keep the Home Fires Burning*, London, 1977, p.55) War posters were intended to be ephemeral and were not intended as archival or historical documents – as a result of this many are incredibly rare.

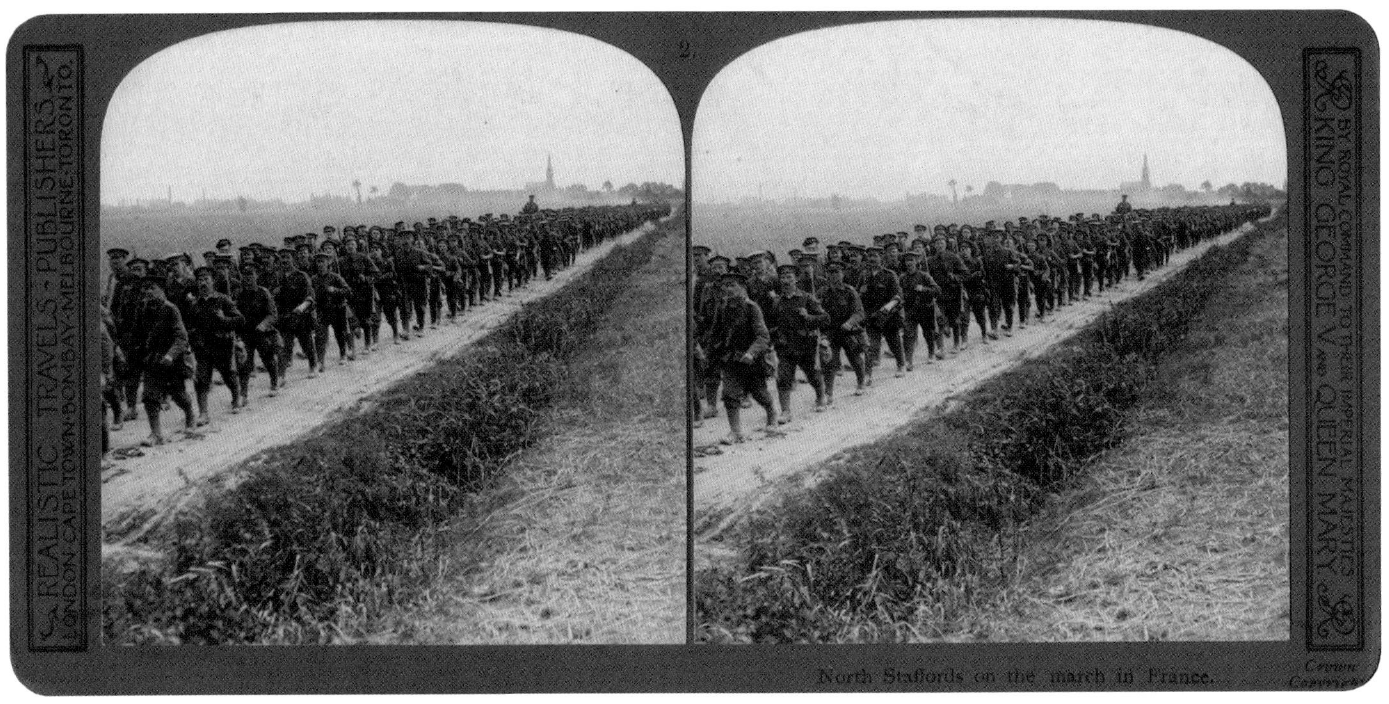

127 – Stereoscopic print: *North Staffords on the march in France.*
 3 ½ x 7 in. (9 x 18 cm), published by Realistic Travels

128 – Canadian School

Here's YOUR chance, IT'S MEN WE WANT, 1915,
Lithographic poster , black ink on yellow paper, 38 x 24 3/4 in. (97 x 63 cm),
Published by the Central Recruiting Committee No. 2 Military Division, Toronto,
Printed by Stone

In 1914 only three thousand men were on the roster of the Regular Canadian Army. An appeal was immediately launched for recruits to join the Canadian Expeditionary Force and, as in Britain, large numbers joined up during the euphoria of the first months of the war. High unemployment, newly-arrived British immigrants and the promise of regular pay, were factors which stimulated recruitment. Although Prime Minister Robert Borden was initially commited to avoiding conscription, as a result of the heavy losses incurred during the Battle of the Somme, Canada desperately needed to replenish its fighting men. On August 29, 1917 the Military Service Act was passed, which subjected all able-bodied males in Canada between the ages of 20 and 45 to compulsory military service. Poster production was generally financed locally appealing to the men to join their district battalions.

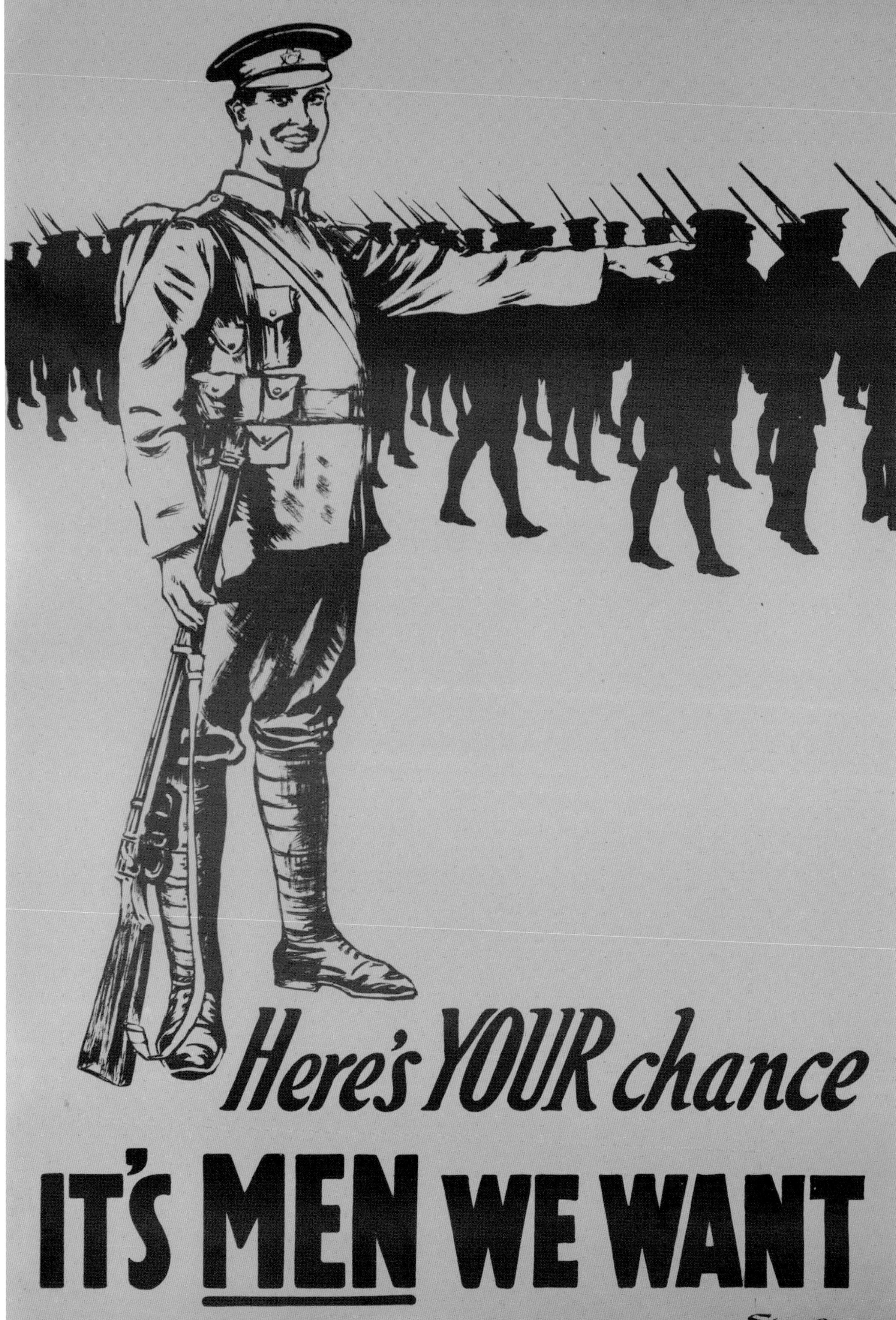

Here's YOUR chance
IT'S MEN WE WANT
Stone Co

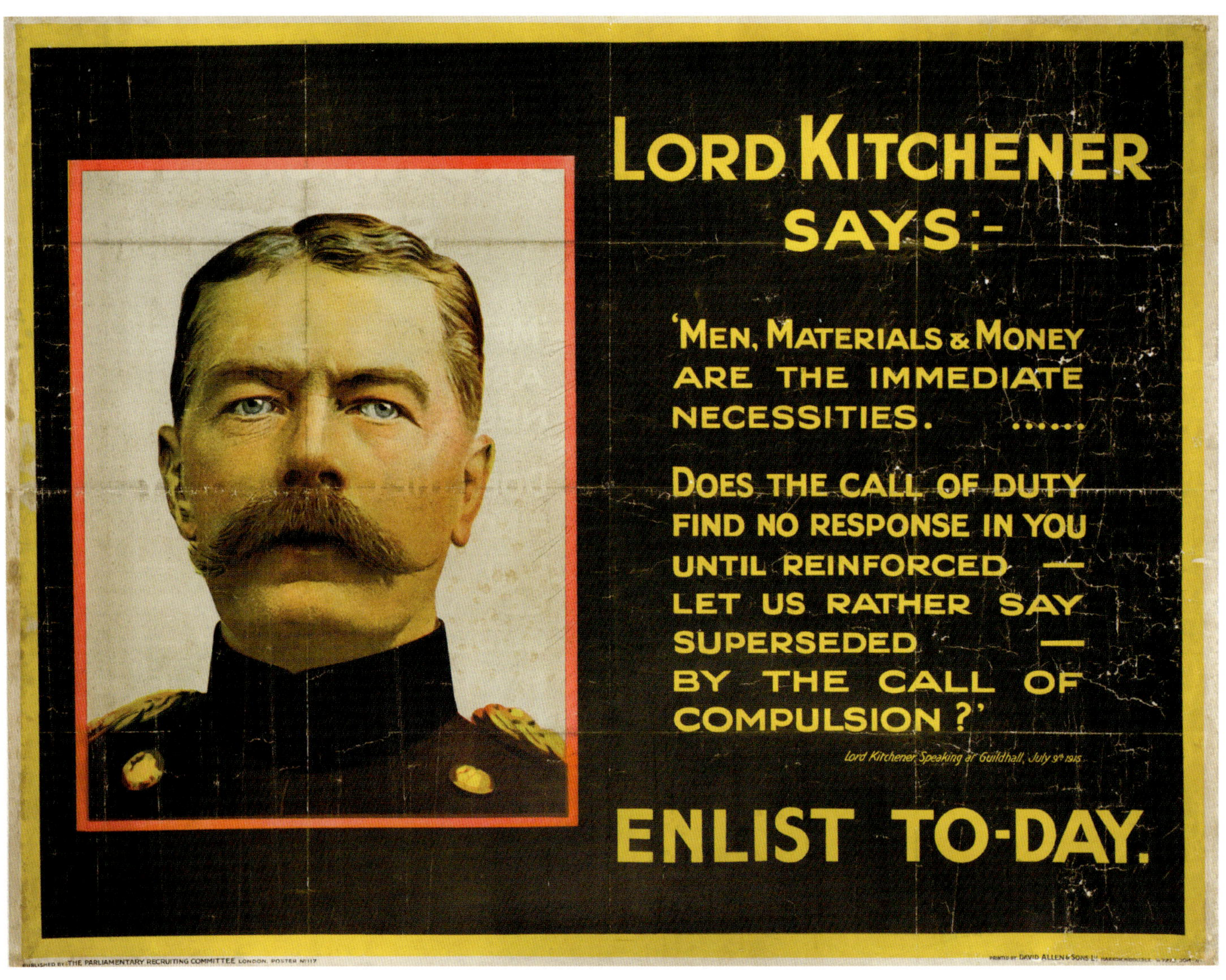

129 – English School

Lord Kitchener Says... Enlist Today, 1915,
Published by The Parliamentary Recruiting Committee, London, Poster no 117, 40 x 50 inches (102 x 127 cm),
Printed by David Allen & Sons

Field Marshal Herbert Horatio Kitchener was appointed Secretary of State for War at the outbreak of hostilities in 1914 and he set about organising a recruitment drive of volunteers for the British Army. Although the designer of this poster is not known the image of Kitchener is taken from a photograph by Alexander Bassano. The text was taken from a speech given by Kitchener at the Guildhall, July 9,1915. The poster was issued in two sizes: 20 ½ x 30 in. (52 x 76 cm) and this rarer one which is nearly twice as large.

130 – Frank Brangwyn   (1867-1956)

Orphelinat des armées (W1096), 1916,
Lithographic poster, 60 x 40 in. (152.5 x 101.4), printed by Avenue Press, London

Brangwyn produced over 80 poster designs during the war. A large proportion of Brangwyn's work during this period was given free of charge to charitable groups such as the Red Cross, The National Institute for the Blind (St Dunstan's Hostel for Blinded Soldiers and Sailors), The Belgian and Allied Aid League and probably *L'Orphelinat des Armées*, an American charity in aid of a French Army Orphanage.

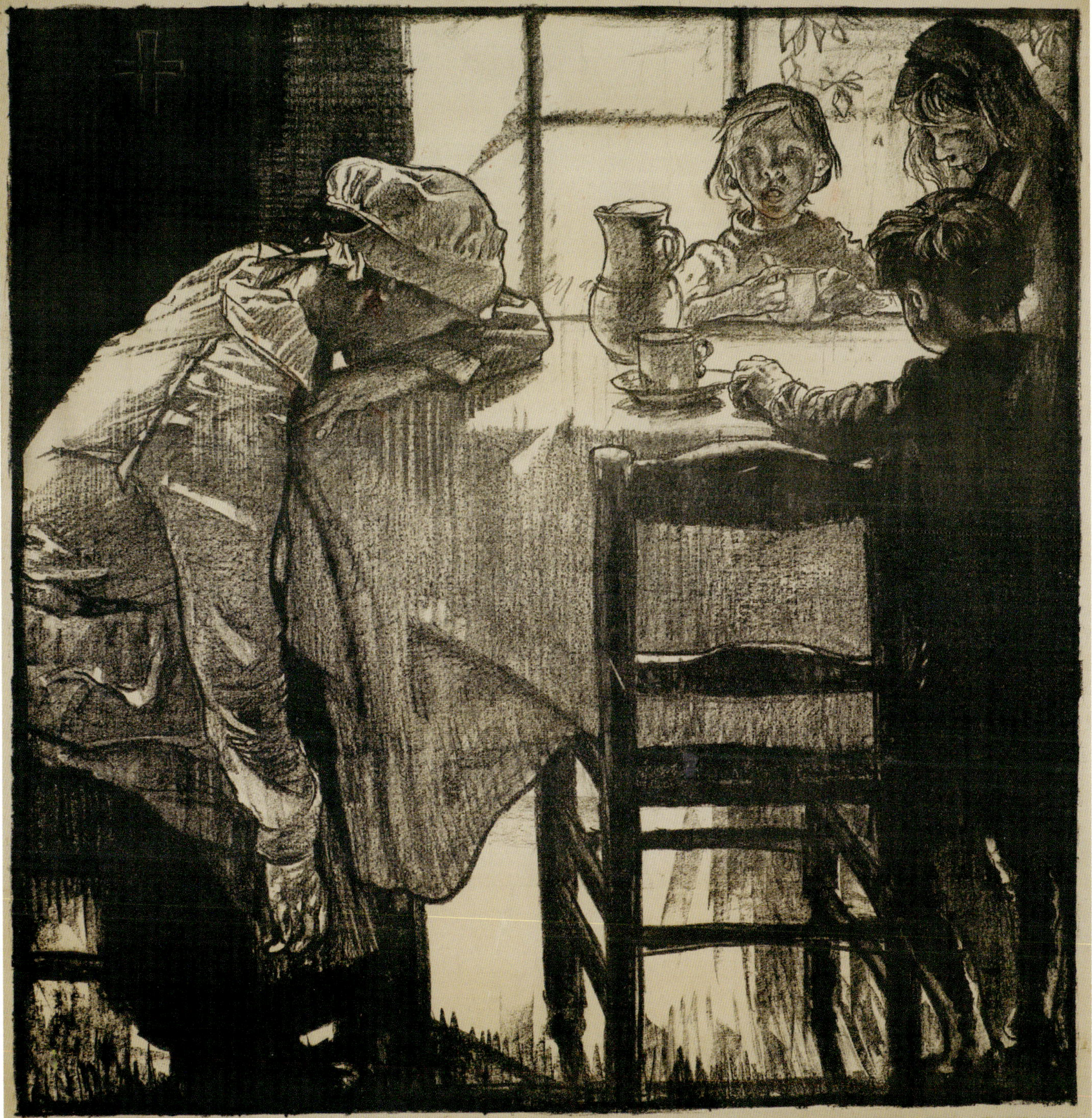

ORPHELINAT
DES ARMÉES

ASSURER AUX PETITS ORPHELINS::
LE FOYER ET LA TENDRESSE MATERNELLE
L'ÉDUCATION AU PAYS. UNE CARRIÈRE
APPROPRIÉE A CHAQUE ENFANT. LA
LEGION DE LEURS PÈRES

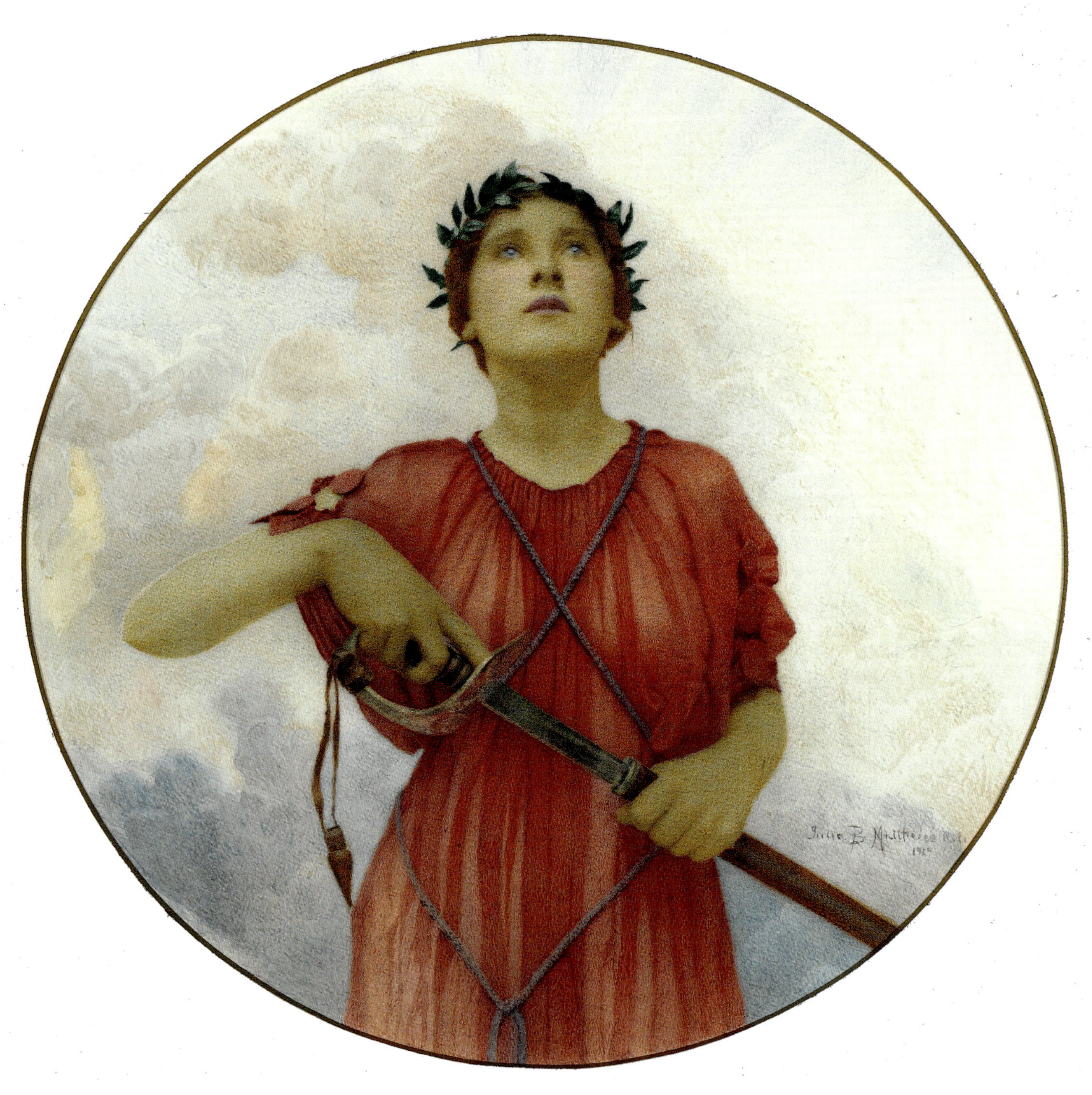

131 – Julia Matthews (d.1948)

Guided by Matchless Fortitude, To Peace and Truth Thy Glorious Way Hast Ploughed, c. 1918,
Watercolour on paper, 11 in. (28 cm.) diameter

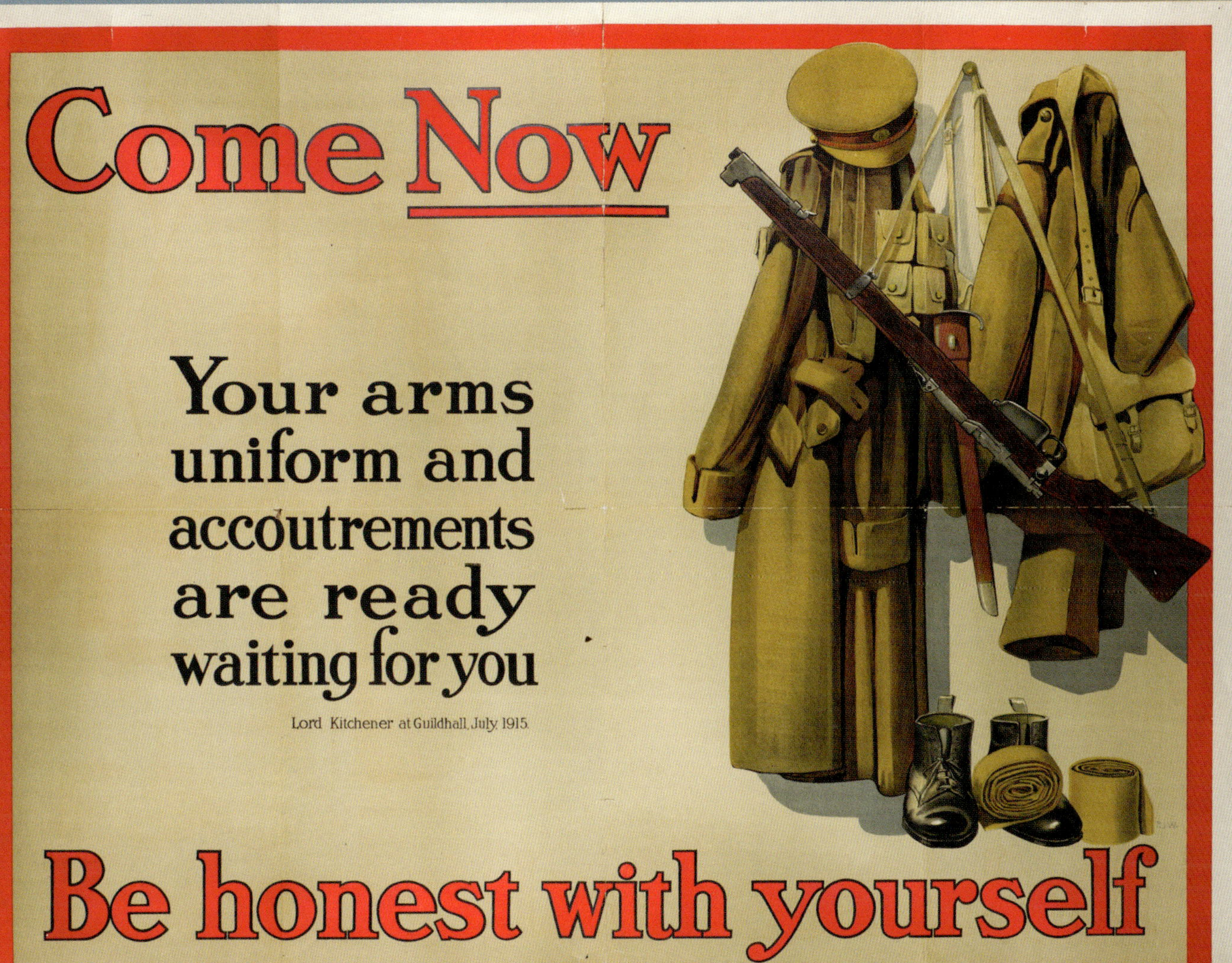

132 – P. J. W.

Come Now Be honest with yourself, 1915
Guildhall July 1914 original Parliamentary Recruiting Committee Poster No 130,
Lithographic poster, 40 x 50 in. (102 x 127 cm),
Printed by David Allen & Sons Ltd, September 1915

This poster was designed uniquely for Ireland. The promise of free uniforms was an incentive for men to enlist.

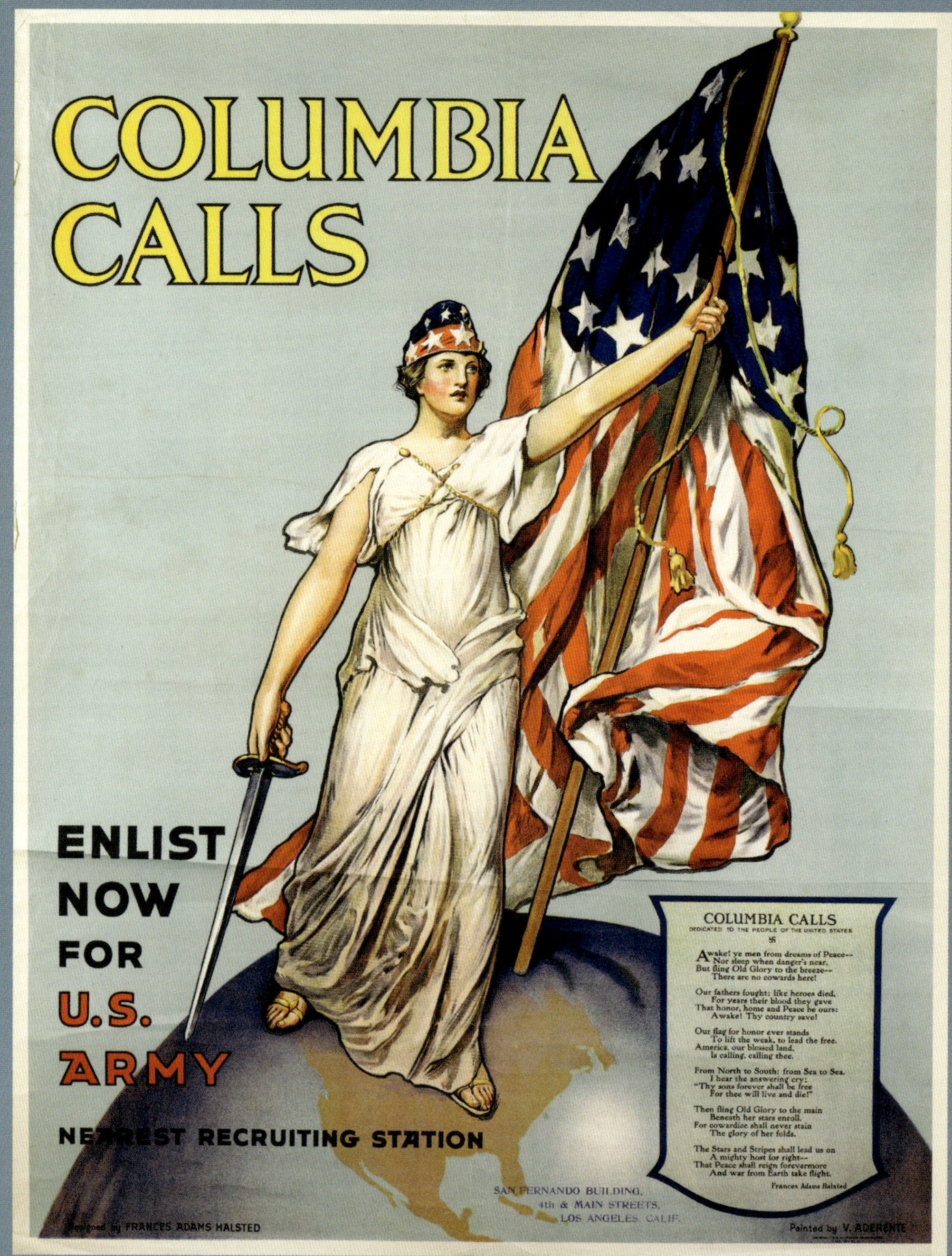

133 – Frances Adams Halsted & Vincent Aderente (1880-1941)

Columbia Calls, c.1916,
Lithographic poster, 30 x 40 in. (76 x 101 cm)

According to a story in the *New York Times* (June 3, 1917), the design of the poster and the poem, both by Frances Adams Halsted, dated from 1916, when Halsted was convinced that war between Germany and the United States was inevitable. After the United States entered the war in the spring of 1917, the U.S. Department of War announced that it was purchasing 500,000 copies of the poster. Halsted pledged that the proceeds would go to the establishment of a home for the orphaned children of American soldiers and sailors. The illustration is by Vincent Aderente, an American muralist who was born in Italy.

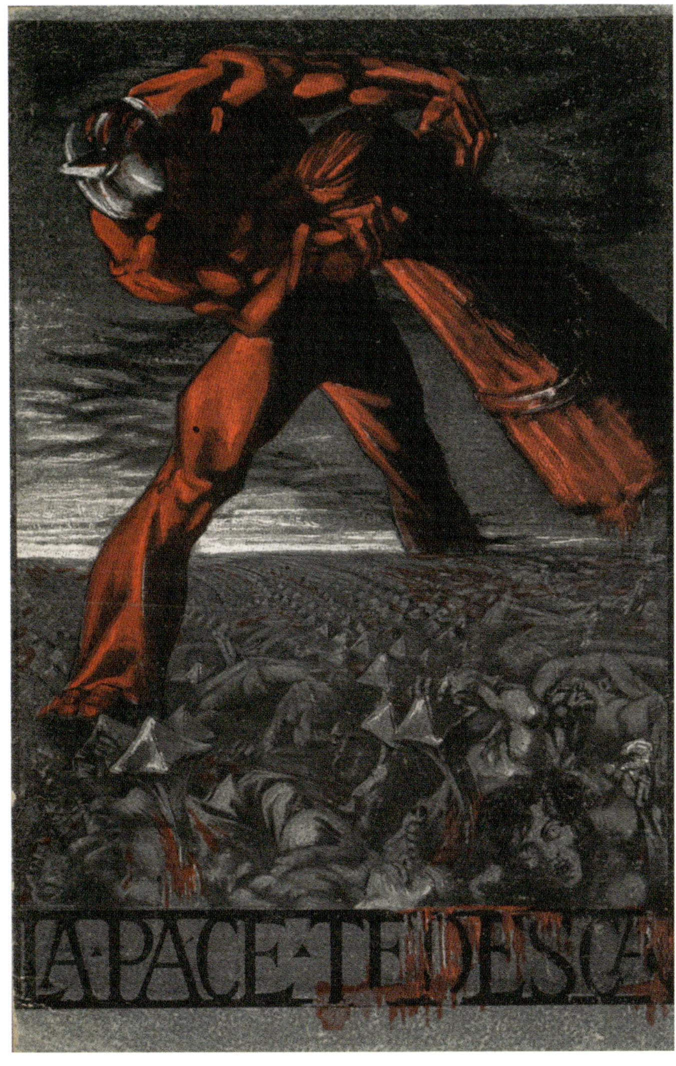

134 – Sergio Canevari

La Pace Tedesca (German Peace), c.1918,
Postcard: 5 ½ x 3 ½ in. (13.8 x 8.8 cm)

The original Italian propaganda poster of this image was published by Bergamo: Instituto italiano d'arti grafiche in 1917 and measured 9 x 6 feet. There are only two known copies, one of which is in the British Library, the other in the Library of Congress. A powerful anti-German image, it depicts a giant, representing Germany, crushing bodies. This image is complementary to another Canevari design entitled *Russian Peace*.

Nominally allied with the Central Powers of the German Empire and the Empire of Austria-Hungary in the Triple Alliance, the Kingdom of Italy refused to join them when the war started in August 1914. Italy entered the war almost a year later, in May 1915, after a period of wavering and secret negotiations with France and Great Britain who agreed to cede territory to Italy if the Allies were victorious.

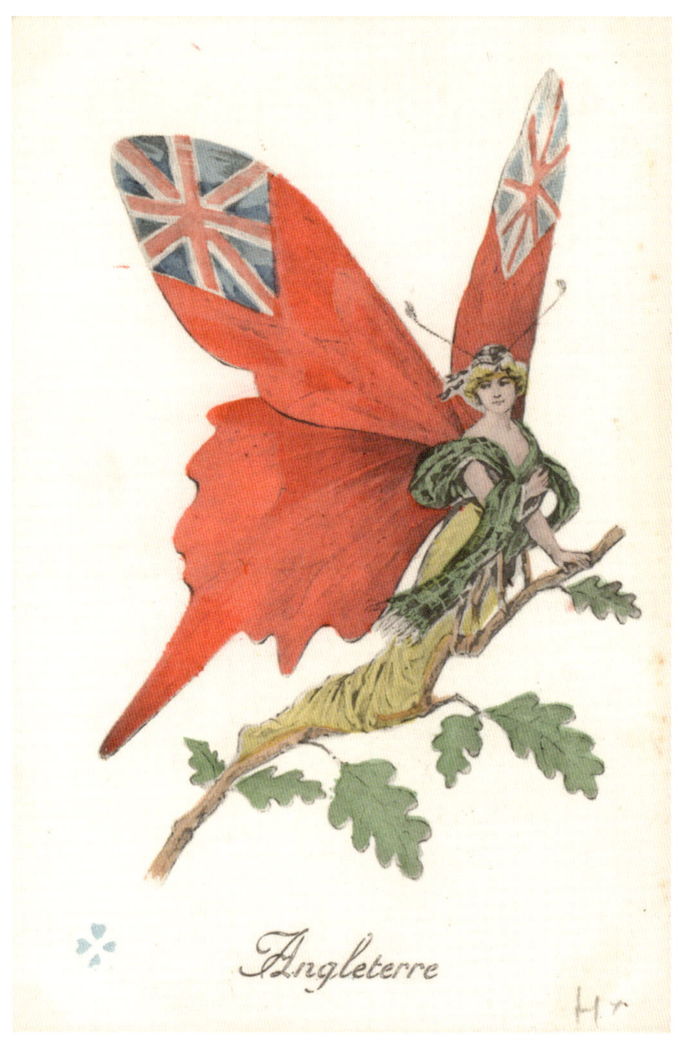

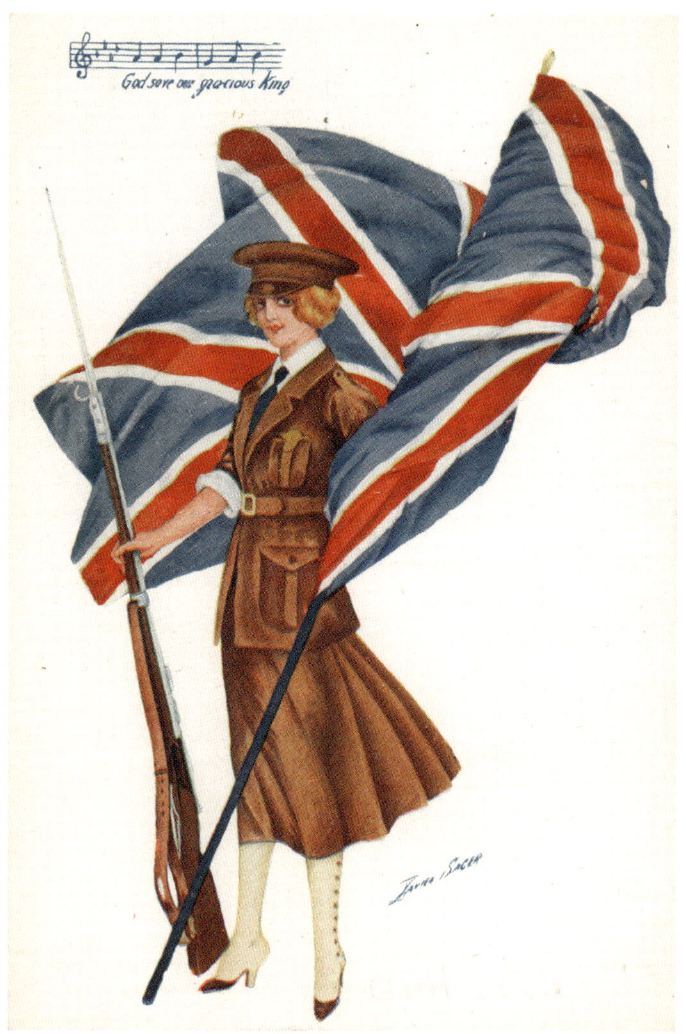

135 – French Postcard

Angleterre,
5 ½ x 3 ½ in. (14 x 9 cm)
Printed by Editions "Aux Alliés" Paris

136 – French Postcard

*God Save Our Glorious King, (*Les hymnes nationaux, par X. Sager),
5 ½ x 3 ½ in. (14 x 9 cm)
Printed by Fantaisies trichromes – A. Noyer – Paris

137 – René Georges Hermann-Paul (1864-1940)

Les Hymnes Alliés, 1917,
Colour lithograph, 19 x 12 ½ in. (48 x 31.5 cm),
Published by Nouvel Essor, Paris

This lithograph celebrates the French-American alliance during the First World War. When the American Expeditionary Forces arrived in France, General John Pershing was said to exclaim, "Lafayette, we have come!"

LES HYMNES ALLIÉS

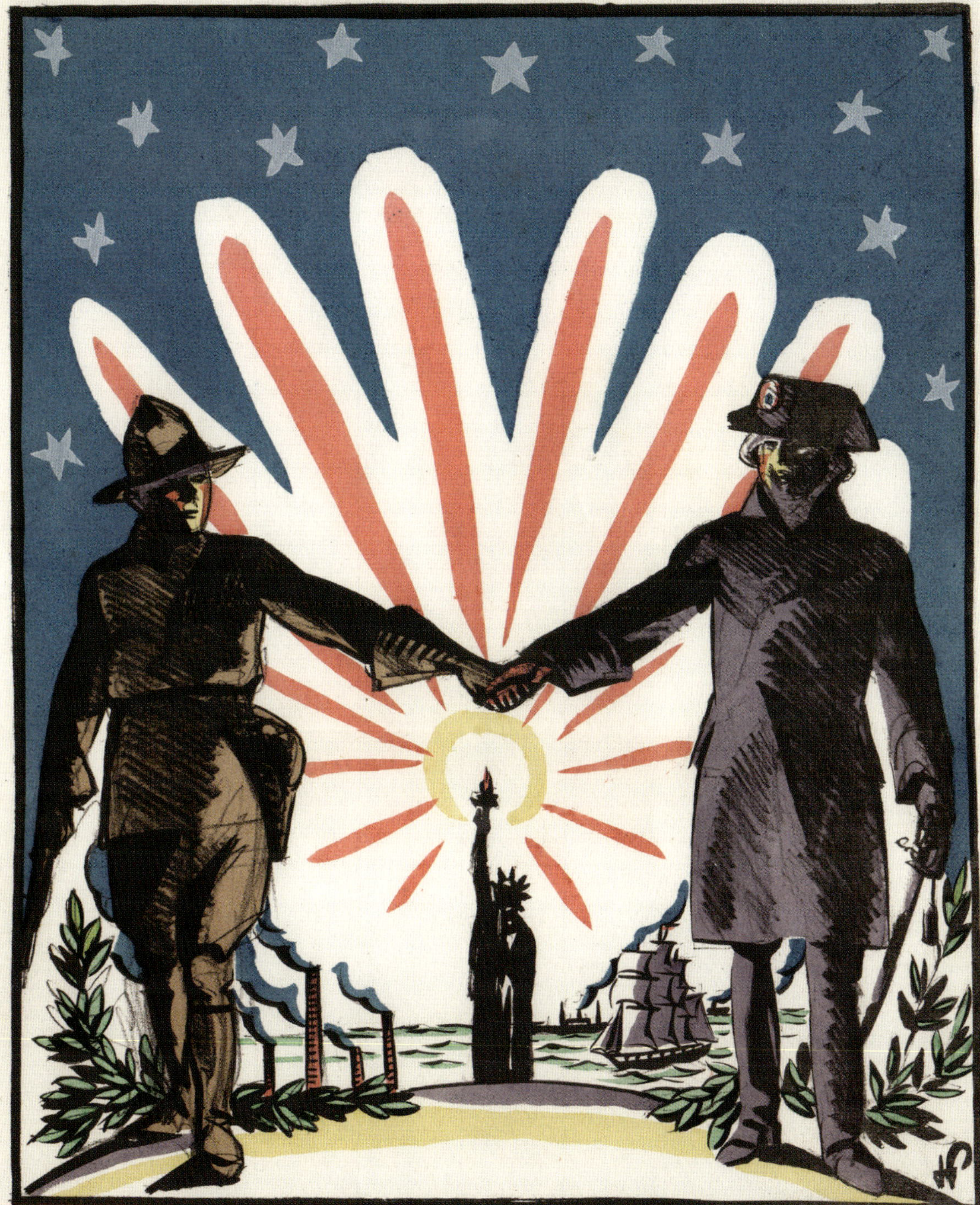

Image de Hermann Paul, tirée à 1.000 exemplaires, Editée à PARIS, par le NOUVEL ESSOR, 40, rue des Sts Pères.

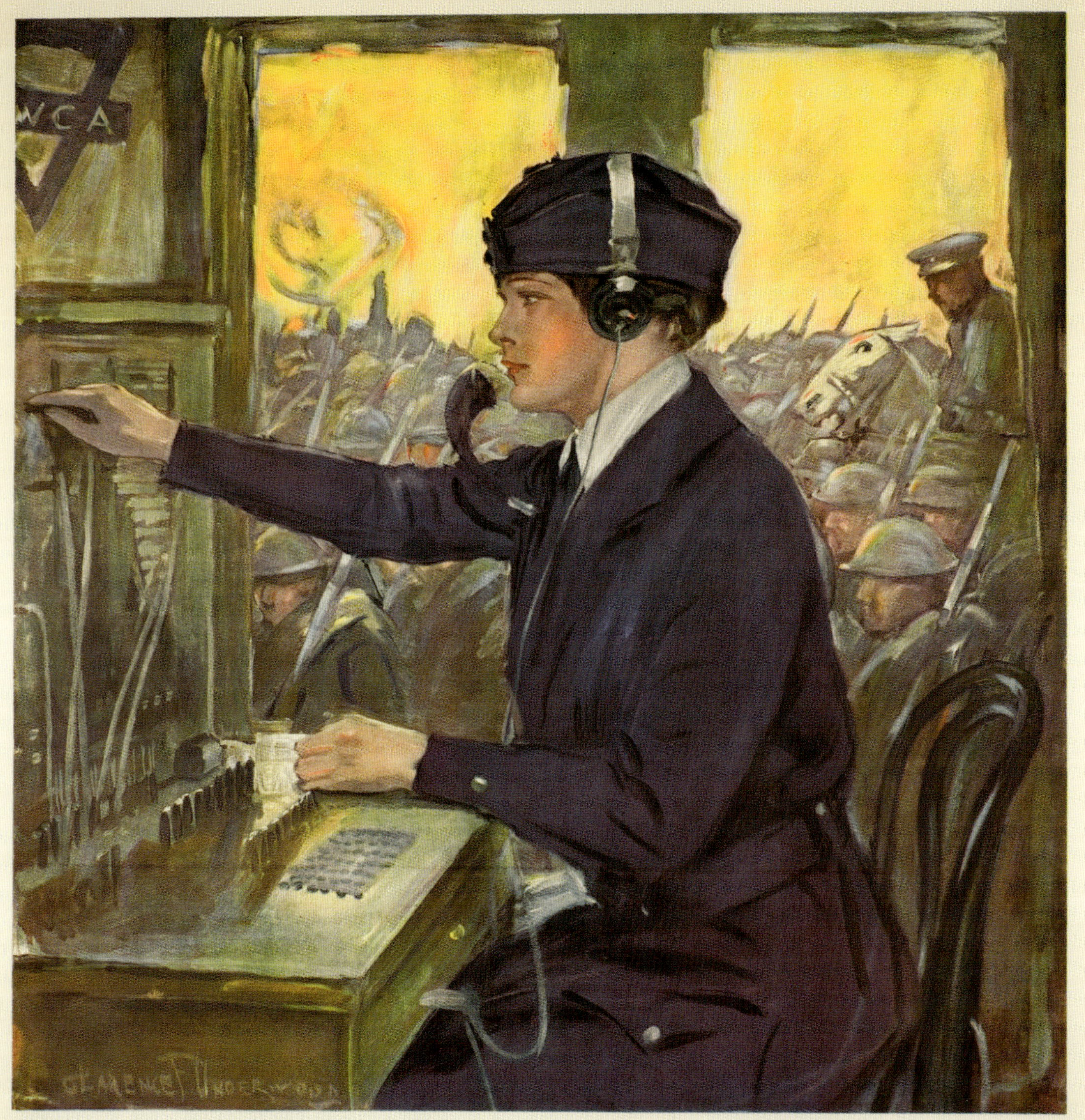

Back our girls over there

Y.W.C.A.

United War Work Campaign

"If the women in the factories stopped work for twenty minutes, the Allies would lose the war."

Field Marshal Joseph Joffre,
in *Proceedings of the national conference on labor conditions*, Society of Industrial Engineers, 1918, p.96

"A person shall not be disqualified by sex or marriage from the exercise of any public function, or from being appointed to or holding any civil or judicial office or post."

The Sex Disqualification (Removal) Act, December 23, 1919.

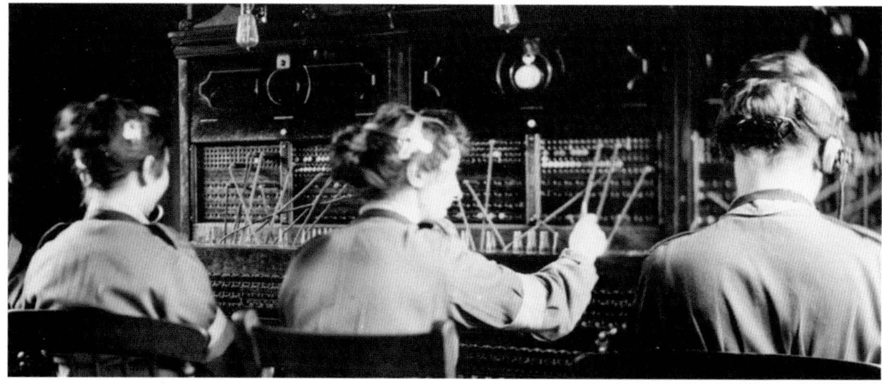

Women telephone operators during the war.

138 – Clarence F. Underwood (1871-1929)

Back our girls over there, 1918, signed in the plate,
Lithographic poster, 26 ⅝ x 19 in. (67.7 x 48.2 cm)

"Hello Girls," as American soldiers called them, were American women who served as telephone operators for John Pershing's forces in Europe. The women were fluent in French and English and were specially trained by the American Telephone and Telegraph Company. The U.S Army recruited and trained 233 female telephone operators to work at the switchboards near the Front in France. In 1979, the U.S. Army finally gave war medals and veteran benefits to the few "Hello Girls" who were still alive.

America produced about 2,500 poster designs and approximately 20 million posters – nearly one for every four citizens – in little more than 2 years. This Young Women's Christian Association poster for the United War Work Campaign shows a woman telephone operator working behind the French Frontline. The United War Work Campaign was a combined effort of several organizations, including the Y.W.C.A., to raise money for the war.

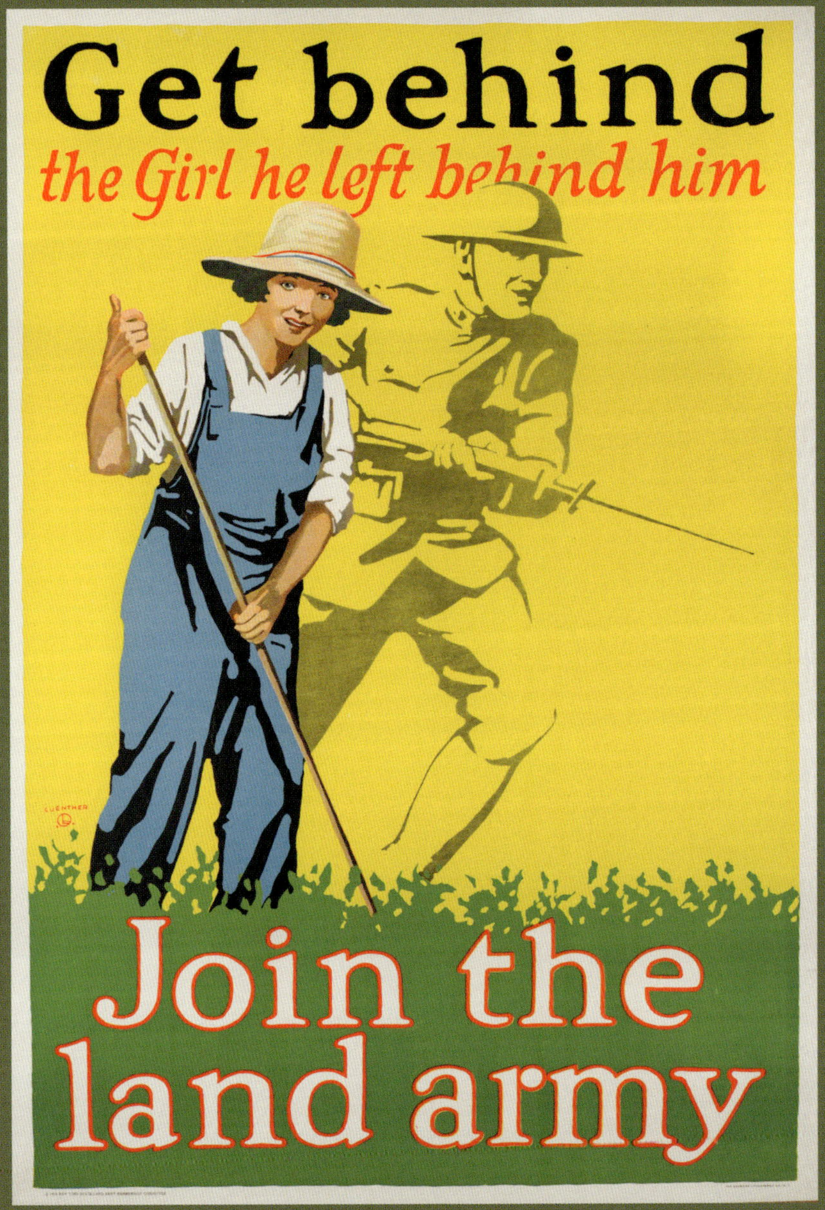

139 – Lambert Guenther (1888-1961)

Get behind the girl he left behind him Join the land army. c.1918, signed in the plate,
Lithograph printed by The American Lithographic Co., 30 x 20 in. (76.2 x 50.8 cm),
Copyright by New York State Land Army Membership Committee

Guenther was born in Germany and emigrated to the US in 1908. He became a naturalised American citizen in 1914. The Woman's Land Army of America (WLAA) – which was modelled on the British Women's Land Army –operated from 1917 to 1921, employing 15,000 - 20,000 women. Many were from towns and cities and college educated, and whole units were associated with colleges. Women who worked for the WLAA were sometimes known as farmerettes. The WLAA was supported by Progressives like Theodore Roosevelt, and was associated with the suffrage movement. In Britain, where there was a shortage of farm labour as men were conscripted into the Forces as well as a need to grow more food due to the threat to supplies caused by German submarines, the Women's Land Army (established in February 1917) boasted over 113,000 members by 1918.

140 – Adolph Treidler (1886-1981)

For Every Fighter a Woman Worker – Care for Her through the YWCA, c.1918, signed in the plate,
Lithographic poster, 40 x 30 in. (101.6 x 76.2 cm), printed by the American Lithographic Company

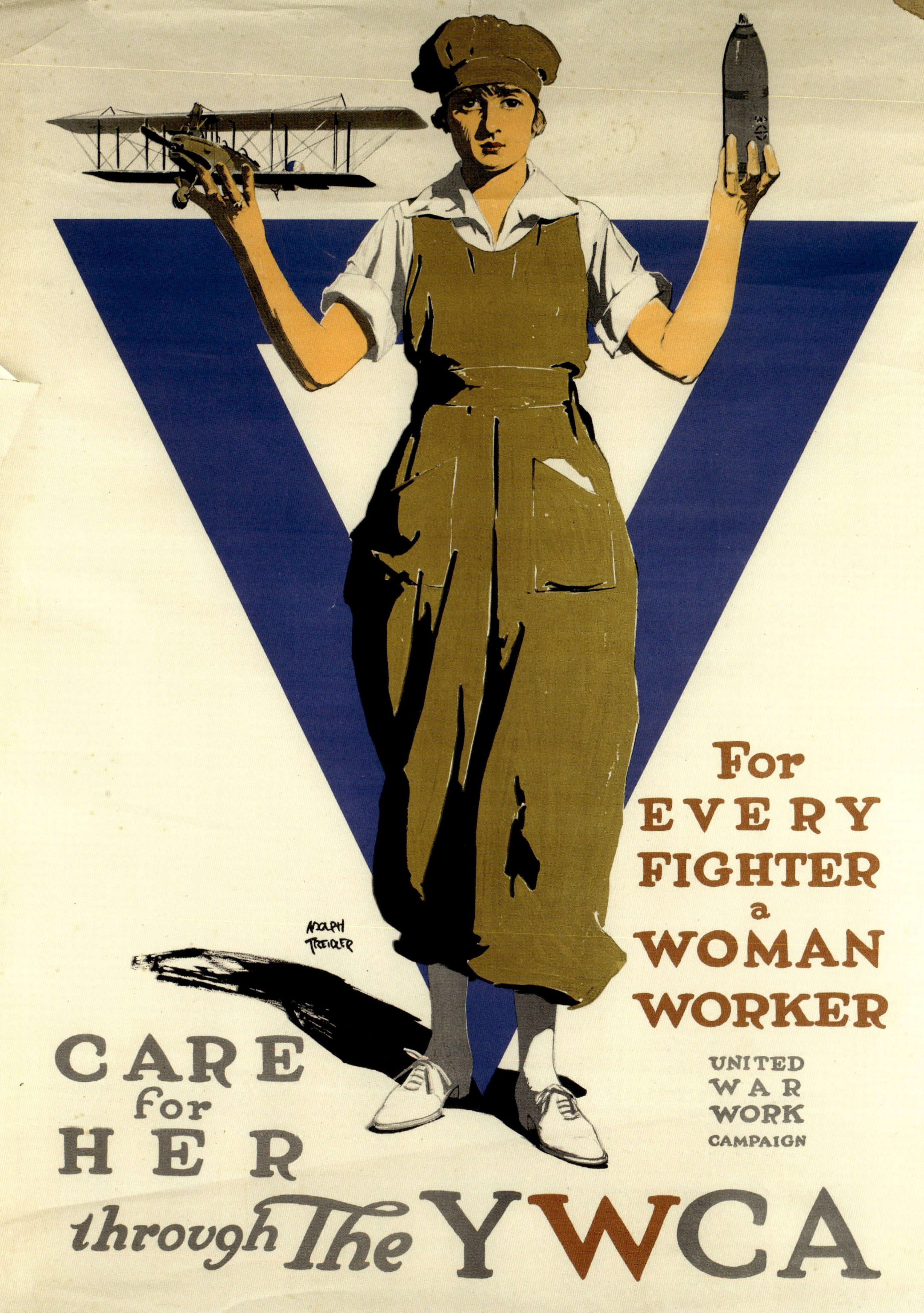
For
EVERY
FIGHTER
a
WOMAN
WORKER
UNITED
WAR
WORK
CAMPAIGN
ADOLPH TREIDLER
CARE
for
HER
through The YWCA

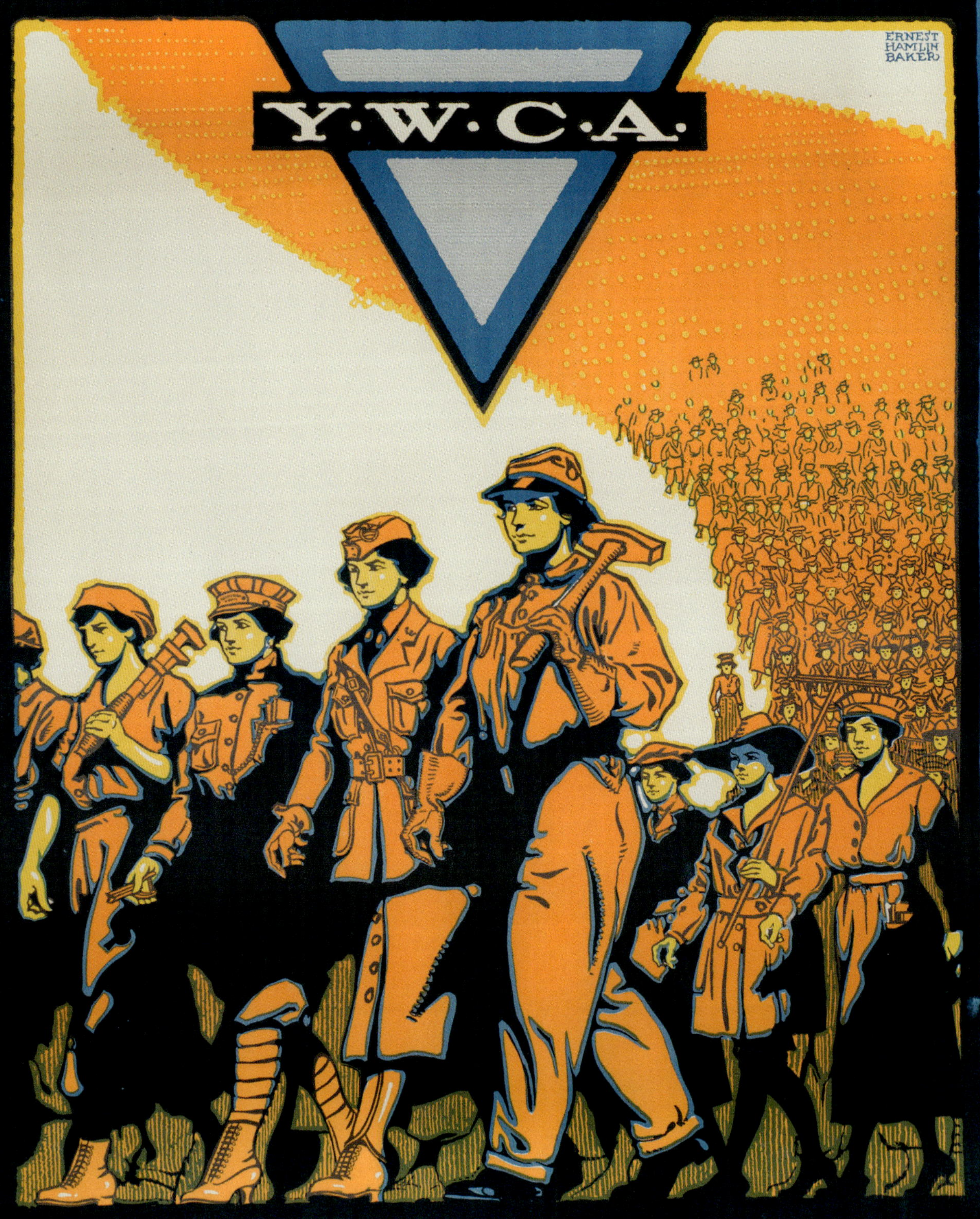
FOR EVERY FIGHTER
A WOMAN WORKER
ERNEST HAMLIN BAKER
Y·W·C·A·
BACK OUR SECOND LINE OF DEFENSE
UNITED WAR WORK CAMPAIGN
THE UNITED STATES PTG. & LITH. CO., N.Y.

142 – Margaret Wrightson (1877-1976)

Mechanic, Women's Army Auxiliary Corps, 1917,
Signed and dated 1917,
Bronze, height: 10 in. (25.4 cm)
Suggestion for a War Memorial exhibited
at the Royal Academy in 1919, No. 1567.

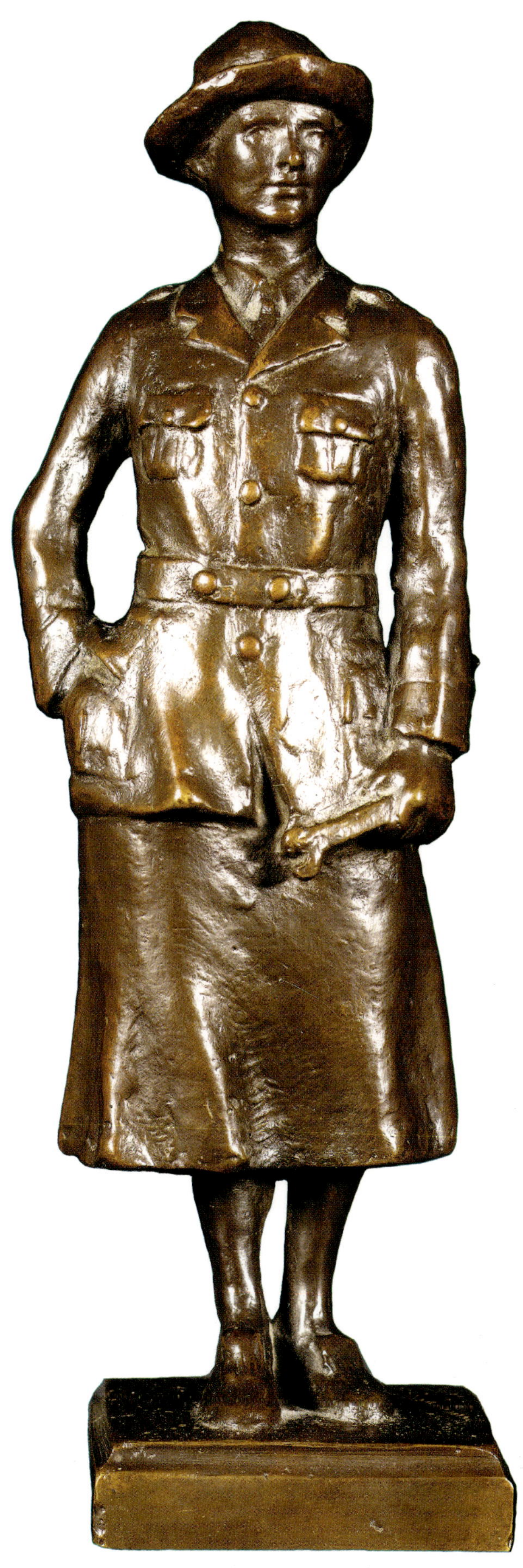

141 – Ernest Hamlin Baker (1889-1975)

For Every Fighter a Woman Worker /
Back Our Second Line of Defense, 1918,
Lithographic poster, 42 ½ x 28 ½ in. (108 x 72 cm),
Printed by the United States Printing and Lith. Co.

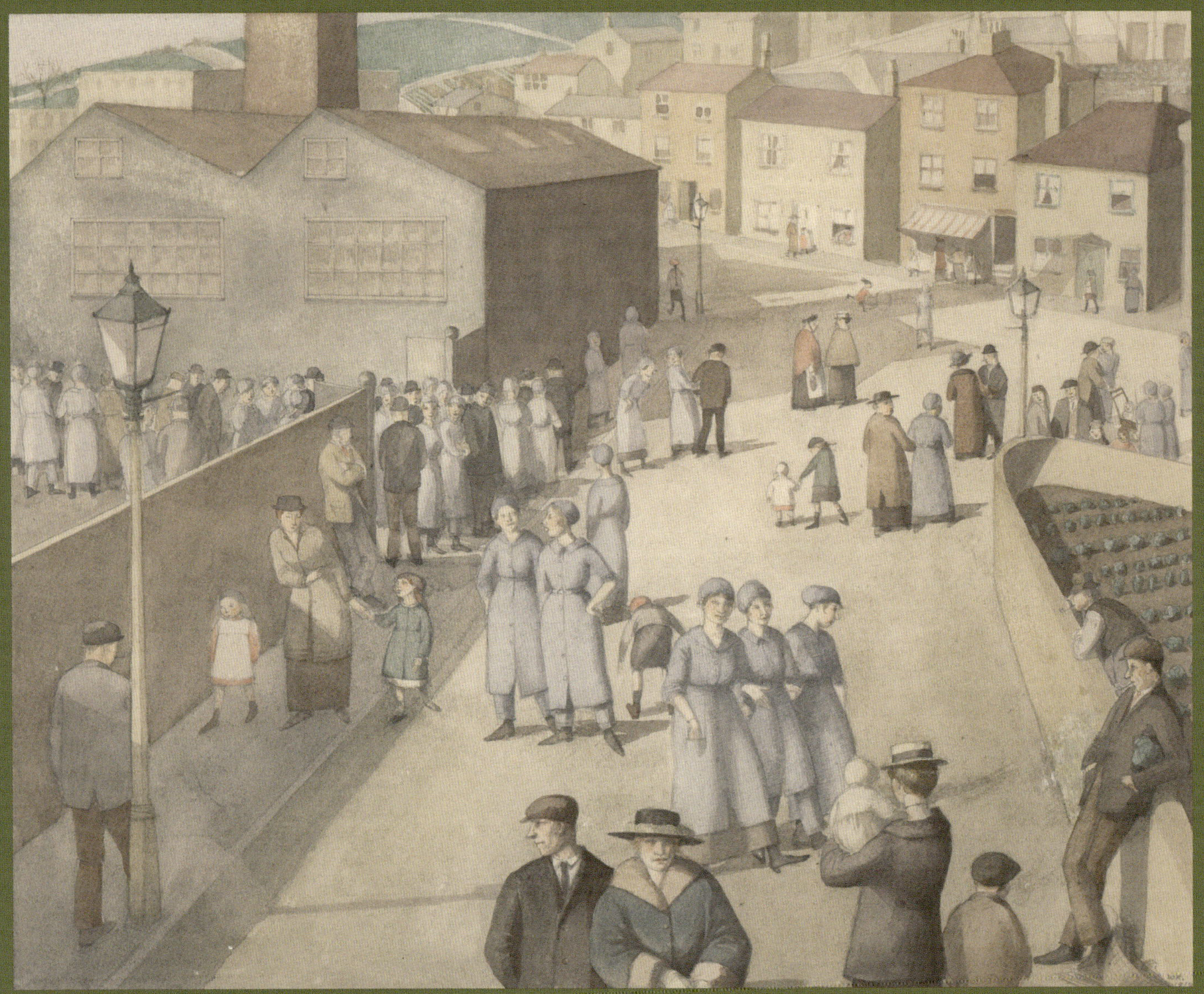

143 – Winifred Knights (1899-1947)

Leaving the Munitions Works, 1919, signed and dated,
Watercolour, 10 ⅝ x 12 ½ in. (27 x 32 cm)
Provenance: Allan Gwynne Jones

By June 1917, roughly 80% of the weaponry and ammunition used by the British Army during the First World War was being made by female munitions workers, known as munitionettes. Often working with hazardous chemicals without adequate protection, munitionettes were also at risk from explosions, particularly in converted premises. Winifred Knights herself was deeply traumatised after witnessing the explosion of a TNT factory in Silvertown on January 19, 1917, which killed 73 people and injured 400.

144 – Lucien Jonas (1880-1947)

Four Years in the Fight. The Women of France. We Owe Them Houses of Cheer, c.1918,
United War Work Campaign. Y.W.C.A.,
Lithographic poster, 42 x 28 in. (106.7 x 71.1 cm), printed by: Strobridge Lith. Co., New York

During the First World War the rapidly expanding war industries led to fundamental changes in the roles played by women. In 1918 nearly three million new women workers were employed in the food, textile and war industries. Taboos and restrictions were removed allowing women to work for the first time in large-scale production industries such as steel mills and logging camps.

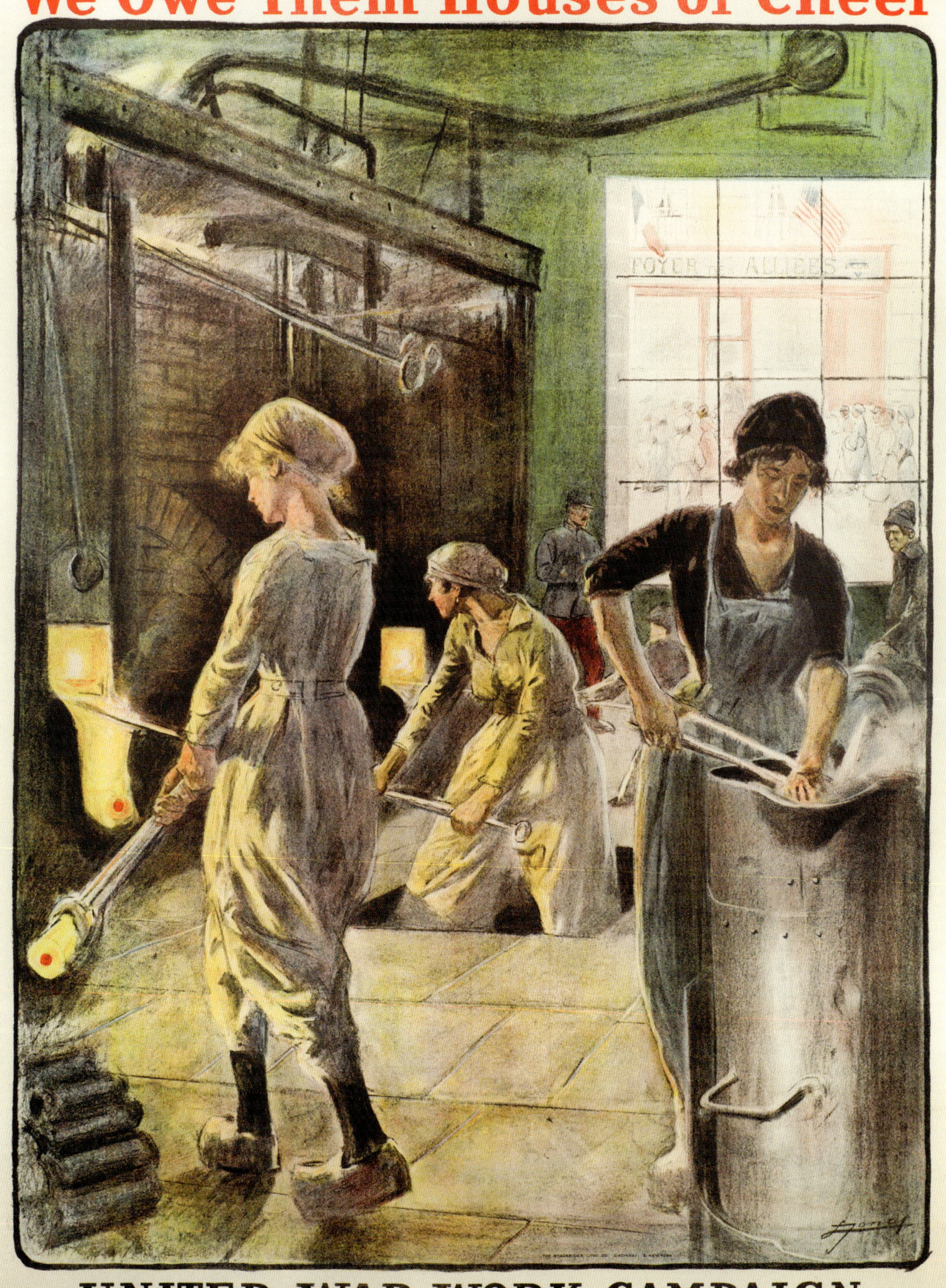

FOUR YEARS IN THE FIGHT
Y.W.C.A.   The Women of France   Y.W.C.A.
We Owe Them Houses of Cheer
UNITED WAR WORK CAMPAIGN

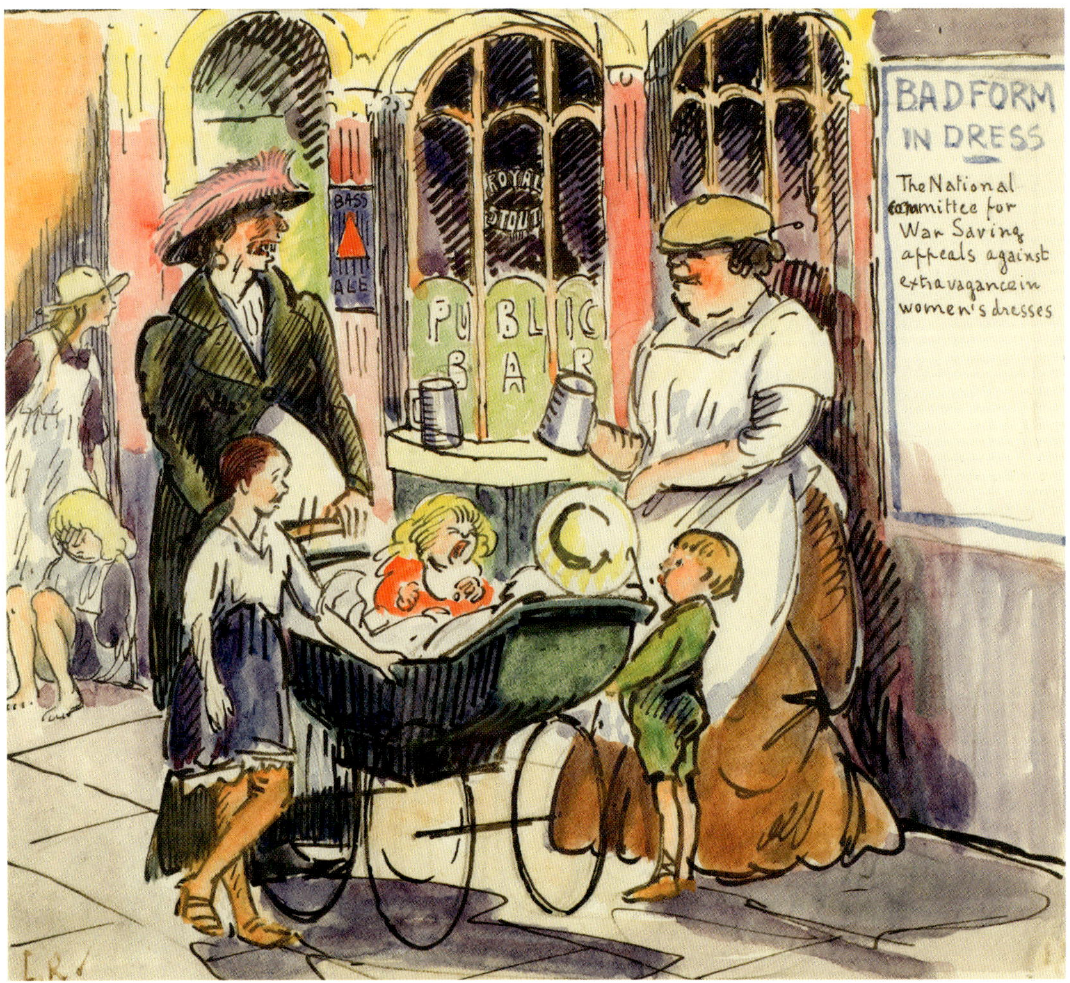

145 – Ludovic-Rodolphe (Rodo) Pissarro (1878-1952)

Bad Form in Dress, c.1915, signed with initials,
Pen and ink, watercolour on paper, 7 x 7 ¼ in. (17.5 x 18.5 cm)
The fourth son of Camille Pissarro, 'Rodo' moved to England at the outbreak of war. Living in West London, he recorded life on the Home Front in a number of witty on-the-spot watercolours.

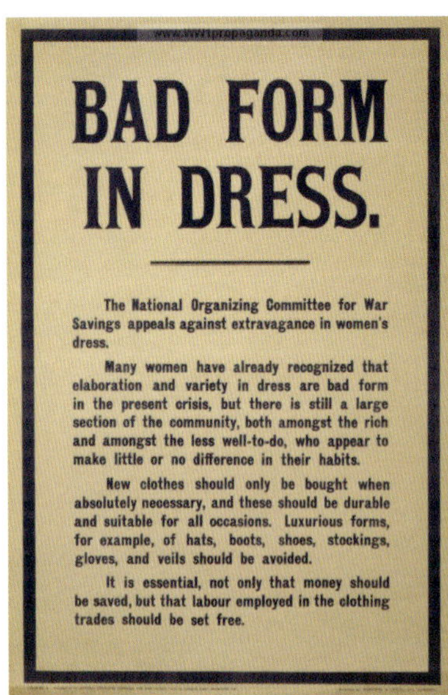

At least two posters produced by the National War Savings Committee (1915) warned women against frivolous dress in this time of need. One read: "To dress extravagantly in war time is worse than bad form, it is unpatriotic."

Left:
"BAD FORM IN DRESS.
The National Organizing Committee for War Savings appeals against extravagance in women's dress.
Many women have already recognized that elaboration and variety in dress are bad form in the present crisis, but there are still a large section of the community, both amongst the rich and amongst the less well-to-do, who appear to make little or no difference in their habits. New clothes should only be bought when absolutely necessary, and these should be durable and suitable for all occasions. Luxurious forms, for example, of hats, boots, shoes, stockings, gloves and veils should be avoided.
It is essential, not only that money should be saved, but that labour employed in the clothing trades should be set free. "

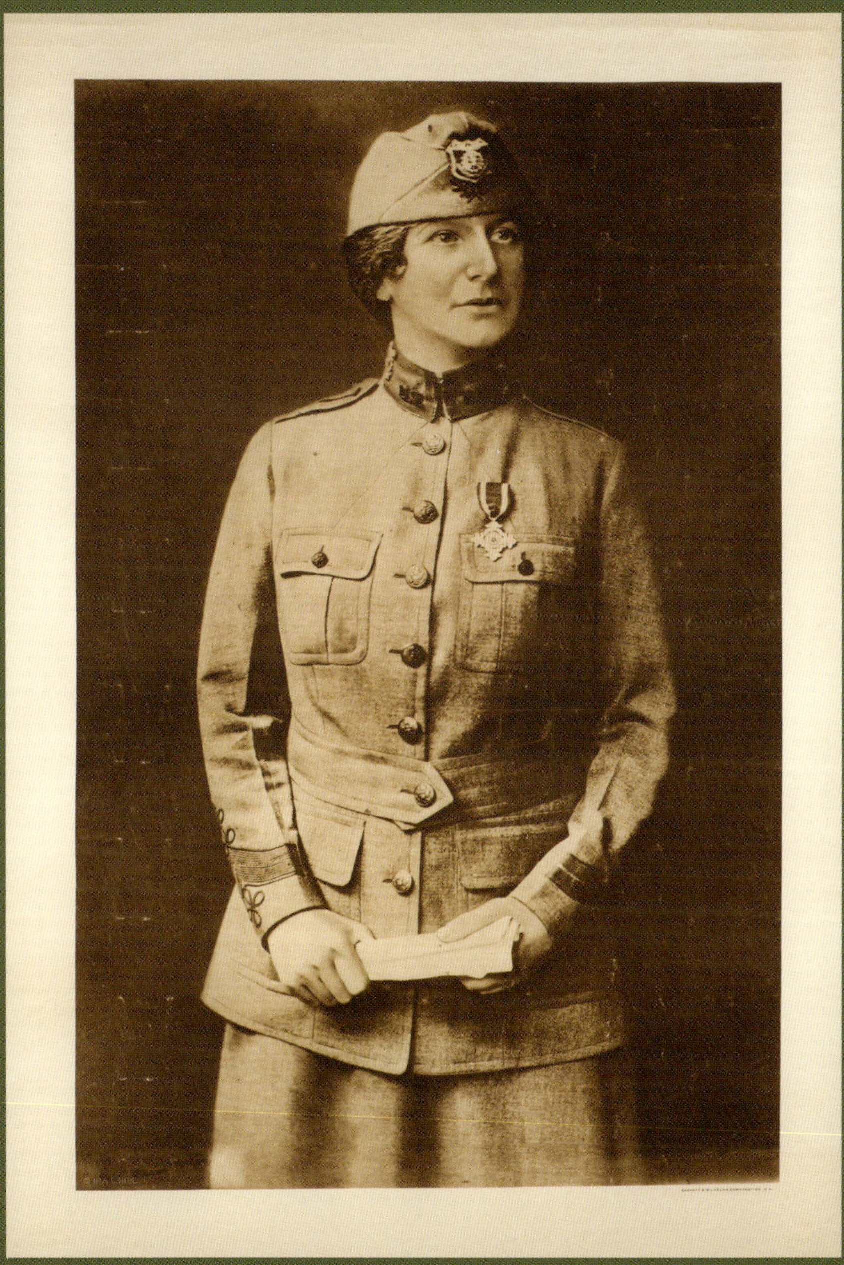

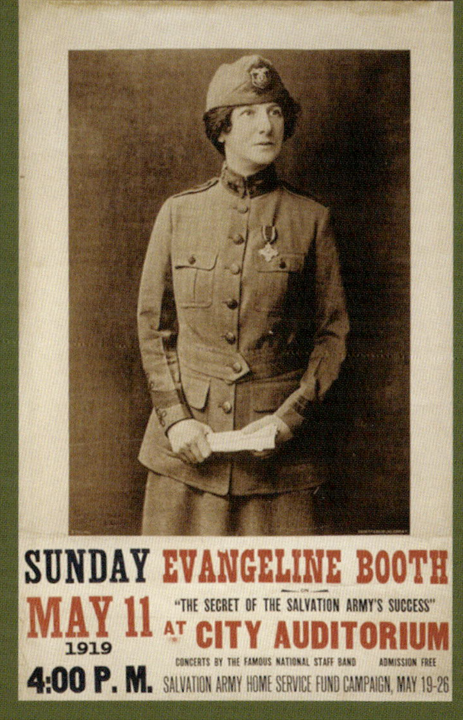

146 – Ira L. Hill   (1877-1947)

Evangeline Booth – Salvation Army, c.1919,
Lithograph, 41 x 27 in. (104 x 69 cm)
Published by Sackett & Willielms Corp, copyright Ira L. Hill

Founded by William Booth (1829-1912), the Salvation Army is best known for its social welfare and charitable services. Booth's daughter, Evangeline (1865-1912), who also had a long and successful career with the organisation, was awarded the Distinguished Service Medal for her efforts to provide aid to U.S. soldiers in Europe during the First World War. Booth became the Salvation Army's first woman General in 1934. This rare large photographic portrait was used for Booth's 1919 lecture tour: *The Secret of the Salvation Army's Success* (above right).

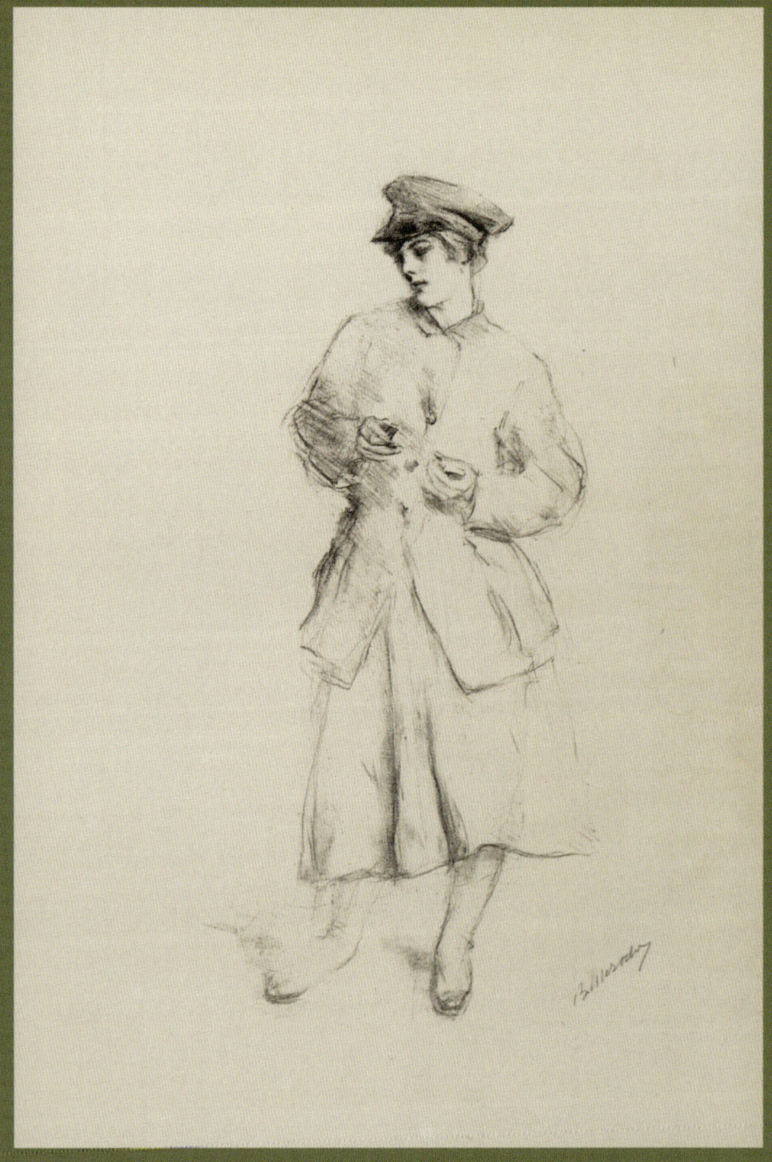

147 – Albert de Belleroche (1864-1944)

Chauffeuse, signed,
Lithograph, 17 ½ x 11 ¼ in. (44.5 x 28.6 cm)

Belleroche used Selfridges' girls as models during the war. Lift attendants are known to have worn unifroms of this kind.

148 – René Georges Hermann-Paul (1864-1940)

Novembre 1914 – Yser, from the *Calendrier de la Guerre (1ère année – août 1914-juillet 1915),* 1916,
Coloured woodcuts, 17 ¾ x 13 ¾ in. (45 x 35cm) each,
Published by Librarie Lutetia [A. Ciavarri, Directeur]

This complete set includes twelve colored woodcuts each representing a month of the first year of the Great War from August 1914 until July 1915. Each month is represented by a place, a battle or an event such as mobilization. Women figure prominently in most of these images.

The Battle of the Yser took place in October 1914 between the towns of Nieuwpoort and Diksmuide along a 35-kilometre long stretch of the Yser river. The front line was held by a large Belgian force which succeeded in halting the German advance, though only after heavy losses. After two months of defeats and retreats, the Battle of Yser finally halted the invasion that gave Germans control of over 95% of Belgian territory. Victory in the battle allowed Belgium to retain control of a tiny part of its territory making King Albert a Belgian national hero and sustaining national pride.

FOLLOWING PAGES:
Décembre 1914 – Enrôlements, Septembre 1914 – Bataille de la Marne, Octobre 1914 – Reims, Mai 1915 – Italie and
Juillet 1915 –Permissionaires

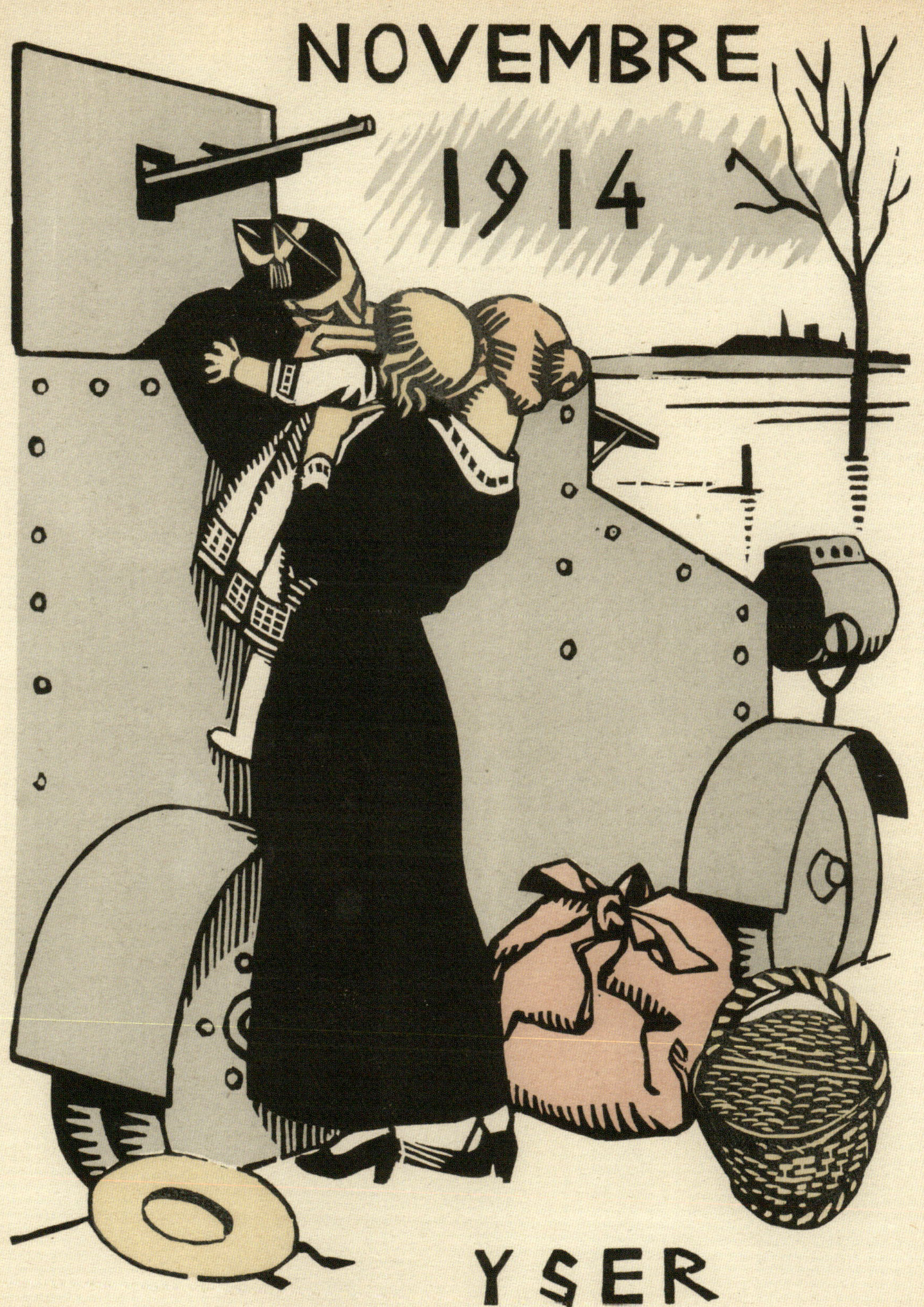

Bois taillé au canif par Hermann-Paul

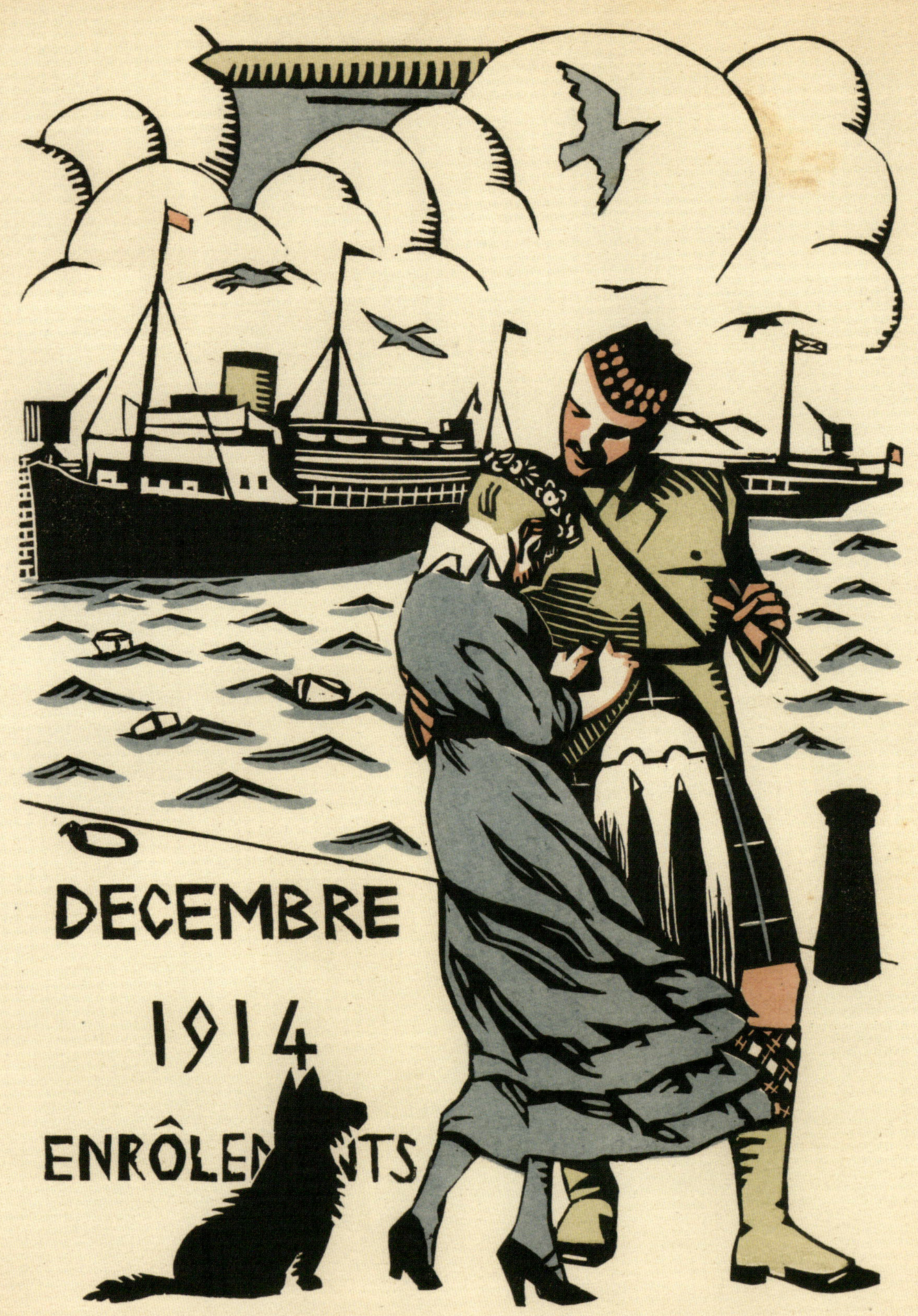

Bois taillé au canif par Hermann-Paul

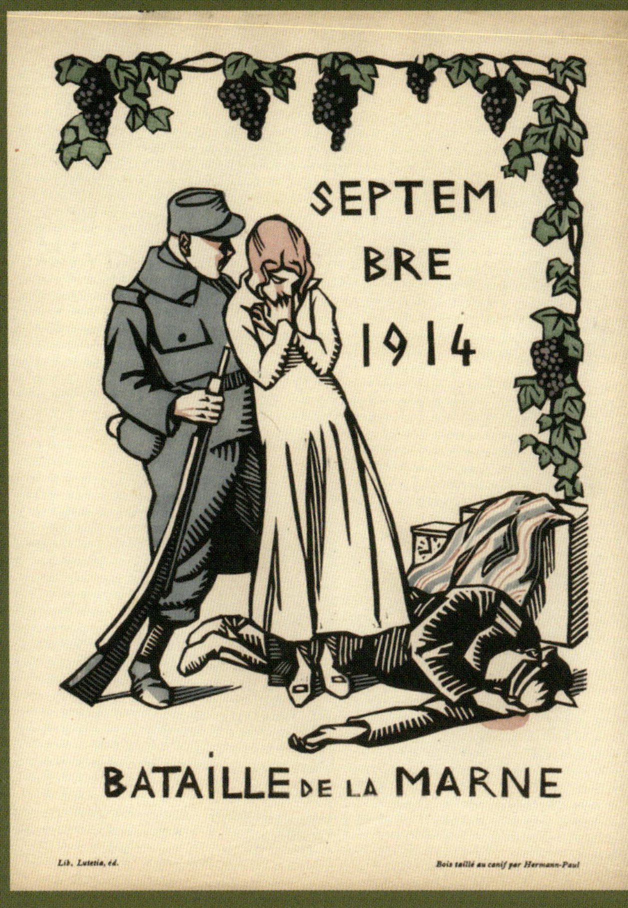

SEPTEM
BRE
1914
BATAILLE DE LA MARNE
Lib. Lutetia, éd.
Bois taillé au canif par Hermann-Paul

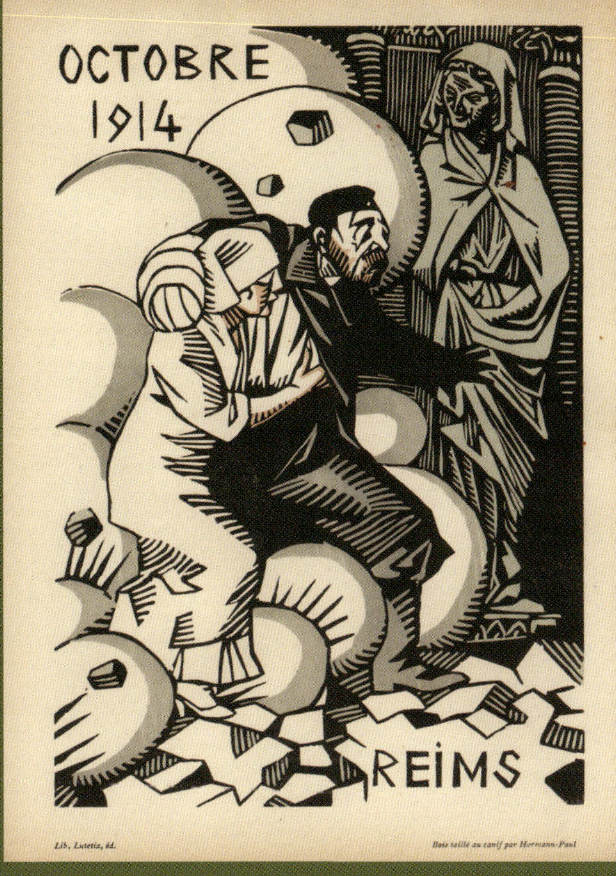

OCTOBRE
1914
REIMS
Lib. Lutetia, éd.
Bois taillé au canif par Hermann-Paul

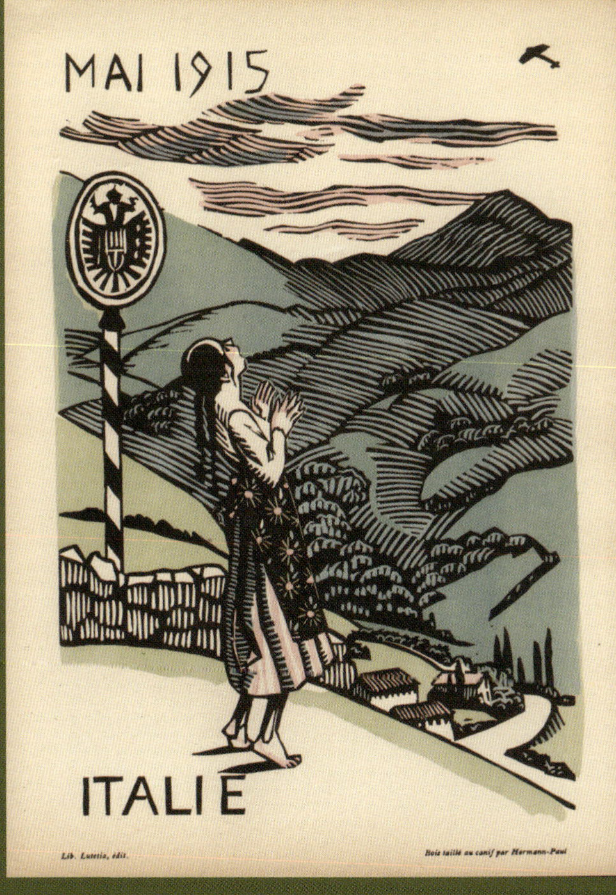

MAI 1915
ITALIE
Lib. Lutetia, édit.
Bois taillé au canif par Hermann-Paul

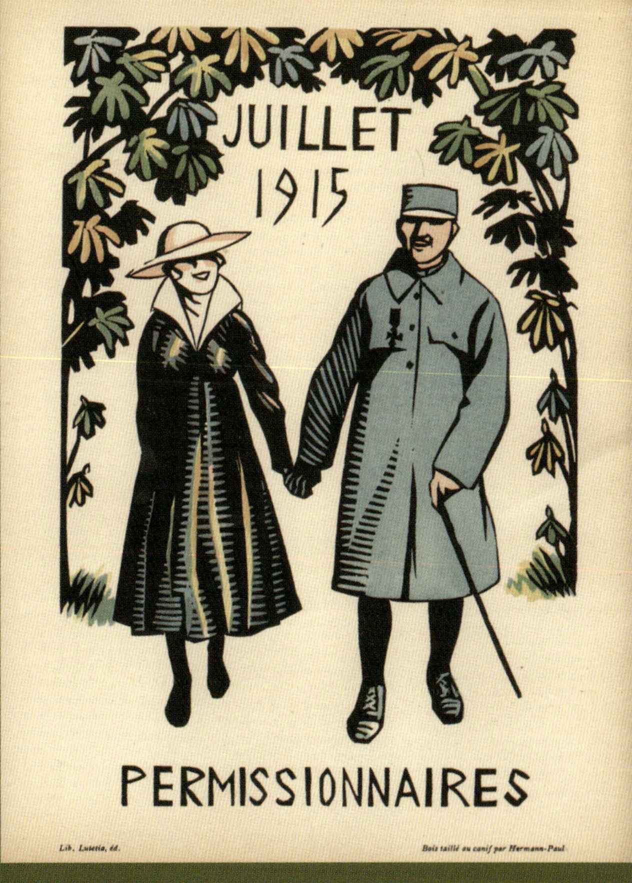

JUILLET
1915
PERMISSIONNAIRES
Lib. Lutetia, éd.
Bois taillé au canif par Hermann-Paul

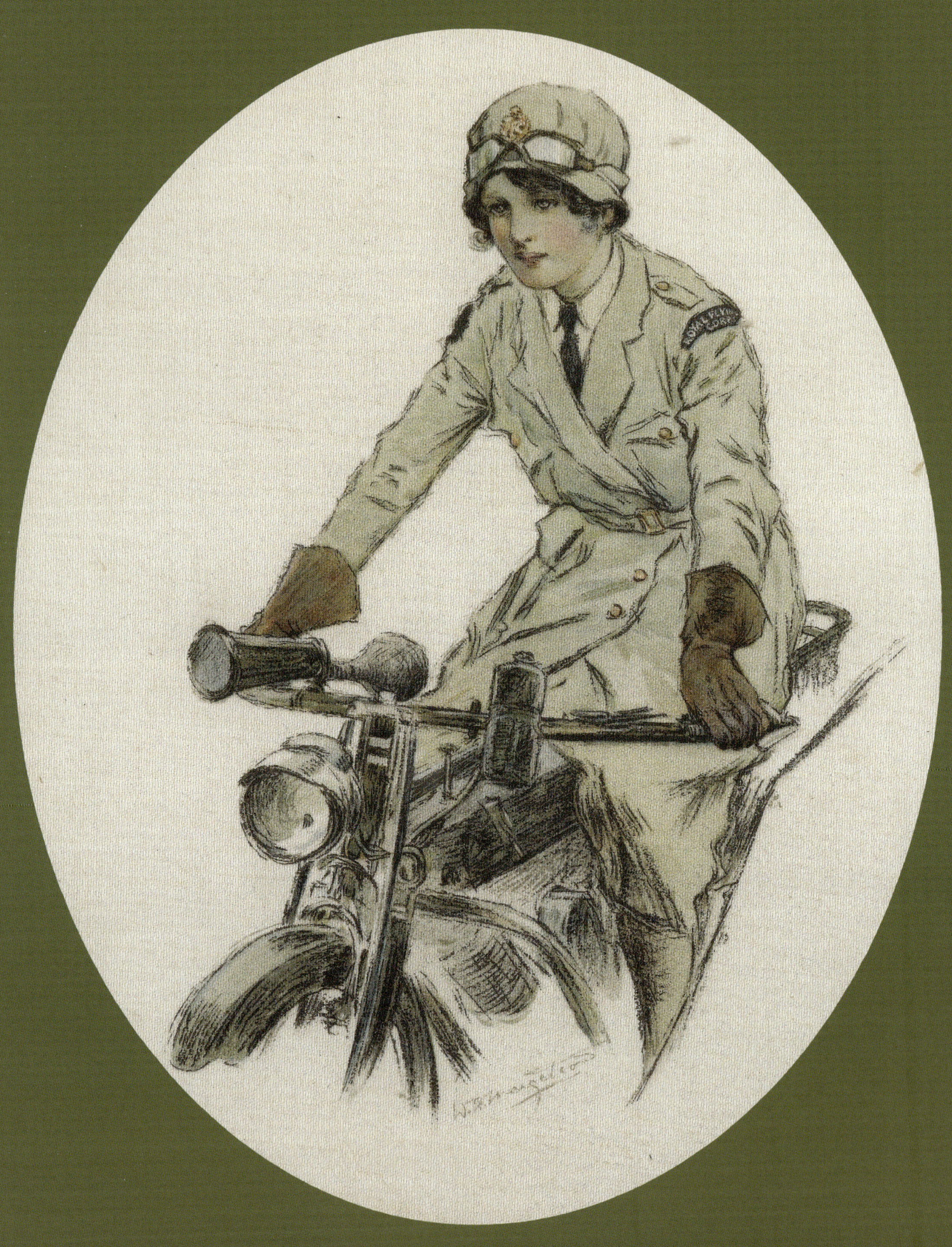

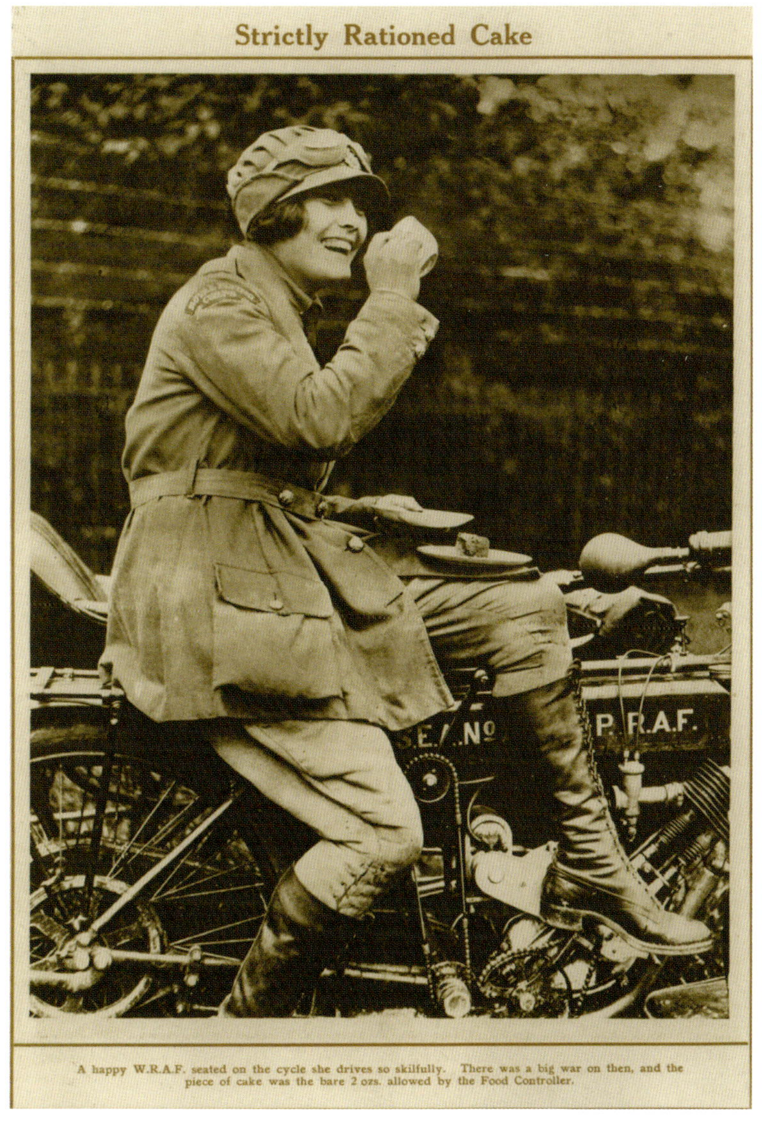

Strictly Rationed Cake, from the catalogue *War in the Air,*
First Exhibition of Royal Air Force Photographs in Colour, c.1918

149 – William Henry Margetson (1861-1940)

Royal Flying Corps Woman Dispatch Rider, c.1917, signed indistinctly,
Lithographic print and watercolour on silk, 6 ½ x 5 ¼ in. (16.5 × 13.4 cm)

This lithograph depicts a member of the Women's Army Auxiliary Corps (WAAC) attached to the Royal Flying Corps, as indicated by the RFC cap badge and shoulder titles. Women began to be enlisted in the WAAC in 1916, and by 1917 the Royal Flying Corp had all-female companies who lived at home and worked in their nearest RFC Unit. The use of motorcycles by the armed forces began during the First World War. One of the more exciting job categories open to women during the war was working as dispatch riders, often making journeys at night, on poor roads and using only acetylene lighting. An identical print is in the collection of the National Army Museum.

INDUSTRY

"All through the war the great armament firms were supplied from the enemy countries. The French and the British sold war materials to the Germans through Switzerland, Holland and the Baltic neutrals, and the Germans supplied optical sights for the British Admiralty. The armament industry, which had helped stimulate the war, made millions out of it."

C.J. Pennethorne Hughes, *An Outline of European History, Part IV: 1815-1918*, London 1935

"If any mourn us in the workshop, say
We died because the shift kept holiday."

Rudyard Kipling, *Batteries Out of Ammunition, Epitaphs of War*, 1922

150 – Adrian Gil-Spear (b.1879)

Workers Lend Your Strength to The Red Triangle : Help the "Y" Help the Fighters Fight
(United War Work Campaign – November 11 to 18), c. 1918,
Lithographic poster, 27 x 21 1/2 in. (69 x 50 cm)

This poster shows a young man lifting a crate box, under the gaze of an older man in a YMCA uniform, whilst a soldier in the shadows marches forward, bayonet out. The message of this poster is that young American men could be part of the war effort by joining the YMCA and participating in the United War Work Campaign.During the war, the U.S. shipped about 7.5 million tons of supplies to France to support the Allied effort. That included 70,000 horses or mules as well as nearly 50,000 trucks, 27,000 freight cars, and 1,800 locomotives. In addition to this, by August 1918 over 1.5 million American soldiers were stationed in Europe.

WORKERS
YMCA
LEND YOUR STRENGTH
TO THE RED TRIANGLE
HELP THE "Y" HELP THE
FIGHTERS FIGHT
UNITED WAR WORK CAMPAIGN — NOVEMBER 11 to 18
Gil Spear

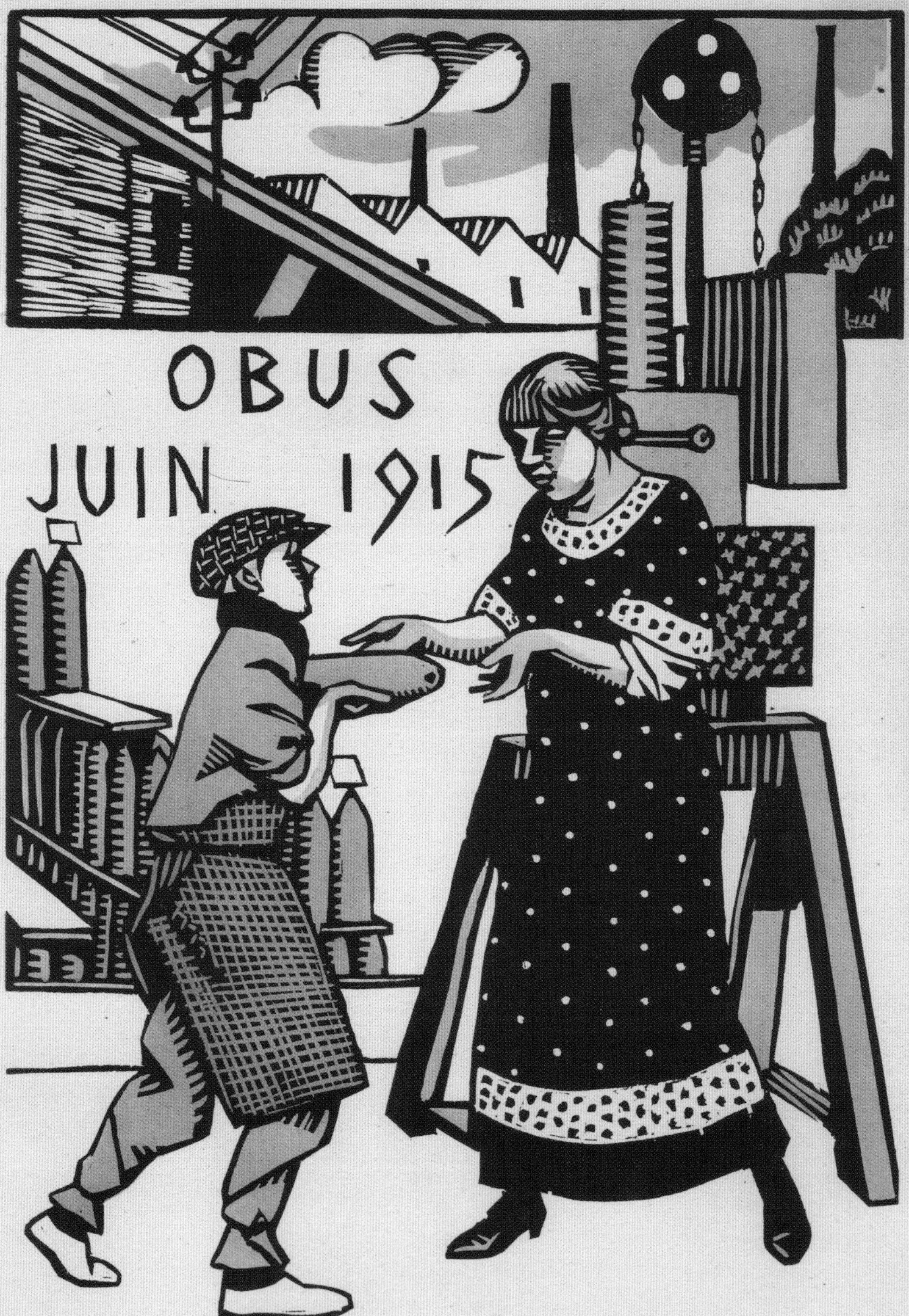

Lib. Lutetia, éd.

Bois taillé au canif par Hermann-Paul

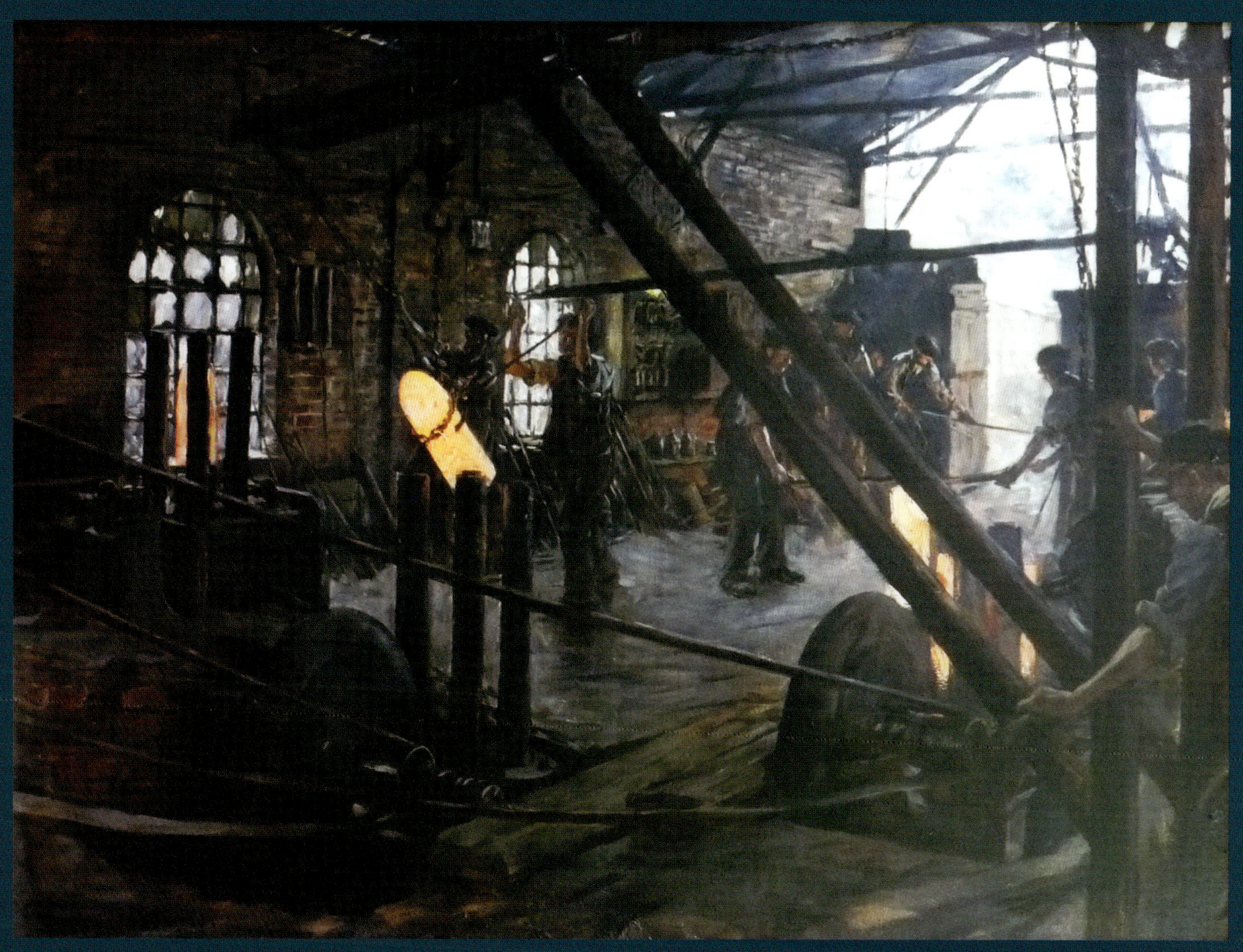

151 – Stanhope Alexander Forbes (1857-1947)
Shell Workers, 1918,
Oil on canvas, 30 x 40 in. (76.2 x 101.6 cm)
Exhibited: Royal Academy, 1919, No. 367

Throughout the war, Stanhope Forbes, who was too old to enlist, painted and exhibited patriotic subjects, many of which were shown at The Royal Academy: examples include *Ought I to Go?*, (No. 417) and *The Steel-workers*, (No. 624) exhibited in 1915, *The Smith's Workshop*, (No. 189) exhibited in 1917 and *Shell Workers* (No. 367) and *The Munition Girls* (No. 119) exhibited in 1919. Many of his industrial subjects, including *Shell Workers*, were commissioned by Sandberg, an Engineering company which wished their contribution to the war effort to be recorded for posterity.

148 – René Georges Hermann-Paul (1864-1940)

Juin 1915 – Obus, from the *Calendrier de la Guerre (1ère année – août 1914-juillet 1915),* 1916,
Coloured woodcuts, 17 ¾ x 13 ¾ in. (45 x 35cm) each,
Published by Librarie Lutetia [A. Ciavarri, Directeur]

In order to supply its armies, the Allies diverted most industrial output to the war effort. With so many men at the Front, women and boys were recruited by the munitions industry to meet demand.

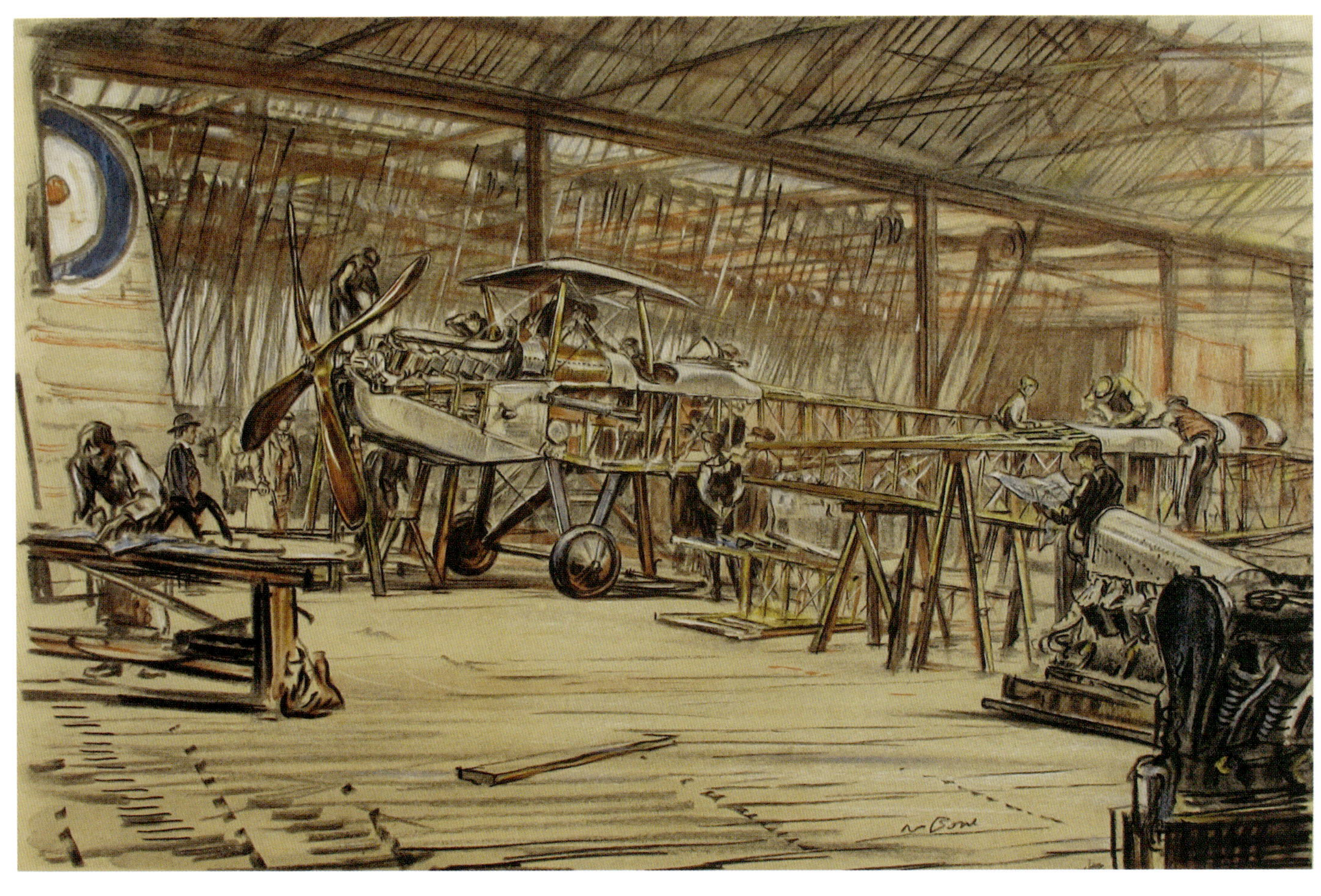

Muirhead Bone (1876-1953)

152 – Erecting Aeroplanes – an RE8, 2-seater reconnaissance plane being built at the Coventry Ordnance Works, February 1917,
Signed in the plate,
Coloured lithograph, 11 x 17 in. (28 x 43 cm)

153 – Mounting a Great Gun, Coventry, February 1917,
Signed in the plate,
Lithograph, 17 x 11 in. (43 x 28 cm)

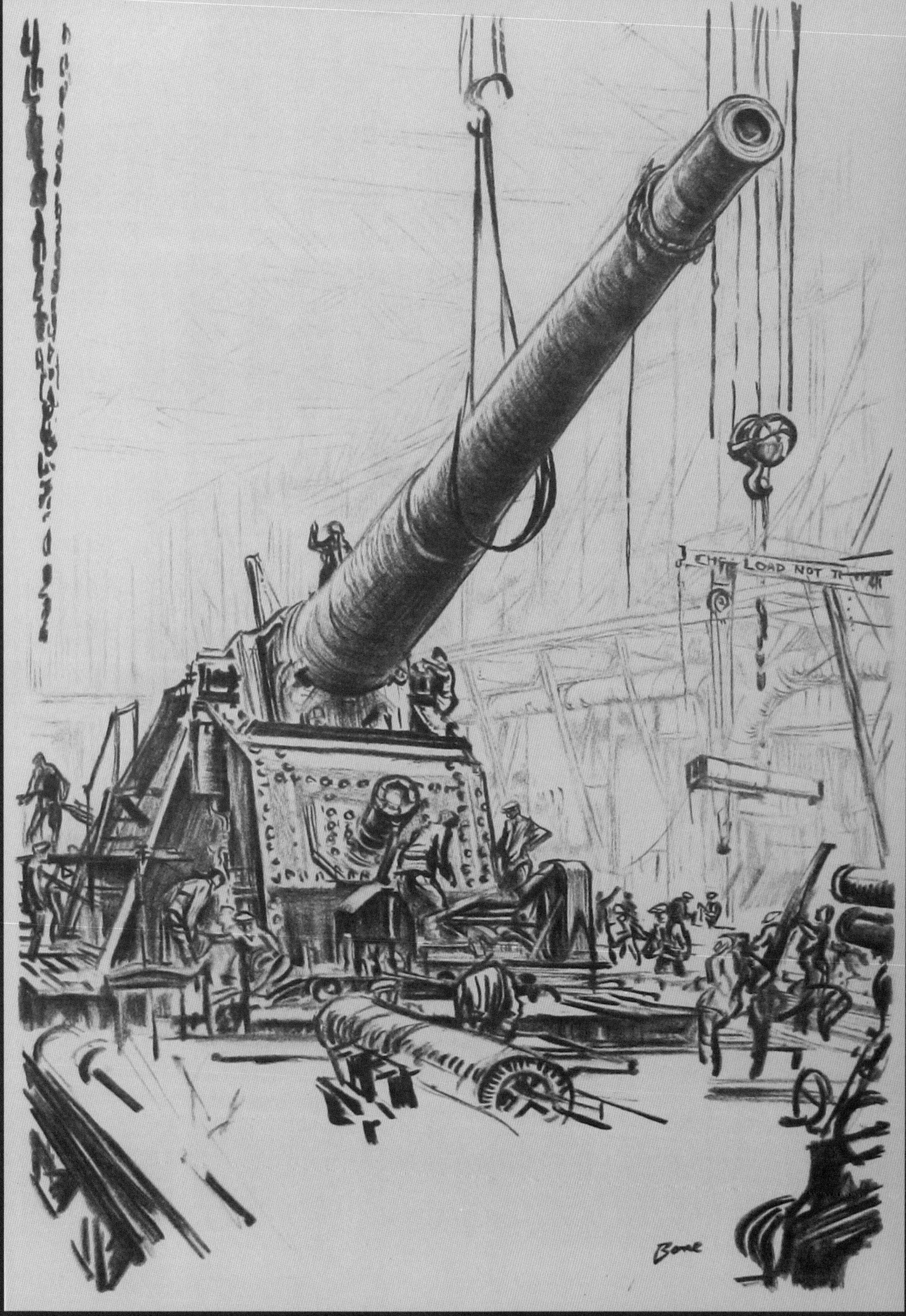
CHE LOAD NOT
Bone

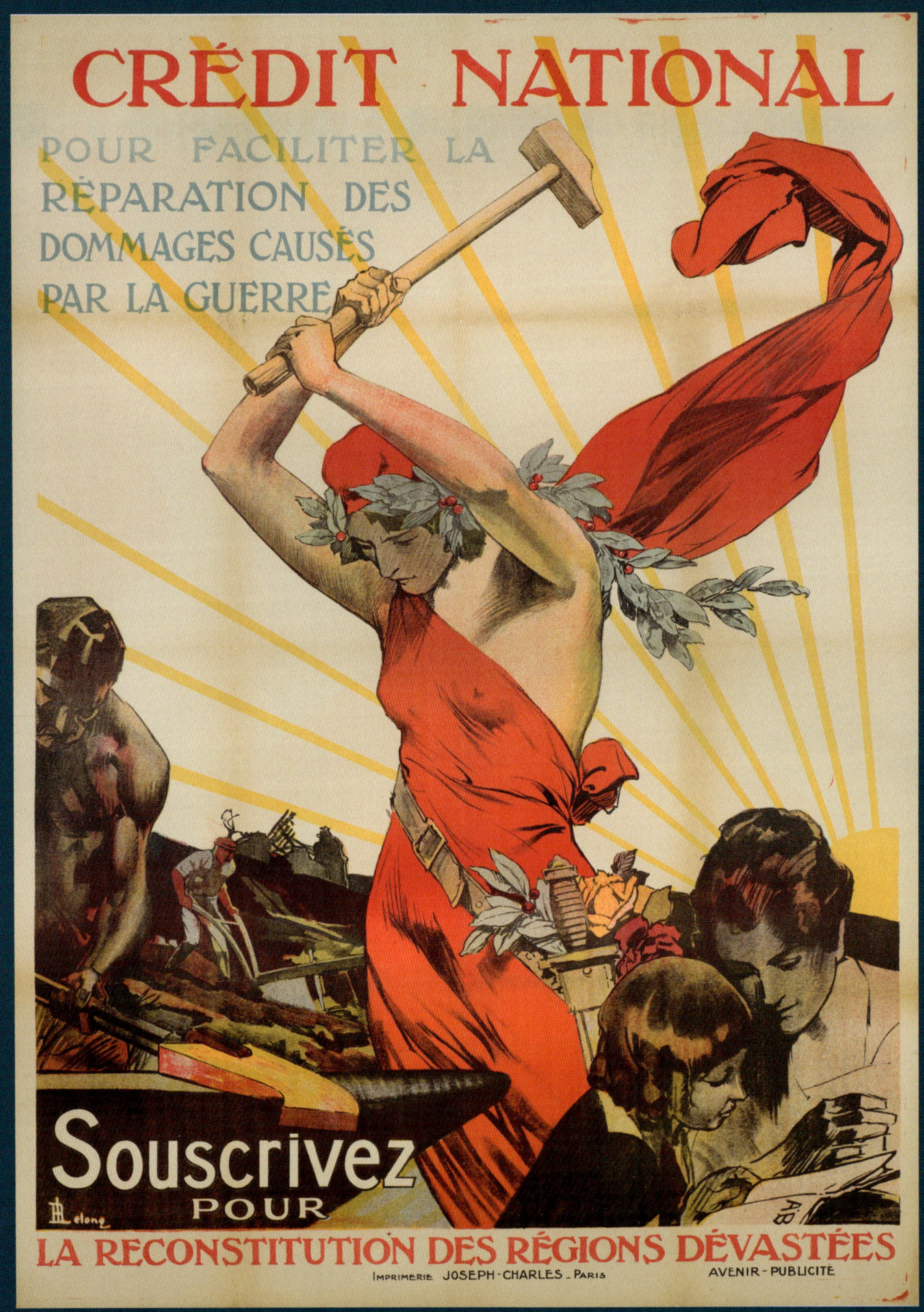

154 – René Lelong (1871-1933)

Crédit National – Souscrivez pour la reconstitution des régions dévastées, c.1920
Inscribed: "Pour facilitez la réparation des dommages causés par la guerre, souscrivez pour la reconstitution des régions dévastées."
Lithographic poster, 47 x 32 in. (119 x 81 cm), printed by Joseph Charles

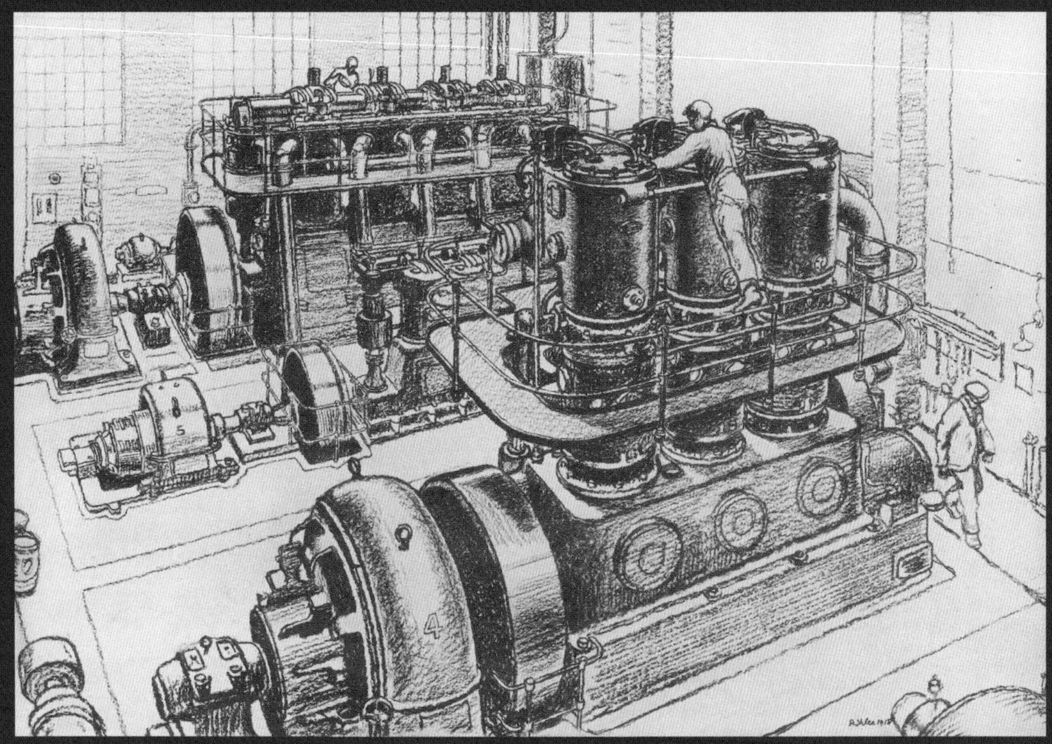

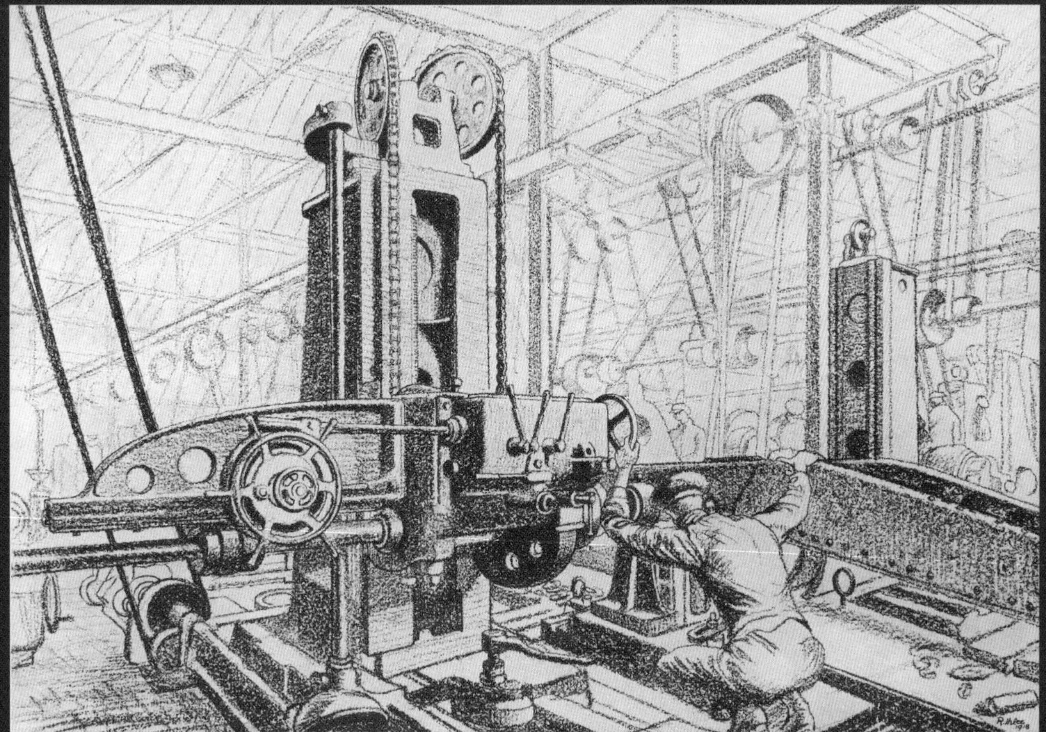

155 – Rudolph Ihlee (1883-1968)

Westwood Works in Peterborough in production during the First World War, 1918, signed in the plate,
Lithographic print, 10 x 13 in. (25 x 33 cm) each

These two lithographs were produced as part of a set of twelve by Rudolph Ihlee when he was working in the Westwood Works Drawing Office in Peterborough in 1918. During the war most of Westwood Works' own production was interrupted and in common with other engineering factories a large part of the workforce – which now included women – was turned over to helping the war effort. Goods produced at Westwood included cordite mixers, field ovens, diesel engines for lorries, tractors and tanks and the 6-inch Howitzer Field Gun.

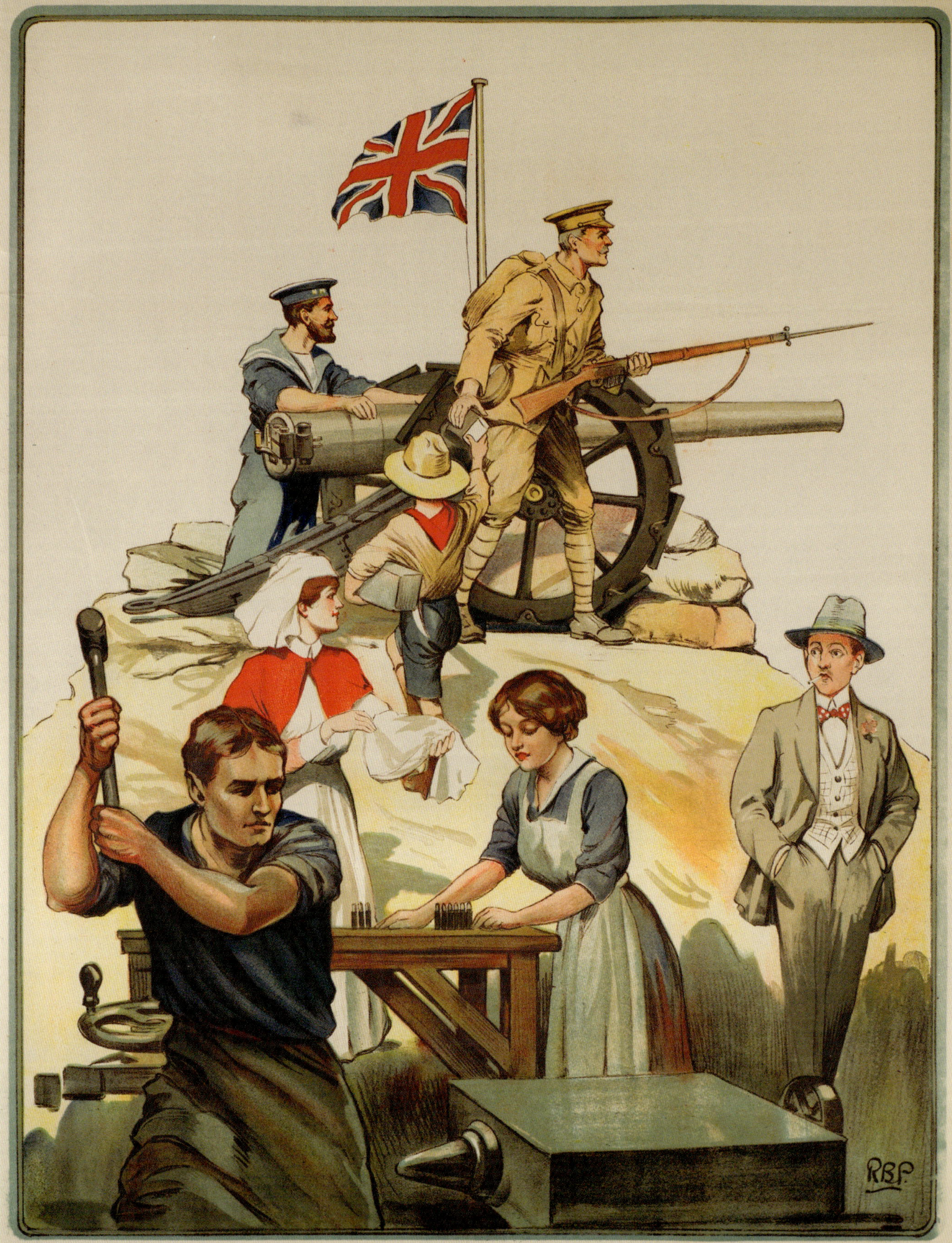
DESIGNED BY LT. GEN. SIR R.S.S. BADEN POWELL.
RBP
Are YOU in this?
PUBLISHED BY THE PARLIAMENTARY RECRUITING COMMITTEE, LONDON. POSTER NO. 112
PRINTED BY JOHNSON, RIDDLE & CO. LTD. LONDON S.E.

PACIFISTS & CONSCIENTIOUS OBJECTORS

"Against the vast majority of my countrymen, even at this moment, in the name of humanity and civilization, I protest against our share in the destruction of Germany. A month ago Europe was a peaceful comity of nations; if an Englishman killed a German, he was hanged. Now, if an Englishman kills a German, or if a German kills an Englishman, he is a patriot, who has deserved well of his country."

Bertrand Russell, in a letter to *The Nation*, August 15, 1914

"I had them placed in special rooms, nude, but with their full army kit on the floor for them to put on as soon as they were minded. There were no blankets or substitute for clothing left in the rooms, which were quite bare. Several of the naked men held out for several hours but they gradually accepted the inevitable. Forty of the conscientious objectors who passed through my hands are now quite willing soldiers."

Lieutenant Colonel Reginald Brook, Commandant, Military Detention Barracks, Wandsworth, London.
The Daily Express, July 4, 1916

156 – Robert Baden-Powell (1857-1941)

Are YOU in this?,
Original Parliamentary Recruiting Committee Poster No. 112, 30 x 20 in. (76 x 51 cm),
Printed by Johnson Riddle, 1915

Whilst this image is usually interpreted as a call for the unity of all classes in a common aim, the well-dressed civilian on the right strolling out of the picture may be interpreted as a Shirker – someone who profiteered from the war and avoided his duty.

Before the First World War there had never been compulsory military service in Britain. The first Military Service Bill was passed into law in January 1916 following the failure of recruitment schemes to gain sufficient volunteers in 1914 and 1915. From March 1916, military service was compulsory for all single men in England, Scotland and Wales aged 18 to 41, except those who were in jobs essential to the war effort, the sole support of dependents, medically unfit, or 'those who could show a conscientious objection'.

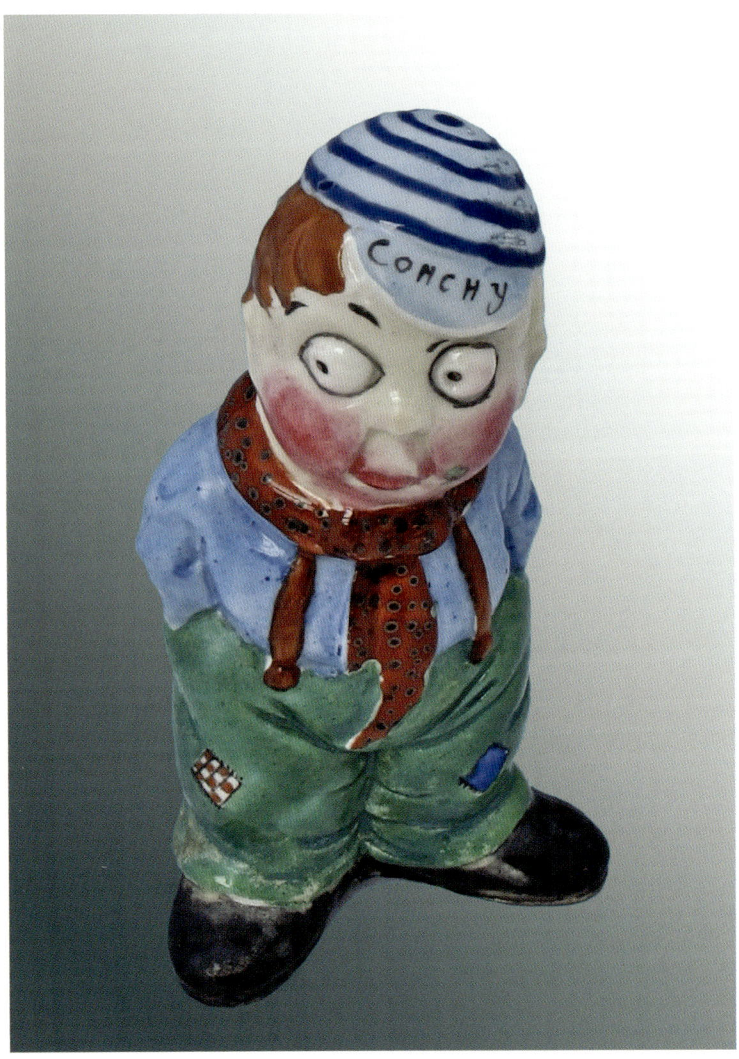

157 – CONCHY
Hand-painted Savoy china (Birks Grotesques),
A Chloe Preston "peek-a-boo" character,
Height: 4 ½ in. (11.5 cm)

There were approximately 16,000 British men on record as conscientious objectors (COs) to armed service during the First World War. This figure does not include men who may have had anti-war sentiments but were either unfit, in reserved occupations, or had joined the Forces anyway. Many of the men who fought did so because of the intense social, political and religious pressure and the terror of being accused of cowardice if they did not.

158 – English School

Which? Have you a reason, or only an excuse, for not enlisting now!,
Lithographic poster, 30 x 19 ¼ in. (76 x 49 cm),
Parliamentary Recruiting Committee poster, printed by the Abbey Press

Thousands fought and died unquestioningly because they felt that they had no choice - propaganda filled every available space, and the patriotic messages of posters were reinforced from the pulpit, by politicians and in newspapers.

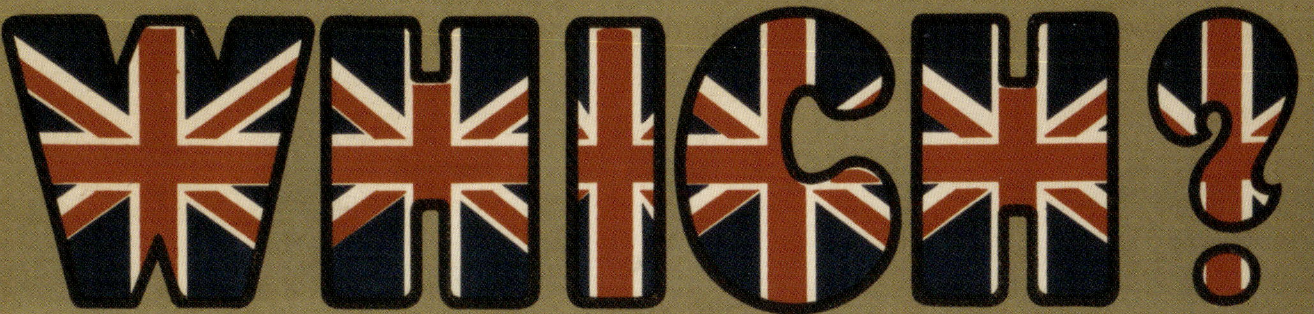

HAVE YOU A
REASON=

OR ONLY AN
EXCUSE~

FOR NOT ENLISTING

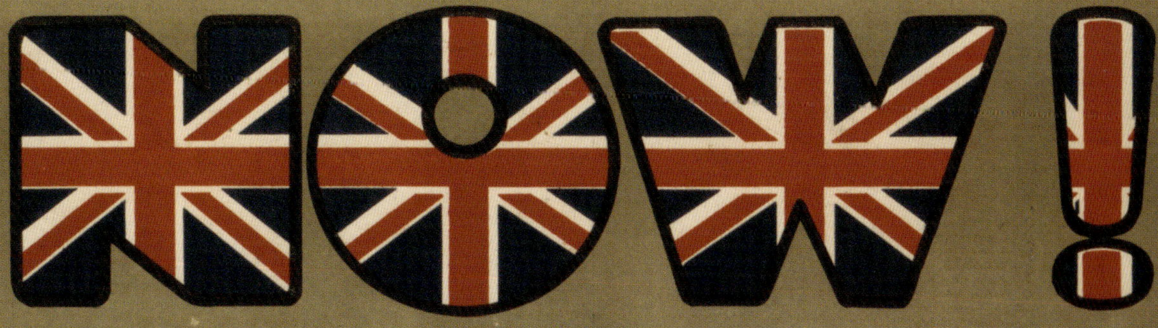

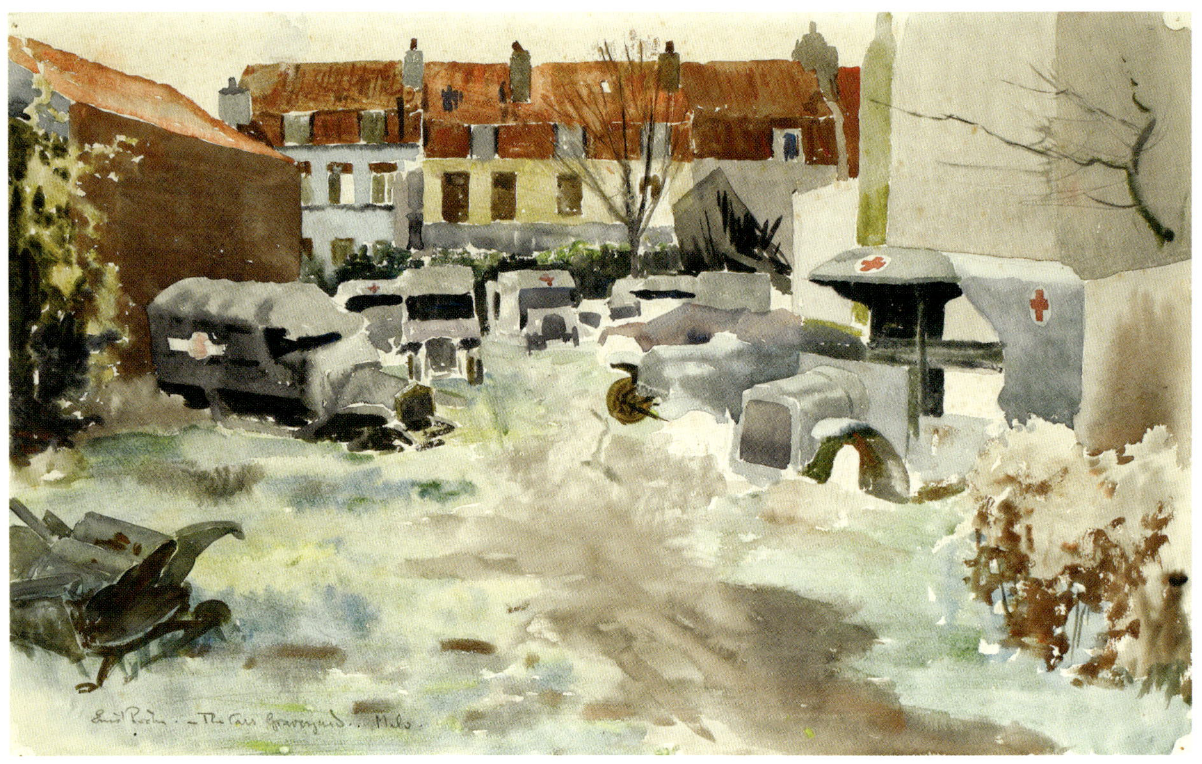

159 – Ernest Procter (1886–1935)

The Cars Graveyard, Malo, c.1919,
Signed, inscribed with title,
Gouache on paper, 12 ¼ x 19 in. (31 x 48.2 cm)

Many conscientious objectors, such as Ernest Procter, served in the Medical Corps, rather than as soldiers. Between 1916-17 Procter worked as an ambulance driver for the Friends' Ambulance Unit (FAU) in Dunkirk, a voluntary organisation founded by individual members of the British Religious Society of Friends (Quakers), in line with their Peace Testimony. The FAU operated from 1914-19 and was chiefly staffed by registered conscientious objectors such as Procter. Altogether it sent more than a thousand men to France and Belgium, where they worked on ambulance convoys and ambulance trains with the French and British armies. Procter later served on the Western Front with two units of the Section Sanitaire Anglaise, at Nieuport Bains and at Verdun. He was appointed Official War Artist for the Ministry of Information from 1918-19.

Rudolph Sauter (1895–1977)

160 – *Low Tide, May 21, 1916* , dated on a label to the reverse,
Pastel on Oakey's Warranted Glass Paper, 6 x 10 in. (15.4 x 25.4 cm),

161 – *Storm Cloud, near Dartmoor, May 1916*
Pastel on Oakey's Warranted Glass Paper, 5 x 6 in. (12.5 x 15. 2 cm)
The paper for these works might have been chosen for its interaction with the medium of pastel or simply because of paper shortages during the war.

From 1918-19 Sauter was interned at Alexandra Palace (used as an internment camp for German and Austrian civilians during the First World War). His father Georg (who had already been interned in Wakefield Prison in 1916) was German by birth. The series of pastels created near Dartmoor in the Spring of 1916, when Sauter was staying with his uncle, the writer John Galsworthy, are far removed from the drama of the Western Front. Entries in Galsworthy's wartime diaries record Sauter as a regular companion. Sauter's internment was to have a significant bearing on Galsworthy's eventual disenchantment with the war.

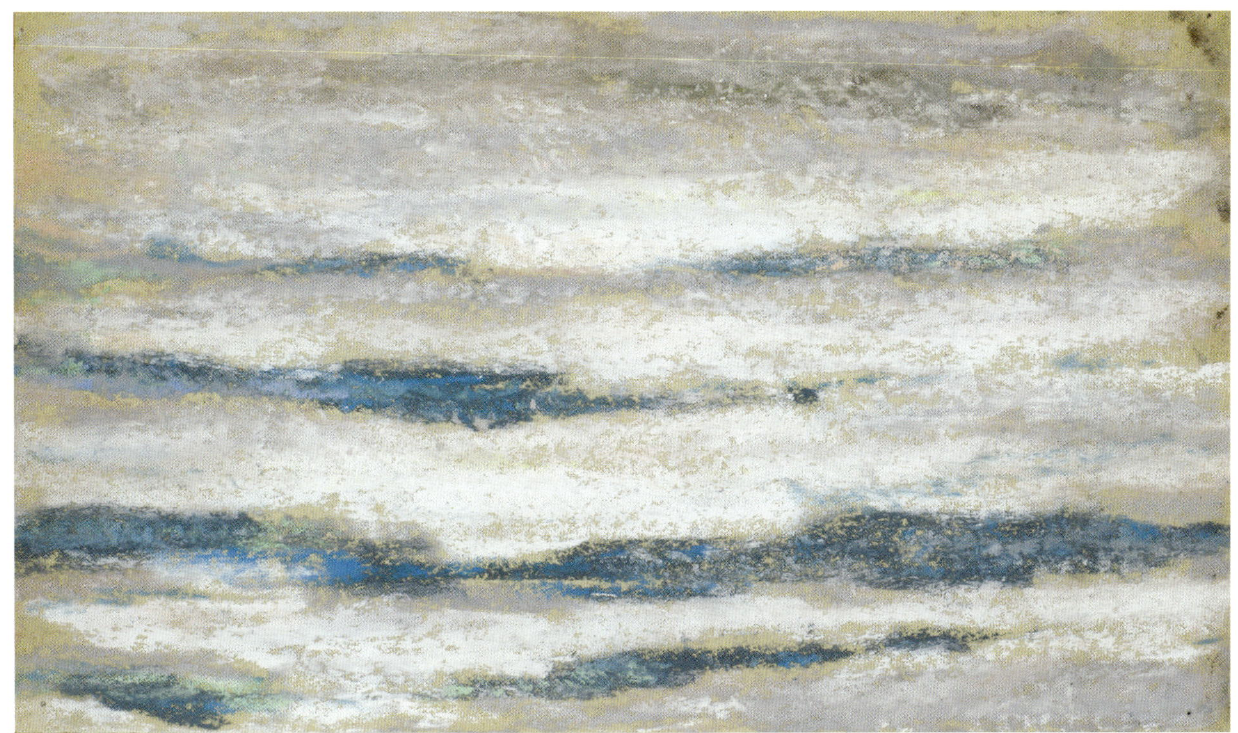

160

161

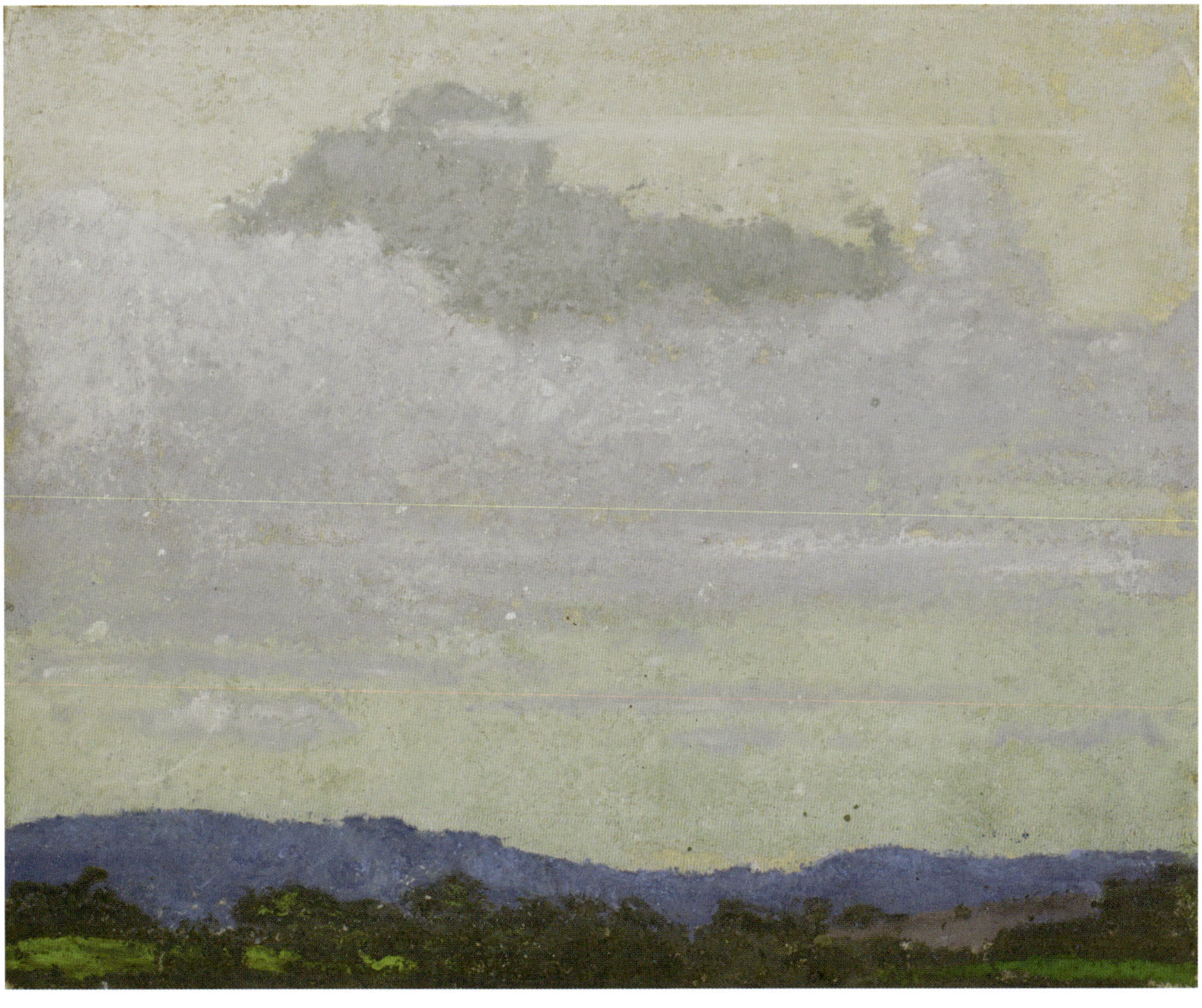

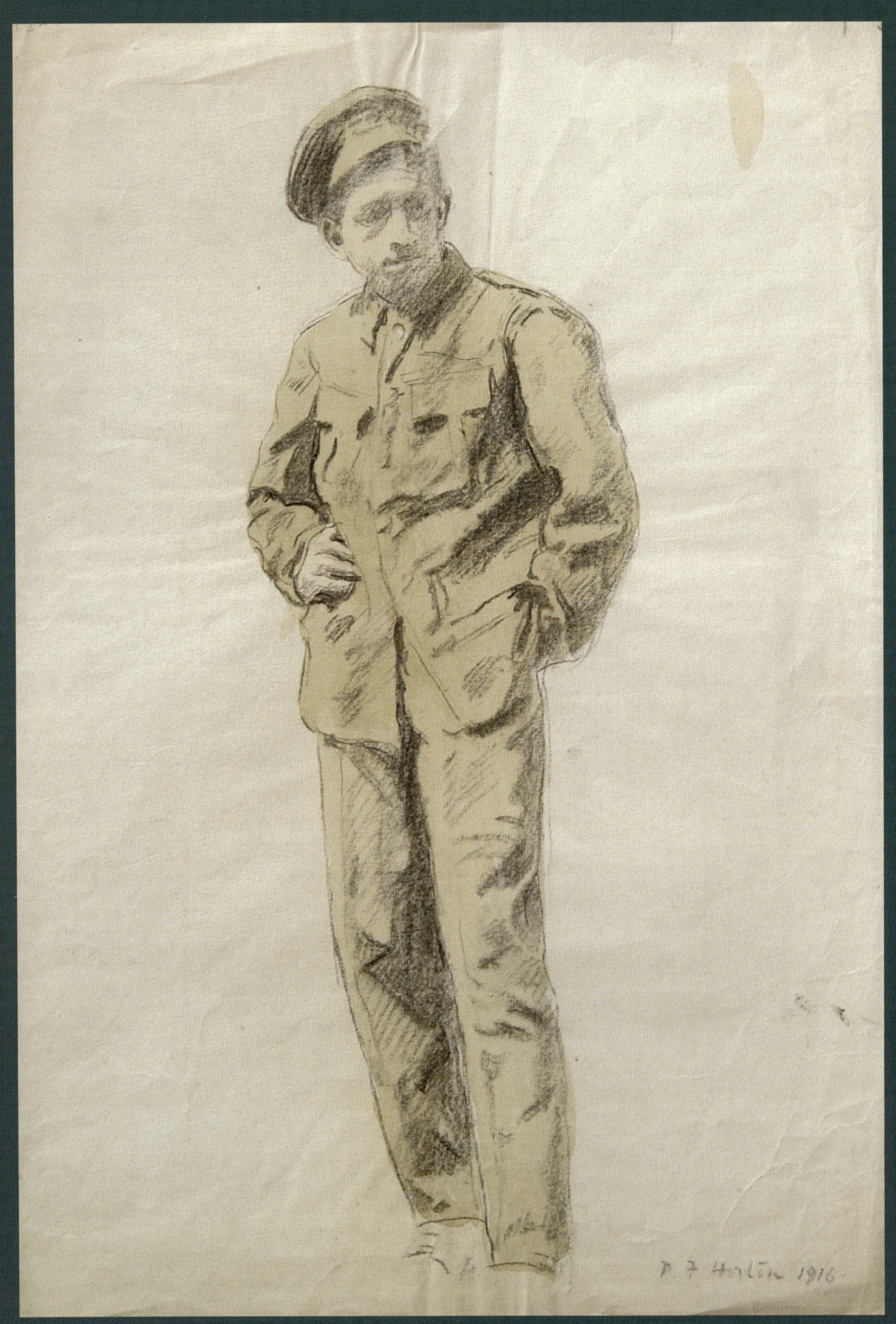

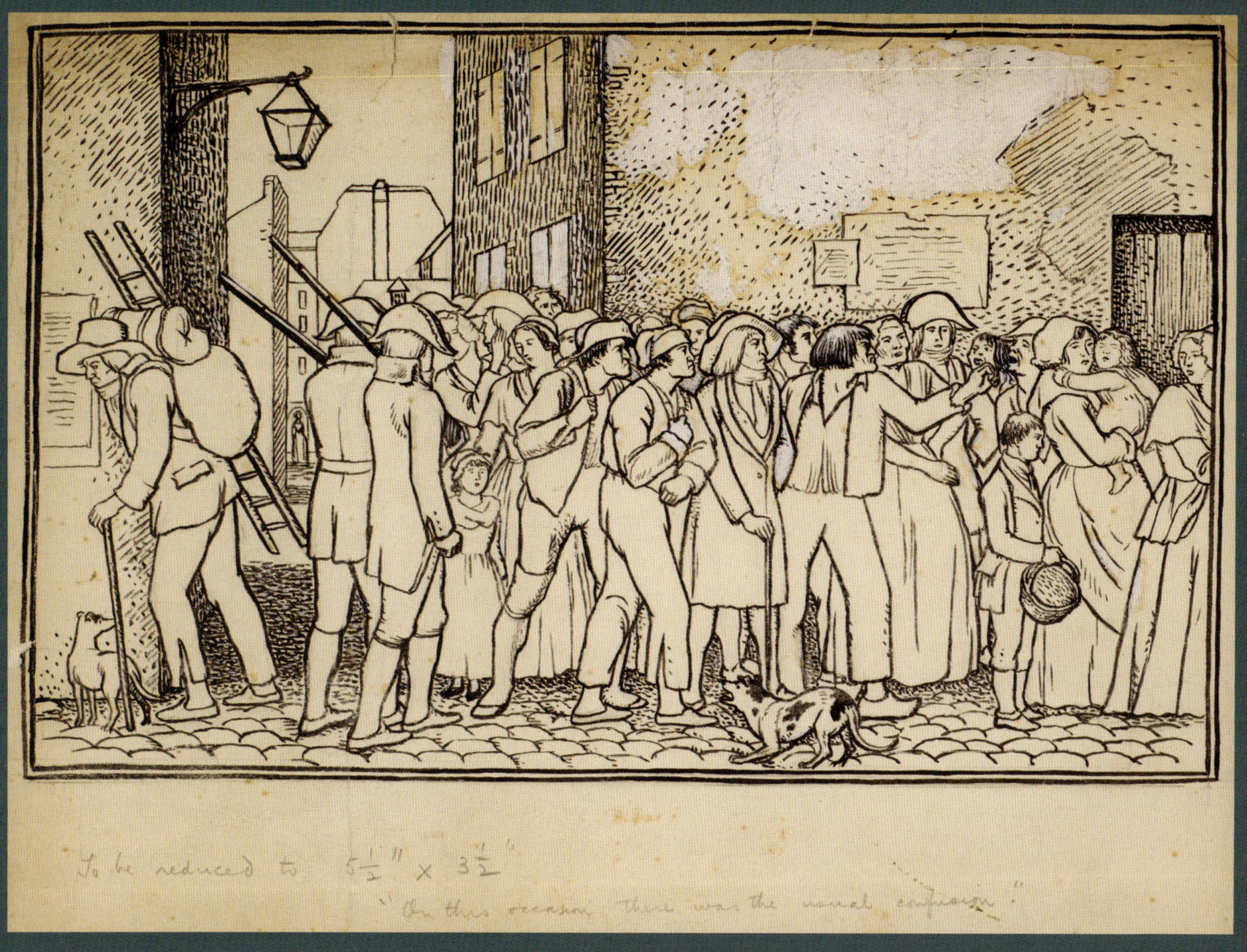

Percy Horton (1897-1970)

163 – *'On this occasion there was the usual confusion'* 1925, in *Labour Weekly*,
Inscribed with title and notes to the printer,
Pen & ink with white highlights on paper, 9 ½ x 12 ½ in. (24.1 x 31.8 cm),
Literature: reproduced in *Labour Weekly*, March 25, 1925

162 – *Portrait of a Private*, 1916, signed and dated,
Watercolour over charcoal on paper, 10 x 14 ¾ in. (25.5 x 37.5 cm)

Percy Horton's training as an artist was interrupted by two years' imprisonment as a conscientious objector during the First World War. Until the end of July 1916 he was under arrest at the depot of his regiment – the Royal Fusiliers 29th Division – at Chichester. On August 1 he arrived in Edinburgh, where he was committed to Calton Jail, initially for thirteen weeks' solitary confinement. The First World War had had a profound effect on the Horton family: Percy's brother Harry was gassed, wounded and shell-shocked in the course of his service in Italy and France with the West Kent Regiment. Horton opposed the First World War as a capitalists' war using the working classes as cannon-fodder. Indeed during the Second World War, his readiness to don uniform demonstrates that armed struggle did not offend him *per se*. At the end of 1917, writing to his father from Edinburgh Royal Infirmary, he observed: 'my portraits are very popular. Everyone wants to have one and they pose so patiently.' Horton seems to have been deprived of paper and pencil on his arrival in Edinburgh, and it seems likely that this sketch was made while the Regiment was still at Chichester.

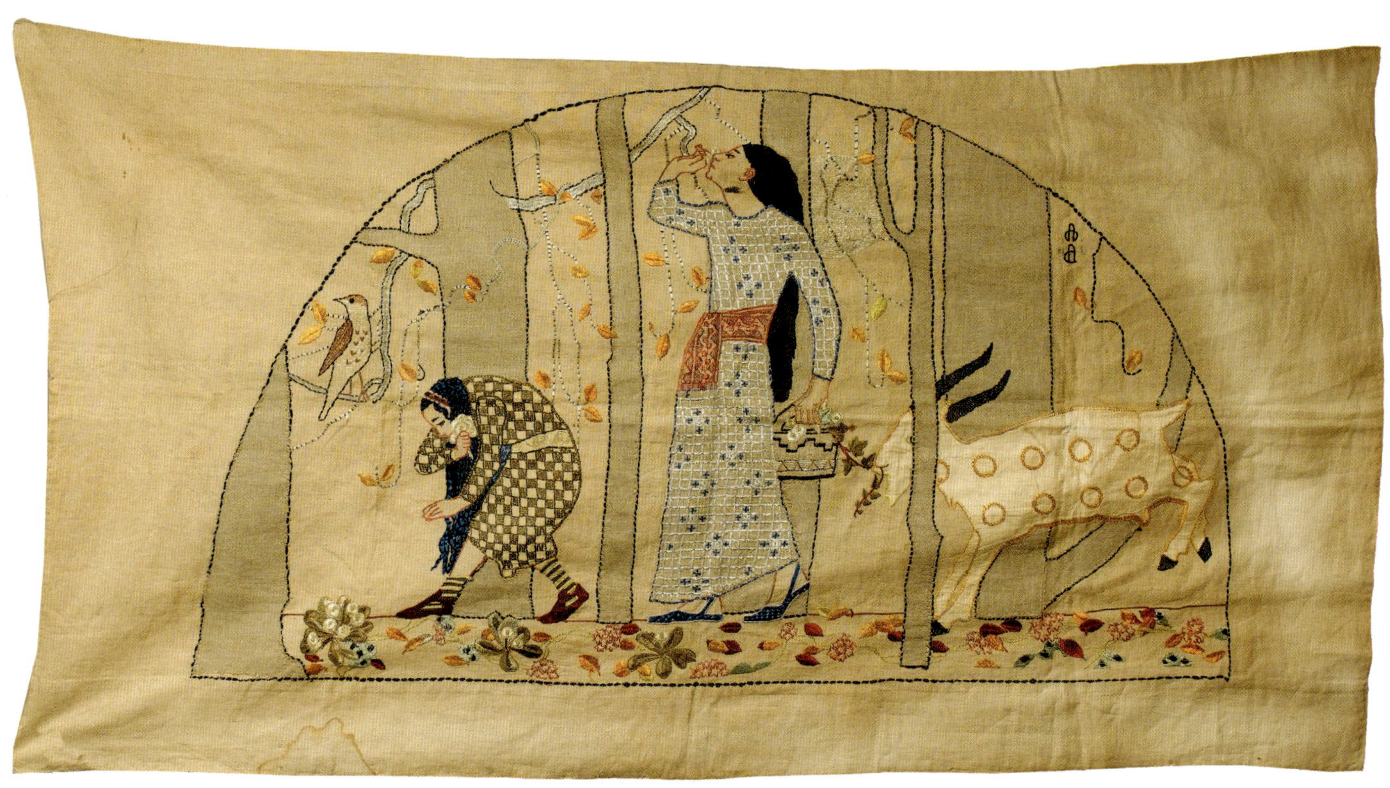

164 – Constance and Maxwell Armfield (1876-1941) (1881-1972)

Damsels in a Wood, 1916,
Signed with each artist's monogram between the date '1916'
Embroidered lunette, silk and woollen threads on rectangular unbleached linen ground, 37 x 76 in. (94 x 193 cm)

Constance and Maxwell Armfield were Quakers. In 1915, on account of their pacifist beliefs, they abandoned England to spend seven years in America. In the autumn of 1916, the year of this panel, the *International Studio* magazine featured a three-page article on the embroidered work the Armfields had exhibited with the National Society of Craftsmen. It is likely that this panel featured in this 1916 exhibition.

165 – Frank Brangwyn (1867–1956)

Peace (Love Amid Ruins) (P1020), 1920, signed in pencil,
Lithograph (trial proof), printed in sepia ink, 10 ½ x 9 in. (26.7 x 22.9 cm),
Literature: Marechal, *Collectie Frank Brangwyn*, 1987, p.189; Libby Horner, *Brangwyn at WAR!*, (Horner and Goldmark, 2014) p.144

The editioned version of this lithograph was printed in black or sepia. This image, showing a woodcutter offering a flower to a baby whilst the mother looks on, with a war torn landscape behind, was intended 'to promote the resurgence of Belgium after the war', (Marechal, *Collectie Frank Brangwyn*, 1987, p.189).

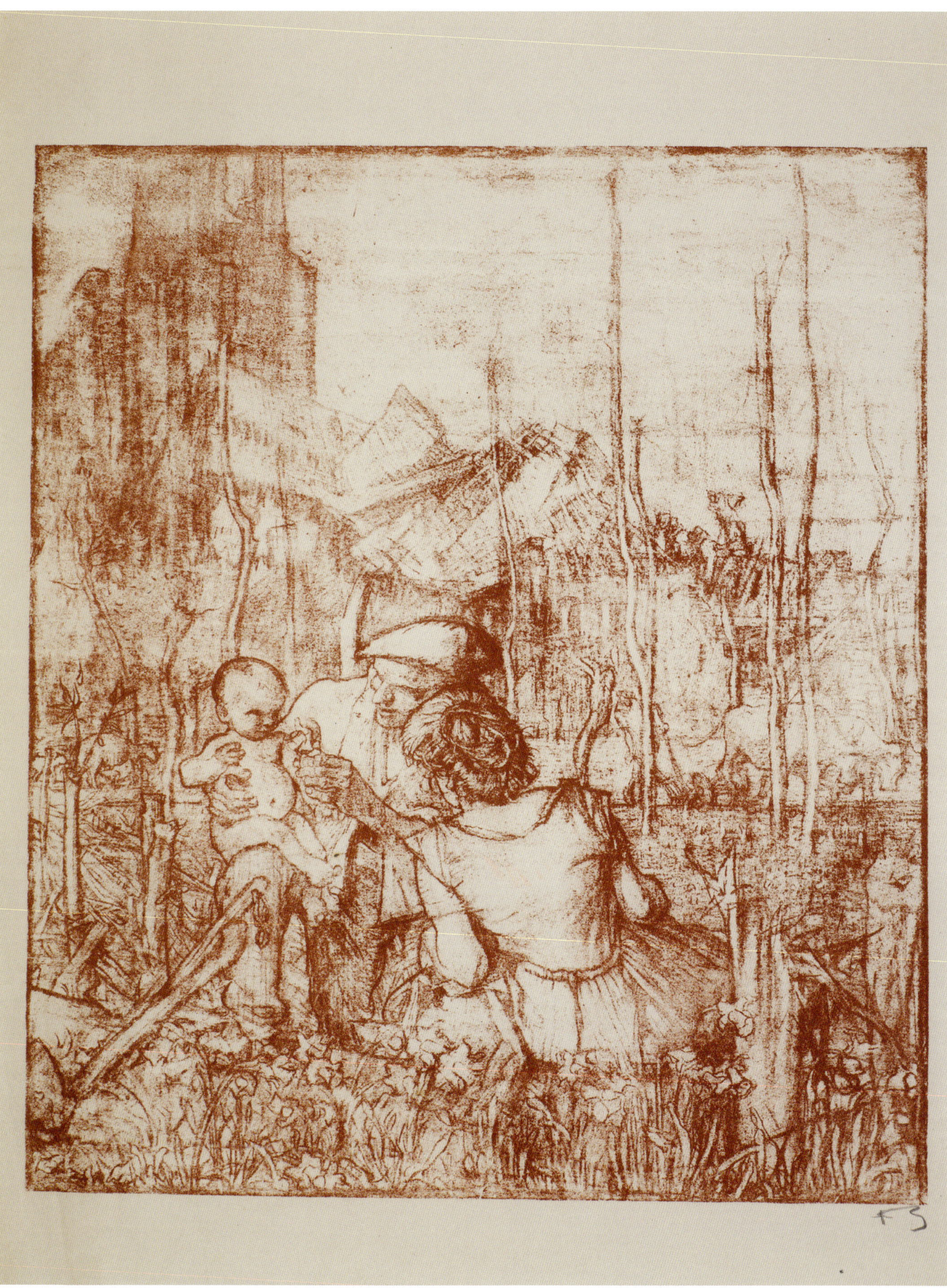

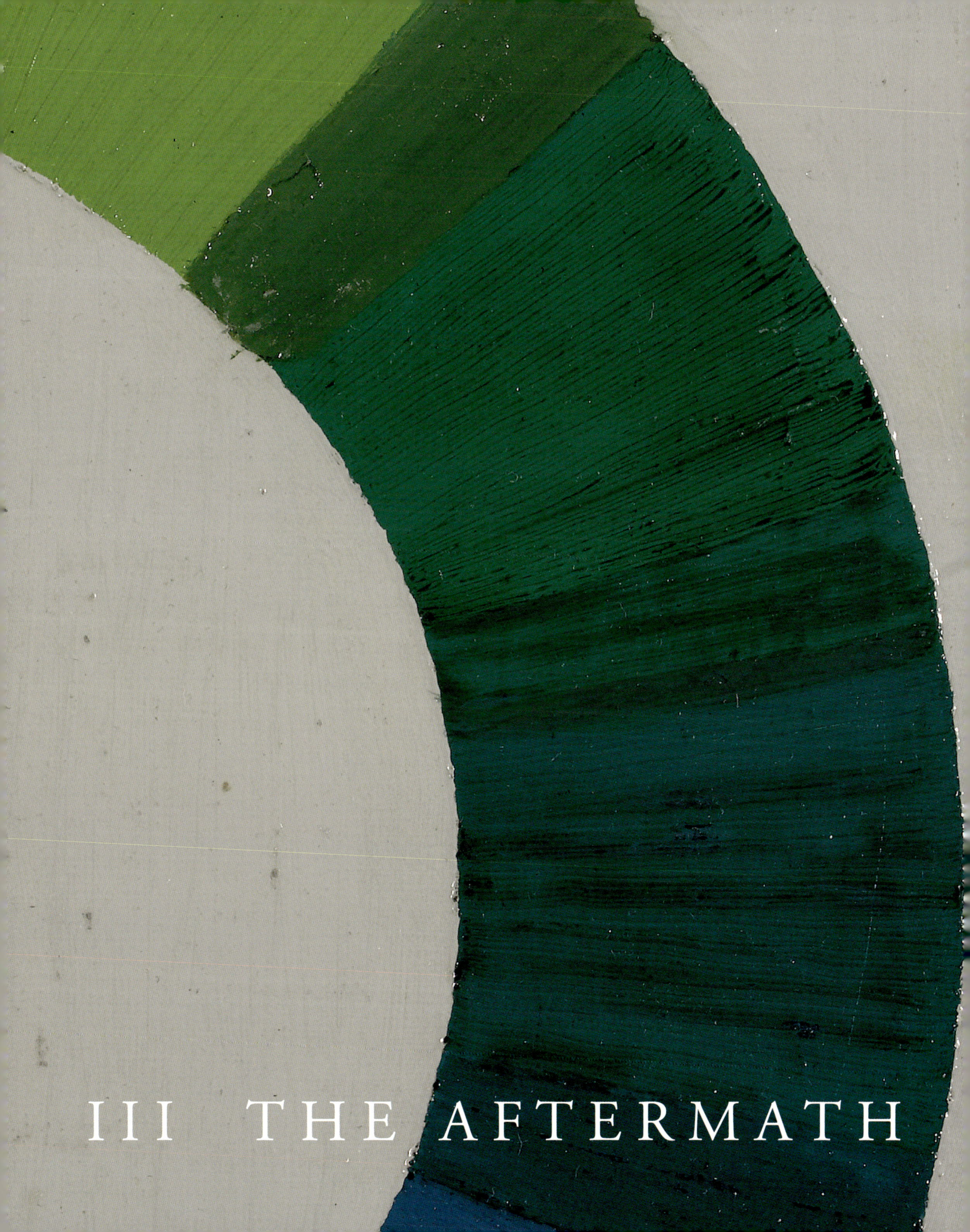
III   THE AFTERMATH

S.—1320 b.   (Established—May, 1900.)
              (Revised—January, 1917.)   Copy

62   **NAVAL SIGNAL.**

| P.O. of Watch— |
| Read by— |
| Reported by— |
| Passed by— |
| Logged by— |
| System— W/T. |
| Date— 11-11-18 |
| Time— 10.56 AM |

FROM— Navy Office (Southend)

To— General

Message received from Admiralty (fullstop) Armistice signed (fullstop) Hostilities are to be suspended forthwith (fullstop) All anti-submarine defensive measures in force to ensure security of men of War at sea or in harbour are to remain in force until further orders. Submarines on the surface are not to be attacked unless their hostile intentions are obvious.

(1014)

M. 1704/00.
Sta. 6/14.
Sta. 596/16.

(6222) 12000/D912 100m pads 12/17ss G & S 109 156

166 – Naval Signal Announcing the Armistice

Wilfrid J. Jenkins - H.M.S. Mersey,
Handwritten Signal, dated 11.11.18., sent at 10.56 a.m. from Navy Office (Southend) to General System W/T (Wireless Transmission), containing a message from The Admiralty concerning the Armistice.

"At eleven o'clock this morning came to an end the cruellest and most terrible war that has ever scourged mankind. I hope we may say that thus, this fateful morning, came to an end all wars."

David Lloyd George, House of Commons, November 11, 1918

"When Marshal Foch heard of the signing of the peace treaty of Versailles he remarked with singular accuracy: 'This is not peace. It is an armistice for twenty years.'"

Winston Churchill, *The Second World War, Vol. 1: The Gathering Storm*, Penguin Classics 2005 edition, p.6

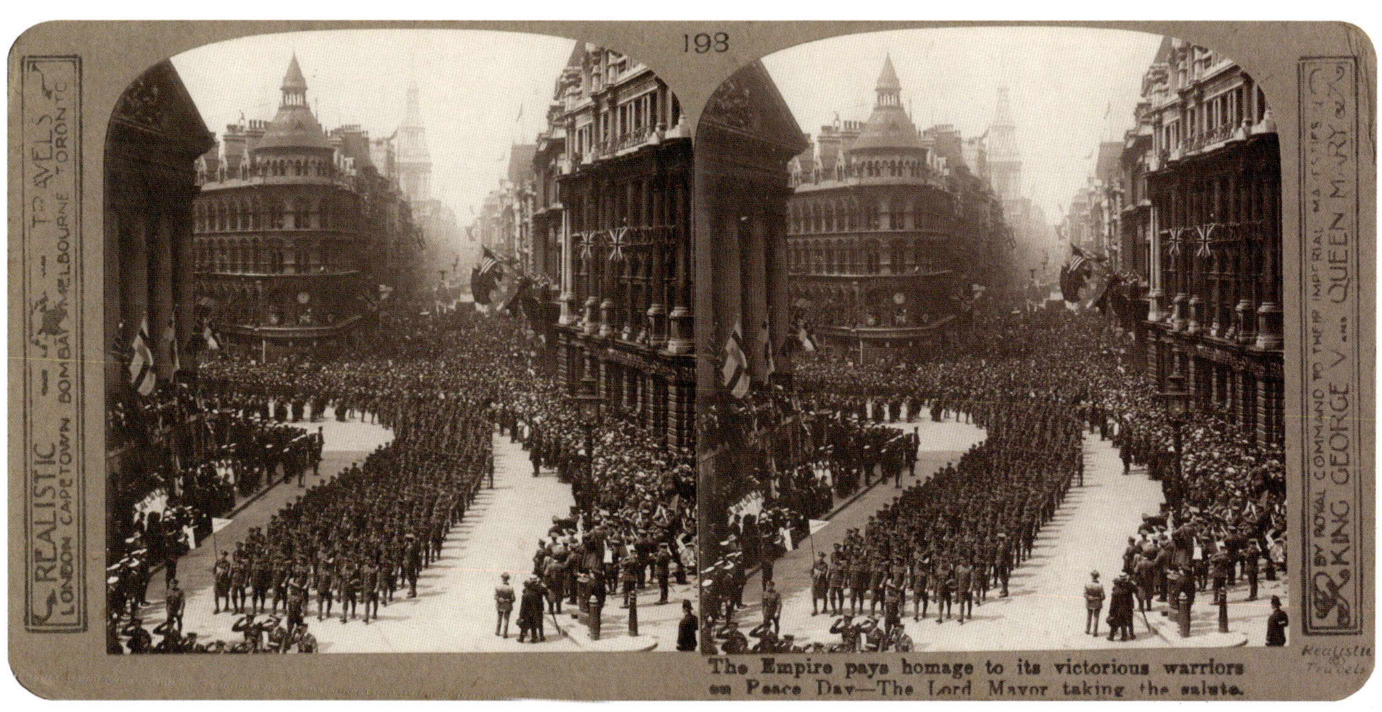

167 – Stereoscopic print: *The Empire pays homage to its victorious warriors on Peace Day – The Lord Mayor taking the salute.* 3 ½ x 7 in. (9 x 18 cm), published by Realistic Travels.

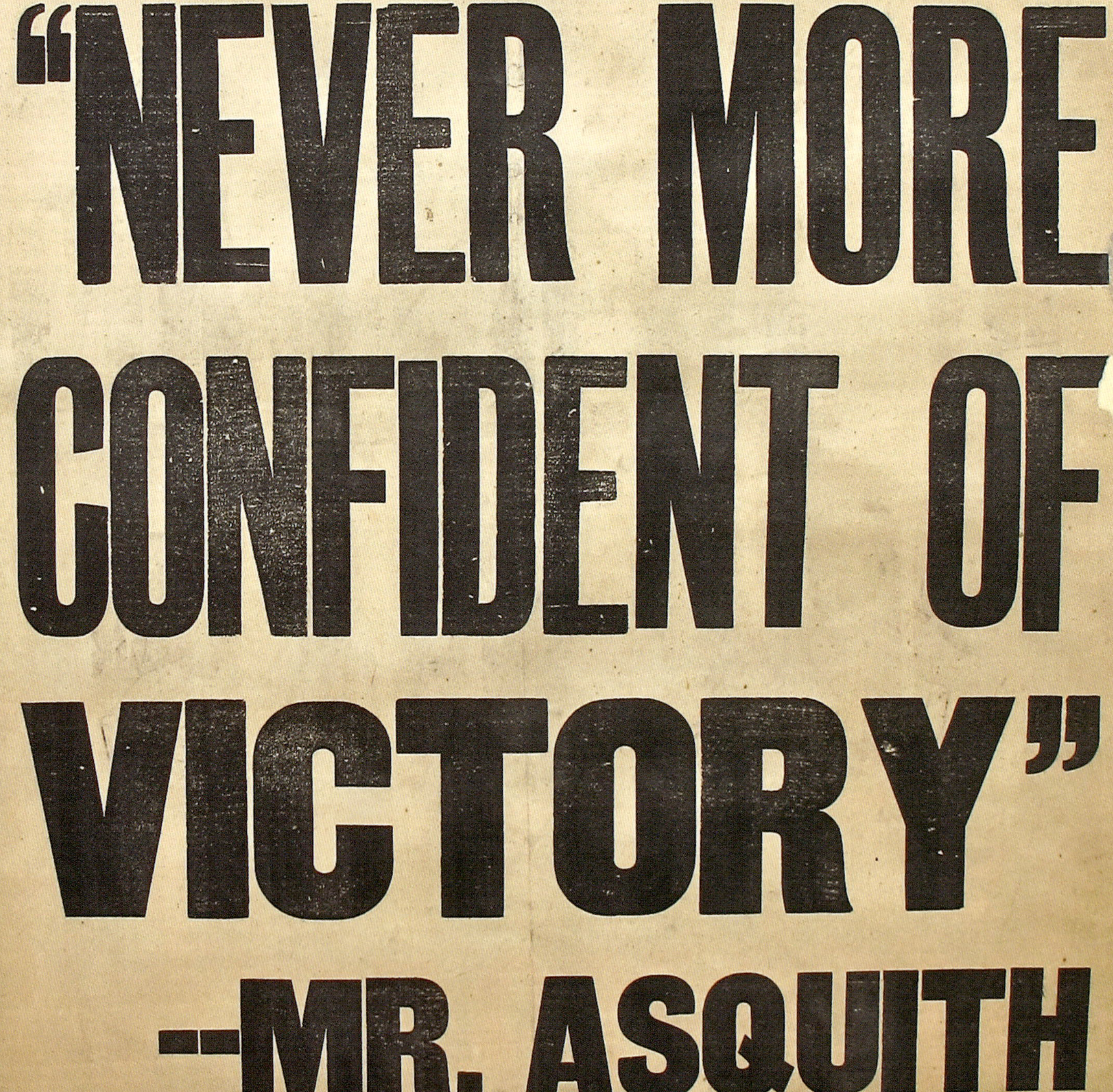

DAILY
Chronicle
½D.
½D.
THURSDAY, JULY 29.
"NEVER MORE
CONFIDENT OF
VICTORY"
--MR. ASQUITH

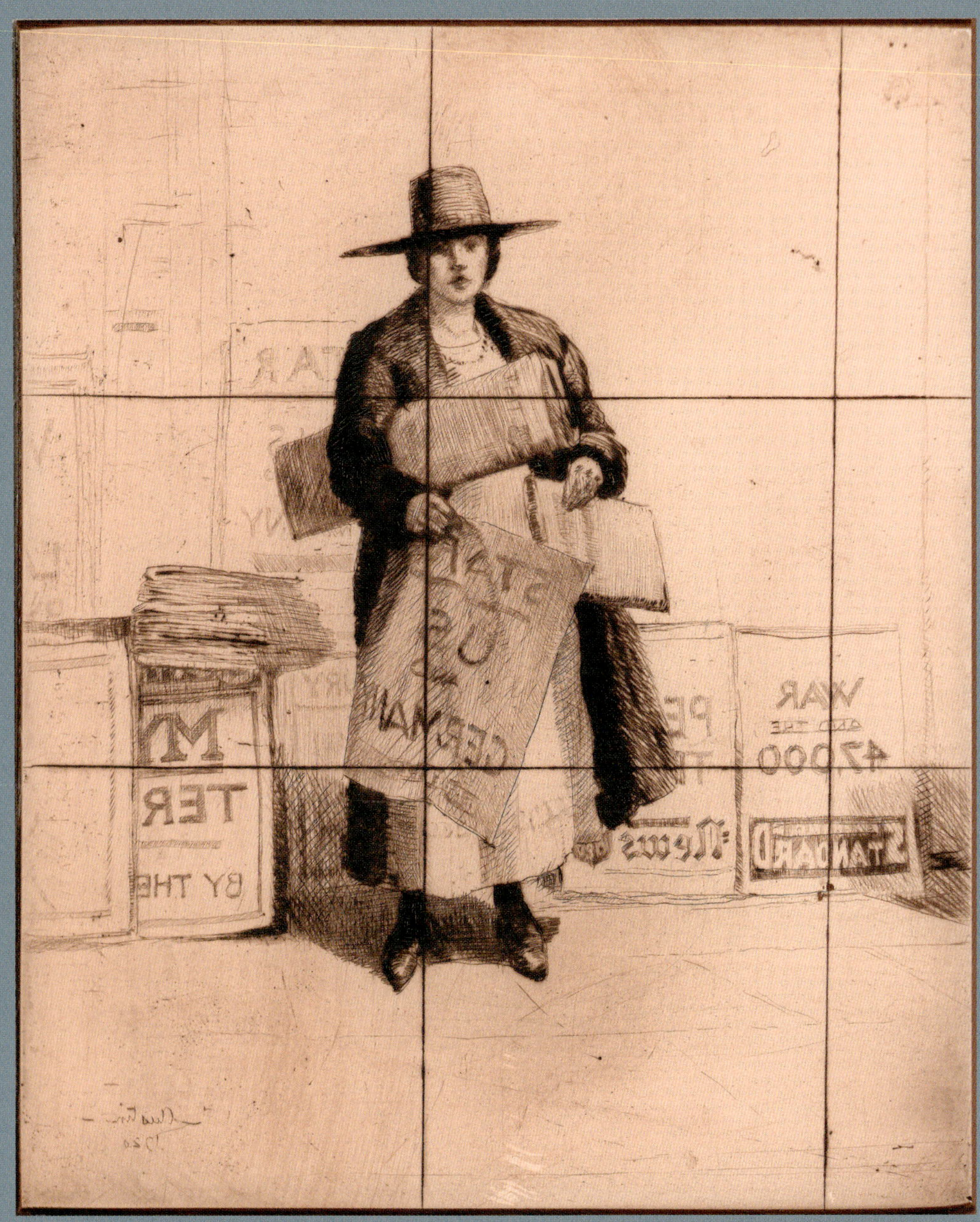

169 – Robert Austin (1895-1973)
Woman selling newspapers announcing Peace Terms, c.1918,
Original copper plate, 5 ¾ x 4 ¾ in. (14.5 x 12 cm)

This picture is likely to date to October 1918 when (on October 5) Germany asked America to negotiate terms. As a precondition for negotiations President Wilson demanded the retreat of Germany from all occupied territories, the cessation of submarine activities and the Kaiser's abdication. Although the Armistice was declared just over one month later on November 11, 1918, negotiations on the terms of the Peace were lengthy and the Armistice was only finally ratified on January 10,1920.

168 – "NEVER MORE CONFIDENT OF VICTORY" – MR. ASQUITH

Original newstand poster from *The Daily Chronicle* dated Thursday, July 29, 1915, 29 ½ x 21 in. (75 x 53.5 cm)

'Over by Christmas' has become a phrase synonymous with the war and the irony of its unintentional longevity. Inspite of the worsening entrenchment (by 1915 there was little hope of a speedy end to hostilities) victory was claimed to be in sight throughout the conflict.

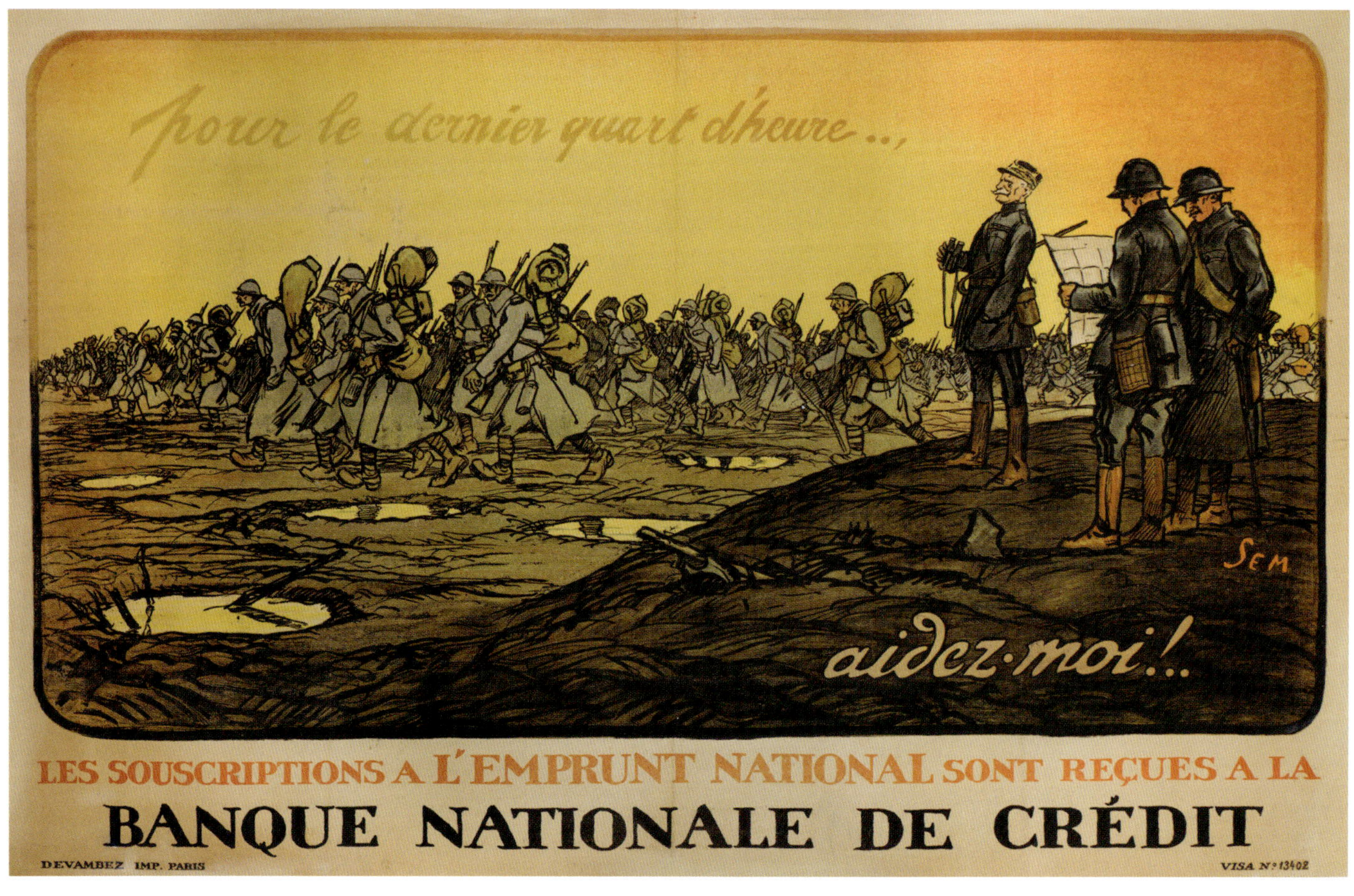

170 – Georges Goursat (1863-1934)

Pour le dernier quart d'heure...aidez-moi! les souscriptions à l'Emprunte National sont reçues à la Banque Nationale de Crédit,
Signed in the plate,
Colour lithographic poster, 31 x 47 ¼ in. (79 x 120 cm)

Maréchal Foch appears overseeing his troops as they march across the battlefield. Foch was appointed Commander in Chief of the Allied armies in 1918. Georges Goursat, known as Sem, was a renowned French caricaturist during the *Belle Epoque*. Aged 51 at the start of the war and therefore too old to fight, Goursat worked as a war correspondent for *Le Journal*. In 1916 and 1918 he published two albums of *Croquis de Guerre* (War sketches) as well as designing posters for war bonds.

171 – Lucien Jonas (1880-1947)
Crédit Commercial de France Souscrivez Pour La Victoire , c.1918,
Lithographic poster, 47 x 31 ¾ in. (119.3 x 80.6 cm,
Printed by Chachoin. Imprimerie, Paris

War loan posters were almost certainly the largest category of posters produced between 1914 and 1919. They appealed to civilians' desire to aid the war effort rather than to any monetary value to be gained and were produced by all major countries and usually issued in series. Subscribers were often given a copy of the actual poster, hence the large number that survive compared to other wartime posters. In France they were known as *Emprunt National*, in America as *Liberty Bonds*, in Canada as *Victory Loans*, and in Britain as *War Loans*.

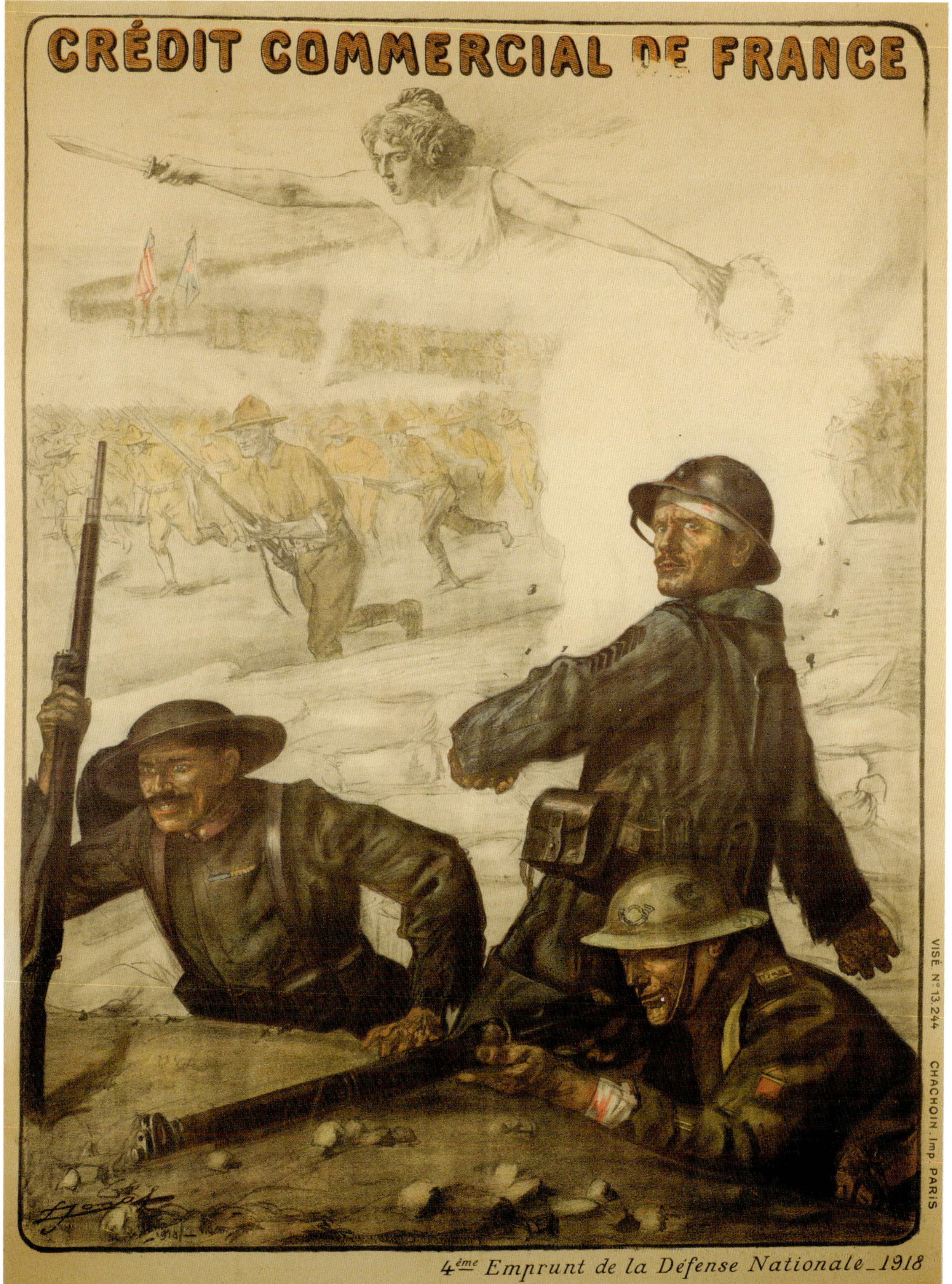

CRÉDIT COMMERCIAL DE FRANCE
VISÉ N° 13.244
CHACHOIN. Imp. PARIS
4ème Emprunt de la Défense Nationale _ 1918
SOUSCRIVEZ POUR LA VICTOIRE
et POUR LE TRIOMPHE DE LA LIBERTÉ

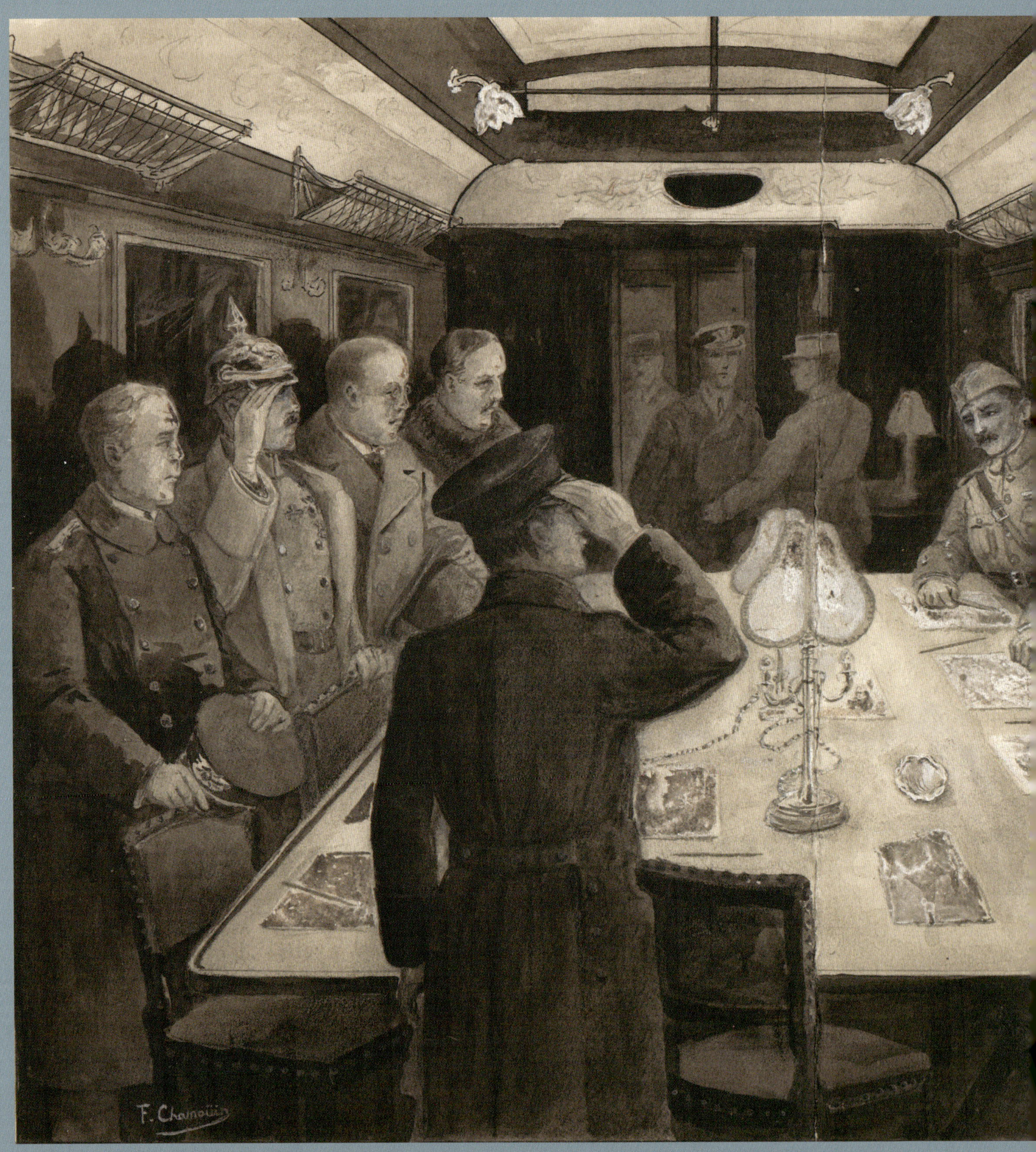

F. Chanoux

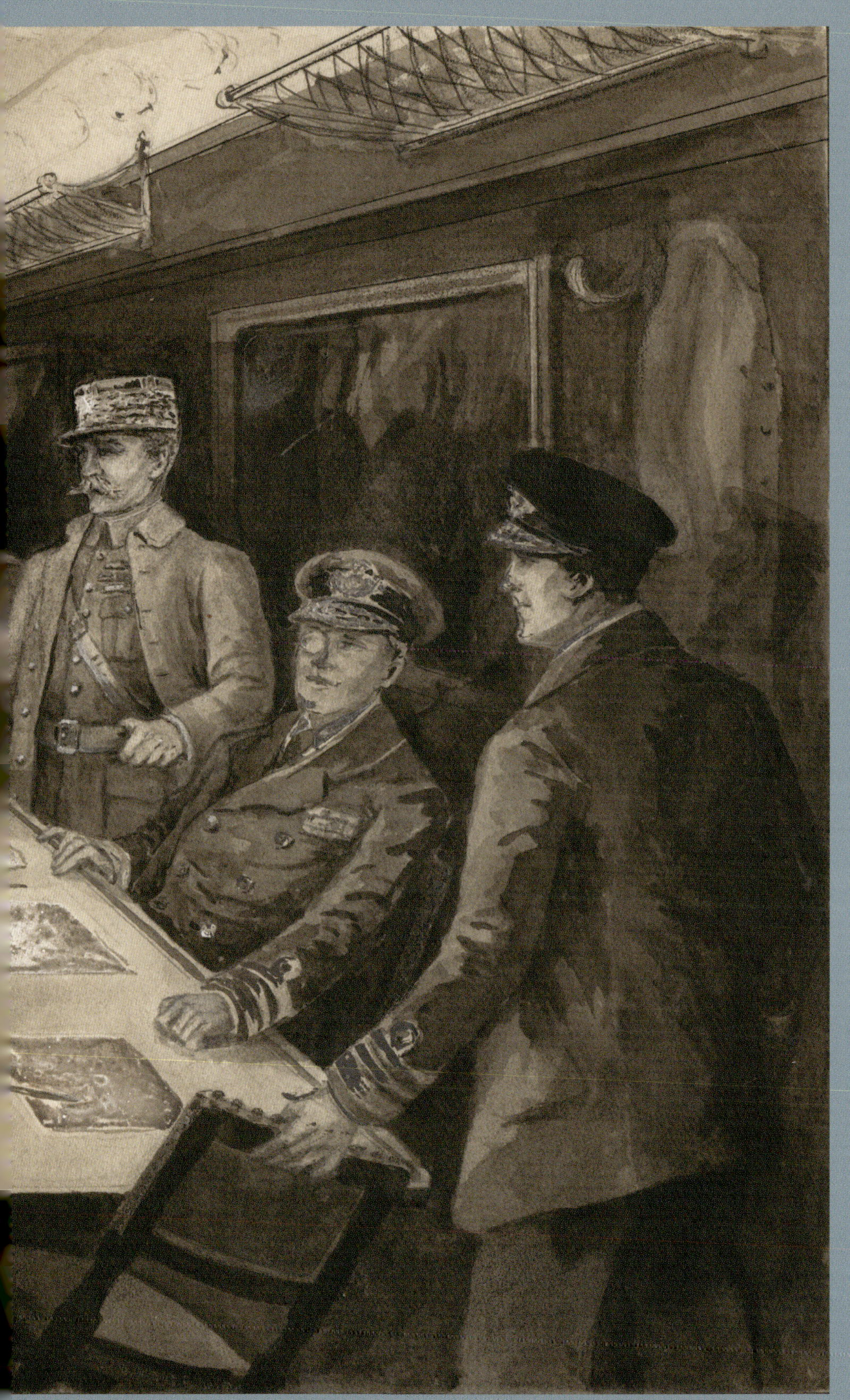

172 – F. Chamouin

The Signing of the Armistice in the carriage of
Maréchal Foch's private train, CIWL #2419
(Compiègne Wagon),
Pencil, ink and watercolour on paper,
8 ½ x 13 ¼ in. (22 x 33.7 cm)

F. Chamouin was an illustrator and as with
many of his designs this watercolour was
reproduced as a post-card.

The signing of The Armistice took place in
Ferdinand Foch's railway carriage in the Forest
of Compiègne, about 60 kilometres north of
Paris. For the Allies, the personnel involved
were entirely military: Marshal Ferdinand
Foch (the Allied Supreme Commander),
First Sea Lord Admiral Rosslyn Wemyss,
(representing Britain) and General Maxime
Weygand, (Foch's Chief of Staff). The German
delegation was led by Matthias Erzberger,
(a civilian politician), Count Alfred von
Oberndorff, (the Foreign Ministry), Major
General Detlev von Winterfeldt, (representing
the Army) and Captain Ernst Vanselow,
(representing the Navy).

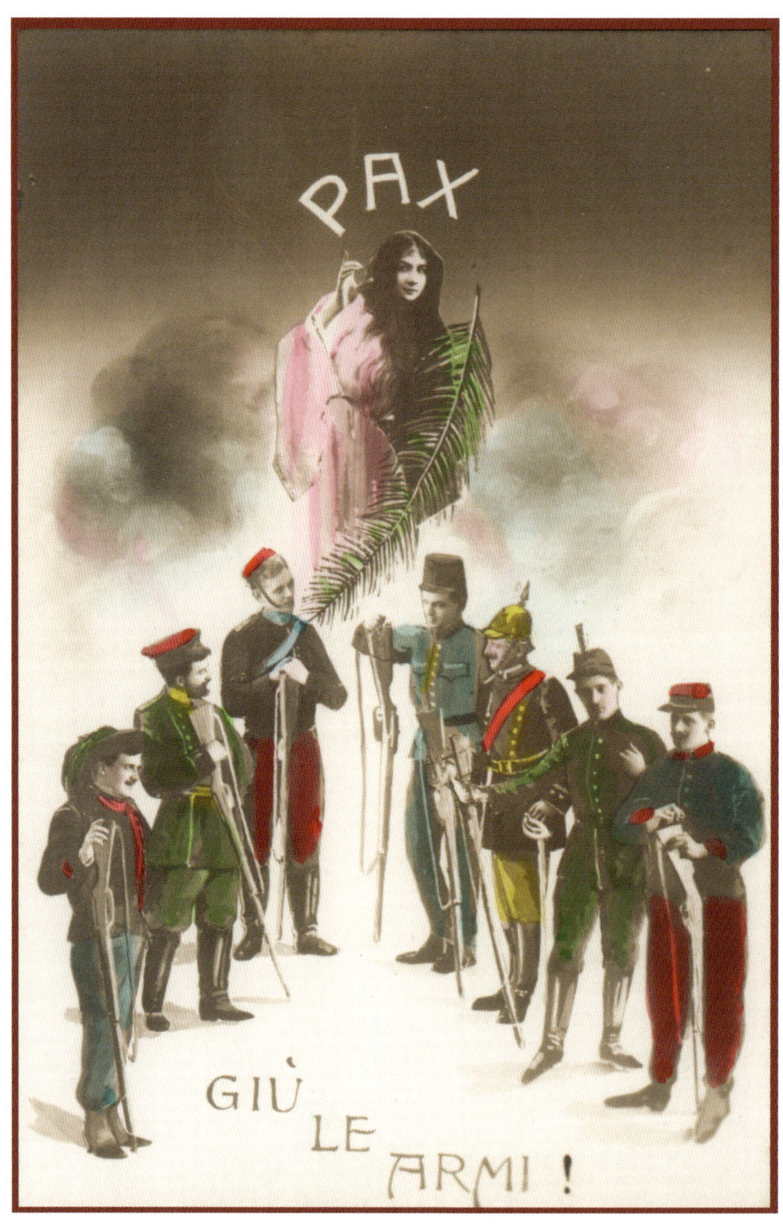

173 – Italian Postcard

PAX - Giù le Armi ! (Pax – Put Down Your Weapons)
5 ½ x 3 ½ in. (13.7 x 8.7 cm)

174 – Bernard Becan (1890-1943)

L'Oeuvre edite, ce que sera LA GRANDE PAIX, c.1917,
Lithographic poster, 45 ½ x 31 in. (115.6 x 78.7 cm),
Published by L'Œuvre de Parrains de Reuilly and printed by Pichot Imprimerie, Paris

This poster relates to H. G. Wells' 88-page book, published in 1917, *Nouvelles anticipations : ce que sera la grande paix*. Wells supported Britain in the First World War despite his many criticisms of British policy, and opposed, in 1916, moves for an early peace. In an essay published in *What is Coming? (A Forecast of Things after the War)*, 1916, Wells acknowledged that he could not understand those British pacifists who were reconciled to "handing over great blocks of the black and coloured races to the [German Empire] to exploit and experiment upon". The extent of his own pacifism depended upon an armed peace, with "England keep[ing] to England and Germany to Germany".

Three young women, representing Britain, the United States of America and France, dance together in a circle, holding hands with another, partially visible, woman.

L'ŒUVRE édite

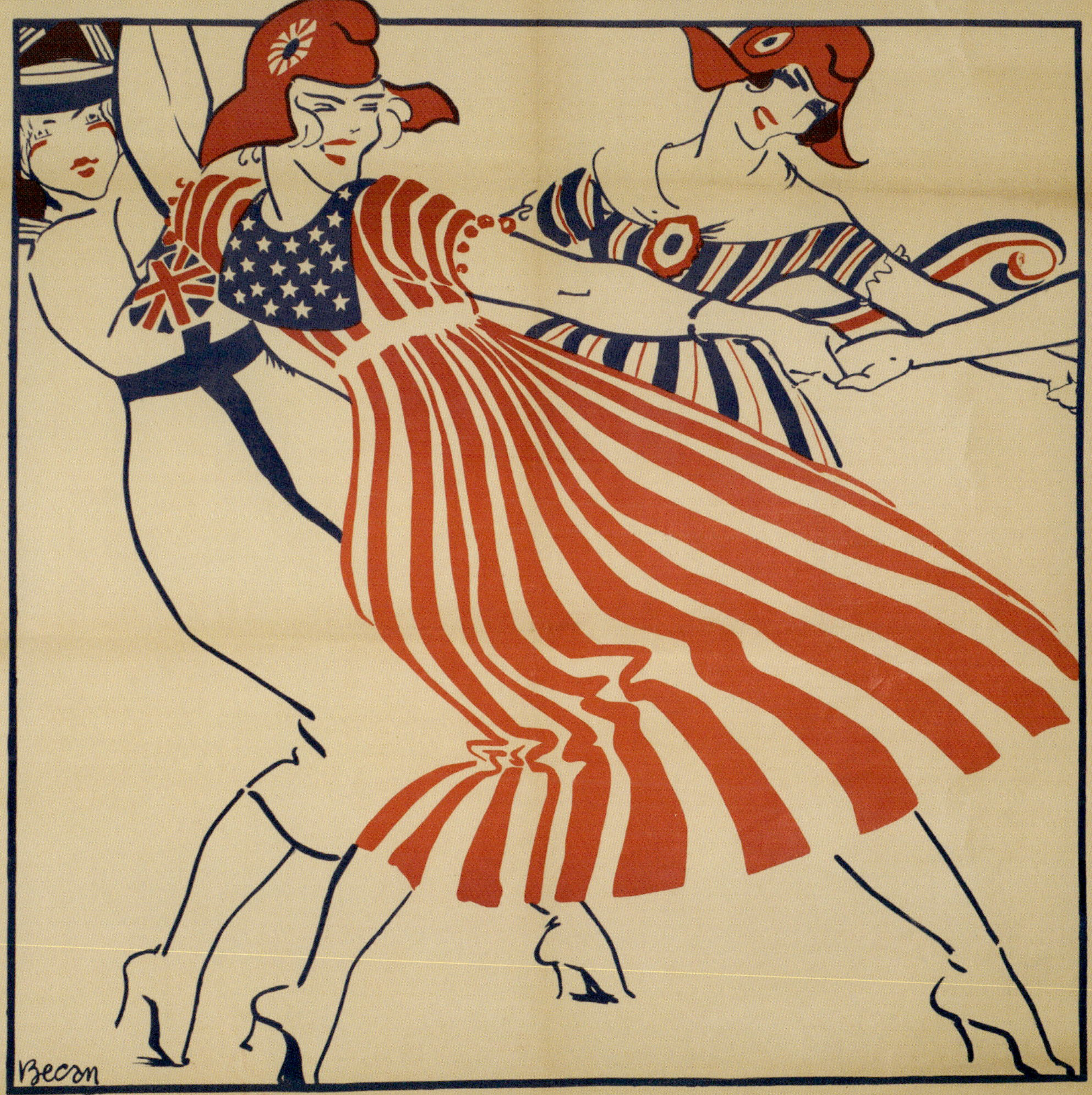
Becan

ce que sera
LA GRANDE PAIX
par H.G. Wells partout: 0f,65
IMP. PICHOT . PARIS.
VISA. 419

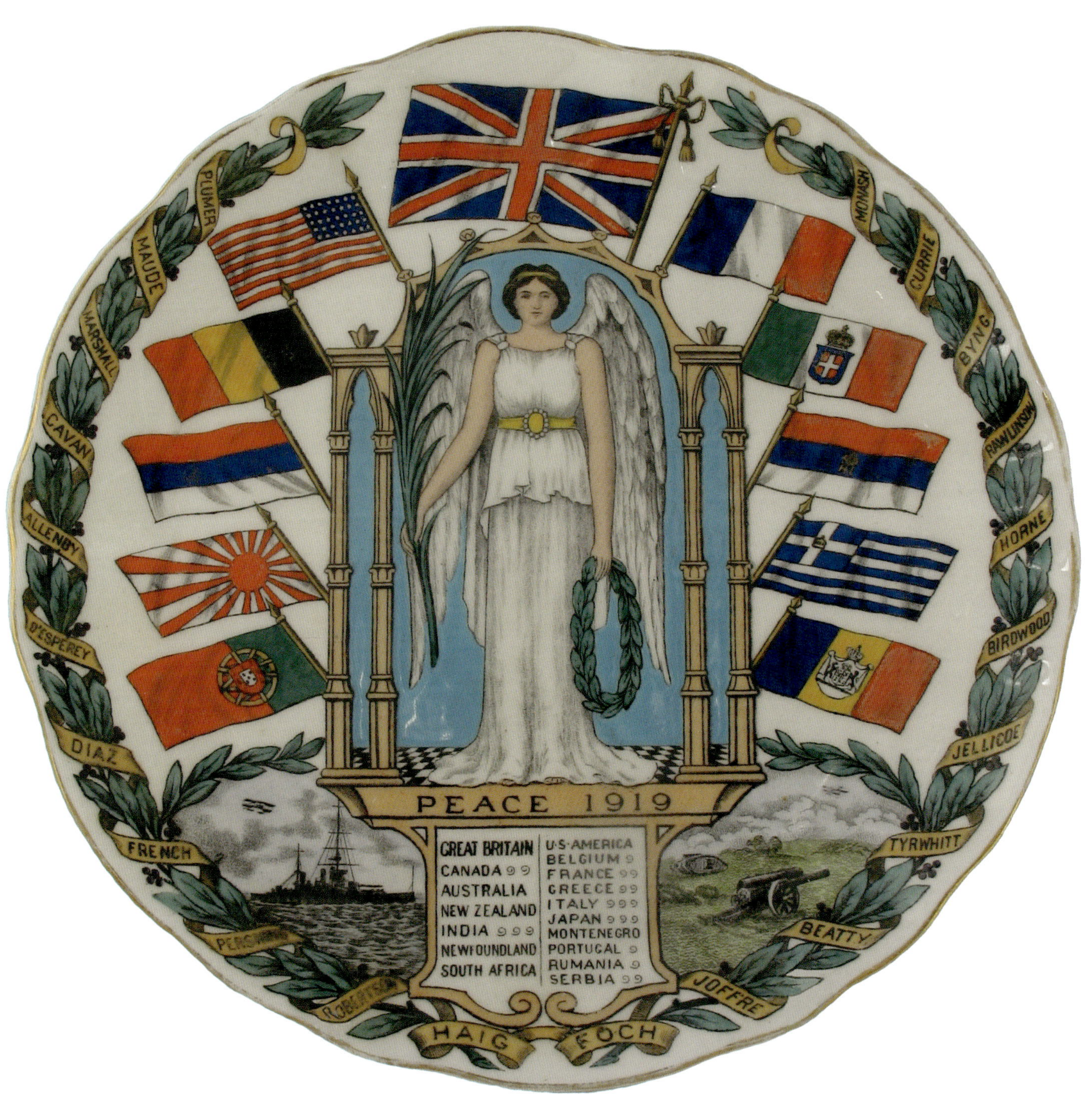

175 – Peace Plate

W. H. Goss "Peace" plate, c.1919,
China – transfer printed ceramic, diameter: 8 in. (20.5 cm)

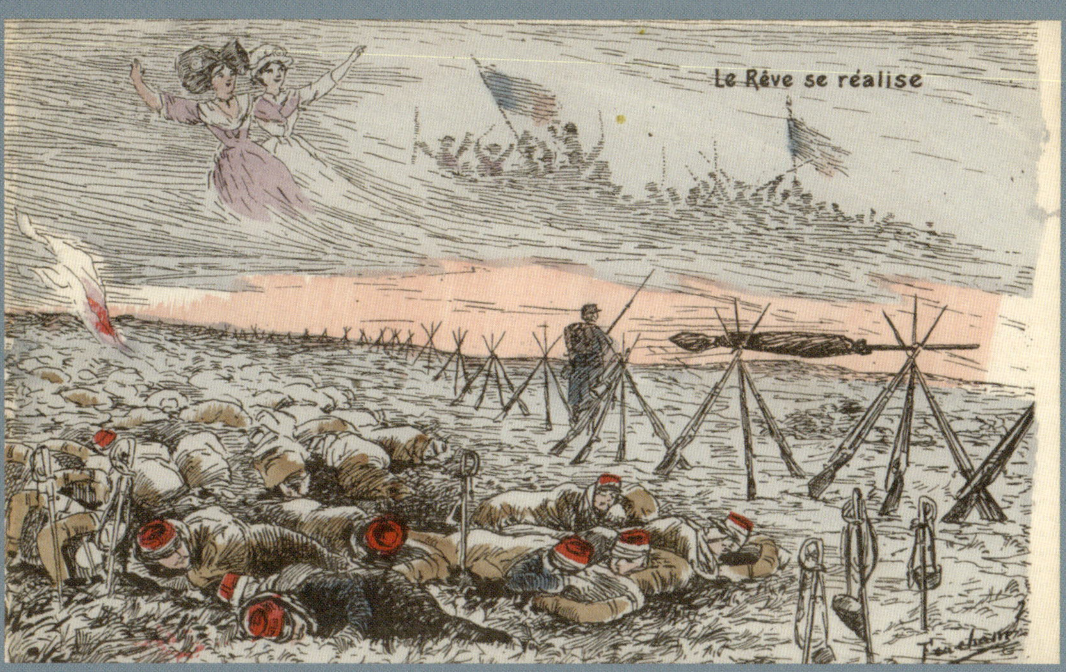

Fercham

176 – Hand-coloured printed postcard: *Le rêve se réalise (The dream comes true)*,
3 ½ x 5 ½ in. (8.8 x 14.1 cm)
Fercham was a pseudonym for an unidentified artist who produced postcards for the postcard publisher L'Hoste (LH).

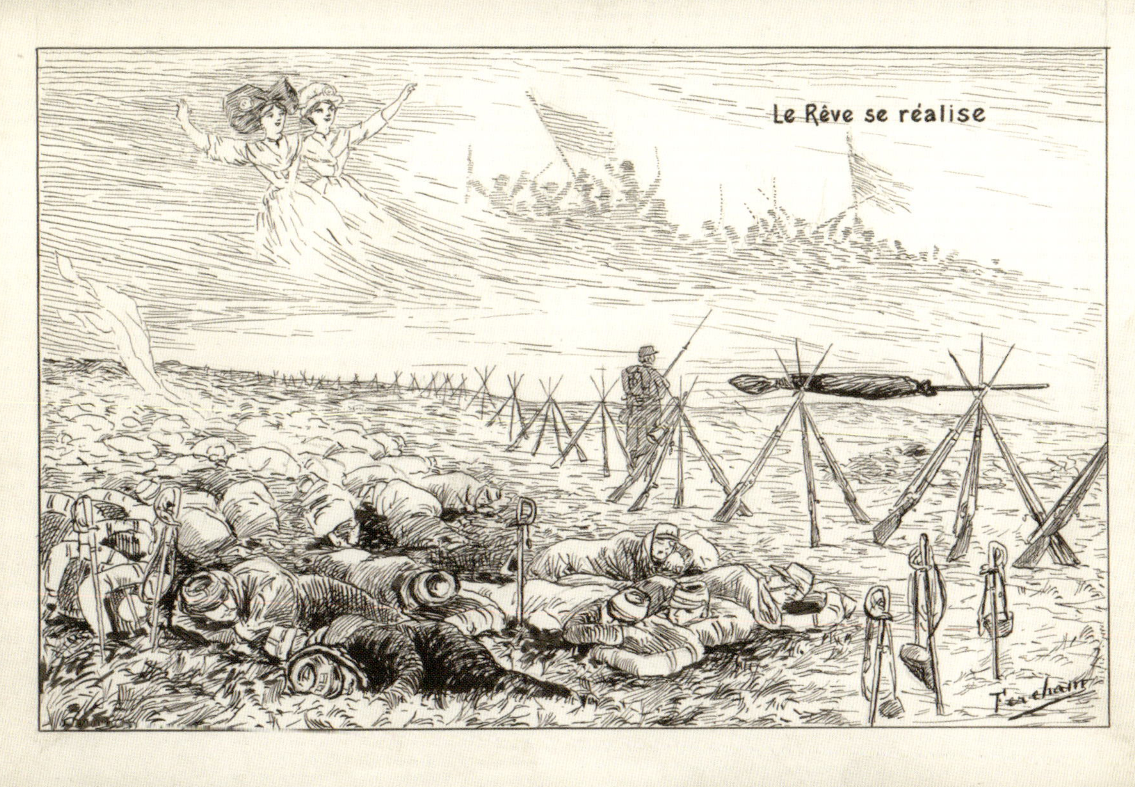

177 – *Le rêve se réalise (The dream comes true)*, c.1918,
Oirginal drawing for postcard design,
Pen & ink on paper, 6 ¼ x 9 in. (16 x 23.2 cm)

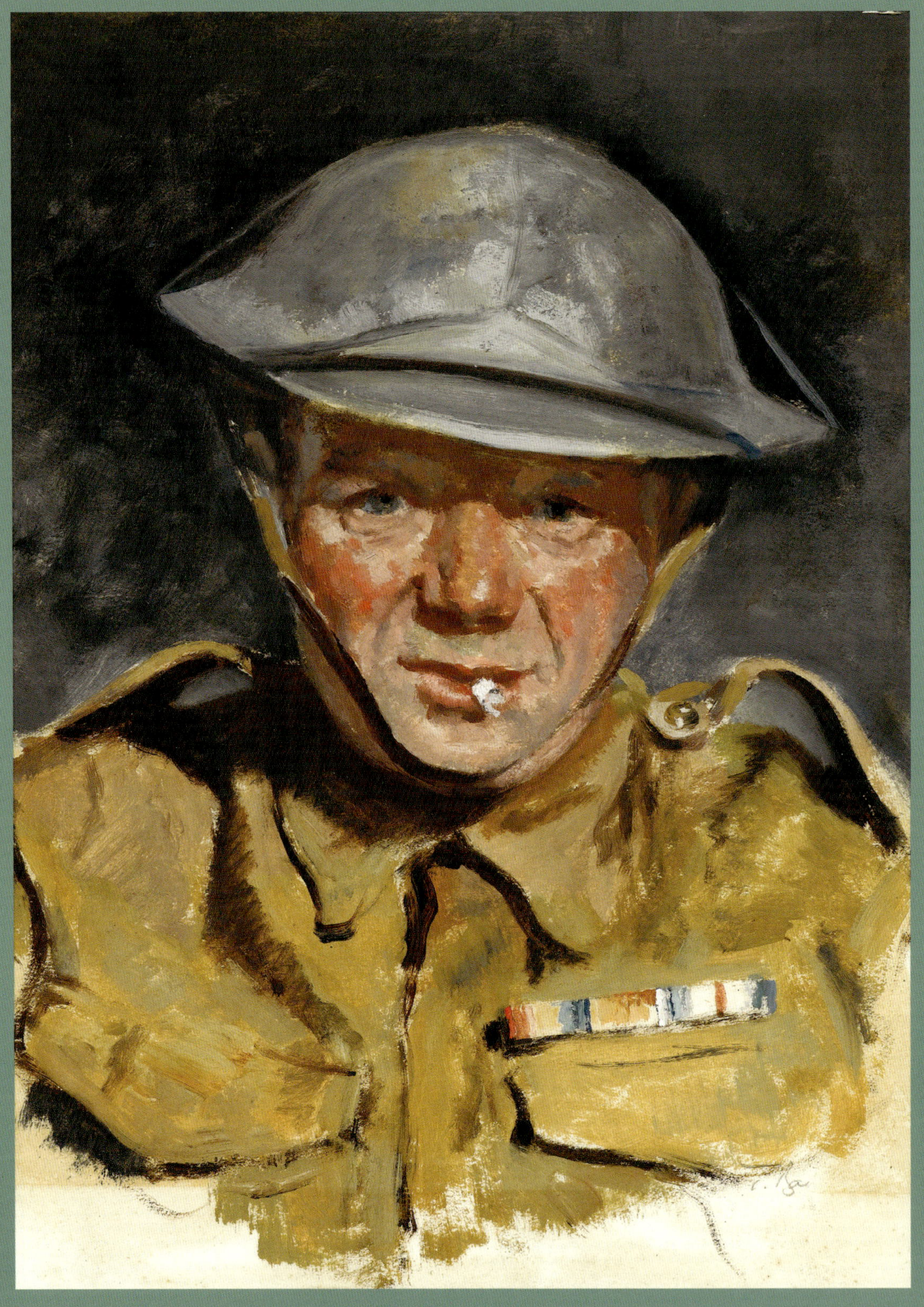

178 – English School

Soldier with First World War decorations, late 1930s, indistinctly signed,
Oil on paper, 14 x 10 ¼ in. (36 x 26 cm)

A number of men (born around the turn of the century) were likely to serve in both World Wars (18 was the age of conscription in the First World War and 41 was the cut off point for conscription in the Second World War). The soldier depicted here is wearing 1937 pattern battledress and Great War medal ribbons.

Laurence Binyon, *For the Fallen*, first published in *The Times*, September 1914

Rudyard Kipling, 'Epitaphs of the War: Common Form', 1919

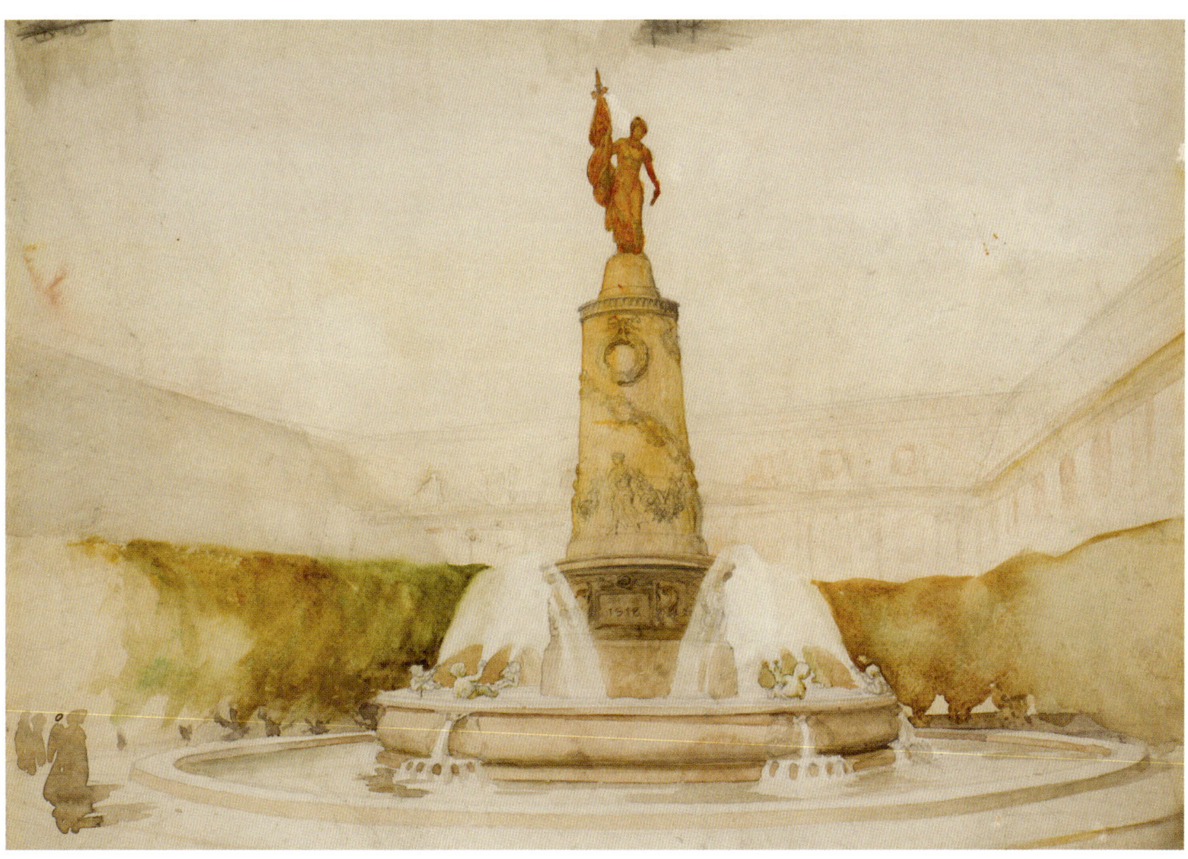

179 – Charles Cundall (1890-1971)

The Meta Sudans in Rome as a War Memorial, early 1920s,
Watercolour on paper, 15 x 21 in. (38 x 53 cm), provenance: The Phoenix Gallery, Lavenham

This watercolour is a 'capriccio', a re-elaboration of the ancient Rome Meta Sudans fountain. The plaque is inscribed with the date 1918 in the manner of a war memorial. The ruins of Meta Sudans survived until 1936 when Mussolini demolished and paved over them to make room for the new traffic circle around the Colosseum. During the war Cundall served with The Artist's Rifles and was invalided out in 1916. As a result of wounds incurred in his right arm, Cundall had to learn to paint with his left hand. In the early 1920s Cundall travelled on his honeymoon through France and Italy when this watercolour is likely to have been produced.

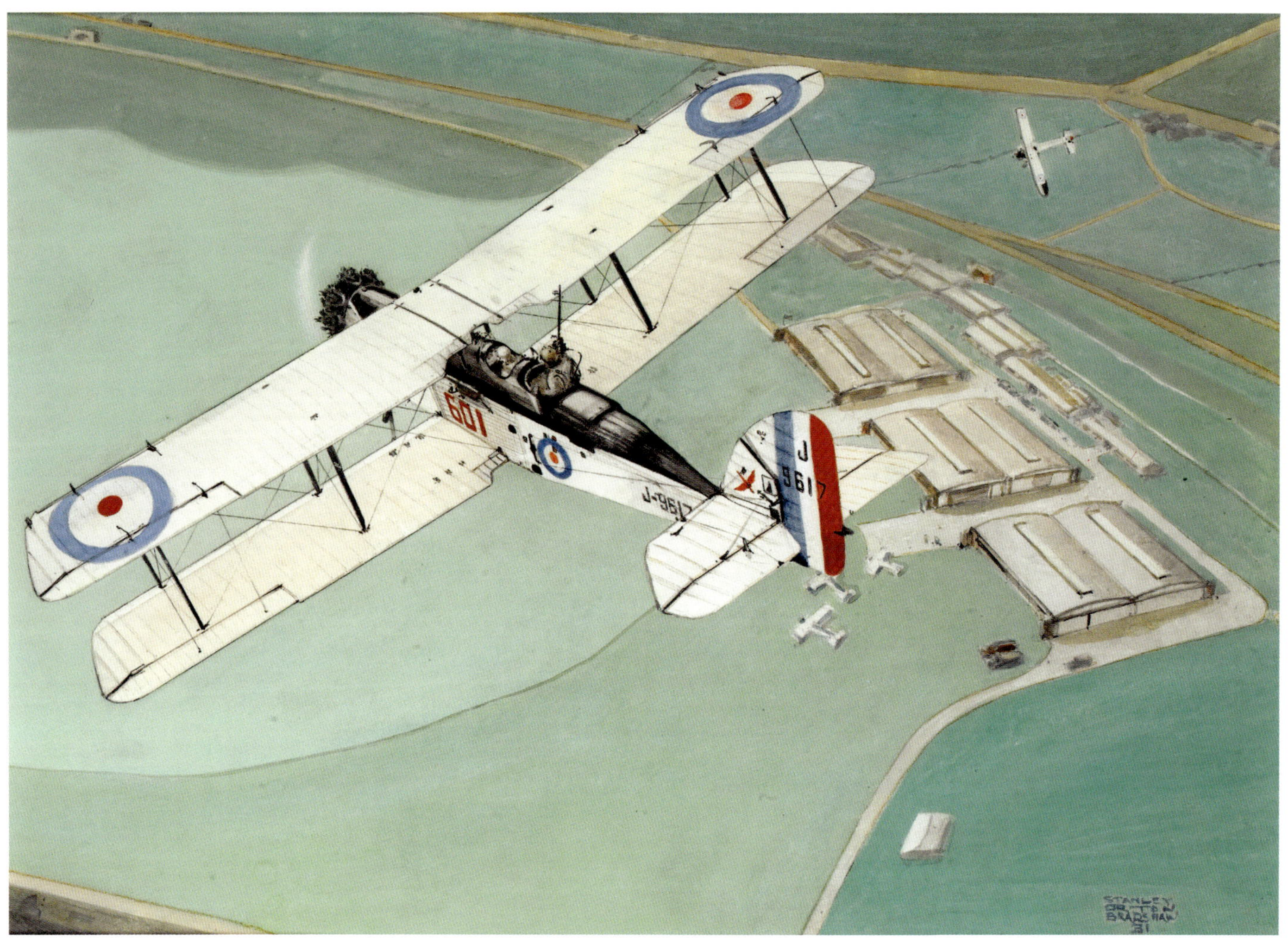

180 – Stanley Orton Bradshaw (1903-1950)

A Westland Wapiti of No. 601 Squadron, Auxiliary Air Force, 1931, signed and dated,
Gouache on paper, 14 x 19 in. (35.5 x 48.2 cm)

The 20-year period between the end of the First World War and the beginning of the Second World War – often referred to as the "Golden Age of Aviation" – saw huge developments in flight as a commercial, military and leisure activity. During this time, the aeroplane changed from a slow, wood-and-wire-framed and fabric-covered biplane to a fast, sleek, all-metal monoplane.

The Westland Wapitii, a British two-seat general purpose military single-engined biplane was in production from 1927 until 1932. Its military usefulness was soon outstripped by the new generation of aeroplanes such as the Hawker Harts developed during the late 1930s.

From November 1929 to June 1933 Westland Wapiti Mks.IIa, VI's were flown by the Millionaires Squadron (No. 601, County of London, Squadron) formed at RAF Northolt in 1925. The aircraft shown in this watercolour, identifiable by the number on the tail J 9617, was commissioned into service in 1929, crash-landed at Brooklands in 1930, repaired and returned to Hendon, remaining in service as a trainer until 1942.

181 – Eric Gill (1882-1940)

Design for a War Memorial, 1925, signed, annotated and dated 26.1.25,
Pencil on paper, 22 x 29 ¾ in. (56 x 75.8 cm)

After the First World War and the setting up of the Imperial War Graves Commission, Gill was asked to make several public war memorials. These include those at Trumpington near Cambridge, Bryantspuddle in Dorset, South Harting in Hampshire, Bisham in Berkshire and Chirk in North Wales. In a letter to the *Burlington Magazine*, (April 1919) Gill objected to 'the strange contention that we are a Christian Empire' and the way that this led to the proposal 'not only to put up crosses at central monuments but even sham altars.' He also expressed dismay at the plans to standardize lettering on memorials and headstones.

The present design for an unrealised war memorial is unusual for its large size and degree of finish. The design includes an exploration of the way that the figures would read from different viewpoints, as well as incorporating Gill's suggestions about where to place the names of the fallen.

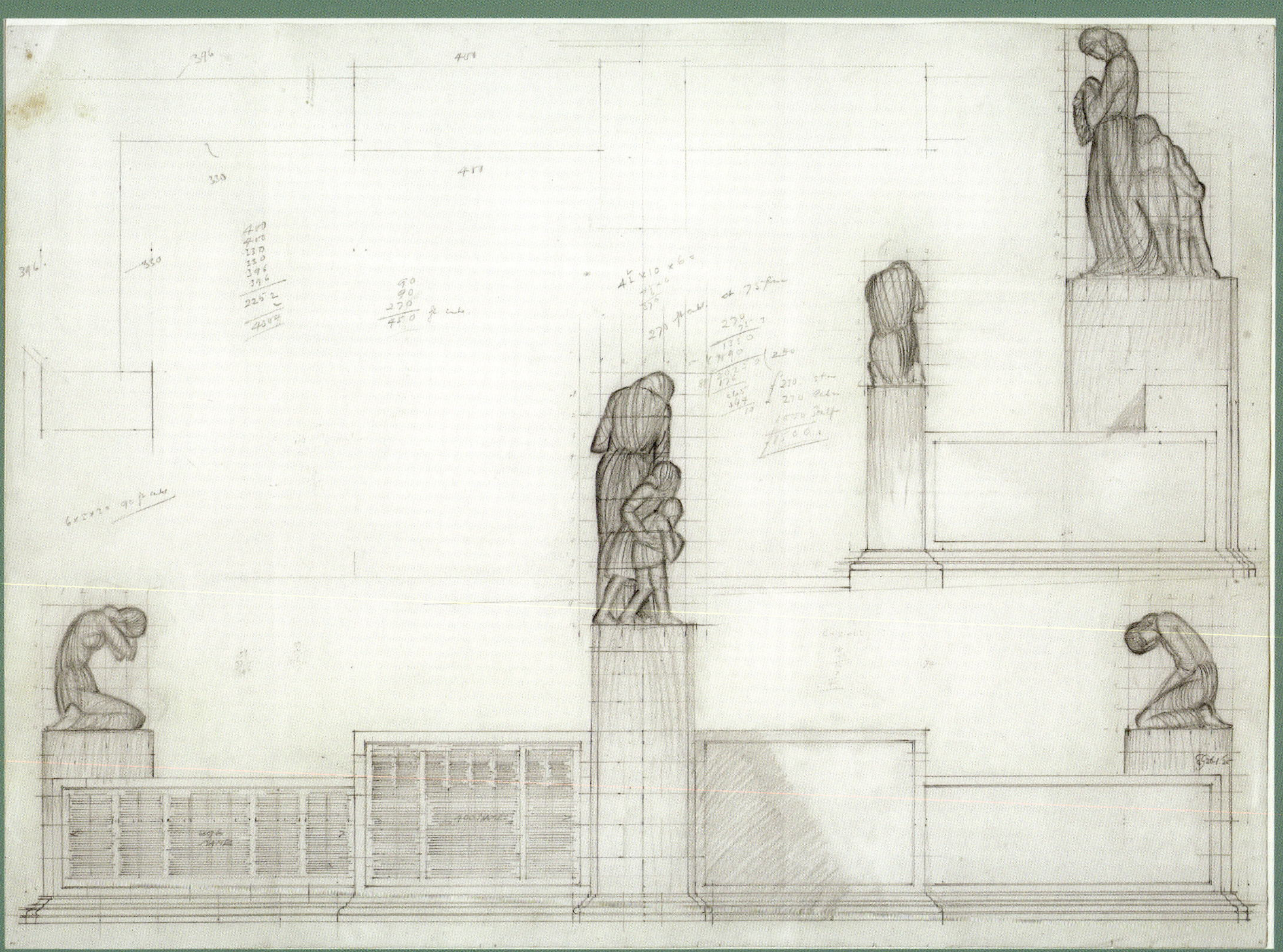

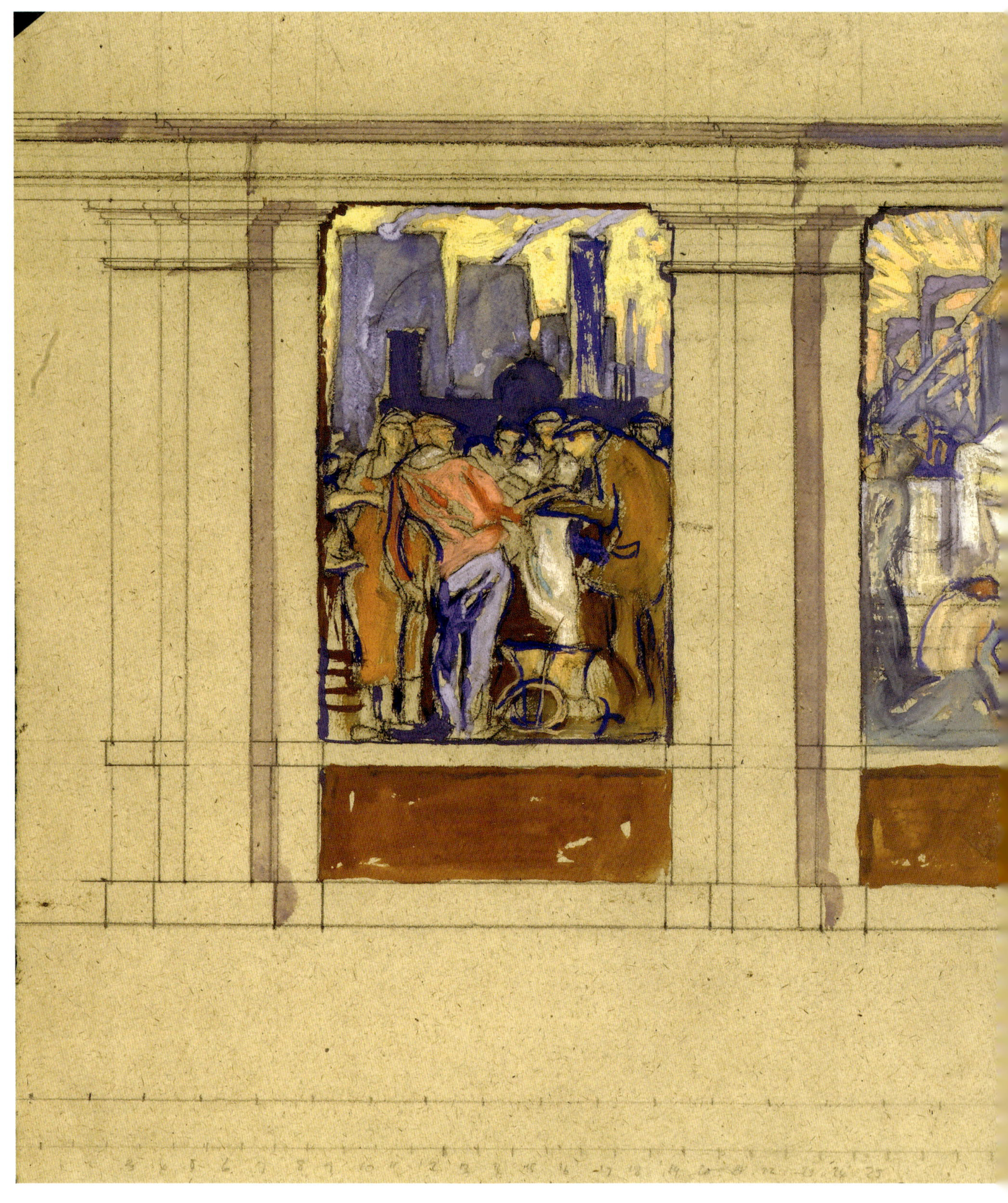

182 – Frank Brangwyn (1867-1956)

Study for Birmingham University War Memorial (M4898), c.1921,
Inscribed 'Birmingham War Memorial in red', illegible inscription above,
Gouache on brown paper, 13 ½ x 22 ¼ in. (34.5 x 57 cm),
Provenance: Ernest Waldron West until 1994; thence by descent.
Literature: Libby Horner, *Brangwyn at WAR!*, (Horner and Goldmark, 2014) p.145

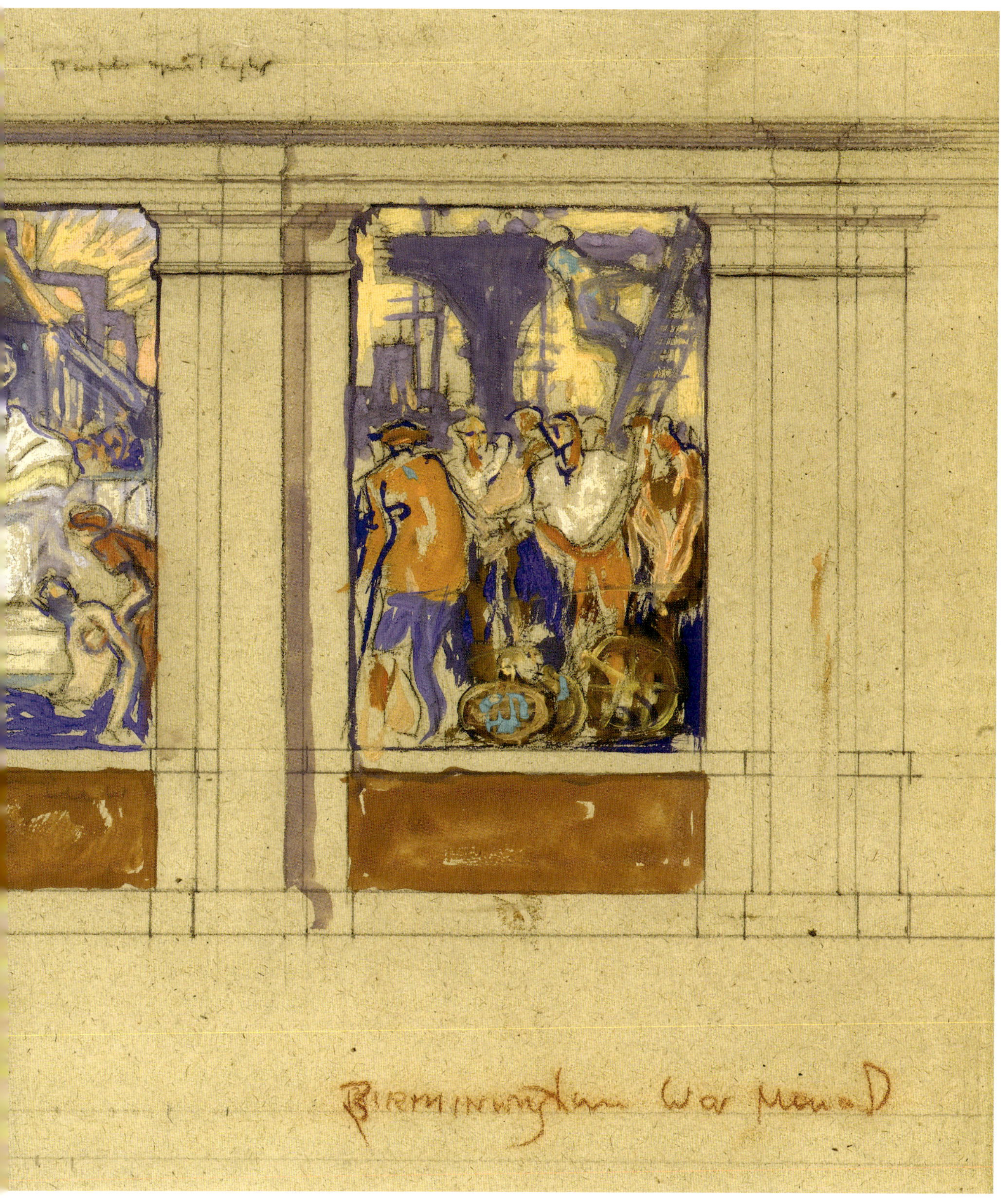

Brangwyn's assistant Frank Alford noted in his diary in July 1921 that Sir Aston Webb discussed with Brangwyn a mosaic memorial to ex-soldiers, consisting of three panels. The project never came to fruition and this is the only known study for it.

Ernest Waldron West (1904-1994), a portrait painter who was born, trained and worked in Worcestershire, was profoundly influenced by Brangwyn. West befriended Brangwyn in the late 1930s and as part of his friendship acquired, over the next two decades, a number of works including this study.

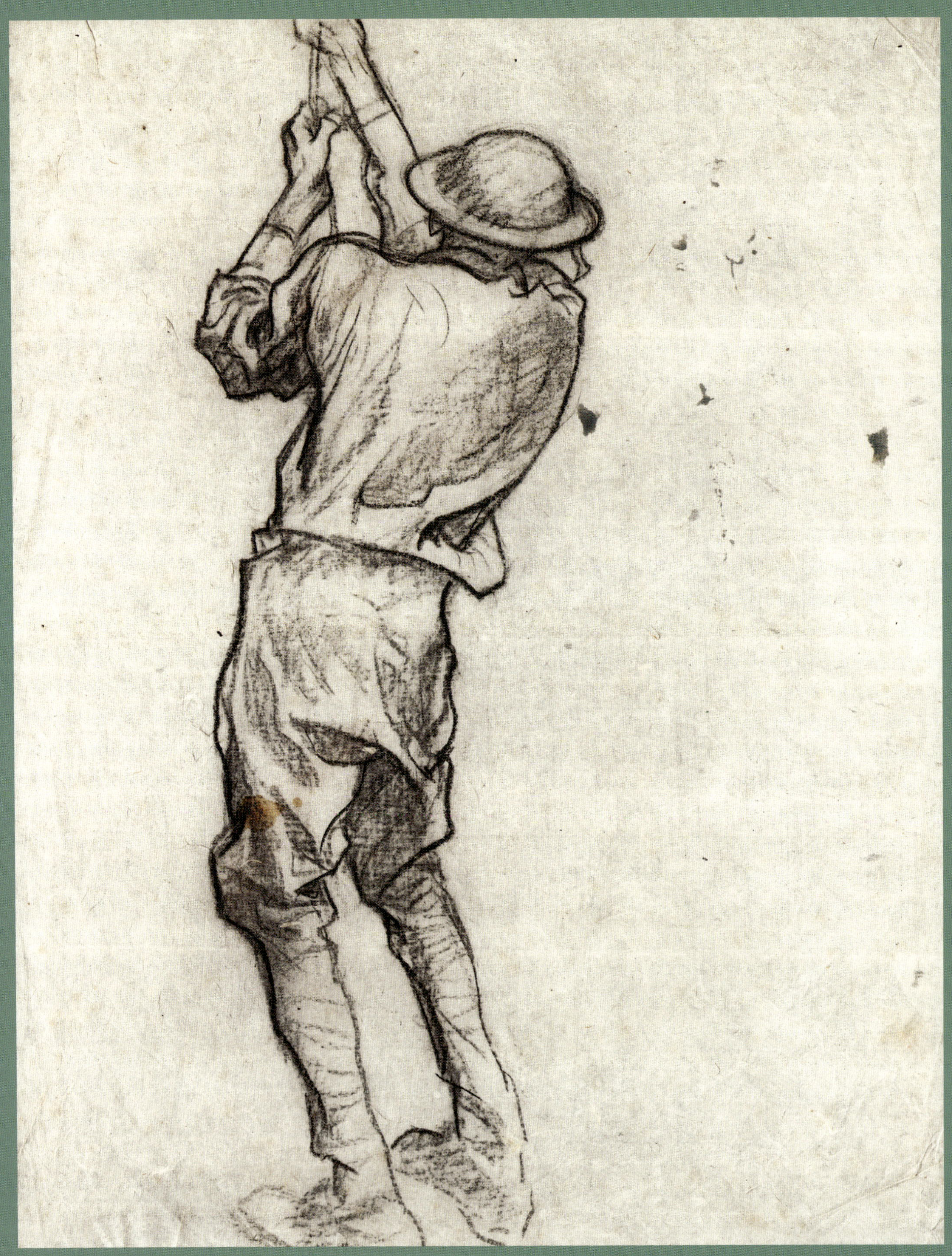

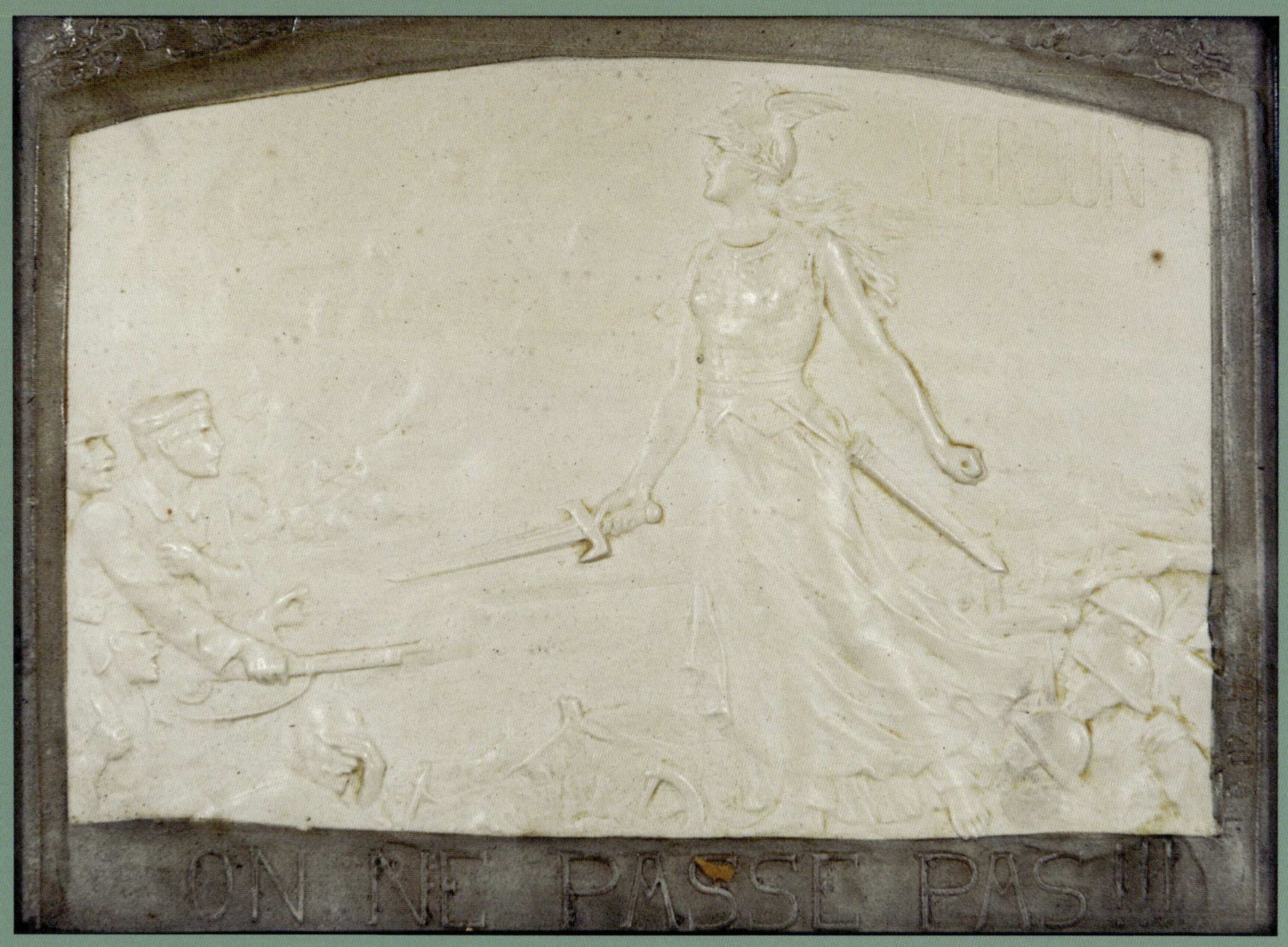

184 – Louis Octave Joseph Mattei (1877-1932)

Verdun – On ne passe pas, c.1917, signed and titled, the original plaster maquette, 8 x 10 ½ in. (20 x 26.5 cm)

The battle of Verdun (February 21 to December 18, 1916) resulted in nearly one million casualties. The inscription on this commemorative plaque is an abbreviated version of Robert Georges Nivelle's celebrated battle-cry "Vous ne les laisserez pas passer, mes camarades". Nivelle, a French Artillery Officer, was given command of the French Second Army in the Battle of Verdun in May 1916, and the counter-offensives he led succeeded in rolling back the German forces in late 1916. He was much criticised however, at the time, for wasting French lives. A French Lieutenant at Verdun who was later killed by a shell, wrote in his diary on May 23, 1916: "Humanity is mad. It must be mad to do what it is doing. What a massacre! What scenes of horror and carnage! I cannot find words to translate my impressions. Hell cannot be so terrible. Men are mad!"

This original plaster maquette would have subsequently been cast in an edition of bronze and sold as a souvenir of one of the longest and most costly battles in human history.

183 – Frank Brangwyn (1867-1956)

Working Soldier (Study for British Empire) (M1145), c.1925,
Black chalk on paper, 18 ¼ x 14 in. (46.5 x 36 cm)
Literature: Libby Horner, *Brangwyn at WAR!*, (Horner and Goldmark, 2014) p.155

From 1924 Brangwyn was occupied with what he regarded as the culmination of his life's work, a mural scheme for the Royal Gallery in the House of Lords, commissioned by Lord Iveagh as a First World War Memorial. The first scheme – which was rejected, and to which this study relates, – showed soldiers and tanks in action. The final scheme, known as *The Empire Panels*, were installed in Brangwyn Hall, Guildhall, Swansea in 1934.

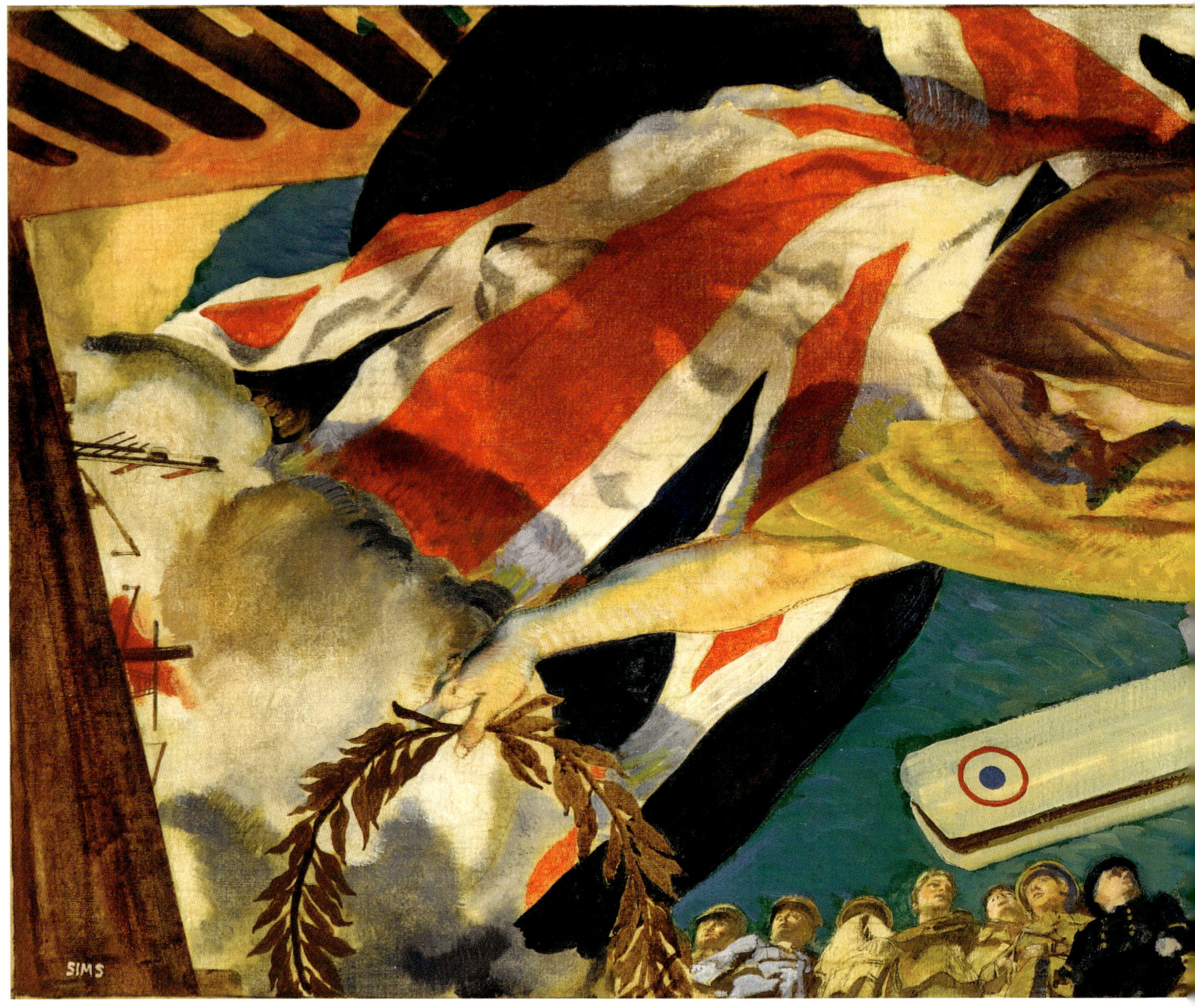

185 – Charles Sims (1873 -1928)

Study for Ceiling painting in the Great Hall of the Institute of Civil Engineers, c.1919, signed,
Oil on canvas, 17 ¹⁵⁄₁₆ x 43 ⅛ in. (45.5 x 109.5 cm)

War memorials, of which there are an estimated 40,000 in Britain, vary hugely in style and form. Some national organisations oversaw schemes, principally the British War Memorials Commitee and The Imperial War Graves Commission, but many memorials were commissioned by local community leaders and other civic groups with relatively little or no central state involvement. These could take the form of memorial windows, murals, plaques, rolls of honour, cenotaphs, or entire memorial buildings.

In 1920 Sims was commissioned to decorate the ceiling of the Institute of Civil Engineers in Great George Street, Westminster. On December 2, 1919 the Institute's Minutes recorded the Council's decision 'that advantage be taken of the opportunity afforded of the cleaning and reinstatement of the Great Hall, and the erection of scaffolding therefore, to complete the architect's original scheme for the decoration of the mouldings of the ceiling … The Council accept the offer of Sir John Griffith the President, to complete the ceiling of the Great Hall

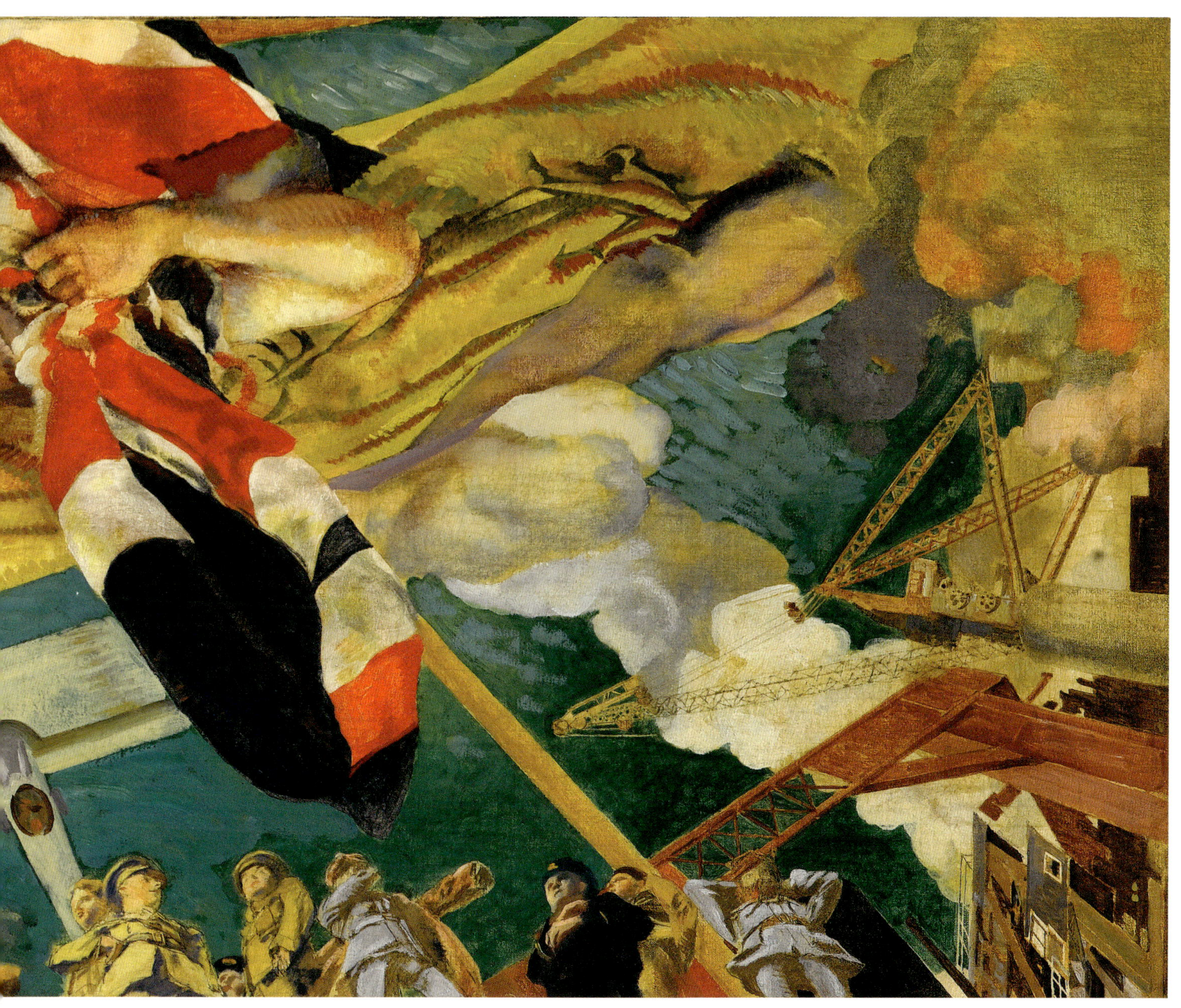

by providing for the decoration of the central panel a painting emblematic of the Civil Engineers' war-time efforts.' The ceiling decoration was part of a commemorative scheme, including a plaque designed by Derwent Wood to record the names of those members killed in the Great War.

Sims's design is enormously inventive. A figure of Victory swoops down, surrounded by a billowing Union Jack and holding the victor's laurels, although it also serves as a wreath for the dead. At the edges people crane their necks to peer upwards, as people looking up at the ceiling would do, and a biplane, emblem of modernity, crosses the composition. Sims was deeply engaged in the process of commemorating the war. His son was killed in the Navy in 1914, and he painted a lamentation that was exhibited at the Royal Academy to great acclaim. In 1918 he travelled to France as an Official War Artist and was there when the guns fell silent for the Armistice. Sims was paid £1,000 for his Civil Engineers ceiling commission. The fully completed canvas exhibited here was perhaps used to show the Council what form the final decoration would take.

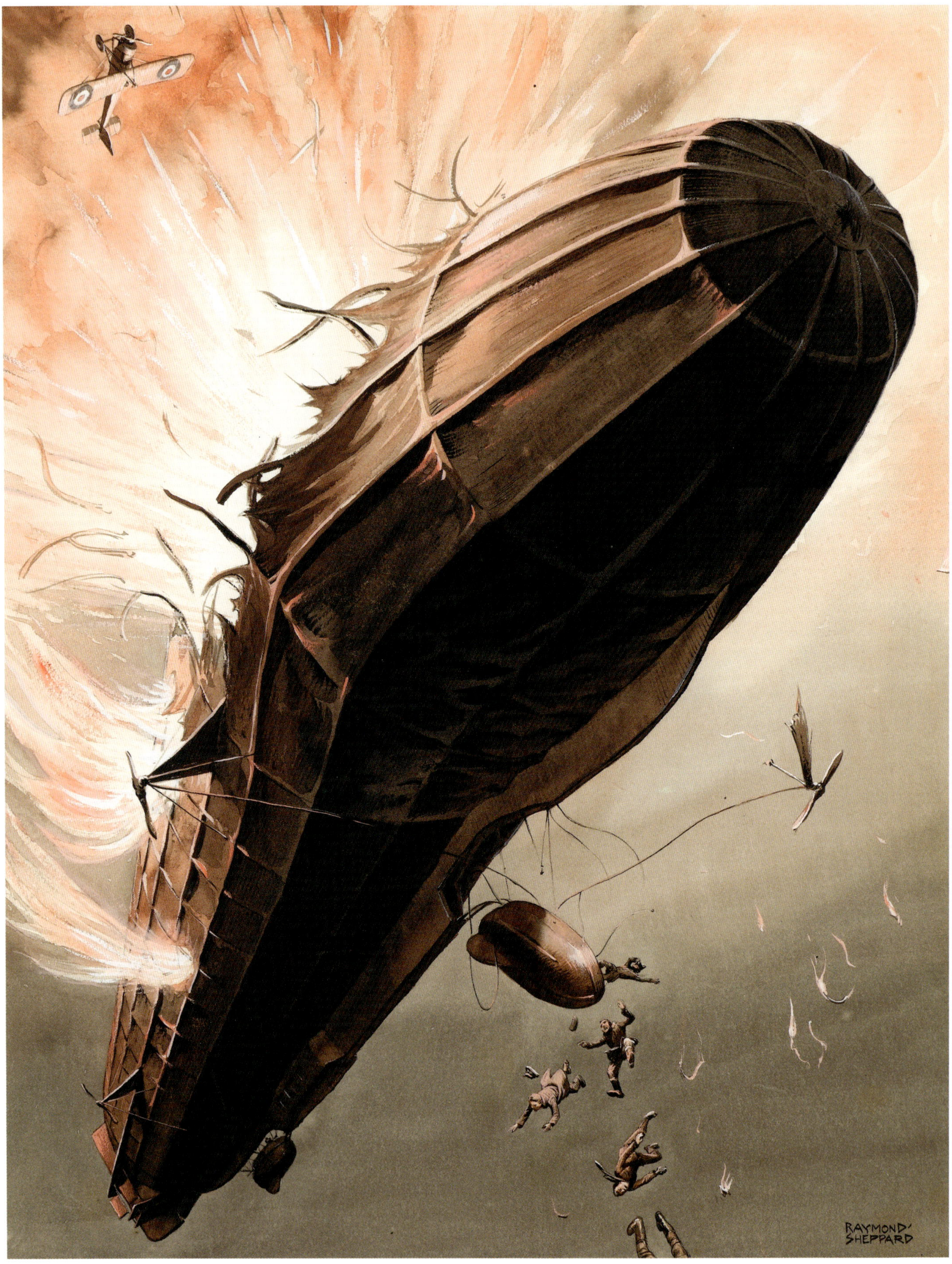
RAYMOND
SHEPPARD

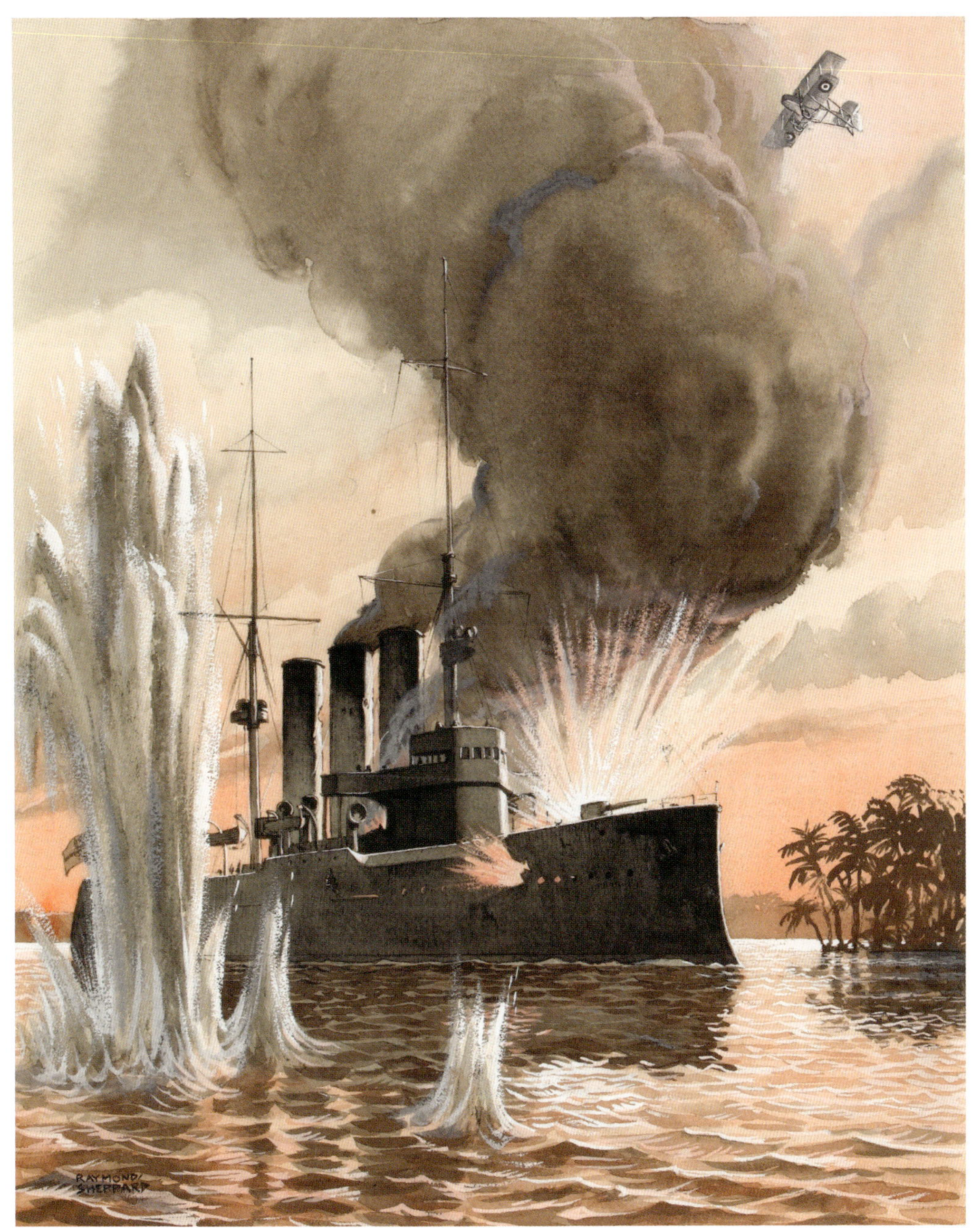

Raymond Sheppard (1913-1958)

187 – *End of a sea raider*, c.1957, signed,
Gouache on card, 16 x 12 in. (30 x 28 cm.)

Having had no direct experience of the First World War, Raymond Sheppard treated its history with a glamorous and nostalgic boys-own vision. His illustrations found a ready audience with the generation recovering from their own experiences of the Second World War, eager for stories about acts of heroism against a common German enemy.

Between 1934 and 1958 Sheppard illustrated well over 100 books, receiving commissions from over 15 publishing houses including Hutchison, Blackie and Son, Macmillan, Oxford University Press and Faber and Faber.

186 – *Reginald Alexander John Warneford Attacking Zeppelin LZ-39*, signed,
Gouache on card, 16 x 12 in. (30 x 28 cm),
Literature: *Raymond Sheppard, Master Illustrator,* Liss Fine Art, November 2010, Cat.83,

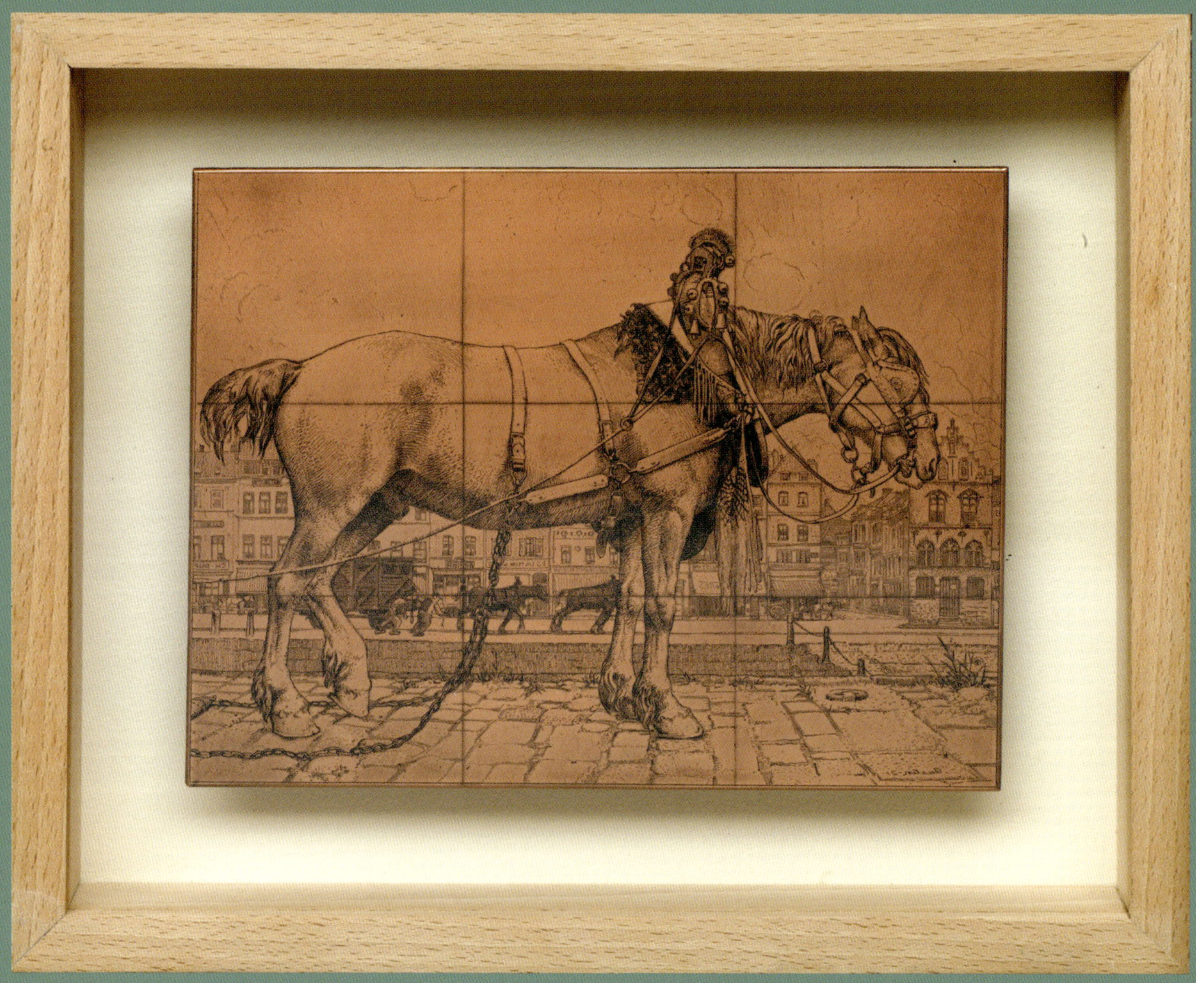

Robert Austin (1895-1973)

188 – *The Horse of Ostend*, 1921,
The original copper plate, cancelled, 5 ⅞ x 7 ⅝ in. (14.8 x 19.2 cm)

During the war, Austin served as a gunner in France. In 1921, he went on a cycling tour of France with Norman Tennant:

"In the long vacation of 1921, we decided to take our cycles over to France and travel down the old battle line to renew our acquaintance with the places where we had been during the war. We landed at Ostend and it was here that [Austin] made the sketch "The Horse of Ostend", with its background of quayside houses.

We cycled westwards to Nieuport, where the old trench system reached the coast …. A short distance to the South lay Ypres, which was slowly beginning to emerge from the devastation caused by 4 years of constant shelling during the war."

Notes from *Robert Austin and Norman Tennant, A Record of Friendship*
The Kylin Press 1982, p10

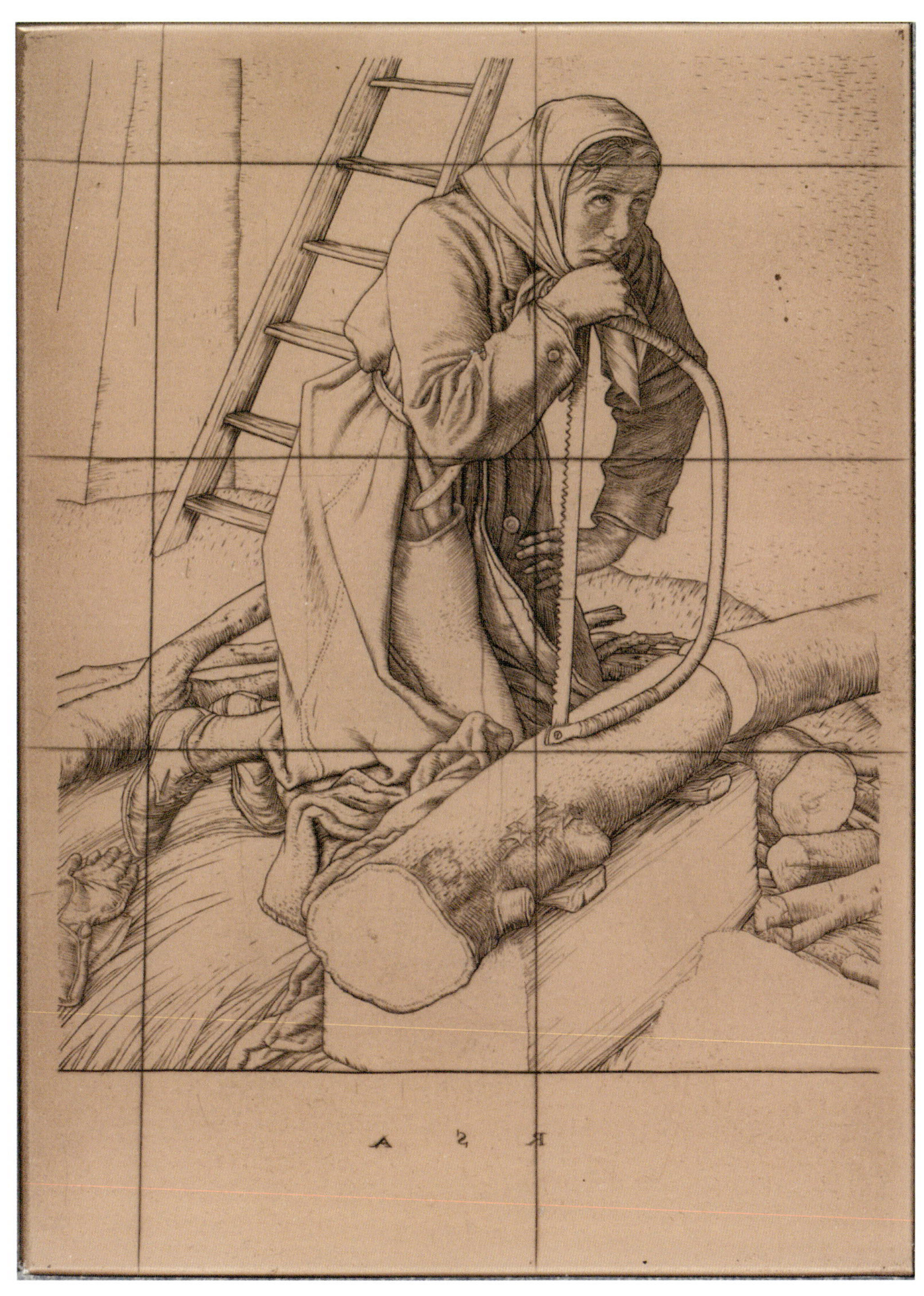

189 – *Widow of a hero,*
Original copper plate, cancelled, 9 ¼ x 7 in. (23.5 x 17.5 cm)

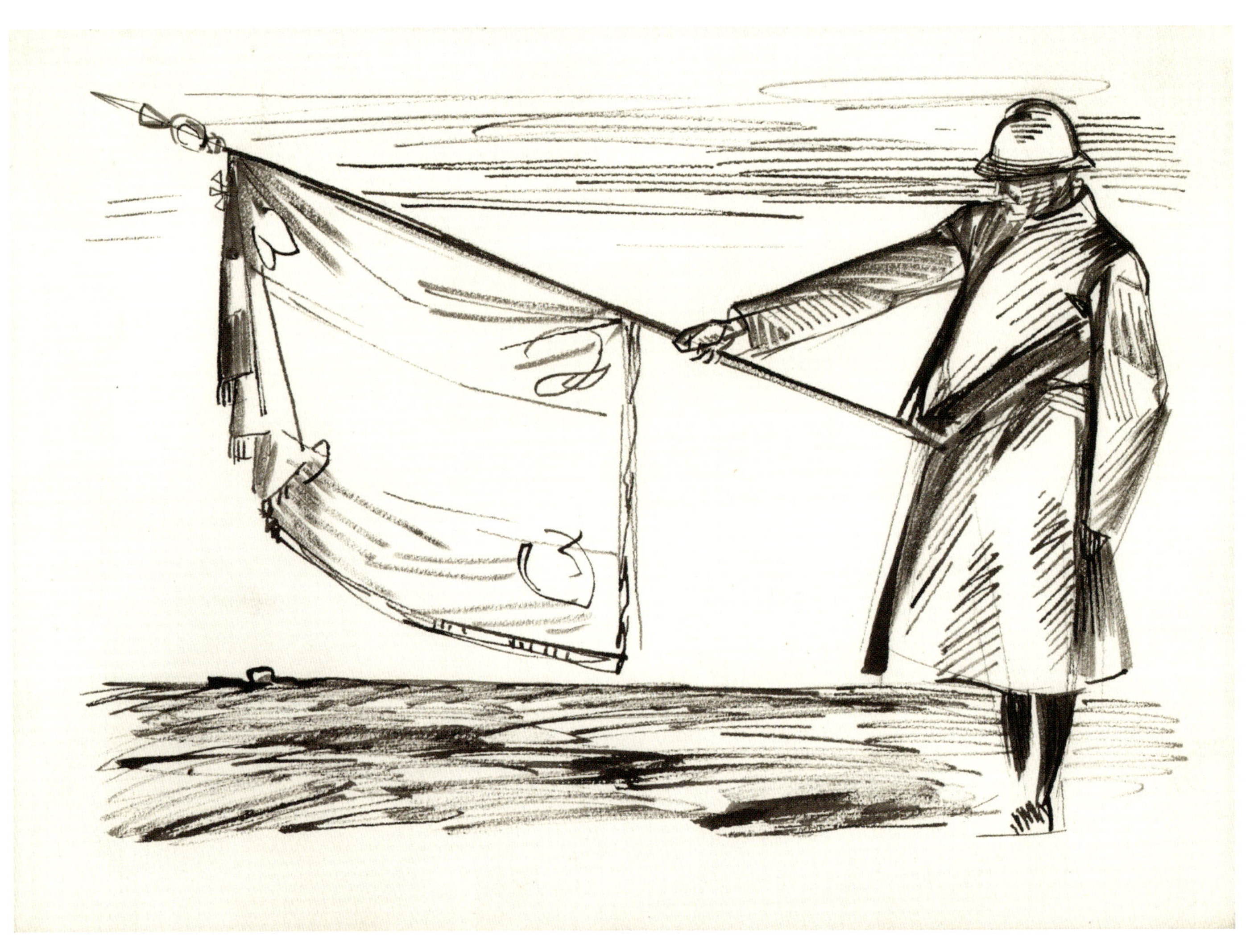

190 – René Georges Hermann-Paul (1864-1940)

Standard Bearer in Mourning,
Pen & ink on paper, 9 ½ x 12 ½ in. (24.1 x 31.8 cm)

This haunting image shows a standard bearer with his standard lowered in tribute to the fallen.

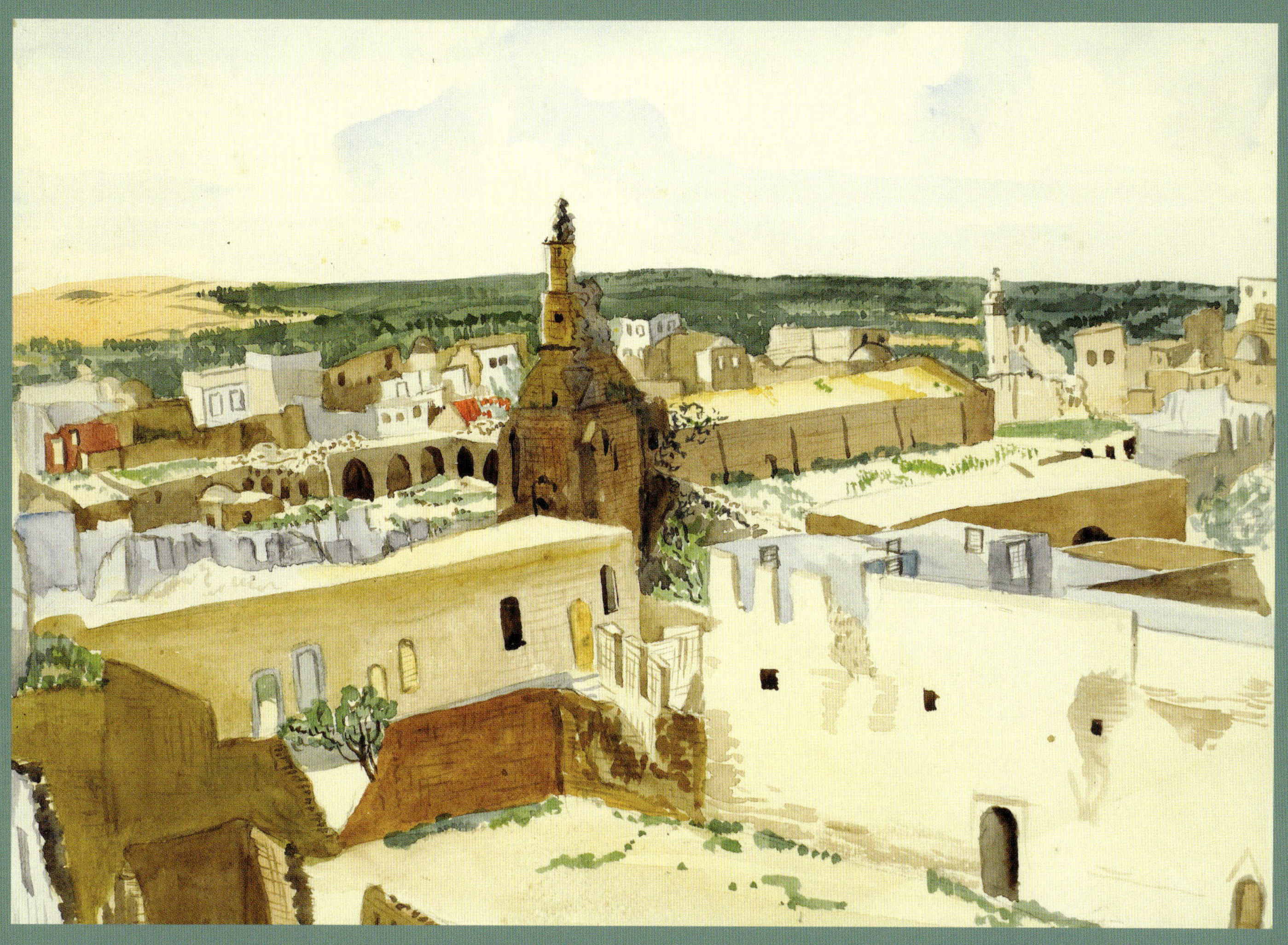

191 – Richard Carline (1896-1980)

Palestine, signed dated and inscribed with title,
Watercolour on paper, 10 ½ x 14 ½ in. (26.5 x 37 cm),
Provenance: acquired directly from the Artist's family

After the war Richard Carline and his brother Sydney were asked to go in their capacity as war artists to the Middle East. There they made numerous sketches from the air and ground of the war-zones in Palestine, Syria, Mesopotamia and Persia in preparation for a series of large oil paintings for the newly-founded Imperial War Museum.

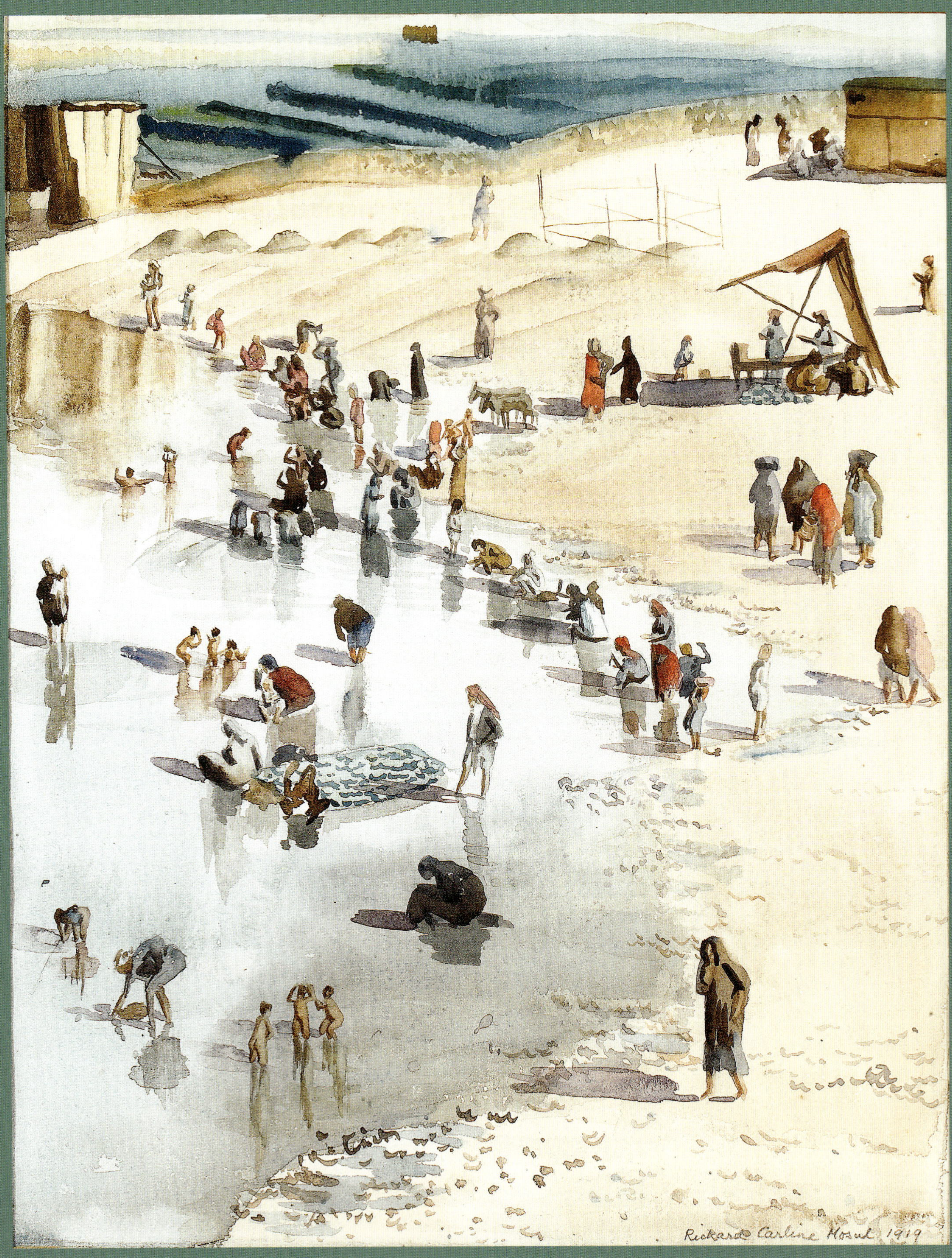

Richard Carline Mosul 1919

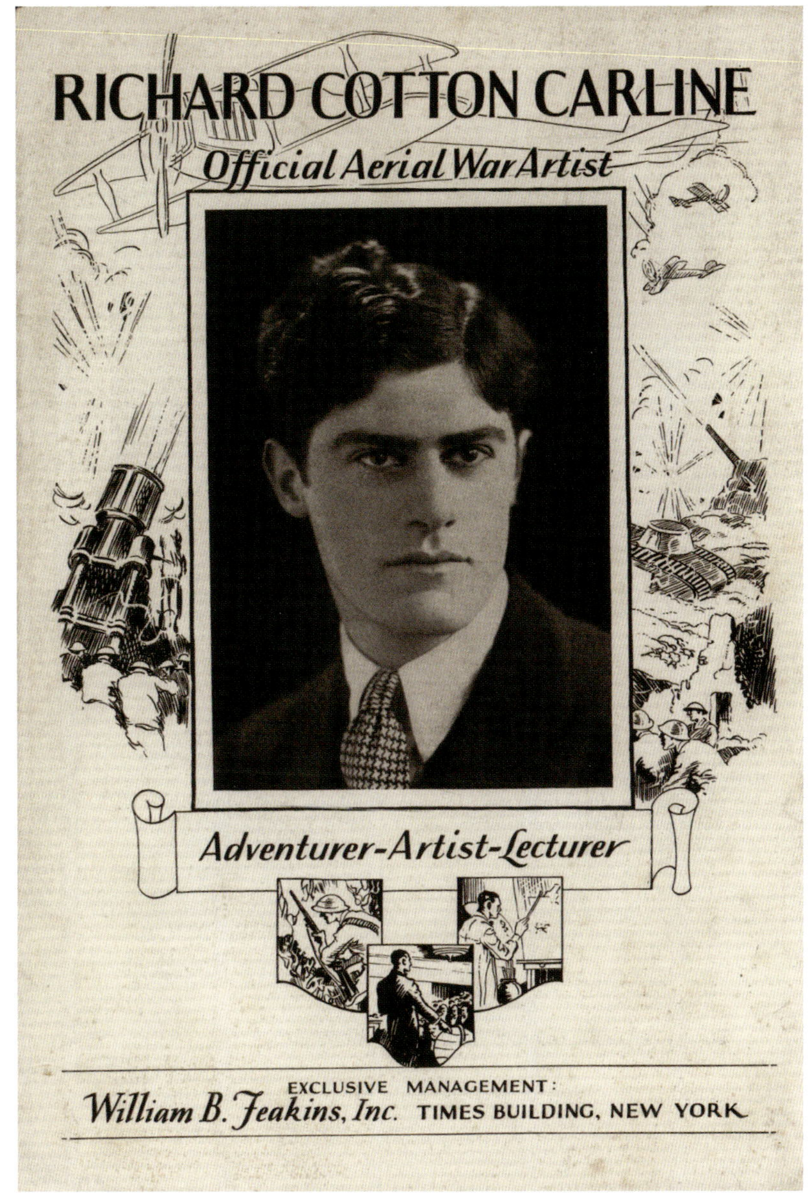

The leaflet which accompanied Richard Carline's USA lecture tour

192 – Richard Carline (1896-1980)

Women and children of Mosul, washing on the banks of the Tigris River, 1919,
Inscribed on the reverse: 'Women washing at Musul Mesopotamia',
Watercolour on paper, 13 x 10 ½ in. (33 x 26.7 cm)

The leaflet accompanying Carline's USA lecture tour states: 'Richard Carline is a pioneer, if not the first airman to realize the possibilities of painting scenes from an aeroplane. He and his brother, Sydney Carline, were commissioned to travel from Egypt to Persia by air and ground, with a view to painting a series of pictures of scenes viewed from an aeroplane. Their wanderings took them through Palestine, Syria, parts of Arabia, to Mosul and Nineveh, across Kurdistan, through Persia and as far as Teheran and the Caspian Sea and India. They visited most of the sites referred to in the Bible, Babylonia and Assyria, and Persia, the sites of the ancient cities of the desert camps of the Bedouins.'

Mosul is situated 400 kilometres north of Baghdad on the west bank of the Tigris River, close to the ruined Assyrian city of Nineveh.

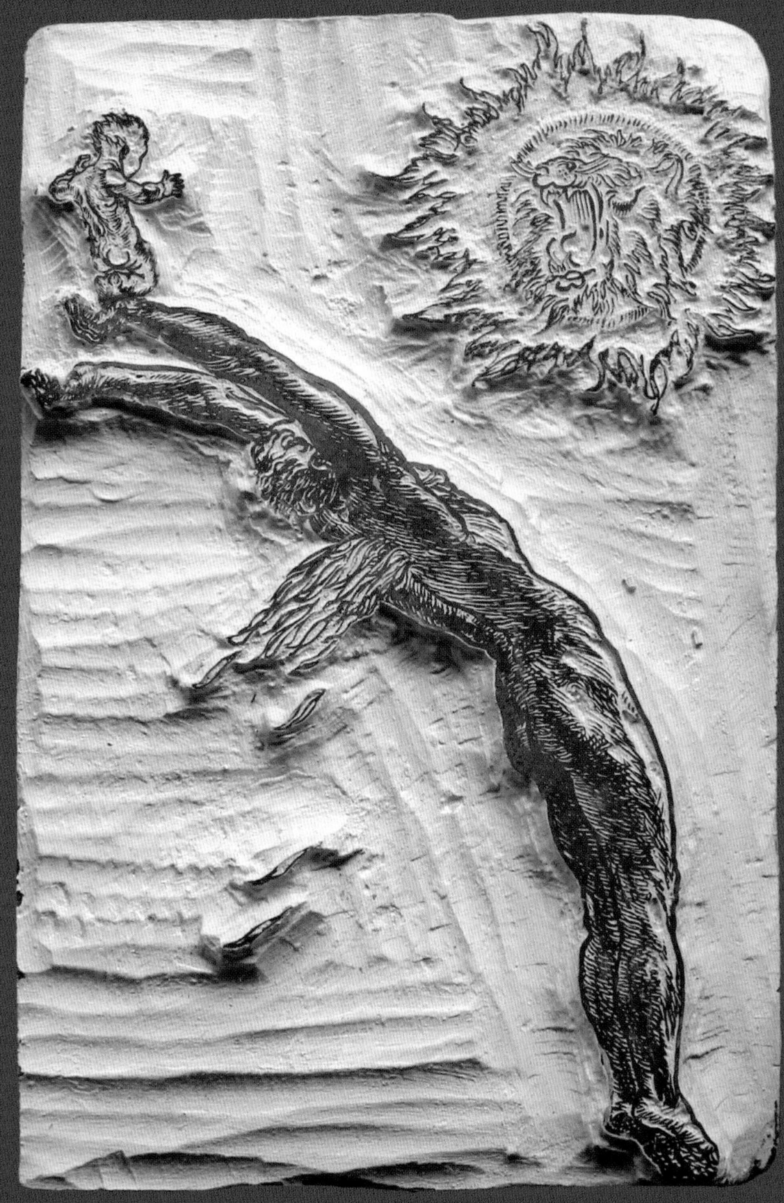

Frederick Carter (1883-1967)

193 – *The Babe of Fire*,
The original woodblock, 4 ¼ x 2 ⅝ in. (10.8 x 6.8 cm)

During the war, Carter produced anti-war cartoons for the Labour Party's *Herald Weekly* and worked as a librarian in the Aeronautical Directorate. His work of the war period and its aftermath has much in common with the imagery of Apollinaire's *The Little Car* (August 31,1914):

We said goodbye to a whole epoch / Furious giants were looming over Europe / The eagles were leaving their eyries expecting the sun / Voracious fishes were swimming up from the abysses / Nations were rushing together to know each other through and through / The dead were trembling with fear in their dark dwellings

During the 1920s, Carter became a mystic and worked on illustrations for D. H. Lawrence's *Apocalypse* (1929).

"And all this mourning has veiled the truth. It's not so much lest we forget, as lest we remember. Because you should realise that so far as the Cenotaph and the Last Post and all that stuff is concerned, there's no better way of forgetting something than by commemorating it."

Alan Bennett, *The History Boys*, 2004

"If we do not end war – war will end us. Eveybody says that, millions of people believe it, and nobody does anything."

H.G. Wells, *The Shape of Things to Come*, 1933

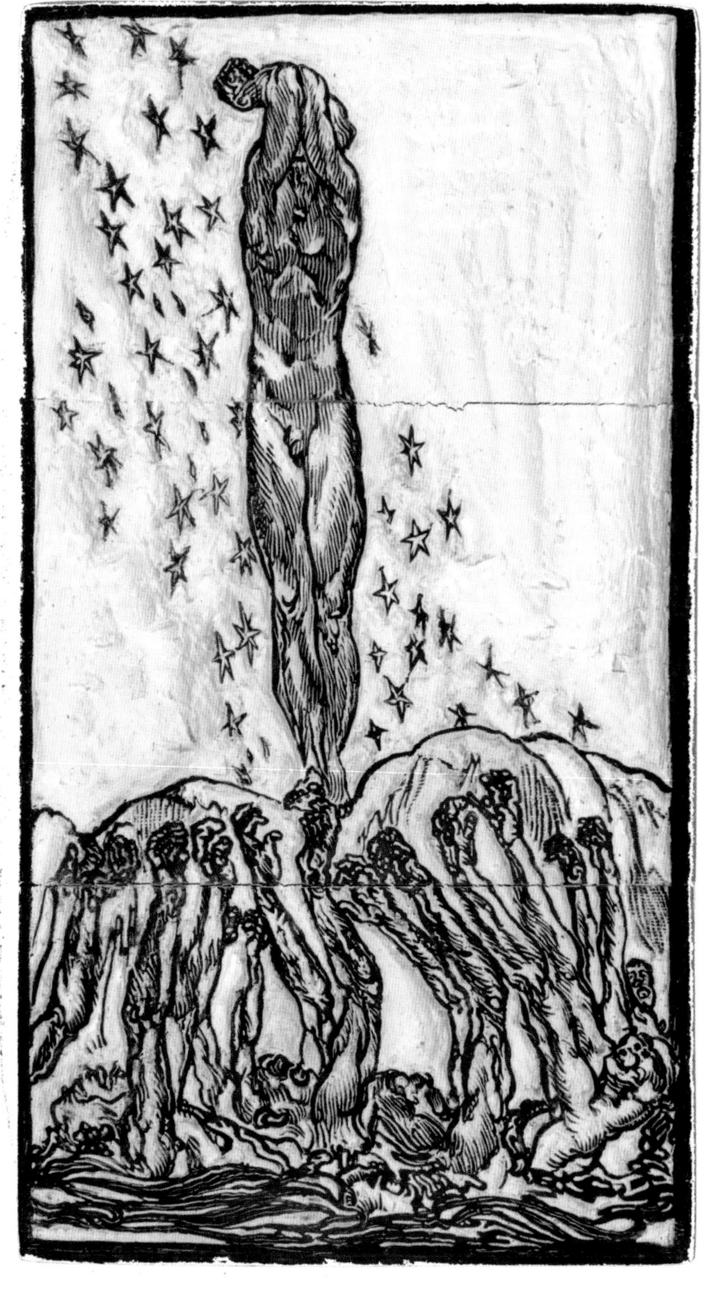

194 – *Escape*, c.1915,
The original wood engraving mounted
with a signed print,
10 ½ x 12 ¼ in. (27 x 31 cm) overall

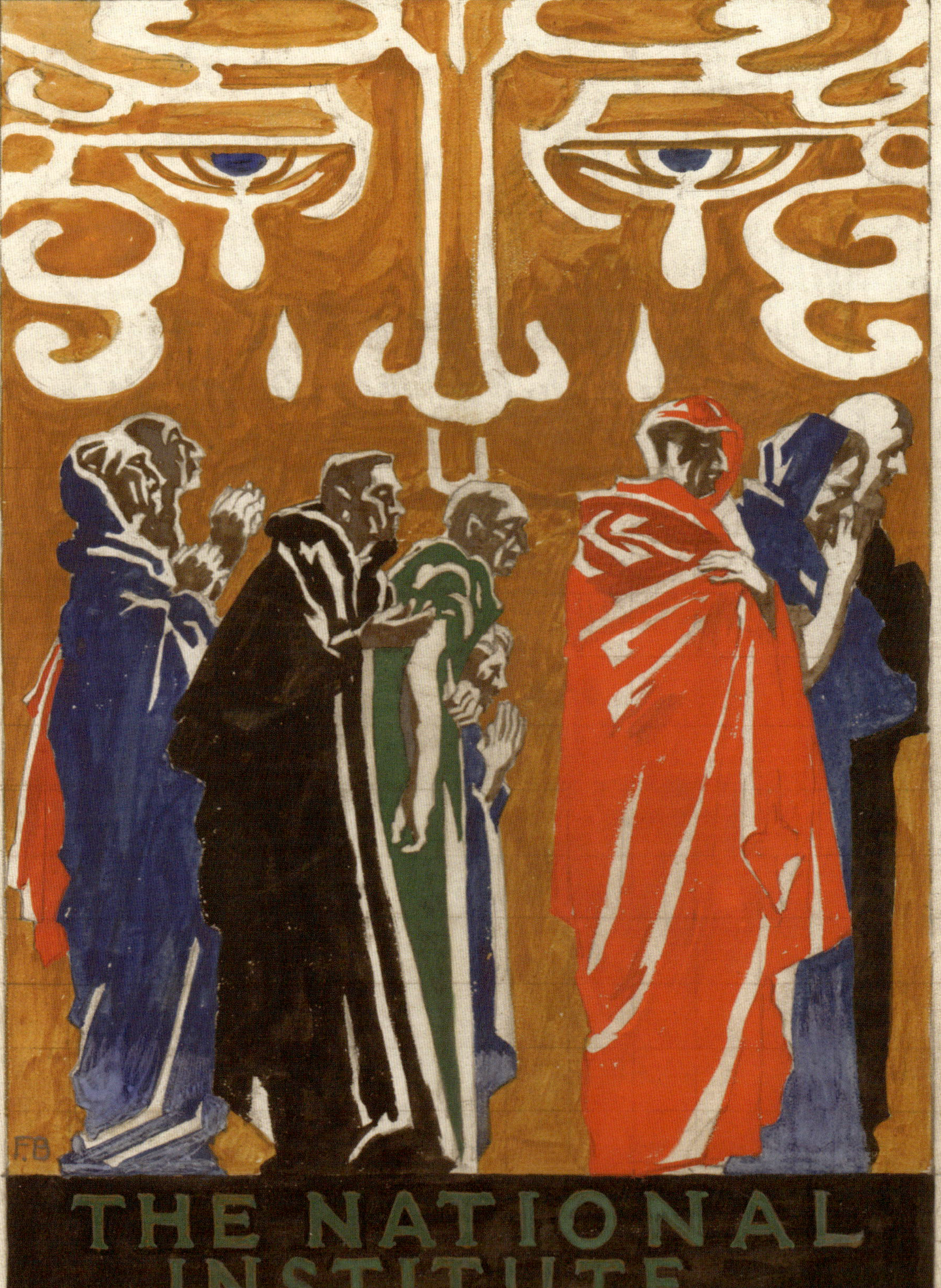
THE NATIONAL
INSTITUTE
FOR THE BLIND

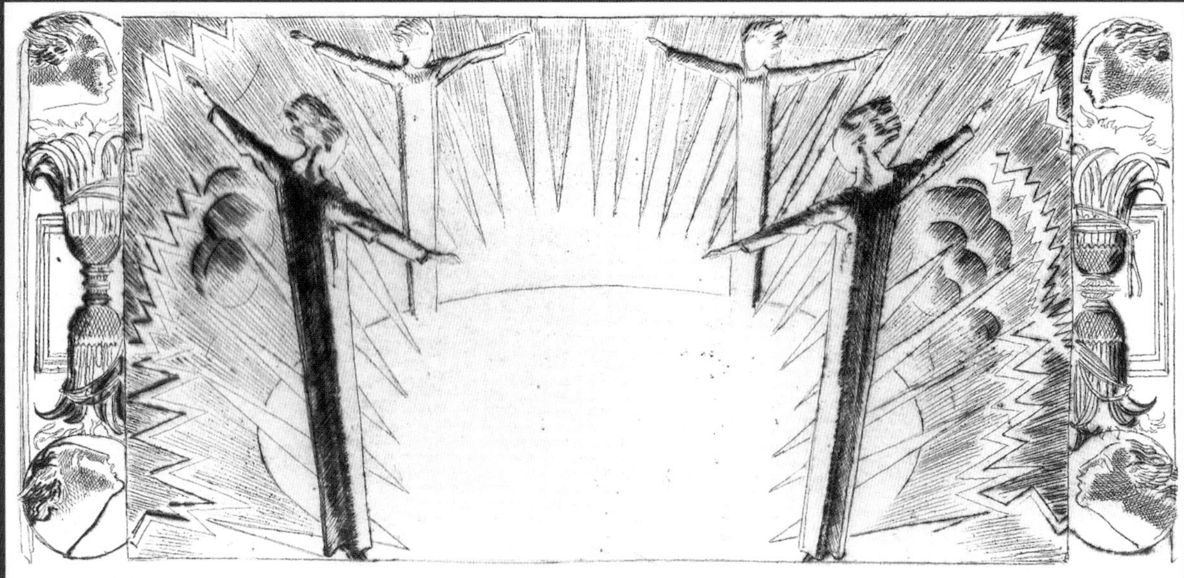

196

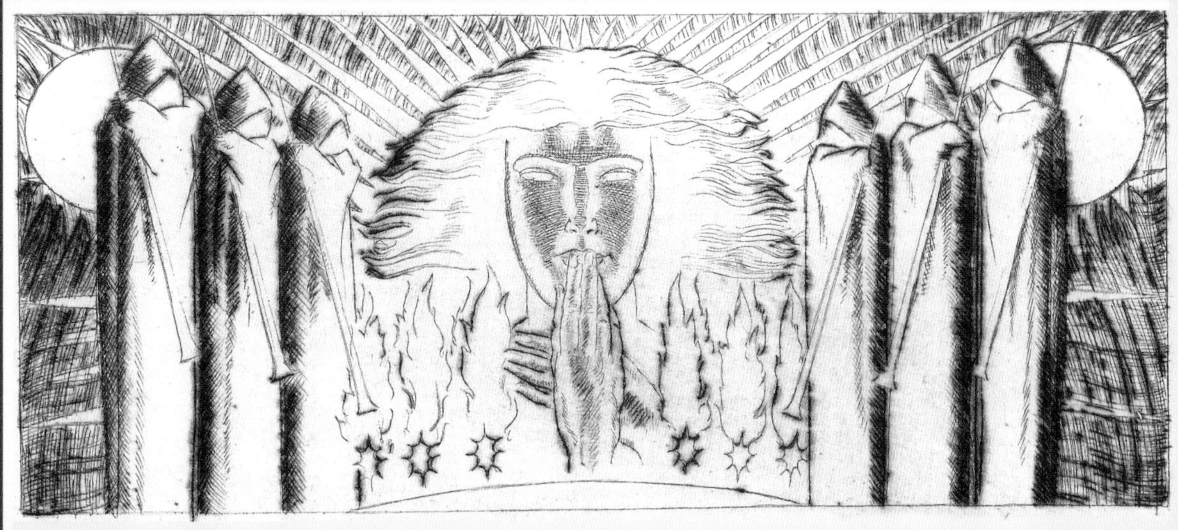

197

Frederick Carter (1883-1967)

196 – *The Four Winds of the Apocalypse*, 1925,
Etching, 4 ⅜ x 7 ¾ in. (11 x 20 cm) (plate size)

197 – *Silence in Heaven*, 1925,
Etching, 4 x 7 ⅜ in. (10 x 19 cm) (plate size)

195 – Frank Brangwyn (1867-1956)

Study for cover "The National Institute for the Blind" (B2910), signed with monograph and signature in pencil,
Pencil and gouache on paper mounted on card, 13 ⅛ x 8 ½ in. (33.5 x 21.7 cm),
Literature: Libby Horner, *Brangwyn at WAR!*, (Horner and Goldmark, 2014) p.88

The war resulted in a huge increase in blindness – partly a consequence of the deployment of chemical warfare. By recalling Rodin's *Burghers of Calais*, (1884) Brangwyn's wartime design explores themes of dignity and sacrifice.

198 – Alan Sorrell (1904-1974)

A Land Fit for Heroes, 1936, signed and dated,
Pen & ink and gouache on paper,
11 ⅝ x 19 ½ in. (32.1 x 49.4 cm),
Provenance: Richard Sorrell

David Lloyd George promised the soldiers who
fought for 'King and Country' that they would
return to a 'land fit for heroes'. The land they
returned to had changed profoundly, yet it met
hardly any of their expectations: of those lucky
enough to return, most collected their civilian
suit, a pair of medals and a small cash payment,
then joined the ranks of those looking, in vain,
for work; others collected a disability pension
but were never able to work again. Sorrell was
fourteen in 1918, and had spent much of a
sickly childhood in a Bath chair; perhaps this
made him more sympathetic towards the victims
of the war. In this harrowing picture, a statue
of Britannia on a pedestal ironically surveys the
scene: a civilian grandee with a hawkish expression
watches a pathetic parade of war-wounded, some
so grey-faced that they seem already to be ghosts.
The picture, a grim foreboding of the carnage to
come, called on Sorrell's memories of the First
World War veterans.

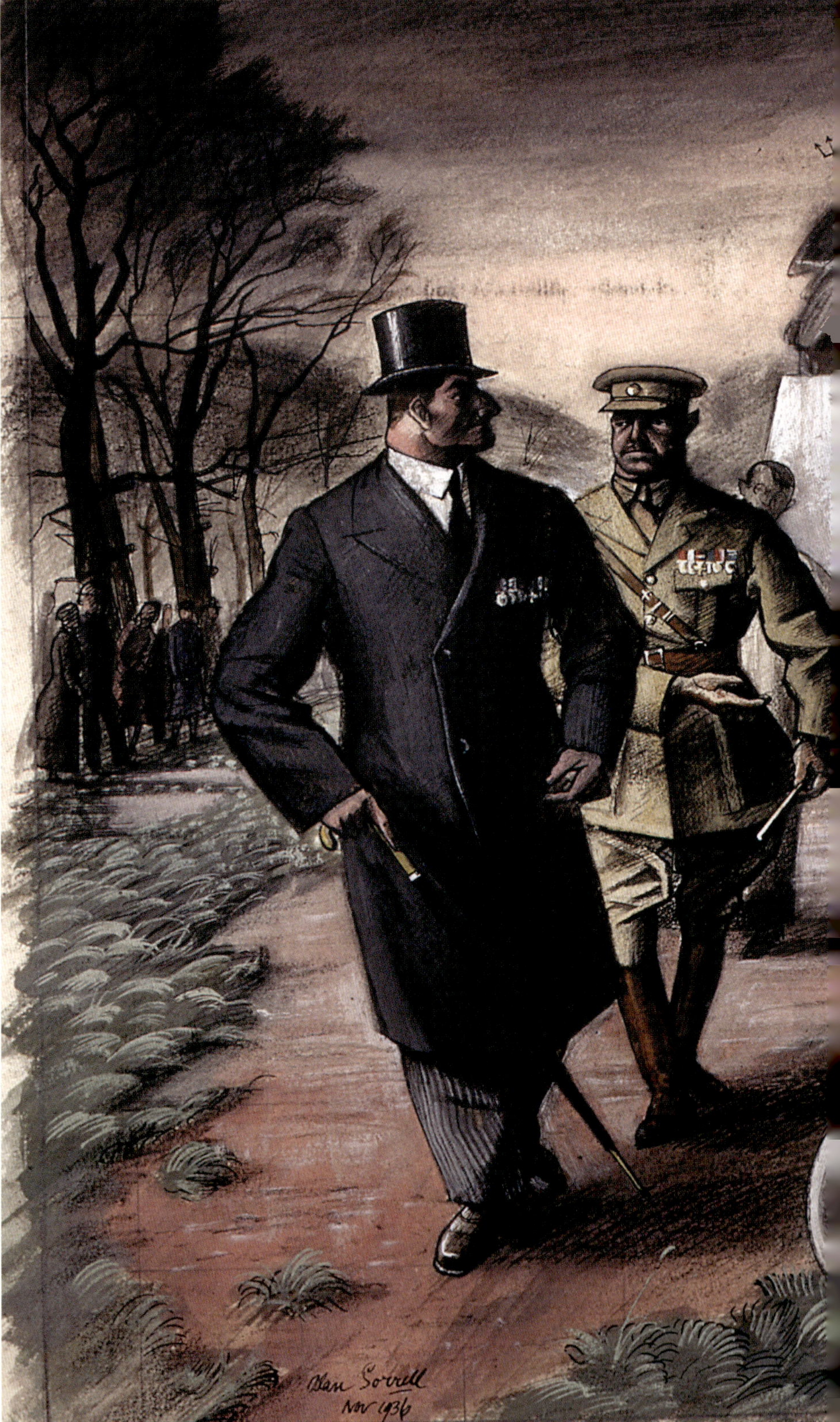

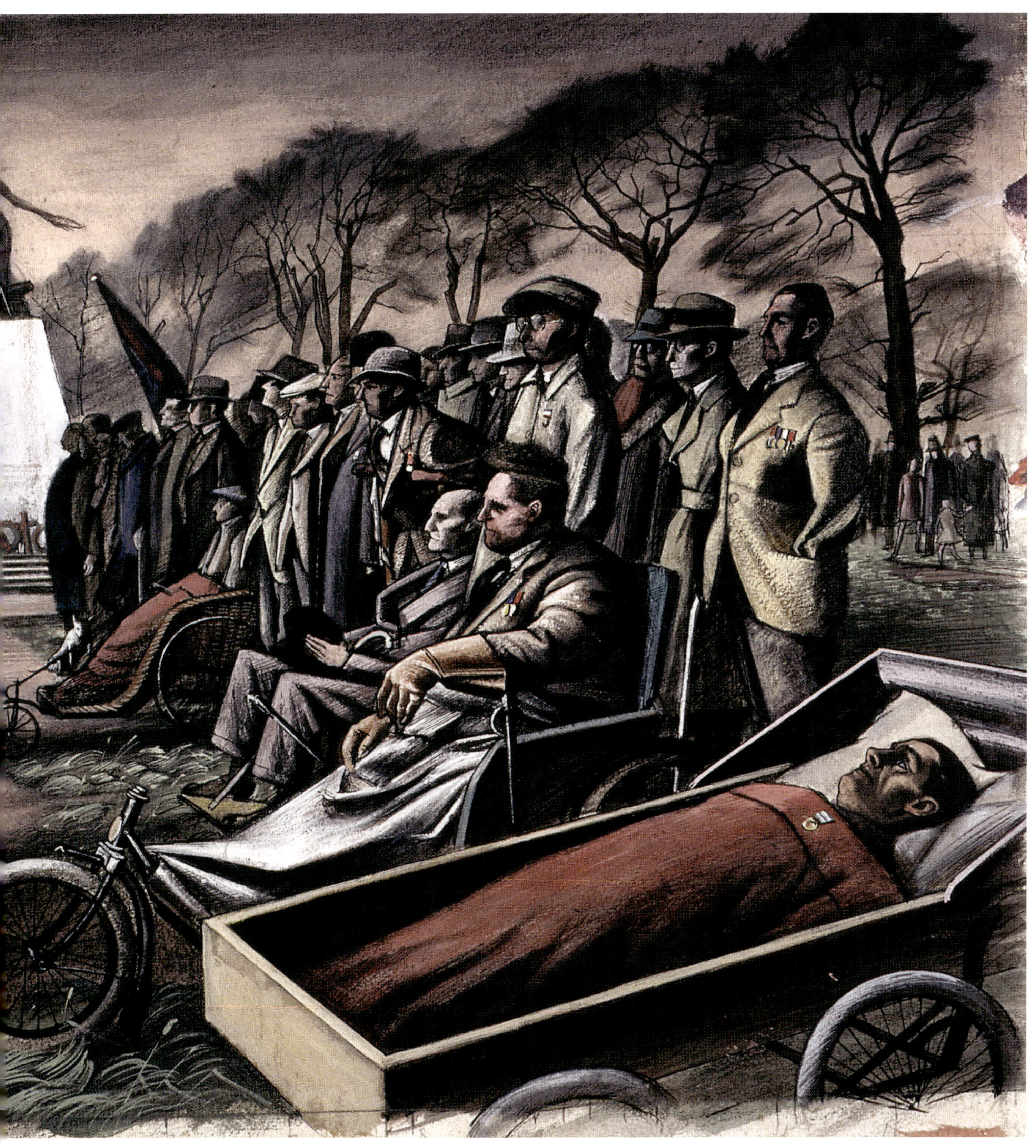

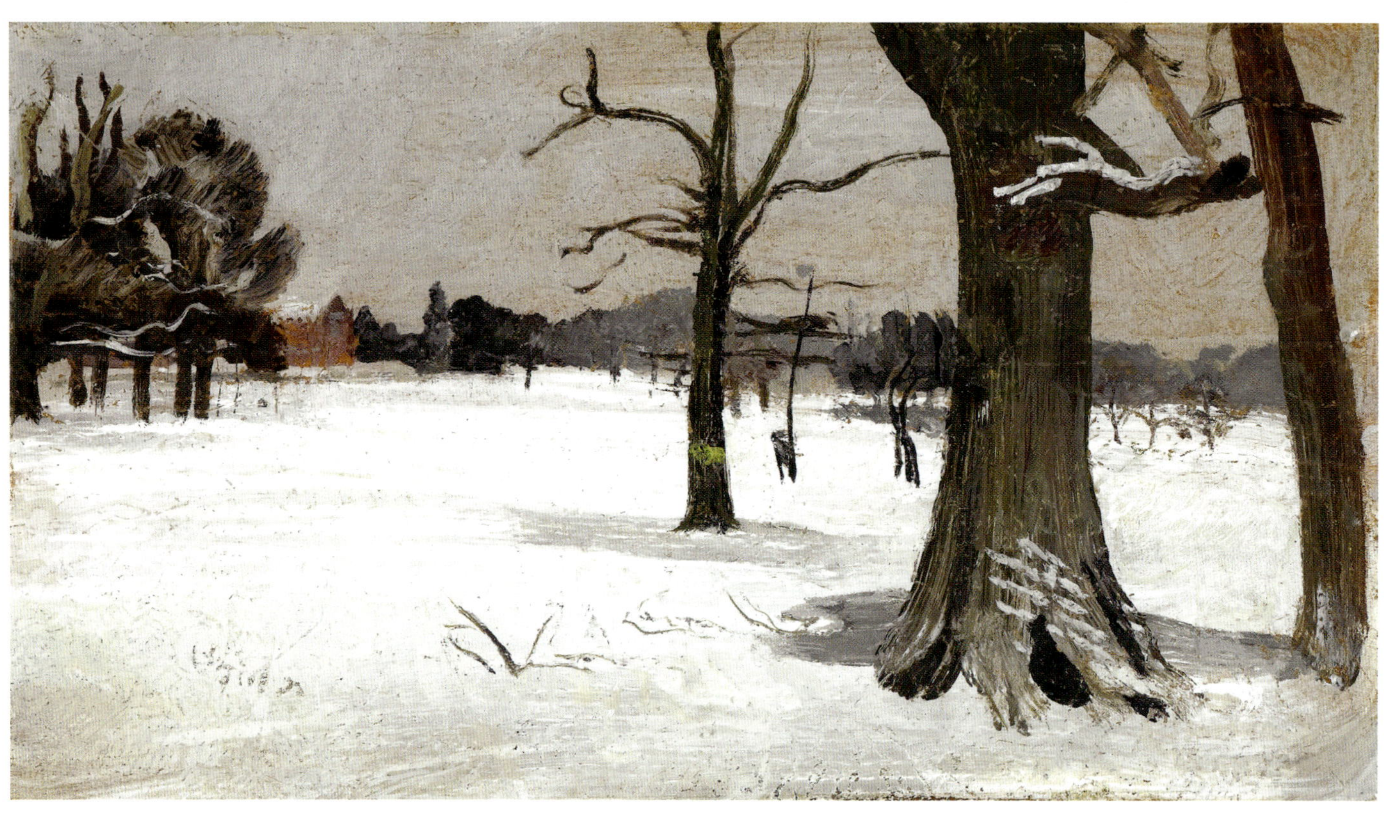

199 – Charles Sims (1873-1928)

Snow scene, c.1918,
Oil on panel, 5 x 8 ½ in. (12.8 x 21.8 cm)

This bleak snow scene is possibly the panel exhibited by Sims at the Royal Academy in 1918 under the title *April Snow*, (533). The First World War proved to be a traumatic experience for Sims; his eldest son was killed in action, and he became unbalanced by the horrors that he had witnessed in France whilst working as an Offical War Artist.

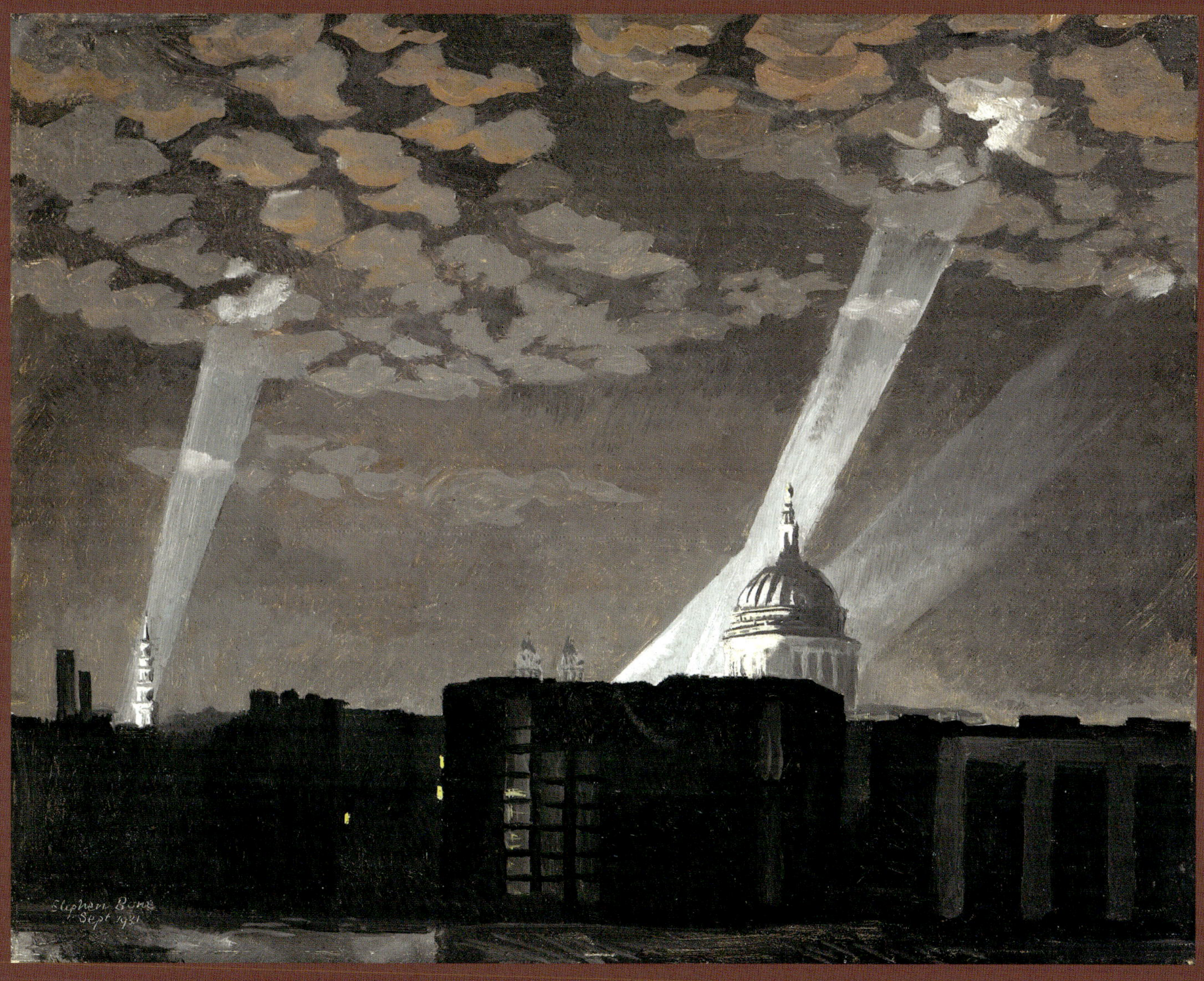

200 – Stephen Bone (1904-1958)

St Paul's and St Bride's Floodlit, Sept. 1931, signed and dated,
Oil on panel, 13 x 16 in. (33 x 40.6 cm)

If it were not dated September 1931, exactly nine years before the first bomb attacks on St Paul's, Stephen Bone's panel might be mistaken for an iconic image of the Second World War. Far from achieving peace, 'the war to end wars', which cost seventeen million lives, was but a terrible prelude to the sixty million deaths resulting from the Second World War.

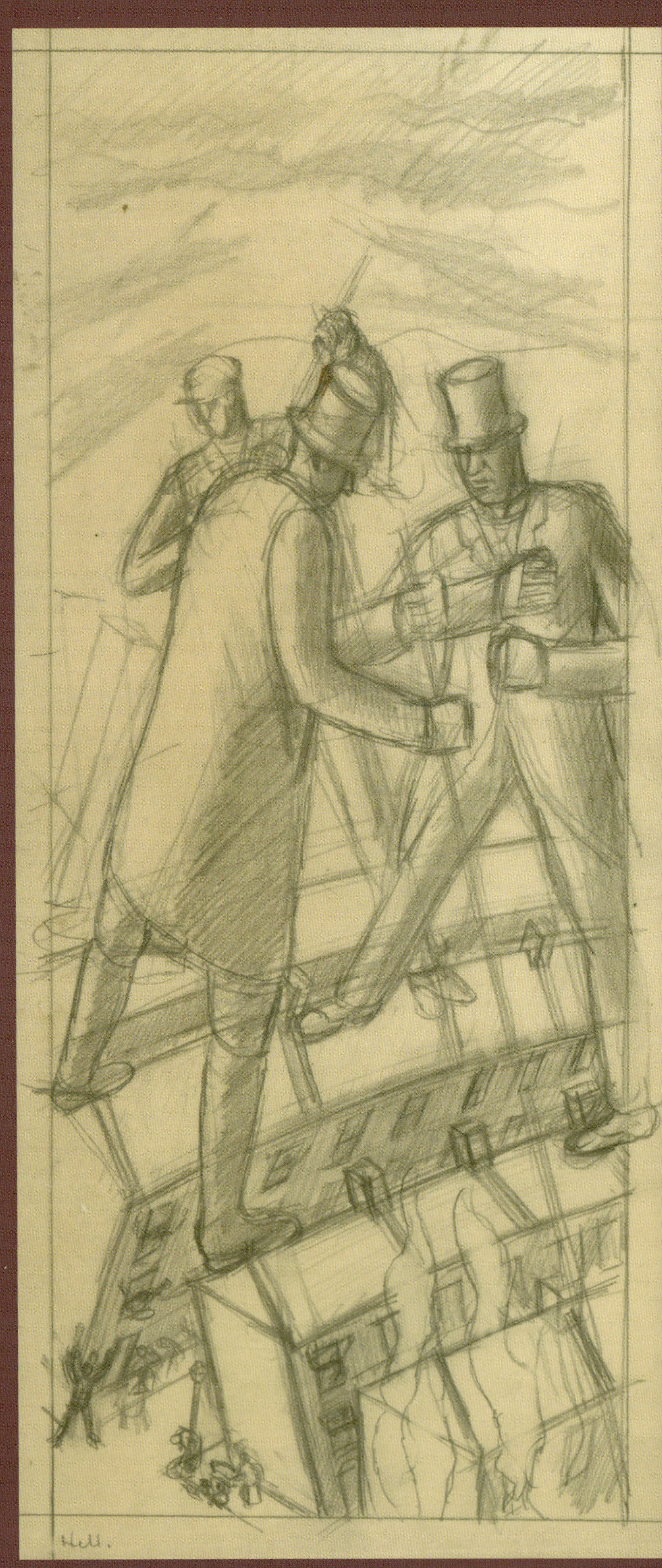

201 – *Hell*,
Inscribed with title,
Pencil on tracing paper,
14 ⅜ x 6 ⅛ in. (36.5 x 15.5 cm.)

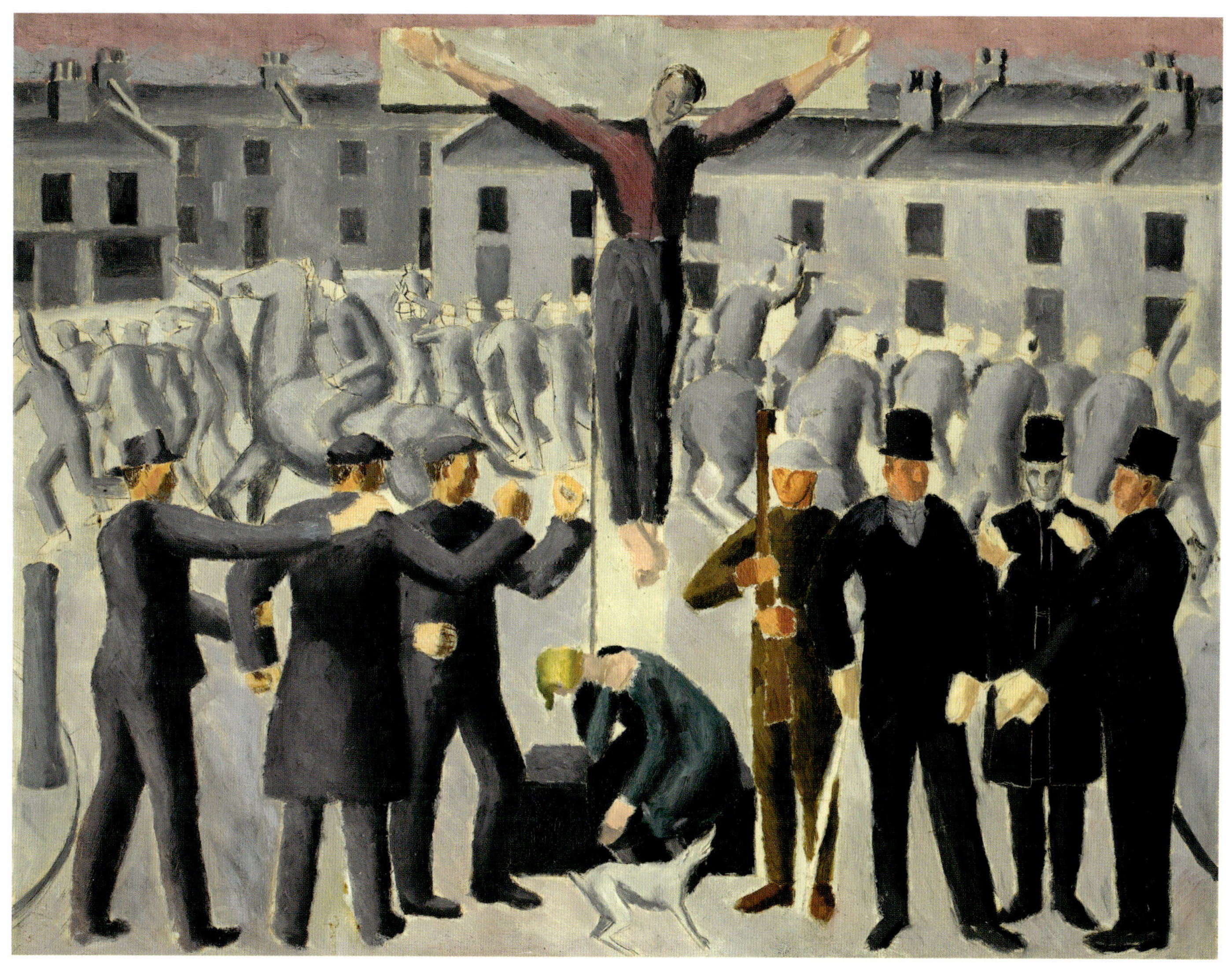

Archibald Ziegler (1903-1971)

202 – *An Allegory of Social Strife,* late 1920s,
Oil over pencil and red crayon on panel, 21 1/8 x 26 5/8 in. (53.5 x 67.7 cm)

One of many bitter legacies of the war was mass unemployment and social unrest. This image, which can be read as a polemical allegory of the sacrifice of the working man as a victim of the ruling classes, recalls the 1926 General Strike which Ziegler would have lived through as a young art student. It depicts the artist himself on the cross. He is flanked on the left by pugnacious workers' leaders and on the right figures representing the Establishment (Socialists and Capitalists). Brow-beaten workers, under attack, fill the background. A soldier stands guard to the Establishment figures, amongst which is a macabre, frock–coated man whose pose and dog-collar alludes possibly to the Church. A study for this right hand group is inscribed by the artist with the title '*Hell*'. Ziegler's striking composition is likely to have inspired Emmanuel Levy's iconic self portrait from 1942, '*Jesus the Jew*'.

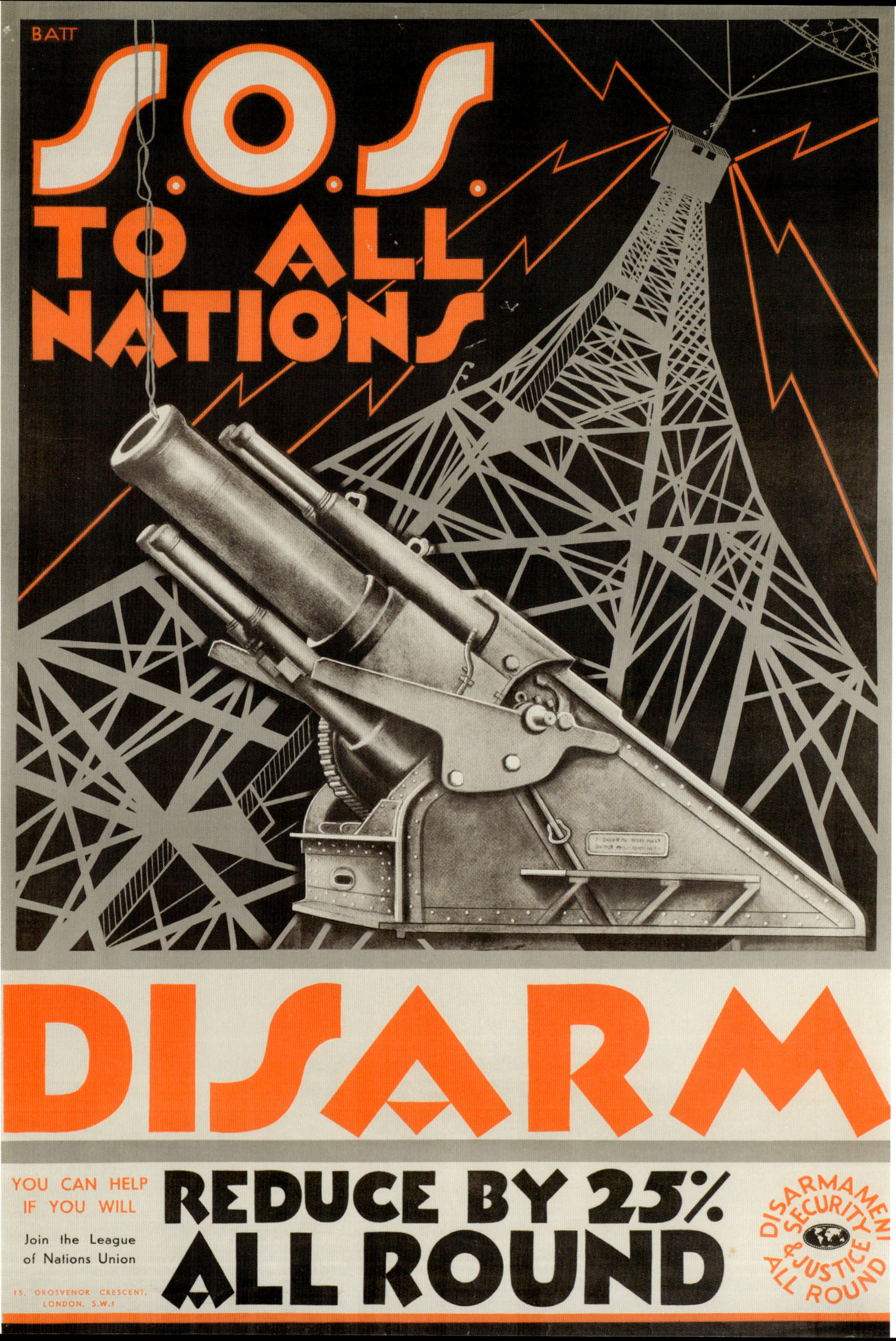

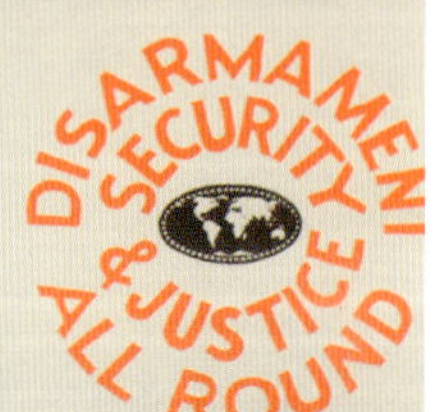
BATT
S.O.S.
TO ALL NATIONS
DISARM
YOU CAN HELP
IF YOU WILL
Join the League
of Nations Union
15, GROSVENOR CRESCENT,
LONDON, S.W.1
REDUCE BY 25%
ALL ROUND
DISARMAMENT
SECURITY
&JUSTICE
ALL ROUND

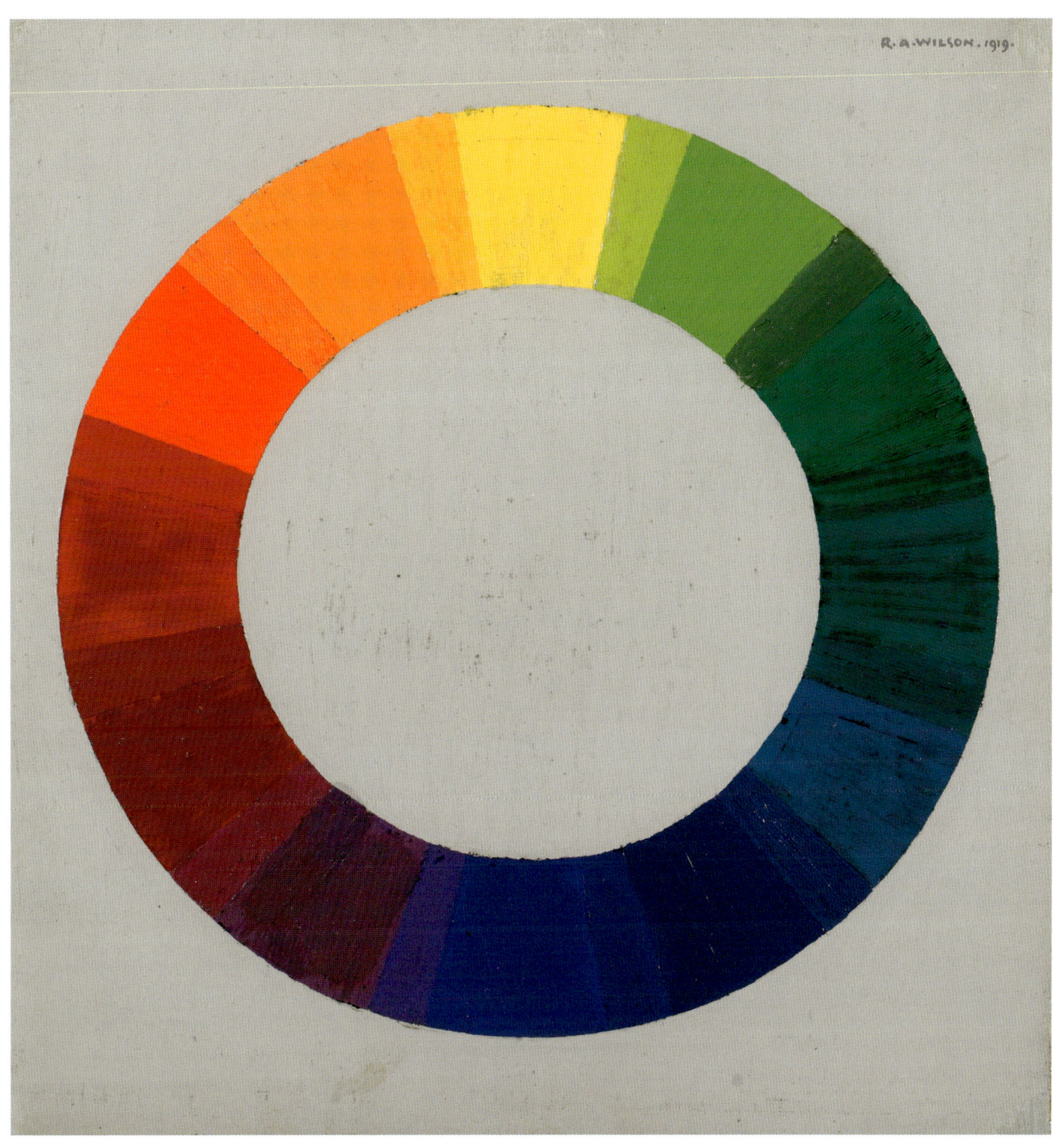

204 – Robert Arthur Wilson (1884–1979)

Colour Wheel, 1919, signed and dated
Oil on canvas, 13 x 12 1/4 in. (33 x 31 cm.),
Literature: *Eye-Music, Kandinsky, Klee and all that Jazz*, Frances Guy, Pallant House, Chichester, 2007, pp. 96-99

'Colour: its meaning and use, logic, mystery, symbolism and power' was the title of a BBC radio broadcast given by Wilson in May 1920. Although *Colour Wheel* shows an awareness of Chevruel's colour theories, its broader symbolism might equally relate to the void left by the war and the power of renewal as suggested by the continuous form of a circle.

203 – Batt

S.O.S. To All Nations – Disarm, League of Nations Union, c.1920,
Lithographic poster, 30 x 20 in. (76 x 51 cm)
The League of Nations Union (LNU) was an organization formed in October 1918 in the United Kingdom to promote International Justice, collective security and a permanent peace between nations based upon the ideals of the League of Nations. The League of Nations was established by the Great Powers as part of the Paris Peace Treaties, the International settlement that followed the First World War.

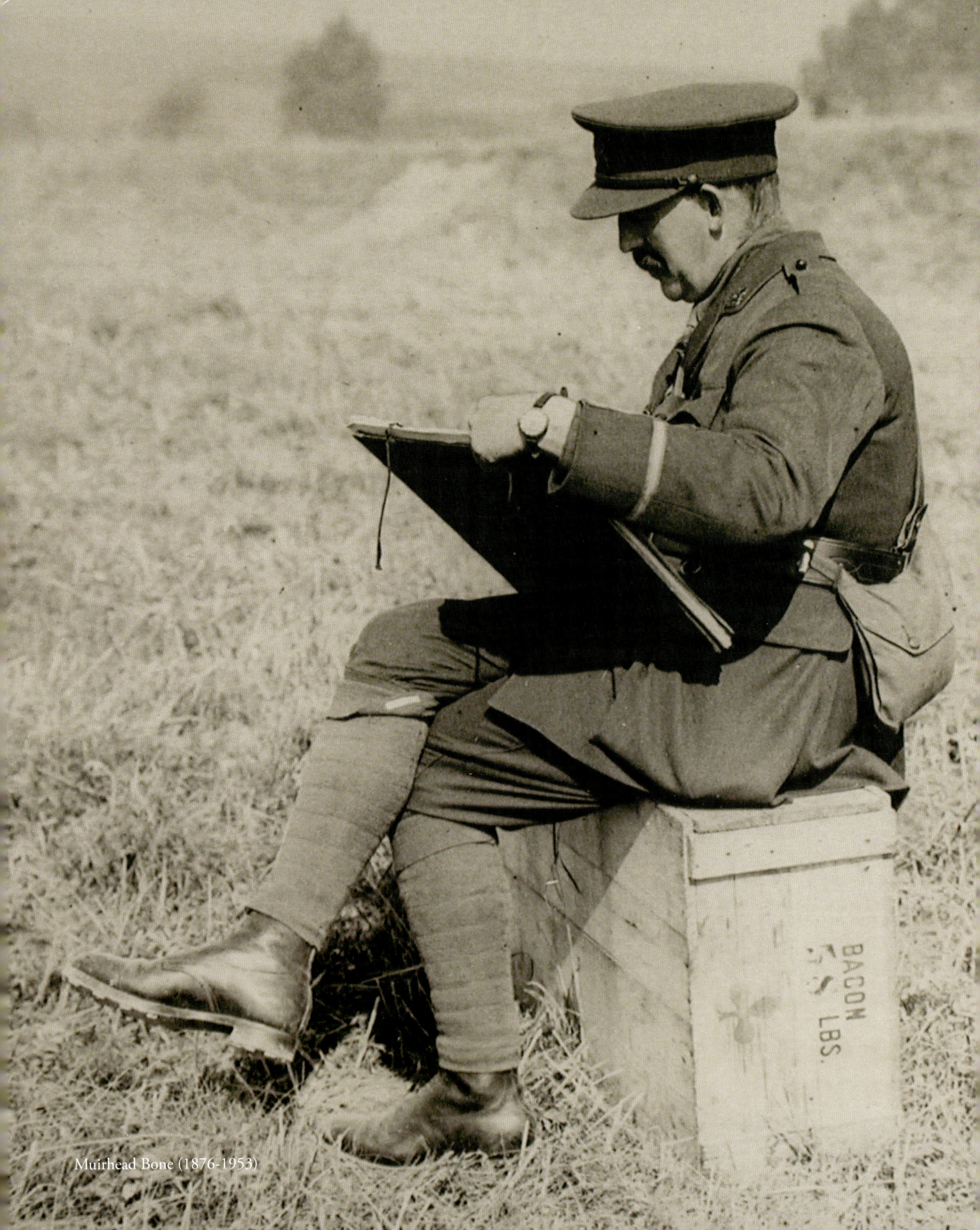

Muirhead Bone (1876-1953)

The numbers which follow each artist's name refer to the page or pages on which his or her work is reproduced.

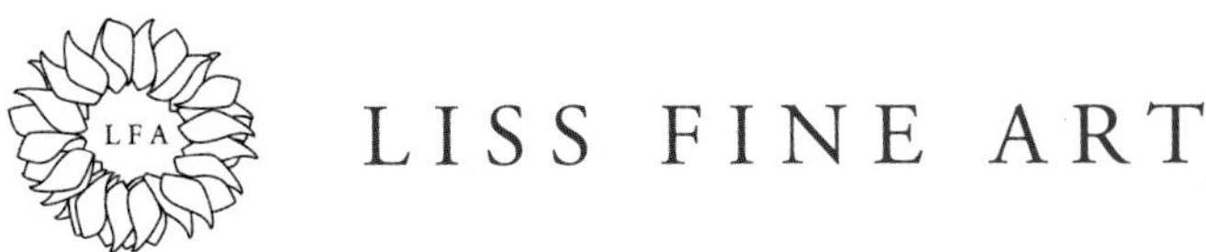

paul@lissfineart.com   sacha@lissfineart.com

Founded in 1991 by Paul Liss and Sacha Llewellyn, Liss Fine Art specialises in the unsung heroes and heroines of British art from 1880 to 1980. During the last 20 years Liss Fine Art have worked in association with museums to develop a series of in-depth exhibitions to encourage the reappraisal of some of the lesser known figures of 20th century British Art.

www.lissfineart.com

Design and Typesetting by David Maes

Text © Sacha Llewellyn, Paul Liss and David & Judith Cohen
Photography: Glynn Clarkson, Petra Hogervorst
Printed by Zenith Media, 2014

ISBN: 978-0-9567139-9-5